BUSINESS TAX AND LAW HANDBOOK

David Bertram

Duncan Taylor

FINANCIAL TIMES MANAGEMENT
128 Long Acre, London WC2E 9AN
Tel: +44 (0) 171 447 2000
Fax: +44 (0) 171 240 5771
Website: www.ftmanagement.com

A Division of Financial Times Professional Limited

First published in Great Britain in 1998

ISBN 0 273 62807 0

British Library Cataloguing in Publication Data
A CIP catalogue record for this book can be obtained
from the British Library

Typeset by M Rules
Printed and bound in Great Britain by Biddles Ltd, Guildford and King's Lynn

*The Publishers' policy is to use paper manufactured
from sustainable forests.*

CONTENTS

Preface xi

Abbreviations xii

1 INTRODUCTION 1

2 COMPUTING PROFITS FOR TAX PURPOSES 8

2.1 How taxable profits are arrived at 8
2.2 Capital allowances 22
2.3 Pre-trading expenditure 41

3 MAIN PRINCIPLES OF CAPITAL GAINS TAX 42

3.1 Basic outline of capital gains tax 42
3.2 Who is subject to capital gains tax? 43
3.3 What assets are chargeable assets? 44
3.4 Which types of transaction may produce a chargeable gain? 45
3.5 Computation of capital gains 49
3.6 Some special problem areas 57

4 CAPITAL GAINS TAX AND BUSINESS TRANSACTIONS 63

4.1 Loans to private businesses 63
4.2 Losses on unquoted shares 65
4.3 Roll-over relief 67
4.4 Relief for reinvestment in unquoted shares 71
4.5 Hold-over relief for gifts of business property 74
4.6 Partners and capital gains 77
4.7 Retirement relief – general provisions 80
4.8 Retirement relief and unincorporated traders 82
4.9 Retirement relief and full-time directors and employees 84

5 OUTLINE OF VAT 87

5.1 Introduction 87
5.2 Legal authorities 89
5.3 Basic principles 90
5.4 Practical implications 95
5.5 Imports, exports and single market 106
5.6 Anti-avoidance measures 107

5.7 Special schemes 109
5.8 Enforcement procedures 111
5.9 Fraud 115
5.10 Appeals 115

6 STAMP DUTY AND BUSINESS TRANSACTIONS 117

6.1 Documents liable to duty 117
6.2 Sanctions where duty is not paid 122
6.3 Avoiding or reducing duty 123

7 CONTRACT LAW 129

7.1 Offer 129
7.2 Acceptance 131
7.3 Consideration 133
7.4 Mistake 135
7.5 Misrepresentation 137
7.6 Duress and undue influence 139
7.7 Terms of contract 142
7.8 Exemption and exclusion clauses 147
7.9 Breach of contract 153
7.10 Frustration 155

8 SALE OF GOODS 158

8.1 Terms implied into a sale of goods contract 158
8.2 Description 159
8.3 Fitness for purpose and quality 159
8.4 Sale by sample 161
8.5 Exclusion of terms implied by ss 13–15 of the 1979 Act 161
8.6 Breach of an implied term 161
8.7 Stipulations of time 162
8.8 Consumer protection 162
8.9 Passing of property and risk 164
8.10 Delivery and acceptance 165
8.11 Remedies of the seller 167
8.12 Remedies of the buyer 168

9 BUSINESS PREMISES 170

9.1 Introduction 170
9.2 Taking business premises 170
9.3 Keeping business premises 186
9.4 Leaving business premises 195

10 EMPLOYMENT LAW **198**

10.1 Introduction 198
10.2 The impact of EC law 199
10.3 Employing the worker: the worker's status 200
10.4 The employee 204
10.5 The contract of employment 205
10.6 The doctrine of restraint of trade 208
10.7 Written particulars of employment 211
10.8 Continuity of employment 214
10.9 Unfair dismissal 216
10.10 Redundancy 234
10.11 Termination of employment 240
10.12 Maternity rights 246
10.13 Statutory sick pay (SSP) 254
10.14 Further statutory payments to employees 255
10.15 Itemised pay statements 257
10.16 Wages: payment and deductions 257
10.17 Sex and race discrimination 260
10.18 Discrimination on grounds of disability 266
10.19 Equal pay 268
10.20 Insolvency of employer 271
10.21 The Transfer of Undertakings (Protection of Employment) Regulations 1981 (TUPE) 272

11 TAX AND EMPLOYEE COMPENSATION **281**

11.1 PAYE 281
11.2 National insurance contributions 284
11.3 Benefits in kind 286
11.4 Travelling, subsistence and entertaining 293
11.5 Company cars 297
11.6 Beneficial loans 301
11.7 Living accommodation 303
11.8 Miscellaneous benefits 305
11.9 End of year returns 308
11.10 Profit-related pay and share schemes 308
11.11 Gifts of shares 309
11.12 Non-approved share options 310
11.13 Profit-sharing schemes 313
11.14 Share option schemes 314
11.15 Executive share option schemes 315
11.16 Special employee shares 316

11.17 Termination payments 317
11.18 How the Inland Revenue ensures compliance 321

12 LIFE ASSURANCE, PENSIONS AND PERMANENT HEALTH INSURANCE 324

12.1 Introduction 324
Part I – The basics 325
12.2 Life assurance 325
12.3 Pensions 331
12.4 Permanent health insurance 338
Part II – The uses 339
12.5 Introduction 339
12.6 Sole traders 340
12.7 Partners 343
12.8 Companies 345

13 HEALTH AND SAFETY 349

13.1 Introduction 349
13.2 Health and Safety at Work Act 1974 349
13.3 Other relevant legislation 353
13.4 Criminal and civil liability 355
13.5 Working conditions 358
13.6 Machinery and equipment 361
13.7 Hazardous fumes and substances 363
13.8 Reporting of injuries, insurance and reducing risks to health 364
13.9 Computers and other display screen equipment 366
13.10 Conclusion 367
13.11 Sources of further information 367

14 GENERAL INSURANCE 368

14.1 The need for insurance cover 368
14.2 Protection 368
14.3 The main compulsory insurance requirements 369
14.4 The insurance intermediary 370
14.5 Types of cover available 372
14.6 Types of policies available 382

15 PARTNERSHIP LAW 384

15.1 What is a partnership? 384
15.2 Limited partnership 385
15.3 Is there an agreement? 386

15.4 The salaried partner 387
15.5 Partnership and third parties 387
15.6 Liability of partners 388
15.7 Partnership agreement 389
15.8 Dissolution and winding-up of a partnership 393
15.9 EEIGs 397

16 HOW AN UNINCORPORATED BUSINESS IS TAXED ON ITS PROFITS 398

Self-employed individuals 399
16.1 Current year basis 399
16.2 Transitional provisions 403
16.3 Capital allowance basis periods 409
Partnerships 410
16.4 Special rules governing assessment of firm's profits 410
16.5 How transitional provisions apply to partnerships 411
16.6 Treatment of other income 412
16.7 Qualifying loans 412
16.8 Anti-avoidance rules 415
Miscellaneous 416
16.9 Relief for trading losses 416
16.10 Post-cessation receipts and expenses 423
Practical aspects and introduction of self-assessment and how it affects self-employed individuals 424
16.11 Outline of new regime 424
16.12 Penalties and interest charges 429
16.13 Achieving finality 432
16.14 How the system operates in 1996–97 432
Annual payments, NIC etc 433
16.15 Miscellaneous practical aspects 433

17 COMPANY LAW 435

17.1 What is a company? 435
17.2 Memorandum of association 438
17.3 Re-registration 440
17.4 After incorporation 442
17.5 Directors 448
17.6 Meetings 457
17.7 Share capital 468

17.8 Dividends 475
17.9 Ultra vires 476
17.10 Auditors 477
17.11 Work permits 479
17.12 Selection of administrative documents to be filed at Companies House 485

18 HOW COMPANIES ARE TAXED 488

18.1 Liability for corporation tax and how 'profits' are defined 488
18.2 Accounting periods, rates and payment of tax 491
18.3 Companies' capital gains 494
18.4 Interest and other charges 495
18.5 Dividends and advance corporation tax 497
18.6 Losses 500
18.7 Groups of companies 503
18.8 Close and investment companies 507
18.9 Double taxation relief on foreign income 509
18.10 Controlled foreign companies and anti-avoidance legislation 511
18.11 Forex transactions 514
18.12 'Pay and file' 519
18.13 Claims and elections 520

19 TAX PLANNING FOR SOLE TRADERS AND PARTNERS 522

Operating as an unincorporated business 523
19.1 Bringing in a partner (and becoming a partner) 523
19.2 Buying out a partner 525
Operating as a limited company 528
19.3 General tax considerations 528
19.4 Possible disadvantages 531
19.5 Other tax aspects 533
19.6 Transferring a business to a company 534
Sale of the business and cessation 539
19.7 Sale 539
19.8 Cessation 541

20 TAX AND THE COMPANY PROPRIETOR 543

20.1 Buying a company 543
20.2 Corporation tax planning 545
20.3 Treatment of remuneration for PAYE and NIC purposes 548

20.4	Benefits in kind	550
20.5	Dividends	550
20.6	Loans to the company	552
20.7	Loans by the company	553
20.8	Sale and purchase of assets by the company	553
20.9	Self-administered pension schemes	556
20.10	Raising business finance	558
20.11	Purchase of own shares	564
20.12	Demergers	567
20.13	Longer term capital gains tax planning	569
20.14	Anti-avoidance legislation	572
20.15	Sale of the company	573
21	**INHERITANCE TAX AND BUSINESS PROPERTY**	**578**
21.1	Persons subject to IHT	578
21.2	When a charge arises	579
21.3	Transfers of value	579
21.4	Gifts which are not transfers of value	581
21.5	Exempt transfers	584
21.6	Potentially exempt transfers	587
21.7	Reservation of benefit	588
21.8	Business property	590
21.9	Agricultural property	591
21.10	Computation of tax on lifetime transfers	592
21.11	Computation of tax payable on death	593
21.12	Handing on the family business/company without attracting IHT	596
GLOSSARY		**602**
INDEX		**613**

PREFACE

We have written this book because we perceived a need for a practical guide for businessmen and their professional advisers. Business tax and law are key subjects for any proprietor, director of a private company and for specialists responsible for particular functions such as personnel managers, company secretaries and finance directors. Such business people are typical clients of accountants and solicitors and we know from long experience that they need to be guided through the complex maze of legislation regulation and common law. Very often we are asked specific questions and we find it essential to put our advice into a broader context—half the battle in practice is to identify all pertinent questions and matters to be addressed. We have therefore endeavoured to produce a handbook which describes and explains the main principles that lie behind topics such as employment law, contracts, health and safety at work and taxation. We have sought to identify problem areas and matters on which specific advice should be taken from a professional adviser who specialises in that particular field.

Practising as an accountant or solicitor has changed beyond recognition over the past 25 years. There will always be a need for a professional adviser who gives general advice, helps clients to identify key questions and then interprets the input from specialists and explains to the client what it means in practice. Both of us see this as our main role. However, the legislation and case law are now so complex that we all now need to take advice from colleagues who specialise in particular areas. We are therefore grateful that a number of our colleagues and partners have contributed chapters, as have Vince Jerrard of Allied Dunbar and Gill Clark of Eagle Star.

We are most grateful to Jilli Smith of Pitman Publishing for all her help and support, and for the work behind the scenes by the various typists involved, in particular Allison White. The continued patience of our respective wives Catherine and Lindsay is also appreciated!

The law is stated as at 31 December 1997.

David Bertram
Duncan Taylor

ABBREVIATIONS

ACAS	Advisory Conciliation and Arbitration Service
ACT	advance corporation tax
ADRs	American Depositary Receipts
AIM	Alternative Investment Market
APPP	Appropriate Personal Pension Plan
CA 1985	Companies Act 1985
CAA 1990	Capital Allowances Act 1990
CFC	controlled foreign company
CGT	capital gains tax
CY basis	current year basis
ECJ	European Court of Justice
EDT	effective date of termination
EIS	Enterprise Investment Scheme
ERA	Employee Rights Act 1996
ESC	extra statutory concession
ETO reason	economic, technical or organisational reason
EU	European Union
EWC	expected week of childbirth
FA	Finance Act
FSAVC	Free Standing Additional Voluntary Contributions
HSE	Health & Safety Executive
HSWA 1974	Health and Safety at Work Act 1974
IBA	industrial buildings allowance
IHT	inheritance tax
IHTA 1984	Inheritance Tax Act 1984
LAPR	Life Assurance Premium Relief
NI	National Insurance
NRE	net relevant earnings
PET	potentially exempt transfer
PHI	permanent health insurance
PPE	personal protective equipment
PPP	Personal Pension Plan
PSO	Pension Schemes Office
PY basis	preceding year basis
QCB	qualifying corporate bond

SERPS	State Earnings Related Pensions Scheme
SDRT	stamp duty reserve tax
SMP	statutory maternity pay
SP	Inland Revenue Statement of Practice
SSAP	Statement of Standard Accounting Practice (issued by the Institute of Chartered Accountants)
SSP	statutory sick pay
TA 1988	Income and Corporation Taxes Act 1988
TCGA 1992	Taxation of Chargeable Gains Act 1992
TMA 1970	Taxes Management Act 1970
TULR(C)A	Trade Union and Labour Relations (Consolidation) Act 1992
TURERA	Trade Union Reform and Employment Rights Act 1978
USM	Unlisted Securities Market
VAT	value added tax
VATA 1994	Value Added Tax Act 1994

1

INTRODUCTION

Being in business is not easy and there is a multitude of legal obligations and reporting requirements. A businessman cannot hope to become an expert overnight but he should not just muddle along; if he does so he is bound to come unstuck.

A detailed study of the subject is beyond the scope of this book. Instead, the authors' intention is to describe the basic principles of business tax and law, and to give examples of how these principles work in practice and highlight those areas where the businessman should take professional advice.

The following are key aspects to bear in mind.

1.1 HOW ARE TAXABLE PROFITS COMPUTED?

It is important to appreciate that accounts which have been drawn up according to commercial principles may need to be adjusted for tax purposes. For example, there is no tax relief for depreciation.

Accounts should be drawn up on the earnings basis, ie a trader's stock or work in progress at his year end should be brought into account in arriving at his profit. Certain expenses are not allowable for tax purposes, for example entertaining or gifts to customers. A provision for a bad debt can be allowable for tax purposes but only if it is a specific provision. Bonus payments to employees can be a tax deductible expense even though they are paid after the end of the year. However, they have to be paid within nine months if tax relief is to be obtained for the year to which the bonuses relate. Pension contributions are tax deductible only if they are actually paid during the accounting period.

Although no tax relief is given for depreciation charged in accounts, relief may be due via the capital allowances system.

1.2 CAPITAL GAINS TAX (CGT)

Chapters 3 and 4 cover CGT as it relates to a businessman. Chapter 3 covers general principles such as what assets are chargeable assets and how a gain is computed for CGT purposes. Particular types of assets such as land and buildings, unquoted shares and foreign property are then discussed. Chapter 4 focuses on various business transactions such as tax relief for a person who has lent money to a businessman where that loan has to be written off, and looks at the circumstances in which income tax relief may be available for a person who has subscribed for shares in an unquoted trading company.

Roll-over relief enables a person who reinvests a capital gain to defer tax. It applies to disposals of land and buildings, goodwill and other similar assets. The relief introduced more recently for reinvestment in unquoted shares is also covered.

Retirement relief may provide for total exemption from tax on gains of up to £250,000 plus half of the excess over £250,000 up to a maximum of £1,000,000. However, there are stringent conditions which need to be satisfied if relief is to be available at all.

1.3 VALUE ADDED TAX (VAT)

VAT affects almost every businessman. Chapter 5 covers the basic rules as well as those which apply to import and export transactions and special schemes available to traders in certain industries. A trader normally needs to account for VAT on a quarterly basis and it is therefore important to understand the procedures properly. The legislation provides certain 'incentives' for traders to comply since interest and penalties may be levied for failure to render returns and pay VAT promptly.

1.4 STAMP DUTY

This tax, established in 1694, is the oldest form of tax in force in the United Kingdom. The general principles are covered in Chapter 6. Professional advice should be sought as liability for stamp duty tends to arise only on certain exceptional (but usually larger) transactions such as the purchase, or taking a lease, of premises.

1.5 CONTRACT LAW

In this increasingly litigious age, it is important to understand the basics of the law of contract. Chapter 7 describes the main principles and deals with the situation where things go wrong, eg one party makes a mistake or suffers loss through misrepresentation. The chapter also covers the Unfair Contract Terms Regulations.

1.6 SALE OF GOODS

Sale of goods law is really part of contract law, but it merits a chapter in its own right. The Sale of Goods Act provides that certain terms are taken as being implied when parties enter into a contract. The chapter also covers matters such as product liability and liability under the Consumer Protection Act.

1.7 BUSINESS TENANCIES

For most businessmen, taking a lease of business premises is their largest single commitment. A lease can be a short- or long-term contract and rent may continue to be payable if the business comes to an end and the premises are no longer needed. Most modern leases contain an obligation on the tenant to return the premises in a fit condition at the end of the lease. It is very important for the tenant to be aware of what he may be letting himself in for. The chapter also takes into account the Landlord and Tenant (Covenants) Act 1995.

1.8 EMPLOYMENT LAW

This is an area of the law where the influence of EU legislation is particularly apparent. Even temporary and part-time employees may acquire significant statutory employment protection rights. It is very important to follow the proper procedures where an employee's work is less than satisfactory or where an employer may need to make the employee redundant.

1.9 EMPLOYEE COMPENSATION

In Chapter 11 the rules which require an employer to deduct tax and withhold NI contributions are set out. The chapter covers matters such as Pay As You Earn—how it works and payments from which PAYE must be withheld. It then goes on to look at benefits in kind, the way in which they are taxed and the returns which must be completed at the end of the year by the employer.

An important element of employee remuneration may consist of profit-related pay or special share schemes and these are covered in some detail. Also discussed are the treatment of redundancy payments and compensation for loss of office, and the way in which the Revenue ensures that the proper procedures are observed. A businessman may encounter the Collector's Audit Division and he may also undergo an investigation by one of the Schedule E Compliance Units—it is important to be prepared.

1.10 LIFE ASSURANCE, PENSIONS AND PERMANENT HEALTH INSURANCE

Chapter 12 covers the basics of life assurance, pensions and permanent health insurance. It details the different types of policy and sets out the legislation governing them. The second part of the chapter considers the uses of life assurance, pensions and permanent health insurance, with particular emphasis on the business needs of sole traders, partners and small companies.

1.11 HEALTH AND SAFETY AT WORK

There is a mass of legislation and European and Government regulation covering health and safety. In some situations, an employer who has transgressed could be exposed to criminal liability. Even in cases where only civil penalties are involved, it is not a matter to be taken lightly as the Health and Safety Executive or the local authority may have the power to compel a person to cease trading until certain work is carried out to ensure that adequate standards are in operation. This chapter offers a basic introduction to this complex area.

1.12 GENERAL INSURANCE

The subject of general insurance is comprehensively examined in Chapter 14. The need for insurance cover is explained and the main compulsory insurance requirements are set out. The different types of cover available, from physical property to liability and indemnity insurances, are described in detail.

1.13 PARTNERSHIP LAW

The Partnership Act was passed in 1890 and has been supplemented by a number of cases which have come before the courts over the last 100 years. Entering into a partnership requires careful consideration as a partner may be jointly and severally liable for all the firm's debts. The position on tax liabilities is changing with the introduction of self-assessment, but this is merely an exception to the general rule. It is therefore crucially important to carefully regulate certain aspects of the firm's financial affairs to ensure that partners who leave it do not avoid their proper share of any problems and liabilities.

1.14 TAXATION OF UNINCORPORATED BUSINESSES

Not only are there special rules which govern the way in which taxable profits are arrived at, there are also special rules covering the way in which self-employed individuals are taxed. The current year basis now applies in most cases, but problems can arise from the transition from the old preceding year basis.

There are also additional complications for partners, over and above the rules which apply to individuals who carry on business on their own account as sole traders.

1.15 COMPANY LAW

It is all too easy for individuals to acquire a company 'off the shelf' from formation agents and to commence trading with little or no understanding of the proper legal procedures. Companies House and the Revenue are increasingly taking a tough line and the well advised businessman needs to understand the basic reporting requirements.

It is also important to make provision in case things start to go wrong or to develop in an unexpected way. Situations are often encountered where a 50 per cent shareholder wishes to disengage from a company and the other shareholder has quite different views on how this should be dealt with. There may be deadlock from a legal view point which is hardly conducive to achieving an orderly and efficient parting of the ways. Similarly, problems may arise if a director is exceeding his authority and committing the company in ways which are not acceptable to his fellow directors. The position is often made worse because proper procedures were not followed in the past (eg there are no formal minutes of directors' meetings at which policy matters were discussed). As in so many areas, legal disputes may arise simply because a situation has arisen which was not envisaged at the outset; we have therefore endeavoured to provide an overview of relevant aspects of company law which need to be borne in mind by individuals who are directors and/or shareholders in private companies.

1.16 HOW COMPANIES ARE TAXED

If a company is formed to carry on a business, it is important to understand how the company will be treated for tax purposes. A return may be required on a quarterly basis for interest and other annual payments paid by the company. Advance corporation tax (ACT) may need to be paid at the end of the quarter in which a dividend is paid. Mainstream corporation tax has to be paid nine months after the year end.

Companies are now on the pay and file system, and over the next few years this will be converted, from a date to be announced, to a self-assessment system for companies. Automatic penalties and interest charges may apply where accounts are filed late with the Revenue.

There are a number of important claims and elections which may need to be made, usually within a set period of either two or six years. The Revenue normally resists late claims unless there are good reasons why the claim was not made in time.

1.17 TAX PLANNING FOR SOLE TRADERS AND PARTNERS

Chapter 19 covers some of the key issues for self-employed businessmen such as the tax implications of bringing in or buying out a partner. The chapter looks at questions such as whether there are tax benefits in transferring a business to a company and the most tax efficient way in which to achieve such a transfer, and some of the tax aspects which need to be considered where an unincorporated business is sold or closed down.

1.18 TAX AND THE COMPANY PROPRIETOR

Tax is an important consideration for shareholder directors. Chapter 20 looks at points to bear in mind when buying a company, the treatment of shareholder directors, the way in which they are assessed on benefits received by them (or by members of their family) and the tax implications of various transactions with the company. Many shareholder directors tend to use their company as a 'money box' and draw cash during the year in anticipation of bonuses which will be declared at the company's AGM—all very well in theory but doing this may infringe company law and give rise to a tax charge for the company and a separate tax charge for the director.

Matters are considered such as the purchase of assets from the company (or sales of assets to the company), the rules affecting self-administered pension schemes, possible ways in which a shareholder may be bought out (purchase of own shares and demergers) and more technical issues such as CGT planning and anti-avoidance legislation.

1.19 INHERITANCE TAX AND BUSINESS PROPERTY

Inheritance tax may take 40 per cent of an individual's assets on his death. But there are special reliefs available for businesses and in particular 100 per cent business property relief for unincorporated businesses and substantial shareholders in private trading companies. However, business relief may not always be available as once again there a number of stringent conditions which need to be satisfied.

2

COMPUTING PROFITS FOR TAX PURPOSES

This chapter covers the way in which a business's taxable profits are ascertained and deals with some of the more common adjustments to accounts which are required for tax purposes. For example, a set of accounts prepared for commercial reasons may include a provision for wear and tear to a building. Such a provision needs to be 'added back'. (As no relief is available for depreciation as such, relief is due only via the capital allowances system.) The chapter covers the following topics:

(1) How taxable profits are arrived at
(2) Capital allowances
(3) Pre-trading expenditure.

2.1 HOW TAXABLE PROFITS ARE ARRIVED AT

2.1.1 Accounts should be prepared on 'earnings basis'

The Revenue's view is that accounts should normally be prepared to reflect a trader's earnings for a year rather than just the cash received. For example, the accounts should include debtors (ie bills which have been issued but which have not been paid by the year end) and work in progress.

The Revenue almost always requires accounts to be prepared on the earnings basis for the first three years of a business. However, the Revenue allows an unincorporated trader to switch to a cash basis thereafter, provided he gives an undertaking that bills for completed work will be issued at regular and frequent intervals (see SP A 27). Where accounts are prepared on the cash basis, this treatment applies to expenses as well as income.

Companies are not normally allowed to use the cash basis.

2.1.2 Sound commercial accountancy principles

The Master of Rolls stated in *Gallagher v Jones* [1993] STC 537, CA that:

> '. . . Subject to any express or implied statutory rule . . . the ordinary way to ascertain the profits or losses of a business is to apply accepted principles of commercial accountancy. That is the very purpose for which such principles are formulated. As has often been pointed out, such principles are not static: they may be modified, refined and elaborated over time as circumstances change and accounting insights sharpen. But so long as such principles remain current and generally accepted they provide the surest answer . . .

In practice, there are two fundamental concepts which underly accounts drawn up on normal commercial accountancy principles:

(1) The *accruals* concept where income and costs are accrued, ie recognised as they are earned or incurred rather than according to when money is received or paid. In general, income (or 'revenue') and costs should be 'matched' so that revenues are set against associated costs and expenses. However, it may sometimes be necessary to depart from this rule because of the 'prudence' concept.
(2) The *prudence* concept requires that revenue and profits should not be anticipated but rather should be recognised only when realised. Moreover, provision should be made for all known liabilities. If necessary, a provision should be made for costs or expenses for which liability has arisen, with the provision being made on an estimated basis in the light of the information available.

Certain types of expenditure are disallowed for tax purposes even though it may be sound accounting practice to deduct such costs in a trader's accounts. However, in *Johnson v Britannia Airways Ltd* [1994] STC 763, the High Court upheld the company's appeal to allow provisions made in its accounts for the future overhaul of jet aircraft. This was done by taking the average cost of the ten most recent overhauls. This was then converted to an average cost per flying hour, taking account of the history of the engine concerned. The provision in the accounts was arrived at by taking the average cost multiplied by the actual hours flown by each engine in the accounting period. The Special Commissioners had held that the provision gave a 'true and fair view' of the company's trading position. This case establishes an important precedent.

2.1.3 Capital expenditure

(TA 1988, s 74(1)(f) and (g))

Capital expenditure is not a cost which may be deducted in arriving at profits for tax purposes. The generally accepted definition of capital expenditure was given by Lord Cave in *Atherton v British Insulated and Helsby Cables Ltd* (1925) 10 TC 155 where he stated:

> '. . . when an expenditure is made . . . with a view to bringing into existence an asset or an advantage for the enduring benefit of a trade . . . there is very good reason (in the absence of special circumstances leading to an opposite conclusion) for treating such an expenditure as properly attributable not to revenue but to capital.'

The definition in the *Atherton* case is only a most general definition, eg the fact that expenditure is recurring expenditure rather than a 'once and for all' outlay does not mean that it is revenue expenditure. Lord Greene MR stated that '. . . if the sum payable is not a revenue payment it cannot be made so by permitting it to be paid by annual instalments' (*Henriksen v Grafton Hotel Ltd* [1942] 24 TC 453). It was also held in that case that an enduring benefit need not be a long-term benefit; expenditure incurred in obtaining a liquor licence for three years was held to provide an enduring benefit which was capital in nature.

Money spent on acquiring an asset to be used for the trade is a capital outlay, whether the asset is a building or something liable to be worn out, such as a machine. The purchase of goodwill is capital expenditure even though there is no tangible asset. Similarly, extensive repairs which had to be carried out before a ship could be used for a company's trade are regarded as capital expenditure (*Law Shipping Co Ltd v CIR* (1923) 12 TC 621, Ct of Sess). However, in *Odeon Associated Theatres Ltd v Jones* (1971) 48 TC 257, CA, the company had acquired several theatres which, because of wartime restrictions, needed repair and redecoration. This had not affected the purchase price and did not restrict their use for public performances. *Law Shipping* was distinguished because the theatres could still be used whereas the ship required a refit to make it seaworthy. A lump sum payment to secure release from an onerous liability, such as a lease at a high rent or a fixed rate loan, is also regarded as capital expenditure.

The Revenue can take this to extremes. In the November 1991 issue of *Tax Bulletin*, the Revenue stated that expenditure on a course attended by a proprietor is regarded as capital expenditure if he attends to acquire new expertise, knowledge or skills. In contrast, where the individual attends merely to update expertise which he already possesses, the expenditure is normally regarded as revenue expenditure.

2.1.4 Expenditure not wholly for the purposes of the trade
(TA 1988, s 74(1)(a))

The legislation requires the expenditure to be incurred 'wholly and exclusively' for the purposes of the trade. Consequently, expenses which are incurred partly for trade purposes and partly for personal reasons are not allowable. For example the Revenue has invoked s 74(1)(a) to disallow the cost of clothing (*Mallalieu v Drummond* – see below) and of meals incurred by a self-employed carpenter working away from home (*Caillebotte v Quinn* [1975] STC 265).

Where an expense is incurred for mixed purposes, the whole amount is disallowed. However, where it can be shown that an *additional* cost was incurred wholly for business reasons, a deduction may be due for this. Consequently, if a trader pays his wife a salary which exceeds the real value of her services as an employee, it is normally only the excess which is disallowed.

Note that the requirement is that the expenditure is incurred wholly for the *purposes* of the trade. This implies that the test which must be satisfied is a subjective, rather than an objective, one. There is support for this in *Bentleys, Stokes & Lowless v Beeson* (1952) 33 TC 491, CA where Romer LJ stated:

> 'If the activity be undertaken with the objective both of promoting business and also with some other purpose, for example, with the object of indulging an independent wish of entertaining a friend . . . then the [requirement] is not satisfied though in the mind of the actor the business motive may predominate . . . *Per contra*, if in truth the sole object is business promotion, the expenditure is not disqualified because the nature of the activity necessarily involves some other result . . .'

Here the costs involved were those of entertaining clients. It was held that the expenditure was allowable even though there was an incidental benefit to the trader who enjoyed the lunch. There is now a statutory disallowance for entertaining expenditure (see 2.1.6 below).

Unfortunately, more recent decisions by the courts have suggested that the proper test may be an objective one. In the case involving the barrister's black dresses (*Mallalieu v Drummond* [1983] STC 665) Lord Brightman stated that:

> ' . . . she needed clothes to travel to work and clothes to wear at work, and I think it is inescapable that one object, though not a conscious motive, was the provision of the clothing that she needed as a human being. I reject the notion that the object of a taxpayer is inevitably limited to the particular conscious motive in mind at the moment of expenditure . . . the motive of which the taxpayer is conscious is of vital significance, but it is not inevitably the only object which the commissioners are entitled to find to exist.'

A similar interpretation lies behind the decision in *Mackinlay v Arthur Young McClelland Moores & Co* [1989] STC 898 which concerned removal expenses borne by the firm for two partners who were relocated within the UK. Lord Oliver stated:

'One is . . . brought back, first, last and all the time to the question whether an expenditure on a partner's removing expenses can be said to be laid out not just partly but exclusively for the purposes of the partnership business. That cannot, in my judgment, be answered simply by ascertaining what was the motive with which the move was undertaken. It is inescapable as it seems to me, that the expenditure, motivated no doubt by the fact of moving house, which in turn was motivated by the desire to put the partner concerned in a better position to further the interests of the firm, was an expenditure serving necessarily and inherently intended to serve the personal interests of the partner in establishing his private residence for himself and his family and it cannot be said to be exclusively for the purposes of the partnership practice.'

2.1.5 Sums recoverable from an insurance policy etc
(TA 1988, s 74(1)(l))

Where a trader can get back from an insurance company the money that he has paid out, there is no deduction due for the expenditure. The same treatment applies where a trader has been indemnified against a particular cost.

2.1.6 Entertaining and gifts to customers
(TA 1988, s 577)

Any expenses for entertaining customers or suppliers which are included in a set of accounts normally need to be added back. There used to be an exception for the cost of entertaining overseas customers but this no longer applies. There is an exception which may apply where the entertaining is provided by a hotelier, restaurateur or by someone else who provides entertainment in the ordinary course of his trade. Staff entertainment is also an allowable expense but the individual employee may be assessed on a benefit in kind.

The cost of gifts to customers, potential customers and to potential introducers is also disallowed unless the gift carries a conspicuous advertisement and is neither food, drink, tobacco or a voucher exchangeable for such goods, nor an item which costs more than £10 per recipient per year.

2.1.7 Illegal payments and fines
(TA 1988, s 577A)

There is a specific provision disallowing illegal payments such as bribes. This also covers payments made in response to threats, menaces, blackmail and other forms of extortion.

Fines and penalties for breach of the law have been disallowed since *IRC v Alexander von Glehn & Co Ltd* (1920) 12 TC 232, CA in which a company was refused a deduction for the costs of settling an action for breach of World War I regulations. The Revenue often invokes this case to disallow parking fines.

2.1.8 Provisions for bad debts

(TA 1988, s 74(1)(j))

A general provision against bad debts is not allowable, but provisions against specific debts are a proper deduction for tax purposes provided that it can be shown that the amount is a reasonable provision. A provision may be allowable even though the debt is subsequently collected: the key question is whether the provision was reasonable at the time that the accounts were drawn up. If this test is satisfied the provision is allowable and the amounts subsequently collected are brought into account as receipts for the year in which they are received.

The Revenue has explained its approach to provisions for bad or doubtful debts in the August 1994 issue of *Tax Bulletin*. Its interpretation is that a trader may be entitled to a deduction provided the following circumstances are satisfied:

- The debt existed at the balance sheet date.
- Before the accounts were finalised, the trader/company directors discovered that the debtor's financial position at the balance sheet date was such that the debt was unlikely to be paid.

The Revenue states that a common example of this is where a debtor goes into administration or liquidation shortly after the balance sheet date and before the date on which the financial statements are approved by the trader. Its occurrence before the accounts were finalised normally sheds light on the debtor's financial position at the balance sheet date. If the period between that date and approval of the accounts is short, it is unlikely that a debtor would have gone from financial good health to insolvency in that period. In these circumstances it is normally reasonable for the trader to regard the debt as doubtful. The acceptable amount of provision depends on the information available.

The Revenue contrasts this with a situation where a debtor is an habitually slow payer and there are no grounds to believe his financial position has changed. Here the Revenue argues that the length of time that a debt has been outstanding is not in itself a sufficient reason to regard the debt as doubtful.

2.1.9 Remuneration not paid within nine months of year end
(FA 1989, s 43)

Bonus payments to employees may be made after the end of a year. If they clearly relate to a period of account, it is normal for the trader's accounts to include a provision at the year end. However, this provision is allowable only if the remuneration is paid within nine months.

2.1.10 Pension contributions for employees
(TA 1988, s 592(4); FA 1993, s 112)

A deduction is due only if the contribution is paid during the course of the trader's year. This applies whether the contribution is paid to an approved or unapproved scheme.

Pension contributions for an unincorporated business proprietor are not an allowable deduction in computing profits, although relief is available as a deduction from taxable profits (see Chapter 12 for details of proprietors' personal pension contributions).

2.1.11 Annual payments
(TA 1988, s 74(1)(p) and (q))

Certain annual payments (eg patent royalties) generally need to be paid net of income tax at the basic rate. The payments are not deductible in arriving at an unincorporated trader's profits which are assessable under Schedule D Case I or II, although they are allowed as a deduction for higher rate purposes. A company can deduct the amounts paid as an annual charge (see 18.4).

2.1.12 Interest

Interest payments on loans taken by partners are allowable (if at all) against the partner's general income (see 16.7). Interest paid by a sole trader or by a partnership may be deducted in arriving at the business's taxable profits provided it passes the 'wholly and exclusively' test (see 2.1.4).

Problems may arise where overdraft interest is charged in a set of accounts and the proprietor's capital account is overdrawn. The Revenue is likely to argue that the interest (or, at any rate, part of it) was incurred not for the purposes of the business but to finance drawings.

It is wrong to assume that interest is always allowable provided the trader's capital account remains in credit. The Revenue has advised:

> 'the disallowance of overdraft interest is not automatically ruled out because a proprietor's capital account is in credit. Essentially, what matters is whether the overdraft has funded private expenditure. It would, for example, be easy enough for a trader to bring his current (or capital) account back into credit by simply up valuing his assets, but that would hardly alter the fact that the overdraft is due to personal expenditure.'

In this situation, advice should be sought from an accountant.

A slightly different treatment arises for partners. The Revenue view is that provided partners' capital accounts remain in credit overall, no restriction for interest applies as it can be reasonably argued the partners with overdrawn accounts are borrowing from those whose accounts are in credit. Note, however, that if partners raise personal loans to finance the firm, there is a disallowance of interest paid by them unless their account remains in credit (see 16.7.1).

2.1.13 Cost of raising business finance
(TA 1988, s 77)

There are often certain costs in raising long-term finance. For many years these costs were regarded as capital expenditure by the Revenue. A statutory deduction is now available provided certain conditions are satisfied:

(1) The costs must be wholly and exclusively incurred in obtaining loan finance, providing security or repaying a loan.
(2) The costs must represent expenditure on professional fees, commissions, advertising, printing or other incidental expenses in relation to raising finance.

In some cases a deduction is available even though the attempt to raise business finance failed.

The Revenue view is that premiums paid on an insurance policy do not qualify, even though the policy may have been taken out at the lender's insistence.

2.1.14 Lease rentals

The way in which lease rentals are treated depends on the type of lease. If it is an 'operating lease' (ie for a period which is less than the asset's anticipated useful life) it is normal for rentals to be deducted in arriving at the profits for the period to which the rentals refer. In practice, most leasing agreements provide for rentals to be payable in advance. For example, if a trader pays lease rentals of £12,000 on 1 December which cover a six-month period, and he makes up accounts to the following 31 March, the amount deducted in arriving at the profits for the year ended 31 March is:

$$\frac{4 \text{ months}}{6 \text{ months}} \times £12{,}000 = £8{,}000$$

The balance is relieved as an expense for the following year.

A different treatment is required where a trader pays rentals under a 'finance lease' (ie a lease agreement under which the trader acquires almost all the benefits of outright ownership). There is a special accounting standard which governs the accounting treatment of such leases, and the Revenue view is that the amount which should be deducted is that charged in the trader's accounts in accordance with SSAP 21.

2.1.15 Lease rentals on expensive cars

(CAA 1990, s 35)

Where a trader uses a leased car or provides a motor car to an employee and the original cost was £12,000 or more, part of the lease rentals must be added back as a disallowable expense. The amount disallowed is the following proportion of the lease rental:

$$\frac{1}{2} \times \frac{(\text{Cost of car} - £12{,}000)}{\text{Cost of car}}$$

Thus, if a car which cost £16,000 is leased for a rental of £2,400 per annum, the amount disallowed is:

$$\frac{1}{2} \times \frac{(£16{,}000 - 12{,}000)}{16{,}000} \times £2{,}400 = £300$$

This treatment does not apply to maintenance costs included in the lease rentals provided they are identified separately under the terms of the leasing agreement.

2.1.16 Hire purchase

Where equipment is acquired under an HP contract, the cost of the equipment counts as capital expenditure (in most cases capital allowances are available). The 'interest' element is apportioned over the term of the contract and relief is given for the amount of interest which relates to the accounting period concerned.

2.1.17 Example – Adjustments for HP contracts

A trader acquires a computer under a three-year HP agreement. The cost of the computer was £12,000, but the trader pays 36 monthly HP payments of £420. The total payments (interest and capital) amount to £15,120.

The interest payable over the three years totals £3,120. This is normally allocated roughly as follows:

Year one	£1,040
Year two	£1,040
Year three	£1,040

An alternative approach is:

Year one	£1,715
Year two	£1,040
Year three	£365

This type of allocation reflects the amount of the HP 'loan' which is outstanding during each year.

2.1.18 Legal and professional expenses

Where an inspector of taxes examines a trader's business accounts, he normally asks for an analysis of any substantial amounts relating to legal and professional expenses. The legal costs of acquiring capital assets and of renewing a lease of more than 50 years are disallowed as capital expenditure. In contrast, legal costs incurred to *protect* a capital asset are generally allowable as a revenue expense.

Professional costs incurred towards tax appeals are not allowable because they relate to tax on profits rather than an expense incurred in earning profits. However, in practice the costs of preparing and agreeing tax computations are usually allowed.

2.1.19 Rent payments and the wholly and exclusively test

Where a trader pays rent on premises but uses only part of them for his trade (perhaps living in the remaining part) only part of the rent is treated as an allowable business expense. Where he rents accommodation which is larger than he requires and he sublets part of it, the Revenue sometimes agrees to treat the lettings as a business activity. This means that the full amount of rent payable by the trader is allowable and the rent received is brought into his accounts as if it were a business receipt. However, the Revenue applies this treatment only in certain restricted circumstances and requires the following conditions to be satisfied:

- The accommodation must be temporarily surplus to current business requirements.
- The premises must be used partly for the business.
- The rental income must be comparatively small.
- The rents must be in respect of the letting of surplus business accommodation only and not of land (eg a car park).

In cases where these conditions are not satisfied, the Revenue normally applies the strict treatment and taxes the rental income received by the trader under Schedule A.

2.1.20 Relief for premiums

(TA 1988, s 87)

A trader may be required to make a lump sum payment (ie a premium) to a landlord to obtain a lease. Where the lease is for a period of less than 50 years, part of the lump sum may be treated as income in the landlord's hands and the trader may claim a deduction for this amount as if it were rent payable over the lease period. There is no relief if the lease is for more than 50 years or if the premium is paid to someone other than the landlord, since such a third party (eg an outgoing tenant) is not subject to income tax under Schedule A.

Sometimes the lease requires a tenant to have certain building work carried out to increase the value of the landlord's interest in the property. The landlord may be assessed under Schedule A on a *notional* premium. Where this applies, the trader can claim a deduction just as if he had been required to pay a premium in cash. However, the notional premium is generally far less than the actual cost of carrying out the work concerned.

2.1.21 Example – Treatment of premiums

B pays a premium of £40,000 for a lease of ten years, 82 per cent (ie £32,800) of which is taxed in the landlord's hands as Schedule A income for the year in which the premium is payable.

B can claim a deduction in his accounts for the ten years as if he had paid rent of £3,280 per annum.

If it were not for TA 1988, s 87, the expenditure would be treated as capital expenditure and would attract no relief.

2.1.22 Repairs and renewals

Problems may arise where the repairs are carried out within 12 months of the trader acquiring the premises as such expenditure may be regarded as capital (see 2.1.3). Thereafter, normal repairs to make good wear and tear are an allowable expense.

The fact that the expenditure has been capitalised in the trader's business balance sheet does not automatically preclude a claim that the costs were in fact genuine repairs and/or renewals and are therefore an allowable expense (although this is not a helpful aspect in negotiating with the Revenue).

The accounting treatment should be examined in some detail. It is not unusual to find a business that has spent £100,000 on refurbishing its premises and the whole cost has been capitalised as additions to the freehold land and buildings. However, for taxation purposes, the expenditure might be split as follows:

Reason for expenditure	*Cost* £	*Tax relief*
Improvements of buildings	40,000	No tax relief
Plant and machinery	35,000	25% Capital allowances (see 2.2.2)
Repairs and renewals	15,000	100% revenue deduction
	90,000	
Unallocated professional costs (architect/quantity surveyor fees)	10,000	See below
	£100,000	

The unallocated professional costs can sometimes be spread across the expenditure incurred (so that following the above example of costs of £10,000, £4,444 would get no allowances, £3,889 would qualify for capital allowances and £1,667 would be included with the cost of repairs); this is a contentious aspect so far as the Revenue is concerned and professional advice should be taken.

2.1.23 Refurbishments

Where a building which has been owned by the taxpayer for some years is refurbished, the Revenue allows certain expenditure to be treated as a trading expense. The Revenue has stated that:

> 'That part of the outlay (on improvements, additions and alterations) which is equal to the cost of any maintenance and repair works obviated by the alterations etc, will be allowed as a deduction, except in cases where (i) the alterations are so extensive as to amount to the reconstruction of the property or (ii) there is a change in the use of the property which would have made such maintenance or repairs unnecessary.'

The Revenue also generally allows the cost of rewiring.

VAT is generally charged on construction costs. Sometimes it is reclaimed as input tax, sometimes not. The rule for capital allowance purposes is very simple and straightforward: if the VAT paid is reclaimed, then only the net expenditure qualifies for relief. However, if the VAT is not reclaimed, capital allowances apply to the VAT inclusive expenditure.

2.1.24 Provisions against liability to pay sums after year end

This is an aspect of accounts to which inspectors of taxes pay particular attention. The Revenue needs to be satisfied that relief is not sought for expenditure which will be incurred only in the future. Consequently, an inspector will almost certainly withhold relief unless he is satisfied that a trader became liable to make the payment concerned before the year end. For example, it is often not possible to secure a deduction for redundancy costs unless the necessary redundancy notices are served by the end of the trader's accounting period (see 2.1.26). Similarly, the Revenue will argue that a provision for an amount which may be due to a client for professional negligence is not allowable unless the client's claim has been admitted by the year end. This interpretation is not free from doubt, but the difficulty of persuading an inspector to adopt a more favourable interpretation should not be underestimated. Professional advice is required if sizable amounts of tax are at issue.

There are sometimes circumstances where a payment will almost certainly be required in the future, although the precise amount has yet to be ascertained. An example contained in a recent Revenue publication concerns an insurance broker who may be required to refund commission to an insurance company if clients allow policies to lapse. The Revenue has accepted that a provision may be allowable in these circumstances provided it is arrived at scientifically by reference to past experience (*Johnston v Britannia Airways Ltd* [1994] STC 763). A 'rough and ready' general provision is not allowable.

2.1.25 Valuation of stock and work in progress

A trader's accounts should include his stock in hand at his year end (unless the cash basis applies). Stock should be valued at the *lower* of cost or net realisable value. Cost should normally include a proportion of overheads. It is not correct to look at stock in total, and take the lower of cost or net realisable value on a 'global' basis: each individual item of stock should be looked at separately.

In strictness, a traders' stock should be valued at the year end on an item-by-item basis. However, accounting convention allows groups of similar items to be considered together and net realisable value is then estimated by applying a formula to the cost of similar items of stock. The formula used normally takes into account factors such as the age and condition, past and expected future demand and the scrap or residual value of the types of stock.

Inspectors accept provisions and write-downs arrived at using formulae provided the formula reflects a realistic appraisal of the future income from the stock concerned and results in the stock being included at a reasonable estimate of its net realisable value. Inspectors are likely to challenge provisions and write-downs based on unrealistic assumptions which produce a significant effect on the tax liability for the year.

Similarly, work in progress should be valued at the year end at the lower of cost or realisable value. Where the accounts relate to a profession, it is not necessary to include in cost the time value of work put in by the sole proprietor or partner since this represents the proprietor's profit rather than a cost incurred in carrying on the profession.

The treatment of long-term work in progress can involve complex issues and should be discussed with the firm's accountant.

2.1.26 Redundancy payments

Under general Case I and II rules, redundancy payments are normally an allowable deduction provided that:

- They are laid out wholly and exclusively for business purposes.
- The payments are not of a capital nature.

Where redundancy payments are made in the course of the discontinuance of a trade they are not admissible as a deduction under normal rules (see *IRC v Anglo Brewing Co Ltd* (1925) 12 TC 803).

Where a sum is not deductible under the general Case I rules, TA 1988, ss 90 and 579 may still provide a deduction for:

- Statutory redundancy payments.
- Additional payments, inadmissible on the *Anglo Brewing* principle, up to three times the statutory payment made.

Timing of deduction

Where a deduction is due under the general rules, the Revenue view is that a provision for future payments may be allowed as a deduction provided that:

- the provision appears in the business's accounts in accordance with generally accepted accounting principles, including those in para 18 of Financial Reporting Standard 3 (where applicable); and
- a definite decision was made during the period of account to proceed with the redundancy programme; and
- the provision was accurately calculated using the degree of hindsight permitted by SSAP 17; and
- payment was made within nine months of the end of the period of account, as required by FA 1989, s 43.

Where the right to a tax deduction is dependent on TA 1988, ss 90 or 579, then relief is due for the period of account in which the payment is made. If the payment is made after the discontinuance of the business, it is regarded for tax relief purposes as if it was made on the last day on which the business was carried on.

2.2 CAPITAL ALLOWANCES

2.2.1 Introduction

A trader is entitled to capital allowances on plant and machinery which is used in the trade. Capital allowances are also available on commercial buildings located in an enterprise zone, agricultural buildings, industrial buildings and hotels, and may be claimed for expenditure on know-how and scientific research expenditure. All these are dealt with differently, and various rates of initial and annual allowances are given.

2.2.2 Allowances for plant and machinery
(CAA 1990, s 24)

Plant and machinery attracts a 25 per cent writing-down allowance. Expenditure is deemed to be incurred when a trader enters into an unconditional contract; it is not necessary that the trader should have actually paid for it or have brought it into use by his year end (there is an exception for plant and machinery which is acquired under an HP contract). Abortive expenditure on plant (eg a deposit paid on machinery which is never actually delivered) may also qualify for allowances (see *Tax Bulletin*, February 1992).

Writing-down allowances are computed on the balance of the 'pool' at the year end. The opening balance of the pool represents the cost of plant and machinery brought forward from previous years, less the capital allowances already received. A trader receives writing-down allowances based on the opening balance, plus the cost of additional plant and machinery acquired during the year, less any disposal proceeds.

2.2.3 Example – Writing-down allowances

A and *B* are in partnership. In their year to 31 March 1996 they acquired plant and machinery at a cost of £30,000 and received capital allowances of £7,500.

During their year ended 31 March 1997, they sell some of this plant for £2,000 and buy new plant for £20,000. Their pool would be as follows:

	£
Written-down value brought forward at 1 April 1996	22,500
Additions during year ended 31 March 1997	20,000
	42,500
Less disposal proceeds	(2,000)
	40,500
Less writing-down allowances (25 per cent)	(10,125)
Written-down value carried forward	30,375

For certain categories of expenditure, and for a limited period only, small and medium-sized businesses benefit from a doubling of the rate of capital allowances in the first year. Thus for expenditure on machinery or plant incurred during the 12 months ended 1 July 1988 the new rate of 50 per cent applies to the first year for which allowances are due. Where, exceptionally, the long life asset rules apply (see 2.2.11) the rate is doubled, from 6 per cent to 12 per cent. For subsequent years, allowances are due on the balance remaining at 25 per cent or 6 per cent as the case may be.

The temporary increase applies to businesses which are small or medium-sized using the Companies Act definitions. These are broadly that it satisfies two of the following conditions:

- a turnover of not more than £11,200,000;
- assets of not more than £5,600,000; and
- not more than 250 employees; or
- the company was small or medium-sized for the previous year.

For companies, the company must be small or medium-sized for the year in which the expenditure is incurred to qualify for the increased rate. If the company is a member of a group, the group as a whole must be small or medium-sized, applying the above criteria. The increased rate also applies to businesses carried on by individuals and partnerships made up of individuals, provided the business would qualify if it were carried on by a company.

The increased rate does not apply to expenditure on machinery and plant for leasing, cars, sea-going ships and railway assets. Nor does it apply to expenditure which is excluded from the rules on long life assets under the transitional rules (broadly long life assets bought on or after 26 November 1996 under a contract entered into before that date).

2.2.4 Definition of disposal proceeds

Disposal proceeds are the proceeds of sale or (where the asset has been damaged, lost or destroyed) the insurance or compensation moneys. Normally, the disposal proceeds to be brought in are limited to the trader's original expenditure on the item of plant concerned. If an item of plant is given away, or retained by the trader for his private use, the disposal value is the market value of the plant.

2.2.5 Assets kept separately from the pool

(CAA 1990, ss 34 and 79)

Certain other assets are kept separate from the pool. One particular category is assets which are used partly for trade purposes and partly for other purposes. For example, a van used by a sole trader for 40 per cent business and 60 per cent private use is deemed to form a separate pool. The trader is entitled to 'scaled down' allowances, ie he receives 40 per cent of the full writing-down allowance and 40 per cent of any balancing allowance. 'Short life' assets are also kept separate (see 2.2.10).

2.2.6 Expensive motor cars

(CAA 1990, ss 34–36)

Motor cars which cost more than £12,000 must be kept separate from the pool. The maximum writing-down allowance for such a car is £3,000, but a balancing allowance (or charge) arises on disposal.

2.2.7 Example – Writing-down allowances for motor cars

A operates an advertising business. He makes up his accounts to 30 April. He is assessed on the current year basis (see 16.2). On 1 May 1997 he acquired a car which costs £30,000 and this is used by an employee. After two years, the car is sold for £10,000.

The car is deemed to be in a separate pool; the position is as follows:

		£
Year 1:	Cost	30,000
	Writing-down allowance for 1997–98	(3,000)
		27,000
Year 2:	Writing-down allowance for 1998–99	(3,000)
		24,000
Year 3:	disposal proceeds	(10,000)
Balancing allowance for 1998–99		14,000

2.2.8 Assets brought into use part way through a year

(CAA 1990, ss 24(2) and 60)

An asset which is acquired towards the end of a trader's accounting period still attracts the full 25 per cent allowance *unless* the trade has not been going for 12 months. In such a case, under s 24(2), the 25 per cent allowance may be scaled down.

2.2.9 Example – Assets bought in year that trade is commenced

B commenced trading on 5 October 1996. On 5 April 1997 he acquired plant and machinery for £60,000.

The capital allowances due to him for 1996–97 are:

$$\frac{6}{12} \times 25\% \times £60{,}000 = \underline{\underline{£7{,}500}}$$

Allowances are normally due where a trader incurred qualifying expenditure by his year end by entering into an unconditional contract to purchase the plant and machinery. He does not need actually to have brought it into use by his year end unless the plant and machinery is acquired under an HP contract.

2.2.10 Short life assets

(CAA 1990, ss 37–38)

Where expenditure is added to the pool, the trader receives writing-down allowances which are likely to get smaller and smaller. For example, a trader invests expenditure of £100,000 on plant in year one. He does not acquire any other plant and machinery for five years. His writing-down allowance in year one is £25,000 (ie 25 per cent of £100,000), £18,750 in year two (ie 25 per cent of the residual £75,000) and so on. By the end of year five, the written-down value will be just under £24,000 but the equipment itself may be worn out and have a scrap value of only, say, £2,000.

To cover this type of situation, the legislation allows for a trader to designate certain assets as short life assets. The cost of these assets is kept in a separate pool and a balancing allowance (or charge) arises on a sale within five years, or on the assets being scrapped by then. If an asset is not sold within that period, the written-down value of the asset is transferred to the pool.

(1) In the above example, if the plant and machinery is actually scrapped at the start of year five and the trader receives no scrap value at all, he receives a balancing allowance of £31,640.

(2) Using the same basic facts, if the plant and machinery is still in use at the end of year five, the written-down value of £23,730 is transferred to the trader's pool of other plant and machinery.

The following cannot be short life assets:

- motor cars
- assets used partly for non-trade purposes
- assets originally acquired for non-trade purposes (for example, assets acquired prior to the trade being commenced)
- ships
- certain assets leased-out in the course of a trade.

An election needs to be made for an asset to be treated as a short life asset. This must be submitted to the inspector within two years of the accounting period in which the short life asset is acquired. The inspector will require sufficient information to be able to identify the assets at a later stage (see SP1/86).

2.2.11 Long life assets

(CAA 1990, ss 38A–38H)

A new, lower rate of writing-down allowance was introduced by FA 1997 for expenditure on long life assets. Under the rules, which apply in general to expenditure on long life assets incurred from 26 November 1996, machinery and plant is treated as a long life asset if its expected useful economic life when new is at least 25 years. This is measured from when it is first used as a fixed asset of a business, until it ceases altogether to be so used by anybody as a fixed asset of a business. When an asset changes hands, it is classified as a long life asset if it was a long life asset in the hands of the first owner, or would have been but for the *de minimis* provisions.

A number of categories of expenditure are specifically excluded from the general definition. Thus long life assets do not include any machinery or plant which is a fixture in, or is used in, a dwelling-house, retail shop, showroom, hotel or office or for ancillary purposes. Also there are specific exclusions for motor or hire cars, sea-going ships (until 2011) and railway assets (until 2011). There is a transitional exception for expenditure contracted for before 26 November 1996 and incurred by 31 December 2000 and to which the long life rules do not apply. Expenditure on long life assets is segregated into a separate pool which qualifies for writing-down allowances at 6 per cent instead of 25 per cent. This categorisation of an asset as long life is irrevocable and it cannot later be reclassified as non-long life.

The new restrictions are unlikely to apply to most small businesses, as there are parallel *de minimis* exclusions for individuals and partnerships and for companies. Thus the long life asset provisions do not apply if expenditure on such assets incurred by a sole trader or partnership of individuals does not exceed £100,000 in a period of 12 months. The *de minimis* limit is proportionately reduced for shorter periods. It is important to note that, if the £100,000 limit is exceeded, the restrictions apply to the whole of the expenditure.

It is also required that the individual, or at least half the partners, must work full time in the business. This is to prevent business being artificially split so as to obtain the higher rate of allowance on expenditure below the *de minimis* threshold. Expenditure on a share in machinery or plant, or on providing machinery or plant for leasing, does not qualify for the *de minimis* exclusion. Where expenditure, under a contract for the purchase of machinery or plant, is to be incurred in more than one period, all of the expenditure is treated as being incurred in the first period.

For companies, the *de minimis* figure of £100,000 is divided equally among the number of associated companies. This is similar to the restriction on the application of the small companies corporation tax rate relief in TA 1988, s 13 (see 18.2.7).

A form of tax avoidance by obtaining a balancing allowance or avoiding a balancing charge is prevented. This is achieved by providing that, when a long life asset is disposed of at less than its written-down value, and it is shown that the main object, or one of the main objects, of the disposal is tax avoidance, the asset is deemed to be disposed of at written-down value.

2.2.12 What is plant and machinery?

Until FA 1994 was enacted, there was no definition of 'plant and machinery' within the Taxes Acts. Even after the introduction of specific legislation, the position remains unclear. The statutory definition focuses mainly on what is *not* plant as it forms part of a building and the Revenue's practice and interpretation are still largely based on decisions handed down by the courts.

The earliest judicial definition was provided in *Yarmouth v France* (1887) 19 QBD 647, in which Lindley LJ stated:

> '. . . in its ordinary sense, it includes whatever apparatus is used by a business man for carrying on his business, not his stock-in-trade which he buys or makes for sale; but all goods or chattels, fixed or moveable, live or dead, which he keeps for permanent employment in his business . . .'

Some items are clearly within this definition (eg typewriters, dictating machines, telephone equipment, computers, manufacturing equipment, vans and other motor vehicles). What is less obvious is that a building may contain items which are plant and machinery. In some cases the plant will have become part of the building (eg a lift). Also, there may be structures which are items of plant (eg a dry dock or a grain silo, or a mezzanine floor put into a factory to create storage space).

The courts have also adopted a 'function' test. In *Jarrold v John Good & Sons Ltd* (1962) 40 TC 681, CA, Pearson LJ stated:

> 'The short question in this case is whether the (partitioning) is part of the premises in which the business is carried on or part of the plant with which the business is carried on . . .'

This judgment distinguishes between expenditure which forms part of the setting from which the trade is carried on (ie not plant) and apparatus with which the business is carried on (ie plant). This functional test has been reiterated in subsequent decisions.

2.2.13 Expenditure on fixtures and fittings

One contentious area involves cosmetic improvements on fixtures and fittings. To qualify for capital allowances, it must be demonstrated that the fixtures and fittings perform a useful function in the trade and are not merely part of the 'setting' in which the trade is carried on.

In the leading case of *IRC v Scottish and Newcastle Breweries Ltd* [1982] STC 296 the proprietors of a chain of hotels and public houses had incurred considerable expenditure on cosmetic improvements including decorative lighting and murals. They claimed that their business was not simply to sell food and drink to the public, but also to provide a pleasant 'atmosphere' or 'ambience' in which those staples of life could be consumed. The purpose of the decorations was to produce that 'atmosphere' and therefore those decorations performed a useful trade function. This approach was upheld by the House of Lords. However, see also *Wimpy International Ltd v Warland* [1988] STC 149 where it was held that mere decorative finishing such as wall and floor tiles cannot be plant.

Bear in mind also that the Special Commissioners have ruled that a painting in a bank's boardroom did not constitute plant. This case was heard some years ago, before the House of Lords' decision in *Scottish and Newcastle*, but is nevertheless still relevant for firms of solicitors and other professional firms who may meet resistance from the Revenue on cosmetic expenditure on rooms used for meetings with clients.

2.2.14 Expenditure on a building

Expenditure on a building does not normally qualify as expenditure on plant and machinery. However, there are exceptions to this general rule and the legislation contains a table which lists items which may still rank as plant and machinery even though they are comprised in a building. Although an asset may appear in the following table, it does not necessarily qualify for capital allowances, but entitlement to allowances is not precluded simply because the asset forms part of a building.

Capital allowances are due on building work which is needed to enable plant and machinery to be installed – this would apply if a floor has to be strengthened to install a computer.

Table 2.1 Assets included in building or structure which may nevertheless qualify as machinery or plant

Assets included in the expression 'building'	*Assets so included, but expenditure may be eligible for allowances*
A Walls, floors, ceilings, doors, gates, shutters, windows and stairs.	1 Electrical, cold water, gas and sewerage systems – (a) provided mainly to meet the particular requirements of the trade, or (b) provided mainly to serve particular machinery or plant used for the purpose of the trade.
	2 Space or water heating systems; powered systems of ventilation, air cooling or air purification; and any ceiling or floor comprised in such systems.
B Mains services, and systems, of water, electricity and gas	3 Manufacturing or processing equipment; storage equipment, including cold rooms; display equipment; and counters, check-outs and similar equipment.
	4 Cookers, washing machines, dishwashers, refrigerators and similar equipment; washbasins, sinks, baths, showers, sanitary ware and similar equipment; and furniture and furnishings.
C Waste disposal systems.	5 Lifts, hoists, escalators and moving walkways.
	6 Sound insulation provided mainly to meet the particular requirements of the trade.

Table 2.1 *Cont.*

Assets included in the expression 'building'	*Assets so included, but expenditure may be eligible for allowances*
D Sewerage and drainage systems.	7 Computer, telecommunication and surveillance systems (including their wiring or other links).
	8 Refrigeration or cooling equipment.
E Shafts or other structures in which lifts, hoists, escalators and moving walkways are installed.	9 Sprinkler equipment and other equipment for extinguishing or containing fire; fire alarm systems.
	10 Burglar alarm systems.
	11 Any machinery (including devices for providing motive power) not within any other item in this column.
F Fire safety systems.	12 Strong rooms in bank or building society premises; safes.
	13 Partition walls, where moveable and intended to be moved in the course of the trade.
	14 Decorative assets provided for the enjoyment of the public in the hotel, restaurant or similar trades.
	15 Advertising hoardings; and signs, displays and similar assets.
	16 Swimming pools (including diving boards, slides and structures on which such boards or slides are mounted).

Generally expenditure on the provision of structure or other assets, as listed in column 1 in Table 2.2 below, or any works involving the alteration of land does not qualify as machinery or plant.

Table 2.2 Assets included in building or structure not qualifying as machinery or plant

Structures and assets	*Assets so included, but expenditure may be eligible for allowances*
A Any tunnel, bridge, viaduct, aqueduct, embankment or cutting.	1 Expenditure on the alteration of land for the purpose only of installing machinery or plant.
B Any way or hard standing, such as a pavement, road, railway or tramway, a park for vehicles or containers, or an airstrip or runway.	2 Expenditure on the provision of dry docks.

Table 2.2 ***Cont.***

Structures and assets	*Assets so included, but expenditure may be eligible for allowances*
	3 Expenditure on the provision of any jetty or similar structure provided mainly to carry machinery or plant.
C Any inland navigation, including a canal or basin or a navigable river.	4 Expenditure on the provision of pipelines or underground ducts or tunnels with a primary purpose of carrying utility conduits.
	5 Expenditure on the provision of towers provided to support floodlights.
D Any dam, reservoir or barrage (including any sluices, gates, generators and other equipment associated with it).	6 Expenditure on the provision of any reservoir incorporated into a water treatment works or on the provision of any service reservoir of treated water for supply within any housing estate or other particular locality.
E Any dock including (a) any harbour, wharf, pier, marina or jetty, and (b) any other structure in or at which vessels may be kept or merchandise or passengers may be shipped or unshipped.	7 Expenditure on the provision of silos provided for temporary storage or on the provision of storage tanks. 8 Expenditure on the provision of slurry pits or silage clamps.
F Any dike, sea wall, weir or drainage ditch.	9 Expenditure on the provision of fish tanks or fish ponds.
G Any structure not within any other item in this column.	10 Expenditure on the provision of rails, sleepers and ballast for a railway or tramway.
	11 Expenditure on the provision of structures and other assets for providing the setting for any ride at an amusement park or exhibition.
	12 Expenditure on the provision of fixed zoo cages.

2.2.15 Expenditure on landlord's and tenant's fixtures

There are detailed rules to give capital allowances on plant and machinery which becomes a fixture in a building. The Court of Appeal's decision in *Stokes v Costain Property Investment Co Ltd* [1984] STC 204 established that capital allowances were not due on expenditure on plant by a tenant where the plant became part of a building and therefore became a landlord's fixture. The reason for this was that the items did not 'belong' to the tenant. This situation was obviously unsatisfactory as tenants are often required to install plant such as lifts, air conditioning and so on. Accordingly, the legislation was amended.

Now, if a person incurs capital expenditure on the provision of machinery or plant for the purpose of a trade, and the machinery or plant becomes a fixture, then, if he has an interest in the building or land of which the fixture is a part, it is treated as belonging to him.

This also applies where such expenditure is incurred for leasing otherwise than in the course of a trade (ie an equipment lessor). However, the rules are modified in such a case. Thus, where an equipment lessor incurs expenditure on machinery or plant which is leased directly or indirectly to an equipment lessee, for the purposes of a trade carried on by the equipment lessee, and the machinery or plant becomes a fixture on which the equipment lessee would have been entitled to an allowance if he had incurred the capital expenditure, the equipment lessor and lessee can elect that the fixture be treated as belonging to the equipment lessor. After 23 July 1996 it is a condition that the lessee be liable for tax, thus reversing the decision in *Melluish v BMI (No 3) Ltd* [1995] STC 964.

From 19 March 1997, allowances are available on fixtures leased to non-taxpayers (eg local authorities) provided that:

(1) the fixture is attached to land, and not a building;
(2) the lessee has an interest in the land;
(3) the lessor can remove the fixture at the end of the lease;
(4) the fixture belongs to the lessor when removed;
(5) the fixture can be re-used elsewhere; and
(6) the lessor treats the lease as an operating lease.

This reverses the decision of the Special Commissioners in *J C Decaux (UK) Ltd v Francis* [1996] STI 1041.

For income tax purposes, the election must be made by the first anniversary of 31 January next following the end of the tax year in which the chargeable period in which the equipment lessor incurs the expenditure falls (ie a period of 22 months after the end of that tax year; this ties in with the latest date by which a tax return must be filed under self-assessment). For corporation tax purposes the time limit is within two years of the end of the accounting period in which the equipment lessor incurs the expenditure. It is, however, not possible to make an election where the equipment lessor and the equipment lessee are connected persons, and where an election has been made the fixture cannot be treated as belonging to the equipment lessee who, typically, being a non-taxpayer, could not make use of the allowances.

After machinery or plant has become a fixture, if a person acquires an existing interest in the land to which the fixture is attached, and the consideration given is treated as capital expenditure on providing the fixture, it is deemed to belong to the purchaser. Furthermore, where machinery or plant has become a fixture, and a lessor, who would otherwise be entitled to an allowance thereon, grants a lease such that the lessee incurs capital expenditure on the fixture, it may, on a joint election by the lessor and lessee, be treated as belonging to the lessee. The election must be made within two years of the grant of the lease; again, it cannot be made between connected persons.

A fixture is treated as belonging to a lessee where, after it has become a fixture, a lessor, who would not himself be entitled to an allowance, grants a lease, or the lessee incurs capital expenditure on the fixture and the fixture has not been used by the lessor or a connected person in his trade.

Where the same or different persons could claim allowances by holding different interests in land, priority is given to whichever interest was held first. If no claim is made in respect of the interest held first, the holder of the other interest may claim.

For disposals made before 25 July 1996, where an interest in land which includes a fixture is acquired, and allowances have been claimed on that asset by a previous owner, the amount on which the new owner can claim allowances is restricted to the disposal value of the last owner to claim allowances. The new owner can claim allowances on installation costs if he incurs them. The effect of this is to limit the allowances which can be claimed on a fixture to its original cost. The original cost is the cost to the person who owned it on 24 July 1996 if he claimed allowances, or otherwise the cost to the first person it belongs to after 24 July 1996 who claims allowances. Where a fixture is sold as a chattel to an unconnected person either before affixation or following severance and before re-affixation, this rule starts with the cost to the first owner after that sale who claims allowances, ignoring the disposal value on that or any previous disposal.

Where an industrial buildings allowance (IBA) has been claimed by a previous owner on expenditure on a fixture, the amount on which machinery and plant allowances can be claimed is limited to the unrelieved expenditure. This is computed by apportioning the residue of the expenditure of the previous owner immediately after the disposal, as defined for IBA purposes, between the fixture and any other property included in the disposal.

Where scientific research allowance has been claimed by a previous owner on expenditure on a fixture, the amount on which machinery and plant allowances can be claimed by a subsequent owner is limited to the unrelieved expenditure. This is the lower of the part of the disposal value and the part of the cost of the previous owner attributable to the fixture, apportioning the disposal value and cost between the fixture and any other property included in the disposal or acquisition respectively.

The normal disposal value rules apply where the person to whom a fixture is treated as belonging ceases to hold the qualifying interest other than on a merger, a new lease of the same land, or the lessee remaining in occupation on the termination of a lease. A fixture is treated as ceasing to belong to the lessor if it is treated as belonging to a lessee; and it is treated as ceasing to belong to a lessee on the termination of his interest in the property, in which case it is treated as beginning to belong to the lessor or licensor. Where a fixture is permanently severed from the land to which it is attached, it is to be treated as ceasing to belong to the deemed owner unless on severance it does actually belong to him.

Where an equipment lessor assigns his rights under the equipment lease, or the lessee's obligations under the lease are terminated, the fixture is treated as ceasing to belong to the equipment lessor. However, the assignee takes over the assignor's rights and the amount paid for the assignment is treated both as the price received for the sale of the fixture by the assignor and as expenditure incurred by the assignee in acquiring the machinery or plant which is the subject of the equipment lease. Any capital sum received by the lessor from the lessee is to be treated both as the sale price of the fixture received by the lessor and as the cost of providing it incurred by the lessee, to whom it is to be treated as belonging thereafter.

Where a fixture is treated as ceasing to belong to any person and the qualifying interest continues, or is merged in another interest, the disposal value is that proportion of the price which on a sale of the qualifying interest in the open market would be treated as capital expenditure on the provision of the fixture. Where the fixture is treated as ceasing to belong to any person and the qualifying interest is a lease which comes to an end or has less than seven years to run, the fixture's open market value is calculated on the assumption that the lease still has seven years to run.

A vendor is treated as having disposed of a fixture for its notional written-down value where it is disposed of for less than that amount as part, or in pursuance, of a scheme or arrangement which has avoidance as its main, or one of its main, objects. The notional written-down value is computed by writing down the cost of the asset at 25 per cent a year, or 6 per cent a year if it is a long life asset (see 2.2.11). Avoidance broadly means obtaining a balancing allowance or avoiding a balancing charge.

If an interest in land to which a fixture is attached is sold or acquired, the purchaser and vendor can jointly elect to determine the amount apportioned to the fixture. This fixes the disposal value to the vendor and the cost to the purchaser. It may not exceed either the cost of the fixture to the vendor or the sum to be apportioned. The remainder of the sum to be apportioned is attributed for capital allowance purposes to the other property included in the sale and is apportioned under CAA 1990, s 150 between that property where necessary.

For Revenue comments on fixtures leases and SP 3/91, see the *Tax Bulletin*, Issue 15, February 1995, p 189, para 8.

2.2.16 Fire safety expenditure
(CAA 1990, s 69)

Certain expenditure on a building can be treated as if it were expenditure on plant and machinery. The condition which must be satisfied is that the expenditure is incurred to comply with the requirements of a fire authority under s 5(4) of the Fire Precautions Act 1971 and to obtain a fire certificate issued under that Act. The Act applies to hotels, boarding houses, factories, shops and offices. However, certain businesses are outside the Act (eg nursing homes) and there are no allowances for fire safety expenditure on such premises unless the work is required under a court order made under s 10 of the Act.

2.2.17 Expenditure on second-hand buildings

When a building changes hands, the new owner is entitled to claim capital allowances on the qualifying fixtures and fittings he has purchased. However, some very complex provisions govern the amount of those allowances. As a general rule:

(1) If the vendor incurred capital expenditure on the relevant fixtures and fittings before 12 July 1984, the purchaser may base his capital allowance claim on the price he (the purchaser) actually paid for them – taken, if necessary, as a proportion of the total price paid for the building – even if (because of inflation) that price was more than the original cost to the vendor of installing them.
(2) If the vendor incurred capital expenditure on the relevant fixtures and fittings after 11 July 1984, the purchaser's claim is generally limited to the lesser of the price actually paid and the vendor's original cost.

It follows from (1) above that worthwhile allowances may be available even on very old buildings. Suppose a company buys a pre-war, unmodernised building from a vendor who has owned the premises since 1955. The purchaser is entitled to say that a proportion of the price he paid was for fixtures and fittings which qualify, as 'plant and machinery', for capital allowances. That proportion is arrived at according to the current value of the fixtures and fittings, not their original cost. In practice, the amount may have to be negotiated and the vendor may have an interest in the matter since he may suffer a balancing charge by reference to the amount apportioned to plant and machinery.

2.2.18 Buildings located in enterprise zones

(CAA 1990, s 1)

Qualifying expenditure on a commercial building located in an enterprise zone can qualify for a 100 per cent initial allowance. A commercial building is defined by s 21(5) as a 'building or structure, other than an industrial building or . . . hotel, which is used for the purposes of a trade, profession or vocation or . . . an office'. The definition specifically excludes a building which is wholly or partly used as a dwellinghouse. Certain conditions must be fulfilled:

(1) The building must have been constructed under an unconditional contract entered into before the enterprise zone came to the end of its designated life.
(2) The building must be acquired unused or within two years of its having been let for the first time.

The part of the purchase price which relates to the cost of the land does not qualify for capital allowances. Plant and machinery contained in the building which have become an integral part of the building may also qualify for the 100 per cent allowance.

The initial allowance can be disclaimed, in whole or in part, and the remaining amount of qualifying expenditure is then available for 25 per cent writing-down allowances on a straight line basis over four years, rather than on the reducing basis which applies for plant and machinery.

2.2.19 Example – capital allowances on buildings in enterprise zone

An enterprise zone building is acquired for £200,000. The land cost is £20,000, so £180,000 qualifies for capital allowances. The purchaser disclaims the whole of the initial allowance. He will then receive annual allowances as follows:

	£
Year of expenditure	45,000
Year 2	45,000
Year 3	45,000
Year 4	45,000

If the purchaser had disclaimed only £80,000, the position would have been:

	£
Year of expenditure	100,000
Initial allowance	45,000
Annual allowance	145,000
Year 2 annual allowance	35,000
Year 3 annual allowance	nil
Year 4 annual allowance	nil

Note that the annual allowances are based on the total qualifying costs, not on the balance left over after deducting the initial allowance.

2.2.20 Example – Disposal of building in enterprise zone

A disposal of an enterprise zone building within 25 years of acquisition gives rise to a balancing charge.

An individual acquires an enterprise zone building in year one and takes the full 100 per cent initial allowance on the qualifying expenditure of £95,000. In year four he disposes of the building.

If he receives disposal proceeds of £75,000, there will be a balancing charge of £75,000. If he receives £120,000 (ie more than the trader's qualifying expenditure) the balancing charge is limited to £95,000.

2.2.21 Industrial buildings

(CAA 1990, s 3)

Qualifying expenditure on an industrial building normally attracts 4 per cent annual allowances. Qualifying expenditure is normally limited to the original cost so that the purchaser of a second-hand building receives allowances based on the amount on which the previous owner qualified for IBA.

Expenditure on an unused building during the year ended 31 October 1993 qualified for an initial allowance of 20 per cent. A balancing charge or allowance may arise on a disposal within 25 years.

2.2.22 Example – Disposal of industrial buildings

An industrial building was acquired in November 1992 for a cost of £250,000. The land element was £20,000. If the purchaser brought the building into use immediately, allowances would be due as follows:

		£
Year 1 –	Qualifying cost	230,000
	Initial allowance	(46,000)
		184,000
Year 1 –	Annual allowance	(9,200)
Residue		174,800
Year 2 –	Annual allowance	(9,200)
Residue		£165,600

If the building is sold at the end of year three, a balancing allowance or charge arises according to whether the proceeds exceed £165,600. If the proceeds were £175,000 there would be a balancing charge of £9,400. If the proceeds were £150,000 there would be a balancing allowance of £15,600. The maximum balancing charge would be £64,400, ie the allowance received in year one and year two.

A purchaser who paid £250,000 would be entitled to allowances on the original qualifying costs of £230,000 and would be able to claim an annual allowance of 1/23 for each of the following 23 years.

2.2.23 Definition of industrial building

(CAA 1990, s 18)

An industrial building is a building or structure which is used for the purpose of a trade consisting of:

(1) the manufacture or processing of goods or materials;
(2) the maintaining or repairing of goods or materials for customers;
(3) the maintaining or repairing of goods or materials owned by the trader himself provided that the relevant trade consists of the manufacture or processing of goods or materials;
(4) the storage of:
    (a) raw materials for manufacture;
    (b) goods to be processed;
    (c) goods manufactured or processed, but not yet delivered to any purchaser; and
    (d) goods on arrival in the United Kingdom; and
(5) the working of mines, oil wells etc or foreign plantations.

In addition, a sports pavilion provided for the welfare of workers employed in any trade qualifies for IBA.

Where part of the building is used for a non-qualifying purpose (eg an office), allowances are still available on the total purchase price provided the non-qualifying part is no more than 25 per cent. Qualifying expenditure is exclusive of the land element in the purchase price.

There are a number of cases on the question of whether a building qualifies as an industrial building; professional advice should be taken.

2.2.24 Hotels

(CAA 1990, ss 7 and 19)

A qualifying hotel attracts IBA. The hotel must fulfil the following conditions:

(1) Accommodation must be provided in a building of a permanent nature.
(2) The hotel must be open for at least four months during April–October.
(3) There must be at least ten bedrooms available for letting to the public in general which must not normally be in the same occupation for more than a month.
(4) The services provided must normally include the provision of breakfast and evening meals, making beds and cleaning rooms.

2.2.25 Agricultural buildings allowances

(CAA 1990, s 123)

The term 'agricultural buildings allowances' is slightly misleading in that the expenditure does not need to be on a building. The allowances are given for expenditure on farmhouses, farm or forestry buildings, cottages, fences, ditches, drainage and sewerage works. The *land* must be used for agricultural purposes.

Expenditure on agricultural buildings qualifies only for a 4 per cent annual allowance (given on a straight line basis rather than on the reducing balance). A balancing allowance or charge may arise on a disposal taking place within a period of 25 years.

2.2.26 Expenditure on 'know-how'

(TA 1988, s 530)

Expenditure on acquiring know-how for use in a trade attracts capital allowances. Writing-down allowances of 25 per cent are given on 'qualifying expenditure' which is the aggregate of any capital expenditure on know-how during the basis period, together with any unused balance of expenditure brought forward from the previous basis period, less any disposal value for know-how which has been sold. 'Qualifying expenditure' is defined as expenditure on any industrial information and techniques of assistance in manufacturing or processing goods or materials, or working or searching for mineral deposits, or which may be relevant to agricultural, forestry or fishing operations. This definition does not cover capital expenditure on commercial know-how which does not assist directly in the manufacturing and processing of goods and materials, eg know-how on how to market, package or distribute a manufactured product.

2.2.27 Expenditure on scientific research

(CAA 1990, ss 136–139)

Expenditure incurred by a trader on scientific research related to his trade attracts scientific research allowances. 'Scientific research' is defined as activities in the fields of natural or applied science for the extension of knowledge. A free booklet (CA4: Allowances for scientific research) which defines the above terms, is available from the Inland Revenue.

Qualifying expenditure

Any current expenditure on research (eg research workers' salaries and fees, cost of materials, and repair and maintenance of equipment) is allowed as revenue expenditure. Similarly, a trader may be able to claim a tax deduction for sums:

(1) paid to an approved scientific research association;
(2) to be used for scientific research which are paid to an approved university, college, research institute or other similar institution.

Capital expenditure

A 100 per cent allowance is given for capital expenditure such as the provision of laboratories, pilot plant, and other research equipment. The expenditure need not be on plant and machinery as defined for capital allowance purposes. Residential accommodation which forms part of a building used for scientific research can also qualify provided its cost is not more than 25 per cent of the cost of the whole building.

The legislation does not impose a balancing charge where a building or item of plant or machinery ceases to be used for scientific research purposes and is then used for some other purpose. However, when the asset concerned is eventually sold, the proceeds must be treated as a trading receipt. Also, where an asset is destroyed, any compensation or insurance proceeds must be brought into account as a trading receipt.

2.3 PRE-TRADING EXPENDITURE

(TA 1988, s 401; CAA 1990, s 83(2))

A person may incur expenditure before he starts to trade such as:

- Rent for business premises
- Rates, insurance, heating and lighting
- Bank charges and interest
- Wages or other payments to employees
- Lease rentals on plant and machinery and office equipment
- Accountancy fees
- Advertising costs.

Expenditure qualifies for relief only if it is incurred within seven years of the date that the trade is commenced. Pre-trading revenue expenditure is treated as having been incurred on the first day of trading. Pre-trading capital expenditure which qualifies for capital allowances is treated as having been incurred at the date the trade is commenced. Capital allowances are then due in the same way as allowances are given for expenditure incurred during the first period of trading.

3

MAIN PRINCIPLES OF CAPITAL GAINS TAX

This chapter covers the following:

(1) Basic outline of capital gains tax
(2) Who is subject to capital gains tax?
(3) What assets are chargeable assets?
(4) Which types of transaction may produce a chargeable gain?
(5) Computation of capital gains
(6) Some special problem areas

3.1 BASIC OUTLINE OF CAPITAL GAINS TAX

An individual's capital gains are assessed for a tax year. The due date for payment of tax is 31 January following the tax year concerned (ie for 1997–98 payment is due on 31 January 1999). The way in which chargeable gains are computed is quite different from the rules which determine assessable income for tax purposes. A range of exemptions and reliefs may apply and there is a major distinction between CGT and income tax in that allowance is made for inflation in computing capital gains.

3.1.1 Annual exemption

(TCGA 1992, s 3)

An individual is entitled to an annual exemption, as follows:

	£
1997–98	6,500
1996–97	6,300
1995–96	6,000
1994–95	5,800
1993–94	5,800
1992–93	5,800

A company is not entitled to an annual exemption.

3.1.2 No gain/loss on spouse transactions
(TCGA 1992, s 58)

There is no chargeable gain on any assets transferred from one spouse to the other, whether by gift or sale. The asset is treated as passing across on a no gain/no loss basis, with the recipient acquiring it at his spouse's cost plus indexation to date (see 3.5.7 on indexation relief). The only exception to this rule is where the couple is separated on a permanent basis.

3.1.3 Losses
(TCGA 1992, s 16)

Losses may also arise. The normal rule is that capital losses cannot be off-set against a person's income but may be carried forward against capital gains of future years. However, losses arising from transactions involving connected persons may only be set against gains arising from transactions with the same person. Brought forward losses do not need to be set against gains which are covered by the annual exemption. However, current year losses must be set against capital gains before using the annual exemption.

3.1.4 Rate of tax for individuals
(TCGA 1992, s 4)

Once an individual's gains for a tax year have been computed (net of any losses), the annual exemption is deducted. The balance is then added to the individual's taxable income and the CGT is normally ascertained by working out the additional income tax which would be payable if the capital gains had been taxable income.

3.1.5 Rate of tax for companies

A company's chargeable gains are taxed as part of its overall profits, with no differentiation from its income. The effective rate of corporation tax on its gains for the financial year 1997–98 (beginning on 1 April 1997) is 31 per cent (full rate), 21 per cent (small companies rate) or 33.5 per cent (marginal small companies rate). See further at 18.2.4.

3.2 WHO IS SUBJECT TO CAPITAL GAINS TAX?

An individual's residence and domicile status may have a crucial bearing on his liability to CGT. He can be liable only if he is resident or ordinarily resident for the year in which relevant disposals take place. Residence and ordinary residence are determined in the same way as for income tax. There is one exception: where a non-resident and non-ordinarily resident person has been carrying on a trade or profession through a branch or agency in the United Kingdom, CGT may be charged on a disposal of assets used in that branch despite the fact that the person would normally be outside the charge on capital gains.

An individual who is resident (or ordinarily resident) and domiciled in the United Kingdom is subject to CGT on gains realised both in this country and abroad. By contrast an individual who is not domiciled in the United Kingdom is charged tax on gains from foreign assets only if the proceeds are brought into this country (or, as the legislation puts it, the gains are 'remitted' to the United Kingdom).

A company is subject to tax on its capital gains if it is resident here or if the gains arise from disposals of assets used in a UK branch or agency (see 18.1.1).

3.3 WHAT ASSETS ARE CHARGEABLE ASSETS?

3.3.1 Assets within scope of CGT

(TCGA 1992, s 21)

Gains on virtually all types of assets are potentially subject to CGT, subject to certain stated exceptions. TCGA 1992, s 21(1) states:

> 'All forms of property shall be assets for the purposes of this Act, whether situated in the United Kingdom or not, including –
>
> (a) options, debts and incorporeal property generally, and
> (b) any currency other than sterling, and
> (c) any form of property created by the person disposing of it, or otherwise coming to be owned without being acquired.'

The asset does not have to be transferable or capable of being assigned. The term 'any form of property' is all embracing. For example, the courts have held that CGT was due on an employer's right to compensation from an employee who wished to be released from his service agreement. In another case, the right to compensation in respect of property expropriated by the USSR in 1940 was held to be a form of property and therefore an asset for CGT purposes. Similarly, the High Court held in *Zim Properties Ltd v Procter* [1985] STC 90 that the right to bring an action before the courts constitutes an asset which can be turned to account by the potential litigant negotiating a compromise and receiving a lump sum.

The conclusion therefore is that virtually all forms of property which can yield a capital sum are subject to CGT unless they are specifically exempt.

3.3.2 What assets are specifically exempt?

The following are the main categories of exempt assets which are relevant in the context of this book.

(1) Chattels which are wasting assets.
(2) Chattels where the sale consideration is less than £6,000. There may be some taper relief where more than £6,000 is received.
(3) Foreign currency acquired for personal expenditure outside the United Kingdom. This includes money spent on the purchase or maintenance of any property situated outside the United Kingdom.
(4) Compensation or damages for wrong or injury suffered in a profession or vocation.
(5) Debts.
(6) Gilt-edged securities and qualifying corporate bonds and any options to acquire or dispose of such investments. A qualifying corporate bond is a loan stock which is not convertible and is not a deep discount or a deep gain security.
(7) Shares held by an individual in a personal equity plan.
(8) Shares issued under the Business Expansion Scheme or Enterprise Investment Scheme (see 20.10.1) provided the BES/EIS relief has not been withdrawn.
(9) Shares held by an individual in a Venture Capital Trust.
(10) Sale by an individual of his principal private residence.
(11) Motor cars (unless not suitable or commonly used for the carriage of passengers).
(12) Woodlands.
(13) Gifts to charities.

No gain is assessable where an asset is exempt. Unfortunately, it follows that no relief is normally given for losses (losses on a disposal of shares in an EIS are an exception to this general rule).

3.4 WHICH TYPES OF TRANSACTION MAY PRODUCE A CHARGEABLE GAIN?

(TCGA 1992, s 28)

The most obvious type of disposal is an outright sale with immediate settlement, but there are many other transactions which count as a disposal for CGT purposes, as discussed in 3.4.1–10 below. The liability to CGT is determined by the tax year in which the date of disposal falls.

3.4.1 Outright sale

The date of disposal is the day on which the unconditional contract is entered into, which may, of course, be different from the date that the vendor receives payment. Where payment is made by instalments, it may be possible to pay CGT over a period of up to eight years if the Revenue is satisfied that hardship would otherwise result (TCGA 1992, s 280).

The Revenue operates a concession where a purchaser defaults and the vendor takes back the asset in satisfaction of the sums due to him (see ESC D18). The disposal is effectively treated as if it has never happened.

3.4.2 Conditional sale

A conditional sale is a contract which does not take effect until a stated condition is satisfied.

3.4.3 Example – Conditional sale

A agrees to purchase *B*'s shares in XYZ Ltd provided the local authority grants planning permission over land owned by XYZ Ltd by April 1995. Under this type of agreement, *B* remains the legal owner of his shares until the condition is satisfied. If the local authority does not in fact grant planning permission, *A* is under no obligation to buy *B*'s shares.

The date of disposal under such contracts is the day that the condition is satisfied and the contract becomes unconditional, eg in this example, the date planning permission is granted.

3.4.4 Exercise of an option
(TCGA 1992, s 144)

A 'call' option is a legally binding agreement between the owner of an asset and a third party under which the owner agrees to sell the asset if the other party decides to exercise his option. The purchase price payable upon the exercise of the option is normally fixed at the outset; this constitutes one of the terms of the option. A 'put' option is one where the other party agrees to buy the asset if the owner decides to exercise an option requiring him to do so.

The grant of either type of option does not constitute a disposal of the asset concerned. This happens only when the option is exercised; the day on which this happens is the date of disposal. In some cases, payment is made for the option to be granted. This is treated as a disposal of a separate asset unless the option is subsequently exercised.

3.4.5 Exchange of property

An agreement to exchange an asset for another is a disposal of the old asset and an acquisition of the new asset. If there is any cash adjustment, this must also be brought into account. For example, if *A* exchanges his holding in EF plc for *B*'s shareholding in GH plc, *A* is treated as if he has disposed of the EF plc shares for the market value of the GH plc shares at the time of the exchange. This type of transaction commonly occurs where an individual transfers portfolio investments to a unit trust in return for units.

Exception for certain share exchanges

There is an important exception to the rule that an exchange constitutes a disposal which may apply where a shareholder takes securities offered to him on a company takeover. Provided the conditions set out in TCGA 1992, s 136 are satisfied, the exchange does not count as a disposal and the securities issued by the acquiring company are deemed to have been derived from the original shares, with the shareholder carrying forward his original acquisition value.

The conditions to be satisfied are that the share exchange is a bona fide commercial transaction and not part of a tax avoidance scheme and either:

(a) the acquiring company secures 25 per cent or more of the target company's ordinary share capital; or
(b) the offer which is made would result in the offeror obtaining control of the target company, if it were to be accepted.

It is possible to obtain advance clearance from the Revenue that the requirements of s 136 are satisfied. A written application should be sent to the Revenue's specialist division and the Revenue has 30 days in which to give clearance or come back for further information. The Revenue, once clearance has been given, cannot subsequently go back on this unless it can show that the information supplied by the taxpayer was incorrect or incomplete.

3.4.6 Example – Exchange of shares on company takeover

B holds 1,000 shares in XYZ plc which he acquired in 1985 for £9,000. Another company, ABC plc, makes a take-over bid and offers all XYZ shareholders a share exchange whereby they receive one ABC share (worth £30 each) for every two XYZ shares that they own. The offer document confirms that agreement has been obtained from the Revenue that TCGA 1992, s 136 applies.

If *B* accepts, he will receive 500 ABC shares worth £15,000. However, he will be deemed to have acquired them in 1985 for £9,000. No disposal is deemed to have occurred on the share exchange.

Professional advice should be taken if the securities offered by way of the share exchange include qualifying corporate bonds (see 3.3.2).

3.4.7 Compulsory acquisition of assets
TCGA 1992, s 22)

The transfer of land to, for example, a local authority exercising its compulsory purchase powers is a disposal for CGT purposes. In some cases, once the compulsory purchase order has been served, contracts are drawn up and the land is transferred under the contract. In such a case, the rules in relation to outright sales and conditional sales apply.

Where the compulsory purchase order is disputed, the date of disposal is normally the earlier of:

(1) the date on which compensation for the acquisition is agreed or otherwise determined; and
(2) the date on which the local authority enters the land in pursuance of its powers.

3.4.8 Sums payable as compensation or proceeds under an insurance policy
(TCGA 1992, s 22)

An asset (for example a building) may be destroyed or damaged and a capital sum is received as compensation for this. In such cases, the asset is deemed to have been disposed of at the date that the capital sum is received. Similarly, where a capital sum is received from an insurance policy following such damage the receipt of the insurance money is treated as constituting a disposal.

3.4.9 Gifts
(TCGA 1992, s 17)

A gift is treated as a disposal at market value (except where it is from one spouse to the other). It was once possible for assets to be transferred at cost, but this general form of hold-over relief was abolished by FA 1989. In some cases the capital gains may still be held over, such as where the gift involves business property or is a chargeable transfer for IHT purposes (see 21.10 on lifetime gifts to discretionary trusts).

A gift is normally a 'bargain not at arm's length' which is treated in the same way as a transaction between connected persons.

3.4.10 Asset destroyed or becoming of negligible value
(TCGA 1992, s 24)

The total destruction or entire loss of an asset constitutes a disposal. This could be physical destruction (eg by fire) or legal/financial destruction (eg bankruptcy or winding-up). The legislation also permits a person to elect that he should be treated as having disposed of an asset which has become of negligible value. Normally, a capital loss arises on such an occasion.

'Negligible value' is interpreted by the Revenue as meaning considerably less than small. For example, the Revenue will only agree that shares, loan stock and other securities are of negligible value on being satisfied that the owner is unlikely to recover anything other than a nominal amount on the liquidation of the company. The mere fact that shares have been suspended or de-listed by the Stock Exchange is not regarded as sufficient.

The legislation provides that a disposal is deemed to take place in the year during which the inspector agrees that the asset has become of negligible value. In practice the Revenue permits a claim to take effect up to two tax years prior to the claim provided that the asset was of negligible value in the prior year (see ESC D28).

3.5 COMPUTATION OF CAPITAL GAINS

3.5.1 Amount to be brought in as disposal value

Market value
(TGCA 1992, s 18)

The general rule is that market value must be used unless the transaction is a bargain at arm's length. In the straightforward situation where a contract is entered into with a third party on a commercial basis, the disposal proceeds are the actual sale proceeds. An individual is not penalised because he has made a bad bargain and sold an asset for less than it is really worth. However, if the bargain is not at arm's length and the individual deliberately sells the asset for an amount which is less than its true value, the legislation requires market value to be substituted. If the disposal is to a connected person such as a relative or the trustee of a family settlement or a family company, there is an automatic assumption that the bargain is not at arm's length and market value will always be substituted for the actual sale proceeds if the two amounts are different.

The two main exceptions to the above are transactions between spouses and gifts to charities and similar bodies. In both of these circumstances, the person making the disposal is deemed to sell at a figure which produces a no gain/no loss situation.

It is also possible to hold-over capital gains in certain circumstances (see 4.5).

Contingent liabilities
(TCGA 1992, s 49)

There may be occasions where the contract requires part of the proceeds to be returned at some time in the future. This is known as a sale with 'contingent liabilities'. For example, suppose a vendor receives £150,000 for the disposal of a plot of land, but is under an obligation to return £60,000 in certain circumstances. Is the capital gain charged on sale proceeds of £150,000 or £90,000? In fact, TCGA 1992, s 49 provides that in these circumstances the capital gain must be computed in the first instance without any deduction for the contingent liability. However, if and when the vendor is required to refund part of the sale proceeds because the contingent liability has become an actual liability, the CGT assessment is adjusted accordingly.

Contingent consideration
(TCGA 1992, s 48)

In a similar way, it is possible that the contract may provide that additional sums may be payable if certain conditions are satisfied in the future. If it is possible to put a value on the further amount of consideration which is 'contingent' (ie which is payable only if certain conditions are satisfied) the full amount which may be received is brought into account at the date of disposal without any discount. If the conditions are not in fact satisfied, so that the further amounts are never received, an adjustment is made when that becomes clear.

The position is different where the contingent consideration cannot be ascertained at the date of disposal (this is normally the situation where the contingent consideration may vary and is not a fixed amount). Basically, the legislation requires that the market value of the right to receive the future consideration should be regarded as the disposal proceeds (*Marren v Ingles* [1980] STC 500, HL). The difference between this amount and the amount eventually received forms a *separate* CGT computation for the year in which the final amount of the actual contingent consideration is determined. The treatment of contingent consideration, especially variable contingent consideration, is complex. It normally arises in relation either to land or shares in private companies. This is an area where it is essential to take professional advice.

Deduction for amounts charged as income
(TCGA 1992, s 31)

In some cases the disposal of an asset by an individual may give rise to an income tax charge. Where this happens, the amount which is charged as income is deducted from the sale proceeds and only the balance is brought into account for CGT purposes. This commonly arises where a private company buys back its own shares from an individual or trustee shareholders and the transaction is treated as a distribution (see 18.5). Unfortunately, the Revenue does not accept that this applies where a corporate shareholder has shares bought back by the company in which it has invested.

3.5.2 What costs are allowable?
(TCGA 1992, s 38)

Certain specific types of expenditure

The legislation permits a limited range of expenses to be deducted in computing capital gains and losses. TCGA 1992, s 38(1) states:

> '. . . the sums allowable as a deduction from the consideration in the computation of the gain accruing to a person on the disposal of an asset shall be restricted to –
>
> (a) the amount or value of the consideration, in money or money's worth, given by him or on his behalf wholly and exclusively for the acquisition of the asset, together with the incidental costs to him of the acquisition or, if the asset was not acquired by him, any expenditure wholly and exclusively incurred by him in providing the asset,
> (b) the amount of any expenditure wholly and exclusively incurred on the asset by him or on his behalf for the purpose of enhancing the value of the asset, being expenditure reflected in the state or nature of the asset at the time of the disposal, and any expenditure wholly and exclusively incurred by him in establishing, preserving or defending his title to, or to a right over, the asset,
> (c) the incidental costs to him of making the disposal.

Incidental costs of acquisition

These are limited to:

(1) fees, commission or remuneration paid to a surveyor, valuer, auctioneer, accountant, agent or legal adviser;

(2) transfer/conveyancing charges (including stamp duty); and
(3) advertising to find a seller.

Enhancement expenditure

The legislation permits a deduction to be claimed for expenditure incurred to enhance the value of the asset provided that such expenditure is reflected in the state or nature of the asset at the time of disposal. The latter condition excludes relief for improvements which have worn out by the time the asset is disposed of. Certain grey areas are worth mentioning:

(1) Initial expenditure by way of repairs to newly acquired property which is let may be allowable if no relief has been given in computing Schedule A income.
(2) Expenditure means money or money's worth. It does not include the value of personal labour or skill.

Incidental costs of disposals

The following expenses may be deductible:

(1) Fees, commission or remuneration for the professional services of a surveyor, valuer, auctioneer, accountant, agent or legal adviser.
(2) Transfer/conveyancing charges (including stamp duty).
(3) Advertising to find a buyer.
(4) Any other costs reasonably incurred in making any valuation or apportionment for CGT purposes, including in particular expenses reasonably incurred in ascertaining market value where this is required. Professional costs incurred in getting a valuation agreed with the Revenue are not allowable.

Part disposals
(TCGA 1992, s 42)

Where a person disposes of part of an asset, the cost is apportioned between the part disposed of and the part retained according to the formula [A ÷ (A + B)] where A is the consideration received or deemed to have been received and B is the market value of the part retained.

3.5.3 Example – Part disposals

B holds 1,000 shares in XYZ Ltd which cost him £10,000. The company is taken over and he receives cash of £5,000 and convertible loan stock issued by the acquiring company worth £15,000 (assume that in this particular case no capital gain arises in respect of the loan stock because it is issued on the occasion of a takeover and the necessary Revenue clearances have been obtained). *B*'s acquisition value is apportioned as follows:

$$£10{,}000 \times \frac{5{,}000}{5{,}000 + 15{,}000} = £2{,}500$$

ie the proportion of acquisition value which relates to the part sold.

£7,500 is treated as the acquisition value of the part retained, ie it is taken into account in computing any gain or loss as and when the loan stock is sold.

Special rules may apply where shares are sold out of a shareholding which includes shares held on 31 March 1982 and shares acquired after that date.

Small capital receipts

(TCGA 1992, s 122)

There are occasions where the formula [A ÷ (A + B)] does not have to be used, and the amount received is simply deducted from the owner's acquisition value. The most common situation of this is where a shareholder sells his entitlement under a rights issue, normally on a nil paid basis. Provided that the amount received is small as compared with the value of the asset, the receipt can be deducted from the owner's acquisition value. 'Small' in this context is interpreted by the Revenue as an amount not exceeding 5 per cent of the market value or £3,000, whichever is the lesser.

Capital sums applied in restoring assets

(TCGA 1992, s 23)

Under normal circumstances, an asset is regarded as having been disposed of for CGT purposes if it is lost or destroyed. However, where a capital sum is received from such an asset (eg the proceeds of an insurance policy), the owner may claim that the asset is not treated as disposed of if at least 95 per cent of the capital sum is spent in restoring the asset.

3.5.4 Assets held at 31 March 1982

(TCGA 1992, s 35 & Scheds 2–3)

General rebasing

The general rule is that where assets were held at 31 March 1982, it is to be assumed that the assets were sold on that date and immediately re-acquired at their market value at that time. This is known as 'rebasing'. The original cost still applies in certain circumstances as the rebasing rule is subject to the following qualifications:

(1) Where the gain since March 1982 is smaller than that measured by reference to original cost (or vice versa), the chargeable gain is confined to that figure.
(2) Where a loss has arisen, the allowable loss is the smaller of the loss measured by reference to original cost and the loss measured by reference to the 31 March 1982 value.
(3) Where a gain arises when one has regard to original cost, but a loss arises when one takes the 31 March 1982 value (or vice versa), the position is regarded as no gain/no loss.

However, even these qualifications are ignored if a universal rebasing election has been made.

Universal rebasing election

Under TCGA 1992, s 35(5), if a person so elects, the rebasing rule is applied to all disposals made by him of assets held on 31 March 1982. In other words, original cost is ignored completely and regard is had only for the value of the assets held at that date. In some cases, making this election will mean that losses can be claimed which would not otherwise be available (because of the no gain/no loss rule).

A universal rebasing election is precisely that, ie if the election is made the rebasing rule is applied to *all* assets held at 31 March 1982. Furthermore, once made, the election is irrevocable.

The legislation requires the election to be made within two years of the end of the year of assessment in which a disposal first takes place of assets which were held both at 6 April 1988 and at 31 March 1982. If no election has been made and assets held at 31 March 1982 have been disposed of during the period 6 April 1988 to 5 April 1993, it is now too late to make the election.

Married persons

The election may be made by each spouse separately. However, where assets pass from one spouse to another and the spouse who received the asset subsequently disposes of it, the gain or loss on that particular asset is governed by whether the spouse who transferred the asset had made the universal rebasing election.

Groups of companies

A universal rebasing election by a member of a group of companies normally applies to all members of that group at the time that the election is made (see 18.7.10).

Assets acquired via a gift made between 1 April 1982 and 5 April 1988

(TCGA 1992, Sched 4)

This section may be relevant where *all* of the following conditions are satisfied:

(1) The asset was acquired as a gift or transfer from a trust during the period 1 April 1982 to 5 April 1988.
(2) The donor held the asset at 31 March 1982.
(3) The donor claimed hold-over relief so that the recipient was deemed to have acquired the asset at the donor's original cost.

When rebasing was first introduced, it was recognised that it would be unfair not to permit some relief where an asset had been transferred prior to 6 April 1988 and the gain had been held over. The person who received such a gift cannot claim rebasing because he did not own the asset concerned at 31 March 1982. To give rough and ready compensation for this, the legislation included provisions so that when the recipient of such a gift made a disposal after 5 April 1988, half of the held-over gain could be 'forgiven' or left out of account.

3.5.5 Example – Transfer prior to 6 April 1988 with held-over gain

A received a gift of shares in August 1986 from his father *B*. At the time of the gift, the shares were worth £180,000. *B*'s acquisition value was only £40,000, and indexation amounted to £10,000. This would normally have meant that *B* would have had a chargeable gain of £130,000. However, he made a claim under the legislation prevailing at the time which permitted the capital gain to be held over. This meant that *B* did not suffer a CGT charge, but *A* was deemed to have acquired the assets with an acquisition value as follows:

	£
Market value at date of gift	180,000
Less held-over gain	(130,000)
Acquisition value	50,000

If *A* disposes of the asset after 5 April 1988, his acquisition value is increased by 50 per cent of £130,000 so that his acquisition value becomes £115,000.

This treatment can also apply to other situations where a gain was rolled over (see 4.3) on a transaction which took place between 1 April 1982 and 5 April 1988 and the transferor held the asset at 31 March 1982.

The 50 per cent relief is not given automatically. A must make a formal claim under Schedule 4 within two years of the end of the tax year in which the disposal takes place.

3.5.6 Other acquisition values

Assets acquired via inheritance or from family trust
(TCGA 1992, ss 62 and 71)

Where a person inherits an asset, he is generally deemed to have acquired it for its market value at the date of the testator's death (ie probate value). There is one exception to this. It is possible to claim a form of relief from IHT where quoted securities have gone down in value after the person has died. Where such relief has been claimed, a corresponding adjustment is made so that the person taking the assets concerned is deemed to have acquired them not at probate value, but at the value actually brought into account for IHT purposes after taking account of the fall in value.

Where assets have been acquired from a trust, the beneficiary's acquisition value is normally the market value at the time that the asset is transferred to him. However, the acquisition value may be lower than this where the trustees have claimed hold-over relief either under the general hold-over relief provisions which prevailed up to 5 April 1989, or under the more restrictive provisions which have applied subsequently.

Deemed acquisition value where income tax charged
(TCGA 1992, ss 120 and 141)

Where an individual is subject to a Schedule E income tax charge when he acquires an asset (for example where he exercises a non-approved share option) he is deemed to have acquired the asset for an amount equal to the value taken into account in computing a Schedule E charge on him. Similarly, where an individual acquires shares by way of a stock dividend (ie where there is a choice between a cash dividend or further shares issued by a UK company) the shares are deemed to be acquired for a consideration equal to the amount brought into account for income tax purposes by reason of the stock dividend. This rule does not apply to companies which receive stock dividends on investments held by them as such a dividend is simply treated as a bonus issue made for no consideration.

3.5.7 Indexation
(TA 1992, s 53–57)

CGT is charged on real capital gains. A person who makes a capital gain is allowed to deduct not only his actual acquisition value, but also a proportion which represents the increase in the RPI between the month of acquisition and the month of disposal. The formula used is [(RD – RI) ÷ RI] where:

RD = retail prices index in month of disposal
RI = retail prices index for March 1982 or month in which expenditure incurred, whichever is the later.

3.5.8 Example – Indexation

A acquired shares in X plc on 1 June 1990 for £35,000. He sells them in January 1995 for £60,000.

He has a capital gain of £25,000 before indexation, and a gain of £19,680 after taking indexation into account. The indexation relief is computed as follows:

$$\text{Cost £35,000} \times \frac{\text{RPI for January 1995} - \text{RPI for June 1990}}{\text{RPI for June 1990}}$$

That is $$\text{£35,000} \times \frac{146.0 - 126.7}{126.7} \quad \text{or £35,000} \times 0.152 = \text{£5,320}$$

The RPI figures are set out in Table 27.7 of the *Allied Dunbar Tax Handbook 1997–98*, p 619.

Restriction to indexation relief

(TCGA 1992, s 55(2A))

Indexation relief may only reduce or extinguish a gain; it cannot convert a gain into a loss or increase a loss.

3.6 SOME SPECIAL PROBLEM AREAS

3.6.1 Land and buildings

The basic principles apply in computing gains on land and buildings as they do for other assets. However, there are certain complications which regularly arise in practice.

Expenditure on improvements

Where a property is disposed of, bear in mind that the acquisition cost includes allowable enhancement expenditure only if the expenditure is reflected in the state of the property at the date of disposal. Thus, beware of a situation where property has a high cost but much of the enhancement expenditure relates to additions or improvements which have been worn out, or which have themselves been replaced.

Disallowed initial repairs

The reverse situation often applies where a property is acquired in a very poor state of repair. Expenditure incurred in bringing it into a fit condition is often disallowed. Such repairs are treated as capital expenditure (see 2.1.3). Where this has happened, the amount disallowed in computing trading profits or Schedule A income can be treated as enhancement expenditure for CGT purposes.

Past expenditure qualified for capital allowances

A trader's expenditure on a building may include sums which have qualified for capital allowances (see 2.2), eg expenditure on installing a lift or carrying out structural work so that a computer can be installed. Such expenditure can be allowed for CGT purposes provided it does not mean that there is a loss.

Leases with less than 50 years to run
(TCGA 1992, s 240 & Sched 8)

Another aspect to bear in mind is that the interest in the property which is being disposed of may be a lease which has less than 50 years to run and is therefore regarded as a wasting asset. Where a person disposes of such an asset, his acquisition value is restricted according to specific rules which effectively write off the cost of a wasting asset over the period of its life.

3.6.2 Example – Disposal of a short lease

A purchased a 20-year lease in 1985 for £100,000. In 1995 she disposes of the lease for £100,000. However, this is not a no gain/no loss situation as the proper calculation is as follows:

		£	£
Disposal proceeds			100,000
Original cost of lease		100,000	
Reduced by $\frac{72.770 - 46.695}{72.770}$	=	(35,832)	
			(64,168)
Gain before indexation			35,832

The figures of 72.770 and 46.695 for 20 and ten-year leases are contained in a table in TCGA 1992 (see *Allied Dunbar Tax Handbook 1997–98* at 14.9.2).

Time apportionment and land held before 6 April 1965
(TCGA 1992, s 35 & Sched 2)

Where a person has owned land or buildings for more than 30 years, it may be possible for any capital gain to be computed on the time apportionment basis. This is not possible if the person has made a universal rebasing election (see 3.5.4) or if the land or buildings have development value when they are sold.

The time apportionment basis operates on the assumption that appreciation has occurred at an even rate over the total period of ownership. Because CGT was first introduced on 6 April 1965, the chargeable gain is computed as follows:

$$\text{Overall gain} \times \frac{\text{Period since 6 April 1965 – date of disposal}}{\text{Total period of ownership}}$$

3.6.3 Example – Where time apportionment basis is beneficial

A sells an agricultural property in March 1998 for £510,000. It was originally acquired in April 1945 for £10,000. Its value at 31 March 1982 was £150,000.

Ignoring indexation, the time apportionment basis produces the following result:

$$\text{£500,000} \times \frac{\text{6 April 1965 – March 1998 (33 years)}}{\text{6 April 1945 – March 1998 (53 years)}} = \text{£311,321}$$

This compares with a gain of £350,000 before indexation if the gain is measured by reference to the 31 March 1982 value.

3.6.4 Unquoted shares

A valuation may be required where a shareholder makes a gift or there is some other disposal which is not a bargain at arm's length and the transaction is treated as a disposal at market value (see 3.5.1). A valuation may also be required at 31 March 1982 where this value may be deducted instead of original cost in computing the person's capital gain (see 3.5.4). In both these situations, it is generally necessary to negotiate with the Revenue's Shares Valuation Division. This division operates according to long established rules which have been upheld by court decisions.

Valuation of minority shareholdings

It must not be assumed that the value of a 10 per cent shareholding is the same as 10 per cent of the value of the company as a whole. A firm distinction is drawn between a 51 per cent or greater shareholding which carries control and a minority shareholding. The Revenue's normal view is that the underlying assets are irrelevant when valuing a small minority shareholding and what matters is the dividend history and the extent to which an investor could reasonably expect the past level of dividends to be maintained in the future.

General principles

One aspect to be borne in mind is that the definition of market value for capital gains purposes is the value for the person who acquires the asset. In this regard, the valuation may differ from that used for IHT purposes (see 21.3.3). Thus, if an individual makes a gift out of his 51 per cent shareholding of shares which add up to 17 per cent of the company's share capital, the disposal is normally deemed to take place at a consideration equal to the market value of a 17 per cent shareholding.

Special rules where series of connected disposals made

There are anti-avoidance provisions designed to prevent a person achieving an advantage by making several separate disposals to connected persons. Basically, the anti-avoidance provisions apply where a person makes several gifts or other disposals to connected persons within a six-year period and the value of the property given away in stages is more, when valued at a totality, than the combined value of the separate gifts.

3.6.5 Example – How a series of gifts may be dealt with

A made five separate gifts of shares in B Ltd to his son. Assume that an 11 per cent shareholding in B Ltd is worth only £20,000 whereas a 55 per cent controlling shareholding has a value of £300,000.

Where the Revenue is able to apply the anti-avoidance legislation, the transactions are linked and the individual is assessed as if he had made a disposal on each occasion on a part of the overall value. Thus, *A* would be deemed to have made five separate disposals on the basis that the deemed disposal proceeds on each occasion amounted to £60,000 (ie ⅕ of the value of a 55 per cent shareholding).

Valuing shareholdings at 31 March 1982

(TCGA 1992, s 20(4)–(9))

When valuing shares it is not normally appropriate to have regard to shares held by a connected person. Thus, if a husband and wife each held 30 per cent of the shares in a company at 31 March 1982, each shareholding should be valued on the basis of a 30 per cent minority shareholding, even though when taken together the husband and wife would have control. However, the Revenue operates an extra statutory concession so that if a husband and wife held 30 per cent each at 31 March 1982, but one spouse later transferred all his or her shares to the other, the 31 March 1982 value may then be based on the rights etc attaching to a 60 per cent shareholding.

The Revenue also has a concession which deals with the converse situation. Suppose that an individual had 51 per cent of the shares in his private company at 31 March 1982, and his wife had 9 per cent. If he gave 21 per cent of his shareholding to his wife with a view to equalising their shareholdings, there could be a disadvantage in that the combined value of the two 30 per cent shareholdings might not equate to the value of a 51 per cent and a 9 per cent shareholding. In these circumstances, the Revenue allows the individual's wife to claim that the 21 per cent shareholding given to her by her husband should have a 31 March 1982 value based on it being part of a 51 per cent controlling shareholding.

Time apportionment basis

The time apportionment method of computing gains (mentioned in 3.6.3) also applies to shares in an unquoted company.

3.6.6 Foreign property

Gains should be computed in sterling

Where a foreign property or shares in a foreign company are disposed of, it is not correct to calculate the gain or loss in foreign currency terms and then convert that into sterling at the time of disposal. Instead, the following formula should be used:

Disposal proceeds converted into sterling at the rates prevailing at the time of the disposal

Less

Acquisition cost of 31 March 1982 value converted into sterling at the exchange rate prevailing at that time

Equals

Gain before indexation.

Borrowings in foreign currency

Often an individual or partnership has financed the acquisition of a foreign property with a foreign currency loan and the foreign currency appreciates against sterling. When a disposal of the property takes place, and the loan is redeemed, the extra cost of repaying the loan is not allowable in computing the capital gain on the disposal of the asset.

3.6.7 Example – Gain on foreign property

A financed the purchase of a warehouse in Germany by borrowing the full purchase price of DM 4m. At that time, the sterling equivalent was £1m (DM 4 = £1). When *A* sells the warehouse for DM 6m, the exchange rate is DM 2.50 = £1.

Overall, *A*'s profit after repaying his loan is DM 2m ie £800,000 when one looks at the exchange rate at the time of disposal. However, for tax purposes, the transaction is broken down as follows:

	£
Sale proceeds (DM 6m converted at DM 2.50 = £1)	2,400,000
Cost (DM 4m converted at DM 4 = £1)	1,000,000
Capital gain before indexation	1,400,000
Extra cost in sterling terms of repaying loan	(600,000)

A will be taxed on his gain of £1.4m (less indexation relief) with no relief for the currency loss on repaying his borrowings.

A currency loss of this nature is also not normally allowable in computing an unincorporated trader's profits although special rules now apply for companies (see 18.11 on *Forex*).

3.6.8 Foreign currency

(TCGA 1992, s 252)

This is regarded as a chargeable asset and a gain (or loss) may arise when the currency is disposed of. Such a disposal may take the form of the foreign currency being spent, or being converted into another foreign currency, or converted into sterling. In each of these situations, the sterling equivalent of the foreign currency at the date of disposal is compared with the sterling equivalent at the date of acquisition.

The one circumstance where foreign currency is an exempt asset is where it was acquired for an individual's personal expenditure abroad.

4

CAPITAL GAINS TAX AND BUSINESS TRANSACTIONS

This chapter focuses on the CGT aspects of various business transactions. It deals with the following matters:

(1) Loans to private businesses
(2) Losses on unquoted shares
(3) Roll-over relief
(4) Relief for reinvestment in unquoted shares
(5) Hold-over relief for gifts of business property
(6) Partners and capital gains
(7) Retirement relief – general provisions
(8) Retirement relief and unincorporated traders
(9) Retirement relief and full-time directors and employees.

4.1 LOANS TO PRIVATE BUSINESSES

A person may make a loan to a sole trader or partnership (an 'unincorporated business') or to a private company, or he may give a guarantee to a bank etc which makes a loan to a business. CGT loss relief may be available if a loan has to be written off or a person is required to make a payment under a bank guarantee that he has given.

4.1.1 Loans to unincorporated businesses (TCGA 1992, s 253)

A CGT loss may be deemed to arise if the Revenue is satisfied that a loan has become irrecoverable. There are various conditions which must be fulfilled:

(1) The borrower must not be the lender's spouse.
(2) The borrower must be resident in the United Kingdom.
(3) The borrower must have used the loan wholly for the purposes of a trade carried on by him. The trade must not have been a trade which consists of (or includes) lending money.

When a claim is submitted, the inspector of taxes must satisfy himself that any outstanding amount of the loan is irrecoverable and that the lender has not assigned his right to recover the loan. Strictly speaking, relief is due only when a claim is made and admitted but, in practice, the Revenue permits claims to be made within two years of a year of assessment provided the other conditions were satisfied at the end of that year of assessment (ESC D36).

4.1.2 Loans to companies

(TCGA 1992, s 253)

Similar provisions apply where a person has made a loan to a company which proves to be irrecoverable. The principal conditions which need to be satisfied are:

(1) the company must be UK resident; and
(2) it must be a trading company.

No relief is due where a company makes a loss on a loan to another company in the same group unless the loan is a debt on security (ie a debenture which is capable of being transferred).

4.1.3 Payments under loan guarantees

(TCGA 1992, s 253(4))

Instead of lending money to a relative or friend or his private company, an individual may have given a guarantee to a bank etc. Similarly, a director of a company may have had to give personal guarantees for bank loans to his company.

Where the borrower cannot repay the loan, the bank calls on the guarantor to pay the amount due. In these circumstances, the guarantor may be able to claim a CGT loss under TCGA 1992, s 253 as if he had made a loan which was irrecoverable. The following conditions must be satisfied to claim such relief:

(1) payment has been made under a guarantee;
(2) the payment should arise from a formal calling in of the guarantee – a voluntary payment attracts no relief;
(3) the original loan met the requirements listed in 4.1.1;
(4) the amount paid under the guarantee cannot be recovered either from the borrower or from a co-guarantor.

Where a company has guaranteed another UK company's borrowings and the money has been used for the borrower's trade, a payment under the guarantee may qualify under s 253. This still applies even if the guarantor and borrower are members of the same group of companies.

4.2 LOSSES ON UNQUOTED SHARES

(TA 1988, s 574)

4.2.1 Special relief for subscribers

From time to time, an individual may invest in a private company, either as a working director/shareholder or perhaps as a 'passive' investor with a minority shareholding. Investments may also be made in companies which, whilst they are public companies as defined by the Companies Act 1985, are not quoted companies.

A loss may arise on a disposal of shares in such a company. If the investor acquired existing shares by purchasing them, the loss is a normal CGT loss and the only way in which it can be relieved is by its being set against capital gains. However, if the individual acquired his shares by *subscribing* for new shares, it may be possible to obtain income tax relief for the loss. Subject to certain conditions, the capital loss may be off-set against the individual's income for the year in which the loss is realised. The following conditions must be satisfied:

(1) The loss must arise from one of the following:
    (a) a sale made at arm's length for full consideration (this rules out a sale to a connected person); or
    (b) a disposal which takes place when the company is wound up; or
    (c) a deemed disposal where the shares have become of negligible value.
(2) There are conditions which relate to the company itself, in particular:
    (a) The company must have been resident in the United Kingdom throughout the period from its incorporation until the date of the individual's disposal of shares.
    (b) The company must not have been a quoted company at any time during the individual's period of ownership. The fact that any class of shares has had a Stock Exchange quote rules out relief under TA 1988, s 574 even though the loss may have arisen on a class of share which did not have a quote.
    (c) The company must be a trading company, or the holding company of a trading group, at the date of disposal or it must have ceased to have been a trading company not more than three years prior to the date of disposal and it must not have been an investment company since that date.
    (d) The company's trade must not have consisted wholly or mainly of dealing in shares, securities, land, trades or commodity futures.
    (e) The company's trade must have been carried on on a commercial basis.

4.2.2 Relief also available for subscriber's spouse

The spouse of a person who subscribed for shares may also claim relief under TA 1988, s 574 where he has acquired the shares in question through an *inter vivos* transfer from his spouse. However, shares which are acquired on the death of a spouse do not entitle the widower/widow to s 574 relief on a subsequent disposal.

4.2.3 Nature of relief

The loss is calculated according to normal CGT principles. If the loss is eligible for relief under TA 1988, s 574, the individual may elect within two years for the loss to be set against his taxable income. The loss may be set either against the individual's taxable income for the year of the loss, or his taxable income for the preceding year. Either claim may be made independently of the other. Where an individual has losses which are available for relief under s 574 and he is also entitled to relief for trading losses (see 16.9), he can choose which losses should be relieved in priority to the other.

Any part of the capital loss which cannot be relieved under s 574 can be carried forward for set-off against capital gains in the normal way.

4.2.4 Similar relief for companies

(TA 1988, s 573)

There is a similar relief for investment companies (see 18.8.5) which realise capital losses. Once again, the shares need to have been acquired by subscription. The shares must not be in a subsidiary company or in an associated company (see 18.2.7).

Once again, the investment company's capital loss must be computed on ordinary CGT principles. If relief is required under TA 1988, s 573, an election must be submitted to the Revenue within two years of the end of the company's accounting period in which the loss is realised. The loss may then be set against the company's income and other profits for that year. If the loss exceeds the company's profits for that period, the excess is carried back and set against profits of the preceding accounting period. Any balance can then be carried forward and set against the investment company's capital gains.

4.3 ROLL-OVER RELIEF

(TCGA 1992, ss 152–160)

Relief may be available where a person disposes of an asset which is used by him in a trade (or in certain circumstances, an asset which is used by his family company) and re-invests in replacement assets used for business purposes. This relief is termed 'roll-over' relief. The gain is said to be rolled over in that it is not charged to tax, but is deducted from the person's acquisition cost of the new assets.

4.3.1 Example – Roll-over relief

A sells a farm for £450,000. His capital gain is £200,000. He starts up a new business and invests £500,000 in a warehouse.

By claiming roll-over relief, *A* avoids having to pay tax on the gain of £200,000. The acquisition cost of his warehouse is reduced as follows:

	£
Annual cost	500,000
Less rolled-over gain	(200,000)
Deemed acquisition cost	300,000

The relief is really a form of deferment since a larger gain will arise on a subsequent disposal of the replacement asset.

4.3.2 Conditions which need to be satisfied

There must be a relevant disposal, although this need not be a sale and could, for example, be a gift or an exchange of assets. The asset that has been disposed of must have been used in a business and must have fallen into one of the following categories:

(1) land and buildings
(2) fixed plant and machinery
(3) ships
(4) goodwill
(5) milk and potato quotas
(6) aircraft
(7) hovercraft, satellites and spacecraft.

The replacement assets must also fall into one of these categories, but not necessarily the same category as the asset which has been sold. Moreover, the asset can be used for a completely different trade. It is not possible to claim roll-over relief on the disposal of shares in a family company, nor is it possible to claim it for expenditure on such shares on the basis that this is replacement expenditure (but see 4.4 regarding a different type of reinvestment relief introduced by FA 1994).

The replacement assets must normally be acquired within a period starting one year before the date of the disposal of the original asset and ending three years after the date of disposal. The time limit can be extended (at the Revenue's discretion) if the acquisition of replacement assets within three years was not possible because of circumstances outside the person's control.

4.3.3 Example – Full relief available only where all sale proceeds reinvested

(TCGA 1992, s 152(3)–(11))

Using the same figures as in 4.3.1, *A* sells his farm for £450,000, making the same capital gain of £200,000. He starts up a new business but invests only £400,000 in the new warehouse. The part of the £450,000 disposal consideration for the farm which is not applied in acquiring the warehouse is £50,000. This is less than the gain which arose on the disposal of the farm and the balance of the gain may be rolled-over. The acquisition value of the warehouse is reduced by £150,000.

4.3.4 Old assets not used for business throughout ownership

If the old asset was not used for business throughout the period of ownership, TCGA 1990, s 152(7) applies as if a part of the asset used for the purposes of the trade was a separate asset to that which had not been wholly used for the purposes of the trade.

4.3.5 Example – Old assets

In April 1995, *B* sells a hotel for a gain, after indexation has been calculated, of £50,000. It had originally been bought in April 1987 but was at first let out as an investment. It was used by *B* for a trade carried on by him only from April 1989. The amount of gain which can be rolled over into the purchase of a new asset is calculated as follows:

$$\text{Chargeable gain £50,000} \times \frac{\text{period of trading use of old asset}}{\text{period of ownership}}$$

This equals £50,000 × 6/8 = £37,500. The balance of £12,500 (£50,000 – £37,500) is a chargeable gain.

4.3.6 Treatment where replacement assets are wasting assets
(TCGA 1992, s 154)

The roll-over relief is modified where the replacement expenditure consists of the purchase of a wasting asset (an asset with an expected useful life of less than 50 years) or an asset which will become a wasting asset within ten years. Plant and machinery is always considered to have a useful life of less than 50 years. Furthermore, the acquisition of a lease with less than 60 years to run will also constitute the acquisition of a wasting asset. Rather paradoxically, the goodwill of a business is not regarded as a wasting asset.

The capital gain in these circumstances is not deferred indefinitely, but becomes chargeable on the first of the following occasions:

(1) the disposal of the replacement asset; or
(2) the asset ceasing to be used in the business; or
(3) the expiry of ten years.

4.3.7 Examples – Roll-over relief on wasting assets

(1) *B* sells a factory and re-invests in a 59-year lease of a warehouse which he uses in his business. In the sixth year the warehouse is let as an investment property. The rolled-over gain would become chargeable in year six.
(2) *C* also rolls over into a 59-year lease. He is still using the property after ten years, but because it has become a wasting asset within that period, the rolled-over gain becomes chargeable in year ten.

4.3.8 Reinvestment in non-wasting assets
(TCGA 1992, s 154(5))

If a person acquires new non-wasting replacement assets during the ten years, the capital gain which was originally rolled over into the purchase of the wasting assets can be transferred to the new replacement assets. Assume in example (1) above that *B* had bought the goodwill of a business in year five. He could transfer his roll-over relief claim to the new asset. No gain would then become chargeable in year six when he lets the warehouse.

4.3.9 Replacement asset must be brought into use

Temperley v Visibell Ltd [1974] STC 64 concerned a company which purchased land to build a factory. In the event, planning permission was refused and the factory was never built. It was held that the intention to use an asset for the trade was not sufficient and the expenditure on the land did not qualify for roll-over relief.

However, where the replacement asset is not brought into use right away, roll-over relief may still be available if the following conditions are satisfied:

(a) the trader proposes to incur capital expenditure for the purpose of enhancing its value;
(b) any work arising from such capital expenditure begins as soon as possible after acquisition, and is completed within a reasonable time;
(c) on completion of the work the asset is taken into use for the purpose of the trade and for no other purpose; and
(d) the asset is not let or used for any non-trading purpose in the period between acquisition and the time it is taken into use for the purpose of the trade.

4.3.10 Acquisition of freehold

The Revenue used to deny roll-over relief where a trader acquired a further interest in an asset already used by him for his trade, eg where a tenant farmer bought the freehold. ESC D25 now provides relief as if the expenditure were on a new asset.

4.3.11 Roll-over relief for partners

Where the asset which is disposed of is owned by a partnership, part of the gain belongs to each partner (see 4.6) and it is up to him whether he claims roll-over relief. Because the replacement asset need not be used by the disponor in the same trade, an individual partner may roll-over by incurring expenditure on his own account whereas other partners may choose not to do so.

Roll-over relief can be secured where the replacement assets are used by a partnership in which the owner is a partner (SP D11).

4.3.12 Assets used by an individual's personal trading company
(TCGA 1992, s 157)

Relief can also be obtained where an individual disposes of a property etc which is used by his 'personal trading company', but only if the replacement asset is acquired by him and is used by the same company. A company is an individual's personal trading company if he personally owns at least 5 per cent of the voting shares. The individual need not be a director of the company – indeed he need not even be employed by it. Also, roll-over relief is not lost because he has charged the company rent.

4.3.13 Assets owned by employee or office-holder

(TCGA 1992, s 158)

An employee or office-holder may claim roll-over relief where he disposes of an asset used in the employment. This condition may apply, for example, to a sub-postmaster who has an 'office' for tax purposes, but who generally owns the sub-post office premises. For further details, see SP5/86.

There are circumstances where these provisions mean that a director of a family company who has sold an asset used by one company, and bought new assets used by another family company, is entitled to roll-over relief. However, this is a difficult area where professional advice is essential.

4.4 RELIEF FOR REINVESTMENT IN UNQUOTED SHARES

(TCGA 1992, s 164A)

It is possible for individuals and trustees to secure reinvestment relief on *any* capital gain made after 29 November 1993 where the gain is reinvested in eligible shares in a qualifying unquoted trading company within a period beginning one year before and ending three years after the disposal which has given rise to the capital gain. A company is a qualifying company only if it carries on a trade (dealing in land and various financial activities are, however, not regarded as qualifying trades for the purpose of this relief).

The relief is clawed back where a company ceases to meet the qualifying conditions within three years of the reinvestment (see 4.4.2–4.4.3 below). The gain is then treated as arising at the point in time when the conditions are breached. A clawback may also arise where the individual who has qualified for reinvestment relief ceases to be resident in the United Kingdom within the three-year period. In such a situation, the individual is deemed to have realised the deferred gain immediately before he ceased to be resident.

The main exclusion for trustees is where the beneficiaries of the trust are not individuals. Companies are not eligible.

4.4.1 Example – How reinvestment relief works

A realises a capital gain of £140,000 on the sale of an investment property on 31 May 1997. In December 1998 he makes a further gain of £260,000 on the sale of shares in his family company. If *A* invests £50,000 in a qualifying company within the three years ending 31 May 2000, he can claim reinvestment relief and the assessment on his 1997–98 capital gain will then be reduced by £50,000.

On the other hand, if he were to invest £150,000 during January 1998 he can claim reinvestment relief of up to £140,000 against the May 1995 gain. He might choose to restrict his claim to £133,500 so as to leave a net gain of £6,500 to use up his 1997–98 CGT annual exemption (see 3.1.1).

A might divide up his reinvestment relief to cover all but £6,500 of his 1997–98 gain and £15,500 of the £260,000 gain made on his disposal during December 1998.

4.4.2 Eligible shares

(TCGA 1992, s 164N(1))

The shares must be ordinary shares and shares which do not carry any preferred rights to dividend or to payment in the event of the company being wound up. They must be ordinary shares in a qualifying company, defined as an unquoted company which exists either:

(a) wholly for the purpose of carrying on one or more qualifying trades; or

(b) for the purpose of holding shares in, and making loans to, qualifying subsidiaries.

A qualifying subsidiary is one which carries on a qualifying trade.

A qualifying company cannot be a subsidiary of another company. On the other hand, the company need not be a UK company, nor must it carry on its trade in the United Kingdom. However, an investment in a foreign company does not qualify for relief unless the company is a 'stand alone' company with no subsidiaries.

A company is regarded as an unquoted company only if it has no shares or securities which are quoted on a recognised stock exchange or dealt in on the USM. Shares which are dealt in on the AIM are regarded as unquoted for this purpose.

4.4.3 Qualifying trades

(TCGA 1992, s 164I)

A qualifying trade is defined as one which does not consist to a substantial extent of the following activities:

(a) dealing in land, commodities or futures, or shares, securities or other financial instruments;
(b) dealing in goods otherwise than in the course of an ordinary trade or wholesale or retail distribution;
(c) banking, insurance, money-lending, debt-factoring, hire-purchase, financing or other financial activities;
(d) leasing (including letting ships on charter or other assets on hire) or receiving royalties or licence fees;
(e) providing legal or accountancy services;
(f) providing services or facilities for a trade carried on by another person (other than a parent company) which consists to any substantial extent of activities within any of the above and in which a controlling interest is held by a person who also has a controlling interest in the trade carried on by the company.

4.4.4 Reinvestment relief for EIS investments

It is possible to secure reinvestment relief through an investment under the EIS (see *Allied Dunbar Tax Handbook 1997–98* at 11.6). Investments made under the EIS are subject to different rules than those which apply above and in particular an investor may not have more than 30 per cent of the company's shares (associates' shareholdings are taken into account for the purposes of this test). Also, EIS relief is due only where an individual subscribes for new shares, whereas reinvestment relief is available where an individual acquires shares from a shareholder.

It is only possible to claim the reinvestment relief for an EIS investment if the gains were realised after 28 November 1994. Subject to that, the rules are the same as for reinvestment relief generally, ie the reinvestment must take place within the period which starts 12 months before and ends three years after the relevant gains were realised.

4.4.5 CGT deferral relief for investments in VCTs

It is possible to secure a form of CGT deferral relief (similar to reinvestment relief) by investing in ordinary shares in a Venture Capital Trust (see *Allied Dunbar Tax Handbook 1997–98* at 11.8). Tax relief is available only where an individual subscribes for new shares on or after 6 April 1995. Again, an individual may claim deferral relief for gains realised within 12 months before and after the date that he takes up his investment in the VCT.

4.5 HOLD-OVER RELIEF FOR GIFTS OF BUSINESS PROPERTY

(TCGA 1992, s 165)

Under the legislation which applied up to 5 April 1989, a UK-resident individual could transfer any asset to another UK-resident person on a no gain/no loss basis by claiming hold-over relief.

4.5.1 Example – Hold-over relief

B transferred shares in X plc to her brother *C* in 1988. They were both resident in the United Kingdom. *B*'s shares were worth £29,000 and her capital gain would normally have been £13,000. By claiming hold-over relief, *B* could avoid having a chargeable gain of £13,000. *C*'s acquisition value was then taken as:

	£
Market value at acquisition	29,000
Less held-over capital gain	(13,000)
	16,000

In 1989, the Chancellor abolished the hold-over relief for gifts in general. However, the same type of hold-over relief can still be claimed on gifts of business property and shares in unquoted trading companies.

4.5.2 Definition of business property

(TCGA 1992, s 165(2))

Business property is defined for these purposes as:

(1) an asset used by the transferor in a trade, profession or vocation;
(2) an asset used by the transferor's personal company in a trade;
(3) an asset used for a trade by a subsidiary of the transferor's family company;
(4) agricultural land which qualifies for IHT agricultural property relief (see 21.9).

Where an asset has been used for non-qualifying purposes for part of the person's period of ownership, only a corresponding part of any capital gain may be held over.

4.5.3 Example – Restriction on hold-over relief

A acquired a property in March 1982 for £190,000. In 1997 it is worth £480,000. Take indexation as 84 per cent.

To begin with, *A* rented it out as an investment and he occupied it for his business only for the period from April 1990 to March 1997. If *A* transfers the property by way of a gift, his capital gain will be:

	£	£
Market value		480,000
Less cost	190,000	
Indexation	160,000	
		(350,000)
		130,000

The maximum part of the gain which may be held over is as follows:

$$\frac{\text{April 1990 to March 1997}}{\text{March 1982 to March 1997}} = \frac{7}{15}$$

Thus only £50,000 of the gain may be held over.

4.5.4 Hold-over relief on shares

The definition of business property also includes:

(1) unquoted shares in a trading company; and
(2) quoted shares if the company concerned is the transferor's personal company (it is very unusual for this condition to be satisfied).

A similar restriction to that illustrated in 4.5.3 may apply on a transfer of shares in an unquoted trading company if that company holds investments or other chargeable assets which are not business assets. The restriction is based on the following formula:

$$\frac{\text{Chargeable assets used in the business}}{\text{Total chargeable assets}}$$

4.5.5 Example – Restriction on hold-over relief

B gives his son his shares in X Ltd. The balance sheet of X Ltd shows assets as follows:

	£
Stock	100,000
Factory	500,000
Investments	500,000
Cash	200,000

Only half of *B*'s capital gain may be held over, ie $\frac{\text{Value of factory}}{\text{Factory and investments}}$

4.5.6 Hold-over relief not available on certain gifts

The legislation provides that hold-over relief is available only if the recipient of the transfer is either UK-resident or ordinarily resident. Moreover, hold-over relief is not available if the recipient is dual resident, and the relevant double taxation agreement has the effect of treating him as if he were not resident in the United Kingdom.

Hold-over relief is also precluded where an individual etc transfers an asset to a UK-resident company which is controlled by persons who are neither UK-resident nor ordinarily resident.

4.5.7 Hold-over relief for transactions which are chargeable transfers for IHT purposes

(TCGA 1992, s 260)

There is a completely separate provision which provides hold-over relief where the disposal is a chargeable transfer for IHT purposes and the recipient is UK-resident or ordinarily resident. The main circumstance where this may apply is where assets are transferred by way of gift etc to a discretionary trust (see 21.10).

Where a transfer of assets comes within both ss 165 and 260 of TCGA 1992, s 260 takes priority. Note that where hold-over relief is available under s 260 on a disposal which is a chargeable transfer for IHT purposes, there is no restriction as in 4.5.3 or 4.5.5 because the asset has not been used for business for the whole of the person's period of ownership, or the property includes non-business assets.

4.5.8 Clawback of hold-over relief

(TCGA 1992, s 168)

Hold-over relief is clawed back if the recipient of the gift etc ceases to be resident within six years. The held-over gain is deemed to arise immediately before he ceases to be resident and, if the individual concerned fails to pay the resultant CGT, the transferor can be held liable.

There is one circumstance where the emigration of the recipient does not give rise to a chargeable gain. If the individual is required to work abroad because of his employment, and he returns to the United Kingdom within three years still owning the asset, the temporary 'emigration' does not count for these purposes.

4.5.9 Practical aspects

In strictness, an individual's capital gain should be formally agreed even though it is held-over. However, if both the transferor and transferee agree, it can be left in abeyance, to be ascertained only as and when the transferee makes a chargeable disposal. See SP8/92.

4.6 PARTNERS AND CAPITAL GAINS

The way in which CGT affects partnership transactions can at times be complex. The Revenue's practice is set out in SP D12 but this is extremely technical and to understand its implications professional advice should be sought. The following paragraphs describe some key aspects.

4.6.1 Partnership's acquisition value

Although individual partners' entitlement to profits may vary from time to time, the partnership's acquisition value for the firm's chargeable assets is not affected unless there are cash payments from one partner to another to acquire a greater interest in the firm or unless assets are revalued as part of the arrangements for changes in profit-sharing.

4.6.2 Assets held by firm at 31 March 1982

The partnership may make a universal rebasing election for the values at 31 March 1982 to be used instead of cost. This is quite separate from the individual partners' position in relation to their personal assets when a disposal of an asset takes place. There may be partners who were not in the partnership at 31 March 1982, but this does not affect the computation of the gain.

4.6.3 Partnership gains divisible amongst partners

Where a partnership asset is sold at a capital gain (or loss), the gain is divided amongst the partners in accordance with their profit-sharing ratios. Each partner is personally assessable on his share of the gain. The partner's actual CGT liability depends on his own situation, ie whether he has other gains for the year, has available losses, can claim roll-over relief or is entitled to retirement relief (see 4.8).

4.6.4 Revaluations

Problems may arise where a partnership has substantial assets which are chargeable assets for CGT purposes and which are worth more than their book value (ie the value at which they are shown in the firm's accounts). A revaluation to bring their book value into line with their market value can produce a liability for individual partners if there is a reduction in their profit-sharing ratios. This commonly happens when existing partners retire or new partners are introduced.

There is no such problem where partners leave or come in and there is no revaluation of assets. In such a case, the remaining or incoming partners normally take over the outgoing partners' acquisition values for the firm's asset.

4.6.5 Example – Retirement of partner

A is a partner in a five partner firm and is entitled to 20 per cent of the profits. He retires and his colleagues then share profits on the basis of 25 per cent each. As part of the arrangements for his retirement, the book value of the firm's office block is increased from £150,000 to its current value of £750,000. The surplus is credited to each partner's account so that *A* is credited with £120,000.

A is treated as if he has realised a gain on the disposal of a one-fifth share of the building. This would be based on the £120,000. The remaining four partners are not treated as having made a disposal. Indeed, they each have made an acquisition of a 5 per cent interest in the building for an outlay of £30,000.

4.6.6 Example – Introduction of new partner

B and *C* are partners. Their premises are included in their firm's balance sheet at £200,000 (original cost), but are actually worth £500,000. *B* and *C* agree to admit *D* as an equal partner in return for his paying in new capital into the firm of £700,000. They revalue the premises before admitting *D* as a partner, and the surplus of £300,000 is credited to their accounts. In this case,

B and *C* are each regarded as having made a disposal of a one-sixth interest in the premises. This is because *D*'s new capital goes into the firm as a whole. After coming in, he effectively owns one-third of all the assets (and is responsible for one-third of the liabilities). The former partners' ownership of the premises has been reduced from 50 per cent to a one-third interest.

4.6.7 Example – Change of partners with no assets revaluation

A and *B* are in partnership. They own premises which have a book value of £94,000 (equal to cost in 1980). *A* retires and is replaced by *C*. The premises are not revalued. Later the premises are sold for £244,000. *B* and *C* are assessed on their share of the gain.

The gain is computed by reference to the original cost (£94,000) or the premises' market value at 31 March 1982, *not* their value at the time that *C* became a partner.

This does *not* apply where the partners are connected persons (perhaps because they are relatives), or where cash payments are made to acquire an interest in the firm. In either of these categories you should seek specialist advice.

4.6.8 Partner leaves after roll-over relief secured on purchase of new asset by firm

A capital gain may arise for a partner on his leaving the firm, even though he receives no consideration from his former partners in return for giving up his interest in the firm beyond being paid out his capital account. Take a situation where there are five partners sharing profits and losses equally. One partner leaves and the remaining four continue. The balance sheet shows the partnership premises as having a cost of £500,000. However, on closer examination, it transpires that some years ago the former partnership premises were disposed of, realising a capital gain of £280,000. Roll-over relief was obtained against this capital gain by reference to the purchase of the current partnership premises.

The Revenue takes the view that the outgoing partner is deemed to have realised a capital gain as follows:

	£
⅕ share in partnership premises (deemed proceeds)	100,000
Less cost (⅕ of cost as adjusted for roll-over relief)	(44,000)
Gain before indexation	56,000

The four continuing partners' base value for CGT purposes is increased by £25,000 each.

4.7 RETIREMENT RELIEF – GENERAL PROVISIONS
(TCGA 1992, s 163)

Where an individual is aged at least 50 and he satisfies the necessary conditions for a period of ten years, he may be entitled to an exemption of £250,000 plus one-half of the next £750,000 capital gains.

4.7.1 Example – Retirement relief

A, who is 52 years old, disposes of his business which he has run for 15 years. He realises gains qualifying for retirement relief of £400,000. The relief is as follows:

	£
Appropriate percentage (100 per cent) of first limit	250,000
Excess of gains over this limit	150,000
Relief on excess at 50 per cent	75,000
Therefore total relief	325,000
Taxable gain	75,000

The relief can be split between gains on disposals of two or more different businesses, but the aggregate relief will be restricted to the £250,000 and £1m limits. In some cases, the gains may arise in different tax years.

4.7.2 Date of disposal for retirement relief

Although the date of disposal for CGT purposes is generally the date that contracts are exchanged, or the point in time that a conditional contract becomes unconditional, the Revenue operates a concession for retirement relief purposes. The key date here is the date that the contract is completed.

4.7.3 Example – Retirement relief by reference to completion date

A is aged 49 and 10 months when he enters into a contract to sell his hotel business. However, the sale is actually completed three months later, just after he has attained age 50. Because of ESC D31, *A* will normally be given retirement relief.

4.7.4 Retirement through ill health

(TCGA 1992, s 164(1)(b))

The legislation provides that retirement relief is also available to an individual who is below age 50 but is required to dispose of his business because ill health makes it impossible for him to carry on. In practice, the Revenue requires claimants to provide a medical certificate, signed by a qualified medical practitioner (whether or not the claimant's own general practitioner). The Board itself takes advice from the Regional Medical Service of the Department of Health, and in some cases a further medical examination by the regional medical officer is required.

The Revenue has made it clear that retirement relief will *not* be given to someone aged below 50 where he has ceased work because of the ill health of someone else, for example his spouse.

4.7.5 Conditions to be satisfied for ten years if full relief to be available

(TCGA 1992, ss 163(4))

The full relief is given only if the individual has satisfied various requirements for a period of ten years but some relief is due provided the qualifying period is at least 12 months. A period is a qualifying period if the individual was in business as a sole trader or partner or he was a full-time officer (eg a director) or employee of a personal trading company. The definition of a personal trading company is the same as in 4.3.12, ie the individual must have at least 5 per cent of the voting rights. Separate periods during which an individual satisfied one of these requirements can normally be aggregated provided there is not an interval between them of more than two years.

For specific requirements in relation to disposals by sole traders, partners and full-time directors and employees of personal trading companies, see 4.8 and 4.9 respectively.

4.7.6 Example – Limited relief

In example 4.7.3, if *A* had owned the business for six years, the relief would be as follows:

	£
Appropriate percentage of £250,000	150,000
Excess of gain over £150,000	250,000
50 per cent thereof	125,000
Total relief	275,000
Taxable gain	125,000

4.7.7 Retirement relief for trustees
(TCGA 1992, s 164(3))

There are certain circumstances where the sale by trustees of family settlements of business property or shares can attract retirement relief. This is an area where professional advice should be taken, but in essence the trustees may be able to utilise unused relief available to a beneficiary (normally a life tenant) who uses land etc which is owned by the trustees for a trade carried on by him. Similarly retirement relief may be due to trustees who hold shares in a company where the beneficiary is a full-time director or employee.

4.8 RETIREMENT RELIEF AND UNINCORPORATED TRADERS

The sale of a business may be broken down for tax purposes into the disposal of distinct assets (ie goodwill and buildings, plant and equipment, stock debtors and cash). The CGT position must be looked at separately for each asset.

4.8.1 Retirement relief for sole traders

The legislation requires that a capital gain should arise on the disposal of a business or part of a business. There have been several cases concerning farmers where the individual concerned has disposed of part of his land. In each of these cases, the courts have held that retirement relief was not due since the asset disposed of was used in the business rather than part of the business itself. A similar point arises if a sole trader sells a warehouse or office block, but continues in business.

In practice, the Revenue resists relief for farmers unless the disposal concerns at least 50 per cent or more of the total area being farmed.

4.8.2 Retirement relief for partners

A gain may attract retirement relief where it arises on a disposal which takes place on the introduction of a new partner or on some other change in profit-sharing ratios combined with a revaluation of partnership assets (see 4.6.4).

In some cases, a partner may own an asset which is used by his firm. Retirement relief is available to cover a gain arising from the disposal of such an asset provided the following conditions are satisfied:

(1) The disposal of the asset must take place as part of the individual's withdrawal from participation in the business carried on by the partnership.
(2) Immediately before the disposal (or the cessation of the business) the asset must have been used for the purposes of the partnership business.
(3) During the whole or part of the period in which the asset has been in the ownership of the individual, the asset must have been used for the purposes of:
   (a) the business; or
   (b) another business carried on by the individual or by a partnership of which the individual concerned was a member.

The amount of retirement relief on the disposal may be restricted where the partner has charged his firm a commercial rent for use of the property.

4.8.3 Example – Restriction on retirement relief where partner has charged rent

A is a partner in a four partner firm, and he takes a 25 per cent share of profits. He owns the offices used by the firm and charges a market rent of £10,000 per annum.

The Revenue ignores the rent that A effectively bears himself, but in this situation only 25 per cent of any capital gain realised on the sale of the offices would qualify for retirement relief. If A had charged only £5,000 (ie less than the market rent of £10,000) the proportion of the gain eligible for retirement relief would be

$$\frac{10{,}000 - 3750}{10{,}000} \quad \text{ie} \quad \frac{5}{8}$$

4.9 RETIREMENT RELIEF AND FULL-TIME DIRECTORS AND EMPLOYEES

(TCGA 1992, ss 163–164)

This section focuses on the way in which the capital gain on the sale of shares in a personal trading company (see 4.3.12) and assets owned privately by the shareholder may qualify for retirement relief.

4.9.1 Full-time working directors and managers

To qualify for retirement relief, it is sufficient for an individual to work for the company on a full-time basis in a managerial or technical capacity.

There is no statutory definition of what full-time means in this context. In practice, it is understood that the Revenue accepts that a director whose normal working week is 30 hours (excluding meal breaks) qualifies for relief. A person is required to devote more or less the whole of his time if that is what his job and service contract involve. Absence through illness does not normally prejudice entitlement to the relief.

In some cases, the individual will be working full-time for a group of related companies. Relief is available where a person is required to devote more or less the whole of his time to the service of a commercial association of companies which carry on businesses and which are of a nature that the business of a company and the associated companies taken together may be reasonably considered to make up a single composite undertaking.

This is an area where professional advice may be required in the light of the circumstances of the particular case.

A director who has retired from full-time employment, but who continues to spend an average of at least ten hours per week in the conduct and management of the company's business, may qualify for relief. However, his entitlement is based on the period of full-time service which he had up to the date of his retirement.

4.9.2 Possible restriction of retirement relief

Where a company has investments as well as business interests, the gain which may attract retirement relief is restricted to the proportion of the gain determined by the following fraction:

$$\frac{\text{Chargeable assets used for business purposes}}{\text{Total chargeable assets}}$$

Where a company has disposed of business assets within six months of a disposal of shares, the individual may elect for the restriction to be computed by reference to the position if the company had not sold the assets concerned.

4.9.3 Example of restriction

D holds all the shares in X Ltd. The balance sheet of X Ltd shows the following assets:

	£
Cash at bank	100,000
Gilts	400,000
Quoted shares	500,000
Factory	1,000,000
	2,000,000

The normal approach would be to treat only a proportion of any gain as qualifying for retirement relief. The proportion would be:

$$\frac{1{,}000{,}000}{1{,}500{,}000} \quad \text{ie} \quad \frac{\text{(Business assets)}}{\text{(chargeable assets)}}$$

The cash and the gilts are not chargeable assets and are therefore left out of the equation altogether.

However, it may be that the company has a chargeable asset which does not feature in the balance sheet (goodwill) and the inclusion of this business asset at its market value may increase the proportion of the gain which qualifies for retirement relief.

4.9.4 Sale of premises etc used by company

An individual who has been a full-time director or employee may own property or some other assets which are used by his personal trading company. Retirement relief may be claimed in respect of a disposal of such assets provided the following conditions are satisfied:

(1) the disposal of the asset must take place as part of the withdrawal of the individual concerned from participation in the business carried on by the company; and
(2) the asset must be in use for the purposes of the company's business at the time of the disposal or it must have been so used at the time that the company's business ceased; and
(3) the asset must have been used in the whole or part of the period in which the individual has owned it for the purposes of:
   (a) the business carried on by the company; or

(b) another business carried on by the individual or by a partnership of which the individual was a member; or
(c) another business carried on by the individual's personal trading company.

Relief is restricted where the individual has charged rent. If a full market rent has been charged, no retirement relief is due whatsoever. If the rent is half of the market rent, half of the gain on the disposal of the property may be eligible for retirement relief.

5

OUTLINE OF VAT

Value added tax was introduced by FA 1972 and became operational on 1 April 1973 when it replaced purchase tax and selective employment tax. In concept, it is a simple tax, although various exclusions from a VAT charge and the EC influence have resulted in a simple concept becoming one of the most complicated taxes of all time. This chapter covers some of the detail of VAT under the following headings:

(1) Introduction
(2) Legal authorities
(3) Basic principles
(4) Practical implications
(5) Imports, exports and single market
(6) Anti-avoidance measures
(7) Special schemes
(8) Enforcement procedures
(9) Fraud
(10) Appeals.

5.1 INTRODUCTION

The introduction of VAT was a pre-condition of the United Kingdom's acceptance into what was then known as the European Economic Community which, as a result of the European Communities Act 1982, has become the European Community and is now commonly referred to as the European Union (EU). Part of the EU philosophy is the harmonisation of taxing statutes, particularly those that affect cross-border trading activities. For example, customs duty is an EU tax and is payable when goods enter the EU. It is charged at the same rate when or wherever the goods enter the Community.

Once customs duty is paid the goods are in free circulation and can move freely between member states without the payment of any further duty or being subject to customs' controls. The legislative authority for customs duty is found in EC Regulations which, once agreed by the EC Commission, have immediate direct effect in each member state.

The harmonisation of VAT has been the subject of much discussion by the EC Commission, which has resulted in the introduction of transitional rules with effect from 1 January 1993, commonly referred to as the Single Market Legislation. The rules implement a degree of harmonisation on the VAT accounting requirements of the movement of goods between member states. The ultimate legal authority for VAT is a number of EC VAT directives, which must be reflected in the national legislation of each member state. To that extent, directives have direct effect. For example, if the national law is not in accordance with a directive and thereby disadvantages the taxpayer, the taxpayer can argue his case in the national court, which must recognise the directive. The ultimate right of appeal lies with the European Court of Justice.

The administration of VAT was given to HM Customs and Excise, which introduced a completely new system of tax enforcement to the majority of businesses and the accounting profession. Customs, which is steeped in the history of duty enforcement, brought with it its practical approach to controlling the taxpayer. For the first time, many businesses and their professional advisers had to justify, face to face with the enforcement agencies (the VAT control officer), what had been declared in the VAT return and the amounts shown in the annual accounts.

In principle, for the majority of businesses VAT is not a tax on profits. It is a tax on the consumer that is collected in stages throughout the business chain and is collected, eventually, by the business person supplying the consumer (ie an individual or a business which is not registered for VAT). If a business fails to charge and account for VAT correctly, it must account for both the VAT and any penalties from its own resources and thereby, by default, VAT becomes a charge on profits. Put simply, the business person is a tax collector.

Within the EU, neutrality is achieved by means of an exemption or zero-rating of goods to other member states and taxing 'acquisitions' in the member state of destination. The VAT paid by the final consumer in any country is therefore the same whether he obtains the goods from his own country or from another EU country.

5.1.1 Example – How the VAT system works

A retailer sells goods for £1,000 excluding VAT and therefore adds £175 (at a UK VAT rate of 17.5 per cent). The retailer pays his supplier £750 plus VAT of £131.25. He has to pay VAT charged on the sale to Customs but is entitled to deduct the VAT paid to his suppliers. Hence the net payment to Customs is £43.75.

5.2 LEGAL AUTHORITIES

There is no single piece of legislation covering the administration and collection of VAT. The VAT legislation is described briefly below.

5.2.1 The VAT Act 1994 (VATA 1994)

This is a consolidation act which brings together VATA 1983 and subsequent Finance Acts amending the original legislation. VATA 1994 deals with the administration of the tax and provides for certain aspects to be dealt with by delegated legislation.

5.2.2 Statutory instruments (SIs)

There are various SIs which deal with particular aspects of VAT administration. The most notable is the Value Added Tax Regulations 1995 (SI No 2518) which deals with a wide range of administrative procedures which must be complied with (eg tax invoices, when they should be issued and the details required to be shown; how to recover VAT when a VAT-registered person is not entitled to a full recovery of VAT paid to its suppliers; special VAT accounting procedures for particular transactions, etc).

5.2.3 Treasury orders

Certain Treasury orders describe, among other things, what is or is not chargeable to VAT and also give legal authority to certain organisations able to recover VAT which would otherwise be irrecoverable. Occasionally, Treasury orders are published in the *London Gazette*.

5.2.4 Customs notices and leaflets

The general principle is that VAT public notices are not part of the law. Certain notices, however, are published pursuant to VATA 1994 and SIs and, thereby, *are* part of the law. As such they have the same status as an Act of Parliament and are legally binding upon the taxpayer. For example, Notice 700 (General Guide) is principally Customs' interpretation of the law, but the section dealing with the maintenance of accounting records is part of the law, as is the Public Notice on the special VAT Retail Schemes (Notice 727).

Customs' leaflets are not strictly part of the law but certain leaflets, which explain the commissioners' requirements for particular types of transactions, are, in practical terms, legally binding. This applies to relatively few of the leaflets, the vast majority being simply the commissioners' interpretation of the law.

5.2.5 EC directives

All VAT law stems from the EC Sixth VAT Directive which has direct effect in all member states through respective national laws. Other directives deal with specific aspects such as that which, on 1 January 1993, introduced VAT harmonisation in the single market and others which provide the right to recover VAT incurred in other countries.

5.3 BASIC PRINCIPLES

The basic rule is that VAT is chargeable on the taxable supply of any goods or services in the United Kingdom when supplied by a taxable person 'in the course or furtherance of any business'.

5.3.1 Supplies

The application of VAT differs depending on whether there is a supply of goods or of services. A supply of goods is where legal title to the whole property is, or is to be, transferred to another person. This includes, for example, the transfer of title in land by means of a freehold sale or a lease exceeding 21 years. Anything which is not a supply of goods which is done for a consideration is a supply of services and, therefore, subject to the VAT regime. A VAT charge only arises where consideration is present and, accordingly, a free supply of services is outside the scope of VAT. Care is required, because what may appear to be free is not necessarily so in real terms and a hidden VAT liability could arise. By Treasury Order, any transaction can be deemed to be a supply of goods and not a supply of services (or vice versa). Examples of supplies of goods which may not be self evident are as follows:

(1) The application to another person's goods of a treatment or process which produces goods (eg the making of a suit by a tailor from the cloth provided by his customer is a supply of goods and not a supply of tailoring services).
(2) The supply of any form of power, heat, refrigeration or ventilation.

A supply is subject to VAT at the standard rate unless the VAT legislation provides for specific relief. VATA 1994 provides for two forms of relief:

(1) Zero rating under s 30 and specified in Sched 8 to the Act.
(2) Exemption under s 31 and specified in Sched 9 to the Act.

Taxable

These are supplies that are subject to VAT at either the zero or the standard (currently 17.5 per cent) rate. Supplies of fuel and power are taxable at 8 per cent (5 per cent when supplied after 31 August 1997) when supplied for domestic use or for use for a charity otherwise than in the course or furtherance of a business.

Zero-rated supplies

The zero-rated supplies are exports of goods to places outside the EU (VATA 1994, s 30) and the 16 groups listed in VATA 1994, Sched 8:

(1) Food for human consumption
(2) Sewerage services and water (but not bottled water)
(3) Books, etc
(4) Talking books for the blind and handicapped, and wireless sets for the blind
(5) Construction and sales of new dwellings
(6) Approved alteration of protected buildings
(7) International services (the services that qualify under this heading were greatly reduced on 1 January 1993)
(8) Transport
(9) Caravans and houseboats
(10) Gold
(11) Bank notes
(12) Drugs, medicines, aids for the handicapped etc
(13) Imports, exports etc
(14) Tax-free shops
(15) Charities (certain supplies to or by charities)
(16) Protective and young children's clothing and footwear.

Exempt

These are supplies that are exempt from VAT by statute, ie those listed in VATA 1994, Sched 9. Exemption and zero-rating must not be confused because the overall effect on a business is totally different. Zero-rating gives entitlement to recover VAT on underlying costs whereas exemption does not (see 5.4.5). The main headings under Sched 9 are:

(1) Land (with some exceptions)
(2) Insurance

(3) Postal services
(4) Betting, gaming and lotteries
(5) Finance
(6) Education (when provided by eligible bodies); this heading also includes supplies by youth clubs
(7) Health and welfare
(8) Burial and cremation
(9) Trade unions and professional bodies
(10) Sports competitions
(11) Works of art etc (in limited circumstances)
(12) Fund-raising events by charities and other qualifying bodies
(13) Cultural services.

Outside the scope

Certain supplies or business activities are 'outside the scope' of VAT. This includes an employee's services to an employer but can also include what, on the face of it, are the organisation's normal trading activities. For example, the supply of goods that are situated outside the United Kingdom, although part of the UK business activities, are outside the scope of UK VAT. Similarly, with effect from 1 January 1993, certain services that are either physically performed or are to be received outside the United Kingdom are deemed to have been supplied outside the United Kingdom and, therefore, outside the scope of UK VAT.

Generally speaking, an organisation's 'outside the scope' activities do not permit the recovery of VAT on related costs. The exception to this general principle is where a VAT-registered person supplies goods or services outside the United Kingdom that would be subject to VAT if made in the United Kingdom. There are also special arrangements for certain services which are exempt in the United Kingdom but the recipient belongs outside the EU.

5.3.2 Business

(VATA 1994, s 94)

A supply for VAT purposes must be made in the course or furtherance of any business. As with supply, the word 'business' has not been defined in the legislation but has been interpreted to have a very wide meaning and covers all organisations that carry on activities in a businesslike way. There are directions in the legislation of what the term encompasses and excludes, for example:

- Business includes any trade, profession or vocation.
- Any act done in the furtherance of a business's termination or disposition, whether or not in connection with its reorganisation or

winding-up, is regarded as a supply in the course or furtherance of a business.

- A body is *not* treated as carrying on a business if its objects are in the public domain and are of a political, religious, philanthropic, philosophical or patriotic nature, and a subscription by members only entitles the member to participate in the management or receive reports on its activities.

In *C & E Commissioners v Apple and Pear Development Council* [1984] STC 296 the decision included the following definition of business:

> 'a business for the purpose of Value Added Tax requires the carrying on of an occupation, function or activity which includes the making of some supplies recognised for Value Added Tax purposes.'

A number of organisations which do not consider themselves to be carrying on a business (such as clubs and associations, charities etc) have to conform with the VAT legislation and, where appropriate, register and account for VAT on their business income.

If it can be demonstrated that the activity is purely and simply a hobby, there is no requirement to charge VAT on any resulting income. An employee's services to an employer in return for a salary meets the 'supply of services' definition but the law specifically provides that such services are not in the course or furtherance of a business and, therefore, are outside the scope of VAT.

Charities

There is no automatic relief from VAT for supplies either to or made by charities. If a charity is carrying on a business activity it is required to register and account for VAT on its business income the same as any commercial organisation. Normally a business activity is one which is concerned with the making of taxable supplies for a consideration. The following is a guide to the business and non-business position of the more common activities of charities.

Non-business activities include:

- Donations, legacies and other voluntary contributions from the public.
- Voluntary services performed free of charge.

Business activities include:

- Grants which are the consideration for services rendered, where a benefit is provided to the grantor.
- Sales of donated goods, but in certain circumstances such sales are relieved of VAT by zero rating.
- Hiring out charity run buildings.

Several income sources could be business or non-business depending on the circumstances. The most common area of difficulty is sponsorship. If a sponsor receives nothing in return for his sponsorship, the donation is outside the scope of VAT. If the contribution is made on condition that the sponsor is promoted or receives some benefit, it is the consideration for a taxable supply.

There is relief from VAT by means of zero rating for certain supplies to charities. These are mainly in the health and welfare area but also include:

- The supply of an advertisement on television or in a newspaper, periodical or journal for educational or fund-raising purposes. The relief has recently been extended to job recruitment advertisements provided the advert publicises the charity objectives.
- The supply of a new building and an extension to an existing building which is otherwise standard rated provided the building is intended solely for use for a relevant residential or relevant charitable (ie non-business) purpose.
- Supplies in the course of constructing a building for use as above.

Clubs and associations

(VATA 1994, s 94(2)(a))

Many local clubs and associations, usually formed by local residents, consider they are not carrying on a business, but this is incorrect. The law specifically provides that the provision of benefits to members in return for a subscription or other payment is a business activity. Similarly certain trade and professional organisations consider they are not in business or qualify for exemption as professional associations and there is no requirement to register for VAT. Such organisations generally provide other benefits to their members and, possibly, non-members which are not within the exemption and, therefore, there may be a liability to register.

Admission to premises

(VATA 1994, s 94(2)(b))

The admission, for payment, of persons to any premises is a business activity. Any person carrying on such an activity is required to register and account for VAT if such income exceeds the registration threshold. To avoid the risk of penalties all clubs, associations, charities and similar organisations should review their activities to ensure that they meet their VAT obligations at the correct time.

5.3.3 Taxable person

In addition to considering the words 'supply' and 'business', it is necessary to consider the meaning of 'taxable person' since VAT is not chargeable on supplies made by non-taxable persons. A taxable person is one who is or is liable to be registered for VAT. In other words, it is not possible to avoid VAT by failing to register. Registration is considered in 5.4.1 below.

'Taxable person' is also defined by art 4 of the EC Sixth Directive as 'any person who independently carries out in any place any economic activity'. 'Economic activity' includes all activities of producers, traders and persons supplying services (including mining and agricultural activities) and professionals' activities. The exploitation of tangible or intangible property to obtain income therefrom on a continuing basis is also considered an economic activity.

5.3.4 Consideration

VAT is chargeable on the consideration provided for a supply. Consideration is important as supplies of services for no consideration are not taxable supplies and therefore outside the scope for VAT.

5.4 PRACTICAL IMPLICATIONS

The administration of VAT is by a system of registration, accounting and the submission of regular returns by the taxpayer and control verification visits by Customs.

5.4.1 Registration

Registration is required where a business or any other organisation makes taxable supplies over a pre-determined limit. The limits, based on gross turnover, are increased each year generally in line with inflation.

It is the person who is registered, not the business activity. Once registered, all business activities must be reflected in the VAT accounting records: for example a VAT-registered sole proprietor carrying on several businesses must include the turnover from all his businesses in his VAT accounts. A company is a separate entity from the individuals who own it and must be registered separately. For VAT purposes, a partnership is a separate entity to the persons who are partners in it.

Currently registration is required when one of the following two conditions is satisfied:

(1) When, at the end of any month, the gross taxable turnover during the previous 12 months, on a rolling basis, exceeds £49,000. Such a liability must be notified within 30 days and registration is effective from the first day of the month following the month in which a liability to notify arose. For example, where taxable turnover in the 12 months to 31 January was, say, £50,000, notification must be made within 30 days and registration is effective from 1 March. VAT has to be accounted for on all income received after 1 March, whether or not it refers to invoices issued on or before 28 February. There is no VAT liability for income received prior to the effective date of registration.

(2) As soon as there are reasonable grounds to believe the value of taxable supplies to be made during the following 30 days will exceed £49,000. Registration is due immediately and will be effective from the beginning of the period.

It is only *taxable* turnover (ie goods or services liable to VAT at either the zero or standard rate) that is taken into consideration when determining whether there is a liability to register. Income which is exempt and outside the scope of VAT is ignored. Supplies of goods which are capital assets of the business are disregarded for the purpose of the registration thresholds, with the exception of standard-rated supplies of interests in land.

Note that self supplies, imported services and acquisitions from the EU all need to be taken into account when determining whether registration is necessary.

Voluntary registration

There is an entitlement to register voluntarily for VAT even if the taxable turnover is below the VAT registration limits. This could be an advantage to an expanding or small business as VAT on costs are recoverable and this, providing the charging of VAT on supplies does not reduce demand for the product, increases profitability. Similarly businesses based in the United Kingdom which do not make any supplies there, but make what would be taxable supplies overseas, are entitled to register and are thereby able to recover VAT on UK costs.

Intending registration

A person is eligible to register for VAT even though he is not yet making taxable supplies. The *Merseyside Cablevision Ltd* case (MAN/85/327; [1987] 3 CMLR 290) has affected radically the rules relating to intending registration. Prior to FA 1988, a person who satisfied Customs that he intended to make taxable supplies from a specified date and would be liable to be registered when he commenced to make taxable supplies could request to be registered and Customs could, subject to such conditions as it thought fit to impose, register him from a date as agreed between them. However, these terms were *ultra vires* the provisions contained in VATA 1983, Sched 1, para 5. This provided taxpayers with a right to registration where the taxpayer is carrying on a business, and there is an intention to make taxable supplies in the course or furtherance of that business.

There appears to be no time limit between the dates on which intending registration takes effect and the first taxable supply is made. Normally this is a matter of several months or perhaps one or two years, as stocks are bought in and premises are prepared.

Applicants for intending registration must satisfy Customs that there is an intention to make taxable supplies. This could mean submitting documentation (ie contracts or purchase invoices).

Group registration

Incorporated companies under common control with a belonging in the United Kingdom may register as a group and if so are treated as a single unit. The main advantage of group treatment is any supplies from one member of the group to another are disregarded for VAT purposes. One company is nominated as representative member and any supplies made by or to the group are treated as being made to or by the representative member. However, each company within the group is jointly and severally liable for any tax due from the representative member. Only one VAT return need be completed showing the consolidated figures for all members of the VAT group.

There are two main conditions for entry into a VAT group:

- *Residence* To meet this test the company must be UK resident (ie belonging) although a non-UK-resident company may become a member of a VAT group provided it has an established place of business in the United Kingdom which would constitute a belonging.
- *Control* All companies in a group must be under the control of the same person or persons. This control can be exercised by a company (which need not be a member of the group itself), an individual or a partnership.

Customs uses the definition of control set out in the Companies Act 1985. Control is held to exist:

- where a company holds the majority voting rights in another;
- where the company is a member of the other company and has the right to appoint or remove the majority of its board of directors;
- where one company has the right to exercise a dominant influence over the other company either by provision in the memorandum or articles of association or by virtue of a control contract;
- where a company is a member of another and, by reason of an agreement with the other members, controls a majority of voting rights in the company.

For an individual or individuals to be considered to have control they must have the same control as if they were a holding company and the rules were applied as above.

In *CCE v Kingfisher plc* [1994] STC 63, the effect of a VAT group registration under s 29 of VATA 1983 (now VATA 1994, s 43) was considered. The Commissioners contended that the effect of group registration was merely to provide a simplified accounting procedure whereby supplies of goods and services intra group were disregarded for VAT purposes, but that group registration did not create a single taxable person. The VAT tribunal decided that the purpose of group registration was to enable the group to be treated as if it were a single body corporate, the different member companies being no more than different departments. On an appeal by the Commissioners to the High Court, the tribunal decision was upheld.

Customs has specific authority to deny entry into a group registration where it considers it necessary to protect the Revenue. With effect from 1 March 1995, Customs has fuller powers to restrict changes in VAT groups, including preventing the removal of a member from the group and its complete disbandment. This is as a direct result of the tribunal's decision in *Thorn Materials Supply Ltd & Thorn Resources Ltd* (LON194/1996A and 1987A) which highlighted a simple loophole to avoid VAT. These powers have been further strengthened in FA 1997.

A VAT group registration may not be identical to an accounting group. Companies within an accounting group, which are not members of a VAT group, must account for VAT on supplies to each other as if they were unconnected.

Applications for group registration should be submitted at least 90 days before the intended date of the registration coming into effect.

5.4.2 De-registration

A registered person, or one who has become liable to be registered, only ceases to be liable to be registered if at any time Customs is satisfied that:

- he has ceased to make taxable supplies;
- the value of taxable supplies in the period of one year then beginning will not exceed specified limits; the current limit is £47,000.

It is a requirement that a person who ceases to make or intends to make taxable supplies must notify Customs within 30 days of the date on which he does so or forms the intention to do so. Notification must be in writing and state the date on which the registered person ceased to make or have the intention of making taxable supplies.

One of the consequences of de-registration is that, subject to certain exceptions, tax must be accounted for on any goods forming part of the business assets which were on hand at the close of business or on the last day of registration. The exceptions include where:

(1) the business is transferred as a going concern to another taxable person;
(2) a taxable person has died, become bankrupt or incapacitated and the business is carried on by another person who is treated as the taxable person;
(3) the tax involved is not more than £250.

In addition, the provisions do not apply to any goods where the taxable person can show that no credit for input tax had been allowed for the supply of goods.

5.4.3 Accounting for VAT

It is a requirement for all taxpayers to maintain a VAT account. The VAT Regulations 1995 (SI No 2518), regs 31–39 set down specifically what is to be included in the account. Separate accounts should be maintained for each tax period, known as prescribed accounting periods, and each account should be split into two portions – tax payable and tax allowable. The tax payable portion should include a total of output tax due for that prescribed accounting period, a total of output tax due on acquisitions from other member states, and corrections and adjustments to the tax payable. The tax allowable portion should include a total of the input tax allowable to the taxable person for that prescribed accounting period including the total allowable for acquisitions from other member states and corrections and adjustments.

VAT returns have to be submitted on a regular basis. Each VAT-registered person is normally allocated a three-monthly VAT accounting period, but it is possible to request a particular VAT period (for example to coincide with the business's financial year). It is also possible to request monthly returns if the business regularly recovers VAT from Customs. There is also a scheme whereby it is possible to make annual returns (see 5.7.4).

The largest VAT-registered businesses (ie those which normally pay more than £2m annually to Customs) are required to make monthly payments on account with a balancing payment when the three-monthly VAT return is submitted. The actual monthly payments are calculated by reference to the VAT liability of a reference year.

Returns must be submitted with full payment by the end of the month following the end of the VAT accounting period (the due date). A failure to submit returns and make full payment by the due date is subject to penalties (see 5.8.2). Taxpayers who make regular payments can apply to use the Credit Transfer Scheme which allows a further seven days for payment.

Where a registered person has failed to make a return for a period or where the return appears to be incomplete or incorrect, Customs is empowered to make an assessment of the amount due and notify it to the registered person. The assessment is usually produced automatically by the VAT Central Unit and estimates the amount based on the taxpayer's previous VAT return history. Where the assessed amount is lower than the actual liability, a further assessment is issued when this fact is discovered, usually by the local VAT control officer.

5.4.4 Output VAT

The VAT chargeable on supplies (known as output tax) made during a period must be declared on the return which is provided automatically each period by Customs. Output VAT is due on all supplies made (normally invoices issued during the period), irrespective of whether the invoices have been paid for. There are special schemes available to ease this particular requirement for certain business classes as explained below. In addition, VAT is due on all money received for supplies made during the period and for which a tax invoice has not been issued (eg scrap sales, vending machine income, emptying telephone boxes, staff canteen sales, and certain deductions from salaries for supplies to staff).

For businesses which do not issue tax invoices, such as retailers, VAT is due on the gross taxable income received during the VAT period.

Tax invoices

A registered taxable person making a standard-rated taxable supply to another taxable person must provide him with a tax invoice. The issue of invoices for zero-rated supplies and for supplies to customers who are not taxable persons is optional. A tax invoice must, unless Customs agrees otherwise, be issued within 30 days after the basic tax point (see below), the time the VAT is due.

The invoices are often addressed to the person who is going to pay them and not to whom the goods and services are supplied. It is important to be aware that this may cause problems as only the person receiving goods or services can recover VAT on the invoice.

The details to be shown on a tax invoice are the:

(1) identifying number;
(2) date of supply (ie tax point);
(3) date of issue;
(4) supplier's name, address and registration number;
(5) name and address of the person to whom the goods or services are supplied;
(6) type of supply;
(7) description;
(8) for each description, quantity or extent of services, rate of tax and amount payable excluding tax;
(9) gross amount payable;
(10) rate of any cash discount offered;
(11) amount of tax chargeable at each rate; and
(12) total amount of tax chargeable.

Tax points

The output tax on a supply of goods or services becomes chargeable at a definite time, called the tax point. The rate of tax charged is the rate in force on the tax point, and the supply must be accounted for on the VAT return which covers the prescribed accounting period in which the tax point occurs. The tax point is also important for recovery of VAT because it determines when a claim for VAT may be made. Particular rules are laid down which determine the tax point in a wide variety of circumstances. Many of the rules are, in principle, common to both supplies of goods and services.

The basic tax point is when VAT becomes due and chargeable and is generally determined at the time:

(1) goods are removed by or made available to the customer;
(2) services are performed (ie completed).

The basic tax point for both goods and services may be overridden by the issue of a tax invoice or the receipt of payment in either of the following circumstances:

(1) Where a tax invoice is issued or payment is received before the basic tax point, this earlier date is taken as the tax point.
(2) Where a tax invoice is issued within 14 days after the basic tax point, the date of the invoice is taken as the tax point. Customs has discretion to allow a longer period than 14 days if requested.

The question of whether the receipt of a payment constitutes a tax point has been considered in various court cases. In *C&E Commrs v Faith Construction* [1989] STC 539 the Court of Appeal held that the word should take its ordinary meaning, so that if the customer's liability has been discharged, and the recipient is left without any right to sue for payment, then a payment has been received, even if that payment is regarded as fettered.

In *C&E Commrs v Moonrakers Guest House Ltd* [1992] STC 544, the High Court held deposits for rooms were taxable when received, even if the booking was subsequently cancelled with the deposit forfeited if the room was not re-let. By contrast, in *Richmond Theatre Management Ltd* the VAT Tribunal decided that the tax point for advance ticket sales was when the performance in question ended. This was because the monies received were said to be held in trust for the customer and were refundable if the performance did not take place or the customer was refused admission. This decision was later overturned by the High Court ((1995) *The Times*, 1 February) which ruled that the customers had allowed the company to make whatever use it wished of the ticket money. Therefore output tax was due at the time of payment.

Note that there are special arrangements which apply to the supply of continuous or periodic services. The tax point is the earlier of the date of issue of a tax invoice or the date a payment is received.

Bad debt relief

There have been a number of amendments to the VAT bad debt relief scheme. These changes take effect from a variety of dates.

If a supply is made after 26 November 1996, and the debtor has not paid the supplier within six months, the unpaid supplier can make a claim for bad debt relief (it is not necessary to show that the customer is formally insolvent, merely that he has not paid). At the same time, the debtor ceases to have the right to claim input tax credit on the supply which he has received but not yet paid for, and must repay the input tax claimed to Customs. If, later, the debtor makes payment to his supplier, then the debtor's input tax claim is restored. However, the supplier must now repay the bad debt relief which he has received.

From 17 December 1996, the six-month period for a claim for bad debt relief is measured from the time when payment for the supply is due (and not from the date of the supply).

From 19 March 1997 it is not necessary for the goods to have passed from the supplier to the customer before the supplier can make a claim for bad debt relief. This is useful if the supplier claims reservation of title (*Romalpa* clause).

From 1 May 1997, if a business is transferred as a going concern and the purchaser takes over the seller's VAT registration (on Form VAT 68), the purchaser takes over the seller's entitlement to bad debt relief. He also has an obligation to repay any bad debt relief if payment is subsequently received from the debtor.

5.4.5 VAT recovery

VAT-registered businesses may offset any VAT paid to suppliers (known as input tax) against the output tax declared, subject to the following conditions:

(1) Goods or services have been *supplied to* and have been, or will be, used by the business to make taxable supplies.
(2) Documentary evidence of the supply received (ie a tax invoice to the business by the supplier) is retained. If there is no tax invoice or other documentary evidence, the VAT officer may refuse claims for input tax, although Customs has discretion to accept alternative evidence.

Supplies of zero-rated goods or services are taxable supplies with an entitlement to recover VAT on related costs; there is no such entitlement for exempt supplies. In addition VAT is not recoverable as input tax on goods or services received by the VAT-registered person which are used for a non-business activity or for private use, or are certainly outside the scope transactions. Many people believe that because a VAT-registered business pays an invoice, there is an entitlement to recover the VAT shown on the invoice. This is not correct and to do so may give rise to penalties.

The recovery of VAT by businesses which make both taxable and exempt supplies is described at 5.4.6.

Subject to certain exceptions, VAT on the purchase of a motor car or on business entertainment expenses is not recoverable as input tax (VAT (Cars) Order 1992 (SI No 3122 and VAT (Input Tax) Order 1992 (SI No 3222)). Note that a question has been raised of whether the United Kingdom is correct in blocking VAT recovery on cars, and the law may be altered.

Motor cars

'Motor car' is defined as a vehicle usually used on public roads with three or more wheels which either:

(1) is constructed solely for the carriage of passengers; or
(2) has roofed accommodation fitted with, or constructed or adapted for the fitting of, windows to the rear of the driver.

The definition is wide and a number of semi-commercial vehicles fall within the definition, eg Land Rovers (see *C&E Commrs v Jeynes t/a Midland International (Hire) Caterers* [1984] STC 30).

VAT is normally recoverable on the acquisition of a motor car where it is:

(1) leased or hired (not a lease purchase);
(2) acquired unused specifically to be sold;
(3) acquired to convert it into a vehicle which is not a motor car;
(4) unused and supplied to a person whose only taxable supply is the hire of motor cars to other taxable persons whose business is predominately the provision of motor cars to disabled persons in respect of a mobility allowance.

In addition, VAT is recoverable on the purchase of motor cars by the following businesses:

(1) self-drive hire companies providing the hiring is to the same person (which may be a company) and is less than 30 consecutive days on any one occasion and 90 days total per annum;
(2) driving schools;
(3) taxi firms;
(4) companies leasing cars to any of the above businesses.

With effect from 1 August 1995, recovery of VAT is allowed on cars purchased wholly for business use. If a car is made available for private use, recovery of input tax remains blocked. The relief generally applies to car leasing companies. Taxpayers leasing cars where there is an element of private use are restricted to a 50 per cent recovery of VAT on the leasing charges. The United Kingdom has applied for a derogation from the European Commission to restrict recovery.

Business entertainment

Business entertainment is not regarded as including staff entertainment, but problems may arise where costs of staff entertainment arise incidentally from the provision of entertainment for clients. Staff entertainment does not include entertainment of self-employed representatives and therefore the VAT is non-recoverable (see *C&E Commrs v Shaklee International* [1981] STC 776).

There are a number of occasions where VAT on promotional activities is classified as business entertaining and the VAT non-recoverable. It includes for example the cost of a box at a racecourse, entertainment at trade fairs, exhibitions etc, subscriptions to squash clubs etc, entertaining shareholders, and entertainment by market research companies who invite people for group discussions.

There are two conflicting court decisions on business entertainment. In each case the issue was whether, where the supply in question was used partly for business entertainment and partly for normal use, the whole of the input tax should be excluded from credit, or whether an apportionment was permissible. In *C&E Commrs v Plant Repair and Services (South Wales) Ltd* [1994] STC 232 it was decided that once it was shown that goods or services were used or to be used for business entertainment purposes, the input tax on the entire supply was non-recoverable. In *Thorn EMI plc v C&E Commrs* [1994] STC 469 the opposite conclusion was reached. It was held that a system of proportional deduction was in order where goods and services were used in part for business use and in part for business entertainment. This decision was upheld in the High Court where the previous ruling in *Plant Repair and Services*, above, was also overturned.

5.4.6 Partial exemption

A business that makes both exempt and taxable supplies is known as partially exempt and is generally unable to recover all VAT paid to its suppliers. However, if the VAT on costs relating, directly and indirectly, to the exempt activities (known as exempt input tax) is below prescribed limits, all the VAT is recoverable in full. The current limits for VAT years commencing on or after 1 December 1994 are that exempt input tax must not exceed £625 per month on average in the VAT year (which ends 31 March, 30 April or 31 May depending on the business's VAT return period). In addition, this exempt input tax must also represent less than 50 per cent of the total input tax incurred by a business on all its purchases and expenses for the period. If these limits should be exceeded in any VAT year, *all* the relevant VAT is irrecoverable.

For VAT years commencing prior to 1 December 1994, the limit was £600 per month on average without the 50 per cent qualification.

There are other minor limits that apply in particular circumstances and certain exempt supplies may be ignored. The rules are complex and it is advisable to obtain professional advice. Full details may be found in the VAT Regulations 1995 (SI No 2518), regs 99–109 and Customs VAT Notice 706.

Input tax which can be directly attributable to taxable supplies can be recovered in full. Input tax wholly attributable to exempt supplies is not recoverable. The purpose of a partial exemption method is to allocate such input tax as cannot be directly related in either taxable or exempt supplies, in a fair and reasonable proportion. The method, known as the standard method, allocates input tax on the basis of a ratio of the value of taxable supplies to the value of total supplies, rounded up to the nearest whole number. This method can be used without obtaining permission from Customs.

The use of any other method requires Customs' agreement. Customs normally approves any method which produces a fair and reasonable result. Other methods available include using a ratio of exempt input tax to total input tax, a ratio of staff generating taxable income to staff generating exempt income, or a ratio of the number of taxable transactions to exempt transactions.

5.5 IMPORTS, EXPORTS AND SINGLE MARKET

The term imports and exports refers only to goods entering or leaving the United Kingdom from or to a place outside the EU.

5.5.1 Imports of goods from outside EU

VAT is due upon the importation of all goods into the United Kingdom which would bear VAT if supplied within the United Kingdom. The VAT may be paid on importation in one of three ways:

(1) via a deferment facility arranged with Customs;
(2) by arrangement with the clearing/shipping agent;
(3) payment in cash or a banker's draft.

The recovery of VAT paid is determined by the same considerations as would apply to any purchase made in the United Kingdom. The evidence required to support input tax deduction on importation is form C79. This is issued by Customs as a certificate detailing the amounts of VAT paid or deferred on importations within the previous calendar month.

5.5.2 Export of goods outside EU

In general, the export of goods from the United Kingdom is zero rated. However, to satisfy Customs that zero rating is appropriate it is necessary to hold some evidence that the goods have been exported. An overseas address on a sales invoice is insufficient.

Customs requires supporting evidence in the form of commercial documentation. If this is not available within three months of the date of zero rating the supply, Customs states that the supply is to be treated as standard rated, and VAT accounted for on the relevant VAT return.

5.5.3 Transactions within the single market

With effect from 1 January 1993, supplies to and from EU member states are not regarded as imports (known as acquisitions) or exports (known as supplies). Businesses must maintain records of all movements of goods and make returns for statistical and control purposes.

No VAT is charged on goods arriving from other EU countries where the UK business's VAT registration number is quoted on the invoice. The recipient of the goods must account for VAT on his next VAT return as if he had supplied them. He must calculate the VAT which would have been payable and include the amount with his normal output tax. The same amount may also be recovered as input tax, subject to the normal rules and restrictions on recovery. If the UK VAT number is not quoted, the supplier charges VAT at source.

Supplies of goods to other EU countries are zero rated, provided that the customer's VAT registration number is shown on the sales invoice. If the customer's number is not shown, VAT must be charged at the rate which would be applicable if the goods had been supplied in the United Kingdom. Persons selling goods to other EU member states must submit an aggregate sales list within 42 days of the end of each period. This must show, for each quarter, the value of goods supplied to each EU customer together with each customer's VAT registration number.

There is a requirement to furnish more detailed information, known as 'intrastat' returns, for acquisitions (known as arrivals) and supplies (known as despatches). The returns must be furnished when the threshold for arrivals or despatches is exceeded. Currently the threshold for both is £150,000. Returns are required monthly and should be lodged within ten working days following the end of the month. The information required on the intrastat is extensive, and reference should be made to Customs Notice 60. Note that intrastat relates only to goods, not services.

5.6 ANTI-AVOIDANCE MEASURES

5.6.1 Business splitting

Where a business activity is divided among a number of legal entities (eg a series of partnerships with a partner common to all) and the reason for the division is to avoid having to account for VAT, Customs may issue a direction informing all the businesses that they are registered as a single unit and that VAT must be accounted for on all taxable income. The direction can only be from a current or future date.

Rules of similar purpose apply to groups of companies (especially if there is a foreign branch, or overseas company involved).

5.6.2 Sales to connected parties

Where a VAT-registered business supplies goods or services at below market value to a connected party which is not entitled to a full recovery of input tax, Customs may direct, within three years following the supply, that the open market value is used.

5.6.3 Self supplies, etc

Prior to 31 March 1995, in certain circumstances, an output VAT charge arises on normal business activities which are not supplies made to third parties, ie on business expenditure (usually referred to as 'self supplies'). The value of such self supplies is taken into consideration when determining a liability to register for VAT; the more important ones are described below. The reasons behind this liability are both anti-avoidance and to reduce possible trade distortion.

Buildings

Where a business constructs, or has constructed, on its own land a new commercial building of a value exceeding £100,000 and the building is used for exempt supplies (eg as a head office of a partially exempt business, an exempt lease or as a doctor's surgery) there is an output VAT liability. The value is the total construction costs plus the value of the land. Note that the self supply on buildings was repealed with effect from 1 March 1995, but there are transitional arrangements for buildings uncompleted at this date.

Stationery

If an exempt, or partially exempt, business prints its own stationery there is an output VAT liability on the total printing cost (including all overheads). If the in-house printing costs of an otherwise exempt business exceed the VAT registration threshold there is a liability to register and account for VAT on such costs.

Reverse charges

Certain professional and intellectual services purchased from overseas persons give rise to an output tax liability on the recipient. The services are deemed to be both supplied by and received by the UK organisation, ie there is an output tax liability and the VAT may also be recovered under the normal rules (restricted if partially exempt). The services include royalty and/or licence payments; financial, insurance, advertising, legal, accountancy and consultancy services; and the hire of staff or equipment. A full list is contained in VATA 1994, Sched 5.

5.6.4 Transfer of a business

Where a business's assets are transferred to another person who intends to use them to carry on the same kind of business as the vendor, the transaction is not subject to a VAT charge. However, where a VAT group which is partially exempt (ie not entitled to a full recovery of input tax) acquires assets in these circumstances, there is a deemed taxable supply by the VAT group and output tax must be accounted for on the VAT group's return. The corresponding input tax is restricted by whatever method has been agreed with the local VAT office.

5.7 SPECIAL SCHEMES

There are a number of special schemes which are either designed to simplify VAT accounting or reduce the VAT liability.

5.7.1 Retail schemes

These schemes are used by retailers, ie those in trade classification Groups 24 (Retail Division) and 28 (Miscellaneous Services). Generally this means those who deal direct with the public on a cash basis and who do not normally issue tax invoices.

5.7.2 Second-hand schemes

There are a number of special second-hand schemes which provide for VAT to be charged on the profit, if any, as opposed to the full selling price. Schemes are available for:

(1) cars;
(2) motor cycles;
(3) caravans/motor caravans;
(4) works of art, antiques and collector's items;
(5) boats and outboard motors;
(6) electronic organs;
(7) aircraft;

(8) firearms; and
(9) horses and ponies.

Special stock recording and detailed records including invoices are required. The scheme was extended from June 1995 to cover virtually all second-hand goods, works of art, antiques and collectors' items except precious metals and gemstones. It is recognised that dealers in low value, high volume goods will have difficulty maintaining the detailed records required. A simplified method of VAT accounts has therefore been introduced, known as 'global accounting'. Under the system 'eligible businesses' (those who cannot maintain the detailed records) are able to account for VAT on the difference between the total of purchases and sales in each tax period rather than on individual items. This scheme can only be used for eligible second-hand goods which have a purchase price of less than £500 per item.

5.7.3 Cash accounting

The general principle is that VAT must be accounted for on all tax invoices issued whether or not the customer/client has paid for the supply. Businesses that cannot use the retail scheme, and whose annual turnover is less than £350,000 (excluding VAT), may use the cash accounting scheme, provided certain conditions are satisfied. The conditions are laid down in regulations as described in Customs Notice 731, which in this respect has the force of law. Output VAT is not due until payment has been received but, similarly, input tax on purchases/expenses cannot be recovered until the supplier has been paid and a receipt obtained.

5.7.4 Annual accounting

To avoid having to submit returns quarterly, businesses with an annual turnover not exceeding £300,000 (excluding VAT) may be authorised, in writing, by Customs to use the annual accounting scheme. Nine payments, based on the previous year's VAT liability, are made by direct debit and a final, balancing payment is made with the VAT return at the end of the second month following the allocated VAT year.

5.7.5 Tour operators' margin scheme

This scheme must be used by any VAT-registered business which supplies packaged travel/accommodation services. As the name implies, VAT is accountable on the margin, if any, on the package's taxable element. Special record keeping and an annual calculation is required.

5.7.6 Agricultural flat rate scheme

Under this scheme, farmers and other agricultural businesses need not register and submit VAT returns to recover VAT on overhead expenses, etc. Instead, the farmer charges VAT at a nominal 4 per cent on all his supplies which he retains (in lieu of input tax) and which the recipient is entitled to recover as input tax under the normal rules. The scheme requires Customs authorisation and is not applicable to all farmers. Farmers who would benefit by more than £3,000 compared to being VAT-registered are not entitled to join the scheme.

5.8 ENFORCEMENT PROCEDURES

5.8.1 VAT visits

Customs regularly visits VAT-registered businesses to verify the returns submitted. Its powers are extensive and include the rights to see any documents, accounts, etc relating to the business activities and to inspect (but not search) the business premises. The frequency of visit depends upon a number of factors such as the business's size, types of business activity and compliance history. Visits can range from half a day every few years for smaller businesses to several weeks a year for multi-nationals.

Where errors are discovered, the visiting officer raises an assessment for VAT previously under-declared and, where appropriate, imposes a penalty and interest charges (see 5.8.2). It is advisable, therefore, to have all assessments independently reviewed. Customs collects over £1,000m by way of additional assessments from approximately 450,000 visits each year, but most visits do not result in assessments being issued. If the accounting records are well kept and independently reviewed regularly no problem should arise at the visit.

5.8.2 Penalties

There are a number of penalty provisions which Customs may impose automatically, and arbitrarily, for a failure to comply with the many complex VAT regulations. These were introduced with the view to improving compliance and reducing the amount of VAT outstanding at any one time.

Late registration

(VATA 1994, s 67(1))

Failure to notify a liability to register at the correct time (see 5.4.1) results in Customs imposing a financial penalty. From 1 January 1995 the penalty is a percentage of the net tax due between the date notification was required and the actual date of notification, as follows:

- Belatedness not exceeding nine months: 5%.
- Belatedness exceeding nine months but not exceeding 18 months: 10%.
- Belatedness exceeding 18 months: 15%.

A penalty is not imposed (or is withdrawn) where there is a reasonable excuse for the late notification. What amounts to a reasonable excuse is constantly explored by VAT tribunals. In *G Davies* (LON/86/174 (2126)) it was held that an understandable error in determining the liability of supplies was a reasonable excuse.

Ignorance (see *Neal v C&E Commrs* [1988] STC 131), overwork or the reliance on another person are not normally reasonable excuses. Appeals have succeeded where, on the facts of a particular case, an appellant took reasonable steps to notify (*S Zoweni* (*t/a The Paper Shop*) (1986) VATTR 133).

Late returns

(FA 1994, s 59)

If one payment is submitted late in any 12-month period, Customs notifies the VAT-registered person that payments submitted late during the following 12 months are subject to a default surcharge. If a payment is submitted late during the 12-month surcharge period, a 2 per cent penalty is imposed and the surcharge period extended for a further 12 months. The surcharge rises for each successive late payment to 5 per cent and by increments of 5 per cent to a maximum of 15 per cent. If payments are submitted by the due dates for 12 months, the business is removed from the default surcharge regime and the cycle starts again. The surcharge is waived if it is assessable at the lower rates and is below a minimum amount (ie £200).

A default surcharge is not imposed until after Customs has issued a Surcharge Liability Notice (SLN). There have been several tribunal hearings on this subject and where the taxpayer has been able to demonstrate that he never received an SLN, the surcharge has been withdrawn.

A default surcharge does not apply if a taxpayer has a reasonable excuse for late submission or payment. It is difficult to satisfy this requirement. The tribunal has accepted that the last minute breakdown of the computer, the unforeseen sickness of the person preparing the return at the time it was due or other such catastrophes constitute a reasonable excuse. If a taxpayer can demonstrate that the return and payment were posted in reasonably sufficient time to reach Customs by the due date, there is a reasonable excuse and a default surcharge is not imposed. Posting the return on the last day of the month, however, results in a default occurring.

Insufficiency of funds is not a reasonable excuse. However, in *C&E Commrs v Steptoe* [1992] STC 727, the Court of Appeal confirmed that where lack of funds was due to an unforeseeable inescapable misfortune, beyond the taxpayer's control, insufficiency of funds was a reasonable excuse for non-payment of VAT. The taxpayer had one major customer who was persistently slow in paying invoices.

Misdeclaration penalty

(FA 1985, s 14)

If a VAT officer discovers an under-declaration which exceeds specified limits, he assesses a serious misdeclaration penalty of 15 per cent of the additional VAT assessed. The penalty, which is based on each individual period (ie it is not cumulative), is imposed where the additional VAT assessed exceeds the lesser of:

(1) £1m; and
(2) 30 per cent of the gross amount of tax due for the appropriate return period.

The gross amount of tax is the total combined input tax and output tax for the period. Prior to the aforementioned date, the basis applied was the true amount of tax, ie the amount payable or repayable. The old basis continues to apply for failure to render VAT return cases where the tax-payer fails to notify the Commissioners within 30 days that an assessment issued centrally is lower than the true liability.

Reasonable excuse

A penalty is not imposed where a taxpayer can establish a reasonable excuse to the satisfaction of Customs or on appeal to a VAT tribunal. In addition, a penalty can be mitigated down to an amount (including nil) by Customs or, on appeal, a tribunal.

In *Clean Car Co Ltd* (90/1381 (5965)) the chairman tried to provide objective guidelines for when an appellant has a reasonable excuse. It was stated that the correct test was whether the taxpayer's actions would have been a reasonable action had it been done by a reasonable trader, conscious of, and intending to comply with, his tax obligations, but having the experience and other relevant attributes of a taxpayer and placed in the taxpayer's actual situation at the relevant time.

Voluntary disclosure

A penalty is not imposed where an error is notified to Customs at a time when a taxpayer has no reason to believe his affairs are being looked into. This condition was imposed very strictly by Customs, but they have since been persuaded that the strict application is creating a disincentive to disclose errors. Under a revised code of practice, errors discovered after a visit date has been arranged, including those disclosed at the start of a visit, and in some cases during and after a visit, are normally accepted as voluntary disclosures.

Tax which would have been lost

This is the amount of understatement of output tax or overstatement of input tax. For prescribed accounting periods beginning prior to 1 June 1994, where for any period there was an understatement of output tax or an overstatement of input tax, allowance for the error could be made in determining the lost tax for the prescribed accounting period concerned. This was as a result of a decision in *C&E Commrs v Peninsular and Oriental Steam Navigation Co C/A 1993* [1994] STC 259.

However, following this case, the VAT legislation was amended to prevent the offsetting against an under-declaration of over-declarations arising in other periods. The change is not retrospective, ie it only has effect for prescribed accounting periods beginning after 1 June 1994. For periods prior to this date, the old legislation remains in force and thus errors discovered in previous periods can be offset.

Interest
(FA 1994, s 74)

An interest charge is imposed on assessments for additional tax issued by VAT visiting officers. The interest rate is the prescribed rate as enacted by Treasury order and is not deductible for income or corporation tax. However, Customs has stated that interest may not be imposed where there is no overall loss of revenue eg where a supplier has failed to charge VAT to a customer who would have been entitled to recover the VAT charge. Customs has indicated that each case is decided on its merits, but that officers have been made aware of the need to consider whether there has been a loss of revenue.

Other penalties

There are a number of other penalty provisions such as failure to maintain or produce records, unauthorised issue of a tax invoice (by non-registered persons), and persistent incorrect returns. There are, in fact, over 60 regulatory offences which could give rise to a penalty.

5.9 FRAUD

In VAT law there are two forms of fraud: civil and criminal.

5.9.1 Civil
(FA 1994, s 60)

If, after an investigation, Customs is satisfied there has been an element of dishonesty, it may seek to impose a civil fraud penalty of 100 per cent of the tax involved. If there has been full co-operation by the taxpayer, Customs, or (on appeal) a VAT tribunal, may reduce the penalty by whatever percentage is considered reasonable. In a civil fraud investigation, Customs has only to prove on a balance of probabilities that a fraud had been committed to impose a penalty.

5.9.2 Criminal
(VATA 1994, s 72)

The more serious cases are dealt with under criminal law with penalties of up to three times the VAT involved, or imprisonment, or both. In these cases Customs must use the criminal rules of evidence, etc and prove beyond reasonable doubt that a fraud has been committed deliberately.

5.10 APPEALS

5.10.1 VAT tribunals

There is a right of appeal to an independent VAT tribunal on a number of matters including:

(1) assessments which are considered to be incorrect or not issued to the Commissioners' best judgement;
(2) liability rulings by Customs in respect of a specified supply;
(3) penalties, other than the interest charged for errors, if there is a reasonable excuse for the error; the law does not define 'reasonable excuse' but does state the insufficiency of funds or the reliance on another is *not* one;
(4) the amount of the reduction, if any, of a penalty for a civil fraud where the taxpayer considers he has provided full co-operation with the investigating officers.

The details of appeal procedures are outside the scope of this book. However, the procedure for lodging an appeal to a VAT tribunal (which must be made within 30 days of the appealable event) is straightforward. It is prudent to obtain professional advice before doing so and it is advisable to be represented at the tribunal hearing, which in many ways resembles a court hearing although less formal.

A VAT tribunal decision may be appealed to a higher court on a point of law and, in limited circumstances, an appeal may be referred to the European Court of Justice for a ruling.

5.10.2 Departmental reviews

Many disputes are settled by negotiations with Customs by formally requesting a departmental review of the disputed ruling/assessment within the 30-day time limit. This allows discussions to continue without the loss of the right to appeal to an independent VAT tribunal. Commissioners, if requested, usually review an assessment after the 30-day limit has expired and will, where appropriate, reduce the amount assessed. In certain circumstances it is also possible to make an application to a VAT tribunal to hear a case that is out of time. It is prudent to take professional advice before lodging an appeal.

6

STAMP DUTY AND BUSINESS TRANSACTIONS

Stamp duty is a tax charged on the documents by which certain types of property are transferred to new owners – eg, it is charged on the conveyance of a freehold property. It is important to emphasise that stamp duty is not charged on the *sale* of a property, but on the *document* by which that property is conveyed to the purchaser.

The relevant document has to be submitted to a Revenue Stamp Office with the appropriate payment. An official stamp is embossed onto the document to confirm that duty has been paid, and it is then returned to the person presenting it for stamping. Documents are usually submitted by post, but they can be presented over the counter at offices in London and Edinburgh and in various cities in England, Wales and Northern Ireland.

The information that a businessman needs on stamp duty falls under the following headings:

(1) Documents liable to duty
(2) Sanctions where duty is not paid
(3) Avoiding or reducing duty.

6.1 DOCUMENTS LIABLE TO DUTY

Stamp duty was first introduced in 1694 and the law has not been redrafted since the Stamp Act of 1891. Numerous amendments have however been made (to block loopholes or to grant new reliefs) and the result is legislation which is archaic, exceptionally complex and difficult to follow, and in which the detailed exceptions are more important than the broad general rules. For example, the scheme of the legislation is not to impose duty on documents implementing the sale of certain types of property, but to impose duty on all documents implementing the sale of *any* type of property and then to provide a series of exceptions.

The practical effect of this legislation is to impose stamp duty on documents implementing:

(a) the sale of shares and other securities;
(b) the sale of freehold land and buildings and the grant or assignment of leases;
(c) the sale of certain types of business property, such as goodwill and patent rights.

This is not a comprehensive list but it does include all the charges likely to be incurred by a business proprietor.

Stamp duty is charged only on sales and not (since 1985) on gifts. Nor is any duty payable when assets are put into trust. However, a sale is defined to include the exchange of property for shares or securities, or the exchange of one block of shares for another. Stamp duty is either charged at a fixed rate (eg 50p) or as a percentage of the value (ie ad valorem duty).

A document should be presented for stamping within 30 days of execution (ie signature). Late stamping attracts a substantial financial penalty (see 6.2).

6.1.1 Sale of shares or other securities

Stamp duty is charged on documents transferring ownership of shares (in both quoted and private companies), debentures, unit trust units and other securities. The rate of duty is 0.5 per cent, rounded up to the next 50p (for example, the duty on a sale for £325 would be £2). British Government stocks ('gilts') and stocks issued by certain international bodies (such as the EC) are exempt from duty. The stamp duty is borne by the purchaser and is shown as a disbursement on the broker's contract note. It counts as part of the cost of the holding for CGT purposes.

Where one block of shares is exchanged for another, the transaction is treated as two sales, so both participants must pay the usual duty. In certain circumstances it is possible for shares to be sold without a stampable document being created. This most commonly happens where a block of shares, traded on the London Stock Exchange, changes hands several times in the space of a few days. In such circumstances, stamp duty reserve tax (SDRT) is charged on the transaction. The SDRT is equal in amount to the stamp duty that would otherwise have been paid and so, from the purchaser's point of view, it is immaterial which tax is paid.

6.1.2 Sale of freehold land and buildings

Stamp duty is charged on the conveyance of freehold land or buildings on a progressive scale of rates of 1 per cent, 1.5 per cent and 2 per cent of the price paid rounded up to the next whole pound, as follows:

Value of property	*Duty on full value*
below £60,000	Nil
£60,001 to £250,000	1.0% (£1 per £100 or part of £100)
£250,001 to £500,000	1.5% (£1.50 per £100 or part of £100)
over £500,000	2.0% (£2 per £100 or part of £100)

Stamp duty is paid by the purchaser, and is calculated in exactly the same way whether the property in question is residential or commercial. In both cases, where the sale price does not exceed £60,000, no duty is payable, but if the sale price is £60,250, the duty is £603. If the sale price is £250,000 the duty is £2,500, but if the sale price were £250,250, the duty is £3,754. If the sale price does is £500,000 the duty is £7,500, but if the sale price were £500,250, the duty is £10,005.

The relevant date is the date the conveyance is executed, not the date it was presented for stamping.

Prior to 8 July 1997, a single rate of 1 per cent applied where the consideration for a property exceeded £60,000. Thus for example, duty on the purchase of a property for £300,000 is now £4,500 (previously £3,000). Duty on the purchase of a property for £700,000 is now £14,000 (previously £7,000).

The new rates apply to transfers after 7 July 1997, except for transfers made under a contract already made before 3 July 1997.

6.1.3 Sale and grant of a lease

The stamp duty payable on an assignment of an existing lease is calculated in exactly the same way as for freehold property. It is the capital sum paid for the lease that determines the amount of stamp duty; the amount of rent payable under the lease is irrelevant.

However, when a new lease is granted, stamp duty is charged *both* on the premium *and* on the annual rent. The new rates apply to the premium in the same way as to purchases. The premium is exempt if it does not exceed £60,000 *and* the annual rent does not exceed £600. The duty on the rent depends on the length of the lease and (subject to minor rounding-up) is:

Length of lease	*Duty (as percentage of annual rent)*
7 years or less	1*
7 years and one day to 35 years	2
35 years and one day to 100 years	12
More than 100 years	24

* Nil if the annual rent does not exceed £500. Also, if a

dwelling is let furnished for less than a year, no stamp duty is payable if the total rent for the period of letting is less than £500. If it is £500 or more, a fixed duty of £1 applies.

The grant of a lease at a premium by one member of a group of companies (see 6.3.8) to another is exempt from this charge provided that the lease is granted after 30 April 1995.

6.1.4 Example – Stamp duty on a lease

A ten-year lease is granted at a premium of £50,000 and an annual rent of £1,000. Because the *rent* exceeds £600, the *premium* is not exempt and the total duty payable is:

Duty on premium: 1 per cent of £50,000	£500
Duty on rent: 2 per cent of £1,000	£20
Total duty payable	£520

6.1.5 Stamp duty and VAT

Sales and rentals of some commercial property may be subject to VAT. In such cases, stamp duty is charged on the VAT-*inclusive* sale price, premium and/or rent. Moreover, in certain circumstances the landlord may have the right to add VAT to the rent at a later date: again, the VAT-inclusive figure must be taken (see SP11/91).

6.1.6 Sub-sales

(Stamp Act 1891, s 58)

Where a person

(a) has entered into a contract to purchase a property and
(b) enters into a sale contract before the original contract has been completed,

and the property is then conveyed to the new purchaser, only the second contract generally attracts ad valorem duty. The original purchase contract is not subject to stamp duty. Thus, if *A* enters into a contract to buy a property for £1m, and then enters into a sub-sale for £1.5m to *B*, stamp duty is payable by *B* only on the conveyance arising out of the contract for sale for £1.5m.

The FA 1984 introduced some restrictions; specialist legal advice should therefore be taken.

6.1.7 Sale of contract

If a purchaser who holds the benefit of a contract which has not been completed sells the benefit of his contract to a third party who then completes the purchase, the transaction is treated in a similar way to a sub-sale. Thus if the contract is for the purchase of a property for £1m, and *A* sells that contract to *B* for £500,000, *B* pays ad valorem duty each on the £500,000 purchase price of the contract and on completing the purchase. Overall he pays 2 per cent of £1.5m.

6.1.8 Sale of goodwill and other business assets

The types of property which may be included in arriving at a business's value for stamp duty purposes include book debts, plant and machinery and stock in trade, goodwill, and copyrights, patents and trade marks. The way in which a contract is drafted may have stamp duty consequences and the advice of an experienced solicitor should be sought. Having said this, the normal position is as follows:

(1) The usual arrangement for book debts is for the purchaser to collect them as agent for the vendor as this means that ownership remains with the person selling the business and so no stamp duty is payable on them. Unless documentation is defective, no stamp duty should be payable on the transfer of plant and machinery and stock in trade as legal title can pass by delivery and the purchaser can therefore acquire a good title without a stampable document. The rate of duty on goodwill, copyrights, patents and trade marks is the same as for land and buildings.
(2) Exemption is available where the value of the transaction does not exceed £60,000, but the sale of a business as a going concern counts as a single transaction. Therefore, if a shopkeeper sells his shop premises for £50,000 and his goodwill for £20,000, the value of the transaction is £70,000 and exemption is not available.

Because the stamp duty definition of a sale includes an exchange of property for shares, the incorporation of a sole trader's or partnership business is treated as a sale of that business in exchange for shares in the new company. Stamp duty is charged according to the value of the shares received by the proprietor or the partners which will, effectively, be an amount equal to the value of the business as a going concern (discussed in greater detail at 6.3.7).

6.1.9 Partnerships

A partnership deed or agreement is not normally liable for stamp duty but special rules may apply for a limited partnership (see 15.2).

Where a person joins a partnership, ad valorem stamp duty is payable on any document transferring an interest in the firm to him from an existing partner on the basis that the document is a conveyance. On the other hand, the contribution of new partnership capital gives rise to no such charge unless an existing partner withdraws capital at the same time (in which case the document for the transaction is regarded as a conveyance which attracts ad valorem duty).

The dissolution of a partnership and the division of the firm's assets do not normally attract ad valorem duty. The exception is if an individual partner takes a greater proportion of certain assets and makes a cash adjustment for this; it is then effectively a type of sale.

6.2 SANCTIONS WHERE DUTY IS NOT PAID

As a general rule, the Revenue cannot enforce the payment of stamp duty by taking court proceedings (although it can enforce the payment of SDRT). Nevertheless, a number of effective sanctions do exist, which mean that in practice it is usually best to ensure that a stampable document is indeed stamped:

(1) Although the Revenue cannot take civil proceedings to enforce payment of stamp duty, it can prosecute a purchaser or lessee who fails to produce for stamping a conveyance of freehold land, or the grant or transfer of a lease for seven years or more. The maximum fine is £1,000.
(2) HM Land Registry will not accept any document which is not duly stamped and it is very unwise not to register a purchase of land or a lease for a term exceeding 21 years at the Registry.
(3) A transfer of shares or debentures cannot be registered unless the transfer document has been properly stamped. (Any purported registration by the company is simply not valid in law.)
(4) An unstamped document will not be accepted in any court proceedings. Such document required in court could always be stamped, but there is a financial penalty of £10 where a document is presented for stamping outside the permitted 30-day period, plus interest at 5 per cent per annum from the time the document should have been stamped, plus a fine equal to the duty.

6.3 AVOIDING OR REDUCING DUTY

6.3.1 Sale of shares or other securities

The opportunities to avoid or mitigate duty are circumscribed by the rule that a company may not register a transfer of shares or debentures unless the transfer document has been duly stamped. Beneficial ownership may, of course, be transferred without any change in the registered owner of the shares (eg where the shares are registered in the name of a nominee company).

6.3.2 Depositary receipts

Beneficial ownership of shares in certain UK-quoted companies, registered in the name of American banks, are traded free of stamp duty in the form of 'American Depositary Receipts' or ADRs. Practical difficulties mean, however, that ADRs are suitable only for institutions such as life assurance companies and pension funds and they are not normally held by private investors. In any event, SDRT is charged at the rate of 1.5 per cent where shares are made the subject of Depositary Receipts arrangements.

6.3.3 Company reconstructions

(FA 1986, s 75)

There is a limited statutory relief for the stamp duty payable on the documentation arising out of certain company reconstructions and mergers without change of ownership: this is an area in which proper professional advice is essential. The basic conditions for relief are that:

(a) the acquiring company issues shares to all the shareholders of the target company;
(b) no other consideration passes other than the assumption or discharge by the acquiring company of liabilities of the target company; and
(c) both companies must be incorporated in the UK.

Furthermore, relief is due only where the following further conditions are satisfied.

(i) The acquisition is effected for bona fide commercial reasons and does not form part of a scheme or arrangement of which the main purposes, or one of the main purposes, is avoidance of liability to stamp duty, income tax, corporation tax or capital gains tax.
(ii) After the acquisition has been made, each shareholder of the target company will be a shareholder of the acquiring company.

(iii) After the acquisition has been made, the proportion of the acquiring company's shares held by any shareholder is the same as the proportion of shares originally held in the target company.

The Stamp Office has indicated that it will regard the requirement of the reconstruction to be effected for bona fide commercial reasons as being satisfied where clearance has been granted under TCGA 1992, s 138 (see 3.4.5).

The procedure for claiming s 75 relief is set out below.

(1) A claim should be made in a letter signed by a responsible officer of the acquiring company eg the secretary or a director or the company's professional advisers.
(2) The letter should include the following information and be accompanied by:
    (a) the name, registered number and authorised and issued capital of the acquiring company at the relevant date;
    (b) the name, registered number and authorised and issued capital of the acquired company at the relevant date;
    (c) details of and the reason for the reconstruction;
    (d) details of the consideration and how it was satisfied;
    (e) whether an application for clearance under TCGA 1992, s 138 or 139 has been made to the Revenue and a copy of any application for clearance together with copies of any correspondence with the Revenue;
    (f) confirmation that the shares in the acquiring company have been issued to the acquired company's registered shareholders and that their names have been entered on the acquiring company's register of members;
    (g) a copy of the certificate of incorporation of all relevant companies and all changes of names;
    (h) particulars of the acquired company's register of members immediately prior to the transaction;
    (i) particulars of the acquired company's register of members immediately after the transaction for which relief is claimed;
    (j) a copy of the agreement or offer document; and
    (k) a copy of the instruments of transfer.
(3) A completed Adjudication Application Form (ADJ 467) stating any related adjudication references known should be sent with the claim to:

    The Controller of Stamps (Adjudication Section)
    West Block
    Barrington Road
    Worthing
    West Sussex BN12 4SF

6.3.4 Loan stock

Where a person takes loan stock as consideration for the sale of an asset, such acquisition does not normally attract duty unless:

(a) the loan capital carries a right of conversion into shares or other securities or to the acquisition of shares or other securities; or
(b) the rate of interest exceeds a reasonable commercial return on the capital's nominal amount; or
(c) the amount of interest is determined to any extent by reference to the results of, or any part of, a business or to the value of any property; or
(d) there is a right to be repaid more than the nominal amount of the loan and that amount is not reasonably comparable with what is generally repayable (in respect of a similar capital's nominal amount) under the terms of issue of loan capital in the Official List of The Stock Exchange.

Any transfer of loan capital which does not come within these exemptions is chargeable at the rate of 0.5 per cent ad valorem.

6.3.5 Sale of land and buildings

One widely used way of mitigating stamp duty was closed by FA 1994. If two owners exchange houses, stamp duty is now payable on the market value of the properties as well as on any cash adjustment. Prior to 8 December 1993, stamp duty was payable only on the cash element in the consideration and even this attracted duty only if it exceeded £60,000.

The Stamp Office has agreed that where the documents are correctly drafted the ad valorem charge can be limited to one property. It appears that if a person transfers property A to another person on the basis that the sale consideration is £x and this is to be satisfied by the other person transferring property B, 1 per cent stamp duty is payable on property A and the transfer of property B attracts only 50p stamp duty. However, very careful drafting is required in cases where there is a cash adjustment rather than a straightforward exchange with no other consideration passing between the parties.

Stamp duty is not charged on that part of the agreed purchase price which is allocated to items such as fixtures and fittings which are left in the property. This is because ownership of such items is transferred not by the conveyance, but by delivery.

To reduce duty, purchasers are sometimes tempted to apportion an unrealistically high percentage of the agreed overall price to the contents – especially where this brings the price allocated to the house itself below the threshold and so avoids duty altogether. The Stamp Office is, of course, alive to this temptation and will refuse to stamp a conveyance if the valuations used cannot be justified.

A suggestion sometimes put forward is that a person can buy the site and then contract separately with the builder for him to carry out the building work. Certainly, if the buyer buys a building plot and then contracts with an unrelated third party for the construction of a house, stamp duty is payable only on the 'site value' price actually paid. *Prudential Assurance Co Ltd v IRC* [1993] 1 WLR 211 indicates that this still applies even if the buyer buys a plot from the builder and then commissions him to construct a building on that site *provided* that the site is conveyed to the purchaser before a substantial start is made on the building work.

Where a long lease at a substantial rent is proposed, it is sometimes possible to save duty by splitting the period between two shorter leases; eg instead of a 50-year lease with stamp duty of 12 per cent of the annual rent (see 6.1.3), at the outset sign two leases, one for 20 years and the second for 30 years (commencing on the expiry of the first), with the duty on each lease then being only 2 per cent of the annual rent. For legal reasons, the first lease must be 21 years or less and so counts as a short lease which cannot be registered at the Land Registry.

6.3.6 Sale of business assets

In general, the ownership of buildings and goodwill can only be transferred by a written document and so duty must be paid. There are however three ways of avoiding or reducing duty, though all three are usually only practicable where vendor and purchaser trust each other completely.

(1) Stamp duty is payable on a *conveyance* of freehold land although the *contract* is sufficient to transfer beneficial ownership to the purchaser. Therefore, if vendor and purchaser sign and exchange contracts, but never 'complete' by conveyance, no duty is payable. This was upheld by the courts in 1889 and the Government has never blocked the loophole. The drawback is that, without a stamped conveyance, the purchase cannot be registered at the Land Registry, and this is why this device is only to be recommended where vendor and purchaser trust each other completely (eg on a sale to a connected company or a sale within a family).

(2) The second method is simply not to stamp the documentation. Though failing to stamp a conveyance or the grant or assignment of a lease is a punishable offence (see 6.2), the only sanction against failure to stamp a transfer of goodwill is the double charge if it later needs to be stamped out of time.

(3) Where substantial amounts of money are at stake, advantage may be taken of the rule that a document executed (signed) outside the United Kingdom need not be stamped until it is brought into the United Kingdom. (The document may be stamped without interest or penalty provided it is presented at a Stamp Office within 30 days of being brought to the United Kingdom, as required under the Stamp Act 1891, s 15.) The usual procedure is to take a day trip to Jersey or Guernsey, sign the documents, and leave them in a local safe deposit or bank vault.

6.3.7 Transfer of a business to a company

Stamp duty is payable where a sole trader's or partnership business is incorporated because the trader or the partnership is treated as having sold the business in exchange for shares in the new company (see 6.1.8). Where the successor company is a limited company, its proprietors must produce to the Registrar of Companies a properly stamped copy of the contract by which the business was sold to the company. It is therefore necessary to pay stamp duty on assets which did not pass by delivery. However, a stamped contract is not required where a business is transferred to an unlimited company (see 17.1.2); it is possible to transfer a business to an unlimited company by means of an unstamped contract (for example, one kept outside the United Kingdom) and then to re-register that company as a limited company.

6.3.8 Intra-group transfers

Statutory exemption from stamp duty applies, subject to conditions, where property is transferred from one member of a group of companies to another. For this purpose, a 'group' consists of a holding company and its 75 per cent subsidiaries. The holding company need not be a UK company. A subsidiary is a 75 per cent subsidiary only if the parent company owns, directly or indirectly, 75 per cent of the subsidiary's ordinary share capital. Until May 1995, the requirement was that the subsidiary should be a 90 per cent subsidiary, but the test was by reference to the nominal value of issued share capital of all classes, not just ordinary shares.

Section 27(3) of FA 1967 provides that, to obtain the relief, the transferee company must provide confirmation that the document giving rise to the intra-group transfer was not executed in pursuance of or in connection with an arrangement whereunder:

(a) the consideration, or any part of the consideration, for the conveyance or transfer was to be provided or received, directly or indirectly, by a person other than a body corporate which at the time of the execution of the instrument was associated with either the transferor or the transferee; or
(b) the said interest was previously transferred or conveyed, directly or indirectly, by such a person; or
(c) the transferor and the transferee were to cease to be associated by reason of a change in the percentage of the issued share capital of the transferee in the beneficial ownership of the transferor or a third body corporate.

7

CONTRACT LAW

NICOLA TOMLINS AND DAVID NIVEN, WEDLAKE SAINT

This chapter covers the main general principles of contract law. A detailed study of contract law is beyond the scope of this book.

In any binding contract there are three major components:

(a) an offer which is made by one party and accepted by the other;
(b) an intention to be legally bound by both parties; and
(c) consideration.

This chapter deals with the following areas of contract law:

(1) Offer
(2) Acceptance
(3) Consideration
(4) Mistake
(5) Misrepresentation
(6) Duress and undue influence
(7) Terms of contract
(8) Exemption and exclusion clauses
(9) Breach of contract
(10) Frustration.

7.1 OFFER

For an offer to be capable of being accepted, and leading to a binding contract, an intention must be shown, on the part of the party making the offer, to be legally bound if the offer is accepted. It may be made to an individual person or to a group of people. It may be expressly made in words or by conduct. Sometimes a party may be bound by his offer even if he can later show that he did not intend to make it to the person who accepted it; it is the impression given to the person who accepted it that is important and account is taken of whether a reasonable man in the circumstances would also have had the same view.

7.1.1 Invitation to treat

It is not uncommon for parties to enter into preliminary discussions prior to a contract being made which include requests for information. These are known as invitations to treat, which generally invite an offer and are sometimes confused with an offer.

For example, in *Harvey v Facey* [1893] AC 552 the plaintiff sent a telegram to the defendant saying 'will you sell us Bumper Hall Pen? Telegraph us lowest cash price'. The court decided that no contract had been formed. This telegram was a request for information which the defendant had supplied in their telegram and not an offer.

Generally speaking, a display of goods on which is indicated the price of those goods for sale, in either a shop window or inside a store, is an invitation to treat. If the customer decides to buy some goods then the action by him to take the goods to the cash till is the offer to buy which can be accepted by the shop owner or his employee.

7.1.2 Advertisements

A newspaper advertisement may show certain goods for sale at certain prices. This is not an offer capable of acceptance. Furthermore, it has been held that circulation of a price list by a wine merchant is merely an invitation to treat (see *Partridge v Crittinden* [1968] 1 WLR 1204). However, there are some circumstances where the advertisement could only be held to relate to one matter and to a certain individual or party of individuals and then it may be an offer. In *Carlill v Carbolic Smoke Ball Co Ltd* [1893] 1 QB 256 the advertisement stated that anyone who purchased a carbolic smoke ball, used it in accordance with the instructions and then suffered from flu would receive £100 from the company. The court held that this was an offer which the defendants had shown themselves to be legally bound by and which was capable of acceptance. Their intention to be bound was confirmed in that they had deposited £1,000 with their bankers to show their sincerity.

7.1.3 Termination of offer

Generally an offer may be terminated at any time before it is accepted. The revocation of an offer must be communicated to the offeree. This need not be done by the offeror himself so long as the offeree knows it has been terminated.

7.1.4 Rejection and counter offers

Where an offer is rejected it is terminated and therefore cannot be accepted. Where an offer is made on new terms which were not contained in the original offer, it may be a rejection accompanied by a counter offer. In *Hyde v Wrench* (1840) 3 Beav 334 *A* offered to sell a farm to *B* for £1,000. *B* replied, offering to buy it for £950. *A* rejected the counter offer so *B* tried to accept *A*'s original offer. It was held that no contract had been made since *B*'s rejection and counter offer terminated *A*'s original offer.

However, in some cases the communication from the offeree may not be regarded as a counter offer but merely a request for more information. An objective test then has to be applied to determine whether a communication is sufficient to be regarded as a counter offer.

7.1.5 Lapse of time

An offer which expressly states that it will last for a specified period of time cannot be accepted once that time has passed. Where the offer is not limited in time, then it only lapses after whatever period of time is considered reasonable in the circumstances.

7.2 ACCEPTANCE

Acceptance of an offer must be final and unqualified and it must be communicated to the offeror. An acknowledgement of the offer is not acceptance of it. Acceptance may be made by conduct, eg where *A* offers to send goods, sends them to *B* and *B* then uses them, *B*'s conduct can be regarded as acceptance.

Where the parties carry on lengthy negotiations it may be difficult to say when exactly an offer is made and accepted. Parties may in fact not agree that an offer has been made and accepted. In these circumstances, a court considers all negotiations and looks to the parties' intentions to establish whether an agreement exists. There may be correspondence between the parties after an offer has been made but before acceptance. Careful examination must be made to determine whether such communication can be regarded as an acceptance or whether it is an attempt to vary terms or introduce new ones.

It is common business practice for one party to wish a contract to be governed by his standard trading conditions. An offer by him may include a statement that both parties should be bound by these terms. The other party's reaction to this determines whether he is bound by these terms.

7.2.1 Cross offers

Where each party concerned makes an offer to the other which mirrors the other's offer, there can be no contract even though the offer is identical. What one party must do on receipt of the other's offer is to contact him and confirm acceptance.

7.2.2 Communication of acceptance

This must be made to the offeror, otherwise no contract exists. The communication need not be made by the offeree. However the third party who communicates the acceptance (eg an agent) must have the authority to do so from the offeree.

An exception to communicating acceptance to the offeror arises where acceptance is by conduct. For example, a tenant may be regarded as accepting an offer of new tenancy by remaining in the property.

7.2.3 Method of acceptance

There is no set method of acceptance, although the offeror may indicate that acceptance can only be made in a certain way; if so, that requirement must be adhered to. Acceptance by an alternative method (eg orally where the offer states that acceptance must be in writing) may not bind the offeror.

The offeror cannot impose acceptance where the offeree is silent.

7.2.4 Acceptance by post

Acceptance by post is effective when the letter is posted, not when the letter is received. If it is not received by the offeror it may still be deemed effective acceptance. Nevertheless, the offeree may have difficulty proving that he had posted the acceptance.

Acceptance by post takes priority over the withdrawal of an offer which may have been posted before the acceptance was, but had not reached the offeree when the acceptance was posted. This is an exception to the general rule that an offer may be withdrawn at any time before the offeror is notified of an acceptance.

7.2.5 Contract to make a contract

In certain cases the parties may have agreed in principle but not sorted out the contract details. Whether a contract exists depends on the terms still left to be agreed. However, it is possible for the parties to be bound by contract to make a contract. This is not the same as an agreement to negotiate because that is too uncertain.

7.2.6 Certainty of terms

Where the terms are vague or uncertain they cannot be binding. This does not necessarily mean that there is no contract since a court may, if it considers it appropriate, merely delete the ambiguous words from the contract (see 7.7.4).

7.2.7 Contractural intention

The parties must have intended to create legal relations. It is not necessary generally to produce evidence to show this: it will normally be inferred. However, where one party alleges that this requirement does not exist, then it is for them to show that it does not.

7.3 CONSIDERATION

A contract is not binding unless it is either made as a deed or supported by some 'consideration'. 'Consideration' is the value by which one party suffers a detriment (promisee) or the other gains (promisor). For example, *A*'s payment to *B* is in consideration of *B*'s promise to deliver the goods to *A*.

The court does not generally concern itself whether adequate consideration has been given – whether a person has paid too little or too much does not affect the contract's validity but it might give rise to a claim by that person against the other. An exception to this general rule would occur where a party may have exercised undue influence on the other to enter the contract and the contract may therefore be regarded as being one-sided (see 7.6).

Consideration may be nominal; for example, a contract in which *A* agrees to buy a valuable business for only £1 is just as valid as if he were to agree to pay £10,000. However, a consideration must be real in that it must have some value in the eyes of the law.

Where a contract is made but the performance of it is utterly impossible, so long as both parties are unaware of that fact the consideration is still likely to be effective.

7.3.1 Past consideration

It is often said that consideration for a promise is given in return for the promise itself. If the act or agreement not to do an act, regarded as a consideration, has already been carried out before the 'promise' is made and independently of it, then it is regarded as being 'past consideration'. In these circumstances the contract is not enforceable.

Where, for example, an employer promises to make a payment to an ex-employee for his past services, the contract is unenforceable unless, perhaps, the ex-employee agreed not to work for a competitor for a certain period after leaving (ie the consideration is his promise not to work for the competitor).

There is an exception to the general rule for past consideration; there is consideration where an act is performed before a promise made where three conditions are satisfied:

(1) the act must be done at the request of the person making the promise;
(2) it must be understood that the payment would be made; and
(3) the payment must in any event be legally recoverable.

The Limitation Act 1980 qualifies the rules relating to past consideration, providing that where a person acknowledges a debt in writing and signs the acknowledgement, the debt is deemed to accrue on that date and no earlier date. This extends the period of limitation and enables a party to sue at a later date than he would otherwise have been able to on a debt. However, where a debt has become statutorily barred, the right to sue is lost and the later acknowledgement cannot revive it.

7.3.2 Agreement not to sue

Where a creditor *A* agrees not to sue *B* in return for a promise by *B* to pay interest or additional interest on the sum involved, the promise by *A* is valid consideration. The agreement may be for a limited period of time (perhaps to allow *B* time to pay) or it may be final and perhaps incorporated in a settlement.

The agreement or forebearance to sue may be implied from a person's actions (eg where a party does not sue even though he has stated to the other to whom he owes the money that he will). However, the forebearance must be accompanied by a promise from the debtor for it to be a consideration. Generally, a person cannot provide consideration by promising to do something that he is already legally obliged to do. However, where he promises to do more than he is legally obliged to do (eg a police force providing a greater degree of protection than it thinks reasonably necessary in the circumstances) then this may be good consideration.

Nevertheless, there are situations where one party's legal obligation to perform something for another can be regarded as consideration to a third party. In *Scotson v Pegg* (1861) 6 H&N 295, *B* contracted *A* to deliver coal to *B* or to *B*'s order. *B* then ordered *A* to deliver the coal to *C* who promised to unload it. *A* sued *C* for failure to unload. It was held that *A*'s delivery was good consideration for *C*'s promise even though he was contractually bound by his contract with *B* to deliver to *C*.

7.4 MISTAKE

The law relating to mistake arises in two situations, ie where:

(1) the two parties concerned have a fundamental difference in what they believe is agreed between them (unilateral mistake);
(2) both parties are agreed on the terms but have entered into it having the same but wrong understanding of the facts (mutual mistake).

The principles relating to mistake are different in common law from those established in equity. However, for the purposes of this text only the common law is dealt with.

The mistake must be with regard to a fundamental part of the contract and must be a mistake of fact as opposed to one of law. A mistake does not always render a contract void. In some situations provisions are made in the contract for what might happen if confusion arises. Therefore the principles relating to mistake operate only if the contract is silent.

7.4.1 Mutual mistake

These circumstances generally render the contract void and it is treated as if it never existed. If the mistake is regarded as being fundamental to the contract, then the contract is set aside. However, where the parties are clearly mistaken but the mistake is not so as to make the contract fundamentally and radically different from what the parties believe the contract to be, the contract is not set aside.

A difficult area arises where there is a mistake in the quality of the subject matter. Whereas mistake in the contract's substance generally renders it void and therefore unenforcable, mistake in the quality of it does not affect the contract's validity. For example where a person buys a 1939 car believing it to be a 1948 car, the validity of the contract is not necessarily affected by this mistake.

7.4.2 Unilateral mistake

This does not mean that any party who is alleged to be in breach of contract can successfully claim that he was mistaken over the terms the other party intended him to contract on and have the contract set aside. Instead, a court always applies an objective test and determines what a reasonable man believed should be agreed. Therefore where the parties are clearly so far apart about what was agreed, a court must say that no contract exists. For example, in a case where an auctioneer was selling hemp and tow, and the auction catalogue did not indicate the difference between the two, the defendant bid for tow thinking it was hemp. The bid was accepted but it was held that no binding contract existed as there was a fundamental difference in what the bidder believed he was bidding for and what was actually on auction.

Where one party is aware of the other's mistake in the agreement then a court is unlikely to hold that that contract is binding. However that mistake must be with regard to a fundamental term of the contract, not merely in, for example, the quality of the subject matter.

7.4.3 Mistake in identity

Where one party believes that the person he has contracted with is someone different from the person whom he actually contracted with, the contract may be set aside. Whether the contract is set aside largely depends on the circumstances and the facts of each case. Such situations often involve fraud on the part of one party deceiving the other.

It is always important to establish whether the mistaken party intended to contract with the person that he wrongly believes the other to be or whether the identity of that person did not materially affect the obligations under the contract.

7.4.4 *Non est factum*

Where a party has been misled into signing or executing a document which is substantially different to that which he intended to sign or execute, is he bound by it? To be successful in getting a transaction set aside, a person must be able to show that the document he thought he was signing was markedly different from the one that he actually did sign. He must have made a fundamental mistake in the character and effect of the document.

Where a person signs a document in blank and hands it to another to complete the blanks and finalise the transaction, he may be able to rely on this doctrine. However, where the details which are completed are not what the signatory believed they would be, but nevertheless they do not change the transaction's subject, then the contract is unlikely to be set aside.

A person trying to have the contract set aside must show that he acted carefully (eg that he was not negligent in any way). The standard to be applied to his actions would be that of a reasonably prudent person.

7.5 MISREPRESENTATION

There are basically three types of misrepresentation: negligent, fraudulent and innocent. Misrepresentation arises from a statement of fact as opposed to a statement of opinion, intention or law. If a statement of opinion later turns out to be unfounded it is not usually enough to have a transaction set aside. However, it is enough where a statement of opinion is clearly intended to be relied on, the same way the statement of fact would be. For example, in *Smith v Land and House Property Corporation* (1884) 28 Ch D 7, the vendor, during a sale of property, described a tenant as 'a most desirable tenant' when he knew that the tenant was substantially in arrears with the rent. In these circumstances the purchaser was not bound by his contract with the vendor.

To successfully claim misrepresentation, a party must be able to show that it was reasonable for him to rely on the other's statements, rather than to rely on his own judgement. It is not always easy to distinguish between statement of fact and statement of the law, although it is important to do so because, whereas the former constitutes representation, the latter does not.

7.5.1 Non-disclosure

This does not generally lead to misrepresentation. Exceptions occur where a certain special relationship exists between the parties.

It is possible to be liable for misrepresentation as a result of a party's conduct. For example, a person who goes into a restaurant and sits down and orders a meal is representing that he has the ability to pay.

If *A* makes a representation to *B* which is true at the time he made it but which later becomes untrue, and he does not communicate this to *B* prior to the contract being entered into, *A*'s failure to tell *B* of the changes amounts to misrepresentation.

7.5.2 Constructive notice

In *Barclays Bank v O'Brien* [1992] 4 All ER 983 the defendant wanted to borrow money from the bank which insisted on security. The security was provided by a charge over property jointly owned by the defendant and his wife, and the bank required her to enter the charge also. The wife gave her consent as a result of a misrepresentation made to her by her husband and under undue influence exerted by the husband on her. The court held that in circumstances where a close relationship arises and the wife's position is not as favourable financially as the husband's, then the bank has constructive notice of the misrepresentation unless it has taken reasonable steps to satisfy itself that the wife entered into the transaction freely and with full knowledge of the facts.

Misrepresentation may be made to a group of persons. However, a plaintiff will only be successful if he can show that he is within the group of people who might be regarded as likely to rely on misrepresentation.

The misrepresentation must have induced a person to enter the contract. Where an estate agent's particulars misrepresented the size of a garage and the buyer had himself examined the property on two occasions, misrepresentation was held not to have induced the plaintiff to enter the contract.

The person who makes a misrepresentation does not have to intend that the other party will rely on the misrepresentation; it is usually sufficient to show that he should have realised that the other party would be likely to.

7.5.3 Damages for misrepresentation

Damages can be recovered as a result of misrepresentation. The extent of damages claimed depends largely on the type of misrepresentation.

Fraudulent misrepresentation

A wronged person may rescind the contract, claim damages or do both. Fraud has been described as being false representation '[which] has been made (1) knowingly or (2) without belief in its truth or (3) recklessly as to whether or not this is true or false' (*Hartelid v Sawyer & McCockin Real Estate Ltd* [1977] WLR 481).

It is sufficient if the maker of the statement suspects that it is inaccurate without actually knowing it to be false. It is not necessary to show that his motive is dishonest.

Negligent misrepresentation

Section 2 of the Misrepresentation Act 1961 provides that where a misrepresentation is made a party can recover damages if he can prove that misrepresentation was fraudulent. The accused party is not held liable, however, if he can show that he had reasonable ground to believe and did believe up to the time the contract was made that the facts represented were true.

Innocent misrepresentation

This is where a misrepresentation is neither fraudulent nor negligent. There is no action for damages. However, where misrepresentation occurred before the contract was made and the misrepresentation becomes a term of the contract, then a party can claim damages.

7.5.4 Other matters

Where a party after discovering a misrepresentation does something to suggest that he does not want to rescind the contract, then he is prevented from doing so. Such actions include allowing a period of time to lapse after the contract was made.

A party cannot contract out of his liability for misrepresentation or any appropriate remedy unless it satisfies the test of reasonableness (see 7.8.4).

7.6 DURESS AND UNDUE INFLUENCE

7.6.1 Duress

Contracts may be alleged to have been entered into as a result of duress on the part of one party. The duress must be such that it prevents the person who complains of it from having a free will to enter the contract voluntarily. The effect of duress is to render a contract void (ie unenforceable) or voidable (ie a party complaining of duress has a choice of whether to affirm the contract or avoid it).

Duress is a combination of pressure and the lack of freedom to choose. Pressure is commonplace in commercial transactions and so long as the party being 'pushed' is not forced to enter without freedom of choice, then it is considered perfectly proper and an everyday commercial activity.

Duress may be exerted on a person through threats of violence or actual threat and imprisonment; on goods (ie unlawful detention of a person's goods, or a threat to detain them); or by 'economic duress'.

Duress administered to a person renders the contract void in serious cases and voidable in others. So far as duress to goods is concerned, a person who handed over money as a result of actual or threat of detention of goods can recover that money from the other party.

Economic duress

One party may exert economic pressure on the other which is such that the latter has no realistic choice but to enter the contract on the terms required by the first party. In *North Ocean Shipping Co Ltd v Hyundai Construction Co Ltd* [1979] QB 705 the shipbuilders who were building a ship threatened, without justification, to terminate the contract unless the other party agreed to increase the price for the work they were doing. The plaintiffs needed the ship urgently and reluctantly agreed. Although they stated that they reserved their rights, at no later stage did they raise any objections. They continued to make stage payments to the shipbuilders and eventually took delivery of the ship. The court decided that economic duress had been used by the shipbuilders and therefore the plaintiffs would have been entitled to refuse to pay 10 per cent and to enforce the original contract if they so wished. However, under the circumstances they were regarded as affirming the new price terms. They should have raised further objections not only throughout the contract when the stage payments were made but more particularly at the time of expected delivery.

Where one person owes another money, the former may offer a lower amount than he actually owes, forcing the other to accept it where perhaps his financial circumstances are such that he has no choice. Such an agreement cannot be forced upon him and he should be entitled to recover the balance he is actually owed. As mentioned above, not all threats can be considered to be duress as some may be commercially legitimate. There seems to be no doubt that where the threat is one to commit an act which is unlawful, it is considered to be duress. However, a threat by a party to break a contract where it can be shown that that threat did not force the other party to enter into the contract may not be considered to be duress. Furthermore, a threat not to supply goods unless a higher price is paid is not duress if it can be shown that the other party could have bought a plentiful supply of those goods elsewhere. Therefore, where the threat to do something is lawful but is clearly in excess of that which is regarded as commercially acceptable, it is held to be duress.

A situation could occur where a party has a right to bring a prosecution lawfully but threatens another party with a prosecution unless that other party enters a contract or agrees to more certain terms. This may be regarded as being duress as a threat amounts to excessive pressure which is not acceptable. Furthermore a court will not condone a situation where a party agrees to anything being done on the basis that a prosecution may be stifled.

In a threat to issue civil proceedings (ie where a party threatens to sue unless the other party agrees to certain clauses) a court will not interfere where a party is in fact threatening to enforce its legal right.

Where a person can show that the other party entered into a contract irrespective of the duress then a contract will be valid. However, it is the person accused of duress who is responsible for showing that the other would have entered the contract anyway.

What is the effect of duress?

The person who is subjected to the duress can normally choose whether he affirms or avoids the contract. If duress has occurred and he has taken no steps to set aside the contract, he may be held to have affirmed it.

7.6.2 Undue influence

This is an equitable doctrine which arose to deal with the situation where donations and gifts are allegedly made as a result of one party exerting unreasonable pressure on another. The basic principle arose to prevent one person profiting from his own fraud or wrongful act. A presumption of undue influence arises where the transaction is manifestly disadvantageous to the person who has been influenced.

Where a special relationship exists (eg with a parent and child or solicitor and client), undue influence is likely to be presumed. Therefore, where one party is shown to be disadvantaged, the presumption arises. Family arrangements are treated far more leniently than, say, a relationship between solicitor and client. However, where a parent has exercised undue influence over a child, the transaction is likely to be set aside.

To rebutt the presumption of undue influence, a party must show that the donor was acting independently of any influence from the donee. Perhaps the best way of showing this is to show that he had received independent advice from a third party. That advice must be such that an honest and competent adviser would give if acting solely in the interests of the donor.

A contract made under undue influence is voidable, and not void. Therefore a donor has the right to decide whether to affirm or avoid the contract. However, a donor may lose the right to set aside the contract if he does something to affirm the contract in any way or leaves matters for such a substantial period of time that he may be deemed to have acquiesced and therefore be bound by the transaction.

7.7 TERMS OF CONTRACT

Assuming that it can be established that a contract has been made, it is important to know what terms of a contract have been agreed upon and are therefore binding on the parties concerned.

Not all contracts are expressed in writing – some may be oral or may have terms which are partly oral or partly in writing. Generally, a party is bound by the terms of an agreement if he has agreed to them being incorporated in writing.

Prior to a contract being agreed, representations may be made by one party to encourage the other to enter into the contract. These representations are not usually considered to be the terms of a contract.

7.7.1 Standard form of contract and incorporation of terms

A party may be keen to show that the terms of agreement are those contained in a pre-prepared standard contract form, perhaps in a ticket or enclosed with a letter containing an offer. These standard terms are very often handed to a person at the time a contract is made. The question of whether the terms are then incorporated into the contract is an important one since the standard form of contract frequently tends to impose obligations on the parties and contains clauses which purport to exclude or limit liability in many situations so far as the party who prepared the conditions is concerned.

The conditions must be brought to the notice of the party who receives them either before or at the time the contract is made. If not, they cannot be incorporated into the contract. In *Olley v Marlborough Court* [1949] 1 KB 532, a person who checked into a hotel found that some of his property had been stolen. He sued the hotel which placed reliance on a notice which disclaimed liability for any lost or stolen article but which was on the back of his bedroom door. On arriving at the hotel when he had signed the hotel register, there had been no mention of any exemption clauses. The court held that the notice was ineffective since it had not been brought to his attention until after the contract had been made.

The conditions must be contained in a document which it would be reasonable for the receiving party to expect to contain conditions. For example, conditions contained on a deck chair hire ticket or a parking ticket issued by an automatic machine from a car park are ineffective for bringing attention to the party receiving it.

It is common that two parties engaged in trade enter into several contracts with each other. Where it can be shown that the parties intended that the conditions which had been used in previous contracts should continue to be used throughout the course of dealing between the parties, then those conditions are likely to be effective in the most recent agreement. Similarly, conditions used in a particular trade or business may be incorporated where both parties are in the same trade and are aware that those conditions are used, even when they do not actually refer to them in the contract between themselves.

It is not essential that the party receiving the conditions should have read them. In order for the other party to rely on them being incorporated, he must be able to show that the person receiving the document knew that there was writing or printed matter on the document and that it contained or referred to the conditions on which he intends to rely. The party intending to rely on the conditions must take reasonable steps to give notice to the other party of the conditions. If the receiving party knew that there was writing or printed matter on the document and sufficient steps were taken to give him notice of the conditions, then even if he did not actually know that it contained conditions, he is still likely to be bound by the contract's terms.

The steps to be taken to give reasonable notice of the conditions depends on the facts of each case. It is not always necessary for a set of conditions to be sent to the person concerned; it may be sufficient that the party seeking to rely on them had made specific mention of any pre-contract documents.

If the term on which a party intends to rely is considered onerous, then he must show that he has taken reasonable steps to bring the effect of that clause to the other party's attention. What a party must do depends on the fact of each case, but the court would have to be satisfied that clear steps were taken to draw the effect of that clause to the other party's attention before it is allowed to be incorporated.

If one party intends to rely on printed notices to bring to the other party's attention certain clauses they must be in a clearly visible place and they must be brought to the party's attention prior to entering into the contract.

7.7.2 What if each party wants to contract on its own terms?

A common situation is where *A* sends to *B* an offer, perhaps asking for supply of goods and/or services, and indicates in that letter that he intends to be bound by his own standard terms and conditions, a copy of which will be enclosed with the letter. *B* then replies, indicating that the order is accepted but that he intends to trade on his own terms only. Whose terms are incorporated into the contract? In the example described, neither of the parties' terms are incorporated. *B*'s reply to the order is regarded as a counter offer and not an acceptance.

If after having received *B*'s counter offer, *A* confirms the order, this may be regarded as being his acceptance to *B*'s counter offer and the contract is governed by *B*'s standard terms. The terms must satisfy all the rules relating to incorporation, such as reasonable notice. If these are satisfied, the terms are likely to govern the contract.

There is surprisingly little case law on this specific area. What often happens is that each party writes to the other indicating that he intends to contract only on his own standard terms. At some stage a contract is made and the difficulty is determining whose conditions apply. It is often described as the 'battle of the forms'.

The general principle that has arisen is known as the 'last shot' doctrine: in other words, a court looks into the communication between the parties and tries to establish at which point one set of conditions was unconditionally accepted by the other party (*Butler Machine Tool Co Ltd v Ex-Cell-o Corp (England) Ltd* [1979] 1 WLR 401). However, subsequent case law has placed slight variations on the principle, and in *British Steel Corp v Cleveland Bridge & Engineering* [1984] 1 All ER 504 the court found it impossible to identify an offer which had been accepted. Even though the goods had been delivered and 'accepted' by the receiving party, it was clear that party would never have agreed to the seller's standard terms. In that case the court found that no contract was concluded.

It is important therefore that any party who intends to contract on his own standard terms should ensure that *all* correspondence and contractual documents contain a copy of, or reference to, his standard terms.

7.7.3 Conditions and warranties

Once it is established that a certain term has been incorporated into a contract, it is important to know whether that term will be classified as a condition or a warranty. A *condition* is an essential stipulation of the contract in which one party guarantees to the other that it is true or that certain promises will be fulfilled. Breach of the condition permits the innocent party, if he wishes, to treat himself as being free from any obligation to be bound by the contract and claim damages for any loss he sustains as a result. A *warranty* is a term of the contract which is not regarded as so essential as a condition. Breach of a warranty does not allow a person to treat the contract as discharged but to claim damages only – even if he has suffered no prejudice by the breach.

Furthermore, certain terms may not be clearly defined as either a condition or a warranty; this third category is often referred to as an intermediate term. The consequence of the breach of that term simply depends on the nature of the breach itself. If the breach is a minor one, it can be remedied by an award of damages. If it is so important or fundamental it affects the whole contract, the contract must be regarded as discharged.

There is a substantial amount of case law which assists in determining whether the term is a condition, warranty or intermediate term. The facts of each case are important in deciding this issue.

7.7.4 Meaning and construction of term

It is important that the terms on which the party intends to rely can be easily understood. Therefore where any technical or unusual words are incorporated into a contract, there should be a clear explanation of their meaning to avoid any ambiguity. If there is ambiguity a court may delete that part of the contract or, if the majority of the contract is not clearly intelligible, all of it.

The court looks at the whole context of an agreement to establish the meaning of any particular term or clause. It is not open to a court to alter the words used or to impose a meaning that it believes the parties ought to have included, unless it is clear that that is actually what the parties had intended. In other words, a court will not rewrite the terms of a contract.

7.7.5 Extrinsic evidence

In an ideal world all the terms which affect a contract will be supported by written evidence in the contract itself.

One party may wish to adduce evidence which is extrinsic to the written contract on the basis that the written terms themselves do not clearly show all the points which were agreed between the parties. If after hearing the evidence a court determines that terms additional to those contained in the document were agreed upon and were intended by the parties to be incorporated into the contract, that contract will consist partly of the terms of the document and partly those outside it. If, however, the court finds that the document is a complete record of the contract, it will reject the extrinsic evidence produced. This latter situation is known as the 'parol evidence rule'. Therefore, where a document appears to be a complete contract, a party will have great difficulty convincing a court that further terms outside the agreement were intended to be incorporated into the contract.

Where certain contracts must by law be evidenced in writing, then any extrinsic oral evidence is likely to be excluded.

7.7.6 Collateral contracts

In certain circumstances, although the party intended to be bound by all the terms in a written document, there may be a collateral contract of agreement outside the main agreement which gives efficacy to matters on which the main contract may be silent. This collateral agreement may be oral. A court may determine that it does have effect and that it runs alongside the main contract.

Although the parole evidence rule stipulates that no extrinsic evidence can be included to affect the main written agreement, there are some exceptions to that rule:

(1) Evidence adduced to determine the written agreement's validity or effectiveness.
(2) Evidence used to determine the agreement's true nature.
(3) Evidence to interpret or explain parts of the written agreement.
(4) Evidence of custom or trade usage.

7.7.7 Implied term

Although it is always hoped that any terms incorporated into the contract are expressed either in writing or openly agreed between the parties before the contract is made, it is possible that terms are implied as being incorporated into the contract. This is particularly so in certain types of contracts (eg sale of goods, landlord and tenant, and employment).

Terms implied into the contract do not necessarily reflect the party's intention, although this is possible. Certain contracts might be silent about particular aspects of the contract. However the court does not imply a meaning simply because it improves the contract, it must be a necessity.

Certain statutes imposed implied terms or a term may be implied from general usage or custom in any particular trade or activity. Similarly, evidence of a previous course of dealing between the parties may give rise to certain terms being implied into the contract.

Where however there is an express term which clearly contradicts that which might be considered to be customary in the circumstances then the general rule is that the express terms will prevail.

7.8 EXEMPTION AND EXCLUSION CLAUSES

It is common for parties to want to exclude or limit their liability in the terms of any contract they enter into. Furthermore, they may want to provide time limits in which the other party can lodge a claim.

Exclusion clauses are generally construed strictly. The court takes into account the circumstances of the case and tries to give effect to what they believe to be the parties' intentions. The words must therefore be clear and unambiguous. Where a clause is ambiguous a court infers whichever meaning favours the party against whom the clause is intended to operate, to the detriment of the party seeking to rely on it. This principle is known as '*contra preferendum*'. It is not possible for any party to exclude every liability and in some circumstances a court is prepared to completely delete an exclusion clause.

Where an exclusion clause is drafted so widely that, if interpreted literally, it defeats the main purpose of the contract, the court attempts to interpret it to reflect the parties' intentions.

7.8.1 Liability for negligence

It is possible to exclude or restrict a party's liability for negligence, but the parties must ensure that the words are clear and it is made certain that they intended to exclude such liability. However, it is not possible, in most cases, to exclude liability for personal injury (see 7.8.4).

7.8.2 Burden of proof

This is placed upon the person who intends to rely on the exemption or exclusion clause. He must show that the clause covers the liability that he intends to restrict or exclude. If he satisfies a court of this, the other party will try to convince the court that the loss or damage that arose eminated from an act or omission which falls outside the scope of the clause.

7.8.3 Exemption clause from third party

A third party (ie one that is not a party to the contract) cannot rely on an exemption clause contained in the contract; the exemption clause is intended to apply to the relationship *vis-à-vis* the parties to the contract. However, a situation could arise, say, where the duty of care owed by *A* to *B* arises as a result of a contract between *B* and *C*. An exemption clause in the contract between *B* and *C* which purports to exclude or restrict liability may be regarded as applying to any liability attaching to *A*. The condition that must be proven is that it was the intention of all the parties that such a clause should apply to *A*'s liability.

7.8.4 Statutory control and exemption clauses

Unfair Contract Terms Act 1977

The Act seeks to control terms contained in the contract (and also non-contractual notices which seek to exclude or restrict liability in tort) where those terms purport to exclude or restrict liability. The Act may make the clause concerned ineffective or it may mean that the clause must satisfy the requirement of reasonableness to be effective.

Dealing as a consumer

The Act draws a distinction between situations where a party deals as a consumer and where he does not. There are three conditions to be satisfied for the party to be regarded as dealing as a consumer:

(1) he must not make the contract in the course of the business or hold himself out as doing so;
(2) the other party must make a contract in the course of a business; and
(3) the goods must be of a type ordinarily supplied for private use or consumption.

A qualification to this rule arose in *R & B Customs Brokers Co Ltd v United Dominions Trust Ltd* [1988] 1 WLR 321. The court held that a freight forwarding company dealt as a consumer when it entered into an agreement with a finance company for the purchase of a motor vehicle which was for a director's personal and business use. The decision was made on the basis that the company had not held itself out as making the contract in the course of a business.

Section 3 of the Act applies to a contract where one of the parties deals as a consumer or on the other party's written standard terms of business. The party cannot by reference to any contract term, except in so far as the term satisfies the test of reasonableness, exclude or restrict any liability in respect of his breach of contract, or claim that he is entitled to render a contractual performance which is substantially different from that which is reasonably expected of him, or render no performance at all for all or some of his contractual obligations.

Section 4 states that a person who deals with a consumer cannot by way of any contract term be made to indemnify another person in respect of any liability for negligence or breach of contract, except in so far as the contract term satisfies the test of reasonableness. Indemnities given by people who do not deal as a consumer are not affected by this section.

Liability for negligence

Section 2 prevents a person excluding or restricting his liability (arising from business liability) for death or personal injury resulting from negligence. Any such clause is totally ineffective. Nor can he exclude or restrict his liability for any other loss or damages which arise out of his negligence unless the term satisfies the test of reasonableness.

Consumer guarantees

Section 5 states that any clause which attempts to exclude or restrict business liability for loss or damage resulting from the negligence of the manufacturer or distributor of any goods is ineffective. 'Goods' for the purpose of this section are those ordinarily supplied for private use or consumption. The loss or damage must arise from the goods being defective whilst in use by a person other than exclusively for business.

'Business liability' is not defined by the Act, but s 1 expands on this phrase as appling to liabilities for breach of any obligations which arise from something which occurs in the course of a person's business or from the occupation of premises used for business purposes.

Sale and hire purchase

Section 6 limits the liability of the person who sells or lets out his goods under hire-purchase agreements to exclude or restrict liability for any of the undertakings implied by the Sale of Goods Act 1979, s 12 or the Supply of Goods (Implied Terms) Act 1973, s 8.

Section 7 applies to other contracts such as those for hire of goods or work and materials. Excluding or restricting any liability arising from descriptions of the goods or their fitness for purpose is ineffective so far as any dealings with a consumer are concerned. In dealings with a person who is not a consumer, the liability can be excluded or restricted only in so far as the term satisfies the test of reasonableness. For any liability for breach of obligations arising out of title, the goods concerned cannot be excluded or restricted by an exemption clause. Furthermore any terms which attempt to exclude or restrict liability for the rights to transfer ownership of or requiring possession of the goods are subject to the test of reasonableness.

To be effective, many of the clauses governed by the Act must satisfy the test of reasonableness. To satisfy the test, s 11 states that 'the term shall have been a fair and reasonable one to be included having regard to the circumstances which were, or ought reasonably to have been, known to or in the contemplation of the parties when the contract was made'. The reasonableness of the term is determined at the time when the contract was made; therefore any facts not known at that time are likely to be irrelevant in determining whether a clause is reasonable.

Schedule 2 lays down guidelines (which are not exhaustive) to assist in determining whether a clause satisfies the test. The guidelines apply to contracts dealing with the sale of goods and hire purchase, and contracts for the supply of goods, but they are often regarded as being of general use in assisting to determine whether a clause is reasonable. The guidelines are as follows:

(a) the strength of the bargaining positions of the parties relative to each other, taking into account . . . alternative means by which the customers requirements could have been met;
(b) whether the customer received an inducement to agree to the term, or in accepting it had an opportunity of entering into a similar contract with other persons, but without having to accept a similar term;
(c) whether the customer knew or ought reasonably to have known of the existence and extent of the term (having regard . . . to any custom of the trade and any previous course of dealing between the parties);
(d) where the term excludes or restricts any relevant liability if some condition is not complied with, whether it was reasonable at the time of the contract to expect that compliance with that condition would be practicable;
(e) whether the goods were manufactured, processed or adapted to the special order of the customer.

Limiting liability

Section 11 provides that where a person, by use of a contract term, seeks to restrict liability to a specified sum and the question arises whether that term satisfies the test of reasonableness, then consideration must be given (without ignoring the guidelines listed above) to:

(1) the resources that he could expect to be available to him to meet the liability if it arises, and
(2) how far it was open to him to cover himself by insurance.

A court must determine whether a clause is reasonable. It cannot re-write the term, nor can it delete words to render what it believes is an 'unreasonable' term, reasonable.

Exceptions

Certain contracts are not affected by ss 2–4 of the 1977 Act (Sched 1). They relate to contracts for insurance: creation or transfer of an interest in land, patents, trademarks and copyright; formation or dissolution of a company or the rights or obligations of its members; and any contract relating to creation or transfer of rights in securities.

Schedule 1 qualifies the Act's effect on any contract of marine salvage or towage, a charter party, and for the carriage of goods by a ship or hovercraft. It further qualifies any contract of employment in that any attempt to exclude liability for negligence will not be effective unless it favours an employee.

Misrepresentation

Section 8 of the 1977 Act provides that where a term or clause attempts to exclude or restrict any liability of or any remedy available to a party arising from a misrepresentation, then that term or clause has no effect in so far as it satisfies the test of reasonableness in s 11.

Unfair Terms in Consumer Contracts Regulations 1994

These regulations (SI No 3159) implement the EC Directive 93/13/EC. The Directive attempts to harmonise for all member states the laws on safeguarding the consumer with regard to unfair terms in contracts. They came into force on 1 July 1995.

The Regulations do not affect the provisions of the Unfair Contract Terms Act 1977; nor do they apply to non-consumer contracts. Therefore in some circumstances a party only has the choice of an action under the 1977 Act.

The Regulations prohibit the use of unfair terms in consumer contracts, whether oral or written. They apply to any term or contract concluded between a seller or supplier and a consumer where the term has not been individually negotiated (ie where it has been drafted in advance and a consumer has not been able to influence the term's content). There are a few exceptions but virtually all pre-formulated contract conditions are governed by the Regulations.

Whereas the 1977 Act applies only to specific types of clauses, the Regulations apply to all clauses of a contract which are not individually negotiated.

Plain intelligible language

Regulation 6 provides that terms must be drafted in plain intelligible language. If there is any doubt about the meaning of a written term, the interpretation which is most favourable to a consumer prevails. By using plain intelligible language, contract provisions relating to definition of the subject matter, the price or remuneration are not subject to any test.

However, these may be factors which must be taken into account in considering whether the term is fair.

The Regulations require that any term satisfies the test of 'unfairness' (unlike the 1977 Act's test of reasonableness). If a term is regarded as unfair then it is not binding on a consumer. However, the Regulations stipulate that although one term may be ineffective, where the balance of the contract can continue without that term, it shall be binding on the parties.

What is unfair?

Under reg 4, 'an unfair term is one which contrary to the requirement of good faith causes a significant imbalance in the parties' rights and obligations under the contract to the detriment of the consumer'. When assessing the unfair nature of a term, the following must be considered:

(1) the nature of the goods and services to which the contract applies;
(2) all the circumstances at the time the contract was concluded; and
(3) all other terms of the contract or of another contract on which that contract may be dependent.

Schedule 3 to the Regulations lists 17 terms which it is stated *may* be unfair. The list, although lengthy, is not exhaustive, and includes the following:

(1) inappropriately excluding or limiting the consumer's legal rights;
(2) irrevocably binding the consumer to terms with which he had no real opportunity of becoming acquainted before the conclusion of the contract;
(3) obliging the consumer to fulfill his obligations where the seller/supplier does not perform his;
(4) enabling the seller/supplier to alter the contract's terms unilaterally without a valid reason specified in the contract.

The examples are guidelines only; each term must be assessed on its own merits.

A court must consider whether the term satisfies the requirement of good faith as stipulated in reg 4. Schedule 2 to the Regulations states that:

> in making an assessment of good faith, regard shall be had in particular to –
>
> (a) the strength of the bargaining positions of the parties;
> (b) whether the consumer had any inducement to agree to the term;
> (c) whether the goods or services were sold or supplied to the special order of the consumer; and
> (d) the extent to which the seller or supplier has dealt fairly and equitably with the consumer.

The test for determining whether a term is unfair is similar to that for reasonableness in the 1977 Act. However, it remains to be seen what interpretation can be placed upon the requirements of the Regulations by the courts.

Exclusions from Regulations

The Regulations do not apply to any employment contract, any contract relating to succession rights or rights under family law, or to the incorporation of companies and partnerships; or to any term which is included to comply with or reflect UK legislation or provisions of international conventions to which the EC member states belong.

7.9 BREACH OF CONTRACT

There are many ways in which a contract can come to an end other than by way of the parties discharging their obligations and promises under the contract's terms. However, perhaps one of the most important is by breach of contract.

A breach of contract generally gives rise to a cause of action for the person who has been aggrieved. This does not mean that whenever there is a breach, the aggrieved person is entitled to treat himself as discharged from any further obligation to accept the other party's performance of his contractual duty or any attempt to perform them. However, the aggrieved party usually prefers this course of action, although in some situations he may wish to treat the contract as continuing. Furthermore, he may decide to waive his rights to treat the contract as discharged, except for the other party's performance even though it is defective, and instead sue for damages.

7.9.1 Affirming the contract

The aggrieved party may treat the contract as continuing, in which case he is said to have 'affirmed' the contract. Affirmation may be express or implied if, with knowledge of the breach and knowledge of his right to choose between the alternatives open to him, he does some unequivocal act which suggests that he intends to go on with the contract regardless of the breach. Nevertheless, by affirming the contract the aggrieved party does not lose his right to claim damages for loss he suffered due to the breach.

An aggrieved party may lose his right to treat the contract as repudiated if he conducts himself in such a way that the other party believes that he does not intend to exercise his right. The aggrieved party must have shown unequivocal representation in either words or conduct that he does not intend to do so. Furthermore, it must be shown that the aggrieved party knew of the circumstances giving rise to the breach and of his right to treat the contract as repudiated. Another condition that must be satisfied is that the party who claims that the other has waived his right has relied to such an extent on the action which he regards as being the waiver, that it is an unjust contract to continue. The facts of each case decide whether a court accepts that an aggrieved party waived his right.

7.9.2 Repudiation must be accepted

Where an aggrieved party decides to treat himself as discharged of his obligation under the contract, he must accept repudiation. Otherwise, the contract continues to exist. In other words, he must indicate to the other party that he considers that that party is in breach and that he intends to treat the contract as repudiated. Once acceptance has been communicated, it cannot then be withdrawn. Therefore, if the parties decide to resume the contract's performance, the contract is regarded as renewed, even if the terms are the same.

7.9.3 What if both parties are in breach?

The effect of this depends on the order of the breaches by each party. If party *A* admits the breach and party *B* follows with an act which is also a breach of contract, then if party *B* informs *A* that he intends to treat the contract as repudiated on the basis of party *A*'s breach, failure to perform does not give rise to a breach of contract to *A*.

If both parties commit a breach of contract simultaneously, it is suggested that neither party is entitled to treat the contract as repudiated.

7.9.4 Anticipatory breach

If one party indicates to the other that he intends to do or not do something which leads a reasonable person to believe that the party does not intend to fulfil his obligations under the contract, this could be regarded as an 'anticipatory breach' of the contract. In these circumstances, the 'aggrieved' party may indicate to the other that he 'accepts' the repudiation and sue for damages immediately, or he may wait and see whether the breach does occur and then sue for damages.

7.10 FRUSTRATION

Despite the best intention of both parties to the contract, an event may occur once the contract is entered into which makes it physically or commercially impossible for the contract to be performed. The principles of frustration were illustrated in *Taylor v Caldwell* (1863) 32 LJQB 164, in which the defendants had agreed to allow the plaintiffs to use a music hall for concerts on four specified nights. Before the first night, but after the contract was made, the music hall was completely destroyed by fire. The defendants were sued but the court held that they were not liable in damages to the plaintiffs. It is not necessary that physical destruction of any subject matter has to take place but merely that an event occurs outside the control of either party and is such that it brings the contract to an immediate end.

A court which is asked to determine whether contracts have been frustrated will try to determine whether the contract's terms are wide enough to enable the contract to continue in the new situation; if it is not, the contract must be regarded as frustrated.

7.10.1 Delay

It is not always easy to determine whether an unexpected delay in the performance of contractual duty gives rise to the contract being frustrated. To amount to frustration, the delay must be unexpected and abnormal in that its effect or length would not be reasonable for the contracting parties to have contemplated it occurring. Much depends on the length of the delay in relation to the nature of the contract and the effect which the delay causes upon the contractual duty. If the delay is held to be within the commercial risks undertaken by the party to the contract, the court will hold that there is no frustration.

7.10.2 Sale of goods

The Sale of Goods Act 1979 makes provision where a certain set of circumstances gives rise to the contract being frustrated. Section 7 provides: 'Where there is an agreement to sell specific goods and subsequently the goods, without any fault on the part of the seller or buyer, perish before the risk passes to the buyer, the agreement is voided.' Apart from this particular set of circumstances, the normal rule relating to frustration applies where it is claimed that an agreement to sell goods has been frustrated.

7.10.3 Consequences of frustration

The common law rules of frustration left various defects in that in a situation where a contract was regarded as being frustrated, a party might not be able to recover the payment that it had already made prior to the frustration. The Law Reform (Frustrated Contracts) Act 1943 applies to contracts which have become 'impossible of performance or being otherwise frustrated'.

Section 1(2) of the Act provides that all sums which have been paid or payable in pursuance of the contract before the time of the frustration shall, in the case of sums actually paid, be recoverable and, in the case of sums payable, cease to be payable. There is a proviso that where the party to whom the sums were paid or are payable incurred expenses before the time of frustration, in performance of the contract, then a court may allow him to retain, or recover, a sum up to the level of the expenses incurred.

Benefit acquired under the contract

Section 1(3) states that where a party has, by reason of any performance of another party under the terms of the contract, obtained a valuable benefit (other than a payment of money) before the contract is frustrated, then a sum can be recovered from him which should not exceed the value of the benefit and should be such a figure as the court thinks fit, having regard to all the circumstances. The 'benefit' is the product of the services supplied, but it might be the services themselves. It is up to the court to place a value on the benefit received. This is not always easy since a small service may result in something of great value to the receiving party, or a substantial service may produce something of little value.

The court must take into account the amount of any expenses incurred, if any, by the party who benefited, including any sum that he paid to any other party and the effect, in relation to the benefit, of the circumstances giving rise to the frustration. In effect, the court must first identify the 'valuable benefit', then place a value upon it, and finally consider the award of a just sum, which cannot be greater in value than the actual benefit obtained.

Severing part of the contract

Section 2(4) provides that a court can sever any part of a contract that it believes is severable and treat it as if it were a separate contract which had not been frustrated. The rest of the contract is therefore regarded as frustrated. The Act has no effect upon the part of the contract which can be regarded as being completely performed.

Excluding the act

Under s 2(3), if it is clear that the parties have anticipated that the frustrating event might occur and have provided for what should happen in the event that it did occur, the Act does not apply. However, where the circumstances are so unusual and the effect so serious that they fall outside the clauses' intention, the Act may not have been excluded.

Where the parties intend to make provision in the event that the contract is frustrated, they must make it very clear what the alternative consequences of frustration are. Otherwise, it is likely that the common law rule will apply which may be detrimental to, for example, the paying party.

Exclusion

Certain types of contract are excluded from the Act and these include charter parties, contracts for the carriage of goods by sea, for insurance and for the sale of specific perishable goods, whether or not the risk passes to the buyer before the date of perishing.

8

SALE OF GOODS

NICOLA TOMLINS AND DAVID NIVEN, WEDLAKE SAINT

The law of contract for sale of goods was consolidated in the Sale of Goods Act 1979, as amended by the Sale and Supply of Goods Act 1994. Provisions relating to contracts for work and materials exist in the Supply of Goods and Services Act 1982. Agreements of hire purchase, condition of sale and credit sale are governed by the Consumer Credit Act 1974 and the Supply of Goods (Implied Terms) Act 1973.

This chapter covers the following areas:

(1) Terms implied into a sale of goods contract
(2) Description
(3) Fitness for purpose and quality
(4) Sale by sample
(5) Exclusion of terms implied by ss 13–15 of the 1979 Act
(6) Breach of an implied term
(7) Stipulations of time
(8) Consumer protection
(9) Passing of property and risk
(10) Delivery and acceptance
(11) Remedies of the seller
(12) Remedies of the buyer.

8.1 TERMS IMPLIED INTO A SALE OF GOODS CONTRACT

Section 12 of the 1979 Act states that there is an implied term on the seller's part that he has a right to sell the goods and, in an agreement to sell, that he has a right to sell the goods at a time when the property is to pass. Furthermore, in a contract for sale (other than that in which the seller intends to transfer only such title as he or a third person may have (and which is governed by ss 3–5)) there is also an implied term in s 12(2) that:

(a) the goods are free, and will remain free until the time when the property is to pass, from any charge or encumbrance not disclosed or known to the buyer before the contract is made, and

(b) the buyer will enjoy quiet possession of the goods except so far as it may be disturbed by the owner or other person entitled to the benefit of any charge or encumbrance so disclosed or known.

The seller need not actually own the goods at any time since he only promises that he can give the appropriate rights to the buyer.

This implied term is regarded as a condition and therefore if it is breached the buyer can treat the contract as repudiated and claim damages. Alternatively, he may affirm the contract and also claim damages. Under s 12(2), these obligations are warranties and give rise to no more than a claim for damages.

The exclusion of the provisions of s 12 is prohibited by s 6 of the Unfair Contract Terms Act 1977.

8.2 DESCRIPTION

Section 13 of the 1979 Act provides that where there is a contract for the sale of goods by description there is an implied term that the goods will correspond with this description. Furthermore, if the sale is by sample as well as by description it is not sufficient that the bulk of the goods corresponds with the sample if the goods do not also correspond with the description. Care must be taken to ensure that the description is as accurate as possible.

8.3 FITNESS FOR PURPOSE AND QUALITY

8.3.1 Fitness for purpose

Section 14 states that where a buyer expressly or impliedly makes known to

(1) the seller who sold him the goods in the course of business, or
(2) the credit broker who had previously sold the goods in the seller, where the buyer is paying all or part of the goods' purchase price in instalments,

the particular purpose for buying the goods, there is an implied condition that the goods are reasonably suited to that purpose. This applies whether or not the goods are commonly supplied for such purpose, but not if the buyer does not, or it is unreasonable for him to, rely on the seller's or credit broker's skill or judgement. A credit broker is defined by s 61(1) as a person who acts in the course of a business of credit brokerage carried on by him, that is a business of effecting introductions of individuals desiring to obtain credit –

(a) to persons carrying on any business so far as it relates to the provision of credit, or
(b) to other persons engaged in credit brokerage.

Where the buyer is required to make the purpose of goods known, he is not required to make it known expressly. For example, where an article can only be for one particular purpose, then it is unnecessary for the buyer to make it clear that he wants the article for that purpose. Where the goods may be used for several purposes it may be necessary, but not definitely, to indicate the intended purpose.

The seller must prove that the buyer did not rely on his judgement. If the seller informs the buyer that he has no knowledge or expertise of the goods being bought or the buyer has more knowledge of the goods than the seller, the buyer cannot make a successful claim against the seller that the goods were not fit for their purpose.

The duty to provide goods which are reasonably fit for their purpose is strict and a party cannot successfully defend a claim by showing that he took all reasonable care. However, a seller is not liable where the goods are used by the buyer for purposes which are outside the range of the purposes which the seller could reasonably foresee.

8.3.2 Quality

The requirement that the quality of the goods sold should be of 'merchantable' quality as required by s 14 of the 1979 Act was amended by the 1994 Act. Section 14 (as amended) now provides that where a seller sells goods in the course of a business, there is an implied term that the goods supplied are of 'satisfactory' quality.

Goods are of satisfactory quality if they meet the standard that a reasonable person would regard as satisfactory, taking into account any description of the goods, the price (if relevant) and all other relevant circumstances. The 1979 Act states that the quality of the goods includes their state and condition, and suggests that some of the things that must be taken into account when considering the quality are:

(i) the fitness for all the purposes for which goods of the kind in question are commonly supplied;
(ii) appearance and finish;
(iii) being free from minor defects;
(iv) safety; and
(v) durability.

This does not apply where the unsatisfactory nature of the goods is specifically drawn to the buyer's attention, or where the buyer examines the goods, before the contract is made. In this case the examination ought to reveal the problem or, where a person is purchasing goods by way of examining a sample, the problem should be apparent on reasonable examination of that sample.

8.4 SALE BY SAMPLE

Section 15 of the 1979 Act applies where by purchasing the bulk of the goods the buyer can place his reliance on examination of a sample. It must be clear that the parties intended that the sample, which is exhibited to the buyer at the time of sale, is a small sample of the goods which the buyer is purchasing. Section 15 states that the bulk *must* correspond with the sample in quality and the buyer must have a reasonable opportunity of comparing the bulk with the sample before he is deemed to have accepted the goods.

Further, s 15 (as amended) states that the goods will be free from any defect which might make their quality unsatisfactory, which might not be apparent on reasonable examination of the sample.

8.5 EXCLUSION OF TERMS IMPLIED BY SS 13–15 OF THE 1979 ACT

Where the buyer is a consumer, as defined in the Unfair Contract Terms Act 1977, the seller cannot exclude or restrict his liability by reference to any contract terms imposed by ss 13–15. For non-consumers liability can be excluded or restricted by way of a term of the contract but only if the term satisfies the 'reasonableness' requirement.

8.6 BREACH OF AN IMPLIED TERM

The terms implied by ss 13–15 of the 1979 Act are conditions and as such an aggrieved party is normally entitled to treat the contract as repudiated and reject the goods. However, the 1994 Act made an important amendment for non-consumers; where the breach on the part of the seller is so slight that it is unreasonable for him to reject the goods, 'the breach is not to be treated as a breach of condition but may be treated as a breach of warranty'. The aggrieved party can claim damages only. This provision only applies unless a contrary intention appears, or is to be implied, from the contract.

8.7 STIPULATIONS OF TIME

Section 10 of the 1979 Act provides that unless a contrary intention appears from the contract's terms, stipulation of time of payment is not deemed to be of the essence of a contract of sale. Whether any other stipulation of time is of the essence of the contract depends on the terms of the contract itself. In other words, late payment does not give rise to an action for damages. However the Act further provides that a court has the power to award interest.

8.8 CONSUMER PROTECTION

8.8.1 Cancellation rights

The Consumer Credit Act 1974 enables a buyer who is a consumer to cancel a contract for sale of goods where that contract is within the definition of a consumer credit agreement within the Act. The agreement itself may be generally defined as a credit agreement where the buyer is not a corporate body and where the credit provided does not exceed £15,000 (other than an exempt agreement), or one which is financed wholly or partially by a loan under a regulated agreement connected with arrangements made between the lender and the seller. The Act stipulates when the right of cancellation arises and how it should be exercised. There is generally a 'cooling off' period which starts when the buyer receives a statutory copy of the credit agreement, so that the consumer is free to decide whether he wishes to enter the contract.

Further provisions exist to protect the consumer from the effects of any contract which arises as a result of 'cold calling' (ie where a consumer receives an unexpected visit from the seller and/or his employees). The Consumer Protection (Cancellation of Contracts Concluded Away from Business Premises) Regulations 1987 allow a 'cooling off' period which permits cancellation and the return of any money to the consumer. The Regulations do not apply to contracts for the supply of food, drink and other goods which are for current consumption, certain contracts concluded on the basis of a trader's catalogue, contracts which do not require the consumer to make total payments exceeding £35.00, and contracts cancellable by virtue of the Consumer Credit Act 1974.

8.8.2 Product liability: Consumer Protection Act 1987

The Act imposes liability on manufacturers and certain other people for death, personal injury and physical damage to property which arises from defective products. The liability imposed does not depend upon proof of negligence and (subject to certain defences) is therefore a strict liability.

The plaintiff must show that the injury or damage suffered was caused by the product and that the product was defective. Once these conditions are satisfied the manufacturer or other person is likely to be liable unless he comes within the defences provided for by the Act. The products covered are virtually all goods.

The following people can be held jointly and severally liable:

(1) the manufacturer of the finished product;
(2) the manufacturer of any part of the product which is defective;
(3) any person who permitted his name or logo to be placed on the product and thereby held himself out to be a producer;
(4) the importer of the product into the EC;
(5) the supplier of the product who may be unable to trace the product back to its manufacturer.

Defence

Section 4 of the 1987 Act sets out six defences which are available, notwithstanding the strict liability imposed. A person is afforded a defence if he can show that:

(1) the defect is attributable to compliance with any requirement imposed by or under any enactment or with any EC obligation; or
(2) he did not at any time supply the product to another; or
(3) the supply of that product by him was otherwise than in the course of his business and that he is not caught within the definition of identifiable people who should be liable; or
(4) the defect complained of did not exist in the product at the relevant time (ie it arose after the time when he supplied the product); or
(5) the state of the technical and scientific knowledge at the time of the supply was such that he would not be able to discover the defect (sometimes known as the 'state of the art' defence); or
(6) the defect was contained in a product which eventually became comprised in a final product and was fully attributable to the final product's design or due to compliance with the requirements made by the final product's producer.

It is also possible for the person being sued to rely on a claim for contributory negligence on the part of the person complaining of the damage.

8.9 PASSING OF PROPERTY AND RISK

Sections 16–20 of the Sale of Goods Act 1979 contain the rules governing the passing of property, in goods sold, from the seller to the buyer. All provisions of ss 16–20 can be varied and in most terms the parties, whether buyer or seller, will want to vary them by way of specific terms in the contract. Section 16 refers to unascertained goods (eg '50 kilograms of flour') and provides that no property in the goods transfers to the buyer unless and until the goods are actually ascertained.

Section 17 provides that for specific or ascertained goods, the property is transferred to the buyer at such time as the parties intend it to be transferred. In other words consideration must be given to the contract's terms, the parties' conduct and the general circumstances of the case.

Section 18 sets out various rules for ascertaining the parties' intention for the time when the property in the goods is to pass to the buyer, in the absence of any contrary intention by the party. They can therefore be excluded by reference to terms in the contract.

Section 19 states that where there is a contract for sale of specific goods (or where goods are subsequently appropriated to the contract) the seller may reserve the right of the goods' disposal until certain conditions are fulfilled. In those circumstances the property in the goods does not pass to the buyer until these conditions are fulfilled.

8.9.1 'Romalpa' clauses; retention of title

This type of clause puts the seller in a more favourable position than he would normally be if the buyer is unable to pay. Under the 1979 Act the property in the goods passes to the buyer when the contract is made, irrespective of the time of payment or delivery. Consequently, a seller is advised to include a clause stipulating that he retains property in the goods supplied until he receives payment. The principle arose as a result of *Aluminium Industrie Vaassen BV v Romalpa Aluminium Ltd* [1976] 1 WLR 676. Such a clause is beneficial to the seller if, for example, the buyer goes into liquidation.

The law has become very complex for this type of clause. The problem generally arises when the goods sold have subsequently been incorporated into another product. It may not therefore be possible to retrieve them.

8.9.2 Passing of the risk

Section 20 of the 1979 Act states that unless it is otherwise agreed in the contract, the goods remain at the seller's risk until the property in them is transferred to the buyer. Then the goods are at the buyer's risk, whether or not delivery has been made.

8.10 DELIVERY AND ACCEPTANCE

8.10.1 Delivery

Detailed rules for delivery of goods are contained in the Sale of Goods Act 1979. Section 29 deals with the place and time of delivery, goods which may be in possession of a third person and expenses incurred in connection with the delivery. Section 30 sets out what might be regarded as a defective, insufficient or excessive delivery. It has been affected by the Sale and Supply of Goods Act 1994 to the extent that s 30(4) (the buyer's right to reject part of the delivery of goods, some which satisfy the contract description) is repealed. Furthermore, a new provision is inserted for situations in which there is a shortfall or excess in the delivery.

Where there is a shortfall the buyer can either reject the delivery, recover the price paid and sue for any loss suffered, or he can accept the quantity delivered, paying for this at the contract rate and recovering any additional money paid; he can also claim damages for breach. Where there is an excess, the buyer can either:

(1) reject the whole of the goods delivered; or
(2) select the correct quantity and reject the rest; or
(3) accept the whole delivery and pay for the excess at the contract rate.

A new provision, inserted by the 1994 Act, states that a buyer who does not deal as a consumer is not entitled to reject the goods where there is a shortfall or an excess if it is so slight that it would be unreasonable for him to do so. The seller must show that a shortfall or excess is so slight that it is unreasonable for the buyer to reject the delivery.

Section 31 deals with delivery by way of instalment (for example, it stipulates when the buyer is not bound to accept delivery by instalments). Section 32 sets out the rules for where delivery is made to a carrier; s 33 makes a buyer take responsibility at the risk of any deterioration in the goods where a seller has agreed to deliver at his own risk to a place other than where they are sold.

All the above rules referred to can be altered by the party by reference to terms of the contract; close consideration should be given to this.

8.10.2 Acceptance

The general rules of acceptance are that where a buyer accepts the goods, he cannot repudiate the contract at a later stage. Therefore any rights he may have had with regard to a breach of condition would then have to be treated as a breach of warranty and would entitle him to claim for damages only.

Section 34(2) of the 1979 Act states that when a seller attempts to deliver goods he must allow the buyer, if requested, a reasonable opportunity of examining them to ascertain whether they conform with the contract and, if appropriate, to compare the bulk of the delivery with the sample. Section 35 (as amended) states that the buyer is deemed to have accepted the goods (except as provided below) when:

(1) he intimates to the seller that he has accepted them;
(2) the goods are delivered to him and he does any act which is inconsistent with the ownership of the seller; or
(3) after a reasonable period of time has passed, he retains the goods without intimating to the seller that he has rejected them.

When considering whether a 'reasonable' time has passed, consideration must be given to whether the buyer has had a reasonable opportunity to examine the goods.

If the buyer has not previously examined the goods, then he is not deemed to have accepted them when they are delivered unless he has a reasonable opportunity to examine them as specified in s 34(2) (see above). Furthermore, where the buyer deals as a consumer, he cannot lose his right to have a reasonable opportunity of examining the goods. Any attempt by the seller to persuade him to contract out of this right will be ineffective.

A buyer is not deemed to have accepted goods merely because he asks for or agrees to them being repaired or where the goods are delivered to another person under a subsale.

Where the contract relates to the making of one or more commercial units, and a buyer accepts any goods included in a unit, he is deemed to have accepted all the goods comprised in that unit.

A right of 'partial rejection' was introduced by the 1994 Act. Where the buyer has the right to reject goods by virtue of the seller's breach which affects some or all of the goods, but he accepts some of the goods including all those unaffected by the breach, he is not regarded as losing his rights to reject the rest. The rule also applies where the buyer is faced with an instalment of goods rather than the entire delivery. Goods are 'affected by a breach' if, as a result of the breach, they do not conform with the contract. The right to partial rejection can be amended or deleted by agreement in the contract.

Section 36 provides that where goods are delivered to the buyer and he refuses to accept them, having the right to do so, he is not bound to return them to the seller; it is sufficient if he intimates to the seller that he refuses to accept them. However, he cannot exercise a lien over the goods to obtain repayment from the seller.

Where the buyer refuses to take delivery within a reasonable time from a request by the seller that he should take delivery, s 37 makes him liable to the seller for any loss which is occasioned by his neglect or refusal to take delivery and also for a reasonable charge for the care and custody of the goods.

8.11 REMEDIES OF THE SELLER

An unpaid seller normally sues the buyer for the price of the goods or for damages for non-acceptance of them. Section 39 of the 1979 Act provides that notwithstanding the property in the goods may have passed to the buyer, the unpaid seller of the goods has a lien on the goods or right to attain the price while he is still in possession of them. Furthermore, where the buyer becomes insolvent, the seller has a right to stop the goods in transit after he has parted possession with them. The Act also gives him a right of resale as defined by s 48. The unpaid seller must be regarded as being in possession of the goods to exercise his right of lien (ie he must retain general control of them).

Section 43 states that the unpaid seller may lose his right to lien or of retention when he delivers the goods to a carrier to transport them to the buyer without reserving the right of the goods' disposal or by his agent lawfully obtaining possession of the goods or by waiving his lien (eg by agreeing to a subsale or when making a new arrangement with the buyer which is inconsistent with his right to a lien). The lien may also be lost if the seller refuses to deliver the goods on some ground other than the buyer's failure to pay. However, an unpaid seller does not waive his lien when he obtains judgment for the price. Only when judgment is satisfied can his lien be defeated.

Where the property and goods do not pass to the buyer, the seller is likely to seek remedy in an action for damages for non-acceptance under s 50 for consequential losses or expenses under s 54 or 37.

Section 50 states that the measure of damages is 'the estimated loss directly and naturally resulting, in the ordinary course of events, from the buyer's breach'. Where there is an available market for the goods in question, the measure of damages is likely to be the difference between the contract price and the market price at the time, if there is one, when the goods ought to have been accepted.

8.12 REMEDIES OF THE BUYER

8.12.1 Damages for non-delivery

Section 51 states that where the seller wrongfully neglects or refuses to deliver the goods, the buyer may maintain an action for damages. The measure of damages is the estimated loss directly and naturally resulting in the ordinary course of events from the seller's breach. Where there is an available market for the goods, the measure of damage is similar to that contained in s 50 (see 8.11 above).

The buyer may also recover interest under s 54 and special damages for additional expenses or, in some circumstances, loss of profit on a resale.

8.12.2 Damages for delay in delivery

Where there is a delay in delivery, the buyer may still accept delivery. If he suffers consequential losses such as additional expenses or loss of profit, he is entitled to sue the seller for such sum which would put him in the financial position he would have been in had the seller made delivery on the expected day.

8.12.3 Damages for defective quality

The buyer may have an action for damages for breach of warranty under s 53 of the Act. He may be entitled to claim damages for diminution in the goods' market value, and for the cost of adaptations or of substituted goods.

Where a buyer, despite having received defective goods, can nevertheless sell the goods to a sub-buyer, his damages should not be reduced by taking the subsale into account. He can rely on the normal measure of damages.

Other items of damage a buyer may wish to claim for are loss of profits under a subsale, wasted expenses; possible fines imposed from the buyer because the goods are defective; and any compensation he may have to pay to a third party because of the defect.

8.12.4 Other remedies of the buyer

Rejection of goods

Where the seller breaches a condition of the contract, the buyer may choose to treat it as terminated, reject the goods and sue the seller for damages (see also 8.10.2 under partial rejection). However where there is a breach of a condition, and the buyer is not a consumer and normally has the right to reject the goods under ss 13–15 of the Sale of Goods Act 1979, but the breach is so slight that it would be unreasonable for him to reject them, then that breach cannot be treated as a breach of condition but may be treated as a breach of warranty. This prevents a non-consumer buyer from objecting to goods in those circumstances. He is entitled to a claim for damages.

The seller must show that the breach is slight. This provision can be deleted or amended by an appropriate clause in the contract.

Recovery of money paid to the seller

Section 54 states that nothing in the Act shall effect the buyer's right to recover money paid, whether or not consideration for the payment of it has failed.

Specific performance

The buyer may wish to insist on the performance being carried out by the seller. Section 52 provides that a court may direct that this should happen. It is always within the court's discretion whether such an order is made. It is not lightly made where the goods are likely to be of an ordinary type and where similar goods could be obtained elsewhere.

Other claims the buyer may wish to make include an application for an injunction, perhaps to prevent the seller from disposing of the goods elsewhere; a declaration from the court of the buyer's position as against his legal rights against the seller; or he may issue proceedings against the seller claiming damages for his wrongful interference with the goods.

9

BUSINESS PREMISES

DUNCAN TAYLOR, WEDLAKE SAINT

9.1 INTRODUCTION

Whether at home, in the office or in the factory, all businesses need premises. The purpose of this chapter is to look at leasehold premises which provide greater flexibility and less capital commitment for most businesses than freehold premises. This chapter also looks at three particular stages relating to business premises, namely acquiring the premises, keeping premises during and at the end of the term and leaving the premises when they are no longer required. We also look at the pitfalls for the unwary.

In this chapter we assume a direct landlord/tenant relationship. There are further complications involving underleases which are not dealt with in this chapter. If in doubt the reader should seek specialist professional advice.

The statutory framework for business tenancies in England and Wales is largely contained in the Landlord and Tenant Act 1954, Part II of which has remained on the statute book for 40 years for the most part untouched. The case law on business tenancies is immense arising largely out of the contrasting commercial pressures of boom and recession. In this chapter the Landlord and Tenant Act 1954, Part II is referred to as 'the 1954 Act'.

The topics covered in this chapter include:

(1) Taking business premises
(2) Keeping business premises
(3) Leaving business premises.

9.2 TAKING BUSINESS PREMISES

9.2.1 What is a business tenancy?

It is important for a tenant to establish whether a tenancy of business premises is 'protected' under the 1954 Act. Subject to certain exceptions as set out below, the 1954 Act applies to 'any tenancy where the property comprised in the tenancy is or includes premises which are occupied by the tenant and are so occupied for the purposes of a business carried on by him or for those and other purposes' (1954 Act, s 23(1)).

In considering whether a tenant is or will be a secure tenant under the 1954 Act it is necessary to dissect s 23(1) and consider its component parts.

Tenancy

There must be a 'tenancy'. This is distinct from a 'licence' to occupy land. The leading case is *Street v Mountford* [1985] AC 809 which (although it is a judgment in respect of residential accommodation) sets out the tests which are clearly applicable to commercial premises. This case is regarded as a watershed in the development of the lease/licence distinction. It came at a time when there was an increasing tendency (in both residential and commercial premises) for contracts to be entered into purporting to be a 'licence to occupy' rather than a tenancy, and thereby avoid the statutory protection that would otherwise be available to the tenant.

Street v Mountford established that a tenancy, as opposed to a licence, is created where there is:

(1) exclusive possession of the premises;
(2) a fixed or periodic term; and
(3) the payment of rent and/or a premium.

The principle test for distinguishing between a lease and licence in business tenancies is that of 'exclusive possession' which is a question of fact in each case to be determined on the evidence.

The court's tendency to find in favour of the tenant where it regards the legal arrangement as a 'sham' has resulted in greater thought being given by landlords to the granting of licences to occupy. Landlords will endeavour to ensure that the tenant will not obtain statutory protection by introducing 'belt and braces' provisions, eg by ensuring that the term of the licence does not exceed six months or by contracting outside the 1954 Act (see 9.2.3 below).

If the tenant does not hold the business premises under a licence, then it is necessary to ascertain whether the business tenancy falls within the definitions set out in s 69(1) of the 1954 Act. This includes any tenancy created:

- by a lease or underlease
- by an agreement for lease or underlease
- in pursuance of any enactment including leases renewed by the 1954 Act.

It is interesting that there is no requirement under the 1954 Act for a rent to be reserved to create a tenancy. However, under s 69(1) of the Act, unless created by statute or court order, the tenancy must be created by some form of agreement. Therefore a *tenancy on sufferance* would not be protected. This arises where a tenant does not have any form of statutory protection but having entered under a valid tenancy remains in occupation, ie holds over without the landlord's permission. Where the landlord has constructed an agreement so that the tenant does not have statutory protection, the tenant cannot benefit by remaining in occupation for a day longer than permitted in an effort to fall within the terms of the 1954 Act.

A '*tenancy at will*' is also excluded from the 1954 Act and arises either expressly or by implication of law. A tenancy at will is a popular method of letting business premises by a landlord for an undefined term.

A tenancy at will is a purely personal relationship which can be determined by either party at any time, although a court would if invited look very carefully at any tenancy to discover whether it is in fact periodic or for a term certain. If it is correctly drafted the tenant will not have the benefit of statutory protection.

There are some tenancies which are excluded from the 1954 Act, namely an *agricultural tenancy*, a tenancy created by a *mining lease* and a *service tenancy*. Nor does it apply to a tenancy granted for a term certain *not exceeding six months* unless (a) the tenancy contains provision for renewing the term or for extending it beyond six months from its beginning; or (b) the tenant has been in occupation for a period which together with any period during which any predecessor in the carrying on of the business carried on by the tenant was in occupation, exceeds 12 months (1954 Act, s 43(3)).

Premises

It is for the benefit of both the landlord and the tenant that the extent of the premises occupied under the tenancy is clearly defined. If not, in extreme circumstances, the tenancy can be void for uncertainty and therefore unenforceable. In the majority of cases the premises occupied by the tenant are clearly defined in the lease and this is confirmed by an inspection of the premises. It follows that the premises comprised in the tenancy must consist of or include premises which are occupied by the business tenant. The definition of premises is not restricted to buildings and includes any land occupied for business purposes: for example, strips of land which were demised to a tenant for the training of racehorses and a field which was used for the purposes of running livery stables and a riding school were accepted as business premises by the court.

Where there is likely to be any conflict or confusion, a *lease plan* is recommended. This is particularly the case where a tenant is taking a suite or floor of offices in a block. Does the tenancy include the kitchen, the toilets or the boiler or are these the landlord's responsibility in terms of cleaning and maintenance? A well drawn plan should avoid any anxiety and expense arising out of such uncertainty.

Using the example of the office block, the lease should provide a clear explanation of the tenant's rights or 'easements' supported by the plan mentioned above, eg the right to use the kitchen and toilets not demised to the tenant and to get in and out of the building. The easement however cannot be occupied, it can only be used so that an easement granted for a term of years will not be protected by the Act even if used for business purposes. In *Land Reclamation Co Ltd v Basildon District Council* [1979] 1 WLR 767 a waste disposal company ran a business on freehold land. However, access could only be gained by its lorries by virtue of a lease for seven years of a right of way over a road. It was held that the company was not entitled to renew its lease which had a critical effect upon the running of the business and the value of the freehold land.

The 1954 Act does apply to an easement granted as part of a tenancy which also includes land and/or buildings so occupied. Again using the example of the office block on renewal of the lease, the 1954 Act applies to protect the tenants' use of the lifts, stairways and entrance hall etc.

9.2.2 Example – easements

A typical example of a right or easement being determinable and thereby making protection under the 1954 Act superfluous is in the case of a restaurant which requires a fire escape over neighbouring premises. Mr and Mrs Smith decide to buy a restaurant on the ground and first floor. They agree to take a lease for 12 years. However, it transpires that the landlord has the benefit of a mere licence to use a fire escape over the premises to the side and rear which is determinable by the owners of the neighbouring property in three years' time on three months' notice. Although in this case the licence is assignable to any subsequent owner of the premises, such as Mr and Mrs Smith, the fact that the neighbouring owners would be entitled to terminate the licence, and thereby force Mr and Mrs Smith to close the business, persuaded Mr and Mrs Smith not to proceed and left the landlord with the option of either running the business himself or letting the premises for a term of no more than three years.

Occupied by the tenant

Only an occupying business tenant is protected by the 1954 Act. If the business tenant only occupies *part* of the premises that are let to him, then statutory protection applies only to that part. Usually there are no difficulties in establishing whether a tenant does occupy the premises, but problems can arise, in particular where there is *seasonal occupation* of premises (eg in holiday resorts). Occupation by the tenant is normally presumed during the out-of-season months provided occupation is reasserted each season on a regular basis. Even solicitors can get it wrong. In the case of *Hancock and Willis v GMS Syndicate Ltd* (1982) 265 EG 473 a firm of solicitors acquired additional accommodation and let out the basement and ground floor of their original building under a licence and used the remainder of the building for the storage of files and for the occasional lunch. The court held that this was insufficient and the 'thread of continuity' had been broken for the purposes of business use and therefore the tenant lost security under the 1954 Act.

Where a tenant is forced to vacate because of the premises' condition or perhaps access to the business premises is prevented due to building works, then it is possible to be out of occupation without losing protection. If there is some compelling reason for temporary absence (eg fire damage) then the 'thread of continuity' is not broken. The court will not be so sympathetic where the reason for non-occupation was due to the fact that the tenant had failed to repair the premises.

'Occupation by the tenant' has come under the spotlight in recent cases involving termination of leases by the tenant (see 9.3 below).

For the purposes of a business

The business premises must be occupied 'for the purposes of a business . . . or for those and other purposes' and therefore it is necessary to consider whether what is being carried on at the premises falls within the meaning of a 'business'.

In s 23(2) of the 1954 Act 'business' is defined as a trade, profession or employment and also includes any activity carried on by a body of persons whether corporate or incorporate. This wide interpretation was held soon after the Act came into being to cover a tennis club in *Addiscombe Garden Estates Ltd v Crabbe* [1958] 1 KB 513 but was held in *Abernethit v AM & J Klieman Ltd* [1970] 1 QB 10 not to cover a Sunday school. According to Harman LJ to apply the 1954 Act to a Sunday school would be to fall into 'the pond of absurdity'. In this case the loft of a house was used for the Sunday school at an unspecified hour every Sunday on a regular basis. Nevertheless the dividing line between a business and a recreation or hobby is a fine one.

Problems do arise with mixed residential/business uses. The tenant must show that the business is a 'significant purpose' of the tenant's occupation of the building. It is a question of law whether the tenant occupies the premises for the purposes of a business carried on by him. In *Royal Life Savings Society v Page* [1978] 1 WLR 1329 a doctor who had consulting rooms in Harley Street, but who occasionally saw patients at his rented home with the landlord's consent, was held to be not protected under the 1954 Act. This is to be contrasted with *Cheryl Investments Ltd v Saldanha* [1978] 1 WLR 1329 where an accountant used his flat for the purposes of a seafood importers without his landlord's knowledge and was held to occupy the premises for the purposes of the 1954 Act.

9.2.3 Outside the 1954 Act – tenancies to which the Act does not apply

The right of occupation of business premises may be unprotected by the 1954 Act because:

(1) it falls outside the tests for protection, eg is a *tenancy at will* or under *sufferance*;
(2) it is within the express exclusions, eg an *agricultural* tenancy, a *mining* lease, a *service* tenancy or for a term certain of *six months or less*; or
(3) it has been terminated in such a way so that protection is ended (see below); or
(4) it is *contracted out* of the 1954 Act.

The letting of business premises 'outside the 1954 Act' has become increasingly popular in recent years where neither the landlord nor the tenant is willing to commit itself in times of economic uncertainty to any long-term commitment or where only one of the parties feels so inclined. The case of *Street v Mountford* made it clear that the licence to occupy route is potentially unsafe for a landlord unless the licence, or for that matter the lease, is contracted out of the 1954 Act.

The parties cannot contract out of the 1954 Act without the benefit of a court order which will only be provided where the court is satisfied that both the landlord and the tenant have taken (or have been provided with the opportunity to take) legal advice. The order must be obtained before the lease is entered into and before the tenant takes possession.

Typically a lease taken outside the 1954 Act by court order is for a relatively short term, ie more than six months and less than, say, 15 years. There is no statutory upper limit (a term for 20 years has been known to be accepted by the court) but the courts may well take a dim view on an application where the proposed term is more than 12 or 15 years. The most common term is three to five years. Although the tenant will not have a statutory right to call for a renewal of the lease in these circumstances, the benefit for the tenant normally arises out of being given an opportunity to negotiate a more favourable rent than if security had been on offer and also less onerous repairing obligations. The tenant should be in a position to ensure that the repair obligations are limited to internal decoration and/or repair only and for the shorter terms may only be required to hand the premises back in no worse a state of condition than they were at the beginning of the term, supported by a schedule of condition and perhaps photographs attached to the lease.

9.2.4 Full repairing and insuring (FRI) leases

In contrast to a recessionary background where a tenant is able to demand a short-term lease and a landlord is willing to grant one, there is a situation where (as we saw in the 1980s) a confident landlord has the upper hand and bargaining power. In this scenario landlords seek tenants who are willing to take full repairing and insuring (FRI) leases typically for a term of 21 years with a 'good covenant'. Although in the nervous 1990s FRI leases became far less common than they were, the signs are that when the economy shows consistent growth and confidence, the 21-year FRI lease may return.

It is clear that any tenant wishing to take on such a long-term contract needs to consider extremely carefully whether it is willing to take on such a potentially onerous liability.

The basis of the appeal of the FRI lease, particularly to the institutions and property companies, lies in the notion of 'privity of contract'. Through the publicity given to recent hard luck cases, privity of contract as regards business tenancies is no longer the mystery it was a decade ago.

9.2.5 Example – Privity of contract in leases

In 1967 Mr and Mrs Williams took a lease on a small industrial unit at a relatively low rent for 21 years. The business prospered and in 1977 after the rent had increased on review comfortably in line with inflation, Mr and Mrs Williams sold their business which provided them with sufficient funds to buy a bungalow by the coast and to invest a lump sum in the bank on which to live on. In 1987 after two more rent reviews the company that took over the lease of the premises from Mr and Mrs Williams went in to liquidation owing £50,000 in rent and service charges to the landlord. The landlord exercised its right under privity of contract to pursue Mr and Mrs Williams as the original tenants for the rent arrears. The capital that they had saved was insufficient to cover the debt and they were forced to sell the bungalow and to take rented accommodation to raise the funds to satisfy the debt.

9.2.6 The Landlord and Tenant (Covenants) Act 1995

On 19 July 1995 the Landlord and Tenant (Covenants) Act 1995 (the 1995 Act) received Royal Assent and radically altered the law of privity in relation to most leases entered into on or after 1 January 1996. The 1995 Act had the effect of abolishing privity of contract in the case of new leases although an outgoing tenant may be required to guarantee the performance of the party taking over the lease, ie its immediate assignee. Such a guarantee is called an *authorised guarantee agreement* (AGA) and is likely to apply in the case of most first assignments of the lease where the landlord's consent is required. This places the onus on the original tenant to find a good covenant that is likely to fulfil its obligations not only in the short term but in the longer term as well. Prior to the 1995 Act the original tenant was mainly concerned to ensure that the first assignee's references were sufficiently strong to prevent the landlord from being able to unreasonably withhold its consent.

In the case of default by the first assignee and eventual disclaimer the original tenant may be required to take up a new lease on the same terms and for the same duration as the original lease.

Therefore where a lease is now assigned the AGA can last only until the assignee (whose liabilities have been guaranteed by the original tenant or his successors in title) is released. The AGA cannot require a tenant to guarantee that anyone else will perform the covenant.

There is a provision in the 1995 Act that relates to both new and existing leases. A landlord who wishes to pursue the original tenant or guarantor must serve a *default notice* under s 17 of the 1995 Act notifying him of the potential claim for what is called a *fixed charge* (ie rent, service charge, liquidated damages and interest) within six months of the current tenant's default.

The default notice is generally accompanied by a letter before action demanding payment of the arrears within a reasonably short period. It also points out if payment is not paid within the required time frame then proceedings will be commenced without further notice to include a claim for interest, court fees and legal expenses.

Once the former tenant or guarantor of a former tenant has received a default notice, he is entitled to take some control over the problem by paying the arrears and other sums demanded in full and calling upon the landlord to grant to him an *overriding lease* of the premises.

This places the former tenant/guarantor in a contractual position between the landlord and the defaulting tenant. The terms of the overriding lease will include all the provisions of the defaulted lease with the exception of any personal covenants given by the defaulter.

Once in possession of the overriding lease the former tenant/guarantor can then take proceedings against the defaulting tenant to recover the arrears discharged by him under the default notice. More usually, the former tenant/guarantor will endeavour to recover possession of the premises to enable him to re-let or possibly retain for his own use.

The 1995 Act also has the effect of amending s 19(1) of the Landlord and Tenant Act 1927 in relation to assignment of commercial leases. Landlords will be able to specify in advance in new leases the circumstances in which consent to an assignment can be withheld or any conditions subject to which consent can be granted. If the provision is worded so that there is no subjective element then the landlord is deemed to be acting reasonably if the agreed terms are adhered to. For example, if there is a requirement that any assignee must be able to produce the most recent set of accounts showing net profits before tax of at least three times the passing rent then this would be acceptable. Alternatively, if the circumstances or conditions are to be determined by an independent third party or by the landlord who is required to act reasonably, this will also be acceptable.

9.2.7 The tenant's covenant

The strength of the tenant's covenant is all important to the landlord. The businessman offering his company as a tenant, whether on taking a new lease or on taking an assignment of an existing lease, may not provide sufficient comfort for the landlord.

This issue has become even more of a concern to the landlord since the implementation of the 1995 Act. Now the tenant, including the original tenant, under a tenancy created since 1 January 1996 remains liable only while the lease remains vested in him unless he has entered into an AGA with the landlord.

The landlord has to ask itself how the quality of the tenant's covenant is to affect the value of its investment. A company listed on the Stock Exchange as a tenant is likely to enhance the value of the freehold. In these circumstances it is unlikely the landlord will require any additional comfort by way of any form of guarantee. If the proposed tenant is a new company, but also part of a group in which the holding company is listed, the listed company may be asked to stand as guarantor.

The more common situation is where the tenant's covenant is not strong enough because the tenant is a company with limited liability. The landlord would generally require some security to persuade it to accept what is on the face of it a second-class covenant. After all, a limited company has by definition limited liability which may not be sufficient to discharge arrears of rent and may be wound up either voluntarily by its members or compulsorily by other creditors, leaving little or no assets to discharge any arrears.

9.2.8 Personal guarantees

It is a standard provision in many commercial leases that on assignment the landlord can require two directors of any assignee company with limited liability to provide personal guarantees to support the assignee's covenant. References should be taken up for the directors (or any other guarantors for that matter) who, if acceptable to the landlord, would be a party to the landlord's licence to assign. Similarly, with a new lease the guarantors would be parties to the new lease. A landlord would normally require two guarantors providing joint and several liability, ie each guarantor can be held responsible for the defaulting tenant's total debt if the landlord chooses. In the economic boom of the mid-1980s, it was common for over-confident businessmen to provide personal guarantees almost without a second thought and they have more recently had to pay the price (often of bankruptcy) for their optimism in the 1990s. As in the case of the 'original tenant' of a lease entered into before 1 January 1996, a landlord will not hesitate to pursue guarantors where there is any chance of recovery of the tenant's indebtedness.

Under the 1995 Act, the guarantors under the AGA are released when the guaranteed tenant is released. Previously (unless released by the landlord or as stated otherwise in the lease) the guarantee subsisted for as long as the term itself.

9.2.9 Rent deposit

Although potentially less onerous since 1 January 1996, a personal guarantee is regarded as being virtually an unlimited guarantee. In a tenants' market the landlord may be willing to accept a lump sum as security, generally representing three or six months' rent. This sum is placed on bank deposit (with interest normally accruing to the tenant) and a deed drawn up between the landlord and tenant records in what circumstances the landlord is entitled to dip into it to withdraw funds.

9.2.10 Example – Rent deposit

A shop is let by *L* to *T* at a rental of £10,000 pa. There is a rent deposit of £2,500 (ie representing three months' rent) which is held in an account run by *L*'s solicitors. The deposit deed provides that 28 days after the quarter day *L* can withdraw the sum of £2,500 without prior notice to *T* if the rent has not been paid. *T* defaults and *L* instructs his solicitors to send him a cheque for this sum. *L*'s solicitors write to *T*'s solicitors demanding the rent deposit account to be reimbursed the sum of £2,500 'forthwith' to avoid proceedings being taken for forfeiture.

The drawback from the landlord's point of view is that once the fund has been used up and assuming the arrears persist there is no guarantee that any excess sums will be recovered. At least in these circumstances the landlord will have had time to consider his options and in the case of an empty building and an insolvent tenant have an opportunity of seeking a new tenant.

The drawback for a tenant, particularly in the case of a new business venture, is the immediate tying up of capital which provides no benefit to the start-up company except nominal interest. The protection of the directors of the new company from the risks of providing personal guarantees usually makes it worthwhile. It may be possible for the tenant to negotiate, within the rent deposit deed, repayment of the fund in certain circumstances, eg after a certain number of years or a good rent payment record, after say three years of net profits of the tenant company exceeding a certain sum such as the annual rent or simply upon assignment of the lease.

9.2.11 Bank guarantees

Previously a bank might on occasion agree to provide a landlord with a guarantee equivalent to, say, six months' rent. The bank then required the tenant to place sufficient funds or other security to support the guarantee. However, as recession took its toll in the late 1980s the number of guarantees being called upon naturally increased at a time when tenants' liabilities already exceeded their assets. Banks will now take some persuading and substantial security before contemplating guarantees. This change in policy has left many tenants considering rent deposits as the only option to the personal guarantee.

9.2.12 Landlords' incentives

During the property recession, commercial landlords have had to be imaginative in securing business tenancies. A number of inducements evolved and landlords became resigned to the fact that they could not always insist on a long 21- or 25-year lease. In a large number of cases it was necessary for financial inducements to be made.

Rent-free periods

Rent-free periods ranging from one week to one year or even more have been offered to tenants particularly in circumstances where landlords are burdened with a surplus of space in a building. The landlord and tenant may agree that this is simply a financial incentive for the tenant to take a lease or to provide the tenant with sufficient breathing space to enable him to pay for the fitting out of the premises. It is important for VAT purposes to distinguish between the two. In *Neville Russell (a firm) v C & E Comrs* (1987) VATTR 194 the landlord agreed a rent-free period to the value of £240,000 to persuade the tenant to enter into a lease. It was held that there were purely commercial reasons for the tenant requiring this rent-free period as he was not sufficiently confident that the business would be able to pay the rent in the short term. In this case the VAT tribunal decided that the rent-free period did not amount to consideration for a standard-rated supply of services by the tenant to the landlord.

Fitting out

In *Neville Russell* above the landlord paid £400,000 to enable the tenant to refurbish the premises and this was held to be a taxable supply. It is therefore imperative that advice is taken from a solicitor or accountant – and if necessary a ruling is obtained from the Commissioners – to establish whether there is a taxable supply. If the rent-free period is linked with the performance of refurbishment works or other services by the tenant which will be of either commercial or financial benefit to the landlord, then this would be regarded as a taxable supply by the tenant to the landlord. However, rent-free periods given to defray fitting-out costs normally fall outside the scope of VAT where the fitting-out work is an obligation upon the tenant which does not directly benefit the landlord.

Reverse premiums

In some cases landlords have paid 'reverse premiums' to tenants to persuade them to take a lease. Again in the *Neville Russell* case, the sum of £300,000 was paid to the tenant by way of a reverse premium. The VAT tribunal held that the reverse premium was paid for the execution of the new lease and was therefore consideration for a taxable supply of services. Accordingly the tenant was liable to account for output tax on the value of the consideration.

Tenant-only break clauses

One inducement that has no VAT impact is a tenant-only break clause. This provides the tenant with an opportunity to determine the lease normally on a fixed date such as the first rent review date. This is particularly welcome in the case where the tenant has a new or relatively new business and also where the landlord has insisted upon a personal guarantee being provided. The tenant has the peace of mind of knowing that if the business does not work out he has an opportunity to terminate the lease in the not too distant future. The only items that the tenant has to worry about are (a) to ensure that sufficient care is taken in serving notice at the right time and on the right person in accordance with the provisions of the break clause in the lease, and (b) to ensure that there are no subsisting breaches of covenant at the time of service of such notice and until termination of the lease.

If the landlord is reluctant to accept the tenant's notice, then the landlord will take every opportunity to keep the tenant 'on the hook'. A landlord may, for example, argue that due to a subsisting (albeit minor) breach of covenant, it is not obliged to accept the notice. The tenant should take care to ensure that the rent is paid on the due date and that at the very least the repair covenant has been complied with if he has any intention of exercising the break provision.

It was held in *Trane (UK) Ltd v Provident Mutual Life Assurance* (1995) 03 EG 128 that the requirement in a lease that the tenant had to observe the tenant's covenants up to the intended termination date had the effect of being what is called a 'condition precedent'. Accordingly any subsisting breach, however minor, would prevent the break clause from being exercised.

In *Trane* the tenant attempted to exercise a 10-year break option in a 25-year lease of industrial premises. The problem was that the tenant was in breach of its repairing obligations, albeit a minor breach. Because of this, the tenant was held not to be entitled to determine the lease. No building is ever going to be in perfect condition at a particular moment. The covenant to repair in this context according to Cooke J was 'to take all proper steps to repair the building once out of repair and to do so with all proper speed and in a reasonable time'. It follows that if a tenant is contemplating exercising a break clause he should instruct his surveyor to prepare a schedule of condition beforehand so that any such problems can be remedied prior to service of the notice and the premises maintained thereafter.

9.2.13 Rent reviews

The purpose of a rent review is to ensure that the landlord continues to receive a market rent for the premises and not simply the historical rent that was fixed at the beginning of the term. This is particularly important where institutional landlords insist upon long 21- or 25-year leases. Although traditionally rents have been fixed by reference to the open market, there have been variations of the theme, particularly in recent years.

Open market rent reviews

In most cases premises are marketed on the basis that except for short leases, rent reviews are generally every three, four or five years of the term. A 'rent review' is shorthand for a reappraisal of the rent for the same premises on the assumption that a willing landlord wishes to grant to a willing tenant the premises in good condition for the original length of term or otherwise the unexpired length of term. Needless to say the formula for rent reviews differs from one lease to the next and often depends on the drafting preferences of the landlord's solicitors. Of course, care does have to be taken by the tenant's solicitor to ensure that the landlord does not have an unfair advantage at the negotiating table on rent review.

Example – Typical scenario of a rent review

The lease provides for a rent review on 29 September. The landlord is required to serve a notice of intention to review the rent not more than six months and not less than three months before the review date. In his notice the landlord having taken the advice of his surveyor suggest an increase to £X to take effect from the rent review date. The tenant acknowledges receipt of the notice but suggests a far smaller rental increase from the current rent of £Y. The lease provides that if one month after service of the notice of intention to review the rent, no rent has been agreed between the landlord and tenant then either party may refer the matter to either an expert or an arbitrator as stated in the rent review formula. In this case the negotiations between the landlord and tenant are unproductive and their respective surveyors are brought in to endeavour to negotiate an agreement.

A starting point for surveyors is often 'comparables'. This is of course far easier in a shopping parade or business park than with restaurants or hotels. The parties may also be obliged to give careful consideration to the wording of the rent review clause to look in particular at the 'assumptions' and the 'disregards'. The parties have to regard the review procedure and the negotiation of the rent as if it were a notional or hypothetical lease and the assumptions behind that hypothetical lease are namely the rent that may be negotiated between 'a willing landlord' and 'a willing tenant' for premises which are 'fit' and 'available for immediate occupation and use'.

The tenant and his surveyor will wish to stress the 'disregards' which are the value elements that the tenant by his very occupation brings to the premises together with any goodwill that the tenant and his business may bring, as well as any improvements being carried out 'otherwise and in pursuance of an obligation to the landlord'.

Despite efforts by the Law Society and the RICS to introduce model forms of rent review, these are not widely used and therefore it is dangerous to assume that any two different leases have identical rent review clauses. Accordingly, rent reviews have proved a minefield for landlords and tenants and in many cases a goldmine for professional advisers.

Until very recently a cornerstone of the rent review formula was the fact that any rent review would be 'upwards only'. Accordingly even in the time of recession if a landlord called for a review, the rent would still go up by, say, £1. As in the case of the recession causing the misery of 'negative equity' for homeowners, so have upwards only rent reviews resulted in premises being 'over rented' where there is no possibility that the 'passing rent' can fall to the 'market rent' on review. If the premises are surplus to requirements then an assignment of that lease becomes virtually impossible unless there are substantial 'inducements' such as rent-free periods and reverse premiums. The tenant may also find that any opportunity for underletting at less than the passing rent is prohibited by the terms of the lease and therefore the landlord can reasonably withhold its consent to any underletting on this basis.

Turnover rents

Rents linked to the turnover of the tenant's business have been in place for many years, particularly in mining leases. It is now a relatively common phenomenon in shopping precincts and also occurs with hotels and restaurants. Turnover rents are also appearing in retail warehouses divided into a series of small units. In this case the landlord is able to monitor each retailer's turnover and the rent that is paid is gauged to that turnover. If the tenant suffers, then so does the landlord and the landlord may feel it incumbent on it to see what it can do to help that tenant's trading. For example, a landlord decided to improve a 1960s shopping precinct by providing a covered area for pedestrians at one end of the precinct where it was previously exposed to the elements and windswept. The effect of this was to secure and in some cases improve the turnover of those shops within the covered area while those outside the covered area began to suffer. As a result of this the landlord extended the covering to all the shops in the precinct for mutual benefit. Another advantage from the tenant's point of view is the saving on professional fees. It follows that the involvement of the professional adviser is likely to be minimal where negotiation is largely unnecessary.

It is worth noting that reference is made to 'turnover' rather than 'profit'. Turnover may be perceived to increase simply as the rate of VAT goes up whereas this may not have a similar effect upon profits. In *Tucker v*

Granada Motorways Services Ltd [1977] 3 All ER 865, the Minister of Transport granted a lease to a tenant of a motorway service area. The tenant paid a fixed rent together with an additional variable rent based upon the takings from the petrol station and catering services. The gross takings included the tobacco duty payable on cigarettes, cigars etc. Accordingly, when tobacco duty rose so did the tenant's rent even though its profit remained the same. Accordingly, it is important that advice is taken on the definition of turnover and as far as possible this should be linked to the actual profit of the business.

Index-linked rents

One advantage of index linking is that both the landlord and the tenant can monitor the rent relatively easily. As in the case of an open market rent review it is often the case that the review date is fixed by reference to an anniversary and, if the formula in the lease is correctly worded, then the new rent will reflect the rate of inflation rather than property values. Although index linking is cheap to operate for the landlord and tenant it may well not reflect the reality of market conditions. If the tenant is in a depressed area where there are a number of empty units around him this would work in his favour in an open market rent review but would have no influence on the RPI. For a unit situated in an affluent and popular area the converse would be the case. Index linking has certainty but often artificiality.

Fixed increases

For shorter leases of anything up to three or five years, the parties may agree to fixed increases perhaps on an annual basis and so expose each party to a certain degree of risk. As in the case of a home buyer locking himself into a fixed rate mortgage, it is likely that one of the two parties may regret such a commitment at some stage in the lease.

Finally, on the subject of rent review, it is worth mentioning an interaction between a landlord's financial inducements and rent reviews. The landlord is anxious that the tenant pays a 'headline rent' on review but disregarding the financial inducements that took place at the beginning of the term. It does not wish for, say, a rent-free period to be taken into account on each and every review date as this would have an effect of depressing the market rent. Accordingly, landlords are now keen to include a further 'disregard' that no account is to be taken of any rent concession made at the commencement of the lease.

9.3 KEEPING BUSINESS PREMISES

The heads of terms are now set out in a lease. The lease has been completed and the tenant is in occupation. Assuming he wants to, how does the tenant ensure that he stays there for as long as he requires the premises?

9.3.1 Requirements of occupation

Implied and express covenants

A lease or tenancy agreement is a contract between the landlord and the tenant. Alongside the express obligations on each party in the lease are various implied obligations. Although it is generally expressly provided for in the lease, there is an implied obligation that the landlord will not interrupt the tenant's undisturbed use or 'quiet enjoyment' of the property. This obligation to provide quiet enjoyment relates to 'unlawful' acts and the landlord would not be in breach if exercising his lawful rights under the lease. For example, in *Owen v Gadd* [1956] 2 QB 99 it was held that the erection of scaffolding outside a shop which obscured its facade at a time when the tenant was hoping for an increase in sales was a breach of the covenant of quiet enjoyment by the landlord. The tenant's remedy would be in damages for loss of trade.

The landlord is also required by implication not to derogate from the grant, ie not to act in such a way as to prevent the tenant from enjoying the benefit of his bargain. In *Johnston and Sons Ltd v Holland* [1988] 1 EGLR 264 the landlord granted a lease of land as an advertising site and thereafter proceeded to erect a hoarding which obscured it.

It is the express covenants (in particular those imposed upon the tenant) which require careful consideration by the tenant and his advisers. It is likely that the bulk of the lease will be made up of the 'tenant's covenants' requiring in particular the rent to be paid on certain days and for the tenant to acknowledge certain obligations and responsibilities. By way of example we now consider a number of typical scenarios relating to these express covenants – namely repair, alterations, user, and 'alienation'.

Repair

The tenant's repair responsibility generally applies either to the whole building or merely the interior, ie internal repair and decoration. As a general rule, the longer the lease the greater the repair responsibility on the tenant. The lease may well state that the tenant is required 'to keep the demised premises in good and substantial (or sometimes 'tenantable') repair'. The definition of 'demised premises' will show whether the repair responsibility is full repairing or simply internal. There is also likely to be a requirement on the tenant to decorate the demised premises on fixed dates. It is possible the tenant's adviser has endeavoured to limit the tenant's liability by providing for amendments in the repair covenant, eg by a schedule of condition which is attached to the lease providing evidence of the repair of the premises at the beginning of the term by reference to descriptions/photographs etc. The tenant may also wish to exclude 'fair wear and tear', particularly in short-term leases where the tenant does not wish to be responsible for his ordinary and reasonable use of the premises or the effect of the elements on the premises.

If the tenant neglects his duties, the landlord is entitled to seek a remedy against the tenant which in this case is for the premises to be put back into the condition they would have been had the repair covenant been fully fulfilled by the tenant. Modern leases generally provide the landlord with the power to enter the premises to carry out these works at the tenant's cost. The landlord's claim would be for a *debt* against the tenant. The alternative of suing for *damages* is more complex. For example, if the lease was granted for seven years or more (and at the time of service of the landlord's notice of dilapidations or a s 146 notice there are three or more years of that term unexpired) then the tenant is entitled to the protection provided by the Leasehold Property (Repairs) Act 1938. In this case leave of court is required before the landlord can enforce a right to damages or forfeiture and the onus is on the landlord to establish a ground to secure leave of the court. If, however, the tenant does nothing once notified of the repairs and fails to secure the protection of the 1938 Act, the landlord's ultimate remedy is in forfeiture, ie recovering possession.

Alterations

It is common for a lease to provide that no alterations can be carried out to the premises except internal alterations which require the landlord's consent. In this case there is an 'absolute' covenant against external alterations, building of extensions etc and a 'qualified' covenant against internal alterations. In the case of the absolute prohibition, this does not prevent the tenant from requesting the landlord for consent. The landlord is of course entitled to refuse permission and is not under any obligation to justify its refusal. Equally, the landlord may agree to the alteration (which would be evidenced by a suitable licence) on the basis of receipt of an appropriate premium.

If the tenant wished to erect internal partitioning then the landlord would not be able to withhold his consent unreasonably. This is the case whether or not the words 'such consent not to be unreasonably withheld' is included by virtue of s 19(2) of the Landlord and Tenant Act 1927. The

1927 Act provides that not only cannot the landlord unreasonably withhold his consent, but also that the landlord cannot demand a premium for so doing, apart from a reasonable sum 'in respect of any damage to or diminution in the value of the premises' or any legal or other expenses incurred in providing its consent. Again this would be evidenced by a licence to alter. Typically the licence will provide that the tenant must comply with all planning and any other statutory obligations in carrying out the alterations and reserve the right in favour of the landlord to require the tenant to reinstate the premises to their previous condition either on assignment or at the end of the term. In the case of an unauthorised alteration the landlord will be entitled to serve a s 146 notice on the tenant and if the tenant does not comply, then the landlord can either peaceably re-enter the premises to forfeit the lease or commence proceedings for forfeiture.

User

User covenants are either expressed positively (eg only 'to use the demised premises as [. . .]') or negatively ('not to use the demised premises except as [. . .] and for no other purpose'). The user may express specific terms and refer to the proposed use of that tenant, or express broad terms and, for example, refer to the most recent Use Classes Order. As in the case of alterations there may an absolute restriction against change of use or a qualified restriction. In this case however there is no statutory implication that consent is not to be unreasonably withheld. However, if the landlord does grant his consent the conditions to which the landlord is entitled to impose on the tenant are limited by s 19(3) of the Landlord and Tenant Act 1927. Should the landlord decide to withhold consent, then there is little more the tenant can do. In the event of breach of this covenant the landlord is entitled to obtain an injunction to stop an unauthorised use where it is clear that damages are not an adequate remedy. In addition the lease may include an express right for the landlord to enter the premises to remedy the consequences of the tenant's breach. The landlord could also sue for damages.

Alienation

Let us assume that the tenant wishes to remain in occupation, but has space surplus to requirements. In his lease it is likely there is an absolute or qualified prohibition against underletting part of the premises or sharing occupation. The likelihood, however, is that there is an absolute restriction and therefore the landlord is entitled to refuse consent without having to justify his decision. In the event of breach of this restriction by the tenant this constitutes an irremediable breach as is the carrying out of alterations without consent. The landlord can either inform the tenant that he intends to re-enter the premises within a reasonable time or require the tenant to vacate the premises within a reasonable time and in default of which the landlord will re-enter.

What is the position where there is non-payment of rent? In this case it is not necessary for the landlord to serve a s 146 notice. A letter before action advising the tenant of the arrears and demanding payment within a certain time is sufficient before court proceedings are commenced. It is a remediable breach and therefore the tenant can be required to discharge all arrears as well as costs within a short period such as seven days before forfeiture takes place.

9.3.2 Expiry of the lease

We now look at the position on the expiry of the contractual term of a lease within the 1954 Act. Where the tenant does *not* have security (eg a lease which is excluded from the 1954 Act by court order), the tenant is *not* entitled to remain in occupation beyond the expiry of the contractual term. This is not always so under the 1954 Act. The assumption is made in this part of the chapter that the tenant wishes to remain in occupation.

Right to renew

A tenant protected under the 1954 Act has an automatic right to renew his tenancy at the current market rent. As long as the tenancy meets the definition referred to in s 23(1) of the 1954 Act (see 9.2.1 above), then until statutory notices are served by either the landlord or the tenant, the lease continues indefinitely. This is assuming that the premises continue to be occupied by the tenant for business purposes (see 9.4.1 below). In this case the tenant is 'holding over'. While the tenant is holding over, the terms of the expired contractual tenancy continue as before (eg the same rent, same repair responsibilities etc).

If the tenant is no longer in occupation for business purposes then he will have no automatic right to renew the lease. He may also be able to argue that the lease has been determined even if no notice by either the landlord or the tenant has been served (see 9.4.1 below).

At a time of falling rents it may well suit the landlord to 'overlook' serving any notice to determine the lease. If it is likely that on a renewal the market rent will be less than the passing rent under the current lease, there may be no point for the landlord to determine the lease. It follows that at a time of economic growth a landlord may suffer significant losses in rental income if he fails to serve his notice in good time. Although a landlord could apply for an 'interim rent' to be determined by the court it often falls some way short of the market rent that is eventually negotiated and hence is rarely the complete answer. At a time when the commercial property market is relatively stagnant there is often a stand-off between landlords and tenants in many business premises. The landlord is not confident that it will be able to negotiate any increase in the rent on renewal and the tenant is equally not inclined to commit himself to a new lease during times of uncertainty. In the meantime the lease continues on the same terms.

The landlord's notice

Under s 25(1) of the 1954 Act 'The landlord may terminate a tenancy to which this Part of this Act applies by a notice given to the tenant in the prescribed form specifying the date at which the tenancy is to come to an end . . .'. The date specified in the notice must be not less than six months and not more than 12 months from the date the notice is issued.

9.3.3 Example – Landlord's notice

If a lease is due to expire on 25 December 1998 and the landlord wishes it to be determined on that date, a notice must be served before 24 June 1998 and after 25 December 1997. It is not fatal if a notice is not served in this example by 24 June 1998. If the matter was overlooked a notice could be served say in August 1998, citing the date for determination as 1 March 1999, ie at least six months ahead. In the meantime the tenant continues paying the rent at the current rate. The same principle applies if the notice has not been served by 25 December 1998.

Tenant's response to landlord's notice

A notice served by the landlord under s 25 will state that within two months after the date of the notice the tenant must advise the landlord in writing whether at the date of termination he is willing to give up possession of the property. If the tenant wishes to renew but does nothing to respond to the s 25 notice within the two months, the tenant may lose all rights to renew. It is essential upon receipt of any notice under the 1954 Act that a tenant takes advice from either a surveyor or solicitor familiar with the Act who can advise upon or deal with the response for the tenant. Within four months from the date of the landlord's notice the tenant must commence proceedings in the court for a new tenancy unless a new lease has been granted in the interim. If the tenant fails to do so, he may lose all rights of renewal under the 1954 Act. Where the landlord and the tenant have taken all the correct steps and proceedings have commenced, then the question of whether a new lease is granted is a matter of negotiation. Failing agreement, the court will take such decisions as it thinks best not only whether a tenancy shall be granted, but also with regard to the terms of a tenancy.

Tenant's request for a new tenancy

It is possible for the tenant to take the initiative which in the days of the rising market was called a 'pre-emptive strike'. If a tenant is certain he wishes to renew (particularly in a situation where the market rent is likely to be less than the passing rent) the tenant has power to terminate the contractual tenancy. A tenant is entitled to serve a notice under s 26 of the 1954 Act which, as in the case of s 25, may be served not more than 12 months and not less than six months before the date of termination. The tenant has to propose the terms of the new lease (eg rent, length of term etc), and a s 26 notice cannot be served if the landlord has already served a s 25 notice. Within two months of the date of the tenant's notice the landlord must give notice to the tenant whether he will oppose an application to the court for the grant of a new tenancy. If the landlord does oppose, then the grounds for such a position must be stated. The ground that is referred to is significant in that it determines whether any compensation is payable to the tenant (see 9.3.4 below).

If the landlord fails to respond to the notice within the two-month period, it cannot prevent the grant of a new lease on the basis of the statutory grounds of opposition.

Application to the court for a new tenancy

Under s 24(1) of the 1954 Act

> the tenant . . . may apply to the court for a new tenancy –
> (a) if the landlord has given notice under [section 25 of this Act] to terminate the tenancy, or
> (b) if the tenant has made a request for a new tenancy in accordance with section twenty-six of this Act.

The application should be made not less than two months and not more than four months after the giving of either of the above notices. It is vital that these time constraints are adhered to as failure to do so may deny a tenant premises from which to operate. It is not surprising therefore that missed time limits under the 1954 Act are one of the most common forms of negligence claims against solicitors!

The application can be made to the High Court or the local county court. In the application the tenant must give details of the proposals for the new tenancy and the landlord must provide an answer to this application within a fixed time period, generally 14 days unless the landlord has agreed an extension with the tenant and the court. In the majority of cases this is as far as the court procedure goes. Often the summons issued by the court provides for a date to be fixed to enable negotiations to continue between the parties. This is assuming that the landlord is happy for the renewal to take place. However, the landlord can oppose the application.

Landlord's opposition to renewal

There are seven specified grounds under which a landlord can oppose an application to renew. The landlord must state the ground or grounds on which he objects in his notice terminating the tenancy or (as the case may be) in his reply to the tenant's request for a new tenancy. One landlord tried to get around this detail by referring to every single ground in his notice but this was rejected by the court.

The grounds for opposition are set out in s 30(1) of the Act and are as follows:

Disrepair

'The tenant ought not to be granted a new tenancy in view of the state of repair' due to a breach of the tenant's obligations under his lease. It was held in *Lyons v Central Commercial Properties London Ltd* [1958] 1 WLR 869 that 'the neglect of repair to which the section refers should be substantial'. A court has a discretion to consider the seriousness of the breach, the tenant's overall conduct and the reasons for the breach which has arisen. No compensation is payable to the tenant if the landlord is successful in establishing this ground (s 30(1)(a)).

Rent arrears

'The tenant ought not to be granted a new tenancy in view of his persistent delay in paying rent . . .' Again the court must exercise its discretion in deciding whether this ground has been established. If the court feels that the landlord should not be required to experience the problems and expense of recovering the rent if the lease were renewed, then the landlord's application may well be granted. No compensation is payable to the tenant if the landlord is successful in establishing this ground (s 30(1)(b)).

Breaches of other obligations

'The tenant ought not to be granted a new tenancy in view of other substantial breaches by him of his obligations under the current tenancy, or for any other reason connected with the tenant's use or management of the holding.' This provides a wider ground for the landlord to oppose renewal in that, for example, it could include breaches of planning regulations. The question that the court asks is whether the landlord's interest has been prejudiced by the breach. No compensation is payable to the tenant if the landlord is successful in establishing this ground (s 30(1)(c)).

Alternative accommodation

'The landlord has offered and is willing to provide or secure the provision of alternative accommodation for the tenant . . .' The alternative accommodation must be available on terms that are reasonable having regard to the provisions of the current tenancy and to all other relevant circumstances. This ground is rarely cited and there are few reported cases. No compensation is payable to the tenant if the landlord is successful in establishing this ground (s 30(1)(d)).

Uneconomic subletting

'Where the current tenancy was created by the sub-letting of part . . . [and] that the aggregate of the rents reasonably obtainable on separate lettings of the holding and the remainder of that property would be substantially less than the rent reasonably obtainable on a letting of that property as a whole.' This is the least common ground and is a purely financial one. It is only open to the 'competent landlord' if he is a superior landlord and is not available to the immediate landlord. The court will agree to this ground if the landlord, by letting the tenanted premises together with the rest of the property in the head lease as a single unit, could expect more rent than by letting the individual units separately (s 30(1)(e)).

Demolition or reconstruction

'The landlord intends to demolish or reconstruct the premises comprised in the holding or a substantial part of those premises or to carry out substantial work of construction on the holding or part thereof and that he could not reasonably do so without obtaining possession of the holding.' This is a common ground for opposition by a landlord. Its intention to carry out these works must be genuine and established at the date of the hearing. Considerable case law exists for whether the landlord had the necessary intention (eg it is often recommended that a landlord which is also a company passes a formal board resolution referring to the intention to demolish or reconstruct the premises). The landlord also needs to show a legal and financial ability to proceed (ie legal in the sense of planning consent and financial in the sense of either having the finance or being able to raise it from a third party). The landlord will not be successful if it merely wishes to recover possession to sell the premises to a developer who wishes to demolish or reconstruct. The landlord must have complete control of the work to be done to the holding. There is nothing to stop a landlord then selling the site once the building has been demolished or reconstructed by it (s 30(1)(f)).

Own occupation

'On the termination of the current tenancy the landlord intends to occupy the holding for the purposes, or partly for the purposes, of a business to be carried on by him therein or as his residence.' There is 'a five-year rule' to be satisfied, namely that the landlord cannot rely on this ground if his interest was purchased or created within five years ending with the termination of the current tenancy. If the landlord himself has granted the tenancy then the five-year rule does not apply. The landlord will have the same problems in establishing 'intention' as under s 30(1)(f) above. The landlord's occupation does not have to be immediate upon the termination of the lease, so long as it is within a reasonable time after the end of the term; nor does the landlord have to occupy all of the premises – a substantial part will normally be sufficient. Note that this ground can also be used if the landlord wishes to occupy the premises as his own residence, although there are few if any reported cases on this (s 30(1)(g)).

9.3.4 Compensation

Compensation for non-renewal

Where the landlord is successful in denying the tenant a new lease on one of the last three grounds referred to above, ie uneconomic sub-letting, demolition and reconstruction or owner occupation, compensation is payable to the tenant.

The amount of the compensation is based on the rateable value of the holding multiplied by an 'appropriate multiplier' as prescribed by the Secretary of State for the Environment made by statutory instrument. The rateable value is ascertained at the date of the service of the s 25 or s 26 notice so that the multiplier is *one* except in a case in which the tenant elects to be paid compensation by reference to the rateable value of the holding on 31 March 1990, in which case the multiplier is *eight*. The tenant will make this election if the holding includes a residential element, but cannot do otherwise.

The compensation is doubled if for the 14 years ending with the date of termination of the current tenancy all or part of the premises have been occupied for business purposes and on any change of occupier each is a successor to his predecessor's business. Any agreement in the lease to exclude or reduce compensation where the occupation for carrying on the business has lasted for five years prior to the date when a tenant is to quit is void under s 38(2) of the 1954 Act.

Compensation for misrepresentation

If the court refuses an order for a grant of a new tenancy under s 55 of the 1954 Act, and the court is satisfied that this was due to 'misrepresentation or the concealment of material facts', the court may order the landlord to pay compensation to the tenant for the damage or loss sustained.

Compensation in the case of compulsory acquisition

Under the Land Compensation Act 1973, s 47 compensation would be payable where an authority compulsorily acquires property subject to a business tenancy and a tenant's right to renew is denied. The compensation payable will not be less than the compensation which would have been payable under the 1954 Act.

Compensation where renewal refused under s 57 or s 58

Where a certificate under s 57 or s 58 is issued in favour of a government department, local authority, statutory undertaker or a development corporation then compensation is payable. Statutory undertakers include for example suppliers of electricity, gas, telecommunications etc, the British Airports Authority and the Post Office. Section 57 has also been extended to include NHS health authorities and the National Trust. The amount of the compensation is assessed as for compensation on termination under s 30 of the 1954 Act.

9.4 LEAVING BUSINESS PREMISES

9.4.1 Tenant's notice to determine

Until recently it was possible to state with some confidence that a tenant cannot walk away from his obligations under a lease simply by giving up possession and surrendering the keys to the landlord at the end of the term. Although by giving up possession he is also giving up his rights as a tenant in respect of renewal (see 9.2.2 under 'Occupied by the tenant' above), it did not affect his responsibility to pay the rent and comply with his repair obligations. The decision of the Court of Appeal in *Esselte v Pearl Assurance plc* (1997) 02 EG 124 (see below) has thrown an unexpected lifeline to tenants.

If the contractual expiry date is a year or less away, then the tenant can take action to ensure that the lease does not last a day longer than necessary. If the lease is contracted out of the 1954 Act by court order (see 9.2.3 above), then neither party is required to serve notice and the lease will determine on the contractual expiry date.

Whether or not a landlord has served a s 25 notice (and provided the tenant has been in occupation under the tenancy for at least one month) he can give not less than three months' notice to end the lease on its contractual expiry date (1954 Act, s 27). A s 27 notice cannot be served after a tenant's request for a new tenancy has been served on the landlord unless procedure under the s 26 notice has been followed by formal discontinuance through the court.

If there is less than three months to go before the contractual expiry date, a tenant can still serve notice under s 27(2) of the 1954 Act by giving not less than three months' notice to expire on a quarter day *after* its contractual expiry date. The notice under s 27(2) may be served before the contractual expiry date (in anticipation of the lease being continued under the Act) or after the contractual expiry date. See the example below.

9.4.2 Example – Notice to determine less than three months before the contractual expiry date

Where the contractual expiry date is 25 December 1998, the tenant can serve a s 27(1) notice to expire on 25 December 1998, on any day up to 24 September 1998. After that day, the earliest date that the lease can be determined using s 27(2) is the following quarter day, namely 25 March 1999.

Prior to the *Esselte* case, it was believed that unless the tenant served notice under s 27(1) before the lease ended, he could end it only serving notice under s 27(2). The decision in *Esselte* showed otherwise.

The tenant, Pearl, took a lease of the premises in Guild House, Peterborough from Esselte and British Sugar for a term of five years expiring on 14 February 1993. Pearl were in the process of relocating to a new head-office in Peterborough. Guild House was a short-term arrangement and the staff were able to move into their new building by 3 December 1992. The premises were vacated and totally cleared out by 5 February 1993.

Pearl served a s 27(2) notice to take effect in June 1994 but later argued that their obligation to pay rent ceased on 14 February 1993 when they gave up possession and were no longer carrying on business in the premises. The Court of Appeal agreed. Nevertheless this is not a recommended course of action and service of a formal notice under s 27 of the 1954 Act is advisable.

If, during the course of the renewal procedure, the tenant decides to discontinue or withdraw proceedings or abandon an appeal, then the termination date under s 64(1) of the 1954 Act is three months after the tenant takes such action.

9.4.3 Other disposal options

Many businesses have found that their premises become surplus to requirements long before the contractual expiry date of the lease and therefore have to look at the options that are available to mitigate the expense of having unwanted leasehold premises. The main options to be considered are as follows.

Assignment

The best solution is to assign the benefit of the lease. This is assuming that any assignee is willing to pay the rent that is being paid. The tenant may have to offer some of the incentives referred to above (eg reverse premiums) to encourage an assignee to take over the lease, subject of course to the landlord's consent being forthcoming. Under the 1995 Act the tenant may well have to guarantee the assignees performance by way of an AGA.

Underletting

If the lease permits and particularly if the premises are 'over rented', an underletting of part or the whole may be considered. The tenant remains responsible for paying the rent under the head lease while collecting a rent himself from his under-tenant. This rent may only go part of the way towards paying the head rent, but at least mitigates the loss. Again the head landlord will wish to be satisfied as to the underlessee's covenant as if he were a direct tenant. The head landlord will always want to know, eg in the event that the head tenant becomes insolvent and the head lease is forfeited, that the underlessee who steps into the head tenant's shoes will be able to pay the rent etc.

Surrender

If neither of the above options arise, then apart from paying rent on an empty building, the tenant's only option is to go cap in hand to the landlord and see whether a surrender can be negotiated. Inevitably, the landlord will seek a premium (as well as payment of his legal costs) based normally upon a multiplier of the annual rental. In most cases the tenant has no negotiating leverage and is at the mercy of the landlord who may well be unwilling to relinquish his right to receive rent, particularly if there is little chance of re-letting quickly at a comparable rent. The tenant should take advice and assistance of a local surveyor on the negotiations in respect of the premium for surrender but if the landlord is not willing to negotiate the tenant has little option but to pay the rent, particularly in the case where the tenant is an individual or a personal guarantee has been provided.

10

EMPLOYMENT LAW

ANDREW KENNEDY, WEDLAKE SAINT

10.1 INTRODUCTION

Over recent years domestic employment law has undergone a metamorphosis with the result that a considerable body of law now exists governing the relationship between an employer and its workforce. EC legislation and ECJ decisions have had an increasing influence on domestic employment law and this trend is set to continue. Over a similar period the number of disputes coming before industrial tribunals has risen steadily.

It is therefore important for employers to be aware of this complex body of law that governs all employment relationship aspects from recruitment to termination (and in some instances beyond). This chapter concentrates on the areas governing the individual employment relationship as they affect the rights and obligations between employer and employee. It does not attempt to deal with collective employment law except where this affects individual employment law in such areas as redundancy and transfer of undertakings.

This chapter deals with employment law under the following headings:

(1) The impact of EC law
(2) Employing the worker: the worker's status
(3) The employee
(4) The contract of employment
(5) The doctrine of restraint of trade
(6) Written particulars of employment
(7) Continuity of employment
(8) Unfair dismissal
(9) Redundancy
(10) Termination of employment
(11) Maternity rights
(12) Statutory sick pay
(13) Further statutory payments to employees
(14) Itemised pay statements

(15) Wages: payments and deductions
(16) Sex and race discrimination
(17) Discrimination on grounds of disability
(18) Equal pay
(19) Insolvency of employer
(20) Transfer of Undertakings (Protection of Employment) Regulations 1981

10.2 THE IMPACT OF EC LAW

EC law has had a profound effect on UK employment law and the rights afforded to individual employees. It is therefore important to have an understanding of the way EC law operates and impacts upon both employers and employees in the UK.

Much of the law affecting UK employers has been implemented to give effect to EC legislation. Indeed, in certain circumstances, employees may be able to rely directly upon the provisions of EC law to enforce rights, where they would have no claim under UK law. The main sources of EC law are:

- *The provisions of the Treaty of Rome 1957* One of the most important provisions of the Treaty in the employment law field is art 119 which provides that men and women should receive equal pay for equal work (see 10.19 below).
- *Legislation in the form of directives* Directives take the form of instructions to countries that are members of the EC (including the UK) to pass national legislation, by a specified date, to implement each directive's provisions.

Certain provisions of EC law have what is known as 'direct effect'. This means that individuals can rely directly on directly-effective EC law in the UK courts. In order for direct effect to be established the provision of EC law must be unconditional, clear and precise. The most important directly-effective provision of EC law is art 119.

In contrast to art 119, directives do not have general direct effect and therefore cannot generally be relied upon by individuals directly in UK courts. However, directives have direct effect where the individual seeking to rely on directive's terms is employed by the State, or by a body that is 'an emanation of the State', in effect public sector employees. However, in contrast to public sector employees, those employed in the private sector are unable to rely on a directive's provisions. However, they may have a claim against the UK government for its failure to implement fully the provisions of any directive into national legislation by the specified date. See *Francovich v Italian Republic* [1992] IRLR 84.

Furthermore, it has been held that the national courts must, as far as is possible, interpret national law in the light of the wording and purpose of any relevant EC directive. This is the case whether the national law was passed before or after the adoption of the directive. This is known as 'the purposive approach'. However, this approach should only be adopted where the national legislation can be interpreted consistently with the directive without distorting the meaning of the domestic legislation itself.

Some of the most important provisions in the context of employment law are:

(1) Equal pay – art 119 and the Equal Pay Directive.
(2) Sex discrimination – Equal Treatment Directive.
(3) Transfer of undertakings – Acquired Rights Directive.
(4) Maternity rights – Pregnant Workers Directive.
(5) Contracts of employment – Proof of Employment Directive.

The importance of EC law in the field of UK employment law cannot be understated. Throughout this chapter references are made to relevant EC provisions, where appropriate.

10.3 EMPLOYING THE WORKER: THE WORKER'S STATUS

Before the employment relationship commences, the most fundamental question to be considered by the employer is whether the worker is to be an employee. Is the worker to be employed under a contract of service (ie an employee) or a contract for services (an independent contractor)? This distinction is extremely important as it forms the basis of the relationship between the parties and the rights and obligations of both parties arise from it. In practice, the vast majority of workers are employees, but in certain circumstances the employer may not feel this is appropriate. Some of the important consequences of the distinction, by which the employer can make a reasoned decision on the employee's status, are listed below:

Employee rights

- Written Statement of Terms and conditions of employment
- Protection against unfair dismissal
- Entitlement to redundancy pay
- Statutory minimum notice entitlement or agreed contractual notice
- Right to statutory sick pay
- Maternity rights, including statutory maternity pay entitlement
- Not to be discriminated against on grounds of sex, race or disability
- Not to be discriminated against on grounds of membership or non-membership of a trade union

- Time off for trade union activities
- Medical suspension payment entitlement
- Guarantee payment entitlement
- Equal pay
- Protection in connection with a transfer of an undertaking
- Right to be consulted on health and safety issues.

Employee obligations

- To work in accordance with the employer's instructions
- To work with due diligence
- To pay income tax through PAYE
- To pay employee NI contributions.

Self-employed – rights

- Entitlement to contractual benefits
- Not to be discriminated against on grounds of sex, race or disability
- Where appropriate to work within a safe system of work and place.

Self-employed obligations

- To work with due skill and diligence
- To pay own tax under Schedule D
- To pay self-employed NI contributions.

The obligations and consequently the costs placed upon an employer are far greater in relation to an employee. However, balanced against this is the high level of control that an employer has over an employee.

10.3.1 Distinguishing between contract of service and contract for services

Once the employer reaches a decision on the worker's status, it is important to ensure that the status that is intended is actually achieved, as it can be seen from above, a number of factors such as tax and NI obligations and statutory employment protection flow from the definition of the relationship. The mere description of the relationship by the parties as being one of employer/employee or employer/independent contractor is not decisive. The label put on the relation-ship is not conclusive and over the years the courts have developed a number of tests in an attempt to ascertain the true nature of employment relationships.

The tests

Mutuality of obligation

This is one of the more recent tests and was first expounded by the courts in *Nethermere (St Neots) Ltd v Gardiner* [1984] IRLR 240, where it was stated that for there to be a contract of service there must be 'an irreducible minimum of obligation on each side'. There must be an obligation on the employer to provide work for the employee and on the employee to perform such work for the employer. Without this element there could not be a contract of service.

The control test

This was the first test developed by the courts and looked at the level of control exercised by the employer over the worker, not only about the particular work that the worker was required to do but also whether the employer controlled how and when the work should be done. The greater the control the more likely that the worker was to be an employee. This test however was not sufficient when dealing with more skilled workers, such as, for example, brain surgeons, and the courts therefore developed what is known as the integration test.

The integration test

This test was set out by Denning LJ in *Stevenson, Jordan & Harrison Ltd v McDonald and Evans* [1952] 1 TLR 101 and looks at whether the worker is an integral part of the business. The closer the connection between the worker and the business the more likely the worker was to be an employee, whereas an independent contractor was more likely to be merely an accessory to the business.

The multiple test

The case of *Ready Mixed Concrete (South East) Ltd v Minister of Pensions and National Insurance* [1968] 2 QB 497 stated that a contract of service existed if:

(1) The worker agrees, in consideration of a wage or other remuneration, to provide his own work and skill in the performance of some service for his master.
(2) He agrees expressly or impliedly that in performance of the service he is sufficiently subject to the control of the other to make him a master.
(3) All the other provisions of the contract are consistent with it being a contract of service. It is important to note that an obligation to work subject to the other party's control was not to be the overriding factor, if all the other provisions of the contract were inconsistent with a contract of service. Therefore, it was important to look at the relationship as a whole and not isolated factors.

Subsequently, in *Market Investigations Ltd v Minister of Social Security* [1969] 2 QB 173 it was again reiterated that control was not the decisive test and that the most important question to ask was whether 'a person was in business on his own account'.

It was stated in *Hall (Inspector of Taxes) v Lorimar* [1994] 1 All ER 250 that the question of whether a person is in business on his own account, though often helpful in distinguishing between a contract of service and a contract for services, might be of little assistance in the case of a person carrying on a business or profession. In such cases the traditional distinction between an employee and an independent contractor should be borne in mind, namely, the extent to which the individual is dependent or independent of a particular paymaster for the financial exploitation of his talents.

The overview approach

It must be emphasised that there is 'no single path to a correct decision'. As the *Ready Mixed Concrete* and *Market Investigations* decisions show, although control is still an important factor, each case will turn on its own facts. Factors which are important will be:

(1) degree of control;
(2) the chance of profit and the risk of loss;
(3) method and payment of tax;
(4) exclusivity of service;
(5) intention of the parties;
(6) integration of the worker into the business;
(7) the employer's right to suspend and/or dismiss;
(8) whether the worker provides his own equipment;
(9) whether the worker is free to hire his own helpers.

When deciding to take on a worker as an independent contractor, it is essential that legal advice is sought to ensure that the way that the relationship is structured is one of employer/independent contractor. Failing to correctly define the relationship can have financial implications. For example, the Inland Revenue has wide ranging powers to recover tax from an employer who has failed to make the appropriate deductions through the PAYE system as he incorrectly thought that his worker was an independent contractor and therefore responsible for his own tax and national insurance contributions. In doubtful cases, it is always advisable to seek prior clearance from the Revenue as regards the tax treatment.

10.4 THE EMPLOYEE

In many instances, employers may wish to employ employees on a part time, temporary or seasonal basis. Particular matters should be borne in mind when engaging such employees.

10.4.1 Temporary employees

First, it is important to note that where temporary employees obtain the necessary two years' continuous employment, they will attain statutory employment protection rights. There are essentially two types of temporary employees.

First, those that are commonly known as 'temps' who are employed through an employment agency which charges its client a fee from which it pays the temp directly. In this instance the employment agency is to be treated as the primary employer and the agency's client as a secondary or quasi employer. It is unlikely that a claim for unfair dismissal or a redundancy payment in these circumstances would be successful against the secondary employer, and an employee should pursue the primary employer.

Secondly, there are temporary employees who are employed for a certain fixed period. If at the time of employing the temporary employee, the employer informs him that his employment is temporary and is to be terminated on the first employee resuming work, then such termination is likely to be a fair reason for some other substantial reason. The tribunal would then go on to consider whether the employer acted reasonably as defined by s 98(4) and (6) of the Employment Rights Act 1996 (ERA). See 10.9 below.

Under ERA, s 106, where an employer employs a temporary replacement to cover an employee who is absent because of pregnancy, childbirth or medical suspension, if at the time of employing the temporary replacement the employer informs the employee in writing that his employment will be terminated on the resumption of work by the other employee, then such a dismissal is deemed to be fair for some other substantial reason and, as above, the tribunal will go on to assess reasonableness in accordance with s 57(3).

10.4.2 Seasonal employees

These are employees who are taken on for a limited period of time, to cover, for example, busy periods in the tourism industry for the summer months. Seasonal employees, subject to the necessary qualifying conditions, are entitled to all the normal employment protection rights. Accordingly, their contracts can only be terminated on the employer providing them with the statutory minimum notice requirement (if there is not a longer contractual period).

There is one particular area of concern which employers should bear in mind when engaging seasonal employees. If the period between seasons of work is short and the particular worker is habitually re-engaged then continuity of employment may be preserved in accordance with the rules dealing with absence due to temporary cessation of work (see 10.8.2 below). This is obviously important with a view to the employee gaining statutory employment protection rights, especially the right to claim unfair dismissal and a redundancy payment.

10.4.3 Part-time employees

Although until 1995 part-time employees' rights to employment protection were limited, now part-time employees enjoy the same rights as full-time employees.

10.4.4 Directors

Directors are not automatically employees of a company. However, a director who is paid a salary and devotes his whole time and attention to the business of the company, will normally work under a contract of employment and be an employee.

A director's contract must be approved by the company's board and under the Companies Act 1985, s 319 a company is prohibited from entering into a contract with a director which it cannot terminate by notice (or can only terminate in specified circumstances) for a period exceeding five years, unless the term has been approved by a resolution of the company in general meeting. Any term not so approved is void and is deemed to be replaced by a term entitling the company to terminate on reasonable notice.

For a fuller discussion of the role of directors, see 17.5 below.

10.5 THE CONTRACT OF EMPLOYMENT

The contract of employment governs the relationship between the employer and the employee. Although in practice a single document is referred to as 'the contract of employment' in reality the contract need not be in writing but can be oral. Indeed a contract can, and in most instances does, include terms expressly agreed between the parties, implied terms, terms implied by custom and practice or arrangement and terms incorporated into a contract from other documents such as collective agreements (where a collective agreement contains terms appropriate for incorporation into an individual contract).

10.5.1 The terms of the contract

Express terms

These are terms which the parties specifically agree upon between themselves.

Implied terms

Frequently many terms of a contract of employment are left unspecified, but nevertheless are implied into the contract. This occurs where implied terms are necessary to give effect to the contract or if such terms are customary in a particular trade or are a usual arrangement for a particular employer. There are terms which are commonly implied into a contract and which affect both the employer and employee. A number of these are listed below.

Employers' duties

To maintain the relationship of mutual trust and confidence There is a duty on an employer not to destroy the trust and confidence that exists in an employment relationship. Breach of this implied term may entitle the employee to treat himself as having been constructively dismissed (see 10.9.1 below) and bring a claim for unfair dismissal as a result of a fundamental breach of a term of the contract by the employer.

To safeguard the employee's health and safety An employer owes a duty to all his employees to safeguard their health and safety. This includes a duty to provide safe equipment and a safe system of work. For a fuller discussion on health and safety and the employer's duties, see Chapter 13.

To terminate the contract on reasonable notice This term is implied where there is no express agreement between the parties. The contract can be terminated by either party on reasonable notice and what is deemed to be reasonable depends upon the particular employment circumstances. Such an implied notice term applies to both employer and employee.

To provide work In general terms, provided the employer fully remunerates his employee, it is not a breach of contract for the employer not to provide work. However, a term to provide work for an employee is implied where, for example, the level of remuneration is dependent upon the amount of work done or where an employee has particular skills which will deteriorate through lack of use.

Employee duties

Fidelity An employee is under a duty to act faithfully on behalf of his employer and to act in the interests of his employer's business. For example, the employee must be honest and not steal from his employer. It is also a breach of the implied duty of fidelity for an employee to compete with his employer's business whilst still employed. However, where an employee merely takes steps in his own time to compete at the end of the employment relationship there would not be a breach of the implied contractual duty of fidelity (Ixora Trading Inc v Jones [1990] FSR 251).

Obedience It is an implied term of the contract that an employee obeys his employer's lawful orders; and not to do so is a breach of the contract. However, such a duty extends only to lawful orders – it is not a breach to disobey an unlawful order.

To work with due diligence and care An employee is under a duty to take reasonable care when performing tasks for his employer. Where an employee fails to take reasonable care in the performance of his duties the employer may be vicariously liable for his employee's lack of care (see Chapter 13).

Not to use or disclose trade secrets or confidential information Another breach of the implied duty of fidelity is for an employee to use or disclose to third parties confidential information of his employer during employment. However, in the absence of an express term in the contract, on termination of employment the implied duty is not as extensive as during employment and only extends to information which is not merely confidential but which can be described as a trade secret. The circumstances of each case have to be assessed in deciding whether any information amounts to a trade secret, but in *Faccenda Chicken Ltd v Fowler* [1986] ICR 297 a number of factors were stressed to be important in deciding whether the implied duty of fidelity applied to confidential information after the termination of employment. These factors were as follows:

(1) The nature of the employment – Did the employee work in a business (or part of a business) where he regularly handled sensitive information?

(2) The nature of the information – Was the information such as to be so highly confidential as to amount to a trade secret?
(3) Did the employer impress upon the employee the confidential nature of the information? What was the employer's attitude?
(4) Could the particular information be easily isolated from other information which the employee was free to use or disclose?

Whilst the employment relationship subsists the implied duties on employees are wide ranging. However, on termination of employment apart from the implied duty not to disclose trade secrets an employee is free to set up a competing business and in theory to solicit customers and employees of his former employer. Therefore, in many cases employers will wish to incorporate into employment contracts express covenants restricting an employee's activities on termination.

10.6 THE DOCTRINE OF RESTRAINT OF TRADE

Express covenants in a contract of employment restricting an employee's activities after termination of employment are governed by the doctrine of restraint of trade. Such covenants are *prima facie* void on public policy grounds.

To be valid this type of covenant must be reasonable in both the interests of the parties and of the public (*Nordenfelt v Maxim Nordenfelt* [1894] AC 535). A covenant will only be upheld to the extent that it is reasonably required for the protection of the employer's legitimate interests. A protectable interest must first be established and then the clause must be limited to what is reasonably necessary to protect that interest.

Restraint of trade covenants fall into two main categories.

10.6.1 Non-competition covenants

Although any attempt by an employer to prevent a former employee from competing against him by inserting into that employee's contract a blanket non-competition covenant after termination will not be upheld by the courts, an employer is free to seek to uphold a covenant restricting an employee from working for a trade rival. Such a covenant is likely to be upheld provided it is limited to a reasonable period of time (*Littlewoods Organisation Ltd v Harris* [1977] 1 WLR 1472). A reasonable period of time is likely in most circumstances to be one not exceeding one year after termination.

Employers can also seek to prohibit a former employee from working in the same business as that for which he worked for his former employer within a specific geographical area and for a specific period of time. Such clauses are extremely restrictive and are only upheld by the courts where the employer can show that he has a large concentration of customers within a particular area that it is necessary for him to protect. If the employer can show this, the covenant is still only reasonable to the extent that the area it seeks to cover is limited and that the covenant runs only for a certain length of time. It is important to remember that a valid covenant covering a particular radius in one part of the country may not be valid covering the same radius in another area. Contrast a highly populated urban area with a rural area with a low population level (*Scorer v Seymour-Johns* [1966] 3 All ER 347, CA).

10.6.2 Non-solicitation covenants

Such a covenant will seek to restrict the former employee from soliciting his former employer's customers or clients. Again such covenants must be reasonable in relation to the time that they run and should be limited to those customers with which the former employee dealt with.

Furthermore, it was standard practice for employers to include a covenant in contracts prohibiting the poaching of fellow employees. However, following the Court of Appeal decision in *Hanover Insurance Brokers Ltd v Schapiro* [1994] IRLR 82, such covenants are generally unenforceable. In order to try and enforce such a covenant, it should be limited to very senior employees or those employees who have a particular expertise that it is necessary for the employer to protect and should only cover individuals who were employees at the same time as the departing employee.

Also, covenants were frequently specified to apply however the contract was terminated. Again, recently, this has been held to be too wide and covenants are only enforceable if a contract is terminated lawfully (*Living Design (Home Improvements) Ltd v Davidson* [1994] IRLR 69).

The drafting of restrictive covenants is extremely tricky and legal advice should be sought on every occasion. The above is only a brief summary of the relevant law and failure to carefully consider with appropriate advice when drafting covenants may result in them being unenforceable, because they are too wide in nature.

In certain circumstances the courts are willing to sever an unenforceable covenant or part of a covenant providing that what remains makes sense without the need for modifying the wording and that the sense of the contract itself is not altered. However, it is far preferable to insert into a contract a correctly drafted limited covenant which is likely to be upheld by the courts than to seek reliance on a widely drafted covenant which will fail and cannot at a later stage be altered.

If an employer, after termination of an employee's contract, wishes to rely upon any express covenants contained within that contract there are two remedies available:

(1) *An injunction*. This is the usual and most effective remedy by an employer seeking to enforce a term of the employment contract. An application for an injunction can be made once evidence of any breach has come to light and a successful application will result in the employee being restrained from breaching any of the terms of the covenant.
(2) *Damages*. An employer can also bring a claim against his employee for damages for breach of contract or breach of confidence. In such cases the employer, in order to recover damages, has to show that he has incurred a loss. There is also a potential claim against the employee's new employer for inducing the breach of contract, if the new employer was aware of the employee's breach.

10.6.3 Intellectual property rights

A complex body of law exists to deal with intellectual property rights that arise during the course of the employment relationship. This legislation governs copyright, patent and design rights.

The right of copyright is governed by the Copyright, Designs and Patents Act 1988. Section 11(2) of the Act states that, subject to contrary agreement, the first owner of any copyright in a work made by an employee during the course of his employment is his employer.

The Patents Act 1977 governs the protection of an original invention capable of industrial application by means of a patent. Section 39 of that Act states that an invention made by an employee belongs to his employer if:

(1) it was made in the course of the employee's normal duties; or
(2) it arises out of duties specifically assigned to him, in circumstances where an invention might reasonably be expected to result from the performance of those duties; or
(3) it was made in the course of the employee's duties and at that time the employee had, because of the nature of his duties and the particular responsibilities arising from them, a special obligation to further the interest of his employer's undertaking.

Further, s 40 of the 1977 Act states that in certain circumstances, where a patent is granted in relation to an invention made by an employee, but which belongs to an employer, and the patent is of outstanding benefit to the employer, compensation may be payable to the employee. The object of the compensation is to award the employee with a fair share of the benefit that the employer has derived or can be reasonably expected to derive from the patent.

Finally, s 42 of the 1977 Act states that any attempt by an employer to diminish the employee's rights in relation to inventions is unenforceable.

The Copyright, Designs and Patents Act 1988 introduced for the first time a design right. Section 215(3) of the 1988 Act states that where a design is created by an employee in the course of his employment, the employer is the first owner of the design right.

10.7 WRITTEN PARTICULARS OF EMPLOYMENT

A contract of employment contains both express and implied terms and need not be set out in writing (see 10.4).

However, under s 1 of the ERA an employer is now under a duty to provide each employee (whose employment is to continue for more than one month) with a written statement of certain terms and conditions of his contract of employment within two months of the commencement of employment. This new provision, however, does not apply to an employee whose employment had begun with the employer prior to the date when the provision came into force (30 November 1993). However, such employees have a right to ask for a statement in the new form either before or within three months of termination of employment and the employer must comply with the request within two months of such request being made.

The written statement must contain the following specific information.

(1) The names of both the employer and the employee.
(2) The date employment began.
(3) The date continuous employment began (if applicable).
(4) The employee's job title or a brief description of the job.
(5) The place or places of work.
(6) The scale or rate of remuneration together with payment intervals and the method of calculating remuneration.
(7) The hours of work.
(8) Holiday entitlement (including public holidays) and holiday pay containing sufficient information to enable an employee to calculate entitlement to accrued holiday pay on termination of employment.

These details must be provided in a single document that is known as the principal statement. Further additional information which must be provided must include:

(1) Terms and conditions for sickness, injury and sick pay.
(2) Pensions.
(3) Length of notice required from both employer and employee to terminate the contract.
(4) Where the employment is not intended to be permanent, the period for which it is expected to continue, or if for a fixed term the date when that term will end.
(5) Details of any collective agreements which directly affect the terms and conditions of the employment.
(6) Disciplinary rules and procedures, together with details of a person to whom an employee can appeal against any disciplinary decision.
(7) Details of a person whom an employee can approach seeking redress of any grievance relating to his employment.

These further provisions may be contained in other documentation which either the employee has reasonable opportunity of reading in the course of his employment or which are made reasonably accessible to him in some other way.

Where there are no provisions relating to any of the matters listed above, this fact must be stated in the written statement.

10.7.1 Changes to statement of terms and conditions of employment

Where there is a change to any of the terms contained in the written statement, the employer is under an obligation at the earliest opportunity, and in any event not later than one month after the change, to provide the employee with a written statement containing particulars of the change. It is important for the employer when altering an employee's contractual terms to remember that as a general rule this should only be done with the employee's consent. A unilateral variation by the employer will constitute a breach of contract and may give rise to unfair dismissal claims (see 10.9 and in particular 10.9.10).

10.7.2 Employees working overseas

Where an employee is required to work outside the United Kingdom for a period of more than one month, the employer must provide details of the period for which the employee has to work outside the United Kingdom, the currency in which he will be paid, details of any additional remuneration and benefit and any conditions that relate to his return to the United Kingdom.

10.7.3 Unlawful terms

A contract must not contain any term which is unlawful or contrary to public policy, for example, contracts entered into knowingly with a view to defrauding the Revenue or contracts for an immoral purpose.

10.7.4 Remedies for failure to provide written particulars

If an employee has not been provided with a written statement under ERA, s 1, or if the written statement provided raises a query as to certain terms or conditions that should have been included or referred to in it, the employee can make a complaint to an industrial tribunal. Where there is no express or implied agreement concerning a particular term, a tribunal, if it considers the complaint well founded, will state the particulars which should have been given and the employer is then deemed to have provided a statement containing such particulars. Thereafter, if the employer has been in breach of any of those terms, the employee can bring an appropriate action against the employer. There is no right to claim compensation for failure on the part of an employer to provide a written statement.

A claim before the tribunal can be brought by any employee who has more than 13 weeks continuous employment. Where the employment has been terminated, the complaint must be brought within three months of the date of the termination of the employment or within such further period as the tribunal considers reasonable where it was not reasonably practicable for the employee to bring the application within the three-month time limit.

Therefore, an employer is under a duty to provide a minimum statement of certain terms of employment. However, although the written minimum statement is relied upon in many cases, there is benefit to be obtained by the employer in providing a more detailed contract of employment. The employer can make provision for such matters as restraint of trade clauses (the importance of which is noted at 10.5 above) and any other special rules which that particular type of business may require.

Furthermore, under ERA, s 13 it is unlawful for an employer to make deductions from an employee's wages unless such deduction is required or permitted by a statutory or contractual provision, or the worker has given his prior written consent to the deduction. Therefore, incorporation into the contract of a term entitling the employer to make deductions from an employee's wages in certain circumstances ensures that the employer does not breach the Wages Act provisions (see 10.16 below).

Finally, as a matter of good practice, an employer should ensure that his employees sign a copy of their contract of employment to prove receipt.

10.8 CONTINUITY OF EMPLOYMENT

A number of statutory employment protection rights are dependent upon the employee having worked continuously under a contract of employment for a minimum period of time.

The main statutory employment rights which are subject to a qualifying period of continuous employment are as follows:

Right	*Qualifying period*
Redundancy payment	Two years
Unfair dismissal	Two years
Statement of written reasons for dismissal	Two years
The right to up to 40 weeks' maternity leave	Two years
Statutory maternity pay	26 weeks before the beginning of the 14th week before the expected week of confinement
Written particulars of employment	Two months
Minimum notice period	One month
Guarantee payment	One month ending with the day before the workless day or more than three months if engaged on a fixed term or specific task contract for three months or less
Medical suspension payment	One month ending on the day before suspension begins or more than three months if engaged on a fixed term or specific task contract for three months or less

An employee's period of continuous employment is determined on a week by week basis, although it is the total number of calendar months or years of employment attained that is important for qualifying periods or statutory rights. The period begins with the day on which the employee actually commences work and ends on the day that is to be ascertained in accordance with the appropriate rules. In most cases this will be the last day the employee works. Once an employee has commenced work there is, subject to contrary evidence, a presumption that employment is continuous. Therefore, it is important to look at the rules for calculating what weeks count towards a period of continuous employment and under what circumstances continuity will be broken.

10.8.1 Weeks which count

The ERA set out detailed rules regarding what weeks counted in calculating an employee's period of continuous employment. Continuous employment is calculated in the same way for part-time and full-time employees, irrespective of hours worked.

Any week during which an employee's relations with his employer are governed by a contract of employment count in calculating continuity.

10.8.2 Periods where no contract of employment exists

Periods in which there is no contract of employment may nevertheless count as periods of employment for continuous employment purposes. The situations in which continuity of employment are preserved are set out below. If in any week the employee is for the whole or the part of that week:

(1) incapable of work in consequence of illness or injury, a period of not more than 26 weeks under this provision counts in preserved continuity;
(2) absent from work on account of a temporary cessation of work, this covers the situation where an employee is habitually re-engaged by an employer and the periods of no employment in between are relatively short;
(3) absent from work in circumstances such that, by arrangement or custom, he is regarded as continuing in the employment of his employer for all or any purpose, this would cover such instances as where an employee is absent on unpaid leave;
(4) absent from work wholly or partly because of pregnancy or childbirth, and furthermore in relation to the right to return to work after absence for pregnancy or childbirth, if an employee exercises her right to return in accordance with ERA, s 71 (see 10.12.4 below), all weeks during that period of absence count in calculating continuity.

Further instances in which continuity is preserved are as follows:

(1) Under ERA, ss 94 (unfair dismissal) and 193 (redundancy payment) when employment is terminated in a situation where notice should have been given, but was not, and as a result the employee did not attain the qualifying condition of two years' service for claims for unfair dismissal or a redundancy payment, the employee's employment is treated as continuing until the expiry of the statutory minimum notice period that that employee would have been entitled to.

(2) Section 210(5) of ERA applies to preserve continuity of employment where an employee's contract of employment is renewed or he is re-engaged under a new contract of employment in pursuance of an offer made by his employer before the ending of his employment under a previous contract or within four weeks thereafter.
(3) An employee who is dismissed and then reinstated or re-engaged pursuant to an industrial tribunal award or by a settlement through ACAS has continuity preserved, notwith-standing the period between dismissal and reinstatement.
(4) On the transfer of a trade or business from one person to another, the period of employment of an employee with the transferor company counts as a period of employment with the transferee company and consequently continuity of employment is preserved (see 10.21 below).
(5) If an employee's employment is transferred to another employer who at the time the employee enters his employment is an 'associated' employer of the former employer, again that employee's continuity of employment is preserved. Employers are treated as associated if one is a company of which the other (directly or indirectly) has control, or if both are companies of which a third person (directly or indirectly) has control.

10.8.3 Weeks which do not count but which do not break continuity

Certain weeks do not count in the calculation of continuous employment, but do not operate so as to break continuity. Where an employee's period of employment includes intervals which do not count in calculating continuity, but which do not break it, the commencement of the employee's continuous employment is treated as having been postponed by the number of days which do not count. Circumstances where these rules apply are:

(1) any week during which an employee takes part in a strike or is absent from work because of a lock-out;
(2) any week during which an employee is employed overseas.

This applies only in calculating the qualifying period and amount for redundancy payment purposes.

10.9 UNFAIR DISMISSAL

Sections 94–110 of ERA concern the right of an employee, subject to certain qualifying conditions, not to be unfairly dismissed by his employer. An affected employee may bring a claim of unfair dismissal before an industrial tribunal. If the claim is successful, the tribunal may order the employer to reinstate or re-engage the employee and/or to pay compensation.

The interpretation of the law of unfair dismissal has resulted in substantial case law, but many decisions can only be explained on their own specific facts. However, the decisions do give guidance and reference has been made to leading cases in particular areas of unfair dismissal law.

10.9.1 The basis of a claim

Pre-conditions

In order for the employee to be able to bring a claim for unfair dismissal before a tribunal he must first show that he was employed by the employer under a contract of employment; that he was dismissed by the employer; and that he has attained the necessary two- year period of continuous employment.

Certain employees are excluded from bringing a claim, for example when the employee is over the normal retirement age in the particular employment in question; or he is working abroad; or he has been dismissed in connection with a lock-out or strike. The burden of proof rests with the employee to show that he satisfies the necessary qualifying conditions.

Dismissal by the employer

Sections 95 and 136 of ERA state that an employee is to be treated as having been dismissed if and only if:

(1) the contract under which he is employed by the employer is terminated by the employer with or without notice; or
(2) where under that contract he is employed for a fixed term and that term expires without being renewed under the same contract; or
(3) the employee terminates that contract with or without notice, in circumstances in which he is entitled to terminate the contract without notice by reason of the employer's conduct (what is known as 'constructive dismissal').

Termination by the employer

It is important to note that once an employer gives notice of dismissal to an employee, as a general rule this cannot be withdrawn without the employee's consent. Likewise, the same principle applies to notice of resignation given by the employee.

Expiry of a fixed term contract

The expiry of a fixed term contract which is not renewed by the employer is a dismissal for unfair dismissal purposes. However, under ERA, s 197 an employer and employee can agree in writing to exclude the employee's right to claim unfair dismissal arising out of the non-renewal of the contract where the employee is employed under a fixed term of one year or more. If it is intended to exclude such rights, provision should be made in the contract of employment itself.

Constructive dismissal

Constructive dismissal occurs where an employer has committed a repudiatory breach of the employee's contract of employment, which entitles the employee to resign. The leading case in this area is the Court of Appeal decision in *Western Excavating (ECC) Ltd v Sharp* [1978] IRLR 27. There must be an intention by the employer to break one or more of the essential terms of the employee's employment. It is not sufficient that the employer has merely acted unreasonably.

The repudiatory breach by the employer need not be of an express term of the contract, but could be a breach of an implied term such as that of mutual trust and confidence (see 10.5.1 above). Examples of actions by an employer which may justify an employee claiming constructive dismissal are a unilateral reduction in an employee's pay or a substantial change in the nature of the employee's job.

It is important that an employee must not affirm the breach of contract by his employer by delaying his resignation for a substantial period of time or by doing some other act which is inconsistent with his acceptance of the breach.

10.9.2 Qualifying period

An employee must have been continuously employed for a period of at least two years at the effective date of termination (EDT) to be able to bring a claim for unfair dismissal. The period of continuous employment is calculated from the date of commencement to the effective date of termination. The EDT is defined in ERA, s 97(1) as:

(1) where an employee's employment is terminated by notice, either by the employer or the employee himself, the date on which that notice expires;
(2) where an employee's employment is terminated without notice, the date on which that termination takes effect;

(3) where an employee is employed under a fixed term contract which expires without the term being renewed, the date on which that term expires.

In most instances the EDT is the date on which the employee finishes work. However, where an employee is dismissed without notice or with notice that is less than the statutory minimum, the EDT is the date on which the minimum statutory notice would have expired if it had been given (see 10.8.2 above). Accordingly, an employee who is dismissed without notice one week short of attaining two years' continuous employment is nevertheless, under the operation of this rule, deemed as having two years' continuous employment and therefore is entitled to bring a claim for unfair dismissal.

10.9.3 The reasons for dismissal

Once the employee has established that he has been dismissed and that he satisfies the other qualifying conditions, the burden of proof switches to the employer to show:

(1) the reason or the principal reason for the dismissal; and
(2) that reason was one of the *prima facie* fair reasons set out in ERA, s 98.

Section 98 sets out the following *prima facie* fair reasons for dismissal:

(1) a reason related to the capability or qualifications of the employee to carry out the particular job which he was employed to do;
(2) a reason relating to the employee's conduct;
(3) the employee's redundancy;
(4) that the employee could not continue in his position without contravening a duty or restriction imposed by or under an enactment;
(5) some other substantial reason of a kind such as to justify the dismissal of an employee holding the position which that employee held.

10.9.4 Fairness – has the employer acted reasonably?

If the employer has established one of the *prima facie* fair reasons set out in ERA, s 98, the industrial tribunal will then go on to consider the question of whether the dismissal was fair or unfair in all the circumstances of the particular case (having regard to equity and the substantial merits of the case). The question is whether the employer acted reasonably in treating the reason for dismissal as a sufficient reason for dismissing the employee.

The burden of proof does not rest on either party, but it is for the tribunal to be satisfied that the employer acted reasonably when dismissing the employee. A leading case on this point is *Iceland Frozen Foods Ltd v Jones* (1982) IRLR 439, in which the EAT stated that it was the function of an industrial tribunal to determine whether in the particular circumstances of each case the decision by the employer to dismiss the employee fell within the band of reasonable responses which a reasonable employer might have adopted. If the dismissal falls within the band, then it is fair; if it does not, then it is unfair. It is not for the tribunal, in judging whether the employer acted reasonably, to substitute for the employer's decision what they believe the right course of action should have been. In many instances one employer might have dismissed whereas another might have taken some other form of disciplinary action, but either decision could fall within the band of reasonable responses.

It is also for an employer, to show that he has acted reasonably, to have adopted fair procedures when taking a decision to dismiss an employee. Until the House of Lords' decision in *Polkey v AE Dayton Services Ltd* [1988] ICR 142, it was believed that if the employer had adopted an unfair procedure in dismissing an employee, but established that if he adopted a fair procedure, the employee would still have been dismissed, then that dismissal could still be fair. However, in *Polkey* the House of Lords held that this was the wrong approach and that fair procedures must be followed regardless of whether or not a failure to do so would in fact not affect the ultimate outcome.

10.9.5 Automatically unfair dismissals

Certain dismissals are deemed to be automatically unfair and are not subject to the reasonableness tests set out in ERA, s 98(4). Also in certain cases, an employee may be able to bring a complaint despite the fact that he does not satisfy the necessary qualifying condition regarding continuous employment:

Trade union related dismissals

It is automatically unfair for an employer to dismiss an employee for either:

(1) being or proposing to become a member of an independent trade union; or
(2) refusing to join or remain a member of a trade union; or
(3) taking part or proposing to take part in union related activities at an appropriate time, ie outside working hours or within working hours if agreed with the employer.

An employee can bring a claim under this heading irrespective of the fact that he may not have two years' continuous service or that he may be over the age of 65 or the normal retiring age in his employment. In such a case, the burden of proof rests upon the employee to show that the reason for the dismissal was union related. However, if he does satisfy the necessary qualifying conditions, it is for the employer to prove the reason for dismissal in the usual way.

Maternity related dismissals

Under ERA, s 99(*f*), it is automatically unfair for an employer to dismiss any woman irrespective of her hours of work or length of service if the sole or principal reason for her dismissal is that she was pregnant or was for any other maternity related reason. For further discussion, see 10.12.7 below.

Health and safety related dismissals

Section 100 of ERA now makes it automatically unfair for an employer to dismiss an employee for certain health and safety reasons. Again, no qualifying period of employment is required.

Assertion of statutory rights

Under ERA, s 104, it is automatically unfair to dismiss an employee if the reason or principal reason for the dismissal was the allegation by an employee that his employer had infringed a statutory right or that the employee had brought proceedings to enforce a particular right. The relevant statutory rights include, for example, claims made under ERA, s 13 (Protection of wages) are claims to a written statement of terms under ERA, s 1. Again, no qualifying period of employment is required.

Spent convictions

Where under the Rehabilitation of Offenders Act 1974 a conviction has been spent, it is automatically unfair for an employer to dismiss an employee for failure to disclose such a spent conviction.

Transfer of undertaking related dismissals

It is automatically unfair to dismiss an employee where that dismissal is for a reason connected with the transfer of an undertaking unless such dismissal can be justified as being for an ETO reason entailing changes in the workforce (see 10.21 below).

Redundancy – unfair reasons for selection

It is automatically unfair for an employee to be selected for redundancy because he is a trade union member or has refused to become one, or an employee is selected for redundancy because she is pregnant; or where the employee is selected for redundancy in breach of an agreed practice or customary arrangement.

10.9.6 Grounds for dismissal

Capability

Capability is defined as being assessed by reference to skill, aptitude, health or any other physical or mental quality. Capability falls into two classes: (1) the inability of an employee to carry out his particular job to the required standard (ie incompetence), and (2) ill health.

Incompetence

In incompetency cases it is important for the employer to show:

(a) what was required of the employee;
(b) that the employee was aware of what was required; and
(c) that he fell short of the required standard.

Complaints about an employee's incompetence must relate to 'work of the kind which he was employed by the employer to do'. Therefore, in certain circumstances a single act of incompetence or negligence may be sufficient to justify dismissal in some cases. For example, in *Alidair Ltd v Taylor* [1978] ICR 445 an airline pilot who landed his aircraft negligently so as to put the lives of his passengers at risk was fairly dismissed by his employer in view of his gross incompetence and the potentially calamitous consequences that his actions could have had.

However, most incompetency cases involve a number of relatively minor incidents, which taken in isolation are relatively unimportant but which accumulated over a sufficient period of time may constitute a reason for dismissal. In cases of this kind, it is important for an employer to adopt a fair procedure in dealing with the employee and such procedure should include the following steps:

(1) Where an employee falls short of the required standards, the employer should arrange a meeting with him (and his representative) at which he should be informed of the areas in which he is falling short of those standards and the time period during which his performance must improve. The employee should also be told that if the required improvement does not occur, he will receive a formal written warning and that if after that time further improvement is not seen, the ultimate sanction of dismissal may be considered.

(2) If no improvement is apparent, the employee should be called to a second meeting, together with his representative, at which he should be warned of the areas in which he has failed to improve and he should be given the opportunity to explain why there has been no improvement. The employee should be given a formal written warning. At the conclusion of that meeting he should be informed that he will be given a further period in which to improve, but that if there is no substantial improvement within that time then such failure will result in his dismissal.
(3) When no further improvement occurs, a third meeting should be called at which the employer should be given the opportunity to state his case and notice of dismissal will be given. The employee should then be given the opportunity to appeal against the decision to dismiss him.

In certain circumstances, the employer should consider further training for the employee. If the employee can show that the reason for his incompetence is that the employer failed to provide adequate training or adequate tools to perform the task satisfactorily, then a dismissal may well be unfair. The provision of further training and supervision is particularly important where an employee has been recently promoted. Furthermore, an employer should consider whether he has other work available to which the employee would be better suited.

Whether an employer follows all the procedural steps outlined above depends upon the circumstances of each particular case. In the case of a senior employee, he should reasonably be expected to be aware of the standards that are required of him and therefore several warnings may not be appropriate. However, it is advisable that, except in cases of clear gross incompetence, warnings should always be provided.

Illness

Frustration Where ill health may make future performance of the employment contract impossible, the contract may be frustrated and there will be no dismissal of the employee. However, frustration of a contract is rare in these circumstances. For a discussion of the law relating to frustration of contracts, see 10.11.1 below.

Long-term sickness As it is not normally difficult to show that the reason for dismissal was ill health, attention is generally focused on whether the employer acted reasonably in treating ill health absenteeism as sufficient grounds for dismissal. Therefore, of primary importance is the adoption by the employer of a fair procedure.

Before dismissing an employee for ill health the employer should be aware of the current medical position. With the employee's consent, he should obtain a report from the employee's doctor and in many circumstances also have the employee examined, with his consent, by the employer's own doctor.

In *Spencer v Paragon Wallpapers Ltd* [1976] IRLR 373 and *East Lindsey District Council v Daubney* [1977] ICR 566 various principles were set out which would indicate a fair procedure had been adopted in relation to the dismissal of an employee on ill health grounds. The employer having informed himself of the employee's medical condition should consider the following factors:

(1) The nature of the illness.
(2) The likelihood of the illness recurring.
(3) The requirements of his business and the need for the job to be done. Is it essential, because of the nature of the job, that the position needs to be filled quickly, or can the remaining employees cover the work for a period of time?
(4) The employee's past sickness record.
(5) Whether there is an alternative position within the company which would be more suitable to the employee.

Also throughout the period of illness the employer should consult with the employee on a regular basis. Failure to consult with the employee will in most cases render a dismissal unfair.

Persistent short-term absenteeism In cases where there is persistent short-term absenteeism due to unrelated illnesses, a medical examination may not be appropriate. In such circumstances the employee should be told what level of attendance he is expected to attain and be warned that if there is no improvement within a set period, this may result in his dismissal. The situation should then be monitored for a period of time (*International Sports Company Ltd v Thompson* [1980] IRLR 340).

Misconduct

Cases of misconduct fall into two categories: first single acts of misconduct not sufficient by themselves to justify dismissal, and secondly gross misconduct which may entitle an employer to dismiss an employee summarily (without notice). Examples of categories of gross misconduct would include theft, fraud, deliberate falsification of records, fighting, serious incapability through alcohol, being under the influence of illegal drugs, serious negligence which causes loss, damage or injury and serious acts of insubordination. Whereas any of the above examples may justify summary dismissal, in contrast a one-off incident of bad timekeeping would not.

It was stated in *British Home Stores Ltd v Burchell* [1980] ICR 303 that where an employer dismisses an employee for misconduct, the employer must establish that he had a belief that the employee was guilty of misconduct. Furthermore, the employer must have had reasonable grounds for that belief, and that in forming that reasonable belief he had carried out a reasonable investigation into all the circumstances of the matter.

Accordingly, it can be seen that the burden of proof in such cases is not as high as the burden of proof of reasonable doubt in a criminal court. Therefore, if an employer has a reasonable belief that one of a number of employees is guilty of dishonesty and following a full and proper investigation into the matter it cannot identify the particular employee responsible, it may be reasonable for the employer to dismiss all those who could have been responsible (*Frames Snooker Centre v Boyce* [1992] IRLR 472).

Furthermore, in cases where an employee is arrested by the police and criminal charges are pending, an employer does not have to wait for the outcome of the criminal case before deciding what action to take. If the employer carries out his own investigation and as a result dismisses the employee for dishonesty, such dismissal may be held to be reasonable, even if the employee is subsequently acquitted at trial.

The conduct for which an employee is dismissed usually relates to his behaviour during his employment. However, in certain instances behaviour outside of employment may affect his continued employment. For example, a teacher who has a conviction for indecent assault on a child, even though such conviction was for an offence outside his normal working hours, may be unsuitable to continue on his employment.

10.9.7 Dismissal procedures

Even in cases of serious misconduct, it is important that employers follow a fair procedure when dealing with cases of misconduct by employees. Failure to follow a fair procedure is likely to result in the dismissal being unfair. It is therefore important for all employers to have properly set out disciplinary procedures.

Two publications by ACAS set out certain steps which should be included in fair disciplinary procedures. These two publications are the ACAS 1977 Code of Practice on Disciplinary Practice and Procedures in Work and the 1987 Advisory Handbook *Discipline at Work*.

Paragraph 10 of the 1977 Code states that procedures should:

(1) Be in writing.
(2) Specify to whom they apply.
(3) Provide for matters to be dealt with quickly.
(4) Indicate the disciplinary actions which may be taken.

(5) Specify the levels of management which have the authority to take the various forms of disciplinary action, ensuring that immediate superiors do not normally have the power to dismiss without reference to senior management.
(6) Provide for individuals to be informed of the complaints against them and to be given an opportunity to state their case before decisions are reached.
(7) Give individuals the right to be accompanied by a trade union representative or by a fellow employee of their choice.
(8) Ensure that, except for gross misconduct, no employees are dismissed for a first breach of discipline.
(9) Ensure that disciplinary action is not taken until the case has been carefully investigated.
(10) Ensure that individuals are given an explanation for any penalty imposed.
(11) Provide for a right of appeal and specify the procedure to be followed.

When a matter of misconduct arises, the incident should be fully investigated immediately and witness statements taken if appropriate. Where witness statements are taken and these are the main evidence which are relied upon in taking disciplinary action against an employee it is appropriate for copies of the statements to be provided to the employee in question.

In cases of suspected serious misconduct, an employer should consider a brief period of suspension with pay. However, it is important to note that unless there is express provision in an employer's disciplinary procedures which are incorporated into a contract of employment, the employer does not have the right to suspend an employee. In the absence of this being an express term of the contract, any suspension is a fundamental breach of the contract of employment by the employer which entitles the employee to resign and claim constructive dismissal.

Before a disciplinary decision is taken, a hearing should be held at which the employee is given an opportunity to state his case. He should be given the opportunity of having a fellow employee or trade union representative present at the meeting.

An employer, before deciding on the appropriate penalty, must take account of the employee's record and any other relevant factors. It is good practice for an employer to adjourn the hearing to consider a case before giving his decision. Once a decision has been made, this should be notified to the employee in writing and the employee should be informed of his right of appeal. The letter should state how the appeal should be made and to whom. Any appeal should be conducted by a member of senior management who has not been involved in the previous decision or investigation.

It is essential that records are kept of all disciplinary proceedings and copies of letters are retained on an employee's personnel file as this will be important evidence should an unfair dismissal claim be made to an industrial tribunal.

10.9.8 Redundancy

Where the reason or the principal reason for an employee's dismissal is redundancy it may be unfair in two circumstances.

First, a dismissal is automatically unfair if the circumstances constituting the redundancy applied equally to one or more employees in the same undertaking who held positions similar to that held by the dismissed employee and who have not been dismissed by the employer, and the reason for the selection for dismissal was either

(i) trade union related,
(ii) health and safety related,
(iii) related to an assertion by him of his statutory rights,
(iv) maternity related, or
(v) he was selected in contravention of a customary arrangement or agreed redundancy procedure and there were no special reasons justifying a departure from that arrangement or procedure.

Secondly, where the dismissal is not automatically unfair under the above principle, it may be still be unfair in that it does not fulfil the reasonableness tests contained in ERA, s 98(4). For example, the failure to consult may render a dismissal unfair (see 10.10.3 below).

In *Williams v Compair Maxam Ltd* [1982] ICR 156 the EAT sought to lay down certain principles on which a fair selection procedure for redundancy should be based. These principles were laid down in a case where there was a recognised trade union, but are generally accepted as good practice (although failure to follow all the steps would not necessarily render a dismissal unfair). The employer should:

(1) give as much warning as possible of impending redundancies to enable the employees concerned or the recognised trade union (if appropriate) to take early steps to inform themselves of the relevant facts, consider possible alternative solutions and, if necessary, find alternative employment;
(2) consult the recognised trade union (if appropriate) of the best means by which the desired result can be achieved fairly and with as little hardship to the employees as possible;

(3) seek to establish criteria for selection which so far as possible do not depend solely upon the opinion of the person making the selection, but can be objectively checked against such matters as attendance record, efficiency at the job, experience or length of service;
(4) ensure that the selection is made fairly in accordance with those criteria;
(5) see whether instead of dismissing an employee he can offer him alternative employment.

However, these principles should now be considered in the light of TULR(C)A, s 188, which imposes more onerous consultation duties upon an employer (see 10.10.3 below).

It is important to emphasise that the necessity for consultation before redundancy notices are sent out is extremely important. Consultation must take place with both the affected employees and also the recognised trade union (if relevant). It would be very rare for a redundancy dismissal to be held to be fair where there has been no consultation.

10.9.9 Contravention of any enactment – illegality

If an employee is dismissed by his employer because the employee could not continue to work in the position he held without breaking the law, such dismissal will be for a *prima facie* fair reason. This must be a matter of fact; it is not enough that the employer genuinely believes that he would be breaking the law by continuing to employ the employee.

The employer must still act reasonably in all the circumstances, having regard to the size and administrative resources of his organisation. An employer should arrange a meeting at which the employee should be informed of the situation and invited to express his views. In appropriate cases an employer should consider whether it or an associated company has a suitable vacancy which the employee can be offered instead.

A common example of a fair dismissal under this head would be where it is an integral part of an employee's job to drive a motor vehicle and he has been disqualified from holding a valid licence.

10.9.10 Some other substantial reason

Section 98 of ERA provides a 'catch all' potentially fair reason for dismissal which is for 'some other substantial reason of a kind such as to justify the dismissal of an employee holding the position which that employee held'. The employer is required to show only that the other substantial reason for dismissal was a potentially fair one. Once the reason has been established, the industrial tribunal must then decide whether the employer acted reasonably under s 98(4) in dismissing for that reason.

The most common example of a *prima facie* fair dismissal falling within this category is where an employer has had to undergo a necessary reorganisation of his business. This may apply in cases, for example, where as a result of the reorganisation he has had to alter his employees' terms and conditions of employment. Usually such alteration would be a fundamental breach of the contract of employment entitling the employee to resign and claim constructive dismissal. However, if the employer can show that it was *prima facie* fair because of the necessity of the business reorganisation, then the tribunal will go on to consider whether the employer had acted reasonably in accordance with all the circumstances under s 98(4).

10.9.11 Remedies

Procedure

Where an employee considers that he has been unfairly dismissed, providing that he satisfies the necessary qualifying conditions, he should present a claim for unfair dismissal to an industrial tribunal within three months of the effective date of termination. The tribunal has a discretion to allow a complaint outside the three month time limit if it considers that it was not reasonably practicable for the employee to bring the claim within the appropriate time limit.

Tribunal awards

If a tribunal considers that an employee has been unfairly dismissed, it must then decide which remedy is appropriate. There are three basic remedies available, as follows:

Reinstatement

This is an order that the employer should treat the employee in all respects as if he had not been dismissed. If the tribunal makes a reinstatement order the employee is entitled not only to be restored to his previous position with the company, but also to an amount equal to the salary he would have received had he continued to be employed, together with any benefits he would have been entitled to (eg Christmas bonus, wage increase). The tribunal in making such an order must spell out the relevant terms and conditions which apply to the employee and the date by which reinstatement is to take effect.

Re-engagement

This is an order that the employee be re-engaged by the employer (or the employer's successor or an associated employer) in employment that is comparable to that from which he was dismissed or in other suitable employment. If the tribunal makes such an order it must state the employer's identity, the nature of the employment, the rate of pay, the amount of arrears of pay which the employee is entitled to and other benefits and privileges which must be restored to the employee, and the date on which the re-engagement order is to take effect.

Reinstatement and re-engagement

In considering whether to make both orders, the tribunal must consider a number of factors including whether the employee wishes to be reinstated and whether it is practicable for an employer to comply with an order for reinstatement or re-engagement. In most instances such orders are not appropriate because the working relationship has broken down so completely that it is not practicable to expect the employer and the employee to work together again.

Additional tribunal award

If a reinstatement or re-engagement order is made by an industrial tribunal and an employer fails to comply with it this may result in the employee being given an additional award, unless the employer can show that it was not reasonably practicable for him to comply with the order. The additional award is normally between 13 and 26 weeks' pay in such cases except where the dismissal was on the grounds of sex or race, in which case the additional compensation is an amount between 26 and 52 weeks' pay. A week's pay is subject to the statutory limit of £210. The award may exceed these limits, where necessary, to enable the award to fully compensate for the loss suffered from the date the employee was dismissed to the date he should have been reinstated.

Special award

Where an employee is dismissed for a trade union related reason (see 10.9.5 above), and has applied for an order for reinstatement or re-engagement and such an order is either not made or not complied with, then the employee is entitled to a special award.

Where an order is not made, the special award will be a week's pay (subject to the statutory maximum of £210) multiplied by 104, or £13,400, whichever is greater. The figure must not exceed £26,800.

Where an order for reinstatement or re-engagement is made, but is not complied with, then unless the employer can satisfy the tribunal that it was not reasonably practicable for him to comply with the order, the special award will be one week's pay multiplied by 156 or £20,100, whichever is the greater. In this instance there is no upper limit.

Compensation

Compensation for unfair dismissal has two elements: a basic award and a compensatory award.

Basic award

The basic award is calculated in the same way as a redundancy payment and is dependent upon the employee's gross weekly pay, length of service and age at the date of termination. The amount of a week's pay is subject to a statutory maximum of £210 and the maximum number of years to be taken into account is 20.

The number of complete years of continuous employment are taken into account in calculating the basic award. Consequently, the employee receives:

(1) One and a half week's pay for each full year of employment in which the employee was not below the age of 41.
(2) One week's pay for each full year of employment in which the employee was not aged between 22–40.
(3) Half a week's pay for each year of employment not falling within (1) or (2) above.

Consequently the maximum basic award is $20 \times 1\frac{1}{2} \times 210 = £6{,}300$.

The basic award may be reduced in four circumstances:

(a) where the employee's conduct before dismissal or before being given notice of dismissal was such that it was just and equitable to reduce the award;
(b) where the employee has already received a redundancy payment in relation to the same dismissal;
(c) the employee has unreasonably refused an offer of reinstatement;
(d) the employee is aged 64 on his effective date of termination, in which case the basic award is reduced by $\frac{1}{12}$ for each whole month during which the employee has been employed since his 64th birthday.

Compensatory award

The compensatory award is intended to restore the employee to the position which he had prior to his dismissal. The amount of compensation is such sum as the tribunal considers just and equitable in all the circumstances, having regard to the loss sustained by the employee as a consequence of the dismissal that loss can be attributed to action taken by the employer.

In assessing the compensatory award the main heads of compensation (see *Norton Tool Co Ltd v Tewson* [1972] ICR 501) are:

(1) *Loss of earnings* from the date of dismissal to the date of the tribunal hearing. This figure is calculated net of tax and NI contributions, and any payment in lieu of notice that the employee received is taken into account. Also, if an employee has found a new job, his earnings in that new employment are also taken into account.
(2) *Future loss of earnings*. If an employee is still unemployed at the date of the hearing, or is earning less than he previously earned, the tribunal will award a sum for future loss of earnings for such period as it considers reasonable.
(3) *Loss of benefits in kind*. These would include such things as loss of company car, medical insurance and free or subsidised accommodation. In calculating the loss suffered by an employee as a result of losing such benefits, the correct approach in calculating the loss is the cost to the employee in replacing the lost benefits.

    In calculating the loss of benefit of using a company car, reference can be made to AA guidelines. See *Shore v Downs Surgical plc* [1984] ICR 532.
(4) *Loss of pension rights*.
(5) *Loss of statutory rights*. The tribunal awards a nominal figure for loss of the protection from unfair dismissal or the right to a redundancy payment for the first two years of any new employment. The usual figure awarded in this respect is £200.
(6) Expenses reasonably incurred as a result of the dismissal. In *Leech v Berger Jonsen and Nicholson Ltd* [1972] IRLR 58, expenses incurred in looking for new employment were a recoverable loss.

A tribunal may also award compensation for loss of the accrued right to the statutory minimum period of notice.

Reduction of the compensatory award

A tribunal may reduce the level of any compensatory award for the following reasons:

(1) *Contributory fault*. Where a tribunal finds that an employee has to any extent caused or contributed to his own dismissal by his actions it reduces the amount of the compensatory award by such proportion as it considers just and equitable (see *W Devis & Sons Ltd v Atkins* [1977] ICR 662). In rare cases the reduction may be as much as 100 per cent.
(2) *Where the employee has failed to take reasonable steps to mitigate his loss*. The employee is under a duty to mitigate his loss. He should therefore take all reasonable steps to find alternative employment. If he does not do so, this may be taken into account in reducing the compensatory award. It is important to note that an employee is not obliged to accept the first job offered irrespective of pay and conditions.

(3) *Where the tribunal considers a reduction just and equitable*. The tribunal has the power to reduce the compensatory award to reflect general considerations of fairness. The cases where tribunals may decide that it is just and equitable to reduce compensation under this head can be divided roughly into two groups:
   (a) where, by the time of the hearing, the employer can show that the employee is guilty of misconduct which would have merited dismissal, even if the employer did not know about that misconduct at the time of the dismissal; and
   (b) where the employee could have been fairly dismissed at a later date or if the employer had followed a fair pro-cedure. See *Chaplin v HJ Rawlinson Ltd* [1991] ICR 553.

The maximum compensatory award is £11,300. In calculating the compensatory award, the tribunal must first calculate what the employee's losses are and must then apply any appropriate reductions. If the figure reached is still above £11,300, then the award should be reduced to the maximum of £11,300. For example, where a tribunal considers an employee's losses to be £20,000 but that he was 20 per cent responsible for his own dismissal, the award will be reduced to £15,000. As this is above the statutory maximum the employee will only receive £11,300.

The recoupment provisions

If an employee who has brought a claim for unfair dismissal has received unemployment benefit, job seekers allowance or income support between the date of his dismissal and the industrial tribunal hearing, the employer may be ordered by the Department of Employment, in a recoupment notice, to pay part of the compensation awarded not to the employee but to the Department of Employment or DSS so that the benefit money can be recovered.

Interest on tribunal awards

Industrial tribunal compensation awards now carry interest which starts to run 42 days after the tribunal's written decision is sent to the parties.

10.9.12 Settlement

An employer may wish to settle a claim for unfair dismissal rather than proceed to a hearing. In order for any agreement that is reached with the employer to be binding it must be in one of the following forms:

(1) An agreement reached through the auspices of an ACAS conciliation officer. Once a complaint of unfair dismissal has been presented, an ACAS conciliation officer is appointed to the case to conciliate between the employer and the employee (or their representatives) to

establish whether a settlement is possible. Any agreement to settle should be recorded in writing and on a form designed for the purpose (form COT3). Once the COT3 has been signed by both parties and the settlement sum paid, an employee is then precluded from bringing any further claims to an industrial tribunal.

(2) Compromise agreement. Under ERA, s 203, an unfair dismissal claim may be settled if the conditions governing a statutory compromise agreement are fulfilled. The most important of these conditions are that the agreement must be in writing and the employee must have received independent legal advice from a qualified lawyer as to the terms and effects of the proposed agreement and, in particular, its effect on the employee's ability to pursue his rights before an industrial tribunal. If the conditions are not fully satisfied, the employee will not be precluded from bringing further claims. The following claims can also be settled by means of a compromise agreement:

- itemised pay statements
- guarantee payments
- medical suspension pay
- time off for public duties
- time off for training while under redundancy notice
- time off for ante-natal care
- written reasons for dismissal
- unlawful deduction from pay under the ERA 1996
- sex discrimination
- race discrimination
- equal pay
- rights not to suffer a detriment in health and safety cases
- rights to alternative work and pay in maternity suspension cases.

10.10 REDUNDANCY

An employee who is dismissed by his employer in certain circumstances is entitled to a redundancy payment as set out in ERA, s 139(1). To qualify for a redundancy payment an employee must satisfy certain qualifying conditions.

10.10.1 Qualifying conditions

To be entitled to a redundancy payment, a person must be:

(a) An employee Only employees are entitled to redundancy payments. The burden is upon the person applying for the payment to show

that he is an employee. He must have been continuously employed for a period of two years ending with the relevant date. The relevant date is defined in the same way as the effective date of termination for unfair dismissal purposes. However, for redundancy purposes an employee is not entitled to count any period of employment before his 18th birthday in calculating his period of continuous employment.

Also, as for unfair dismissal purposes, where an employee has been dismissed with no notice or less than the statutory minimum period of notice, the relevant date for the purpose of calculating continuous employment is extended to the date upon which the statutory minimum notice would have expired had it been given (see 10.8.2 above).

(b) Dismissed The employee must have been dismissed. The statutory definition of dismissal for redundancy payment purposes is the same as that for unfair dismissal (see 10.9.1 above). The employee must have been dismissed by reason of redundancy. Section 139(1) of ERA contains the definition of redundancy and provides that an employee who is dismissed shall be taken to have been dismissed by reason of redundancy if the dismissal is attributable wholly or mainly to:

> '(a) the fact that his employer has ceased, or intends to cease, to carry on the business for the purposes of which the employee was employed by him or has ceased or intends to cease to carry on that business in the place where the employee was so employed; or
> (b) the fact that the requirements of that business for employees to carry out work of a particular kind in the place where he was so employed have ceased or diminished or are expected to cease or diminish.'

Sub-paragraph (a) covers the situation in which the place of business where the employee could be required to work under his contract is shut. Therefore, where the contract contained a mobility clause entitling the employer to transfer an employee, it was thought that the employer could invoke the mobility clause to transfer the employee from the workplace which had closed down to one where there was work. If the employee refused, he could then be dismissed for misconduct and a redundancy payment avoided.

However, following the EAT decision in *Bass Leisure Ltd v Thomas* [1994] IRLR 104, this approach has been doubted. It was held that an employee's place of work is not wherever an employer can require him to work under his contract. A factual enquiry should be undertaken to ascertain where the employee's true place of work is and if work has ceased there, and the employee is dismissed, he is redundant and can claim a redundancy payment. The exception would be when the new location represents suitable alternative employment which the employee unreasonably refuses (see (g) below).

Sub-paragraph (b) refers to circumstances of a reduction in the business requirements for employees to carry out work of a particular kind, (ie the employer has a surplus of labour). It is important to note that there is no requirement for the work to reduce, but only a requirement that the number of employees carrying out that particular work can be reduced. This would be the case where an employer ascertains that there is over-manning.

(c) Below retirement age To claim a redundancy payment the employee must be below the age of 65 or the normal retiring age in the business in which he is employed. For employees over the age of 64 the amount of any redundancy payment payable is reduced by 1/12 for each month by which his age exceeds 64.

(d) Not ordinarily working outside Great Britain

(e) Must not have contracted out of his rights to claim a redundancy payment Where an employee is employed under a fixed term contract for a minimum of two years and he has agreed in writing to contract out of his right to a redundancy payment, then he is dismissed on the expiry of that fixed term without it being renewed, and he is not entitled to a redundancy payment.

(f) Eligible Certain employees such as civil servants and other public employees are specifically excluded from the right to a redundancy payment.

(g) Redundant without an offer of suitable alternative employment An employee who has been offered employment either on the same terms and conditions as he previously enjoyed or has been offered suitable alternative employment and he has in either case unreasonably refused the new offer of employment, loses his right to a redundancy payment. The offer of alternative employment must be made by his original employer or an associated employer before his previous employment comes to an end and must start immediately upon the ending of his previous employment or within four weeks thereof.

Where the terms and conditions of the new contract differ wholly or partly from those which the employee previously enjoyed, then he is entitled to a statutory trial period of four weeks, which can be extended by mutual agreement, in which to decide whether the alternative employment is suitable.

Where the employee accepts the offer of alternative employment there is no redundancy situation. However, he may reject the new offer of employment if it is not suitable and, provided the rejection is reasonable, he is entitled to a redundancy payment.

10.10.2 The redundancy selection process

Once an employer has decided that a redundancy situation exists he must then implement that redundancy. It is important that when implementing a redundancy an employer adopts a fair procedure. Failure to do so can result in an employee who satisfies the necessary qualifying conditions bringing a claim for unfair dismissal.

An unfair dismissal may result where an employer has selected an employee or employees for redundancy in contravention of a customary arrangement or agreed selection procedure. Where such an arrangement or procedure exists the employer must adhere to it. Furthermore, an employer must not select an employee for redundancy for an inadmissible reason such as his membership of or participation in the affairs of a trade union. In these circumstances a selection for redundancy is automatically unfair.

Where there is no customary arrangement or agreed procedure, the employer is free to use his own selection criteria, which must be reasonable and properly applied. One of the standard criteria for selection is that known as 'last in, first out', but other factors which may also be considered are the type of skills of an employee for which there is a continuing employment need and the suitability of individual employees to perform those tasks; the employee's competence, and his past conduct.

10.10.3 Consultation and notification requirements

Section 188 of TULR(C)A, as amended by TURERA 1993, imposes stringent obligations on employers to notify and consult with recognised trade unions on impending redundancies. An employer who proposes to dismiss any employees as redundant must consult at the earliest opportunity with any recognised trade union that represents any employee who falls within the class of employees to be made redundant. A recognised trade union is one that an employer recognises for the purposes of collective bargaining.

The employer must begin consultations before giving individual notices of dismissal and the consultation must continue over a sufficient period of time to allow the union representatives to consider the proposals put to them. For the purposes of the consultation the employer must disclose in writing the following information:

(1) The reasons for the proposed redundancies.
(2) The number and type of employees whom it is proposed to make redundant.
(3) The total number of such employees employed by the employer.
(4) The proposed selection criteria.

(5) The proposed method of carrying out the dismissals having particular regard to any agreed procedure.
(6) The proposed method of calculating the amount of any redundancy payment (other than the statutory entitlement).

Furthermore, where an employer is proposing to dismiss more than 100 employees at any one place of work, within a period of 90 days or less, then such consultation must begin at least 90 days before the first of those dismissals takes effect. Where more than ten employees are to be made redundant within a period of 30 days, consultation must begin at least 30 days before the first dismissal takes effect.

Following the amendments made by TURERA the consultation must include consultation about ways of avoiding the dismissals completely or reducing the number of employees to be dismissed and mitigating the consequences of any dismissal. The obligation is upon the employer to undertake consultation with a view to trying to reach agreement with the union representatives.

The protective award

Where an employer fails to comply with any of the above consultation requirements, the trade union can bring a claim to an industrial tribunal within three months of the date on which the dismissal takes effect or in such further period as the tribunal considers reasonable where it was not reasonably practicable for the complaint to be presented within the three-month period. Unless the employer can show that there were special circumstances which rendered it not reasonably practicable for him to comply with the consultation requirements, the tribunal will make a declaration that the complaint is well founded and may also make a protective award. If the tribunal decides to make a protective award it specifies a protected period during which payments should have been made to the employees who have been dismissed or whom it is proposed to dismiss. The length of the protected period is what the tribunal considers to be just and equitable in all the circumstances. The maximum protected period is 90 days where 90 days' consultation was required, 30 days where 30 days' consultation was required and up to 28 days in any other circumstance.

Even where an employer does not recognise a trade union, it is still under a duty to consult with each individual employee whom it proposes to make redundant. Consultation is one of the basic principles of fairness and the failure by an employer to warn and consult his affected employees will in most circumstances make any dismissal for redundancy unfair.

Notification to the Department of Employment

Even where no trade union is recognised, an employer must also notify the Department of Employment of its intention to effect redundancies within the same limits as those required for consultation with recognised trade unions.

10.10.4 Redundancy checklist

The following is a checklist that an employer should consider before implementing any redundancies:

(1) Once the decision to make redundancies has been made the employer should first consult with any recognised trade union representatives, bearing in mind the appropriate time limits, and should provide them with all the appropriate information. Where there is no recognised trade union, the employer should consult with the individual employees.
(2) He should notify the Department of Employment where appropriate, again bearing in mind the appropriate time limit.
(3) Having decided on the numbers to be made redundant he should invite volunteers for redundancy.
(4) He should then establish the selection criteria with the agreement (if possible) of the recognised union. He should consider whether the numbers of employees to be made redundant can be reduced and should also consider whether there is any suitable alternative employment within the company or associated company for the affected employees.
(5) He should consult with the individual affected employees.
(6) He should then send out the notices of dismissal informing the employees of their impending redundancies. He should allow the affected employees time off to look for other employment.

10.10.5 Claim for a redundancy payment

The claim for a redundancy payment must be made within six months of the relevant date by either submitting a claim in writing to the employer claiming a redundancy payment, or by bringing a claim for a redundancy payment to the industrial tribunal, or by submitting an unfair dismissal complaint. If a claim is not brought within six months the tribunal has a limited discretion to allow a claim to be brought within a further six months.

10.10.6 Calculation of the redundancy payment

The redundancy payment is calculated along similar lines to that of the basic award for unfair dismissal purposes. It is therefore calculated by multiplying one week's gross pay (subject to the statutory maximum of £210) by a factor depending upon the employee's age and the number of completed years of service (subject to the statutory maximum of 20 years). Therefore:

(1) for every year during the whole of which the employee is aged 41 or over – a multiplier of one and a half;
(2) for every year during the whole of which the employee is aged between 22 and 40 – a multiplier of one;
(3) for every year during the whole of which the employee is aged between 18 and 21 – a multiplier of one half.

The employer should give the employee a statement showing how the redundancy payment has been calculated.

Finally, it should be remembered that in addition to any statutory redundancy payment, an employee may be entitled to a contractual redundancy payment under his contract of employment and will also be entitled to work out his notice period or be paid in lieu of notice.

10.11 TERMINATION OF EMPLOYMENT

There are two kinds of claim potentially available to an employee on termination of his contract of employment:

(1) unfair dismissal;
(2) a redundancy payment; and
(3) a claim for damages for wrongful dismissal derived from the common law relating to contract.

10.11.1 Lawful methods of termination

A claim for wrongful dismissal arises where an employer has terminated an employee's employment in breach of the employee's contract. However, a claim for wrongful dismissal does not arise where the contract is terminated in accordance with one of five common law methods:

By agreement

An employer and employee may agree to terminate the contract of employment and thereby release each other from their obligations.

However, any agreement is void if it purports to exclude the rights conferred on all employees by employment protection legislation (eg unfair dismissal/redundancy).

By effluxion of time

A fixed term contract or a contract to perform a specified task automatically terminates at the end of the term or when the task is completed.

By notice

A contract of employment usually contains an express term setting out the notice period. Where, however, the contract fails to specify a notice period then the contract is deemed to be terminable by either party giving reasonable notice. What amounts to reasonable notice depends on the particular circumstances of the employment concerned. Such factors which are taken into account in deciding what is a reasonable notice period are: the type of job; the employee's status; the period by which the employee's pay is calculated; and any custom or practice which is established in the industry or profession.

Whatever period of notice is specified it must not be less than the statutory minimum period of notice laid down by ERA, s 86. This states that where an employee is continuously employed for at least one month but less than two years he is entitled to one week's notice. Thereafter he is entitled to one week's notice for each complete year of employment up to a maximum of 12 weeks' notice, after 12 years' employment.

Following repudiatory breach

Following a repudiatory breach of the employment contract an employee can be dismissed immediately without notice. This is known as summary dismissal. Typical examples of conduct which may entitle an employer to dismiss summarily include theft by an employee of his employer's property and gross insubordination.

Frustration

A contract is frustrated where its performance becomes impossible or substantially different from that which the parties envisaged at the time of entering into the agreement by reason of an unforeseen event which has occurred and which is not the fault of either party. Where the contract is held to be frustrated, there is no dismissal and therefore there can be no claim for wrongful dismissal, unfair dismissal or a redundancy payment. The question of whether a contract has been frustrated most frequently occurs in the cases of illness and imprisonment, although it must be said that the doctrine of frustration is not frequently applied in illness cases.

10.11.2 Written reasons for dismissal

Under ERA, s 92 an employee is entitled to be provided by his employer, within 14 days of his request, with written reasons for his dismissal. The statement giving the written reasons is admissible in evidence at any proceedings and it is therefore important that the statement is consistent with the employer's case before an industrial tribunal. An employee must have two years' continuous employment to be entitled to written reasons for dismissal.

Where a request for written reasons for dismissal has been made by an employee and the employer has failed to comply, an employee can bring a claim to an industrial tribunal on the grounds that his employer has unreasonably failed to provide written reasons for his dismissal or that the reasons given are inadequate or untrue. The claim must be brought within three months from the effective date of termination of the employment. This period can be extended if the tribunal is satisfied that it was not reasonably practicable to bring the claim within that period.

If the tribunal finds the claim well founded it may make a declaration as to what it believes the employer's reasons were for dismissing the employee, and will award a sum equal to the amount of two weeks' pay (not subject to the statutory maximum of £210 per week).

10.11.3 Wrongful dismissal

Where an employer dismisses an employee in breach of his contractual or statutory obligations to give that employee notice or any other contractual obligation, it may become liable to pay the employee damages for breach of contract. Examples of actions by an employer which can lead to a claim for damages for wrongful dismissal are as follows:

(1) Where an employer terminates an employee's contract without proper notice, either contractual or statutory.
(2) Where an employer terminates a fixed term contract before the expiry of the term. However, it is usual to make provision in a fixed term contract for earlier termination by including a provision that the contract may be terminated by either side giving a specified period of notice.
(3) A claim for wrongful dismissal can arise when an employer is found to have repudiated the contract in breach of one of the fundamental contractual obligations. Repudiation occurs where an employer, by his conduct, displays an intention not to be bound by the contract. For example, where an employer insists on imposing new terms and conditions on an employee without that employee's consent, this can amount to a breach of a fundamental term of the contract

entitling the employee to treat the contract as discharged and then sue his employer for wrongful dismissal for breach of contract.

(4) Disciplinary procedures may form part of a contract of employment. If an employer dismisses an employee without following contractual disciplinary procedures this may amount to a serious breach of contract (*Boyo v Lambeth LBC* [1994] ICR 727, CA).

10.11.4 Damages for wrongful dismissal

Once an employee has established that he has been dismissed in breach of contract or without being given the proper statutory minimum period of notice, he must then show that he has suffered loss as a result of the breach by the employer.

The employee's remedy for his employer's breach of contract is damages, the aim of which is to place the employee in the same situation he would have been in if the contract had been properly performed. The amount of damages that an employee receives is based upon the amount of pay and other fringe benefits (such as company car, pension and medical insurance) that he would have been entitled to had the employer complied with his contractual and statutory obligations. Therefore, the courts cannot award compensation beyond the time when the contract could have been brought to an end by the employer in accordance with its terms. For example, in the case of a fixed term contract where the fixed term is for a period of five years and the contract is brought to an end after three years, the employee is entitled to compensation for pay and fringe benefits for the unexpired two-year term.

As stated, an award of damages is based upon contractual entitlements. Therefore benefits that are merely discretionary should be excluded from a damages calculation (*Lavarack v Woods of Colchester Ltd* [1967] 1 QB 278).

Where an employer has dismissed an employee in breach of the disciplinary procedures laid down in the contract of employment, the level of damages are based on the length of time it would have taken for the employment to be terminated lawfully by the employer if he had followed the correct disciplinary procedures.

10.11.5 Mitigation

An employee must take all reasonable steps to mitigate his loss by seeking other employment. If he fails to take such steps his level of damages may be reduced accordingly. If the employee finds alternative employment then such payments that he receives are taken into account in reducing the level of any compensation that he may be entitled to. Furthermore, statutory benefits received are taken into account in assessing damages.

10.11.6 Accelerated receipt

A further deduction in the level of compensation may be made under this heading. This is particularly relevant where an employee on a long fixed term contract is wrongfully dismissed after the contract has run only a short period of time. For example, where an employee is employed under a five-year fixed term contract and is dismissed after only one year then he is entitled to receive his pay for the further four remaining years. However, by awarding such a large lump sum which could be invested to produce an income, the employee is actually better off than he would have been if the contract had been properly performed. Therefore, as the courts do not allow an employee to make a profit, a deduction is made to account for the employee receiving the money in advance, and having the opportunity to benefit by investment.

10.11.7 Interest

Interest may be awarded on the damages from the date when the cause of action arose to the date of judgment, or in the case of payment made before that date, the date of payment.

10.11.8 Payment in lieu of notice

An employer who intends to dismiss an employee may in certain circumstances consider it desirable that the employee should not work out his notice period. The employer pays that employee in lieu of notice instead.

There has been considerable case law over recent years concerning whether a payment in lieu of notice is taxable. Where the contract of employment expressly provides that an employer may pay an employee in lieu of notice then such a right constitutes an 'emolument' of the employment and therefore is subject to deduction for tax and national insurance in the normal way.

However, where there is no express contractual provision for payment in lieu of notice, then it can be said that a payment in lieu of notice is compensation for loss of office and therefore as not paid in connection with the contract of employment, it is not subject to tax and national insurance and can be paid gross.

If a non-contractual payment in lieu of notice is held to be compensation, it is tax free. However, it may in any event be subject to tax under the rules regarding payments on loss of office (commonly known as 'golden handshakes'). These rules provide that where the total amount paid to an employee on the termination of his employment (including any redundancy payment) exceeds £30,000, then the balance above £30,000 is taxable.

Should an employer include an express right to pay in lieu of notice in an employee's contract?

Where there is an express right to pay in lieu of notice, then any such payment will be fully taxable. Furthermore, where there is an express payment in lieu clause, and an employer dismisses an employee by making a payment in lieu, it was held in *Abrahams v Performing Right Society* (1995) *The Independent*, 25 May that the employee is not under a duty to mitigate his loss (see 10.11.5 above). The employee is therefore entitled to be paid for the whole of his notice period. This is because a payment in lieu is not treated as a claim for damages (as the employer has the express right to lawfully terminate by making a payment in lieu), but is rather a debt due under the contract. Therefore, where the employee is under a long notice period or on a fixed term contract where there is a lengthy period of the contract still unexpired, the amount due may be substantial, where there is no duty on the employee to mitigate.

However, an express payment in lieu clause is extremely important where an employee is subject to restrictive covenants. Where an employer dismisses an employee by making a payment in lieu, he is in breach of contract unless the contract expressly allows termination with a payment in lieu. If not, the breach by the employer prohibits him from enforcing clauses in the contract intended to survive termination, such as restrictive covenants (see *General Billposting Co Ltd v Atkinson* [1909] AC 118.

10.11.9 Wrongful dismissal claims – procedure

Until 11 July 1994, all actions for wrongful dismissal had to be brought in the county court or High Court. The time limit for such actions was the normal limitation period of six years from the date of the breach of contract.

Since 11 July 1994 an alternative procedure is now available via the industrial tribunals. The tribunals have a limited jurisdiction to hear breach of contract claims, but the maximum that a tribunal can award in respect any one claim or any number of claims relating to the same contract is £25,000.

A breach of contract claim is brought by presenting an Originating Application to an industrial tribunal within three months of the effective date of termination of the contract.

There is therefore now a dual procedure available to employees in bringing breach of contract claims. It may be that employees will still bring breach of contract claims in the county court as they will be entitled to their costs from the employer should they be successful, whereas they will not if the claim is in an Industrial Tribunal.

10.12 MATERNITY RIGHTS

This is an extremely complex area of the law and it is possible to give here only an outline of the rights protecting pregnant employees. Not only is the law relating to statutory maternity leave and maternity pay relevant, but also the law relating to sex discrimination and equal pay. Furthermore, individual employees' own terms and conditions of employment may be more favourable than the statutory minimum protection. All references in this section are to EP(C)A as amended by TURERA.

10.12.1 Time off for ante-natal care

An employee who is pregnant and who, on the advice of a registered medical practitioner, registered midwife or registered health visitor, has made an appointment to attend at any place for the purpose of receiving ante-natal care, has the right not to be unreasonably refused time off during her working hours to enable her to keep the appointment. The employee also has the right to be paid for that period of absence at the appropriate hourly rate. There is no minimum qualifying period for employees to attain this right.

An example where an employer can reasonably refuse to allow an employee time off to attend an ante-natal class could be in respect of a part-time employee who could be expected to attend when not at work. Where an employer has unreasonably refused an employee time off for ante-natal care or where he has failed to pay the employee the amount due to her while attending the ante-natal appointment, the employee may present a complaint to an industrial tribunal. If the complaint is well founded the tribunal will make a declaration to that effect and can order the employer to pay to the employee the amount of money which would have been due under the statutory provisions.

10.12.2 Maternity leave

As a result of the 'Pregnant Workers' Directive, new rules were introduced by TURERA so that since 16 October 1994 all women expecting a baby have the right to 14 weeks' statutory maternity leave. This right applies to all women irrespective of their length of service or the number of hours they work each week. Furthermore, employees who have more than two years' continuous employment can delay their return to work for up to 29 weeks after the beginning of the week in which their baby was born.

During the 14-week maternity leave period all employment rights other than 'remuneration' must be preserved. There is no statutory definition of remuneration and its scope is uncertain, but it is obvious that it covers the normal wage, commission and bonus payments, if these are contractual.

To identify the maternity leave period the employer must have regard to two sets of rules governing both its start date and when it ends. The commencement of the maternity leave period is usually within the particular woman's control as it is the date on which she notifies her employer as the date she wishes her maternity leave to begin. This date must not be before the eleventh week before the expected week of childbirth (EWC). A woman is not, however, free to choose the start date of her maternity leave where she is absent from work wholly or partly because of pregnancy or childbirth after the beginning of the sixth week before the EWC. In this instance the maternity leave period is triggered on the first day of absence.

10.12.3 Notice requirements

To preserve her right to continue to enjoy the benefit of her usual terms and conditions of employment, apart from remuneration, a woman must comply with certain notice requirements. She must notify her employer of the date on which she intends her maternity leave to begin, at least 21 days before that date, or if that is not reasonably practicable, as soon as is practicable. Where the first day of absence wholly or partly because of pregnancy or childbirth occurs, either before the notified leave date or before the woman has had the opportunity to inform her employer of such a date, and the maternity leave period is triggered by a pregnancy related absence in the six weeks before the EWC, the employee must notify her employer as soon as is reasonably practicable that she is absent for a pregnancy related reason.

Where the maternity leave period is triggered by the baby's birth, either before the notified leave date or before a leave date has been notified, again as soon as is reasonably practicable the woman must notify her employer that she has given birth. Furthermore, a woman must inform her employer at least 21 days before the beginning of her maternity leave period, or if that is not reasonably practicable as soon as is practicable, that she is pregnant and of the EWC, or of the date of birth if that has already occurred. Also, if requested by her employer, she must produce for inspection a certificate from either a registered medical practitioner or registered midwife, stating the EWC.

Women who satisfy the appropriate qualifying condition of two years' continuous employment at the beginning of the eleventh week before the EWC are entitled to delay their return to work for up to 29 weeks, beginning with the week of the baby's birth. The right to this extended maternity leave is only available provided the notice requirements detailed above are complied with. During this extended maternity leave period, an employee's rights are governed by the terms of her individual contract of employment.

10.12.4 The right to return to work

Employees with less than two years' service

All employees who fall within this category can return to their original job on exactly the same terms and conditions as before they commenced their maternity leave at the end of their 14-week maternity leave period. They are under no obligation to give their employer notice of their return to work, unless they intend to exercise this right before the end of their maternity leave period in which instance at least seven days' notice is required.

Employees with more than two years' service

Employees in this category have the right to return to their original job or to work of the same nature on terms and conditions that are no less favourable than those which were applied to them prior to their maternity leave. An employee who intends to return to work at the end of her extended maternity leave period of 29 weeks after the week of the baby's birth must give her employer 21 days' notice of her intention to return. Her notified date of return can be postponed by the employer for up to four weeks after the notified return date for any reason whilst an employee may postpone her return if she is unfit to work for up to four weeks beyond the extended maternity leave absence of 29 weeks.

10.12.5 Statutory maternity pay (SMP)

Most women are entitled to SMP during their maternity leave. This benefit is administered and paid directly to eligible employees by their employers. The following is a brief summary of the complex SMP provisions; for greater detail reference should be made to the appropriate DSS leaflet NI257, *Employers Guide to Statutory Maternity Pay*.

Eligibility

To be eligible for SMP an employee must:

(1) be pregnant and have ceased work wholly or partly because of pregnancy or childbirth;
(2) must have 26 weeks' continuous employment ending with the fifteenth week before the EWC;
(3) must have reached or given birth before reaching the eleventh week before the EWC;
(4) must have normal weekly earnings of at least £57 per week in the eight weeks ending with the fifteenth week before the EWC.

Period and rate of payment

SMP is payable for 18 weeks. Therefore if a woman returns to work at the end of her 14-week statutory maternity leave period, no further SMP is payable.

The maternity pay period starts no earlier than 11 weeks before the EWC, or if a woman works beyond this then the week following the week in which she stops work. Where, however, a woman is absent from work wholly or partly because of pregnancy or confinement in the six weeks before her EWC then the maternity pay period commences in the week on which that day falls.

For the first six weeks of the maternity pay period, SMP is payable at 90 per cent of the employee's normal weekly earnings or £52.50, whichever is higher. Thereafter, SMP is payable at the rate of £52.50.

Recovery of SMP by the employer

An employer can recover up to 92 per cent of SMP paid by making appropriate equivalent deductions from its NI contributions. Where, however, an employer's total NI contribution bill is £20,000 per annum or less SMP is reimbursed at the rate of 104 per cent.

10.12.6 Maternity allowance

Where an employee is not eligible for SMP, she may be entitled to maternity allowance if she has worked and paid NI contributions for 26 weeks in a 66-week period before the week in which her baby is due. The rate of maternity allowance is currently £52.50 for women who are in work in the fifteenth week before their EWC, or otherwise at the rate of £44.55.

10.12.7 Protection from dismissal on the grounds of pregnancy or maternity related reasons

Under ERA, s 99, it is automatically unfair for an employer to dismiss any woman, irrespective of her hours of work or length of service, if the sole or principal reason for her dismissal is one of the following:

(1) That she is pregnant or is dismissed for any other reason connected with her pregnancy.
(2) She is dismissed at any time during her 14-week maternity leave period and the sole or principal reason for that dismissal is that she has given birth or is for any other reason connected with her having given birth.
(3) She is dismissed at the end of her maternity leave period and the sole or principal reason for her dismissal is that she was away from work during her maternity leave period, or that she had the benefit of her usual terms and conditions (excluding remuneration) during her maternity leave period.
(4) She is dismissed because she has given birth or for any other reason connected with her having given birth within four weeks of the end of her maternity leave period. The woman must submit a medical certificate during her maternity leave period which states that she will be incapable of work at the end of her maternity leave period by reason of ill health. Also at the date of the dismissal the incapability must continue and the certificate must remain current.
(5) The sole or principal reason for her dismissal is a requirement or recommendation to suspend her on health and safety grounds.
(6) She is made redundant during her maternity leave period and is not offered a suitable alternative available vacancy.

The new s 60 gives women greatly increased rights for protection from dismissal on the grounds of pregnancy or for a reason related to pregnancy. A claim under s 60 must be brought within three months of the dismissal or such other period as the tribunal considers reasonable if it was not reasonably practicable to bring the claim within three months.

10.12.8 The right to return to work and dismissal

If at the end of a woman's extended maternity leave (ie up to 29 weeks after the week of the birth) an employer refuses to allow the woman to return to work there will be a deemed dismissal under ERA, s 96 on the date that she had notified her employer that she wished to return to work. The employer then has to establish that the reason why the woman was not permitted to return fell within one of the *prima facie* fair reasons for dismissal contained in ERA, s 98. If the tribunal considers that the dismissal was for one of the maternity related reasons set out in ERA, s 96 the dismissal is automatically unfair.

There are two situations in which a woman will in any event lose her right to return to work after extended maternity absence. These are:

(1) If her employer can show that it has fewer than six employees and it was not reasonably practicable for it to allow the woman back or to offer her suitable and appropriate alternative work.
(2) If the employer can show that it was not reasonably practicable for a reason other than redundancy to give her her old job back, and he offered her suitable and appropriate alternative work which she has either accepted or unreasonably refused.

It should be noted that the onus lies on the employer to show that there was no suitable and appropriate alternative work.

10.12.9 Redundancy and maternity dismissal protection

Where a redundancy situation arises during a woman's maternity leave, the employer is entitled to make that woman redundant provided that the reason for her redundancy is not a maternity related one. However, the employer is under a duty to offer the woman any suitable and appropriate alternative work which is available, failing which the redundancy related dismissal is automatically unfair. Again, the obligation is on the employer to show that there was no suitable and appropriate alternative work. Where this is the case, the woman is nevertheless entitled to a redundancy payment, providing of course she has the necessary two years' continuous employment.

Also, even if the woman does not have the right to claim that the redundancy was for a s 60 reason and therefore automatically unfair, if she has the two years' continuous employment she may nevertheless bring an 'ordinary' unfair dismissal complaint on the grounds that her selection for redundancy was unfair.

10.12.10 Written reasons for dismissal

Where a woman is dismissed while she is pregnant or where the dismissal ends her maternity leave period, she is automatically entitled to written reasons for her dismissal, irrespective of her hours of work or length of service.

10.12.11 Maternity protection and health and safety

Employers are under a general duty to take reasonable care for the health and safety of their employees. These duties are laid down both in common law and in statute; for a fuller discussion on an employer's health and safety obligations in general see Chapter 13. Employers should also make reference to guidelines issued by the HSE.

Under ERA, s 99 it is automatically unfair for an employee to be dismissed if the reason for doing so was a requirement or recommendation to suspend that employee on health and safety grounds, irrespective of the employee's hours or length of service. As a result of the implementation of the Pregnant Workers Directive by the Management of Health & Safety at Work (Amendment) Regulations 1994, further stringent obligations are laid upon employers in relation to the health and safety of new or expectant mothers in their employment.

Under these amended regulations an employer, whose workforce includes women of child-bearing age, is under an obligation to carry out risk assessments in relation to that risk group. Where any risks are identified, an employer must take preventative or protective measures to avoid those risks. If these measures will not be effective in avoiding such risks, then the employer must alter the woman's working conditions or hours of work. Furthermore, if this alteration is not reasonable or still does not avoid the risks, then the employer must offer the woman any suitable alternative work which is available. If no alternative work is available, the woman must be suspended from work on full pay.

Where there is suitable alternative work available, and the employer fails to offer it to the affected employee, she has the right to bring a complaint to an industrial tribunal. Such a claim must be brought within three months beginning with the first day of the suspension or if this was not reasonably practicable within such time as the tribunal considers reasonably practicable. Where the complaint is upheld the tribunal can award such compensation as it considers just and equitable.

Where a woman is suspended on the grounds that there is no suitable alternative work and the employer fails to pay her her full remuneration during the suspension period, again she can bring a complaint to an industrial tribunal within three months, or such further period as the tribunal considers is reasonably practicable.

If a pregnant woman works nights and it is necessary for her to be moved off night work for health and safety reasons, the employer must ensure that this is done.

There are further specific regulations which place obligations upon employers in relation to pregnant workers. Employers are advised to contact their local Health & Safety Office for advice if they have any queries as to their obligations in this respect.

10.12.12 Maternity rights and inter-relationship with sex discrimination law

Although the dismissal of a woman for pregnancy or for a pregnancy related reason is automatically unfair under ERA, s 99, a woman may also be able to obtain a remedy under the Sex Discrimination Act where she is either refused employment or treated unfavourably as a result of her pregnancy. As there is no statutory cap on the amount of compensation for sex discrimination – from a compensation point of view it may well be desirable to bring a claim under the Sex Discrimination Act rather than under s 99 where the statutory limit on unfair dismissal compensation of £11,300 applies.

Until recently, it was established law that where a pregnant employee was treated unfavourably, she had to show that she was treated less favourably for a reason connected with her pregnancy than a man would have been treated in such circumstances if he had been ill. However, in *Webb v EMO Air Cargo (UK) Ltd* [1994] IRLR 482, the ECJ ruled that it was contrary to the Equal Treatment Directive to compare a woman who was unavailable for work due to pregnancy to a man who would be unavailable for work for medical or other reasons. If the woman is treated unfavourably because she is pregnant this amounts to direct sex discrimination under EC law irrespective of how a man was or would have been treated had his employment had similar consequences (eg he had been absent from work on sickness grounds for a similar period to a woman's absence for a pregnancy related reason).

The case has now been returned to the House of Lords for the court to decide whether the Sex Discrimination Act can be construed in accordance with EC law as interpreted by the ECJ. The law relating to maternity rights in general and its inter-relationship with the law of sex discrimination is complex. Legal advice should be sought by employers when dealing with maternity related issues.

10.13 STATUTORY SICK PAY (SSP)

Where an employee is absent from work due to sickness he may be entitled to:

(1) contractual sick pay as set out in his written statement of terms and conditions of employment;
(2) SSP.

There are numerous regulations governing this complex area, but the main provisions are contained in the Social Security Contributions and Benefits Act 1992.

10.13.1 Qualifications for SSP

The main requirements for an employee to be entitled to SSP are that he must:

(1) have four or more consecutive qualifying days of sickness;
(2) notify his absence to his employer;
(3) supply evidence of his incapacity for work. This is usually agreed between the employer and employee and normally involves a self-certification by the employee for periods of absence of four to seven days and thereafter a doctor's certificate.

There are a number of employees who are excluded from the right to SSP and these include those employees who have been taken on for a specified period of three months or less; an employee who is pregnant and who is off sick during the maternity pay period; an employee who already has been paid 28 weeks' SSP during a three-year period of entitlement, and an employee who is over state pension age on the first day of sickness.

10.13.2 The period of payment

As mentioned above an employee is only entitled to SSP once he has been absent for four or more qualifying days. This period is known as a period of incapacity for work. SSP is therefore payable on the fourth qualifying day and thereafter until either the employee has reached his full entitlement of 28 weeks' SSP or returns to work. An employer's liability to pay SSP ends once the employee has received 28 weeks' SSP during a three-year period.

Once the employee's entitlement to SSP has terminated, if the employee is still sick, he will then be entitled to state benefits.

10.13.3 The amount payable

Employees who earn less than the lower weekly earnings limit for NI liability (£62) are not entitled to SSP. There is one rate of SSP – £55.70 – payable to all qualifying employees.

An employer is entitled to recover any amount by which the payments of SSP made by him in any month exceed 13 per cent of the amount of the employer's liabilities for NI contributions payments in respect of that month.

Where an employee also has a contractual right to sick pay, an employer is well advised to include within an employee's written statement of terms and conditions that he is only entitled to contractual sick pay as is appropriate to top up wages to the normal level of remuneration after payment of SSP or any sickness benefit received afterwards.

An employer is obliged to keep minimum information on record for SSP purposes for at least three years. Furthermore, when an employee leaves in certain circumstances an employer is under a duty to issue the employee with a 'leaver's statement'.

The statutory sick pay rules and regulations are extremely complex and failure to comply with them can amount to a criminal offence. This section is only a summary of some of the more important rules relating to SSP. When dealing with these complicated issues employers should refer to DSS booklets on SSP and seek legal advice.

10.14 FURTHER STATUTORY PAYMENTS TO EMPLOYEES

10.14.1 Medical suspension payment

Where an employee is suspended from work on medical grounds in compliance with any law or regulation concerning workers' health and safety, that employee may be entitled to be paid by his employer during each week of the period of suspension for a maximum of 26 weeks. To claim such a payment the employee must have been continuously employed for a period of one month ending with the day before that on which the suspension begins.

It should be noted that an employee who is employed either:

(1) under a contract for a fixed term of three months or less, or
(2) under a contract made in contemplation of the performance of a specific task which is not expected to last for more than three months,

is not entitled to a medical suspension payment unless he has been continuously employed for a period of more than three months ending with the day before the day on which the suspension begins. An employee is not entitled to such a payment where either he is absent from work because of illness during the period where such a payment would be due or is offered suitable alternative work which he unreasonably refused to perform.

If an employer fails to pay a medical suspension payment where due, an employee can bring a claim to an industrial tribunal within three months of the date on which the claim for a payment was made, or within such further reasonable period, if the tribunal considers it not reasonably practicable to bring the claim within the three-month time limit. If the complaint is well founded, the tribunal will make an order for the employer to pay the employee the amount considered to be due.

10.14.2 Guarantee payments

Where an employee, on any day which in accordance with his contract of employment he is normally required to work, is not provided with work by his employer by reason of either:

(1) a diminution in the requirements of the employer's business for work of the kind which the employee is employed to do, or
(2) any other occurrence affecting the normal working of the employer's business in relation to work of the kind which the employee is employed to do,

that employee may, subject to certain exceptions, be entitled to a guarantee payment. The qualifying conditions are the same as those for a medical suspension payment. An employee is not entitled to a guarantee payment where the employer's failure to provide work is as a result of a strike, lock-out or other industrial action, not necessarily involving the employee concerned.

An employee is not entitled to a guarantee payment for a workless day if his employer has offered to provide alternative work for that day which is suitable in all the circumstances and the employee has unreasonably refused the offer or he does not comply with reasonable requirements imposed by his employer with a view to ensuring that his services are available.

Amount of payment

There are detailed rules governing the calculation of guarantee payments. However, at present the maximum amount of any guarantee payment is £14.10 per day and such payment cannot exceed five days in any period of three months.

Where an employer fails to make payment to an employee, that employee may present a claim to an industrial tribunal. The time limit for presenting the claim is the same as for a medical suspension payment. If the tribunal finds the complaint well founded, it will order the employer to pay the amount of the guarantee payment to the employee that is found to be due.

10.15 ITEMISED PAY STATEMENTS

An employee is, subject to certain statutory exceptions, entitled to a written pay statement from his employer detailing:

(1) the gross amount of salary;
(2) the amount of any variable or fixed deductions from that amount and the reasons for which they are made; this can however be done under a separate statement of fixed deductions;
(3) the net amount of wages;
(4) where parts of the net amount are paid in different ways, the amount and method of each part payment.

If an employer does not provide an employee with a pay statement, the employee can apply to an industrial tribunal and the tribunal can make a declaration concerning the particulars to be included in any statement. Furthermore, where the tribunal finds that any unnotified deductions have been made from the employee's pay, during the period of 13 weeks immediately preceding the date of the application made by the employee, the tribunal may award a sum not exceeding the amount of the unnotified deductions during that period.

An application can be brought at any time whilst employment continues or within three months after the termination of employment. The tribunal does not have the power to extend the time limit in any circumstances.

10.16 WAGES: PAYMENT AND DEDUCTIONS

The payment of wages is governed by an individual's contract of employment. If there is no express term governing how wages are to be paid, then payment is determined by an implied term and such implied term is likely to be that which is customary for the payment of wages in a particular industry.

10.16.1 Deduction from wages

Under the ERA, s 13 an employer is not entitled to deduct sums from an employee's wages unless either:

(1) such deduction is required or permitted by a statutory or contractual provision; or
(2) the worker has given his prior written consent to the deduction.

Therefore, if in certain circumstances an employer wishes to make deductions from an employee's wages, the right for him to do so should, for the sake of clarity, be in writing and contained within the contract, a copy of which should be given to the employee.

It is important to note that the provisions of the ERA 1996 apply not only to employees, but also to persons working under a contract for services. The following deductions are excluded from the operation of the provisions:

(1) deductions made to reimburse an employer for any overpayment of wages or expenses;
(2) deductions made pursuant to any statutory disciplinary proceedings;
(3) statutory payments due to a public authority;
(4) sums payable to third parties, made either pursuant to a contractual term to which the worker has agreed in writing or to which he has otherwise given his previous written agreement or consent (the most common example of this would be trade union dues);
(5) deductions made as a result of participation in a strike or other industrial action;
(6) deductions made for the purpose of satisfying a court or tribunal order for the payment of an amount by a worker to his employer; this requires the worker's prior written agreement or consent.

The definition of wages for ERA purposes includes all sums payable to a worker in connection with his employment including any fees, bonuses, commission and holiday pay or other emoluments referable to his employment.

There are however a number of payments that are specifically excluded from the wages definition and these include advances under loan agreements or by way of an advance of wages; payments for expenses incurred in carrying out employment; payments by way of pension, allowance or gratuity in connection with the worker's retirement or as compensation for loss of office; any payment in relation to the worker's redundancy; or any payment otherwise than in the worker's capacity as a worker.

10.16.2 Retail workers

Special rules regarding wage deductions apply to retail workers. The employer of such a worker cannot deduct wages for cash shortages or stock deficiencies that amount to more than one-tenth of the worker's gross wages payable on a particular pay day. An employer must make any deduction below that limit not more than 12 months after the date on which he discovered the shortage or deficiency or ought reasonably to have discovered it.

The employer of a retail worker cannot receive any payment from the worker on account of a cash shortage or stock deficiency unless he has:

(1) notified the worker in writing of his total liability in respect of that shortage or deficiency, and
(2) made a demand for payment which is both in writing and on a pay day.

The demand must be made not earlier than the first pay day after the date of the written notification and not later than 12 months after the date when the employer discovered the shortage or deficiency or ought reasonably to have done so. As stated above, the amount demanded must not exceed one-tenth of the worker's gross wages payable on the particular pay day.

The restriction of deductions to one-tenth of gross wages does not apply to deductions from a final wages payment.

10.16.3 Worker's remedy for unlawful deduction

The worker's remedy is by way of complaint to an industrial tribunal. The complaint must be brought within three months of the date of the deduction, or within such further period if it was not reasonably practicable for the complaint to be brought within the time limit. If the tribunal finds that the complaint is well founded, a declaration is made to that effect and the employer is ordered to repay to the worker the amount of the deduction.

It is important for employers to note that where sums have been wrongfully deducted and they have been ordered by a tribunal to repay such sums to an employee, the employer cannot at a later stage seek to recover those same sums by lawful means, even if the sums were properly owing to the employer. It is therefore important for employers to ensure that they deduct money correctly on the first occasion to ensure that any sums owing to them will be recovered.

10.17 SEX AND RACE DISCRIMINATION

Discrimination on the grounds of sex or marital status is made unlawful by the Sex Discrimination Act 1975; discrimination on racial grounds is unlawful under the Race Relations Act 1976. Both Acts make discrimination unlawful in every stage of employment, from recruitment to dismissal. Furthermore, the Acts apply to self-employed workers as well as employees. (Disability discrimination is dealt with at 10.18 below.)

10.17.1 Recruitment

Discrimination can occur in recruitment in a number of ways – either in the arrangements that an employer makes for determining who should be offered employment (ie job specifications), or in the terms on which an employer offers employment, or by the employer directly refusing or omitting to offer employment. For example, a question at interview to a female employee as to whether she has any plans to start a family could amount to sex discrimination.

It is important for employers to ensure that any of their staff who are involved in conducting job interviews should be aware of the potential pitfalls. The Equal Opportunities Commission has issued a Code of Practice for the elimination of discrimination on the grounds of sex and marriage through the promotion of equality of opportunity in employment. In recruitment situations, it suggests that the following considerations should be borne in mind:

(1) Applications from both men and women should be processed in the same way.
(2) There should not be separate lists of male and female applicants, or those that are married and those that are single.
(3) Any questions asked at interview should relate to the requirements of the job.
(4) Questions about plans for marriage or family intentions are liable to be interpreted as discriminatory.
(5) There should be proper training of staff involved in conducting interviews so that potential discriminatory questions can be avoided.
(6) Records should be kept showing the reasons why particular applicants were or were not appointed. Such records could prove to be important evidence if queries ever arose.

Once employment has commenced, discrimination can occur in a number of ways, either in the terms of the employment afforded to an employee or the denial or limited provision afforded to an employee regarding access to promotional opportunities, training facilities or any other benefits or by subjecting a person to any detriment, or by dismissing them.

10.17.2 Types of discrimination

Discrimination can occur in three ways: directly, indirectly, or by victimisation.

In ascertaining whether there has been discrimination, the position of the person alleging discrimination is compared with someone of similar ability and qualifications in a similar situation. In all circumstances 'like will be compared with like'.

10.17.3 Direct discrimination

Direct discrimination occurs where a person is treated less favourably than another on the grounds of sex, marital status or racial grounds. It is important to note that the employer's intentions are irrelevant. Therefore, even if the employer feels that he is acting in the best interests of the person concerned, if that person is treated less favourably by the employer, then there is direct discrimination. The test is simply one of whether the treatment was less favourable. In *R v Birmingham City Council ex parte EOC* [1989] IRLR 173, HL denying girls the same number of places in selective secondary education as boys amounted to direct discrimination. It was not necessary to show that selective education was more desirable than non-selective education.

10.17.4 Indirect discrimination

Indirect discrimination occurs where an employer applies a requirement or condition which applies equally to all persons, but:

(1) the proportion of women, married persons or persons of a particular race who can comply with that condition is considerably smaller than the proportion of men, unmarried persons or persons not within that race; and
(2) the employer cannot show that condition to be justifiable irrespective of the sex, marital status or race of the person to whom it is applied; and
(3) the requirement is to that person's detriment because he or she cannot comply with it.

In considering whether an employer has indirectly discriminated against an employee, it is necessary to consider carefully the different concepts involved in the above definition of indirect discrimination.

First, a requirement or condition imposed by the employer must operate as a bar preventing the employee concerned from obtaining what is sought. For example, in *Home Office v Holmes* [1984] IRLR 299 an obligation on an employee to work full time was held to be a requirement for the purposes of the definition of indirect discrimination.

Secondly, when deciding whether the requirement or condition has had a disproportionate impact on one particular sex or racial group, it is necessary to define the appropriate pool for comparing members of one sex or racial group with members of the other sex or another racial group. The choice of the appropriate pool for comparison is a question of fact for an industrial tribunal and will turn on the particular circumstances of each case. However, the Court of Appeal in *Jones v University of Manchester* [1993] IRLR 218 indicated that any pool for comparison should be defined broadly, so as to cover all men and women to whom the employer applied or would apply the requirement.

In deciding whether a particular employee 'can comply' with a requirement or condition, the question is not whether the employee is physically able to comply but whether he can in practice comply, having regard to custom and usual behaviour. For example, in *Mandla v Lee* [1983] IRLR 209 the House of Lords rejected an argument that Sikh employees could comply with a prohibition on wearing turbans, as in accordance with custom and cultural conditions they could not comply, although theoretically they could have done.

Thirdly, the requirement or condition must be shown to operate to the particular employee's detriment because he cannot comply with it. This is an objective test and it would be sufficient for the employee concerned to show that he could not comply with the requirement or condition at the time when his claim arises.

The test of justifiability

Even when the above requirements are satisfied, an employer may still avoid liability for indirect discrimination if it can show that the requirement or condition was justifiable irrespective of sex or race.

The question of whether a particular discriminatory condition is justifiable depends upon an objective test. The correct approach was stated by the ECJ in *Bilka-Kaufhaus GmbH v Weber von Hartz* [1987] ICR 110. The employer in order to justify a discriminatory practice must put forward objective economic grounds relating to the management of the business. The practice must also be necessary and in proportion to the objectives pursued by the employer. It is a matter for determination by an industrial tribunal on the facts of each case when striking a balance between the requirement's discriminatory effect and what are the employer's reasonable needs. For example, in *Singh v Rowntree Mackintosh Ltd* [1979] ICR 554, the employer imposed the rule that none of his employees could have beards. This condition effectively excluded Sikhs from employment at the company and Mr Singh complained of indirect discrimination. The tribunal held that indeed the condition was discriminatory, but that it was justifiable on the grounds of hygiene.

Two examples where an employer has been held to indirectly discriminate against an employee are as follows:

(1) A refusal by an employer to allow a request from an employee returning from maternity leave to work on a part-time basis after the birth of her baby amounted to indirect sex discrimination, even though the employee had worked on a full-time basis prior to maternity leave. The employer could not justify the requirement of full-time work as it needed only to have made a relatively minor adjustment within the organisation of its department to accommodate the employee's request for part-time work (*Guthrie v Royal Bank of Scotland* (Case No 31796/86), 10 March 1987).
(2) A blanket mobility clause imposed on all staff may amount to indirect sex discrimination as it is likely to have a disproportionate adverse effect on women. This is because women tend to earn less than their husbands and a higher proportion of women than men would find it impossible to relocate as their husbands, the main breadwinners, could not realistically give up their jobs (*Meade-Hill & The National Union of Civil and Public Servants v The British Council* (1995) *The Times*, 7 April 1995).

10.17.5 Victimisation

It is also unlawful for an employer to treat any person less favourably than another due to the fact that that person brings proceedings, gives evidence or information or takes or threatens to take any action, or makes any allegation concerning his employer with reference to either the Sex Discrimination Act, the Disability Discrimination Act, the Race Relations Act or the Equal Pay Act 1970.

10.17.6 Genuine occupational qualification

An employer also has a defence to an allegation of sex or race discrimination where he can show that the discrimination is as a result of a genuine occupational qualification. Therefore, if the defence can be established, an employer can discriminate in relation to advertisements, interviewing procedures and in job offers. Once the employment relationship has been established, again if the defence is available, an employer can refuse individual opportunities for promotion, training or transfer.

In the context of sex discrimination, a genuine occupational qualification can be established where, for example, the essential nature of the job calls for a man for reasons of physiology. This does not relate to physical strength or stamina but would, for example, apply in the case of an employer seeking male models or in the case of theatrical performances, for reasons of authenticity, male actors. It can also be a genuine occupational qualification where the need for the job to be held by a man is important in order to preserve decency or privacy.

In the context of race discrimination, an example of a genuine occupational qualification would be where for reasons of authenticity an employer may require members of only one race, for example Indian waiters in an Indian restaurant.

10.17.7 Liability for discriminatory acts

Both the individual concerned and his employer are liable for discriminatory acts carried out by an employee during the course of his employment, whether or not those acts are done with the employer's knowledge or approval. However, an employer does have a defence to vicarious liability where he can show that he has taken such steps as were reasonably practicable to prevent an employee from doing such acts during the course of his employment. It is therefore important for an employer to be seen to be pro-active in this field. If allegations of discriminatory acts are brought to his attention he should deal with these immediately.

10.17.8 Remedies

An individual who is alleging sex or race discrimination can bring a complaint to an industrial tribunal. Such complaint must be brought within three months of the discriminatory act. However, a tribunal can consider an application out of time if it considers that it is just and equitable to do so.

If the complaint is well founded, the industrial tribunal can make a declaration declaring the complainant's and the employer's rights in relation to the act of discrimination which has been complained about. For example, the declaration can state that certain training facilities should be made available to an employee. Furthermore, an award of compensation can be made. The amount of compensation awarded may include a sum for injury to feelings which results from the employee's knowledge that it was a discriminatory act which brought about the employer's action. Until *Marshall v Southampton & South West Hampshire Regional Health Authority (No 2)* [1993] IRLR 445, there was a maximum limit of £11,000 on the amount of compensation recoverable in discrimination cases. However, this case held that it was inconsistent with EC law (ie the Equal Treatment Directive) for there to be a limit on compensation when this bore no relation to the loss that had actually been suffered. Following this decision, the UK government enacted amending legislation so that the maximum limit has now been removed for both sex and race discrimination cases. Furthermore, as a result of *Marshall (No 2)*, amending legislation has been introduced to give an industrial tribunal power to award interest on compensation.

Finally, a tribunal can make a recommendation that the employer within a specified period of time takes such action as appears to be practicable for the purpose of obviating or reducing the adverse effect on the complainant of any act of discrimination to which the complaint relates.

10.17.9 The role of the Equal Opportunities Commission and the Commission for Racial Equality

The Commissions are both extremely active in the fields of sex and race discrimination. They have the power to carry out formal investigations and as a result of those investigations serve non-discrimination orders on employers. Such an order is made if a Commission is satisfied that an employer has committed or is committing a discriminatory act or maintaining a discriminatory practice. The terms of the non-discrimination notice require the employer to cease committing such acts and institute any necessary changes in any of its practices to avoid any discriminatory effects. If this order is not complied with, it can be enforced in a county court. The Commissions also adopt a pro-active role in advising individuals about their rights in relation to discriminatory matters. Where appropriate, they can support individuals in claims against an employer.

Where a person has brought a claim for discrimination to an industrial tribunal, they can serve on the employer concerned a questionnaire that has been compiled by the Commissions. If then an employer does not answer the questions on the questionnaire or provides inadequate answers, its replies can be taken into account in the tribunal proceedings and a tribunal has the discretion to draw adverse inferences from them.

Finally, in relation to disabled employees, there is a disability discrimination bill that is presently passing its way through Parliament and it is anticipated that it will be enacted towards the end of 1995. The bill, if enacted in its present form, will outlaw discrimination against disabled workers.

The field of potential discriminatory acts is very wide and extends from recruitment right through training, promotion, transfer, redundancy selection procedures through to dismissal. In all cases an employer should consider carefully whether action that it proposes to take could have a potential discriminatory effect. Legal advice is important in this area and should certainly be sought, for instance before the placing of job advertisements in local or national newspapers.

10.18 DISCRIMINATION ON GROUNDS OF DISABILITY

On 2 December 1996 the Disability Discrimination Act (DDA) came into effect. This introduced a new category of discrimination making it unlawful for employers (with certain exceptions (see 10.18.5)) to discriminate against those with disabilities.

The key elements of the DDA that are relevant to employers are that:

(a) it is now unlawful to discriminate against current or prospective employees with disabilities because of a reason relating to that disability; and
(b) the DDA obliges employers to make reasonable adjustments if their employment arrangements or premises place the disabled employee or disabled applicant at a substantial disadvantage.

As with the RDA and SDA there is no qualifying period of employment before a claim may be presented and that the Tribunals are able to award unlimited compensation for discrimination.

10.18.1 Definition of 'disability'

The definition of 'disability' is particularly wide and goes beyond those who are registered as disabled to include all persons who have a 'physical or mental impairment which has a substantial and long-term adverse effect on [that person's] ability to carry out normal day-to-day activities'.

The meaning of 'mental' or 'physical' impairment is intentionally not specifically defined by the DDA so that the Act is able to potentially cover all physical and mental impairments. However, certain conditions are excluded from the DDA by virtue of reg 4 of the Disability Discrimination (Meaning of Disability) Regulations 1996. Excluded conditions include kleptomania, pyromania, a tendency to physical or sexual abuse of other persons, exhibitionism, voyeurism, hay fever and addiction to alcohol, nicotine or other drugs.

To be a substantial and long-term condition, it must either:

(a) have lasted at least 12 months;
(b) be likely to last at least 12 months; or
(c) be likely to last for the rest of the lifetime of that person.

To affect normal day-to-day activities the condition must affect at least one of the following activities:

- Mobility
- Manual dexterity
- Physical co-ordination
- Continence
- Ability to lift, carry or otherwise move everyday objects
- Speech, hearing and sight
- Memory or ability to concentrate, learn or understand perception of the risk of physical danger
- Severe disfigurement is also treated as having a substantial and long-term adverse effect on the person's ability to carry out normal day-to-day activities.

10.18.2 Types of discrimination

As opposed to the SDA and the RDA, which cover three types of discrimination (direct, indirect and victimisation) the DDA only defines discrimination as (1) direct discrimination (s 5) and (2) victimisation (s 55).

Direct discrimination is defined in a similar way to that of the RDA and SDA (see 10.17.3) as is victimisation (see 10.17.5). However, the DDA has also introduced a new obligation on an employer that is specific to the realms of disability discrimination. This is the employer's duty to make reasonable adjustments in order to accommodate the disabled person (s 6).

10.18.3 Employer's duty to make reasonable adjustments

Under DDA, s 6(1) the employer is required to take such steps as are reasonable in all the circumstances to prevent the disabled person from being placed at a substantial disadvantage compared to others. Examples of steps that an employer would be expected to take are, for example, altering premises (such as providing ramps and widening doorways for wheelchair access), altering working hours or allocating certain duties to another person. The list of steps that an employer may be expected to take is not exhaustive but an employer is only expected to make such adjustments that are reasonable in the circumstances.

In determining whether an action is reasonable in the circumstances s 6(4) provides that an employer should consider:

A. The extent to which taking the step would prevent the effect in question;
B. The extent to which it is practicable for the employer to take the step;
C. The financial and other costs which would be incurred by the employer in taking the step and the extent to which taking it would disrupt any of its activities;
D. The extent of the employer's financial or other resources;
E. The availability to the employer of financial or other assistance with respect to taking the step.

Note that the duty to make reasonable adjustments does not mean an employer has to act in anticipation of employing persons with disabilities. The employer only has to make the adjustments if he employs or is considering employing a disabled person.

10.18.4 Remedies

The remedies under the DDA are similar to those available for SDA and RDA claims (see 10.11.8).

10.18.5 Exemptions

Certain employers are exempt from the requirements of the DDA. The main exemption is for employers who employ less than 20 people. However, note that DDA, s 68(1) classifies apprentices and self-employed workers as employees.

Also beyond the realms of the Act are partners. Although employees of a partnership that has more than 20 employees will be protected by the DDA, the partners themselves are not given such protection.

Other exemptions include police officers, persons working in the armed forces, firefighters and prison officers.

10.19 EQUAL PAY

The Equal Pay Act 1970, as amended, sets out the domestic provisions underpinning a woman's right to equal pay to that of a man (or vice versa) for like work or work rated as equivalent or work of equal value. EU law is also very important in this area, especially art 119 of the EC Treaty which sets out the principle that men and women are entitled to equal pay for equal work. Article 119 can be enforced directly by individuals in the UK courts. There is also the Equal Pay Directive which can be used as an aid in construing domestic law, where this falls short of EC law requirements. The Directive prohibits discrimination between men and women when it comes to levels of pay for the same work or work of equal value.

It is important to note that, in line with the Sex Discrimination Act 1975 and the Race Relations Act 1976, the Equal Pay Act 1970 applies to the self-employed as well as employees.

All complaints regarding discrimination in contractual pay or benefits should be brought under the Equal Pay Act and not the Sex Discrimination Act.

The Equal Pay Act deems an equality clause to be included in a woman's contract, where it is not incorporated expressly. Such a clause operates so that if a term in a woman's contract is less favourable to her than a similar term in a man's contract, then the appropriate term in the woman's contract is modified so as to make it as favourable as the term in the man's contract. Also, if a woman's contract does not include a beneficial term which is within a man's contract, then again the woman's contract is modified to include that term.

The equality clause applies not only to pay but to all terms and conditions of employment.

10.19.1 Like work

A woman is treated as employed on like work to that of a man if her work is the same or of a broadly similar nature to that of a man's, and any differences in the work are not of practical importance in relation to the performance of her contract. As to what amounts to a difference of practical importance, this depends upon the facts of each particular case, but regard will be had to the nature, extent and the frequency with which such differences occur in practice. However, if the difference is merely incidental to the main employment, such difference is not of practical importance.

10.19.2 Work rated as equivalent

A woman can claim equal pay even if not employed on like work if, after a job evaluation study has been carried out, the woman's job has been rated as equivalent to a man's in terms of the demand made on the worker. There are various headings for evaluation within such a scheme such as effort, skill and decision. All job evaluation schemes must be carried out on an objective basis and if as a result of the scheme the woman's work has been rated as equivalent, the woman is entitled to equal pay. If, however, the work has not been rated as equivalent, her case for equal pay may fail. However, a woman may challenge a job evaluation scheme if it is discriminatory in itself.

10.19.3 Work of equal value

Even if a woman is not employed on like work or work that has been rated as equivalent under a job evaluation scheme, she may now claim equal pay if her work is of equal value to that of a man's. Equal value is assessed in relation to the demands placed upon a worker under headings such as effort, skill and responsibility. It is important to note that a claim can still be brought under this heading even if a man is paid the same as a woman for doing like work, but there is another man doing a different job who is paid more but the work is deemed to be of equal value.

10.19.4 The comparator

The basis of any claim for equal pay is that of a comparison between a man and a woman (or vice versa). The comparator must be a person of the opposite sex employed in the same employment (or in the employment of an associated employer) at the same place of work, or at another place if there are common terms and conditions of employment observed at the different places of work. Also, under art 119 of the EC Treaty a comparison can be made with a previous employee who has subsequently left the employment.

10.19.5 The material factor defence

Even if a woman has succeeded in showing that she is entitled to equal pay as she is performing either like work, work rated as equivalent or work of equal value, it is possible for an employer to justify the difference between the man's and the woman's contract by showing that the variation is genuinely due to a material factor which is not the difference in sex. In *Rainey v The Greater Glasgow Health Board* [1987] ICR 129 it was held that in establishing the material factor defence, the material difference need not be restricted to the personal qualities of the employee and the relevant comparator, but can extend to other factors such as market forces.

10.19.6 Remedies

Any claim under the Equal Pay Act 1970 must be brought before an industrial tribunal. If the claim is successful, the woman is entitled to the insertion of an equality clause into her contract of employment which then entitles her to be paid at the same rate as that of her male comparator. The woman is also entitled to recover arrears of wages for up to two years before the commencement of proceedings. Industrial tribunals also have a discretion to award interest on the amount of any award of compensation; this to be calculated with effect from the date of the discriminatory act. Even if equality has been achieved at the time of the application, arrears of pay may be awarded for any inequality that existed during the preceding two years.

10.20 INSOLVENCY OF EMPLOYER

On an employer becoming insolvent, it is likely that a number, if not all, of the employees will have outstanding claims. Under the Insolvency Act 1986 certain claims by employees are treated as preferential debts. However, in many cases there will be insufficient funds to meet even those preferential debts and consequently an employee may be left in an unsatisfactory position. However, employees now have the right to make an application to the Secretary of State for Employment for payments from the National Insurance Fund. These debts include:

(1) Up to eight weeks' arrears of pay. For these purposes, pay includes a guarantee payment, a medical suspension payment, remuneration under a protective award and any payment for time off from work which is permitted by statute.
(2) A payment in respect of the statutory minimum period of notice.
(3) Up to six weeks holiday pay relating to the previous 12 months.
(4) A basic award for unfair dismissal.

There is a statutory limit of £210 per week that is payable in respect of each debt.

10.20.1 Redundancy payments

An employee can also make a claim against the National Insurance Fund where he claims that his employer is liable to pay him a redundancy payment and that his employer is insolvent and that the whole or part of his redundancy payment remains unpaid.

10.20.2 Occupational pension schemes

The Secretary of State may also make payments out of the National Insurance Fund into an occupational pension scheme, where an employer has become insolvent and at the time of the insolvency there were unpaid relevant contributions that had to be paid by the employer into the scheme.

10.20.3 Remedy

Where an employee has applied for payment from the National Insurance Fund and his application has been refused, he may present a complaint to an industrial tribunal either that the Secretary of State has failed to make any payment or that the amount of any payment made is less than the amount that should have been paid. The complaint should be brought within three months of the date on which the Secretary of State's decision is given to the employee, or if the tribunal considers that it was not reasonably practicable to bring a complaint within that time, within such further period as is considered reasonable.

If the complaint is well founded, a declaration is made to that effect and the amount that is due from the Fund is stated.

10.21 THE TRANSFER OF UNDERTAKINGS (PROTECTION OF EMPLOYMENT) REGULATIONS 1981 (TUPE)

The TUPE Regulations, which implement the Acquired Rights Directive, are designed to protect the rights of employees on a change of employer, whether such change results from a takeover or merger or a contracting out situation. The UK courts when construing the TUPE Regulations adopt a purposive approach in line with the Acquired Rights Directive and ECJ decisions (see 10.2 above).

10.21.1 Application

The Regulations apply whenever there is a transfer from one person to another of an undertaking or part of an undertaking which is situated in the United Kingdom immediately before the transfer. For there to be a relevant transfer there must be a transfer of an undertaking or part of an undertaking as a 'going concern'.

It was originally thought that, therefore, the TUPE Regulations only applied to undertakings which were commercial ventures. However, following the case of *Dr Sophie Redmond Stichting v Bartol* [1992] IRLR 366 the exclusion of undertakings that were not in the nature of a commercial venture from the operation of the TUPE Regulations was contrary to the Acquired Rights Directive. Accordingly, the Regulations were amended by TURERA so that this inconsistency with the Directive was removed.

In deciding whether there has been a transfer to which the Regulations will apply, the ECJ in *Spijkers v Gebroeders Benedik Abbatoir CV*

[1986] 2 CMLR 296 stated that the important question is whether the entity retains its identity after the transfer. Is there a separate identifiable economic entity which is transferred and which is continued after the transfer by the new employer in substantially the same manner?

In answering this question, the circumstances of each particular case should be examined, but a number of useful guidelines are:

(a) the type of undertaking in question;
(b) whether tangible assets, such as buildings and stock, transfer;
(c) whether goodwill transfers;
(d) whether customers transfer;
(e) whether there is an intention to transfer employees;
(f) whether there is any suspension in the carrying on of the activities, and if so for what period of time;
(g) the degree of similarity of the activities carried on before and after the transfer.

There has been considerable litigation as to whether there is a transfer of an undertaking to which the Regulations apply when a service which has previously been carried on 'in house' is 'outsourced' to an external contractor or when a new contractor takes over the provision of those services from the previous contractor. Case law indicates that such circumstances can amount to a transfer falling within the ambit of the Regulations (see *Rask v ISS Kantineservice (A/S)* [1993] IRLR 133 (the contracting-out of an in-house catering service to a private contractor); *Kenny v South Manchester College* [1993] IRLR 265 (contracting-out of the provision of prison education services); and *Dines v Initial Health Care Services Ltd* [1994] IRLR 336 (change of contractor for the provision of hospital cleaning services after competitive tendering)).

The law relating to transfers is constantly developing and will cover many scenarios. There can be a transfer to which the Regulations apply even where there is no transfer of assets or customers. For example in *Kenny v South Manchester College* [1993] IRLR 265, on the College successfully tendering to provide prison education services, there was a relevant transfer for the purposes of the Regulations, despite the fact that the premises, books and other items required to provide the education services would remain the property of the Home Office or the local education authority. Nevertheless, the Regulations applied as the education department in the prison was a clearly identifiable entity and would continue after the transfer in substantially the same manner as it did beforehand.

Furthermore, in *Schmidt v Spar Und Leuhkasse Der Fruheren* [1994] IRLR 303, it was confirmed that the Acquired Rights Directive, and as a consequence TUPE, can apply to a business or operation carried on by just one person.

However, the test laid down in *Spijkers* (of whether there is a separate economic entity which is in existence after the transfer, carrying on the same economic or similar activity as it carried on prior to the transfer) will be the decisive criterion in deciding whether there has been a transfer to which TUPE applies. In *Isles of Scilly Council v Brintel Helicopters Ltd* [1995] IRLR 6, it was stated that the question of retention of identity could be supplemented by enquiring whether the job previously done by the employee was still in existence after the transfer.

In this context, it is important to note that TUPE only applies to a transfer from one legal person to another. Therefore, the Regulations will not apply where there is merely a change in ownership by way of share transfer.

There have also been a number of recent developments that affect the application of TUPE. The recent case of *Süzen* [1997] IRLR 255 has transformed the general approach to transfers. This case involved the transfer of a school cleaning contract from one contractor to another. The employer who won the contract dismissed its employees and the question arose whether the transfer of the cleaning activity to a new contractor equated to the transfer of an undertaking.

The case was referred to the ECJ which held that a transfer of activities does not, in itself, constitute a transfer of undertaking.

This ruling has since been accepted by the Court of Appeal in *Betts v Brintel Helicopters Ltd* [1997] IRLR 361, in which the court drew a distinction between labour intensive activities and other types of activities. The court suggested that with labour intensive activities, if the activity continued with 'substantially the same staff after the alleged transfer the court may well conclude that the undertaking was transferred . . .'. This effectively takes the ruling in *Süzen* one step further, as where an undertaking is transferred with 'substantially the same staff' as before the transfer then there may very well have been a transfer regulated by TUPE. We have yet to see how case-law in this area develops, and although employers may see these decisions as a way of avoiding TUPE it must be remembered that all of the circumstances of the transfer should be considered before concluding that a transfer is not regulated by TUPE.

10.21.2 Operation

The most important consequence of a transfer to which the Regulations apply is contained in reg 5 which provides that those employees employed in the undertaking immediately before it is transferred are transferred to the new employer (the transferee) on the same terms and conditions of employment that they enjoyed with their previous employer (the transferor). Subject to certain limited exceptions, all the transferors rights, powers, duties and liabilities under or in connection with the contract of any transferring employee is transferred to the transferee. Furthermore, anything done by the transferor in respect of a transferring employee is deemed to have been done by the transferee. Accordingly, the transferee inherits:

(1) all existing contractual terms, both express and implied;
(2) liabilities for past breaches of contract;
(3) statutory liabilities such as unfair dismissal compensation, redundancy payments and claims for compensation under discrimination legislation;
(4) continuous employment with the transferor;
(5) tortious liability, such as liability for personal injuries.

However, the transferee does not inherit criminal liability and liabilities relating to the provisions of occupational pension schemes which relate to old age, invalidity or survivor's benefits. In *Walden Engineering Co Ltd v Warrener* [1993] IRLR 420, an argument that transferring employees should be entitled to equivalent pension benefits after the transfer was specifically rejected.

10.21.3 'Immediately before the transfer'

An employee only transfers to the transferee company if he is employed by the transferor 'immediately before the transfer'. Until the House of Lords' decision in *Lister v Forth Dry Dock and Engineering Co Ltd (in Receivership)* [1989] IRLR 161, there had been considerable case law regarding the meaning of the phrase 'immediately before'. If a transferor was to dismiss certain employees, for example, three hours before a transfer would this avoid the application of the Regulations?

The House of Lords, in the *Lister* case, adopted a purposive approach in construing reg 5 of the TUPE Regulations and stated that it referred not only to a person employed immediately before the transfer, but also to an individual 'who would have been so employed if he had not been unfairly dismissed for a reason that was connected with the transfer which was not an economic, technical or organisational reason entailing changes in the workforce' (see 10.21.4). Therefore, if the transferor dismisses employees prior to a transfer, but for reasons connected with it, the TUPE Regulations will bite.

10.21.4 Unfair dismissals and business transfers

Regulation 8 provides that a dismissal, the reason or principal reason for which is the transfer or a reason connected with it, is automatically unfair whether the dismissal occurs before or after the transfer. However, reg 8(2) provides a defence for an employer where the dismissal is because of an 'economic, technical or organisational reason entailing changes in the workforce of either the transferor or the transferee before or after the transfer'. Where the dismissal can be shown to be for such an 'ETO reason' this does not make the dismissal automatically fair, but the tribunal will go on to consider whether the dismissal was fair and reasonable in all the circumstances in accordance with the reasonableness tests under EP(C)A, s 57(3).

Under the Regulations an employee must bring a claim for unfair dismissal within three months of the date he was dismissed.

A dismissed employee may also have claims for a redundancy payment or wrongful dismissal.

10.21.5 What amounts to an ETO reason?

An employer can establish a defence to a transfer related dismissal if it can show that it was for an ETO reason entailing changes in the workforce. In *Wheeler v Patel* [1987] ICR 631, it was stated that an economic reason must relate to the conduct of the business itself. Therefore, a dismissal which is made to facilitate a transfer or which is made at the request of the transferee does not amount to a relevant economic reason.

The ETO reason must also entail 'a change in the workforce'. In *Berriman v Delabok Slate Ltd* [1985] ICR 546, this phrase was held to mean a change in the number of employees or a change in the functions that the employees are required to perform. It does not cover the situation where an employer merely dismisses those employees who do not agree to changes in their terms and conditions of employment. Therefore, where an employer seeks to harmonise the terms and conditions of the transferring workforce with those of its present employees, any such attempt at harmonisation is connected with the transfer and does not amount to an ETO defence. However, where a number of employees are not required by the transferee, and in a non-transfer situation would be deemed to be redundant, then the ETO defence should apply.

10.21.6 Redundancy payments

Where an employee is automatically transferred to the transferee in accordance with the Regulations, he is not dismissed by the transferor and therefore is not entitled to a redundancy payment. However, where an employee is either dismissed by the transferor before the transfer for a genuine redundancy reason or where following the transfer, the transferee dismisses the employee for a genuine redundancy reason, the employee is still entitled to a redundancy payment, even though the dismissal is for an ETO reason connected with the transfer.

10.21.7 Avoiding the Regulations

Regulation 12 provides that any agreement that attempts to exclude or limit the operation of the Regulations is invalid. However, in any transfer documentation, it is usual for the transferor and the transferee to agree certain warranties and indemnities that provide who is liable for payment of any sums deemed to be payable as a consequence of any transfer related dismissal, or any liability that may transfer as a result of the operation of the Regulations.

From an employee's point of view, following *Katsikas v Konstantinidis* [1993] IRLR 179, an employee cannot be forced to transfer to a new employer against his will. Accordingly, following amendments to reg 5 by TURERA, an employee's contract is not transferred if the employee informs either the transferor or the transferee that he objects to becoming employed by the transferee. However, it is unlikely that an employee would exercise this right to object as the Regulations further provide that if an employee exercises his right to object, then his contract of employment is automatically terminated and he is not treated as having been dismissed by the transferor and therefore is not be entitled to any compensation.

10.21.8 Collective agreements and trade union recognition

Regulation 6 provides that any collective agreement which has been made between a transferor and a trade union which is recognised by the transferor, and which applies to transferring employees, continues to have effect after the transfer as if made by the transferee with the relevant trade union. However, the effect of this regulation is minimal as collective agreements are unenforceable unless the contrary is stated in the agreement itself.

Furthermore, reg 9 provides that where, after a transfer, the undertaking transferred retains an identity distinct from the remainder of the transferee's undertaking, any trade union which the transferor recognised with regard to the transferring employees is deemed to be recognised also by the transferee. Again, the effect of reg 9 is minimal as there is no legislation enforcing trade union recognition and an employer is free to withdraw recognition at any time.

10.21.9 Provision of information and consultation with trade unions

Regulation 10 imposes an obligation on both the transferor and the transferee to inform and consult with recognised trade unions in relation to a transfer of an undertaking. This obligation applies to a trade union that is recognised in respect of employees of both the transferor and the transferee who are to be affected by the transfer.The fact that the Regulations only require the transferor or transferee to inform and consult recognised trade unions was held in *EC Commission v United Kingdom of Great Britain and Northern Ireland* [1994] IRLR 412 to be incompatible with the Acquired Rights Directive, as it does not provide for a procedure for designating employee representatives where an employer refuses to recognise a trade union. The obligation to inform and consult should extend to undertakings where there is no recognised trade union. The position in the UK will therefore have to be altered, but it remains to be seen how this will be done. The employer of affected employees must provide the recognised unions with the following information:

(1) the fact that a relevant transfer is to take place;
(2) when the transfer is to take place;
(3) the reasons for the transfer;
(4) the legal, economic and social implications for the affected employees;
(5) the measures which the employer envisages taking in relation to those employees or if no measures are envisaged, then that fact; and
(6) where the employer is the transferor, the measures that the transferee envisages that it will take in relation to those employees automatically transferring to it on the transfer and, again, if no measures are envisaged, that fact.

The duty to inform recognised trade unions of the above facts applies in every case, but the obligation to consult applies only where an employer envisages that it will be taking measures in respect of its employees in connection with the transfer. Following an amendment to the Regulations laid down in TURERA, the consultation process must be carried out with a view to seeking the trade union's agreement to the measures to be taken. This is analogous to the provision concerning collective redundancies.

The information about the transfer must be provided to the recognised trade union long enough before the transfer to enable consultation to take place. There are no specific time limits stipulated, but it is important to ensure that the information is provided early enough to enable a meaningful dialogue. However, where there are 'special circumstances' which render it not reasonably practical for an employer to comply with the duty to inform, it is sufficient for an employer to show that he took all reasonable steps to comply with the duty. A situation is unlikely to amount to a 'special circumstance' unless there is, for example, an unforeseen emergency which requires the transfer to be expedited.

Where an employer fails to inform or consult in accordance with reg 10, the recognised union concerned can bring a complaint to an industrial tribunal within three months of the transfer or within such reasonable time thereafter, if it was not reasonably practicable to bring the complaint within three months. Where the tribunal considers the complaint well founded it will make a declaration to this effect and may order the employer to pay up to four weeks' pay as compensation to each employee affected.

10.21.10 References

An employer is under no legal duty to provide a reference for an employee (*Gallear v J F Watson & Son Ltd* [1979] IRLR 306). However, where an employer agrees to provide a reference, it should exercise great care when compiling that reference.

In *Spring v Guardian Assurance* [1994] IRLR 460, the House of Lords held that employers owe a duty of care to employees in respect of the preparation of a reference. Whilst, when providing a reference to a prospective employer, the former employer does so for the benefit of that person, it also does so to assist the employee who has to rely on his former employer to exercise due skill and care. The implication of this decision is that it is now far easier for employees to challenge references given by a former employer if he can show that the employer has not taken all reasonable care in compiling a reference.

An employee may also have actions in defamation or malicious falsehood where his previous employer provides an inaccurate reference. However, these claims are far more difficult to prove and are not very common.

Further more, when an employer supplies a reference to a prospective employer, he will owe that employer a duty to exercise a reasonable degree of care and skill to ensure that the reference is accurate and not misleading (see *Hedley Byrne and Co Ltd v Heller and Partners Ltd* [1963] AC 465). Consequently, if the prospective employer suffers loss as a result of its reliance on an inaccurate reference, the old employer may be held liable to pay damages on account of its negligence, if the mistake was due to carelessness.

An employer, when providing a reference, may therefore include a disclaimer of any liability arising out of a result of a potential new employer relying on the reference. However, any such disclaimer is subject to the provisions of the Unfair Contract Terms Act 1977, and will only be enforceable if the disclaimer is reasonable.

10.21.11 Summary

The TUPE Regulations and associated EC legislation are extremely complex. At the time of the introduction of the Regulations in 1981, it was possible to exclude most cases from their operation. However, the starting point now must always be that the Regulations do apply. The facts of each situation can then be looked into to see whether the operation of the Regulations can be excluded, although today it is unusual to find many situations which do not fall within the scope of the Regulations.

Where a merger or takeover of a business or a change of contractor providing certain circumstances is envisaged, legal advice should be taken as the operation of the Regulations have significant consequences and could affect whether such a transaction is finalised.

Finally, there is at present a new draft of the Acquired Rights Directive, which makes a number of important amendments to the directive. However, it is not clear at this stage if and when the new provisions will be implemented.

11

TAX AND EMPLOYEE COMPENSATION

In this chapter, we deal with an employer's obligations to operate PAYE and national insurance contributions and we also cover the tax treatment of benefits in kind and other forms of employee compensation. The chapter is set out under the following main headings:

(1) PAYE
(2) National insurance contributions
(3) Benefits in kind
(4) Travelling, subsistence and entertaining
(5) Company cars
(6) Beneficial loans
(7) Living accommodation
(8) Miscellaneous benefits
(9) End of year returns
(10) Profit-related pay and share schemes
(11) Gifts of shares
(12) Non-approved share options
(13) Profit-sharing schemes
(14) Share option schemes
(15) Executive share option schemes
(16) Special employee shares
(17) Termination payments
(18) How the Inland Revenue ensures compliance.

11.1 PAYE

All payments of 'emoluments' by a person carrying on business in the United Kingdom are subject to PAYE (pay as you earn). The following are listed in the Revenue publication *Employer's Guide to PAYE* as payments to directors and employees from which PAYE should be deducted:

(1) Salary
(2) Wages
(3) Fees

(4) Overtime
(5) Bonus
(6) Commission
(7) Pension
(8) Honoraria
(9) Pay during sickness or other absence from work
(10) Holiday pay
(11) Christmas boxes in cash
(12) Employee's income tax borne by the employer
(13) Payments for the cost of travelling between the employee's home and his normal place of employment
(14) Payments for time spent in travelling
(15) Cash payments for meals
(16) Payments in lieu of benefits in kind
(17) Certain lump sum payments made on retirement or removal from employment
(18) Certain sums received from the trustees of approved profit sharing schemes
(19) Gratuities or service charges paid out by the employer.

On the other hand, PAYE cannot be deducted from certain benefits even though they are regarded as taxable income. The *Employer's Guide* states that the following are income from which tax cannot be deducted:

(a) Living accommodation provided rent free or at a reduced rent
(b) Gifts in kind such as Christmas hampers
(c) Luncheon vouchers up to 15p per day
(d) Employee's liabilities borne by the employer
(e) Income in the form of company shares.

Employers are also required to account for PAYE when they pay their staff in 'tradeable assets' such as gold bars or commodities, or with non-marketable assets where the employer has made arrangements for the employee to convert them into cash.

11.1.1 Operation of PAYE

The Inland Revenue issues code numbers which determine the amount of PAYE deductions. Such code numbers are based on the latest information available to the Revenue and are intended to ensure that the amounts withheld under PAYE approximate closely to the individual's actual liability. Nevertheless, deduction of tax under PAYE is provisional in that if the actual liability exceeds the amount withheld under PAYE, the Revenue may collect the balance. It can do this either by issuing a code to take increased PAYE deductions in subsequent years or by raising an assessment to collect all the tax in one go.

Although the top rate of tax is 40 per cent, the Revenue may issue 'K' codes under which increased deductions may be made of up to 50 per cent of an individual's pay. The principle behind K codes is that notional pay is added to an employee's actual pay, and PAYE is operated accordingly. This is intended to cover the situation where the benefits in kind which are taxable exceed a person's allowances.

Amounts deducted in arriving at pay

(TA 1988, s 202)

Contributions made by an employee to an approved retirement benefit scheme and contributions of up to £900 to a payroll giving scheme ('give as you earn') are deducted from an individual's salary in arriving at taxable pay for the purposes of both PAYE and Schedule E. Profit-related pay must also be left out of account provided that it does not exceed the limits which are set out in 11.10 below.

Note that national insurance contributions (NIC) are based on pay *before* such amounts are deducted (see 11.2 below).

The point in time at which PAYE should be applied can, in certain circumstances, be earlier than the date of actual payment.

11.1.2 Accounting to the Revenue for PAYE

Regulations impose an obligation on the employer to pay tax deducted under PAYE to the Collector of Taxes or Accounts office within 14 days of the end of the tax month in which the deduction was required. Employers with a monthly liability below £600 may choose to account for such deductions on a quarterly basis instead.

The Collector is provided with powers to recover such amounts of PAYE and NIC which are overdue. Further provisions enable such sums to be recovered from the employee rather than employer in certain circumstances.

It is also worth remembering that where an employer has not paid over the PAYE tax to the Collector of Taxes within 14 days of the end of the year of assessment (ie by 19 April), that unpaid tax or NIC automatically carries interest from 19 April until the date of payment.

11.1.3 End of year returns

In addition to paying over the tax and NIC, the employer is required to submit certain documents to the Inspector of Taxes providing details of the employees, their emoluments and tax and NIC due. Individuals' end of year summaries (form P14) and the employer's end of year return or annual return (form P35) are required to be submitted by 19 May following the end of the year to which they relate. Penalties may be charged for late submission. Additional documents may be required where, for example, payments are made to casuals or where students have been employed.

11.2 NATIONAL INSURANCE CONTRIBUTIONS

11.2.1 Employers are liable to deduct contributions

Employers are required to deduct NIC from their employees' earnings and pay this over to the Collector of Taxes at the same time as they account for PAYE.

11.2.2 Employees' contributions

Individuals who are employed are liable for Class 1 NIC ('primary contributions'). No contribution is payable unless the employee earns at least £62 a week. If he earns £62 or more, contributions are charged at 2 per cent on the first £62 plus 10 per cent of earnings between £62 and £465 a week. No contribution is payable on earnings in excess of £465 (the 'upper limit'). Lower contributions apply if the individual is contracted out of SERPS.

Contributions are normally assessed by reference to weekly earnings but if the employee is paid less frequently, contributions are calculated on the corresponding figures for a monthly basis or whatever other period is covered by the payment of salary to the individual.

Where an individual has a period of unemployment during a year, this does not affect his liability when he resumes employment. Each 'earnings period' is looked at in isolation and there is no general principle which corresponds to that used for income tax whereby a tax year is looked at as a whole. There is a slight exception to this for company directors (see 2.3.2) but this is basically an anti-avoidance provision.

Women who married before 7 April 1977 and who have chosen to pay a reduced rate are subject to pay NIC of only 3.85 per cent. This right is lost if the woman is divorced but is not lost if she is widowed.

11.2.3 Employer's contributions

In addition to the contributions paid by the employee, employers are also required to pay contributions ('secondary contributions'). There is no ceiling on the amount of an employee's earnings which attract secondary contributions.

Employers may also be liable for Class 1A contributions where the employee has a car which is available for private use. The amount of the scale benefit as used for income tax purposes is treated as if it were additional earnings subject to secondary contributions. A further charge may arise if the employee is provided with fuel for private mileage, with the Class 1A charge again being based on the scale benefit used for income tax purposes. It is important to note that there is no corresponding liability for employees' contributions on these benefits.

11.2.4 Definition of earnings for NIC purposes

Earnings for national insurance purposes include all cash remuneration. Contributions are also payable on sick pay, holiday pay etc. The definition of earnings is quite different from that used for income tax purposes. For example, NIC is assessed on individual's pay before superannuation contributions and before any charitable donations made under a payroll deduction scheme. Profit-related pay is another type of earnings which may be exempt for income tax purposes, but gives rise to a liability for NIC.

Where an employer settles his employee's pecuniary liabilities, the sum paid is treated as earnings for national insurance purposes even though it is not pay for PAYE purposes. In general, no contributions are payable for benefits in kind. However, there is an exception to this for certain types of benefits in kind which can easily be converted into cash. For example, the Contributions Agency takes the view that premium bonds and national savings certificates are earnings for national insurance purposes because they may be encashed by the holder surrendering them.

Vouchers are not normally regarded as earnings provided they are exchangeable only for goods and may not be surrendered for cash. However, the Contributions Agency is looking very closely at arrangements in which a wide variety of vouchers (which are accepted by retailers and suppliers) are offered, and it would be wise to take professional advice.

11.2.5 Anti-avoidance rules

Financial instruments such as gilts, unit trusts, quoted shares etc, are treated as earnings for national insurance purposes, as are derivative instruments such as warrants and options. Gold bullion and other commodities and vouchers exchangeable for gold or commodities are within the charge, as are fine wine and gemstones. Finally, the rule that PAYE should be applied to the transfer of assets where the employer has made arrangements for the employees to realise cash (see 11.1.1) now applies to NIC.

Where an employer acquires an insurance policy such as an investment bond and transfers it to an employee, the value of the policy is regarded as earnings for national insurance purposes.

11.3 BENEFITS IN KIND

11.3.1 General rules

The legislation distinguishes between 'P11D employees' (ie directors and employees earning £8,500 or more per annum) and other employees. An employer is required to submit form P11D in respect of each P11D employee who may then be assessed on the cost to the employer of benefits in kind received by them. Other employees are normally taxed on benefits only if they are convertible into cash.

Directors are normally within the P11D regime, regardless of whether their remuneration reaches or exceeds the £8,500 limit. An employee falls within the P11D category where remuneration, *together with benefits and reimbursed expenses*, is £8,500 per annum or more. Such employees were formerly called 'higher paid' employees. The threshold of £8,500 was set in 1979 and, in accordance with the Government's intentions that all employees should pay income tax on the whole of their earnings, whether received in cash or in kind, this limit has not been increased. By 1989 the term 'higher paid' had become inappropriate and consequently, while there was no change made in the level of the threshold, references to higher paid employees were deleted from the legislation.

Employees are treated as earning £8,500 or more if they are remunerated *at the rate of* £8,500 per annum or more. For example, a person whose employment began on 1 January 1997 and who had received a salary of £2,000 and reimbursed expenses of £200 by 6 April 1997 would be within the P11D category as the total amount of £2,200 would give an annual rate greater than £8,500.

Unless a dispensation applies, all reimbursed expenses and other benefits have to be reported on form P11D and count towards the £8,500 limit, even though they may be justified as being for business purposes and no taxable benefit in kind ultimately arises.

Dispensations

The Revenue may grant a dispensation so that certain reimbursed expenses need not be reported on form P11D. This is clearly useful in reducing administration and accounting work and, wherever possible, employers should apply for a dispensation. The expenses covered by it will be set out by the Revenue and any expenses not covered must still be reported. Any changes in the method of reimbursing expenses or scales of allowances must be notified to the Revenue.

11.3.2 Benefits which may result in a tax charge for non-P11D employees

The general rule is that employees who are not within the P11D category are assessable only on benefits capable of being converted into cash or on any benefits provided through an employer meeting an employee's own personal liability. This principle has been modified to some extent so that, for instance, credit vouchers are an assessable benefit even if the employee is not within the P11D category. However, the principle continues to hold good with regard to benefits such as the provision of a company car, free use of assets, beneficial loans etc.

Table 11.1 below sets out the position.

Table 11.1 Treatment of benefits received by non-P11D employees

	Taxable	*Non-taxable*
Benefits capable of being turned to pecuniary account ie convertible to cash	✔	
Luncheon vouchers in excess of 15p per working day	✔	
Credit tokens and vouchers	✔	
Transport vouchers (ie any ticket, pass or other document or token intended to enable a person to obtain passenger transport services)	✔	
Living accommodation	✔	
Payment of employees' personal liabilities	✔	
Company cars		✔
Free use of assets		✔
Beneficial loans		✔
Medical insurance		✔

11.3.3 Tax treatment of specific benefits where received by non-P11D employee

Benefits capable of being converted into cash

Where the benefit is convertible into cash, the measure of assessable benefit is the amount of cash which could be realised, not the cost to the employer. For example, an employee provided with a new suit by the employer would be taxable only on its second-hand value.

Payment of employee's personal liabilities

A liability arises where the employer pays a personal liability of the employee. This includes such items as home heating and lighting bills and water rates, but special rules apply where the employee is in representative accommodation (see 11.4.8).

Credit tokens and vouchers

(TA 1988, s 142)

The taxable amount on credit tokens and vouchers is the cost to the employer of providing them. Vouchers other than cheque vouchers are deemed to be taxable emoluments as and when they are *allocated* to a particular employee, not when they are *used* by that employee.

Transport vouchers

(TA 1988, s 141)

There is specific legislation to ensure that season tickets provided by employers are taxable. Once again, the measure of the assessable benefit is the cost to the employer of providing the voucher.

Living accommodation

(TA 1988, s 145)

The assessable amount is the greater of the gross rateable value of the property or the rent payable by the employer, less any amount made good by the employee. Following the abolition of domestic rates, estimated values are used for new or substantially altered properties. No assessable benefit arises where the employee occupies representative accommodation (see 11.3.5 below).

11.3.4 Benefits not taxable for any category of employees

There are certain benefits that are not usually taxable even when the employee is within the P11D category. The most common items are:

(1) directors' and officers' insurance;
(2) incidental overnight expenses allowances;
(3) retirement benefits;
(4) luncheon vouchers (up to 15p per day);
(5) staff canteen and dining facilities;
(6) sports facilities;
(7) workplace nurseries and crèches;
(8) rail strike costs;
(9) removal expenses;
(10) long service awards;
(11) awards under suggestion schemes;
(12) use of a pooled car;
(13) the provision of representative accommodation;
(14) re-training.

Retirement benefits

Payments by an employer to an *approved* occupational pension scheme to secure retirement benefits for an employee do not give rise to an income tax liability for that employee. Payments into a non-approved scheme are taxable as additional remuneration for the year that the employer makes the relevant contribution. To secure approval, a pension scheme must be established for the sole purpose of providing 'relevant benefits' (ie pensions, death-in-service payments, and widows' and dependants' pensions). In addition, an employee's contributions must not exceed 15 per cent of his remuneration. The pension benefits payable by an approved scheme must not exceed certain limits. Pension schemes are covered in more detail in Chapter 12.

Luncheon vouchers

Non-transferable luncheon vouchers (ie vouchers which are not capable of being exchanged for cash) are exempt from income tax up to a limit of 15p per working day. Vouchers for larger amounts are partly exempt, with the excess over 15p being taxable in full, whether or not the employee is within the P11D category.

Staff canteen and dining facilities

No taxable benefit in kind arises where the canteen etc is used by all staff. Furthermore, the use of a separate room by directors and more senior staff does not prejudice this exemption, unless the meals provided are superior. The Revenue may also accept, in certain cases, that facilities provided by the employer for staff to use a local restaurant may come within the definition of a 'canteen', provided that *all* staff are eligible to use these facilities on the same terms.

There are requirements which need to be strictly observed. For example, there must be no voucher or form of identification which employees need to produce on entering the restaurant. Furthermore, the Inland Revenue may try to withhold exemption from directors and employees earning £8,500 or more who use such a restaurant facility.

Sports facilities
(FA 1993, s 75)

No taxable benefit arises on the use or availability of sports facilities owned by the employer. Similarly, no taxable benefit generally arises where an employer takes out corporate membership of an outside sports club so that *all* the employees are able to use the club's facilities. An assessment will, however, be made if the employer takes out a subscription for a particular director or employee earning £8,500 or more, or if the subscription covers a small group of such employees and directors.

Workplace nurseries and crèches

Employees are exempt from income tax on the benefit derived from the use of a workplace nursery provided by the employer. The exemption applies only to nurseries run by employers alone or jointly with other employers or bodies, either at the workplace or elsewhere. The provision by an employer of cash allowances to employees for childcare, or the direct meeting of an employee's childcare bills by an employer, are taxable benefits.

Relocation expenses
(FA 1993, s 76)

Section 191A and Sched 11A of TA 1988 provide for a ceiling of £8,000 for the amount which may be paid tax free for any one move. It is not necessary for the individual to dispose of his former residence in order to qualify for the exemption. Payments made to compensate employees for losses on the sale of their old houses are now regarded as taxable. Many practitioners still regard this as debatable and base their arguments on a 1959 decision by the House of Lords, *Hochstrasser v Mayes* [1960] AC 376.

From 5 April 1998 relocation expenses are to be subject to NIC to the extent that they exceed £8,000.

Long service awards

Awards to directors and employees to mark long service are exempt provided the period of service is at least 20 years and no similar award has been given to the employee within the previous ten years. The gift must not consist of cash and the cost should not exceed £20 per year of service. An Inland Revenue concession has extended the exemption to gifts of shares in the company which employs the individual or in another group company.

Awards under suggestion schemes

(Extra-Statutory Concession A57)

Provided the employee concerned is not engaged in research work, he may receive a tax-free payment under a firm's suggestion scheme. The making of suggestions should not, however, be regarded as part of the employee's job. The size of the award should also be within certain limits (ie £25 or less where the suggestion, although not implemented, has intrinsic value). Where the suggestion *is* implemented, the amount should be related to the expected net financial benefit to the employer. The current limits are:

(1) 50 per cent of the expected net financial benefit during the first year of implementation, or
(2) 10 per cent of the expected net financial benefit over a period of up to five years.

There is an overriding maximum of £5,000. Any amount in excess of £5,000 is taxable.

Pool cars

(TA 1988, s 159)

No tax charge arises by reason of the use of a pooled car. A car qualifies as a pooled car only if *all* the following conditions are satisfied:

(1) It is available for, and used by, more than one employee and is not ordinarily used by any one of them to the exclusion of the others.
(2) Any private use of the car by an employee is merely incidental to its business use.
(3) It is not normally kept overnight at or near the residence of any of the employees unless it is kept on premises occupied by the employer.

These requirements are strictly interpreted. Note that a car only qualifies as a pooled car *for a tax year*. There is a danger therefore in a car being taken out of pooled use and allotted to a specific employee towards the end of a tax year. As the car now no longer qualifies as a pooled car, any employee who has had the car available for private use during the same tax year may be assessed. Therefore, if the car is ordinarily parked overnight near the home of one of the users, it will not qualify as a pooled car and will create tax problems for any other employees who use it.

Representative accommodation

(TA 1988, s 145(4))

Living accommodation qualifies as representative accommodation if *any one* of the following conditions is satisfied:

(1) It is necessary for the performance of the employee's duties that he should reside in the accommodation.
(2) The accommodation is provided for the better performance of the employee's duties and it is customary to provide accommodation for such employees.
(3) The employee has to live in the accommodation because of a special threat to his security.

The exemption under the first two conditions is usually only available to directors who (together with their associates) hold 5 per cent or less of the company's ordinary share capital and are full-time working directors. Where the employer pays for heating, lighting, repairs, maintenance etc, the representative occupiers cannot be assessed in respect of such benefits on more than 10 per cent of their emoluments of the employment.

Re-training

(TA 1988, ss 588–589)

Where an employer pays the cost of a course undertaken by an employee (or former employee) for the purpose of providing him with skills for future employment elsewhere (or self-employment), the cost of the course can be a deductible expense of the employer, and may not be a taxable benefit of the employee.

Sandwich courses

(Statement of Practice SP4/86, re-issued November 1992)

Where an employee is released by his employer to take a full-time educational course at a university, technical college or similar educational institution which is open to the public at large, payments for periods of attendance may be treated as exempt from income tax. There are various conditions which attach to this exemption, ie:

(1) The course must last for at least one academic year with an average of at least 20 weeks of full-time attendance.
(2) The rate of payment must not exceed the greater of £7,000 and the rate of payment that an individual would have received had he been granted a public grant.

Where the rate of payment exceeds the above limits, the full amount is taxable but where the amount of payment is increased during a course, only subsequent payments are taxable.

11.4 TRAVELLING, SUBSISTENCE AND ENTERTAINING

11.4.1 General rules

Travel between home and the ordinary place of work does not rank as business travel. Where an individual is 'on call' and assumes the responsibilities of the employment upon leaving home, it may be possible to argue that home to work travel is business and not private travel, but this usually applies only in exceptional cases.

It was intended that, from 5 April 1998, a new concept of 'triangular travel' so that additional cost incurred in travelling to a client's premises rather than the normal place of work was to be allowable. However, following representations that the new scheme was unworkable, further changes are to be made in FA 1998.

In order to secure tax relief on reimbursed travelling expenses, the employee must keep adequate records so as to distinguish business from non-business travel. Ideally, expenses claims to the employer should show the actual cost of such travel and, if the employer is to obtain a dispensation, the Revenue needs to be satisfied that such internal controls exist.

Mileage allowances should not be so large as to create a 'profit' element which would of course be taxable. The Revenue has introduced a Fixed Profit Car Scheme setting maximum rates of reimbursement which can be treated as tax free. These are *reduced* when the business mileage exceeds 4,000 miles per annum. The rates from 6 April 1997 are:

	Amount per mile	
Engine size	*Up to 4,000 miles*	*Over 4,000 miles*
Up to 1000 cc	28p	17p
1001–1500 cc	35p	20p

1501–2000 cc	45p	25p
Over 2000 cc	63p	36p

Where reimbursement is not linked to engine size, the rates are 40p up to 4,000 miles per annum and 22.5p thereafter. Provided these rates are not exceeded and mileage is for business purposes, no benefit in kind will arise. Interest paid on a loan taken out for the purchase of a car used for business purposes may qualify for tax relief. Relief for such interest is not included in Fixed Profit Car Scheme rates and needs to be claimed separately.

11.4.2 Subsistence

The Revenue view is that it is strictly only the extra costs of living away from home which are allowable. If there are continuing financial commitments at home, the whole cost of living away from home is normally allowed. This concession is not available if the employee has no permanent residence, for example an unmarried person who normally lives in a hotel or club and who gives up that accommodation when away on a business trip. There is a specific exemption where an employee performs his duties wholly overseas and needs board and lodging abroad in order to do so.

There is, however, a statutory *de minimis* exclusion for incidental overnight expenses, where an individual is away from home on a 'qualifying absence' and the expenses, which would not otherwise be deductible, do not exceed a £5 nightly maximum for absences elsewhere in the United Kingdom and £10 if the absence is abroad (TA 1988, s 200A).

11.4.3 Overseas travelling expenses
(TA 1988, ss 192–193)

Where some or all of the duties of an employment are performed abroad, the expenses of travelling to and from the UK to carry out these duties are specifically regarded as having been necessarily incurred in the performance of the overseas employment. It follows, therefore, that if those expenses are reimbursed by the employer, no benefit in kind arises. Recent legislative changes have relaxed the rules further, so that, while the employee is serving abroad, the employer may pay for an unlimited number of journeys made by the employee to and from the UK without any tax charge arising. However, these journeys must be made wholly and exclusively for the purpose of performing the duties of the employment.

Moreover, where an employee travels between places where different jobs are performed, and one or more of these jobs is performed wholly or partly overseas, the expenses incurred in travelling overseas are also deemed to be necessarily incurred in performing the duties carried out overseas, so that once again no benefit in kind arises. In many cases, there is dual purpose in travelling and a taxable benefit in kind arises on the private element. Consequently, where travel expenses relate partly to a foreign holiday taken at the end of the business trip, there would be a taxable benefit in kind.

Similarly, a benefit in kind may be assessed on some or all of the expense where a spouse accompanies a director or employee and where this is not necessary for business purposes.

Maintenance of records

A director or employee who travels overseas should be able to substantiate a claim that expenses were necessarily incurred for business purposes by producing details of the expenses and the time spent away from home. A brief itinerary should be available where travel is undertaken within the overseas country or countries. The Revenue normally expects that an employer will properly control expenditure but in certain cases it may wish to see receipted bills or other vouchers.

11.4.4 Spouse's travelling and subsistence expenses

Where a spouse or other member of the family accompanies the director or employee abroad on a business trip, it is helpful in satisfying the Revenue that no benefit in kind arises if the board of directors minute their decision that the director should be so accompanied. However, this is not generally sufficient in itself and it is necessary to show that the spouse or other relative was able to perform certain tasks which could not be performed by the director.

It may be possible to show this if the spouse has some practical qualification, for example an ability to speak the foreign language concerned. A relative's expenses might also be allowable where the director or employee is in poor health and to travel alone would be impracticable or unreasonable. Where the individual's presence is for the purpose of accompanying his or her spouse at business entertainment functions, the expenses of the trip may be disallowed in calculating the employer's tax liability under the entertainment legislation, even though the expenses may be allowable in determining the employee's tax liability.

11.4.5 Employees working overseas – family visits
(TA 1988, s 194)

Where an employee is abroad for a continuous period of 60 days or more, there is an exemption for amounts borne by the employer for travelling expenses for visits by the employee's spouse and minor children. The exemption is only available for two journeys by the same person in each direction in a tax year. There is no relief if the employee ultimately bears the expense personally.

11.4.6 Entertaining expenses and round-sum allowances

It is not uncommon for directors or employees to have a round-sum allowance to cover such things as travelling, subsistence and entertaining. In the case of travelling and subsistence, the allowance counts as the taxable income of the director or employee, but a tax deduction may be claimed for any part of the allowance which can be shown to have been spent for business purposes. It is very important to have a record-keeping system which enables such claims to be substantiated. It may be better for the employer to dispense with round-sum allowances and reimburse the director or employee for properly substantiated expenditure. In this way, no benefit in kind should arise.

In the case of entertaining expenditure, the situation is rather more complex. If an employer reimburses a director's or employee's entertaining expenditure or pays a round-sum allowance which is specifically intended for entertaining, the expense to the employer is disallowed for tax purposes. The reimbursement or allowance is entered on the director's or employee's P11D but a deduction may be claimed for all the expenditure which is for genuine business purposes. If, on the other hand, the director or employee is given a round-sum allowance not specifically designated as being for entertaining, there is no question of the allowance being disallowed in the employer's tax computation. However, the director or employee would only escape liability on any part of the allowance which could be shown to have been used for business expenditure *other than* entertainment.

11.4.7 Private use of company vans
(TA 1988, ss 159AA–159AC and Sched 6A))

An employee may be assessed on a standard amount of £500 per year for private use of a company van. The amount is reduced to £350 for vans which are four or more years old at the end of the tax year. Any vehicles in excess of 3.5 tons are exempt from tax altogether (unless the vehicle is used wholly or mainly for the employee's private purposes). Where an employee has two or more vans made available for private use at the same time, tax is charged on the scale figure for each van. The standard amount will be reduced *pro rata* where the van is only available part of the year. A reduction is made for any contributions made by the employee towards the private use. Where a van is shared amongst several employees, the standard amount is apportioned among the employees.

11.5 COMPANY CARS

11.5.1 Car benefits

(TA 1988, ss 157, 168A–168G and Sched 6)

The taxable benefit is based on the list price of the car at the time that it was first registered, and not on the cost of the car. The taxable benefit is 35 per cent of the list price which includes delivery charges, standard accessories and optional accessories fitted when the car was first made available to the employee. A separate addition to the list price is also made where accessories are fitted after the car has been made available, but accessories with a list price of less than £100 and accessories installed before 1 August 1993 are left out of account. Where the car is at least four years old at the end of the tax year the benefit is reduced by one-third.

Where the list price of a vehicle exceeds £80,000, the excess is not taken into account.

Where a car is more than 15 years old at the end of the tax year, the car has a market value of at least £15,000 and the market value exceeds the list price, the benefit in kind is calculated by reference to the market value rather than original list price.

The assessable benefit is reduced by one-third where there is at least 2,500 business miles per annum. There is a reduction of a further one-third where the business mileage is at least 18,000 miles per annum.

Prima facie, if an employee is offered a car in return for a reduction in salary, he may well be taxable under Schedule E on the amount of remuneration foregone (*Heaton v Bell* (1969) 46 TC 211, HL). However this charge is specifically prevented by TA 1988, s 157A.

11.5.2 Tax treatment of employee contributions

Contributions made by an employee towards the cost of the car can be deducted from the list price, subject to a maximum deduction of £5,000.

11.5.3 Example – Employee contributions to company cars

Two employees are entitled to company cars. One contributed £4,000 towards a car with a list price of £18,000 while the other contributed £11,000 towards a car with a list price of £25,000. Their assessable benefits in kind for 1998/99 are:

	A	*B*
	£	£
List price	18,000	25,000
Less capital contribution income of:		
(A) amount contributed	(4,000)	
(B) deduction for capital contribution limited to		(5,000)
	14,000	20,000
35% thereof	4,900	7,000
Assessable benefits	4,900	7,000

Annual payments made by employees for private use of a car may still reduce the assessable benefit on a £1 for £1 basis. In the above example, B would have been better off if he had reduced his initial capital contribution and made annual payments in return for being allowed to use the vehicle for private purposes.

11.5.4 Returns

So as to enable coding notices to be amended to reflect changes in an employee's car benefit, employers have to submit returns for directors or employees who either:

(1) have a car provided for the first time;
(2) change vehicles;
(3) have the use of an additional car;
(4) have the use of a car withdrawn;
(5) qualify to be assessed on an existing car either by being appointed a director, or by coming within the 'higher paid' employee category.

Returns, using Inland Revenue form P46 (car), should be returned on a quarterly basis covering the following periods:

Period of return	*Latest date for submission*
6 April to 5 July	2 August
6 July to 5 October	2 November
6 October to 5 January	2 February
6 January to 5 April	3 May

The return provides details as to the make of car, engine size, list price, accessories, capital contributions and anticipated annual business mileage.

The maximum penalty for failing to submit a return by the due date is £300 plus £60 per day until the return is submitted.

The maximum penalty for submitting an incorrect return, either fraudulently or negligently, is £3,000.

11.5.5 Private petrol

(TA 1988, s 158)

An additional scale benefit applies where an employer provides private petrol for use in a car to which a scale benefit charge arises. The scale charge depends entirely on engine size. The scale for 1997/98 is as follows:

Engine size	*Petrol*	*Diesel*
	£	£
Up to 1400 cc	800	740
1401 to 2000 cc	1,010	740
More than 2000 cc	1,490	940

The scale figures apply regardless of the amount of private fuel provided. If *any* is provided, the fuel scale charge always applies unless the employee reimburses his employer for the full cost. In some cases it may be cost effective for an employee to do this and the position should therefore be reviewed before the start of each new tax year.

11.5.6 Other related costs

The scale benefit does not cover the salary of a chauffeur. If a director is allocated a chauffeur, the full cost to the employer of providing the chauffeur should be included on the director's form P11D and will therefore be potentially assessable as a benefit in kind (subject to a claim for business mileage).

11.5.7 Car parking spaces

(TA 1988, s 197A)

The provision of a car parking space at or near the employee's place of work is not a taxable benefit. Where, however, an employee pays for car parking himself, he cannot claim a deduction for those charges.

11.5.8 Mobile telephones
(TA 1988, s 159A)

Tax is charged on a standard amount of £200 per year per telephone unless the employee is required to make good the whole cost of any private use. The Revenue interprets these provisions so that the requirement to make good the full costs of private calls must exist throughout the year. It is therefore wise to ensure that the internal arrangements are sufficient to meet this requirement.

11.5.9 Free use of assets
(TA 1988, s 156)

A taxable benefit arises where an asset is made available by an employer for use by a director or P11D employee. The annual benefit is 20 per cent of the asset's market value when it was *first* made available for use by the employee. Assets which may be involved include yachts, furniture, television sets, stereo equipment, company vans etc, ie virtually any asset apart from living accommodation and company cars. If the employer rents or hires the item concerned for a sum in excess of 20 per cent of the asset's original market value, the higher rental charge is substituted as the assessable benefit. A deduction is allowed for any contribution or rental payable by the employee.

A further charge may arise if the ownership of assets is eventually transferred to the employee. The amount may be determined either by the market value of the asset at the time of transfer of ownership, or, where a higher figure results, by the original cost of the asset at the time it was first made available as a benefit for *any* person, less any amounts already charged as benefits in connection with the availability of the asset.

The second alternative does not apply to cars.

11.5.10 Example – Transfer of assets

A company provides an employee with the use of a yacht which costs £40,000 with the employee paying a rental of £2,000 per annum. After two years the yacht is sold to the employee for its second-hand market value of £20,000. The assessable benefit would be:

	Benefit £
Year one	
£40,000 × 20 per cent	8,000
Less rental paid	2,000
	6,000

Year two	
40,000 × 20 per cent	8,000
Less rental paid	2,000
	6,000
Year three	
Cost of yacht	40,000
Less benefits assessed in years one and two	(12,000)
Amounts paid by employee	(24,000)
	4,000

Where an asset, previously made available to an individual, is transferred at no cost to him (or to another employee), at a time when its market value is still high, it is possible that the overall effect is that the total cost of the benefit for tax purposes exceeds the original cost. In other cases, the rules may operate to impose a high benefit charge upon the transfer of an asset despite the value of the asset having rapidly depreciated during the period of use.

Such rules must therefore be carefully considered when planning the provision of an asset for use by an employee or arranging for its transfer to the employee. It may be that transfer of ownership should be avoided where assets have a relatively short useful life if a tax-efficient remuneration package is desired.

11.5.11 Example – Ownership of assets

A company provides employees with the use of suits which remain the property of the company. The suits cost £200 and have a useful life of two years, after which they are scrapped.

An employee could therefore have an effective benefit of £200 but would be charged tax on only £40 for each of the two tax years.

11.6 BENEFICIAL LOANS

(TA 1988, s 160)

11.6.1 Type of loans which are caught

A charge generally arises for directors and P11D employees on the annual value of beneficial loan arrangements. The annual value of a loan is taken as interest at the 'official rate' less the amount of interest (if any) paid by the employee. The official rate is revised regularly to keep pace with movements in interest rates generally. An additional taxable benefit arises if the loan is subsequently written off or forgiven.

The beneficial loan provisions can also apply if a loan is made to a member of an employee's family.

Moreover, the Revenue is able to assess benefits even though there may be no formal loan, where credit has been involved. In particular, a director who overdraws his current account with the company is regarded as having obtained a loan and is subject to an assessment.

Almost all loans by employers (and persons connected with them) are caught as the legislation deems such loans to have been given by reason of the employment. Until 6 April 1994, there was only a single exception in that this rule did not apply where the employee was related to the employer and it could be shown that the loan was given for family reasons. There were no other exceptions and there have been cases where bank employees etc have paid a normal commercial rate of interest on money lent to them, but have been assessed on a benefit because the interest they have paid has been less than the official rate.

For 1994–95 and subsequent years, loans made by an employer whose business includes the lending of money to the general public do not give rise to a charge on the employees provided the loans are made on similar terms to the public.

11.6.2 Beneficial loans used for a qualifying purpose

No charge arises on a cheap loan where the money which has been borrowed has been applied for a qualifying purpose, eg for the purchase of shares in a close company in which the individual has a material interest or where he is employed full time in the conduct and management of the company's business.

11.6.3 *De minimis* exemption

There is an exemption for all cheap or interest-free loans made to an individual employee which do not exceed £5,000. This figure excludes loans which qualify for tax relief such as loans of up to £30,000 for house purchase.

11.6.4 Employee loans written off

If the loan is written off, the amount forgiven is treated as assessable income for that year even if the person concerned is no longer employed by that company. The only exception here is if the loan is forgiven on the death of the employee.

Some care needs to be taken if it is decided to clear a loan by making an *ex gratia* or compensation payment to an employee upon the termination of the employment. An income tax liability arises if the loan is formally written off. On the other hand, no liability normally arises if the employee receives a cheque as an *ex gratia* or compensation payment and uses that sum to clear his outstanding loan. It is recommended that professional advice be taken in such circumstances.

11.7 LIVING ACCOMMODATION

(TA 1988, ss 145–146)

11.7.1 Introduction

The income tax charge which generally applies where an employee is provided with accommodation (unless it is representative accommodation—see 11.3.5) depends on whether the property is owned or rented by the employer. In the past, where the employer owned the property, the assessable amount was usually the gross annual value for rating purposes. Despite the abolition of domestic rates, this treatment continues to apply for properties on existing rating lists. For new properties, and those where there have been major improvements, the Revenue makes an estimate of what the gross annual value would have been had rates continued.

Where the property is rented by the employer, the assessable amount is the greater of the rent paid and the annual value as above. In addition a charge may arise on the annual value of any furniture and fixtures, and on any occupier's expenses borne by the company such as water rates, decorations, gardener's wages etc.

An additional charge may arise where the employer paid more than £75,000 to acquire the property. The amount assessable is a percentage of the excess of the cost of the property over £75,000. The percentage to be applied is the official rate of interest used for beneficial loans (see 11.9) as at the *beginning* of the tax year.

11.7.2 Example – Charge on living accommodation in excess of £75,000

A company director occupies a property owned by the company which has a gross annual value of £2,000. The cost of the property in 1989 was £100,000.
The director is assessed on the following amount for 1995–96:

	£
Gross annual value	2,000
£25,000 × 8% =	2,000
	4,000

11.7.3 Properties owned for more than six years

Where the property is made available to an employee and it has been owned by the company for at least six years, the figure taken into account in computing the additional charge is the market value at the time it was made available rather than the cost. The actual cost (including improvements) to the employer is still used to determine whether the provisions will apply. Consequently, properties whose actual cost was less than £75,000 (including the cost of any improvements) are not within the scope of this additional charge even if their market value exceeds £75,000. Where the actual cost exceeded £75,000, the additional charge is based on the market value.

11.7.4 Example – Charge on living accommodation purchased over six years ago

In Example 11.7.2, assume that the company has owned the property for more than six years and that in May 1994, when the director first occupies it, the market value is £200,000. As the original cost of the property exceeded £75,000, the director is assessed on the following amount for 1997–98:

	£
Gross annual value	2,000
£125,000 × (say) 8% =	10,000
	12,000

11.7.5 Possible reduction in assessable amount

It may be possible to reduce the assessable amount where the employee is required to occupy a property which is larger than would normally be needed for his or her own purposes. In *Westcott v Bryan* (1969) 45 TC 476 a director was required to live in a large house so that he could entertain customers. He was allowed a reduction in the assessable amount to cover the relevant proportion of the annual value and the running expenses.

Some care is needed if it is intended to claim relief in this way. This claim succeeded because the house was larger than needed for the director and his family. It would not have succeeded had the property merely been more expensive than he would have chosen. It was also helpful that the directors of the company had approved board minutes setting out their requirement and the business reason for it.

Holiday accommodation and foreign properties

Some employers buy holiday flats or cottages etc for use by staff. In practice, the Revenue generally apportions the assessable amount for the year amongst those employees who have occupied the property. The assessment can be reduced by letting the accommodation to third parties when it is not required by directors and employees. A practical problem arises with regard to overseas properties. Because there is no rateable value, the benefit is the annual rent which the property would normally command on the open market.

11.8 MISCELLANEOUS BENEFITS

11.8.1 Council tax

Where an employer pays the council tax on behalf of an employee, this is normally chargeable as part of the employee's remuneration package, resulting in a charge to both income tax and NIC. The one exception to this is where the employee is a representative occupier (see 11.3.5).

11.8.2 Medical insurance

(TA 1988, s 155(6))

The cost of medical insurance is normally assessable on P11D employees. Where the employer has a group scheme, a proportion of the total premiums is related to individual employees. There is an exception in that the premiums are exempt to the extent that they provide cover for an employee working outside the UK.

11.8.3 Telephone rental

The Revenue treats the full amount of the rental paid by the employer as a taxable benefit in kind even though the telephone may be partly (or mainly) used for business calls. The decision in *Lucas v Cattell* (1972) 48 TC 353 was that the expenditure on rental had a dual purpose (ie that a telephone is intended to be used for both business and personal use) and therefore no part of it was allowable.

11.8.4 Club subscriptions

A benefit in kind is deemed to arise where an employer pays or reimburses an employee's subscription to a club, even though the employee may only belong to the club in order to entertain the employer's customers.

11.8.5 In-house tax and financial advice

This is a type of expenditure which the Revenue has ignored in the past, but is now treating this as a benefit in kind where the cost can clearly be allocated to particular employees. Similarly the Revenue will seek to assess directors on a benefit in kind where work on their personal taxation affairs has been carried out by the company's auditors, the cost being recovered in whole or in part from the company.

11.8.6 Christmas parties and other annual functions
(Extra-Statutory Concession A70)

The Revenue has said that it will not assess a benefit in respect of 'modest' expenditure on a Christmas party for staff, provided the party is open to all staff. The limit for expenditure to be regarded as modest in this context is currently £75 per head. Although this rule is generally attributed to Christmas parties, it may apply to a function at another time of year.

Where there is more than one annual function and their total costs per head exceed £75, the functions that total £75 or less are not taxed. All other functions are taxed in full.

11.8.7 Legal fees

There may be expenditure which is incurred for the benefit of the company's business but nevertheless is deemed to give rise to a benefit in kind. A leading case in this connection concerned a director of a company who was accused of dangerous driving. It was necessary for the company's business that he should not be imprisoned and the company paid his legal expenses. Although the lawyers engaged by the company were more expensive than the director would have used himself, the expenditure by the company was treated as a benefit in kind.

11.8.8 Outplacement counselling
(TA 1988, s 589B)

The value of outplacement services provided to employees made redundant is exempt from income tax. Such services may include assistance with CVs, job searches, office equipment provisions and advice on interview skills. These types of costs are not treated as part of a termination payment (see 11.17).

11.8.9 Goods and services provided at a discount to the normal price ('in-house benefits')

Where employees are allowed to purchase goods or services from their employer, no tax charge arises provided they pay an amount equal to the employer's cost. The House of Lords decided in November 1992 that 'cost' meant marginal cost, not average cost (*Pepper v Hart* [1992] STC 898). This normally produces a significantly lower benefit.

Following this, the Revenue published a statement in January 1993 setting out its practice for the future with regard to teachers, employees within the transport industry and other employees who receive goods or services from their employer. The relevant press release stated that Treasury Ministers had the matter under review but, in the event, the decision has not been disturbed.

The Revenue has stated that the decision in *Pepper v Hart* means that:

(1) rail or bus travel by employees on terms which do not displace fare-paying passengers involves no or negligible additional costs;
(2) goods sold at a discount which leave employees paying at least the wholesale price involve no or negligible net benefit;
(3) where teachers pay 15 per cent or more of a school's normal fees, there is no net benefit;

(4) professional services which do not require additional employees or partners (eg legal and financial services) have no or negligible cost to the employer (provided the employee meets the cost of any disbursements).

11.9 END OF YEAR RETURNS

Form P11D can be obtained from the local Revenue office. The form needs to be submitted by 6 June following the end of the tax year. If the forms are submitted late there can be a penalty of up to £300 for each late return, and a continuing daily penalty of up to £60 may be imposed under similar procedures as for forms P35/P14. Penalties up to £3,000 may be charged for each incorrectly completed return.

11.10 PROFIT-RELATED PAY AND SHARE SCHEMES

(TA 1988, ss 169–171)

The rules on profit-related pay schemes (PRP) are complex in so far as they concern the companies which set up a scheme. They are relatively straightforward from the point of view of the employee.

11.10.1 PRP exempt from income tax

Where an individual receives profit-related pay under a registered scheme, all or part of the PRP is exempt from income tax. The exemption is available on the lowest of:

(1) 20 per cent of total remuneration for the year;
(2) £4,000;
(3) the actual PRP received in the tax year.

Where an individual participates in more than one PRP scheme, the £4,000 exemption has to be divided between the amounts payable under each PRP scheme.

PRP is being phased out over the period from 1 January 1998 to 31 December 1999. The exemption limit in (2) is:

(a) from 1 January 1998 to 31 December 1998 – £2,000;
(b) from 1 January 1999 to 31 December 1999 – £1,000.

For profit periods beginning after 31 December 1999, the relief is withdrawn altogether, and all existing registrations cease to have effect (FA 1997, s 61).

Profit-related pay forms part of a director or employee's earnings for NIC.

11.10.2 Conditions required for PRP scheme to be registered

The following conditions need to be satisfied before the Revenue will register a profit-related pay scheme:

(1) The scheme rules should provide for at least 80 per cent of relevant employees to participate. Relevant employees are those who are in the pay unit concerned (these need not necessarily be the company as a whole but could, for example, be a division within the company).
(2) The PRP legislation requires that employees must participate 'on similar terms'. This does not necessarily mean that all employees should receive the same amount (although a scheme could be established on such a basis). Instead, the scheme rules may provide for payments to vary in order to reflect the following factors:
   (a) levels of remuneration;
   (b) length of service;
   (c) hours worked;
   (d) other similar objective factors.
(3) Individuals who have more than a 25 per cent shareholding in a company (either alone or taken together with associates) cannot participate in a PRP scheme.

11.11 GIFTS OF SHARES

A gift of shares to an employee is normally a taxable benefit, with the tax charge being based on the market value of the shares. If the shares are given to the employee by a shareholder, he is normally treated as if he had made a disposal of the shares at their market value, and he may therefore be liable for capital gains tax.

The tax position where an employee is allowed to subscribe for new shares at an undervalue is broadly the same. The employee is taxed on the difference between the amount that he pays to subscribe for the shares and their market value. However, dealing with matters in this way usually avoids any capital gains tax problems for the shareholders (since there is no disposal by the existing shareholders or the company, merely an issue of new shares).

A company normally needs to report the acquisition of shares by an employee within 30 days of the end of the tax year.

11.12 NON-APPROVED SHARE OPTIONS

11.12.1 Introduction

A Schedule E income tax charge may arise on the exercise of a share option or on the growth in value of shares which have been acquired by reason of the individual's office or employment (and, in particular, shares in dependent subsidiaries). The legislation was introduced on a piece-meal basis and it is often difficult to discern any clear or logical structure or principles which underly the legislation.

11.12.2 Non-approved share options

(TA 1988, s 135)

A tax charge may arise on either the grant or the exercise of the option.

Grant of the option

A charge may arise only if the option has a potential life of more than seven years. Even if the option is capable of being exercised more than seven years later, the Revenue is unlikely to assess a value greater than the difference between the value of the shares at the time the option is granted and the aggregate of the amount (if any) paid for the grant of option and the amount payable under the option.

Exercise of the option

A person who is subject to tax under Schedule E Case I may be subject to an income tax charge when he exercises a non-approved share option which has been granted to him by reason of his office or employment. The charge is not dependent upon his selling the shares but arises on any profit or gain that he is deemed to have made by exercising the option. Normally the profit is simply the difference between the market value of the shares at the time that he exercises his option and the price payable under the option.

Profit related pay scheme: mandatory requirements

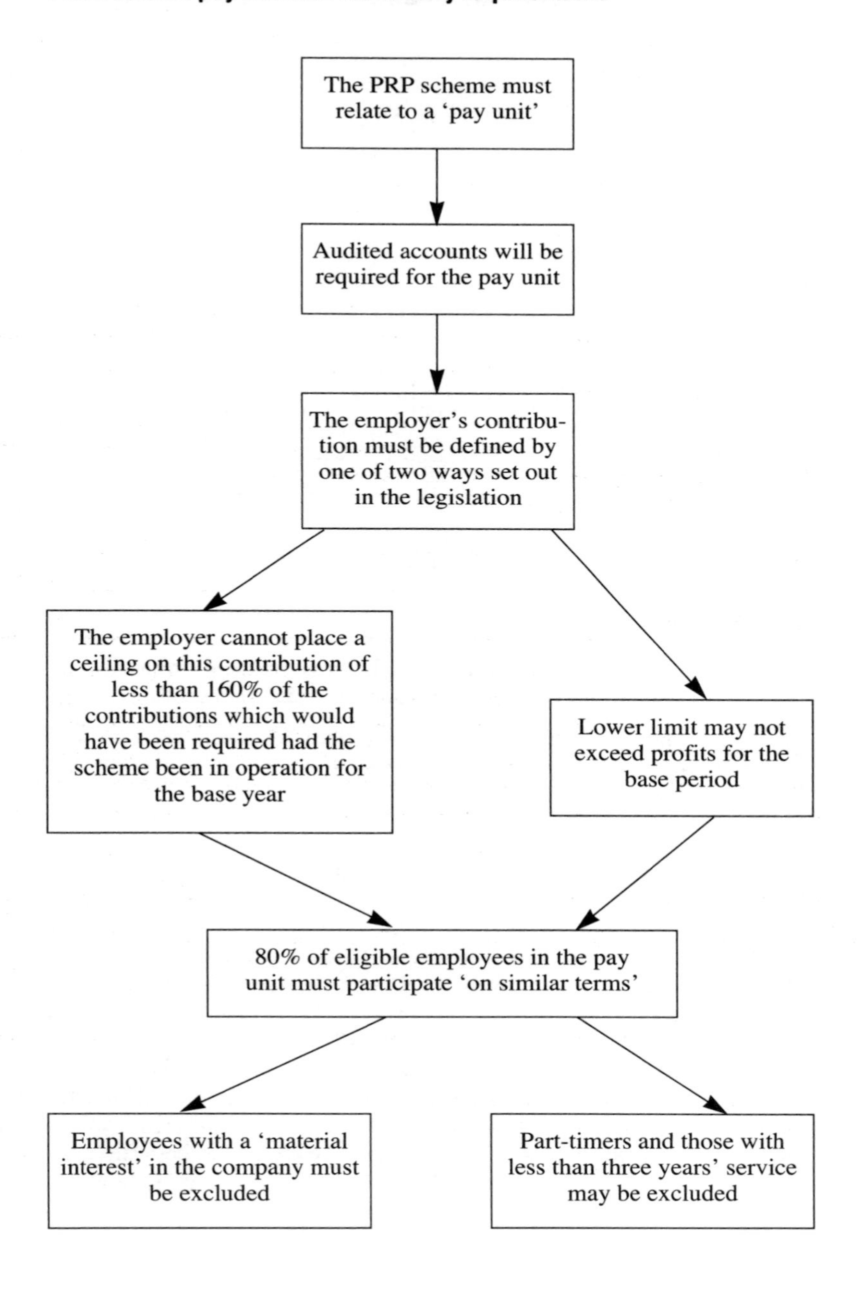

11.12.3 Example – Exercise of share options

A was granted an option to acquire 1,000 shares in XYZ Ltd at a price of £2 per share. After five years have elapsed, he exercises the option and pays £2,000 to acquire the 1,000 shares. By this time the shares have grown in value to £5 per share.

A will be assessed for the year in which he exercises the option. His profit will be assessed as £3,000, ie:

	£
Market value of 1,000 shares	5,000
Less amount paid	2,000
	3,000

Where the option was granted before 6 April 1984, the tax payable may be paid by instalments over five years provided the individual makes a formal election under TA 1988, s 137. The election must be made within 60 days of the end of the tax year in which the option is exercised.

11.12.4 Residence status of the employee

No charge arises under these provisions if the employee was not resident and ordinarily resident in the UK at the date that the option was granted. This is because the individual has to be UK-resident and ordinarily resident if he is to be chargeable to tax under Schedule E Case I.

The charge, however, still arises where an individual who was resident and ordinarily resident when the option was *granted* ceases to be UK-resident before the option is *exercised*.

11.12.5 Other employee share options
(TA 1988, s 162)

Where an individual exercises an option which was granted to him as an employee, but at a time when he was not chargeable to tax under Schedule E Case I, and he retains the shares, an income tax charge may arise on the eventual disposal of the shares. The legislation on beneficial loans contains deeming provisions which treat the difference between the shares' market value at the time that the option is exercised and the amount payable to exercise the option as if it were a loan. On a subsequent sale or disposal of the shares the loan is deemed to be written off and a Schedule E charge arises if the individual is resident in the UK at that time.

11.12.6 Returns by employer

A company which grants an option to an employee must make a return within 30 days of the end of the tax year.

11.13 PROFIT-SHARING SCHEMES
(TA 1988, ss 186–187)

These operate by means of a trust, with the trustees receiving payments from the company's profits to enable them to buy shares on behalf of the employees. In computing its profits, the company should get a deduction for the sums paid so long as the trustees apply the money in accordance with the approved scheme rules. The amount which may be appropriated to an employee under the scheme cannot exceed £3,000 or, if greater, 10 per cent of the employee's remuneration for PAYE purposes, with an overall limit of £8,000.

The employee is entitled to dividends paid on the shares during the period of retention by the trustees. The trustees *must* retain the shares for a period of two years; if the shares are then retained by the trustees for a further three years, there is no income tax charge on the employee. If they are sold by the employee within three years of appropriation, an income tax charge arises based on the percentage of the 'locked-in value' ie the lower of the market value of the shares when they were appropriated by the trust fund or the sale proceeds. The percentages are as follows:

Date of disposal	*Appropriate %*
Before release date	100
After cessation of employment due to injury, disability or redundancy	50
After relevant age*	50
Excess or unauthorised shares	50

*ie the applicable pensionable age

Provided that the shares are held in trust for three years, normally the only liability arising to the employee is to capital gains tax when he disposes of the shares appropriated to him. The capital gains liability arises on the difference between the disposal proceeds of these shares less their open market value on the day on which they were appropriated to him. The growth in value from the date of acquisition by the trust to the date of appropriation is tax free.

11.13.1 Examples – Disposals of shares in a profit sharing scheme

(1) In March 1994, the trustees of an approved scheme appropriated 500 £1 shares to an employee at a time when the market value was £1.25 each. The locked-in value is therefore 500 at £1.25 = £625.

In June 1996 the shares are sold for £2.35 each. The sale was made between years four and five and consequently an income tax liability arises based on 50 per cent of the locked-in value, ie £312.50.

(2) The facts are as in example (1) but the sale is delayed until June 1997. The sale is after the end of year five; therefore there is no Schedule E liability. A capital gains tax charge could arise on a disposal of the shares. The gain is the difference between £2.35 per share and £1.25 as adjusted for indexation.

11.14 SHARE OPTION SCHEMES

11.14.1 Introduction

There are two main types of approved share option schemes for employees: save as you earn (SAYE) linked share option schemes and executive share option schemes.

Approved SAYE linked share option schemes were introduced in 1980. The main features of these schemes are that there is a limit on the value of the shares which may be allocated to an employee and that participation in the scheme must be open to all full-time employees who have completed five years' service.

In 1984 the government introduced a further category of approved share options intended to cover special arrangements for senior executives. The maximum amounts involved are much more generous and there is no requirement that the option be granted to all employees.

It is possible for an employer to establish both types of scheme and, indeed, to grant non-approved share options as well.

11.14.2 SAYE option schemes

These schemes entail the grant of an option for employees to purchase company shares at a price which must not be 'manifestly less' than 80 per cent of their market value at the time that the options are granted. The employee is required to take out an SAYE linked savings scheme (maximum £250 per month) and may use the proceeds to exercise the share option either five or seven years later, depending on the rules of the particular scheme. No income tax liability arises on the grant of the options or upon their exercise. Capital gains tax is charged on an eventual disposal of the shares.

11.15 EXECUTIVE SHARE OPTION SCHEMES

The general principle is that an income tax charge may arise on the exercise of a share option, but certain approved share option schemes may be established which avoid such an income tax liability. Capital gains tax may still apply but only on a subsequent disposal of the shares concerned. However, following the Greenbury report, the tax benefits only apply to a restricted extent for options granted after 17 July 1995.

11.15.1 Conditions for approval

In order to receive Revenue approval, the following conditions must be satisfied:

(1) Participation in the scheme must be open only to full-time directors or employees or to part-time employees working at least 20 hours a week. Part-time directors may not participate in this scheme. The Revenue has indicated that it regards a director who works 25 hours per week as full time. The employer may choose which of the employees are to be permitted to participate in the scheme.
(2) Where the employer is a close company, no participant must own (or be entitled to acquire as a result of the grant of the option) more than 10 per cent of the company's shares. Furthermore no individual who has owned more than 10 per cent of the company's shares within the previous 12 months is able to participate.
(3) The price at which the option is to be exercised must not be 'manifestly less' than the value of the shares at the time that the option is granted. With effect from 1 January 1992, it became possible for options to be granted at a discount of up to 15 per cent of the market value of shares at the time of granting where the company also operates an approved profit-sharing scheme or savings-related share option scheme.
For options granted from 29 April 1996, the discount feature is no longer available, and it is only necessary to compare the aggregate consideration and the market value.
(4) There is a limit on the number of shares over which a particular employee may be granted options. The scheme must limit the employee's options to shares with a market value at the time that the options are granted which does not exceed £30,000. Remuneration

for PAYE purposes excludes benefits in kind and reimbursed expenses and is after deducting contributions to an approved pensions scheme.

(5) The shares issued under the scheme must be fully paid ordinary shares of the company or its parent company. They must either be shares quoted on a recognised stock exchange or shares in a non-close company which is controlled by a quoted company or shares in a company not under the control of another company.

(6) Options must not be transferable and must be exercisable only between three and ten years after they are granted. There is an income tax charge on individuals who exercise options under the scheme more than once every three years. This three-year time limit is waived if a director or employee dies, in which case the option must be exercised by the personal representatives within one year of death.

11.16 SPECIAL EMPLOYEE SHARES

There are circumstances where a tax charge may arise on the disposal of shares, or on their being made more valuable by the removal of restrictions. The relevant legislation particularly needs to be borne in mind where the director or employee has acquired shares in a company which is a subsidiary of another company.

Liability to income tax under Schedule E may arise:

(1) when any restrictions affecting the employee's shares are removed; or
(2) when the shareholder receives any special benefit by virtue of ownership; or
(3) where the shares are in a 'dependent subsidiary'.

11.16.1 Shares in a dependent subsidiary

A company which is a subsidiary is deemed to be a dependent subsidiary unless the directors certify each year that it is not a dependent subsidiary and the auditors confirm their agreement to this. A company is regarded as a dependent subsidiary if there is any significant amount of trading with the parent company or another member of the group.

Where an employee holds shares in a dependent subsidiary, a tax charge may arise on the growth in the value which takes place at the earliest of the following times:

(1) the time when he actually disposes of the shares;
(2) the date that the company ceases to be a dependent subsidiary;
(3) the expiry of seven years from the date of acquisition.

A charge may arise even though the company was not a dependent subsidiary when the person acquired his shares if it subsequently becomes a dependent subsidiary.

11.17 TERMINATION PAYMENTS

11.17.1 Redundancy payments
(TA 1988, s 579)

A statutory redundancy payment made under the Employment Rights Act 1996 is exempt from tax although it may need to be taken into account in computing the tax payable on a termination payment (see 11.17.3–11.17.4).

Payment to an employee under a non-statutory redundancy scheme is generally treated by the Revenue as exempt under Statement of Practice SP1/81 where the following conditions are satisfied:

(1) Payments are made only on account of redundancy as defined in the Employment Rights Act 1996, s 166.
(2) The individual has at least two years' continuous service.
(3) Payments are made to all relevant employees and not merely to a selected group of employees.
(4) The payments are not excessively large in relation to earnings and length of service.

In *Mairs v Haughey* [1993] STC 569, the Revenue sought to tax a payment made to an employee for giving up contingent redundancy rights. The Revenue argued that the payment constituted an emolument of the employment, but it was held that a redundancy payment is not an emolument and a lump sum paid in lieu of a right to receive such a redundancy payment is equally not an emolument.

This case has also cast doubt on the view generally held within the Revenue that a termination payment is always taxable where the employee is contractually entitled to it. Statement of Practice SP1/94 was issued after *Mairs v Haughey*.

11.17.2 Ex gratia payments

There has been concern that *ex gratia* payments may be subject to tax under Schedule E as unapproved retirement benefits taxable under TA 1988, s 596A. If this charge arises, the amount received is taxed in full under Schedule E. The Revenue issued a statement of practice in October 1991 (SP 13/91) and has subsequently clarified the position. An *ex gratia* payment is normally regarded as a retirement benefit taxable under s 596A only where it is paid in connection with an individual's retirement. The Revenue has also given the following guidelines on hypothetical situations:

(1) A person who has worked for a company for 20 years leaves at age 54 to take a senior executive position in another company – 'golden handshake'.
(2) A long-service employee leaves to take a senior executive position in another company at the age of 60 – borderline, probably retirement.
(3) A division of a company is sold and the 55-year-old manager responsible for running it leaves to take a job with the purchaser – 'golden handshake'.
(4) A person in his 50s has a heart attack and is advised by his doctor to leave and seek a less stressful position – 'golden handshake'.
(5) An employee aged 35 is involved in an accident and suffers disabilities that make him unable to continue with his job – 'golden handshake'.
(6) An employee aged 50 leaves to take a job nearer home to be able to nurse her aged parents – borderline, 'golden handshake'. If the employee did not take a new job, or was nearer normal retirement age, this situation would be treated as retirement.

Ex gratia payments not caught under TA 1988, s 596A are normally treated in the same way as compensation for loss of office (see below).

11.17.3 Compensation for loss of office

Golden handshakes and other termination payments

(TA 1988, s 148)

Introduction

Where a director's or employee's contract of service is terminated, it may be possible for a compensation payment to be made which is either wholly or partly tax free *provided* the employee is not entitled to the compensation under a contract of service. Where the individual receives compensation, under a term of his contract of employment, the Revenue's view is that it is taxable under Schedule E in the usual way. A payment made to a director as compensation for accepting a reduced salary or any other variation of his service contract is not regarded as a termination payment, and the amount received is normally taxable in full.

Exemptions from the charge under TA 1988, s 148

There are various types of termination payment which are exempt:

Payments made because of death or disability (TA 1988, s 188) A termination payment which arises where an employment is terminated because of death, injury or disability is exempt. Disability covers not only a condition arising from a sudden affliction but also a continuing incapacity to perform the duties of an office or employment because of the culmination of a process of deterioration of physical or mental health caused by chronic illness (see Statement of Practice SP10/81).

Contributions to an approved retirement benefit scheme A special contribution by an employer into an approved retirement benefit scheme is not taxable as a termination payment.

Foreign service (TA 1988, s 188(3)) A lump sum termination payment is not taxable where the employment has constituted foreign service which exceeds the following limits:

(1) three-quarters of the whole period of service;
(2) the last ten years;
(3) one-half of the period of service provided that this amounted to at least 20 years and subject to at least ten of the last 20 years of service being foreign service.

'Foreign' service is defined as meaning a period of service during which the earnings were not assessable under Schedule E Case I either because the individual was not UK resident or because the 100 per cent deduction was available because the period spent working overseas exceeded 365 days (see *Allied Dunbar Tax Handbook 1997–98,* para 3.21).

Basic £30,000 exemption

(TA 1988, s 188(4))

Where a termination payment is not wholly exempt, the first £30,000 is normally free from tax and only the balance is chargeable. Where an individual receives both statutory redundancy payments and a termination payment, the amount of the statutory redundancy payments uses up part of the £30,000 exemption and only the balance is available to cover part of the termination payment.

Employment includes a period of foreign service

The £30,000 exemption may be increased where the employment has included 'foreign service'.

11.17.4 Example – Increased exemption due to foreign service

B was non-resident in the UK from 1976 to 1984. He then qualified for the 100 per cent deduction from 1984 until 1986, so that he was not subject to UK tax on his salary even though he was resident. In December 1997 he retires and receives compensation of £80,000.

The exemption is found by using the fraction:

$$\frac{\text{Foreign service}}{\text{Total period of employment}} \quad \text{ie in this case} \quad \frac{10 \text{ years}}{21 \text{ years}}$$

This fraction is applied to the amount of the golden handshake after deduction of the £30,000 exemption. The taxable amount would be arrived at as follows:

	£
Compensation	80,000
Less 'normal exemption'	30,000
	50,000
$^{10}/_{21}$ thereof	23,809
Taxable amount	26,191

Year for which a termination payment may be taxed

The time when a termination payment is made does not affect the tax liability as it is treated as taxable income for the year in which the employment is terminated.

11.17.5 Payments for restrictive covenants

A payment made to an employee in return for his giving a restrictive covenant is chargeable to tax under Schedule E (TA 1988, s 313). The employer should operate PAYE.

11.18 HOW THE INLAND REVENUE ENSURES COMPLIANCE

11.18.1 The Collector's audit division

The division exists to monitor the operation of tax deduction and payment under the PAYE and construction industry sub-contractors schemes and to monitor NIC compliance.

Method of operation

The Collector of Taxes has a statutory right to inspect documents and records relating to tax deductions. This does not mean Collectors have an automatic right of entry to business or other premises but given their power to inspect documents such a right of entry must to a certain extent follow on. The PAYE Regulations give the Collector the power to specify that the documents should be made available for inspection at a reasonable time at:

- A place agreed by the employer and Collector.
- In default of such agreement, the place in the UK where the documents are normally kept.
- In default of such a normal place, the employer's principal place of business in the UK.

There is no statutory limit to the number of years for which the Collector may ask for documents or records, but the employer is only obliged to keep records for three years after the end of the year to which they relate. It could therefore be said that it is safe for the employer to destroy records after that period has elapsed. The argument against this is that if the Collector finds irregularities in the records for the three most recent years it would be extremely difficult for the employer to refute the suggestions that similar irregularities took place in earlier years. It is therefore advisable that records should be kept for a minimum of six years.

The Inland Revenue's booklet IR 71 entitled 'PAYE Inspections' provides brief information on the way in which such inspections are undertaken, whilst IR 109 explains how settlements are negotiated at the end of an inspection.

Problem areas

From his previous experience of investigations, and knowledge of the type of business the records of which are being examined, the Collector can identify, in advance, those areas which are likely to be a fruitful source of additional liability. The areas most commonly investigated are:

(1) casuals;
(2) part-timers;
(3) bonuses (eg at Christmas);
(4) round-sum expense allowances including entertaining;
(5) directors emoluments of all types;
(6) payments out of petty cash;
(7) termination payments;
(8) self-employed consultants, out-workers etc.

The Collector will check for failure, or under-deduction, of tax either deliberately or through ignorance, as well as being concerned (and this applies particularly to directors) with the timing of deductions. His responsibility extends to Class 1 and 1A NIC as well as to income tax.

Where employers engage sub-contractors in the construction industry the inspection also covers the operation of the Construction Industry Tax Deduction Scheme.

Settlement

Provided the employer agrees with the Collector's conclusions, the unpaid tax and NIC are quantified and the employer is asked to make an offer in settlement of that tax, interest, and possibly penalties.

11.18.2 Role of Schedule E compliance units

While the monitoring of compliance with PAYE and NIC regulations is officially the responsibility of the Collector's PAYE audit teams, visits are increasingly made to employers by Schedule E compliance units.

The units specialise in reviewing the provision of expenses and benefits to directors, and employees earning £8,500 or more per annum. Reviews of P11Ds therefore form a large part of their work. Officers also examine employees' own tax returns however, and focus on aspects of the employer's records which indicate or suggest the provision of benefits which have not been declared.

Compliance visits

During the visit, the employer is asked about the possible provision of benefits by third parties to employees or payment of salaries direct to third parties. Questions may also be asked about the provision of inducement and termination payments. The status of individuals treated as casual employees and as self-employed may also be explored.

The principal inquiries however focus upon an examination of the provision of expenses and benefits to directors or employees and members of their family or household with a view to identifying benefits previously undeclared or undervalued.

Settlements

As with PAYE audit inspections, minor errors may result in settlements confined to that year. In other cases settlements, to include in some cases penalties and interest, may cover the previous six years, with earlier years' adjustments estimated on the basis of the errors discovered for the one year reviewed.

The tax liabilities exposed are normally employee liabilities. In the majority of cases both the Revenue and employer are keen to settle matters in such a way that the employer meets the additional liability.

Care should be taken in such cases to ensure that employee's tax rates are taken into account in computing the tax due, although use of a composite rate may sometimes be administratively beneficial and prove acceptable to the Revenue.

While in strictness the liabilities should be grossed up to take into account the additional benefit of the employer meeting the employee's tax liability, the Revenue may be persuaded to forego this for the sake of a quick settlement with the employer as opposed to raising separate Schedule E assessments on all employees involved.

At the close of their inquiries steps are taken to ensure the employer's procedures are now acceptable, and employers should take the opportunity to review existing dispensations, or apply for new dispensations.

Prior to 1996–97, employers who wished to settle employee's liabilities on a range of minor benefits in kind and incidental expenses entered into informal, non-statutory arrangements known as 'annual voluntary settlements'. These arrangements now have a statutory footing under TA 1988, s 206A and are known as 'PAYE settlement arrangements'.

12

LIFE ASSURANCE, PENSIONS AND PERMANENT HEALTH INSURANCE

VINCE JERRARD, ALLIED DUNBAR ASSURANCE

12.1 INTRODUCTION

Although the fine print can appear daunting, life assurance, pension and permanent health insurance policies are really just evidence of a contract between the policyholder and the company issuing the policy. In exchange for payment of a contribution or premium, the company promises to make one or more specified payments in certain defined circumstances.

Depending on the type of contract entered into, the payment from the company may be, for example, a lump sum on the death of an individual, an income in retirement for a pensioner, or a replacement income for a person prevented from earning by reason of sickness or disability. Despite the technical appearance of many of these policies (often due to complex tax rules offering relief on payment of premiums or benefits), it is useful to bear in mind the essential simplicity of the idea: payment of premiums (usually regular payments) to the company in exchange for the guarantee or expectation of payments back on the happening of some future event.

With life assurance contracts, there must be an 'insurable interest' before a policy can be effected. Broadly, before a person can effect a life policy he must be able to demonstrate that the death of the person whose life is being insured will cause him financial loss. In addition the amount of the assurance must not exceed the amount of that loss.

Individuals have an automatic and unlimited insurable interest in their own life and the life of their spouse. In other cases an insurable interest must be demonstrated before a person can effect a policy on someone else's life (a 'life of another' policy).

This chapter, in Part I, looks at the contracts themselves and gives an outline of the rules which apply to them. Part II then goes on to consider some basic uses of the contracts with reference to sole traders, partners and small companies.

PART I – THE BASICS

12.2 LIFE ASSURANCE

12.2.1 Types of policy

There are three basic types of life assurance policy:

(1) whole of life policies;
(2) endowment policies;
(3) term policies.

Whole of life policies are protection-orientated policies which pay the guaranteed sum assured on the death of the life assured, whenever death occurs. As such, they are most appropriate where long-term protection is needed, for example to meet the inheritance tax liability on an individual's death or to protect the family from the consequences of the 'breadwinner's' death. Whole of life policies may, over the years, also acquire significant cash values, although they are not primarily investment vehicles.

Endowment policies pay a guaranteed sum on the death of the life assured during the policy term, or on survival to the end of the term. Such policies provide a valuable mixture of protection and investment and are often used in conjunction with a mortgage to provide for a lump sum which will pay off the loan at the end of the mortgage term, or on the borrower's prior death.

Term assurance policies pay a guaranteed sum assured only if death occurs before the end of the term. They are for protection purposes only and usually provide no return to the policyholder if the life assured survives the policy term. Term assurance policies are usually the cheapest form of life assurance protection. The cover provided by them can be widened by use of renewal or conversion options. A renewal option allows the policyholder to renew the policy at the end of the original term, without further evidence of health being required. A conversion option allows a policyholder to turn his policy into a whole of life assurance or an endowment policy, free of underwriting, should his needs change. A convertible term assurance is particularly useful if the need is for life assurance protection for the whole of the individual's life but it is not possible to afford a whole of life policy at the time. Term assurance policies can also be effected under some pensions legislation (see 12.3.5).

These policies have the advantage of tax relief on the premiums paid.

A development in the United Kingdom in recent years has been what is commonly called 'dread disease' or 'critical illness' protection. This cover is usually written as an additional benefit to a whole life, endowment or term policy and provides for payment of the sum assured on the life assured suffering one of the several specified diseases or events. Typical dread diseases and events are heart attack, stroke, cancer, major organ transplant, certain types of heart surgery and total permanent disability.

12.2.2 Traditional and unit-linked policies

There are two bases on which policies are offered.

Traditional policy

Under a traditional policy the life assurance company estimates future mortality experience, investment return and company expenses. Using these factors the actuary determines the premium rate for a given sum assured, both of which are then guaranteed by the company. As the assumptions made by the company are, of necessity, conservative, the premiums may often be higher than necessary. To counter this, traditional companies developed 'with profits' policies so that those contracts could share in the extra profits being made by the life company.

Extra profits are allocated to the policy by means of bonuses, either during the policy's term (reversionary bonuses) or on the policy's maturity (terminal bonuses). Once a bonus has been allocated it cannot be taken away, although the level of future bonuses is not guaranteed.

In 1997 the Government started a consultation process on its proposals for the new Individual Savings Account (ISA), an investment vehicle to stimulate savings, particularly among the lower paid and those who do not currently have any significant savings. Life assurance is proposed to be included as an asset capable of being held in an ISA but only to the extent of £1000 contribution per annum (against an annual contribution of up to £5000). Representations on the proposals can be made until 31 January and, no doubt, the position of life assurance in the ISA – and the extent to which it can participate – will be the subject of a number of representations.

Unit-linked policies

These are a more recent innovation introduced to the United Kingdom in the 1960s. They offer fewer guarantees to the policyholder. Premiums are invested in pooled investment funds maintained by the life company and the policy's performance is linked directly to the fund's actual performance. Freed from having to set up the policy with long-term investment guarantees, the company can adopt an investment policy which is not unduly conservative and so may be able to provide a more realistic level of cover from the outset. The direct linking of the policy and the investment performance of the underlying fund also mean that the policyholder is not subject to the company's discretion in deciding the level of bonuses it should declare.

As unit-linked policies do not usually carry the same investment guarantees as traditional contracts, they usually incorporate the system of reviews by which the company can ensure that the policy stays 'on track'. A review compares the original assumptions about mortality, expenses and investment return with the actual performance achieved. Unfavourable performance usually leads to an increase in premium and favourable performance to an increase in benefits.

12.2.3 Qualifying and non-qualifying policies

The other main method of categorising life assurance contracts is according to whether they are 'qualifying' or 'non-qualifying'. This categorisation arises solely for the purpose of the taxation of the policy proceeds.

The qualifying rules are detailed and complex but, very broadly speaking, a qualifying policy is a regular premium policy with a minimum duration of ten years. The premiums remain fairly level and the sum assured satisfies certain minimum requirements to ensure that it provides a realistic level of life cover protection. Qualifying policies are certified as such by the Revenue, a process known as pre-certification.

The 1994 Budget announced impending changes to the life policy tax regime, with an implementation date of May 1996. After a postponement of the implementation schedule, consultation on the Revenue proposals closed in April 1997. The stated intention was to remove pre-certification and to simplify and modernise the current regime but the proposals set out in the Consultation Document attracted widespread concern among many in the industry for their complexity, the likely high cost of implementation and their failure adequately to protect the legitimate expectations of existing policyholders, particularly in the areas of part surrenders (see 12.2.5) and the taxation of trust-held policies. At the end of 1997 the Revenue confirmed that the proposed radical changes to the policy tax regime would not be implemented. Instead, legislation is expected in FA 1998 to address the specific issues of the taxation of trusts (specifically, so called 'dead settler trusts'), personalised portfolio bonds and the fiscal representation in the UK of offshore insurance companies; all areas where the Revenue believes current legislation is deficient and abuse can exist.

12.2.4 The advantages of qualifying policies

Premiums paid under qualifying policies issued before 14 March 1984 attracted Life Assurance Premium Relief (LAPR). Qualifying policies issued before that date continue to benefit from LAPR provided that neither the benefits secured are increased nor the term extended after that date.

Subject to meeting the conditions for LAPR, relief was given at approximately half of the basic rate of income tax in force at the time, on up to the greater of 1/6th of the policyholder's income or £1,500 pa. Where LAPR is still available, it applies at the rate of 12½% for the year 1997/98.

The other key advantage of qualifying policies concerns the taxation of policy proceeds. In general, the proceeds from a qualifying policy are entirely free of tax, provided premiums are kept up for at least 10 years (or three-quarters of the term of an endowment policy, if less).

12.2.5 Tax treatment of policies

While a policy is in force all the tax on income and gains attributable to the policy is the responsibility of the life company which pays tax on them according to its own corporate taxation position.

The life company

Life companies are generally taxed on the excess of the investment income realised capital gain over the management expenses (the 'I–E' basis). For proprietory companies there is a formula to determine the proportion of income and gains to be allocated to policyholders and shareholders, the former's share being taxed at 23 per cent (20 per cent for income from directly held equities) and the latter's share at 31 per cent.

The individual policyholder

The taxation of the individual in connection with income tax and life assurance policies revolves around the concept of the 'chargeable event'. For non-qualifying policies the five chargeable events are:

(1) death of the life assured;
(2) the maturity of the policy;
(3) the total surrender of the policy;
(4) the assignment of the policy for money or money's worth (eg the sale of the policy);
(5) excesses (the system of 'excesses' allows partial surrenders each year of up to 5 per cent of the premiums paid, on a cumulative basis, up to a total of 100 per cent of the premiums paid; only if the cumulative 5 per cent 'allowances' are exceeded does a chargeable event occur).

Chargeable events in the case of qualifying policies are the same as those listed above but with the following amendments:

(1) death or maturity is a chargeable event only if the policy has previously been paid-up within the first 10 years (or three-quarters of the term of an endowment policy, if less);
(2) a surrender or an assignment for money or money's worth or an excess is a chargeable event only if it occurs before the expiry of 10 years (or three-quarters of the term of an endowment policy, if less) or if the policy was made paid-up within that period.

Assignments between spouses or as security for debts are not chargeable events and nor are payments of critical illness claims.

As far as the policyholder is concerned, in most cases life assurance policies (qualifying or not) are free of any personal liability to CGT. Only if the policy is in the hands of someone other than the original owner who gave consideration for it (ie who bought it or gave something of value for it) are proceeds liable to CGT.

Company-owned policies

Special rules apply to post-13 March 1989 policies owned by companies, those assigned to secure a debt owed by a company and those held on trusts created by a company. Broadly speaking, such policies are treated as non-qualifying policies and so may give rise to a tax charge on death, maturity, surrender, part withdrawal or assignment for money or money's worth.

However, policies which would otherwise be qualifying endowments receive more favourable treatment in respect of calculation of the chargeable gain, in certain circumstances where the policy has, throughout its term, been issued to secure a loan to the company which was used to purchase land (or construct, extend or improve buildings) used for the purposes of the company's trade.

12.2.6 Gain on the happening of a chargeable event

Where a chargeable event occurs the gain arising on the event must be computed. The calculation depends on the event's nature but, broadly speaking, it is the investment profit made under the policy, taking into account previous capital benefits enjoyed and the total premiums paid. Any extra amount received by way of death benefit is mortality profit and is not included in the gain for tax purposes.

The rules for calculating the gain as a result of an excess following a withdrawal or partial surrender are somewhat different and take into account the 5 per cent allowable withdrawals. The more favourable treatment for company-owned policies referred to in the previous section is that the amount of the loan (or the lowest amount of the loan during the policy term) is used in place of the sum of total premiums paid when calculating the chargeable gain. Thus, if the loan has remained constant during the policy term and the policy proceeds do not exceed the loan, there is no chargeable gain.

12.2.7 Taxing gains on chargeable events

In outline, tax is payable on a chargeable gain as follows:

(1) Gains made on life policies do not give rise to a tax liability at the basic rate of income tax. Accordingly if the taxpayer's income, including the gain, does not fall into the higher rate tax band there is no income tax charge on the gain.
(2) If the policyholder's income (including any chargeable gain) is taxable at the higher rate, the gain made on the life policy is liable to tax at 17 per cent (the higher rate of 40 per cent, less the basic rate of 23 per cent).
(3) As the gain has accrued over the life of the policy, it would be rather harsh to treat the total gain as the taxpayer's income in the year of receipt. This could push him into the higher rate tax band in that year despite a relatively low income level. Therefore, a measure of relief is afforded by a process known as 'top-slicing'. This involves calculating the rate of tax appropriate to a part of the total gain (a 'slice') and then applying that rate of tax to the whole of the gain.
(4) The taxpayer is usually the policyholder. Exceptions to this are that if the policy is held on trust the charge falls upon the settlor (ie the person who established the trust); if the policy is owned by or held on trusts created, or held as security for a debt owed, by a company, the amount of the gain is treated as part of the company's Schedule D Case VI income (and top-slicing relief does not apply).

Further details of the qualifying rules and taxation of life policies can be found in the *Allied Dunbar Tax Handbook*.

12.3 PENSIONS

12.3.1 Introduction

Pensions are usually regarded as one of the most attractive investments available. Within limits, contributions are deductible at the highest rate of tax paid by the contributor; the underlying pension funds grow, in the main, free of UK taxes on income and gains; and in most cases the pension plan can provide a tax-free cash lump sum to the planholder together with a retirement income in 'old age'.

Over the years UK pensions legislation has undergone substantial reform and development. The Social Security Act 1986 created the framework for the new 'Personal Pensions' and 'Free-Standing Additional Voluntary Contribution Schemes'; reduced the benefits provided by the State Earnings Related Pensions Scheme (SERPS); increased the scope for individuals to contract out of SERPS; and removed the ability of Occupational Pension Schemes to require compulsory membership for employees.

The legislation also allowed, for the first time, banks, building societies and unit trust groups to offer pension plans.

The Budget of July 1997 introduced further radical reform, this time by virtue of tax changes to the treatment of pension funds. It is now no longer possible for such funds to reclaim the Advance Corporation Tax (ACT) paid by a company when it pays a dividend. This could reduce the overall return from an average pension fund by about 0.8 per cent per annum and will have real consequences for pensions funding by companies and individuals in the medium to long term.

The Government has also announced a wide-ranging review of all aspects of pension provision, including the basic State pension, SERPs and private and occupational pension schemes. The review aims to publish the Government's proposals, for further consultation, in the first part of 1998.

12.3.2 The state pension scheme

The benefit the state provides to those in retirement falls into two main parts: the basic retirement pension and the supplementary earnings related pension.

Everyone is entitled to the basic retirement pension, subject to payment of the necessary national insurance (NI) contributions. Currently, for a married man with earnings at the national average level, the aim is to provide a basic pension of approximately 20 per cent of his final earnings level.

SERPS was introduced in April 1978 to provide an additional state pension which is based on earnings (within certain limits) rather than the flat benefit provided by the retirement pension. SERPS also provides a widow's benefit if a husband dies after retirement and also, in certain circumstances, if he dies before retirement. SERPS is funded by the higher rate NI contributions payable by both employers and employees. The self-employed do not contribute towards, or benefit from, SERPS.

In recent years the state pension scheme has come under pressure from increases in life expectancy and large numbers of retired people in the population. These concerns have led the Government to reduce the benefits under SERPS. Those reaching state retirement age in or after the year 2010 will receive a pension of only 20 per cent of their relevant earnings, instead of the 25 per cent originally intended, and the relevant earnings to be taken into account will be the average of lifetime earnings and not the best 20 years of earnings, as was the original rule for SERPS.

A sliding scale will operate for those retiring between the years 2000 and 2010.

12.3.3 Contracting-in and contracting-out

Those who are participating in SERPS (ie employees earning more than the lower threshold for standard rate NI contributions) are said to be 'contracted-in' to SERPS. Since SERPS was introduced it has been possible to opt out of the scheme (referred to as 'contracting-out') in which case NI contributions are reduced for both the employer and employee but with the loss of SERPS benefits.

The original rules only permitted contracting-out through an occupational pension scheme established by an employer, and only where that scheme provided certain guaranteed pension benefits which were broadly equivalent to the SERPS entitlement the employee was giving up.

Contracting-out is possible through an occupational scheme providing a level of benefits at least broadly equivalent to the SERPS benefits being up or through a contracted-out money purchase occupational scheme (COMPS), or an appropriate personal pension plan (APPP) used by an employee not in an occupational scheme or a member of a contracted-in occupational scheme.

With APPPs the individual and the employer continue to make full NI contributions and the DSS make payments which are age related direct to the relevant pension plan. Contracting-out through an occupational scheme means lower NI contributions for employer and employee but the employer is required to make payment of the NI reduction to the occupational scheme with further age related payments made by the DSS.

If the individual is contracting-out on a money-purchase basis these NI reductions are known as 'protected rights contributions' and the fund built up from them must be used to purchase protected rights benefits. It is these benefits which, in effect, replace the SERPS being lost through contracting-out and they are treated more restrictively than benefits built up through the employer's or employee's additional contributions. For example, a protected rights pension cannot commence before state retirement age and cannot be commuted for cash.

Whether contracting-out of SERPS is advisable is a decision to be taken by each employee according to his or her personal circumstances. The key factors to be taken into account are the individual's age, sex, earnings and attitude to risk. The decision has to be reviewed each year before the end of the tax year.

12.3.4 Occupational pension schemes

These are schemes sponsored by an employer and to which the employer must make a contribution. Schemes are established on one of two bases: either money-purchase or final salary (often called defined benefit schemes).

With defined benefit schemes the employee is guaranteed a level of pension benefit based on a fraction (typically 1/60th or 1/80th) of his final salary, multiplied by the number of years' pensionable service. A money-purchase scheme does not carry a guarantee of a specific level of pension but invests the contributions and uses the accumulated fund to provide whatever pension can be purchased with the fund at retirement.

To be tax efficient an occupational pension scheme should be approved by the Pension Schemes Office (PSO) which is a branch of the Inland Revenue. 'Approval' prevents contributions paid by the employer being taxed in the employee's hands but the preferable status of 'exempt approval' offers significant further benefits. An exempt approved scheme is able to invest in a fund free of all UK income and capital taxes (although the fund can no longer reclaim ACT paid on company dividens); the employee can claim tax relief on contributions he makes to the scheme; and employers' contributions are deductible business expenses.

Contributions

In general, there are no specific limits on the amount of contributions which can be paid into an occupational scheme but monitoring is necessary to ensure that the scheme does not become 'over-funded'. In other words, contributions may have to be limited if projected funds in the scheme are likely to exceed the amount necessary to meet its obligations. (See below under 'Benefits' for details of the remuneration cap introduced in 1989 for some scheme members.)

Employees may make personal contributions (of up to 15 per cent of 'eligible' remuneration) to the scheme. This may be done on a voluntary basis (by way of additional voluntary contributions to the scheme or by the employee effecting his own Free Standing AVC plan) but the scheme may require some personal contribution from the employee as a condition of membership.

Benefits

To be exempt approved, the scheme must be set up under irrevocable trust for the sole purpose of providing 'relevant benefits'. These are benefits such as an income in retirement, the option to commute part of that income for a lump sum, an income for the employee's widow etc. As a result of the generous tax benefits available to such schemes, there are strict limits on the benefits which may be provided. For example, the maximum pension which can be provided to the scheme member is usually two-thirds of final remuneration and the minimum period of service required to achieve this level of benefits is now 20 years.

A pension for a spouse or dependant can also be provided of up to two-thirds of the deceased member's maximum pension at normal retirement date. A similar pension can be provided on death after retirement.

An employee's pension can be commuted for a lump sum, also based on final salary and years of service. The maximum lump sum is 3/80ths of final salary for each year of service up to 40 years' service or 2.25 times the pension available before commutation, if greater.

The FA 1989 introduced new rules for members of schemes established on or after 14 March 1989 and members joining older schemes after 31 May 1989. For such members no benefits can be provided for any remuneration in excess of a specific amount (increased in line with the RPI) which is £84,000 for 1997/98. This remuneration 'cap' restricts funding of such schemes (by the employer and by the employees' personal contributions) as well as payment of the various benefits the scheme can provide.

Schemes may also provide a lump sum of up to four times final remuneration (capped where necessary) on the death, in service, of the employee. This can be paid together with a refund of any personal contributions paid by the employee. It is usually possible to pay the death benefits free of inheritance tax.

The eligibility, contribution and benefit rules changed more than once in the late 1980s and some members of existing schemes will have had their positions protected from some of the subsequent changes. Further details can be found in the *Allied Dunbar Pensions Handbook*.

Top-up occupational schemes

The FA 1989 also introduced the concept of unapproved top-up occupational pension schemes. These schemes, for example, allow employers to provide highly paid employees with pension benefits in respect of salary which exceeds the earnings cap, and to provide more than the usual maximum pension benefits.

12.3.5 Personal pensions

Prior to October 1987 the main personal plan was the retirement annuity contract (also called section 226 plans). In October 1987 FSAVC schemes were introduced, enabling an occupational scheme member to effect his own top-up pension as an alternative to making personal voluntary contributions to the employer's scheme. In July 1988 the section 226 plans were replaced by the new personal pension plans.

The wider scope of the PPPs and the ability of individual employees to use them to contract out of SERPS means that the individual has never before had such a wide choice of pension planning opportunities.

Retirement annuity contracts

Although it has not been possible to effect a retirement annuity contract since 30 June 1988, plans in force by that date are allowed to continue.

An individual was eligible for one of these plans if he had relevant earnings. These are earnings which do not carry pension rights, eg the earnings of sole traders, the self-employed, partners and employees in non-pensionable employment. Controlling directors of investment companies are excluded from eligibility.

Unlike occupational schemes, these 'section 226' contracts are not controlled by reference to the maximum benefits which can be provided; rather, restrictions are applied to the amount of contributions which can be made. The contribution limit is 17.5 per cent of net relevant earnings, with larger percentages applicable for those over 50 (up to a maximum of 27.5 per cent for those aged over 60). Net relevant earnings (NRE) are, broadly speaking, an individual's earnings after deduction of any business expenses. The earnings cap applicable to other schemes does not apply. Contributions made to these plans up to the limits are fully tax-deductible and the funds in which the plans invest are free of all UK income and capital taxes. Employers are not able to pay contributions to employees' section 226 contracts and they cannot be used to contract out of SERPS.

The plans are issued on a money-purchase basis, the fund accumulated at retirement being used to provide a lifetime annuity for the planholder. The planholder need not actually retire to take the benefits from these plans but the benefits must be paid between the ages of 60 and 75 (earlier for some specified occupations).

The annuity paid can be in various different forms, guaranteed or not, flat rate or increasing etc. If the planholder dies before taking his annuity a lump sum can be paid, not exceeding the contributions made to the plan plus a reasonable amount of interest or bonuses. Alternatively, an annuity can be paid to the individual's widow or dependants. Annuities can also be effected on a 'joint life basis' for the planholder and spouse, so that the annuity payments continue until the surviving spouse's death. The annuity is treated as earned income when it is paid, and the planholder can elect to commute part of his annuity at retirement. This commutation permits a maximum lump sum of three times the remaining annual annuity, but limited to a £150,000 lump sum per contract for contracts entered into on or after 17 March 1987.

In addition to pension benefits, such plans can provide life assurance protection. The maximum contribution which can be used to provide life cover is 5 per cent of NRE (any such contribution is taken into account in determining the overall contribution limit applicable to the individual).

Death benefits payable under such plans can be assigned or put in trust so that payments of benefits on death can be arranged in a way effective for inheritance tax planning.

If, in any year, an individual pays less in contributions to a plan than would be permitted, it is possible to carry forward the shortfall in contributions for up to six years. It is also possible to 'carry back' a contribution to the previous tax year (and sometimes the year before that).

Personal pension plans

These plans were introduced on 1 July 1988. In many ways they are more flexible than the section 226 contracts which they replaced. For example, employers may make contributions to an employee's PPP; an 'appropriate' PPP can be used by employees to contract out of SERPS; and benefits can be taken between the ages of 50 and 75 (earlier for some specified occupations). Employees' contributions to PPPs are payable net of basic rate income tax under the pension relief at source (PRAS) rules.

PPPs are, like section 226 contracts, money-purchase arrangements with controls on the maximum contributions which can be made. Where an employer contributes to an employee's PPP, the employer's contributions must be taken into account in determining the employee's maximum permissible contributions.

With effect from 1989/90 the maximum contributions allowed (as a percentage of net relevant earnings) are:

Age at beginning of year of assessment	%
below 36	17½
36–45	20
46–50	25
Age at beginning of year of assessment	%
51–55	30
56–60	35
61+	40

However, PPPs are also, with effect from 1989/90, subject to a similar income cap to that referred to in relation to occupational pension schemes (see 12.3.4) and earnings over the appropriate limit must be ignored in calculating entitlement to pay contributions. The benefits provided by a PPP are, again, very similar to those available under a section 226 plan including the use of up to 5 per cent of net relevant earnings to provide life assurance protection, but the tax-free cash which can be taken is a maximum of 25 per cent of the fund.

It is possible to defer taking an annuity but still receive income withdrawals from the fund.

12.3.6 Moving between different types of pension arrangement

If a self-employed individual effects a PPP but then moves into employment, for example a sole trader incorporating his business, he can continue with his PPP. The same is true with an employee who has a PPP and moves into self-employment. In some cases, however, it is not possible to continue with the same pension plan; for example an employee who is a member of an occupational scheme cannot remain in that scheme if he becomes self-employed. Similarly, if a person with a PPP joins an employer's occupational scheme he cannot continue to pay contributions into the PPP if he has no continuing source of relevant earnings.

In those cases where a change of status affects pension planning it is usually possible for a transfer payment to be made from one scheme to another. Many companies offer such transfers on preferential terms, particularly where the individual is moving between the occupational and personal pension regimes.

Further details of pension plans and planning can be found in the *Allied Dunbar Pensions Handbook*.

12.4 PERMANENT HEALTH INSURANCE

Typically, permanent health insurance (PHI) policies are a means of providing a replacement income if an individual is unable to work through illness or disability. Policies are usually available to those aged between 16 and 60 and cover usually ends no later than the normal retirement date for the individual's occupation.

In the event of sickness or disability the policy usually provides for a deferment period and payment of benefits only commence at the end of this period. Deferment periods may be between one month and one year (usually selected by the policyholder at the outset) and are valuable to the company offering the policy because they reduce the number of short-term claims they have to meet. The longer the deferment period, the cheaper the policy. In some cases, especially those occupations where short-term illnesses affect earnings almost immediately (eg professional sportsmen), the company may decline to offer policies with very short deferred periods.

The benefits payable under the policy are usually limited to approximately 75 per cent of the individual's pre-claim earnings, often taking into account any benefits received from the State and any other policy during the period of claim. Limiting the maximum benefit in this way provides the incentive to the individual to return to work as soon as possible.

Benefits paid by such policies are usually taxable as unearned income in the individual's hands but the Revenue allows a 'tax holiday' during which payments are not taxed. The tax holiday, since April 1994, is a period of 12 months starting from an entitlement to claim benefits under any such policy, not 12 months under each such policy. No tax holiday is allowed unless the benefit compensates for loss of income from employment or self-employment. Once taxable, benefits are paid after deduction of basic rate tax in most cases, but there are exemptions allowing payments to be made gross by the life company, for example where the policy is taken out by an employer to enable it to continue to pay a salary to its employee during periods of absence through ill health.

One of the most important things about PHI policies is the definition of 'disability' which is used in the policy. Under some policies a person is not treated as being disabled if he can do any part of his former job. Others may not treat a person as disabled if he is capable of doing some other job for which he is reasonably suited, even if he is completely unable to do his previous job.

The most flexible PHI policies allow the level of benefit to be increased as salary increases and also give the policyholder the option of paying a higher contribution in exchange for disability income which increases to offer protection against inflation during the period of disability.

PART II – THE USES

12.5 INTRODUCTION

In this second part of the chapter the uses of life assurance, pensions and permanent health insurance are considered with particular emphasis on the business needs of sole traders, partners and small companies. The chapter does not consider more personal uses of life assurance but it is most important that they are not overlooked.

Life assurance is a unique product in the paying of a lump sum on an individual's death at some unknown time in the future. As such it plays a vital role in protection of the family on the breadwinner's death and loss of the family's income. The inclusion of 'critical illness' benefits can also be extremely beneficial as a breadwinner's serious illness can have just as severe an impact as his or her death.

Although most people can see the need for life assurance on the family breadwinner's life, it should not be forgotten that many people are only able to go out and earn an income because their partners are devoting themselves to looking after children and the family home. The non-earning partner's death or serious illness can also cause major financial difficulties such as the need for boarding school fees, a cleaner, a nanny – perhaps even the need for the surviving partner to give up work to look after the family.

Life assurance is also important in inheritance tax planning, being able to provide a fund from which the liability may be met, thus preserving the deceased's estate intact.

Life assurance may be used as a means of investment, even though qualifying endowment policies and single premium savings bonds may have advantages for the individual investor and, in some cases, corporate investment.

12.6 SOLE TRADERS

12.6.1 Life assurance

Keyman assurance – loss of profits

Although the sole trader himself usually is the driving force behind the business's profitability, there may be cases in which an employee is also essential to the undertaking's well-being. Where the death or disability of such a key person would weaken the business's profitability or reduce its capital value as a going concern, the business's owner should consider effecting a life policy (with dread disease benefit) on the keyman's life. The individual's status usually satisfies the requirement for an insurable interest, providing this sum assured is reasonable in view of the keyman's value to the business.

Receipt of the policy proceeds on the life assured's death or disability does not normally constitute a chargeable event, and so does not trigger a tax charge on the policy, if the policy is a qualifying policy. However, it is important to consider whether the policy is an asset owned by the sole trader personally or is a business asset. This determines the ultimate tax treatment of both the premiums paid and the sums received.

If the policy is a business asset contributions paid to it, in general, are tax-deductible provided:

(a) the policy is a short-term assurance; and
(b) the insurance is intended to meet the loss of profit resulting from the employee's death; and
(c) the sole relationship between the policyholder and the life assured is that of employer and employee.

These principles were laid down in a statement in 1944 by the then Chancellor of the Exchequer, Sir John Anderson. In general, the first requirement is an indication that premiums paid on a policy with a term of more than five years will not be tax-deductible.

If premiums are tax-deductible, this usually means that the policy proceeds are, in turn, taxable as a trading receipt of the business. If the premiums do not attract tax relief, usually the proceeds are received as a capital sum, taxable (through Revenue practice) only under the policy tax regime as discussed in 12.2.5. In cases of doubt it may be wise to contact the local tax inspector.

Security for loans

If a sole trader has to borrow money for business purposes, the lender may often require assignment of a life policy on the sole trader as security. The policy should ensure that such loans are repaid on the sole trader's death. Premiums are unlikely to be tax-deductible as a business expense because the plan's purpose is to satisfy a capital liability so that the premiums are not an income expense at all.

Insurance for redundancy payments

If a sole trader's business ceases on his death, his personal representatives are liable for making redundancy payments to eligible employees (see 10.9.8). The amount of any payment depends on various factors, such as salary level and length of service, but for a sole trader employing several staff, such payments could be a significant burden on his estate.

12.6.2 Pensions

For the sole trader

Pension provision for a sole trader must now be through a PPP if no section 226 contract had been effected prior to July 1988. As a sole trader is not an employee, occupational pension schemes are not available and the question of contracting-out of SERPS does not arise.

It should be remembered that the individual can effect life assurance protection through a PPP. This can provide term assurance cover at very competitive rates, because the premiums are tax-deductible, but paying for life cover in this way does lead to a reduction in the contributions which are going towards pension benefits.

For his employees

For a sole trader's employees the choice is wider. The employer could establish an occupational scheme for his staff or, in the absence of an employer's scheme, the employees could effect PPPs for themselves. Most sole traders do not want to assume the responsibility of establishing and running an occupational pension scheme but may well be able to make contributions to their employees' PPPs. Some pension providers offer a group PPP arrangement which is particularly suitable in these circumstances. Members of staff still own individual plans but some aspects of the administration are centralised. If the employer does decide to set up an occupational scheme for his employees, a money-purchase arrangement is likely to be preferable because of the absence of long-term guarantees which have to be met by the employer.

Employees should consider whether contracting-out of SERPS will be beneficial to them. This can be effected in a variety of ways: the employer may offer contracting-out under the main occupational scheme; those in a contracted-in occupational scheme may be able to contract out of SERPS by means of an APPP in the restricted form described at 12.3.4; or the PPPs taken out by those not in the occupational scheme can be used to contract out on an individual basis.

If the sole trader's spouse is employed in the business, he or she is like any other employee as far as pension planning opportunities are concerned, but may be treated more favourably by the employer.

For the sole trader's spouse

If the spouse is not employed in the business, consideration should be given as to whether this could be done, especially if the spouse is not otherwise employed.

The salary paid by the sole trader is deductible at his top rate of tax and, if it is less than the wife's personal allowance and the lower rate for NI contributions, no income tax or NI contributions have to be made by either husband or wife in respect of that salary. Of course, it must be possible to justify the employment and the salary being paid by reference to the duties undertaken by the wife.

Once the wife is employed in this way, she could contribute to a PPP, or an occupational scheme could be set up for her by her husband. Although the occupational scheme may be a little more expensive to run and, if it is an insurance company scheme, may have higher minimum contribution levels, it usually offers the chance to provide higher pension benefits for the wife than would a PPP, where the contribution is limited to a percentage of a salary.

To obtain the benefit of tax relief through PPP contributions, the wife should earn more than her tax allowances, but this could lead to payment of NI. In such cases, it may be better for the husband, as employer, to make the PPP contributions for her.

12.6.3 Permanent health insurance

For the sole trader

It is often the case that if the sole trader is not able to work, the business soon becomes unprofitable. Although state benefits do exist (the sickness and incapacity benefits) they are designed more to avoid poverty than to maintain an individual's standard of living. Accordingly, a PHI policy is one of the first things which the sole trader should consider.

For his employees

A sole trader's employees are will usually be entitled to the same state benefits (with the addition of statutory sick pay) but may be treated more favourably under the terms of their contract of employment.

If the employer has undertaken to maintain the full, or a proportion of, salary during periods of sickness, he should consider effecting a PHI policy on the employee's life, so as to 're-insure' the liability for continuing salary. Benefit received from the policy by the employer is taxable as a trading receipt but normally deductible as a trading expense when paid to the employee. There would be no 'tax holiday' on the payments in these circumstances.

Even if the employer has not agreed to maintain salary payments beyond that required by statute, he may still consider effecting a PHI policy on key employees to maintain the profitability of the business during their absence from work.

12.7 PARTNERS

12.7.1 Life assurance

The majority of the uses of life assurance applicable to sole traders also apply to partners. Perhaps the main difference with partnerships is that they are more likely to involve key people and that consideration should be given to the partnership's future on the death of one of the partners.

Quite apart from loss of a deceased partner's earning potential, the surviving partners may, subject to the provisions of the Partnership Deed, be faced with having to pay the beneficiaries the value of the deceased's partnership share. For partners who have made no provision, this burden can be acute and might necessitate expensive borrowing or even the sale of vital partnership assets.

Life assurance can help in these circumstances. The partners can set up an arrangement so that each of them has life cover which is paid to the survivors on his death. The survivors then have the funds to pay the deceased partner's share to his heirs, without affecting other aspects of the business's viability.

This partnership assurance arrangement may be achieved by each partner owning a life assurance policy on the life of every other partner, but this can be unwieldy and expensive where there are more than three or four partners. An alternative is for each partner to effect a policy on his own life and write it in trust for the benefit of the other partners.

Both sorts of arrangement should be accompanied by a cross-option agreement by which the surviving partners can compel the deceased's personal representatives to sell the deceased's partnership share to them and vice versa. The cross-option agreement can also contain further provisions to deal with the valuation of the partnership share, time for payment, the destination of surplus policy proceeds and payment of additional capital, should the policy proceeds be insufficient.

A policy incorporating critical illness benefits can also be particularly useful in partnership arrangements where a partner's serious illness can have effects equally severe as his or her death.

12.7.2 Pensions

For the partners

The pension planning routes available to partners are the same as those available to the sole trader, ie a PPP from 1 July 1988 or through a section 226 contract effected before that time. The life cover which can be provided under such pension arrangements can be extremely useful for partnership assurance planning as it provides tax relief on the life cover contributions, at the individual's top rate of income tax. However, these plans are term assurances which must end no later than the individual's 75th birthday, although most life companies will give favourable consideration to a partner applying for a new life policy on the termination of life cover under a pension scheme with that same office.

For their employees

For partnership employees the position is the same as for employees of a sole trader (see 12.6.2); see also that paragraph for the comments made on spouses which also apply to those employed by the partnership.

12.7.3 Permanent health insurance

Partners are in much the same position as sole traders when considering PHI policies (see 12.6.3). A partnership may be better placed to absorb the loss of profits resulting from a partner's long-term absence through injury or illness but a PHI policy can secure the position still further. A policy can be taken out by each partner for his own benefit with the Partnership Deed providing for a corresponding reduction in that partner's share of profits for the period of absence. Alternatively, policies can be owned by all the partners as partnership assets to replace the income at the partnership level. The former method has the advantage of the availability of a tax holiday and of putting this provision into the hands of each individual.

12.8 COMPANIES

12.8.1 Life assurance

Keyman assurance

Keyman assurance is particularly important for small companies where, for example, the managing director, sales director etc may be fundamental to the business's profitability and continuance.

Frequently, small companies effecting keyman policies are not able to obtain tax relief on the premiums but are not taxed on the proceeds other than through the life policy taxation regime (see 12.2.5). This is because the keyman being insured has a material interest in the company so that the relationship between the life assured and the policyholder is not only that of employee and employer.

In the absence of such an interest in the company on the keyman's part, deductibility of premiums might be achieved if the policy is a short-term assurance. A policy of this nature might be appropriate in the early days of the company's existence (for example, where it is expected that the company will grow sufficiently over the next five years so as to absorb the loss of the keyman after that time). Although keyman policies are caught by the new rules described in 12.2.5, the high level of life cover being provided usually means that any investment profit under the policy will be small, so that any tax charge on a chargeable event will not cause undue difficulties.

Loan protection and repayment

A form of keyman assurance might also be appropriate where the company is obtaining a loan and the lender requires a life policy on a key executive by way of additional security. Even where the lender has not required a life policy as security for a loan, life assurance has a key role to play in company borrowings. Although the company is usually the borrower, it is common for lenders to require a personal guarantee from one or more directors to ensure repayment of any loan.

By having to give a personal guarantee the director is losing one of the main benefits of trading through a company – that of limited personal liability. Bearing in mind that a key person's death in the company organisation may well precipitate profitability difficulties and so make a calling in of the loan more likely, this is another good reason to effect life assurance on the lives of key individuals. Receipt of the policy proceeds will enable the company to repay its borrowings and so free the guarantor's personal estate from the potential liability.

Repayment of loans should also be considered for any company overdraft which could be called in on a key person's death and in relation to directors' loan accounts where the director's estate may require repayment on the director's death.

Note that the rules described in 12.2.5 mean that policies effected after 13 March 1989 (or older policies which are varied after that date to increase their benefits or extend their term) are treated as if they were non-qualifying and may give rise to a chargeable gain unless they are qualifying endowments and have been used to secure specific types of borrowing.

Key shareholder assurance

Another aspect of small companies which needs to be considered is that of transfer of shares on the death of one of the shareholders. In many cases small companies do not declare dividends on the shares, but those involved in the running of the company draw benefits by way of salary and directors' fees. On a director's death, those inheriting the deceased's shares may find that they have a minority shareholding in the company. The shares may be producing no dividends and may be insufficient to enable the new shareholder to become a director. In such a case the shares may be virtually unsaleable except to the other shareholders who may be able to use their position to depress the value of the shares.

Although in exceptional cases minority shareholders may have some rights against an oppressive majority under company law, the problem can be tackled by life assurance arrangements in at least two specific ways.

The company could effect life policies on the individual shareholders so that, on a shareholder's death, it receives a capital sum to buy the shares from the deceased's heirs. It has been possible for companies to buy their own shares since 1982. An agreement can be entered into between the shareholders and the company itself in which various matters can be addressed; for example, options can be given to both sides to require a sale or purchase of the shares and to determine the method of calculating a fair price for them. The existence of such options usually creates the necessary insurable interest to sustain the life assurance. However, the deceased's personal representatives may have difficulty in enforcing their option to require the company to buy the deceased's shares in some circumstances, eg where the purchase price is to come out of the company's capital. In addition, there are various legal procedures to be gone through before an agreement to buy a company's own shares can be set up and further clearances from the Revenue need to be obtained when the purchase is made to ensure there are no adverse tax consequences.

An alternative and relatively simple method of arranging a share purchase scheme is to establish an arrangement similar to that used for partnership assurance (see 12.7.1). In this way each shareholder effects a policy on the life of each of the others, or each effects a policy on his own life and puts it in trust for the benefit of the other shareholders. The life policies are accompanied by a cross-option agreement which enables both the deceased's personal representatives and the surviving shareholders to enforce the sale and purchase of the deceased's shares and tackles such questions as valuation of the shares etc.

12.8.2 Pensions

For directors and other top executives

The company's directors may plan for their own pension benefits through an occupational scheme or a PPP. In most cases the directors and key executives join a company occupational scheme to enable them to maximise their pension benefits in a tax-efficient way. PPPs with direct contributions from the company are also efficient for the purposes of income tax and NI contributions, but the limit on the PPP contributions which can be made usually favours the choice of an occupational scheme.

Life assurance protection can be provided under either type of scheme. Usually it is possible to provide a higher sum assured under a PPP (where the maximum life cover contribution is 5 per cent of net relevant earnings) than under an occupational scheme where the maximum sum assured is four times' salary. Despite this, the occupational scheme is often preferable as the provision of life assurance under the PPP reduces the maximum amount which can be paid towards the pension benefits.

For other employees

The choices are very much the same as for the employees of sole traders and partners. If the company does not want to make pension provision for its staff through an occupational scheme, they can plan for themselves by effecting PPPs. The company may choose to make contributions to its employees' PPPs. A group PPP arrangement could be 'sponsored' by the company if it wishes to indicate a greater commitment to the provision of pensions for its employees.

For spouses of the directors

The comments made in 12.6.2 apply equally to employment of, and pensions for, spouses of directors and top executives of small companies.

12.8.3 Permanent health insurance

As with sole traders and partnerships, the smaller the company the more vulnerable it is to the long-term absence of a key individual. The company may effect PHI policies on its directors and top executives either to enable the company to maintain payment of salary or to cushion the company itself from the possible loss of income due to the key person's absence. The question of whether premiums paid on such a policy are tax deductible for the company is not entirely clear.

Despite the policy's long-term nature it seems likely that premiums paid by a company on a PHI policy on an employee, to enable the company to maintain payment of salary to the employee during a period of disability, should be tax-deductible. Certainly it appears that the receipt of payment by the company from the policy would be taxable in the company's hands (although matched by tax relief on the payment of the salary) even though the payment would be made gross by the life company. In cases of doubt, companies should consult their local tax inspector.

13

HEALTH AND SAFETY

NICOLA TOMLINS, WEDLAKE SAINT

A detailed study of this subject is beyond the scope of this book. Therefore what follows is but a brief outline of a vast and complex area. The reader is advised to refer to specialist books and the legislation on the subject, and to seek legal advice where appropriate.

13.1 INTRODUCTION

Health and safety is the responsibility of employers, employees and anyone else connected with business. However, the onus is on employers to ensure that their work premises and all people using them comply with the statutory requirements.

13.2 HEALTH AND SAFETY AT WORK ACT 1974

This Act is central to health and safety law, and created the Health and Safety Commission and the Health and Safety Executive (HSE). Civil and criminal proceedings can be taken by employers, employees and other parties under the Act.

13.2.1 Employer's duty to employees
(Section 2)

The employer has a general duty 'to ensure, so far as is reasonably practicable, the health, safety and welfare at work of all his employees' (s 2(1)). There are specific provisions which an employer must carry out, but the test of reasonable practice is repeated throughout the Act; an employer should generally balance the probability of the risk to an employee's health and safety against the time and expense of taking extensive measures. Breach of this duty exposes the employer to criminal prosecution.

The employer is required under s 2(2) to:

(1) provide and maintain safe working practices and premises;
(2) arrange for safe methods of using, handling, storing and transporting goods and substances;
(3) inform, instruct, train and supervise employees on health and safety issues;
(4) ensure there is safe access to and egress from the premises at all times; and
(5) provide and maintain a safe working environment, including adequate facilities and arrangements to safeguard employees' welfare.

Section 2(3) requires an employer to prepare and update a written statement of his general health and safety policy and to illustrate how it is implemented into working practices. He must bring the statement to his employees' attention. A recognised trade union can appoint a safety representative to represent the employees' interests; the employer must consult him to ensure his employees' co-operation and to promote, develop and monitor health and safety measures. The representative can require the employer to establish a health and safety committee to monitor the measures.

13.2.2 Duty to people other than employees
(Sections 3–5)

The employer is responsible for the safety of other people who may be affected by his actions. Such people include the general public and visitors. Fumes and waste fall under this provision.

The duty extends to people brought in, for example, to carry out repairs or redecoration.

13.2.3 Manufacturers', etc duty for materials and substances
(Section 6)

Manufacturers, designers, importers and suppliers of any substance used must supply adequate information to anyone handling it in work processes about:

(1) its intended use;
(2) the tests that have been carried out on it; and
(3) how it should be used to prevent health and safety risks.

Materials and substances used to manufacture fairground equipment are subject to further provisions.

13.2.4 Employee's duty
(Section 7)

The employee must:

(1) take reasonable care of his own and other people's health and safety at work, and
(2) co-operate with his employer, managers and statutory provisions to comply with that duty.

Breach of this duty exposes the employee to criminal prosecution.

13.2.5 Interference/misuse and charges for use
(Sections 8 and 9)

No one must intentionally or recklessly interfere with or misuse equipment supplied for health and safety purposes.

An employer cannot expect an employee to pay for any health and safety item. Thus, if the employee must wear protective clothing, the employer must supply it free of charge.

13.2.6 Liability through another person's fault
(Section 36)

A person may be held liable for an incident caused by another's actions, and as a result either or both of them can be charged and convicted.

13.2.7 Enforcement
(Section 20)

Generally, local authorities and HSE inspectors enforce the Act's provisions.

An inspector, at any reasonable time or when there is a suspicion of dangerous practices, can enter any premises with a view to enforcement. He may be accompanied by a police officer if he believes he will be prevented from carrying out his duties, and by anyone else and any equipment needed to assist him with his investigation. He can order that all or any part of the premises be left undisturbed for as long as he needs to investigate them.

He can take measurements, photographs and recordings. He can take samples of items, substances and atmosphere, and order any item or substance to be dismantled or tested if he considers it a danger to health and safety.

If a person of responsibility requests to be present during the inspection, the inspector must allow it unless he believes it would be prejudicial to the State. Where an inspector needs to take articles or substances away for further tests, he must try to take only a sample of it. He can only keep it for as long as it takes to test and examine it; but he can detain it if he feels it is evidence that can be used in proceedings.

The inspector can question any person he reasonably believes can assist him with his enquiries, and have that person sign a declaration of truth. The person questioned can have a representative present (for example, a legal advisor). However, his answers are not admissible in evidence against him or his spouse in proceedings.

The inspector can inspect any books or documents relevant to health and safety, and can take copies of them.

Obstructing an inspector in the course of his duty is an offence punishable by a fine of up to £5,000.

13.2.8 Improvement notices

(Section 21)

An improvement notice is served by the inspector, stating his reasons for doing so, on a person who contravenes a health and safety provision and who is likely to continue or repeat it. That person must remedy the matter within a period specified in the notice. He may appeal against the notice to the industrial tribunal within a period stated in the notice (which must be at least 21 days) from the date it was received. An appeal suspends the notice until it is determined by the tribunal.

13.2.9 Prohibition notices

(Section 21)

An inspector may serve a prohibition notice, stating his reasons, on a responsible person to cease activities which are believed to involve a risk of serious personal injury. The notice specifies the date it is to take effect (ie immediately or after a period of time). The company can appeal to the industrial tribunal within 21 days of receiving the notice. The tribunal may suspend a notice until determination where it considers it safe to do so.

13.2.10 Regulations and approved codes of practice

(Sections 15–17 and 33)

It is an offence to contravene any duty laid down by regulations made under health and safety legislation. Further, approved codes of practice issued by the Health and Safety Commission are admissible in *civil* proceedings as evidence of good practice. Failure to follow a code of practice can be submitted as evidence in *criminal* proceedings to prove the legislation was contravened.

13.3 OTHER RELEVANT LEGISLATION

13.3.1 Factories Act 1961

Much of this Act has been repealed and replaced by the Workplace (Health, Safety and Welfare) Regulations 1992 and the Provision and Use of Work Equipment Regulations 1992 (both 6-pack regulations – see 13.3.3 for a more detailed explanation of this Act).

Factories are defined under s 175 as:

> 'any premises in which, or within the . . . precincts of which, persons are employed in manual labour in any process for or incidental to any of the following purposes . . .:
>
> (a) . . . making . . . any . . . or part of any article; or
> (b) . . . altering, repairing, ornamenting, finishing, cleaning, or washing or the breakup or demolition of any article; or
> (c) . . . adapting [any article] for sale . . .; or
> (d) . . . slaughtering [livestock – ie an abbatoir]; or
> (e) . . . confinement of . . . animals . . . while awaiting slaughter at other premises . . . not maintained primarily for agricultural purposes . . .'

The Act also applies to electrical stations, institutions, docks, quays, ships, building operations and engineering construction works. The local inspector must be notified in writing, at least one month before premises are to be used as such, of the full details of the factory, including its machinery and how it will be used.

All inspections carried out on machinery, equipment, etc must be recorded. The records must be kept for at least two years for inspectors and medical advisers to inspect.

13.3.2 Offices, Shops and Railway Premises Act 1963

Again, much of this Act has been repealed and replaced by the Workplace (Health, Safety and Welfare) Regulations 1992 and the Provision and Use of Work Equipment Regulations 1992 (both 6-pack regulations – see 13.3.3). The Act applies to:

(1) office premises, defined as a whole or part of a building partly, solely or principally used for office purposes such as administration, clerical work, handling money and telephone or telegraph operating;
(2) shops premises, defined as a whole or part of a building which is not a shop, but is used solely or principally for retail or wholesale trade or business; for repairing or treating goods delivered by the public; or for storing and selling solid fuel. Warehouses owned by dock, wharf or quay owners are not included in the definition;
(3) railway premises, defined as a building from which a railway undertaking is carried out or instructed. It does not include offices or shop premises, nor railway staff accommodation, hotels or electrical stations.

The Act does not apply to premises where:

(1) the only employees are the employer's relatives;
(2) the employee resides there as required by his employer;
(3) the hours worked there do not normally exceed 21 hours per week.

An intention to employ people in an office, shop or railway premises must be notified in writing to the HSE or local authority; two copies of the notice must be supplied, and must contain the information required under the Notification of Employment of Persons Order 1964. The relevant abstract of this Act for the premises must be displayed within four weeks of an employee starting work; the abstract is obtained from the HSE on application.

13.3.3 European involvement – the 1992 Regulations

Six regulations were introduced in 1993 to implement certain EC health and safety directives into UK law. Breach of them may render the person liable to civil or criminal prosecution. The regulations are as follows:

(1) Management of Health and Safety at Work Regulations 1992 (SI No 2051);
(2) Workplace (Health, Safety and Welfare) Regulations 1992 (SI No 3004);
(3) Provision and Use of Work Equipment Regulations 1992 (SI No 2932);

(4) Personal Protective Equipment at Work Regulations 1992 (SI No 2966);
(5) Manual Handling Operations Regulations 1992 (SI No 2793); and
(6) Health and Safety (Display Screen Equipment) Regulations 1992 (SI No 2792).

These detailed regulations largely replace the Factories Act 1961 and the Offices, Shops and Railway Premises Act 1963 and place new obligations on the employer. A major change brought in by the regulations is the duty on the employer to make an assessment of the risk to the health and safety of his employees and others who may be affected by his undertaking. He must ascertain the best reasonably practicable way of reducing this risk. Where he employs five or more people he must record his findings. There is not only a general duty on the employer to carry out the assessment but some of the regulations require to be made in relation to specific activities. Codes of practice and/or HSE guidance notes accompany each of the Regulations.

Other regulations have since come into force which are also important (eg the Control of Substances Hazardous to Health (Amendment) Regulations 1992).

13.4 CRIMINAL AND CIVIL LIABILITY

13.4.1 Criminal liability

A prosecution for breach of health and safety requirements is brought, usually, by a local authority or the HSE when it believes it can secure a conviction. An employer, employee, corporate body, director, manager, secretary or other officer can be prosecuted for a breach of the duty imposed. The defendant must seek legal advice before entering a plea to a charge against him. Hearings are held in magistrates' courts or Crown Courts, depending on the seriousness of the offence.

In magistrates' courts, the maximum fine on health and safety convictions is between £2,000–5,000, although for breaches of HSWA 1974, ss 2–6 (see 13.2.1–13.2.3) or contravention of a prohibition notice (see 13.2.9) or a court order this increases to up to £20,000. Very serious offences carry a maximum six-month prison sentence.

Crown courts can impose an unlimited fine or a maximum two-year prison sentence.

13.4.2 Civil liability

Civil proceedings brought against an employer are for claims of breach of statutory duty or negligence.

Breach of statutory duty

A person may have a claim against his employer where he can show that:

(1) he is protected by health and safety provisions;
(2) a provision has been breached; and
(3) the breach has caused him to suffer injury.

Whether the breach caused the injury is a matter of evidence to be considered by the court.

Defence

Before 1945 an employer could avoid liability for breach of statutory duty altogether if he could prove the plaintiff injured himself because of his own negligence. Now, the employer can be found guilty of breach even if the employee's conduct contributed to his own injury, although damages awarded to the employee are likely to be reduced.

However, if the employer can prove that the employee is fully responsible for the breach, he is likely to be found not liable.

Negligence

An employer owes his employees a duty of care to ensure a safe working environment. To prove the employer was negligent, the employee must show that the employer breached that duty, and should have foreseen that in breaching it his injury could – and did – occur.

If it is proved that the event causing the injury could not be reasonably foreseen, the employer is unlikely to be held liable. An employer should anticipate any circumstance where there could be mistakes made or accidental falls or slipping caused because, for example, the employee is distracted, or takes short cuts on a task when under pressure.

The duty of care extends to temporary workers, volunteer workers, visitors and anyone at risk outside the work premises. The duty applies even if the employer delegates to a manager or foreman, or to an outsider such as a consultant (although for the latter he may seek an indemnity from or contribution towards any liability).

Standard of care

An *employer* is expected to have a higher standard of care than his employees. He should have a greater knowledge and expertise and should be more familiar with the job and its surroundings. An *employee* is expected to use the skill and knowledge that his job demands.

The employer should keep up-to-date with work procedures for his trade, and be familiar with HSE pamphlets, approved codes of practice and guidance notes. Failure to do so can prove his negligence.

Employers (and also self-employed persons) are required to carry out risk assessments under the Management of Health and Safety at Work Regulations 1992 (one of the '6-pack' regulations) to minimise health and safety risks. Where five or more people are employed, the assessment results and the arrangements made in the light of them must be recorded and any group of employees at specialist risk must be identified. The assessment must be reviewed as necessary. An employer can appoint one or more persons (depending on the business's size) to help him to comply with his statutory duties; in some circumstances the employer can nominate himself as such a person, or he may use outside experts.

In weighing up the likelihood of accidents occurring with the costs of implementing safety procedures, employers must get the balance right. An employer who can show it is not reasonably practical for him to implement certain measures may not be held liable for failing to implement them.

If, in an action against him, an employer can prove that something intervened in his duty of care to the employee (thus 'breaking the chain of causation'), he may successfully defend the claim of negligence. If the employee contributes to his own injury, damages awarded to him may be reduced accordingly.

13.4.3 Vicarious liability

An employer can be held responsible for any negligent act of his employee which harms another person (including another employee) or causes damage where the employee is 'in the course of his employment'. This does not apply where an employee is on 'a frolic of his own' (such as a practical joke), because it is not a part of the employee's working role.

13.5 WORKING CONDITIONS

13.5.1 Temperature, ventilation and lighting

(Workplace (Health, Safety and Welfare) Regulations 1992, regs 6–8)

The temperature must be over 16°C after one hour in any workroom where substantial sedentary work is carried out, or 13°C where substantial physical work is carried out. These provisions do not apply to waiting rooms (eg in railway stations) or where goods (such as food) may deteriorate, but even so employees must have access to warmth. A thermometer must be provided in the room.

The heating system must not emit fumes into workrooms which may injure or offend the people working there. There must be adequate fresh or purified air and ventilation, and sufficient and suitable natural or artificial light. Windows and skylights must be kept clean and free from obstruction.

13.5.2 Cleanliness and overcrowding

(Workplace (Health, Safety and Welfare) Regulations 1992, regs 9 and 10)

Factories

All fittings and furniture must be kept clean. Dirt and dust must be removed daily from areas where it is known to accumulate. All workshop floors must be washed or swept at least once a week. Unless no mechanical power is used and there are fewer than ten employees, all inside walls, ceilings, partitions and staircases must at least

- every 14 months be washed and, if already whitewashed or colour washed, given a fresh coat, and
- every seven years, where painted, be repainted.

Every employee must have at least 1 cubic metre of working space (unless an exemption certificate provides otherwise) to avoid risk of injury through overcrowding.

Offices, shops and railway premises

The premises and all its fittings and furniture must be kept clean. No dirt or refuse must be allowed to accumulate anywhere a person works or passes through. Floors and steps must be washed or swept at least once a week.

Overcrowding is determined by dividing the measurement of a room's floor in square metres by the number of people employed in it. If the result is less than 3.7, the room is overcrowded.

13.5.3 Floors, passages, stairs and safe access

(Workplace (Health, Safety and Welfare) Regulations 1992, reg 12)

All floors, steps, stairs, passages and gangways must be of sound construction and properly maintained, and must have drainage if they are likely to become wet. They must be kept free from any obstruction or substance to prevent tripping and slipping. Handrails or handholds must be provided on all open-sided stairways. Floor openings must be securely fenced where practicable.

If there is any danger of a person falling more than two metres, fencing or other safety features must be provided, unless there are already secure footholds or handrails in place.

There must be safe means of access to all work areas.

13.5.4 Workstations and seating

(Workplace (Health, Safety and Welfare) Regulations 1992, reg 11)

Workstations must be suitably arranged for the employee and the work being carried out there.

Where work can be carried out whilst seated, the employer must provide seats. Not providing seats in these circumstances is an offence. Chairs for sedentary work must be suitable and, where necessary, adjustable; footrests must be provided if required. (See also 13.9.1 on computer work.)

13.5.5 Toilets

(Workplace (Health, Safety and Welfare) Regulations 1992, reg 20 and Sched 1)

There should be one toilet for every 25 men and for every 25 women. If the total number of staff is not completely divisible by 25, there should be another toilet for the number left over (eg for 79 women staff, there should be four toilets).

Toilets must be adequately ventilated and lit, and kept in a clean and orderly condition.

13.5.6 Washing facilities

(Workplace (Health, Safety and Welfare) Regulations 1992, reg 21)

Adequate washing facilities (including showers where necessary) must be provided for all employees, with hot and cold or warm running water, soap and clean towels or other drying methods. The facilities must be convenient, close to toilets and changing facilities, and kept clean and maintained. Separate facilities should be provided for men and women unless there are single facilities each in a self-contained, lockable room.

13.5.7 Drinking water

(Workplace (Health, Safety and Welfare) Regulations 1992, reg 22)

All staff must have convenient access to drinking water. This can be supplied by the public mains, or stored in a jug or other container and renewed at least daily. Unless the water is supplied by an upward jet, cups must be provided.

13.5.8 Changing facilities and clothes storage

(Workplace (Health, Safety and Welfare) Regulations 1992, regs 23 and 24)

Storage must be provided for clothes not worn during work hours, and where practicable a facility for drying them. There must also be storage and drying facilities for (eg protective) clothing not taken home by the employees. If employees must wear protective clothing or uniforms, changing facilities must be provided with secure storage for their own clothes, which must be separate from their work clothes storage if this is appropriate.

13.5.9 Rest areas

(Workplace (Health, Safety and Welfare) Regulations 1992, reg 25)

Rest facilities must be provided, including an area to eat meals if there is a risk of food becoming contaminated if eaten at the employee's workstation. If employees are expected to eat meals on the work premises, the employer must provide for this (eg a canteen). There must be separate provision for smokers and non-smokers, and facilities available for pregnant women and nursing mothers.

13.5.10 Young persons and women

The local careers officer must be notified in writing within seven days of employing a young person (ie not a child but under 18) in a factory. The employee's full details (including his last school) must be given.

Young persons must be fully trained to operate dangerous machinery, and must not be allowed to clean moving machinery. They and women are prohibited under the Factories Act 1961, s 74 from working in lead manufacture, and are further limited in other areas by ss 128, 131 and 132.

An HSE inspector can serve a notice prohibiting a young person (or any other person) being employed if the job is detrimental to his health. The notice comes into effect from the date specified unless an appointed medical advisor certificates that he is fit to do that job.

13.5.11 Humid factories and underground rooms

(Factories Act 1961, ss 68 and 69)

Factories which produce artificial humidity by steaming or other textile processes must be notified to the inspector when the humidity is first produced. Strict temperature and humidity controls apply.

Underground rooms may be certified by an HSE or local authority inspector as being suitable for storage purposes only.

13.5.12 Fire safety

The Fire Precautions (Workplace) Regulations 1997 came into force on 1 December 1997. They set out criteria for ensuring safety from fire. Many businesses will already meet the criteria. Free advice can be obtained from the local fire brigade.

13.6 MACHINERY AND EQUIPMENT

13.6.1 Safety of machinery

(Provision and Use of Work Equipment Regulations 1992)

All machinery and equipment must be maintained and kept in good repair by trained staff or outside contractors to ensure efficient working order. All maintenance and repairs must be logged; the log must be kept for future inspection. Machinery and equipment includes everything from scissors to lathes.

Parts of machinery which move must be securely fenced or guarded unless it has sufficient safety features or is positioned out of harm's way (an exception which is rarely met). The fencing must effectively protect the employee from the moving parts, and must be of substantial construction, constantly maintained and kept in place while the machinery is in use. This duty is strict; liability is extended to sellers and hirers of such machinery.

The employer must ensure all machinery and equipment can be isolated from its source of energy, and that the method for doing this is clearly indicated and readily accessible.

All staff required to work on machinery or to use equipment must be properly trained and/or supervised by an experienced member of staff to ensure its safe use.

The Regulations also include provisions for supply of health and safety information, temperatures, stability, and markings and warnings.

13.6.2 Hoists and lifts

(Factories Act 1961, ss 22 and 23)

These must be inspected every 6 or 12 months (depending on the type) and the results recorded and kept. The HSE must be notified within 28 days if the equipment cannot be used until repairs are carried out.

Protective gates must be provided to prevent people falling down the hoist or lift shaft, and openings must be securely fenced and maintained. It must be ensured that no person or goods can become trapped between the moving and fixed parts. The maximum working load must be visibly stated and not exceeded.

13.6.3 Lifting methods and machinery

(Factories Act 1961, ss 26 and 27)

Chain slings, rope slings, rings and hooks must be of good construction, sound material, adequate strength and free from patent defect, and must have undergone a strengthening treatment. Each item must have its working load visibly stated on or near it, which must not be exceeded. The equipment must be inspected and tested every six months and the results recorded and kept.

Winches, pulley blocks, transporters and runways must also be of good construction, sound material and free from patent defect, and must be properly maintained. All parts must be inspected every 14 months and the results recorded and kept. If repairs are needed which warrant the equipment unusable, the HSE inspector must be notified within 28 days. The safe working load must be visibly stated.

A driver must be told of anyone working on or near the wheel track of a travelling crane, and must not allow the crane to approach that area to within six metres. A person at risk of being struck by a crane travelling overhead must be warned of its approach.

13.6.4 Steam boilers

(Factories Act 1961, ss 37–39)

Steam boilers must be rendered safe as far as possible. Water-sealed gas holders must be of sound construction and properly maintained, and inspected at least once every two years and the results recorded and kept. A gas holder can only be repaired or demolished under a fully trained person's supervision.

13.6.5 Protective clothing and equipment

(Personal Protective Equipment at Work Regulations 1992)

All protective equipment must be compatible where used together. The employer must assess the level of protective clothing and equipment needed for each employee to ensure his safety. Clothing must fit properly whilst not restricting the employee's ability to carry out his tasks. All clothing and equipment must be maintained and replaced as necessary. Any loss or defect must be reported to the employer immediately.

13.7 HAZARDOUS FUMES AND SUBSTANCES

13.7.1 Dangerous substances

(Factories Act 1961, s 18)

Containers of scalding, corrosive or poisonous liquid must be wherever possible securely covered or fenced to a height of 920 mm to prevent people falling into them. If this is impractical, the employer must still take measures to prevent that risk. Safety provisions apply to ladders or gangways positioned over such containers.

13.7.2 Fumes; lack of oxygen; explosive and flammable substances

(Factories Act 1961, ss 30 and 31)

Breathing and rescue equipment must be provided for employees who could be affected by dangerous fumes or lack of oxygen. Where there is a danger of explosion or inflammable substances, all steps must be taken to prevent this from happening, such as enclosing dangerous areas or providing air vents. This does not apply for machinery installed in the open air.

13.8 REPORTING OF INJURIES, INSURANCE AND REDUCING RISKS TO HEALTH

13.8.1 Compulsory insurance

Employers must take out an approved insurance policy with an authorised insurer against their liability to employees' work-related personal injuries and diseases (Employers' Liability (Compulsory Insurance) Act 1969). This does not apply if the employee is a relative or (unless the legislation states otherwise) is not ordinarily resident in Great Britain. Very few employers (with the exception of those under national ownership or control, or a health service body or city council) are exempted.

Copies of the prescribed insurance certificate must be prominently displayed for the employees' information, and the certificate (or a copy of it) must be produced for inspection when required (see 13.2.7).

Failure to display the certificate is liable on summary conviction in a magistrates' court to a maximum level 3 fine (£1,000). A maximum level 4 fine is applied to an employer who fails to take out necessary insurance.

13.8.2 Reporting injuries, diseases and dangerous occurrences

The employer (or 'responsible person') must follow set procedures when a death, injury, disease or dangerous occurrence (such as collapse of a building or machinery) occurs. A detailed list of injuries and diseases is given in the Reporting of Injuries, Diseases and Dangerous Occurrences Regulations 1995. The relevant authority (usually the HSE) must be notified of the incident immediately (usually by telephone) and must within ten days receive a report on form 2508 or 2508A. A report must also be supplied under the following circumstances:

(1) where the employee is absent through injury for three or more days, within seven days of the accident;
(2) immediately on a death within a year of the accident;
(3) immediately on notification that an industrial disease has been diagnosed;
(4) having already immediately notified the enforcing authority of a gas incident, within 14 days of a death or injury caused by it; and
(5) within 14 days of discovering the death or injury was caused by faulty gas fittings.

Records must be kept for at least three years of all incidents that must be reported and of any forms sent to the enforcing authority. The enforcing authority may ask for extracts of the records from time to time. The authority may ask for further details on a reported incident, such as the equipment used and the qualifications of the persons involved.

There must be procedures in place for evacuating the workplace in the event of, for example, a fire or bomb threat.

13.8.3 Defective equipment

An employee can sue his employer for damages even if the equipment which caused the accident was defective when supplied to the employer. The employer can seek damages from the supplier towards compensating the employee.

13.8.4 Lifting, carrying, etc
(Manual Handling Operations Regulations 1992)

Regulation 2 defines 'manual handling operations' as 'any transporting or supporting of a load [which includes a person, animal or inanimate object] (including . . . lifting, putting down, pushing, pulling, carrying or moving thereof) by hand or by bodily force', which if done incorrectly can cause back injuries and strain. Employers must ensure that the need to handle goods manually is avoided if it involves a risk of injury, and must attempt to inform employees of the precise weight and the heaviest side of each load which must be so handled. Employees must fully use any facility available to assist him.

13.8.5 Information for employees

Employees must be given the opportunity to read HSE issued posters and leaflets, on which the employer must specify the enforcing authority's name and address. Where posters and leaflets are updated, the employer must ensure that the amendments are made to them within six months.

13.8.6 First aid

Adequate first aid equipment and facilities must be provided to minimise injury or illness until help arrives, or to treat minor injuries. Unless exempted by the HSE, the employer must ensure that there are adequate staff trained and able to administer first aid. If the undertaking, for example, is small or the appointed first aider is absent, a member of staff can be appointed merely to take charge of incidents until help arrives. Employees must be aware of where first aid can be obtained, and from whom.

13.9 COMPUTERS AND OTHER DISPLAY SCREEN EQUIPMENT

(Health and Safety (Display Screen Equipment) Regulations 1992)

The Regulations introduced an area of law previously not covered by UK legislation, and cover all employees at risk of a type of injury often associated with keyboard work and poor posture, and to eyesight problems from long periods working at computer and display screens. The guidance notes suggest that an employee who spends more than three hours, continuous or broken, a day at a screen is at risk (although they further suggest that an employer should regard all employees, whether permanent or temporary, using such equipment as falling within these provisions).

13.9.1 Workstations

(Regulations 2–4)

The employer must assess the risk of all workstations and ensure that they meet the requirements laid down in the Regulations. The requirements include the following:

(1) The screen image should not flicker.
(2) Brightness and contrast must be adjustable.
(3) The screen must swivel and tilt easily.
(4) The keyboard must tilt, be separate from the screen and have a matt surface to avoid reflective glare.
(5) The space in front of the keyboard must allow the employee to support his arms.
(6) The desk or table must be large enough to arrange and rearrange all the equipment to suit each user.
(7) The chair must be able to tilt and the back and height adjustable. A footrest must be available to anyone who requires one.
(8) The lighting must prevent reflections and glares on the screen, and the workstation designed to prevent any direct glare from windows or brightly coloured fixtures.
(9) Windows must have adjustable blinds or curtains to reduce the effects of daylight falling on the screen.
(10) The equipment must not produce excess heat which may cause discomfort to the user.

There must be sufficient breaks whilst using the equipment (which can include carrying out other tasks).

13.9.2 Eye tests
(Regulation 5)

The employer must pay for an eye test if the employee requires one; but a prudent employer will offer tests to his employees rather than wait to be asked. An employee who is already employed and is about to use screen equipment for the first time must be offered to have his eyes tested before starting to use it. An employee can decline to take an eye test.

The employer must ensure that the employee has sufficient spectacles or lenses to carry out his screen duties.

13.9.3 Training and information
(Regulations 6 and 7)

An employee must be given adequate health and safety training and information for using a workstation properly (including whenever the workstation is substantially modified).

13.10 CONCLUSION

There are constant developments in the health and safety laws and regulations, and the areas covered in this chapter are but a brief summary of health and safety issues which businesses must be aware of. Further professional advice and investigation is essential to ensure that these areas are fully met and to keep abreast of future developments.

The EU is responsible for many of the changes. For example, two directives look likely to have an impact on UK legislation in the near future: regulations are proposed to implement Directive 94/33/EC (Protection of Young People at Work), and regulations will have to be implemented by the Government to take account of Directive 93/104/EC (Working Time Directive) should the UK's challenge to it to the European Court of Justice fail.

13.11 SOURCES OF FURTHER INFORMATION

Barrett and Howells, *Occupational Health and Safety Law*, 3rd edn (Pitman Publishing, 1997).

Health and Safety Executive – General enquiries: 0541 545500

Publications: 01787 881165

14

GENERAL INSURANCE

GILL CLARK, EAGLE STAR

This chapter covers the following topics:

(1) The need for insurance cover
(2) Protection
(3) The main compulsory insurance requirements
(4) The insurance intermediary
(5) Types of cover available
(6) Types of policies available

14.1 THE NEED FOR INSURANCE COVER

All businesses, whether large or small, have to take risk. It is essential to recognise the uncertain nature of risk. Can the reader appreciate the financial loss which may be incurred as a result of, for example, an extensive factory fire, or a theft? Adequate insurance cover is a fundamental requirement to ensure the continuation of a business in the event of a loss.

14.2 PROTECTION

It is also important to recognise at this early stage that not all risks can be insured but, in return for a known premium, insurance provides for the uncertainty of most losses in a business environment to be transferred to the insurers who arrange cover for thousands of businesses. A business therefore stands to benefit from insuring the risks to which it is subject since insurance can protect its interests by allowing business plans to continue and by facilitating continued production. There is then no need to make contingency plans or tie up capital in the form of reserves to cater for the possibility of a risk actually occurring and causing a loss which could not otherwise be withstood by the business. Insurance can also free the businessman from many of the worries inherent in the running of the business.

14.3 THE MAIN COMPULSORY INSURANCE REQUIREMENTS

Whilst it is good business practice to arrange insurance to protect the business assets and liabilities, there are several forms of insurance which have been made compulsory for most businesses either by UK statutory law or by EC Regulation. These are explained below.

14.3.1 Legislation relating to employers' liability

Employers' Liability (Compulsory Insurance) Act 1969 and Employers' Liability (Compulsory Insurance) General Regulations 1971

The 1969 Act and 1971 General Regulations introduced compulsory employers' liability insurance with effect from 1 January 1972. Most employers (there are some exceptions) carrying on any business in Great Britain must insure, with an authorised insurer, against liability for bodily injury or disease sustained by their employees arising out of and in the course of their employment in Great Britain in that business. Evidence of this insurance must be provided in the form of an insurance certificate which must be displayed in a prominent position at each place of business at which there are employees.

Employers' Liability (Compulsory Insurance) Exemption (Amendment) Regulations 1992

The Third EC Motor Insurance Directive (90/232/EEC) introduced a requirement for motor policies to cover all passengers. Such policies must now cover liability to persons in the employment of the insured when travelling in the course of employment (effective from 1 July 1994). Note that there are liabilities eg to members of the employers' immediate family which are excluded from compulsory employers' liability insurance requirements. These excluded individuals or other exempt bodies must be covered under motor policies from 31 December 1992. This compulsory motor insurance requirement does not extend to the driver of the vehicle who continues to be covered by the employers' liability policy.

14.3.2 Road Traffic Act 1988

This Act consolidated certain legislation relating to road traffic and came into force on 15 May 1989. To comply with an EC Directive on motor insurance, interim regulations gave effect to the Act's requirements from

31 December 1988.

The Act requires that the insurance policy provides unlimited cover for death or bodily injury to a third party (including passengers) and a minimum amount of £250,000 for third party property damage. In practice higher levels of third party property damage are given, usually unlimited for cars and up to £5m for goods vehicles. At present there is no legal requirement for insuring against damage to one's own vehicle.

14.3.3 Statutory examination of engineering plant

By law, many items of plant and machinery (eg pressure systems, power presses, local exhaust ventilation plants, lifts and lifting equipment) must be inspected and certified by a competent person. These examinations are largely in response to the requirements of the Health and Safety at Work Act, and associated legislation.

These services provided by some of the major insurers are sometimes part of a wider policy cover or are on a fee only basis.

14.4 THE INSURANCE INTERMEDIARY

It is possible to purchase insurance in two ways: direct from the insurance company or through an insurance intermediary. As a commercial buyer of insurance, it is recommended that a businessman's insurance requirements are arranged through an insurance intermediary to assist in identifying the risks which confront the business. The variations in policy wording offered by the different insurers further adds to the complexity of arranging insurance cover.

The insurance intermediaries understand the market and know the various types of cover that can be provided, the most competitive premium rates and the best claims services available. The intermediaries' advice is mainly free since they receive remuneration, in the form of commission, from the insurance company. Therefore the businessman does not pay more for using the service of an intermediary than going to the insurance company itself. However, there has been an increasing move towards intermediaries levying fees to clients for their services. This is based on a perceived benefit to the client, of receiving more favourable premiums from the insurance companies, who would not be then including the intermediaries' commission in their terms, and the potential saving in insurance premium tax (IPT).

Intermediaries act as agents for the insured but sometimes have the authority from the insurance companies to issue cover for certain classes of insurance. Intermediaries can be classified as follows.

14.4.1 Insurance broker

A broker is a full-time intermediary and is expected to have a wide knowledge of the insurance market. The Insurance Brokers (Registration) Act 1977 created the Insurance Brokers Registration Council (IBRC) to govern the registration and regulation of insurance brokers. To be registered as a broker, an individual must have:

(1) an approved qualification; and
(2) been employed by an insurance broker or insurance company for at least three years; or
(3) been employed as in (2) above for five years.

14.4.2 Other intermediaries

There are also insurance agents, consultants, financial advisers, or appointed representatives working on either a full- or part-time basis who may not have had such a wide knowledge of the general insurance market as an insurance broker. The agent, for example, may have been an accountant or solicitor who introduced insurance in the course of his main business activity.

Insurers recognise two main categories of non-registered intermediary:

(1) An 'independent intermediary' who acts primarily for his client and is responsible for the advice and service provided.
(2) A 'company agent' who represents up to a maximum of six insurance companies which accept responsibility for his conduct and advice given.

The Association of British Insurers (ABI), introduced a code of practice in 1981 to compliment the Insurance Brokers (Registration) Act by controlling the non-registered intermediaries with the aim of safeguarding consumers' interests. The code was last reviewed in 1993 and is supported by Government. An independent code monitoring committee, comprising ABI members, consumer groups and DTI representation, reports on the operation of the code annually to interested parties, including Government.

14.5 TYPES OF COVER AVAILABLE

There are many areas of a business which require some form of insurance protection. Various forms of cover are available and these range from insurance against loss or damage to the business assets and the financial loss which would follow, to liability and professional indemnity insurances.

14.5.1 Property insurance – 'material damage'

Material damage insurance provides cover for the actual business assets, for example, the buildings, machinery and stock in trade. Various types of material damage cover are available and the following paragraphs give a brief summary of the forms most commonly requested.

Fire and special perils insurance

A basic 'standard fire' policy gives cover for loss or damage following fire, lightning and a limited form of explosion. However, invariably such limited cover is not enough and wider cover is required. This is provided by a 'fire and special perils' policy which covers a range of additional covers as well as fire. These include explosion, aircraft, storm, escape of water, riot, malicious damage and impact by road vehicles or animals. The customer may select the extent of cover he requires.

It is also possible to purchase even wider cover by means of an 'all risks' policy which includes all the above perils together with other 'accidental' damage which gives cover for all damage unless caused by an exclusion stated in the policy. These policies are usually sold on an 'all or nothing' basis rather than a selective basis.

The amount chosen to insure the business assets is known as the 'sum insured' and it is essential that this figure is adequate, otherwise any claim will be proportionately reduced. This is known as 'subject to average'. When fixing the sum insured, an allowance should be made for inflation and possible delays in rebuilding time and obtaining alternative equipment or supplies.

The policy can be taken out on an 'all risks' basis. In addition to fire and special perils, it includes accidental damage or loss not specifically excluded.

It is not sufficient to insure the physical loss or damage to property. It is also essential to insure loss of income following loss or damage and this is provided by means of 'Business Interruption' insurance. Details are explained in 14.5.4.

Theft policy

This provides compensation in the event of the loss of the property insured by theft. It also includes theft damage to buildings. A more detailed description of stock may be necessary, as it is usually this which is attractive to thieves, although it has become more common for computers and computer chips to figure significantly as a target. Commercial theft policies usually require evidence of entry to or exit from premises by forcible and violent means.

Goods in transit insurance

Every business depends upon the movement of goods and documents and as insurance is not provided for business effects under a motor policy, goods in transit insurance is a necessary protection.

An 'all risks' policy is available. If a business owns a small fleet of vehicles, the policy can be arranged to specify the number of vehicles, with individual limits for each vehicle. If a business owns a large fleet of vehicles, it is advised to insure it on 'a declaration basis' whereby the insurance is based on the maximum value in any one vehicle in operation at the inception date of the policy, and a deposit premium charge based on the estimated annual carryings of all vehicles. Any adjustment in the premium is made at each renewal when the actual annual carryings are declared.

A problem arises, however, when goods are sent via a contracted haulier. If the goods are lost or damaged while in the carrier's care, compensation may not automatically be forthcoming as the carrier may be able to prove that he is not liable or, alternatively, can rely on contract conditions to avoid liability.

Various conditions of carriage exist, most notably those resulting from the Road Haulage Association's Standard Conditions of 1991 and the Standard CMR conditions applicable in EC countries. These Conditions should be studied carefully or discussed with an insurance adviser. This being the case, it is advisable that goods are insured under an 'all risks' policy as a carrier's policy ultimately protects the carrier rather than one's business. Such cover can be given on the same policy as for the business's own vehicles, and arranged on a similar basis of maximum any one vehicle and estimated carryings.

If any goods are exported a separate Marine Transit policy may be required.

For goods transported by rail, the liability accepted by the rail authorities is slightly wider than that of the haulage carriers. Even so, additional insurance cover can be arranged at a low premium. This enables any loss or damage to be dealt with by the insurance company and not directly with the rail authorities although it would be expected to first seek whatever compensation is due from such authorities.

The Post Office sets various limits of liability but, as with the above, independent insurance cover can be arranged.

Money insurance

This provides compensation to a business in the event of money being physically stolen or destroyed either at the premises or while being carried to or from a bank. There are various limits which can be arranged. Some companies also provide for compensation if an employee suffers injury from malicious assault while carrying money to or from a bank.

Engineering insurance

An engineering policy provides cover for damage to machinery and can also cover explosion of steam boilers and pressure plant. Cover for electrical and mechanical breakdown is also available for most machinery.

Engineering insurers offer a variety of insurance packages catering for a wide range of machinery and construction risks. Examples include:

(a) machinery breakdown (including loss of profits)
(b) boiler/pressure systems explosion
(c) contract works (eg building and civil engineering, machinery installation)
(d) contractors plant
(e) hired-in machinery and plant
(f) computers and electronic equipment
(g) machinery movement.

Periodic inspection of many types of machinery and plant (eg lifting equipment, pressure systems, local exhaust ventilation, plant power presses) is compulsory by law and most engineering insurers provide such inspection services. Many also offer a range of machinery and health and safety related consultancy services.

It is not sufficient to insure the physical loss or damage to property. It is also essential to insure loss of income following loss or damage and this is provided by means of 'business interruption' insurance (see 14.5.4 below).

14.5.2 Liability insurances

The day-to-day operation of a business, including the ownership of business premises, business vehicles and the manufacture and sale of goods or other services provided, introduces legal responsibilities to employees, the public and to the consumers of the products or services supplied. It is therefore important that all businesses have adequate insurance protection to protect them against the legal liabilities which may arise. These legal liabilities may be imposed by common law, by statute or increasingly by EC regulation. In addition there may be contractual liabilities, some of which may be uninsurable. Penalty clauses are normally uninsurable. Insurers therefore provide employers, public and product liability insurances and professional indemnity insurances to provide protection against these liabilities.

Employers' liability insurance policy

It is compulsory under the terms of the Employers' Liability (Compulsory Insurance) Act 1969 to effect employers' liability insurance. This Act came into force on 1 January 1972. Most employers (there are exceptions) must take out insurance against liability for bodily injury or disease sustained by employees arising out of and in the course of their employment in the UK. An insurance certificate has to be displayed to provide evidence of the insurance being in force.

An employers' liability policy protects the employer against:

(a) his own personal negligence;
(b) his vicarious liability for the acts of his employees;
(c) failure to provide suitable and safe plant, a safe place of work and competent staff;
(d) the personal negligence of employees and their negligence in carrying out their duties;
(e) breach of statutory duty. There are many statutory enactments relating to the health and safety at work of employees, some of which relate specifically to dangerous substances (eg asbestos). The Health and Safety at Work Act 1974 outlines the main statutory duties imposed on the employer. The Management of Health and Safety at Work Regulations 1992 (one of the '6-pack' regulations) require employers to:

    - assess risks to health and safety
    - plan, organise, control, monitor and review measures
    - provide health surveillance
    - appoint competent people
    - set up emergency procedures
    - provide information and training.

    The Regulations give guidance on personal protective equipment provided, manual handling operations and safety requirements relating to display screen equipment (see generally Chapter 13).

The Employers' Liability (Compulsory Insurance) General (Amendment) Regulations 1994 require an employer (which term includes a company and its subsidiaries) to insure and maintain insurance for £2m for claims relating to employees arising out of any one occurrence. Most insurers now offer a limit of liability of £10m, which sum is inclusive of legal costs. Most insurers provide an option to purchase additional protection up to a limit of £25m, although there are facilities to provide even higher limits.

A review of the compulsory employers' liability requirements is at present being undertaken as the 1969 Act has not been reviewed since its inception.

Employers' liability insurance thus provides cover against an award of damages which a business may have to pay for bodily injury or disease sustained by an employee, and also the costs of defending an action brought under the Health and Safety at Work Act 1974.

Public liability insurance policy

This insurance, unlike employers' liability insurance, is not compulsory by law (other than for the owners of riding establishments), but public liability claims carry the same financial threat to a business.

Public liability insurance provides cover for damages or compensation awarded against a company in respect of accidental bodily injury to third parties and accidental loss of or accidental damage to third party property caused in the conduct of the business (eg the negligence of the employer or employees, or perhaps from defects in the properties owned by the business). There are a number of common exceptions within this cover:

- Liabilities arising from the use of motor vehicles where the RTA applies
- Aviation liabilities
- Marine liabilities
- Claims for damage to property belonging to the policyholder or whilst property is in his custody or control
- Loss of or damage to property which is being worked upon
- Liabilities relating to the sale of products
- Any liabilities relating to professional advice provided by the policyholder for a fee.

The policy has a limit of indemnity which applies to any one claim or a series of claims arising from one original cause. In view of the increasing level of awards made by the courts, a business should ensure that its policy provides an adequate limit of indemnity, probably at least £2m. Additional protection is widely available at reasonable additional cost and limits of £5m, £10m and beyond can be arranged.

The policyholder is normally required to pay the first £100 or £250 of any claim.

Product liability insurance policy

Product liability insurance provides protection in respect of the insured's legal liability to pay damages or compensation for accidental bodily injury to third parties, and accidental loss of or accidental damage to third party property caused by goods sold or supplied or contract work executed by the business. The cover does not extend to apply to the cost of recalling, replacing or repairing the product supplied. This is more properly the subject of product guarantee insurance for which there is a limited market.

Product liability cover is usually available only in conjunction with public liability insurance. A limit of indemnity applies to a product liability policy in the aggregate for any one period of insurance. Again significant limits of indemnity are available.

Consumer Protection Act 1987

The objective of s 1 of the Act was to implement the EC Directive concerning liability for defective products (85/374/EEC). The Directive requires all member states to adopt or adapt national laws so as to impose a strict liability system upon the producers of defective products which cause injury to persons or damage to property. The Act became effective on 1 March 1988.

A person who has suffered damage does not have to prove negligence.

Those liable include the manufacturer of a finished product or component; the producer of raw material; or a person who holds himself out to be a producer (eg by putting an own brand label on the article). Where an article is manufactured outside the EC, the importer is also liable.

In view of the liabilities imposed on the producers of goods, importers etc it is important that they are adequately protected by product liability insurance with an adequate indemnity limit.

Good internal procedures are vital including:

- the adequacy of design and development procedures;
- the effectiveness of quality assurance systems;
- emergency plans for product recall if necessary;
- adequate records identifying suppliers, particularly overseas suppliers, so that any claim can be passed down the chain of supply.

Professional indemnity insurance

This type of insurance provides cover for liability arising from a negligent act, error or omission. The cover is not only required by the established professions (eg doctors, architects and solicitors) but anyone working in an advisory capacity. Cover is therefore required by financial advisers, designers of software or laboratories providing testing facilities.

In recent years the liability of professional advisers has been extended by the courts and they can in some circumstances incur liabilities to others with whom they are not in a contractual relationship.

The professional person must act with reasonable skill and care; if he does not do so he incurs a liability to pay compensation or damages which include compensation for financial losses suffered by the claimant.

The insurance cover is normally written on a 'claims made' basis and again, as with product liability insurance, the indemnity limit is normally capped in the aggregate in any one period of insurance.

14.5.3 Motor insurance policies

Any motorised self-propelled vehicles used or kept on a road must be insured for third party liability to meet the requirements of the Road Traffic Act. In addition to this compulsory third party cover a vehicle can also be insured for damage arising from fire and theft; this is known as a 'third party fire and theft' policy. The most common form of cover is the comprehensive policy which includes accidental damage to the employer's own vehicle.

Motor insurance is divided into:

(a) commercial vehicles;
(b) private cars;
(c) motorcycles.

If a business has a number of vehicles, these can be insured as part of a motor fleet policy. This covers all vehicles owned or operated by the business and can also include hired or loaned vehicles, whether they are private cars, goods carrying vehicles or motorcycles.

Comprehensive cover is essential for the small to medium-sized firms which do not have the facilities and resources to repair their own vehicles. If the damage is so severe as to make the vehicle uneconomical to repair, the insurers consider the vehicle to be a 'total loss' and settlement is made on the vehicle's current market value. However, where a car is a total loss and is less than 12 months old at the time of the accident it may be replaced with a new model of the same type. This would not normally apply to leased vehicles or vehicles not purchased as new.

An excess may be applied in which case the business is liable for the first amount of any claim. This is usually in the region of £50 to £250. The excess is usually applicable to young drivers under the age of 25, novices over 25 or as a result of the past driving record of particular drivers.

An employer can agree to pay a voluntary excess in return for a reduced premium. Other factors such as the vehicle type, the business location and past claims experience are taken into account when assessing the premium.

14.5.4 Business interruption insurance

Formerly known as 'consequential loss', this insurance gives protection against pecuniary loss which is almost certain to follow a fire or other physical damage to property. The business interruption policy is designed to protect the profit or other earnings of the business as well as to meet continuing payments for fixed overheads following a loss by a 'peril' insured under the material damage policy. The range of perils insured under a business interruption policy is usually the same as under the material damage policy.

Insurers invariably insist that a material damage policy exists (usually with the same company) and liability admitted under that policy before a payment can be made under a business interruption policy.

The essential features of business interruption insurance are as follows:

Maximum indemnity period

The businessman needs to assess how long it will take to get the business running normally again and also make sure that the cover will allow enough time for rebuilding or re-equiping the business premises and restoring trade to the level it was at before the loss. This is incorporated into the policy as the 'maximum indemnity period'.

Cover under the policy ceases at the end of the period and thus it is important that the indemnity period selected is more than adequate. Obviously, any estimation of the maximum indemnity period requires in-depth calculations and usually either the insurers or insurance intermediary will help in selecting the correct time period.

Careful consideration should also be given to the business's nature, the machinery used and location of staff. A serious interruption, for example, may force staff to leave, machinery may not be available and stock may not be readily replaced. The maximum indemnity period should take account of all these factors so that the possibility of inadequate cover is minimised.

Loss of gross profit

The most common form of business interruption insurance in the market is loss of gross profit on a 'declaration linked' basis. Under this form of cover, there is no sum insured but the premium is based on an estimate of the gross profit (see below) for the coming year, although this figure has to be proportionately increased if the maximum indemnity period is more than 12 months. At the end of the insurance period, this premium is adjusted when the actual gross profit is known, again proportionately increased in line with the maximum indemnity period. This premium adjustment may result in an additional premium to the insurers or a refund due to the insured.

Because the figure chosen is an 'estimate', insurers allow additional cover over that amount, usually 33 per cent, and if in the event of a claim the estimate is found to be inadequate, the claim is not proportionately reduced (ie is not subject to average).

It is still possible to insure profit on an actual basis with a sum insured, but the amount has to be accurate, no additional cover is allowed and the policy is subject to average. If, however, at the end of the period the sum insured was in excess of the gross profit (proportionately increased if necessary), insurers will allow a refund.

Gross profit for insurance purposes is not the figure shown in trading profit and loss accounts but is calculated in line with the definition stated in the policy. Particular attention should be paid to the future expansion of the business. Thus the figure selected should take into account real growth and inflation as well as being proportionately increased in line with the maximum indemnity period.

Other covers available

Other forms of business interruption insurance often asked for are loss of revenue (suitable for hotel or restaurant owners, churches or dental practices), loss of fees (suitable for professional practices such as solicitors) and loss of rent receivable (suitable for property owners).

Extensions of cover

The business may, of course, be affected by losses outside the premises and therefore most business interruption policies are capable of being extended, the most common being:

(1) Denial of access – neighbouring premises damaged by an insured peril may prevent access to the business premises, thus resulting in a loss of earnings.
(2) Failure of public utilities – access or trade prevented as a result of insured damage at the premises of the gas, water or electricity supply company.
(3) Suppliers of goods or services – premises from which the insured obtains essential supplies or services. If supplies are not available from their usual source, production of the business will be curtailed or even halted until supplies are available again or, as is more likely, an alternative source is found, possibly at an increased cost.

Other extensions exist and vary from insurer to insurer depending on the type of business.

Outstanding debit balances

Any business which allows credit for the payment of goods or services relies on its accounting records for the collection of money due. If these records are destroyed by an insured peril customers cannot be traced and the money they are owed may never be collected.

It is possible to cover these outstanding debit balances by means of a 'book debts' policy. As with the business interruption policy, it is essential for a claim to be agreed in respect of these records under the material policy before a claim can be paid under this one.

The sum insured should represent the maximum amount outstanding at any one time. Each month the insured undertakes to provide the actual amount outstanding and at the end of the year the premium is recalculated on the average of these declarations and a refund is allowed to the insured if this is less than the original amount paid. Furthermore, regular declarations facilitate the calculation of the amount payable in the event of a claim.

14.5.5 Other insurances to consider

Fidelity insurance

This type of insurance is centred around fraud or dishonesty on the part of the employees. Cover is provided for loss of money or goods belonging to or held in trust by the employer, caused directly by an act of fraud or dishonesty committed by an employee. As a condition of the policy, fraud or dishonesty has to be perpetrated and discovered during the period for which the risk is on cover, but commonly a discovery period of one to two years after the expiry date of the time period is provided.

In considering the risk, the insurers will wish to know what systems of check and control the employer has put in place to deter and detect such fraud and dishonesty, the frequency of internal and external audits, and the number of employees. Cover is then provided on an annual basis.

The financial impact of fraud from within can pose a serious threat to a business, particularly if, as is often the case, the fraud has continued and remained undiscovered for a long period of time. Fidelity insurance should thus be considered as a viable insurance option.

Credit insurance

This protects a business against bad trade debts and covers the risk that if goods are sold, the purchaser may not pay for them as a result of insolvency. For foreign transactions, the government has set up the Export Credits Guarantee Department, primarily to assist exporting companies against the risk of not being paid. Premiums are charged on a turnover basis or are adjustable according to the amount of debt outstanding at regular intervals.

Legal expenses insurance

The public in general is becoming more litigation conscious and thus there is an even greater likelihood that at some time or other a business may become involved in legal action. Protection is available in the form of legal expenses insurance. For example, costs may be incurred as a result of legal actions brought about by an aggrieved employee who considers that he has been unfairly dismissed. The insurance cover provides financial support to defend or pursue legal rights. The cover extends to include the solicitor's fees and expenses along with any court costs and opponent's costs if appropriate.

14.6 TYPES OF POLICIES AVAILABLE

The insurance policy issued by the insurance company states what risks are covered by the policy, the premium cost, the insured's name and the period of time over which the cover applies.

14.6.1 Single risk policies

Single policies, such as a fire or a burglary policy, are usually more appropriate to the very large organisation. There is thus one policy for fire, one for consequential loss and for various other single risks. The organisation which is large enough financially may opt to retain several risks through self-insurance.

The disadvantage of a single policy is that the system of one premium and one renewal for each risk insured proves costly from the administrative point of view.

14.6.2 Package/combined policies

Single policies do not appeal to smaller businesses such as shops and offices. For smaller manufacturing or distribution businesses, insurance companies can arrange a combined policy. This incorporates separate sections for fire, consequential loss, liability, theft, money etc. The wordings are the same as if separate policies were issued but the business has the advantage of one policy and one renewal premium. There are, however, usually maximum limits on the premium for this type of policy.

Package policies are also available covering a wider range of business classes including property, loss of earnings, money and legal liability cover. The package policy is capable of covering almost all insurance needs. The combination required is selected from all the options available. Various benefits accrue:

(1) Simplified rating structure;
(2) Only one proposal form to complete;
(3) Only one premium and renewal.

The package policy is therefore flexible in accommodating changing business needs. These package policies are ideally suited to shops, hotels and offices, and can also be available for some of the smaller manufacturing and warehouse businesses, although there may be maximum limits on premiums and values.

14.6.3 Other services

A number of insurers are adding extra services to their Commercial Insurance Contracts and these services are another way of increasing the benefits of arranging insurance (eg the provision of helplines to assist on legal matters or to arrange for emergency repair to buildings). In addition a number of insurers provide booklets which can assist you in improving fire and security precautions at the business premises and risk management for vehicles.

Many insurers provide an advisory service relating to employee safety issues and legislation, product safety assessment and environmental studies.

15

PARTNERSHIP LAW

KEITH HATCHICK, SOLICITOR, PARTNER, MARSHALL HATCHICK

Despite the fact that the principal legislation in this area of law dates back to 1890 (the Partnership Act) this form of business relationship continues to be the most important one after that of the private limited company. It is particularly popular for professional services like solicitors, surveyors, architects and accountants and smaller concerns where the rigours of maintaining a company and complying with the legislation are inappropriate.

Aspects of the law of partnership are covered in this chapter as follows:

(1) What is a partnership?
(2) Limited partnership
(3) Is there an agreement?
(4) The salaried partner
(5) Partnership and third parties
(6) Liability of partners
(7) Partnership agreement
(8) Dissolution and winding-up of a partnership.
(9) EEIGs

15.1 WHAT IS A PARTNERSHIP?

Section 1(1) of the Partnership Act 1890 ('the 1890 Act') defines partnership as being the relationship which subsists between persons carrying on a business in common with a view to profit. All forms of company are expressly excluded under s 1(2).

It should be emphasised that partnership is a 'relationship' and does not have a separate legal status (unlike a company). It is the partners themselves who are and remain responsible for the partnership's activities and it is they personally who will if the circumstances require sue or be sued. In other words, whereas a limited company provides the shareholders with limited liability (up to the amount unpaid on their share capital) a partnership gives no such protection to a third party.

This distinction can sometimes be over emphasised since frequently directors/shareholders of small companies will need to have given personal guarantees before banks will contemplate offering such companies loans etc. The giving of such guarantees in effect counteracts the very point of limited liability since if a company fails it may have the same effect as if the partnership failed.

There are at least three different kinds of partnership envisaged by the 1890 Act (s 32) ie one formed:

(1) for a fixed term which when completed results in its dissolution;
(2) for a particular or defined purpose or undertaking, eg a particular sales promotion – as and when completed the partnership is dissolved;
(3) for an indefinite period eg most forms of professional partnership give each partner an ability to terminate on giving the others a period of notice (see 15.8).

15.2 LIMITED PARTNERSHIP

This vehicle has become increasingly important in the context of offshore planning arrangements. The attractions are various and include:

(i) limited liability to certain of the partners;
(ii) it is a registered entity which obtains a Certificate of Registration and a registration number from the Registrar of Companies;
(iii) in the UK it is not automatically subject to UK tax (unlike a UK company): if the management and control is situated overseas, the partnership is deemed to be UK non-resident for tax purposes;
(iv) there are fewer compliance and disclosure requirements than for a company if one of the general partners is an individual.

A limited company must have at least one 'general partner' who remains liable for all the partnership's debts and obligations. This partner may be a company. The remaining partners can be limited partners who are liable to contribute a fixed sum of capital to the partnership and their liability is limited to this extent. There is no statutory minimum capital contribution.

Where there is a limited partnership the partnership agreement must be signed by all (general and limited) partners and notification must be given to the Registrar of Companies (it is not though necessary for the agreement to be filed).

The Limited Partnership Act 1907 is the principal governing legislation. This requires notification to Companies House of its existence and failure to notify converts the limited partnership into a normal partnership in which all partners are completely liable for partnership debts. (The notification form which is required to be completed and sent to the Registrar is called an LP5 and when there are changes these must be notified on an LP6.)

A limited partnership must be formed with a view to making a profit – the holding of investments is not in itself sufficient.

The Department of Trade and Industry has recently published proposals for a professional limited liability partnership with a separate legal personality and limited liability for 'the members'. Under the proposed new scheme members would effectively be agents of a firm and not of each other, and individual members would not be liable for each other's acts. There are a few major safeguards proposed which include the public filing of audited accounts, the availability of a fund on liquidation and minimum standards of conduct through membership of regulated professional bodies.

15.3 IS THERE AN AGREEMENT?

In almost all partnerships there needs to be a partnership deed, ie a contract between the partners setting out the contractual relationship between them. In the past there have been instances where the courts have taken the view that a contract exists even if there is no formal documentation – so long as it can be shown that there was a contractual intention and some form of relationship based upon that intention.

For the purposes of this chapter it is assumed that the partners wish to enter into a written agreement setting out their relationship. Partners are free to agree upon restrictions between themselves, but this cannot effect the rights of a third party unless they have been made a party to the agreement (under the well-defined contractual rules relating to privity of contract).

The partnership deed is a private document between the partners and does not need to appear on a public register (unlike memorandum and articles of association for a private company which require to be registered at Companies House – there is no such public body to which partnerships need report). A further advantage is that financial information relating to the partnership, eg accounts, partners' drawings and general emoluments etc, remain private and not subject to public inspection. A partner is not an employee since partnership being a relationship between partners, no partner is capable of employing himself. A partnership very commonly employs other people and all the partners have authority to make contracts in the course of a partnership business (eg employing people).

15.4 THE SALARIED PARTNER

The salaried partner is an employee of the partnership who is held out to the outside world as being a partner. He (or she) is normally entitled to a fixed remuneration which is not dependent upon profits. A common example of salaried partners is within professional firms where having served apprenticeship it is felt by the equity partners to be appropriate to give an individual the status and prestige of being a partner without the need to consider capital contributions etc. Such a partner's name appears on the notepaper with the other partners and he is able to bind the firm in the same way as any other partner.

It is a question of sometimes great importance whether a person is a partner. The courts have interpreted each case on its own particular circumstances. Irrespective of whether a person is a salaried partner, he is being held out as a partner and as such both he and his fellow partners are jointly and severally liable for his or their actions.

A salaried partner (as a result of his less senior status) is frequently given in the partnership agreement (and if not so given such a partner should insist upon) an indemnity from his fellow partners to compensate him in the event that he suffers liability in his capacity as a partner.

15.5 PARTNERSHIP AND THIRD PARTIES

Since a partnership does not have any separate status under English law it is important to consider in what circumstances a partner is capable of binding his fellow partners and the relationship generally with outsiders.

The basic rule is that a partner is both a principal and an agent for his fellow partners, eg a partner can bind his fellow partners to any contract he signs if acting within his authority. In this way he is binding himself since he is a partner and a principal to that contract, and he is also binding his fellow partners since they are bound under the laws of agency by that contract.

Under s 5 of the 1890 Act it is stated that each partner acts as an agent for the firm. Where a partner does any act in the usual course of business of the kind carried on by the firm he binds the firm and his partners unless that partner has no authority to act for the firm in a particular matter *and the person with whom he is dealing either knows that he has no authority or does not know or believe him to be a partner*.

It is a question of construction and circumstance whether a partnership may be bound under the agency rules. Three factors should be considered:

Nature of the business

An example would be that it is unlikely that a firm of architects could advise upon financial investments whereas a banking partnership may so do. The Court of Appeal considered this question in *United Bank of Kuwait v Hammond* [1983] 3 All ER 418. A solicitor gave false undertakings to the bank concerning money held by the firm on behalf of a client. On the strength of this undertaking the bank advanced money to that client. The court took the view that the solicitor had acted within his ostensible authority in making the allegation since in normal circumstances it would be quite reasonable to expect such funds would fall within the firm's client account as part of normal day-to-day business. The bank was not required to check further since it was reasonable for the partner to be held out by a firm as having such authority.

Carrying on business in the normal way

In one case (*Higgins v Beauchamp* [1914] 3 KB 1192) it was felt that carrying on a cinema business was not in effect a trading business (ie one for purchasing and selling of goods) and therefore a partner could not bind his fellow partner to a debt incurred by him. The carrying on of business in a particular trade or profession can and does over a period of time change and in determining decisions of this nature courts have been flexible.

Knowledge and belief

If a partner has no authority to bind the firm and an outsider dealing with that partner realises it, the partnership cannot be bound by that partner's acts. If a third party does not have knowledge of the partner's lack of authority he can normally rely upon the partner's position as a partner in binding his firm. However, this would not be the case if the outsider did not know or believe that the person he was dealing with was a partner.

15.6 LIABILITY OF PARTNERS

15.6.1 To third parties

Each partner is and remains jointly and severally liable to outsiders for any act or omission committed by any of the partners or their employees in carrying on business. This means that an outsider has a choice of suing all or any of the partners for the full amount of such loss in accordance with normal principles of law. This is irrespective that a person so sued may be a salaried, or indeed a sleeping, partner.

15.6.2 Inter se

Under s 9 of the 1890 Act each partner is liable jointly with other partners for debts and obligations of the firm incurred while he is a partner.

Under s 17 of the 1890 Act a person who becomes a partner does not become liable to creditors of the firm for anything done before he became a partner. Likewise a retiring partner remains liable for debts and obligations incurred before retirement. This rule can be varied if a person either allows himself to be represented as being a partner or represents himself as being one (s 14).

15.7 PARTNERSHIP AGREEMENT

The relationship between partners in a firm is normally set out in writing in a partnership deed. The 1890 Act also contains a number of implied terms. A partnership agreement typically includes details of the following matters:

15.7.1 Good faith

Like company directors it is clear that partners owe a fiduciary duty to each other. The 1890 Act sets out three such duties in ss 28–30, namely:

Honesty and full disclosure

Partners are bound to 'render true accounts and full information of all things affecting the partnership to any partner or his personal representative'. In one case involving a woollen business, a sleeping partner's share was bought for a gross undervalue since only certain assets had been disclosed. It was held that the other partner had been in breach of his fiduciary duty and should be entitled to a proper value (*Law v Law* [1905] 1 Ch 140). In another case involving property development, unbeknown to one of the partners an offer of purchase was turned down by the other. Eventually the property concerned was sold at a lower value. The court took the view that although the partner conducting the sale had used good faith in rejecting the first offer he should have discussed the matter with the other partner and sought additional advice before rejecting it.

No unauthorised personal profit

A partner shall not make a private gain, even if innocent, and should account to his other partners for any profit made. Section 29 states that 'every partner must account to the firm for the benefit derived by him without the consent of the other partners from any transaction concerning the partnership or from any use by him of a partnership property, name or business connection'. This definition is very wide and has been broadly applied by the courts. For example in one case a discount was offered to a partner which would not have been obtainable by the partnership as a whole. Since the partner made a private profit he should have disclosed this profit and have accounted for it to the practice.

No conflict of duty and interest

This is spelt out in s 30 of the Act 1890 which states that 'if a partner, without the consent of the other partners, carries on any business of the same nature as and competing with that of the firm, he must account for and pay over to the firm all profits made by him in that business'.

15.7.2 Management and control

Under s 24(5) of the 1890 Act each partner may take part in the management of the partnership business. This is a corollary of partners having unlimited liability. Note that the limited partner loses his rights to limited liability if he interferes in the business of a partnership. This question of management is also enshrined in s 24(6) which sets out the basic tenet that partners are self-managers in that 'no partner shall be entitled to remuneration for acting in the partnership business'. In larger partnerships it is normal to find at least one partner spending a substantial amount of time in administration and other non-profit-making work and the partnership agreement frequently includes special provisions for such a partner to ensure that his drawings and participation in any profit are not thereby affected. Section 24(6) does not prevent a partnership from making its own arrangements in this respect.

15.7.3 Meetings, reaching decisions etc

There is no rule on how decisions should be reached. There may be a voting system whereby certain partners qualify for a greater number of votes than others. More usually each partner is given one vote with basic decisions being decided upon by simple majority, but with complicated or controversial matters requiring specified majorities (eg 75 per cent or in the case of taking in/expelling a partner, 100 per cent of the votes (other than the partner being so expelled)). The 1890 Act does not codify this (but see 15.7.6 below – s 24(7)) and it is left up to each partnership to agree this as a matter of contractual negotiation. If a partner feels that he is being unfairly treated by the remaining partners he has very limited remedies. If there has been a breach of contract he may be able to sue. It may also be that he can apply for a receiver to be appointed or possibly for a dissolution on just and equitable grounds. There is however no specific statutory protection. It is for this reason that partnership agreements often contain a settlement of disputes mechanism.

15.7.4 Settlement of disputes

It is common for partnership agreements to require disputes to be referred to arbitration. A popular alternative is for the agreement to contain provision for the appointment of an independent third party to act as an expert whose decision shall be binding on all parties (if the parties cannot agree on the appointment of such an independent expert, he would normally be appointed by a third party, eg President for the time being of the Law Society of England and Wales).

15.7.5 Financial provisions

These are probably the most important details from a day-to-day practical view. Under s 24(1) of the 1890 Act it is stated that unless there is contrary agreement all partners are entitled to share equally in the capital and profits of a business and should contribute equally toward the losses (of capital or otherwise) sustained by the firm. Frequently the partnership agreement contains contrary provisions to this to take account of differing roles and participation from each partner. In considering the finances of a partnership it is important to understand the distinction between:

(1) the partnership capital; and
(2) undrawn profits.

Partnership capital means fixed capital which typically is invested in the partnership on its founding or upon new partners being appointed. Upon dissolution or a retirement this is often returned to the partners or the relevant retiring partner with or without the payment of interest. If a partnership is dissolved the amount of surplus over and above the capital is normally deemed to be profit and as such is distributed to the partners in accordance with the profit-sharing rules. In many cases the relevant proportions for a refund of capital are different to those for the division of profits. Each partnership agreement needs to be carefully drawn to ensure that the distinction is clearly provided for. (Section 24 of the Act states other provisions which are frequently incorporated into the partnership agreement, eg under s 24(4) a partner is only entitled to interest on capital when profits have been ascertained. In s 24(3) anything paid over and above capital requirements is entitled to interest at the rate of 5 per cent per annum.)

Of greater importance is the requirement that if one partner is sued for a partnership debt under s 24(2), he is entitled to an indemnity from his fellow partners.

15.7.6 Change of partners

This normally occurs through death, retirement, expulsion or appointment of a new partner. Under s 24(8) unless stated to the contrary (in the partnership agreement), decisions should be taken by majority vote, but where it is proposed to introduce a new partner, s 24(7) requires the consent of all existing partners. Courts have in the past been called upon to interpret a number of provisions regarding nomination and partnership appointments which do not fall within this ambit. The circumstances of each particular case have been considered and the court's ruling has been based on its merits. In one case where a partner had left his partnership to his widow it was deemed that this constituted an assignment of a partner's share and did not entitle the widow to be a partner. Where a partner was entitled to introduce a qualified person as a new partner, subject to the other partners' consent not to be unreasonably withheld, the court ruled that since consent had not been forthcoming the qualified person did not have the right to become a partner (*Re Franklin and Swathling Arbitration* [1929] 1 Ch 238).

In the context of expulsion s 25 states that 'no majority of partners can expel any partner unless a power to do so has been conferred by express agreement between the partners'. In *Walters v Bingham* [1988] 1 FTLR 260 the court was called upon to consider a dissolution provision in the partnership agreement and ruled that there were three questions that should be considered:

(1) Was the expulsion within the ambit of a dissolution provision?
(2) Had the partners exercising the right of expulsion done so in good faith in accordance with the normal partnership duties?
(3) Had the rules of natural justice been complied with, ie had the partner concerned been given details of the precise cause of complaint against him and been given every opportunity to defend himself?

The implication to be drawn is that if all three conditions have been satisfied a court would uphold any such expulsion. Other cases of expulsion which have come before the courts include a refusal to uphold an expulsion clause where the majority were seeking to obtain the partnership share at a discount (*Blisset v Daniel* (1853) 10 Hare 493); the unlawful expulsion of a partner in circumstances where no details of the particular act complained of were given (living with common law wife) (*Barnes v Youngs* [1898] 1 Ch 414); expulsion held to be lawful where a partner was convicted of travelling on a train without a fare and thereby defrauding the railway company and bringing the partnership into disrepute being a breach of his duties as a partner *(Carmichael v Evans* [1904] 1 Ch 486).

The partnership agreement in many instances includes provisions requiring retirement once a partner reaches a specified age or when certain other conditions occur (eg he becomes bankrupt or subject to the Mental Health Acts).

It is common in a partnership agreement for there to be provisions setting out what is required for the introduction of a new partner (the 1890 Act, as mentioned above, requires the consent of all partners and this applies if the partnership agreement does not make another provision). An assignment of partnership does not create a new partner; it merely assigns an existing partner's rights to partnership assets and/or profits to a third party. It may take the form of, for example, a mortgage or an arrangement made upon the divorce of one partner in favour of his former spouse.

In the case of a voluntary assignment the assignee (the person in whom the assignment is in favour) has no right to interfere in the management or administration of the partnership or the assets or acquire the delivery or inspection of any accounts or books. The only interest an assignee would have relates to a share of profits for which the assigning partner may otherwise have been entitled if there had been no assignment. If however the partnership goes into dissolution the assignee has the right to '(i) receive the assignee partner's share and (ii) to receive accounting details verifying the amount of that share from the date of dissolution'.

15.8 DISSOLUTION AND WINDING-UP OF A PARTNERSHIP

This can occur in two circumstances:

(1) where a partnership splits up – in this case a winding-up of the business would be required;
(2) where surviving or continuing partners take over the whole firm – here there needs to be a valuation of the former partner's share of the business.

Dissolution may or may not arise from insolvency.

Frequently partnership agreements spell out the procedure for dissolution. There are at least three common situations which are usually provided for:

(1) Ability to expel a partner – a number of circumstances are expressly included which enable the partners to expel one of their colleagues from the partnership in certain specified situations, eg if the partner concerned is grossly negligent, brings the practice into disrepute or, in a professional practice, becomes barred from continuing to practice in that position. If a partner is charged with an indictable offence, this also enables the others to expel him.
(2) A partner wishes to retire – the agreement usually incorporates a mechanism whereby a partner can hand in his notice. The notice period is often at least six months or a year and expires on a specified date.
(3) Upon death – since the partner's involvement automatically ceases a procedure is usually inserted for the winding-up of his previous involvement.

Even if nothing is specified in the agreement a partner can apply to court for dissolution under s 35 of the 1890 Act. This gives the court the discretion to dissolve a partnership for the following reasons:

(1) Insanity – if a partner becomes a patient under the Mental Health Act 1983.
(2) Where there is permanent incapacity.
(3) If there is prejudicial conduct – this requires proof with regard to the nature of the business that a partner has conducted himself in a manner 'calculated to prejudicially affect the carrying on of the business'.
(4) Where there have been continual breaches of the agreement – the section refers to 'wilfully or persistently committing a breach . . . or otherwise so conducts himself in matters relating to partnership business that it is not practicable for the other partners to carry on the business in partnership with him'.
(5) If a business is being carried on at a loss – there must be some proof in this circumstance that making a profit is not possible.
(6) If just and equitable – this depends on the particular circum-stances presented to court, eg refusal to hold partner meetings, unresolvable dispute (ie where trust and mutual confidence have irretrievably broken down).

15.8.1 Appointment of receiver

In a dissolution it is possible for a receiver to be appointed at the court's discretion. Unlike company law the receiver appointed is responsible to act in the best interests of all the partners. Courts do not usually authorise the appointment of a receiver where there is only a partial dissolution. (There would therefore need to be a winding-up of the complete partnership as opposed to the buying out of the retiring partner.)

The partnership agreement usually specifies what should occur on dissolution. There is likely to be a valuation of each partner's share (where there is a winding-up) or the respective outgoing partners' shares (where there is a partial dissolution). The valuation needs to take into account such sums which may be owing to creditors etc. It also needs to apply a method for the valuation of goodwill (see 15.8.3 below).

The 1890 Act contains a number of basic provisions for dealing with dissolution:

Section 39

This requires all debts and liabilities of the firm to be paid before the distribution of any surplus (after deducting anything due by the partners to the firm) and gives the right of any partner to apply to court to wind up the business and affairs of the firm.

Section 37

On a dissolution or partial dissolution of a partnership any partner may make a public notice of the dissolution and has a right to require other partners to concur with this action. (It is important to remember that a retiring/former partner is liable for debts incurred after departure unless he complies with a notice provision under s 36 and avoids being represented as a partner (s 14) (see 15.6.2 above)). Normally it is prudent for such a partner to inform the firm's existing clients of his departure and put a notice to that effect in the *London* (or *Edinburgh*) *Gazette*. A further prudent precaution would be for him to ensure that all headed notepaper has been properly altered and any stocks of old paper destroyed.

15.8.2 Assets valuation on dissolution

It is usual for the partnership agreement to contain criteria for the valuation of business assets of the partnership on dissolution, requiring the use of the firm's accountant (or an independent one).

15.8.3 Goodwill

This has been defined as being the difference between the value of a business as a going concern and the value of its assets. Like any other business a partnership over a period of time attracts goodwill which can and often does form part of partnership assets. In certain isolated cases it is illegal to sell goodwill, eg s 54 of the National Health Service Act 1977 which forbids the sale of an NHS practice's goodwill. The sale of goodwill is important in assessing how much a new partner may need to pay on joining a partnership and how much the continuing partners may need to pay on the retirement of a partner. The valuation of goodwill is normally conducted by a firm of accountants and the procedure and criteria to be adopted are time consuming and complicated. It is for this reason that professional partnerships are often disposed to value goodwill at nil. This not only prevents argument as to the valuation, but also reduces the amount of time spent in settling outstanding affairs.

15.8.4 Sharing profits after dissolution

Section 42(1) of the 1890 Act states that on partial dissolution the surviving/continuing partners should in the absence of any agreement to the contrary share profits made since dissolution which are attributable to the partners' share of partnership assets. Alternatively such partner or his estate has a right to interest at the rate of 5 per cent per annum on the amount of his share of partnership assets. A partnership agreement may give continuing partners the right to buy out the former partners in accordance with laid down procedures and valuation provisions, but this would need to be expressly incorporated into the provisions of the agreement.

15.8.5 Insolvency

Assuming the partners are personally solvent, s 44 of the 1890 Act sets out the order of priority for repayment of partnership debts and requires the partners if necessary to contribute in the same proportions that they are entitled to share profits.

The order in which funds should be applied is:

(1) payment of debts and liabilities of the firm to persons, not partners;
(2) payment of each partner rateably of sums due to him from the firm for drawings (not capital);
(3) payment of each partner rateably of amounts due in repayment of capital; and
(4) division of any residue among the partners in the proportion in which the profits are divisible.

Where one or more of the partners are insolvent it is more complicated. It is outside the scope of this chapter to consider this matter in any detail, but there are a number of options open to creditors, eg wind up the partnership, wind up the partnership and bring petitions against insolvent partners (and ultimately bankruptcy), bring an action against the individual partners without winding up the firm or bring proceedings against one or more partners without involving others or the firm itself.

15.9 EEIGS

In order to harmonise the laws of member states and each UK Companies Act, the United Kingdom has acceded to the community in seeking to achieve this aim by incorporating various EEC directives into UK legislation. Some areas however have been otherwise treated. For example in 1985, EC Council Regulation 2137/85 was promulgated providing for the European economic interest grouping (more commonly referred to as EEIGs). This was loosely modelled on a French example. Its aim is to enable existing businesses in different member states to form an autonomous body for the provision of common services ancillary to the main activities of its members. All profits made belong to the members of EEIG and they are all jointly and severally liable for any liability.

EEIGs are formed by a written contract between the members. This needs to be registered in the member state in which the official address is situated.

The United Kingdom has added to the Regulation in the form of the European Economic Interest Grouping Regulations 1989 under which Companies House is responsible as the registering body. There is provision set out in the Companies Act 1985 and the Insolvency Act 1986 which are applicable.

There are not many examples of EEIGs, but in England there have been a number of firms of solicitors who have used EEIGs as a means of association with lawyers elsewhere in the community.

16

HOW AN UNINCORPORATED BUSINESS IS TAXED ON ITS PROFITS

This chapter discusses the tax treatment of a 'sole trader' (ie an individual carrying on business on his own account) and partnerships. These are 'unincorporated' businesses, as opposed to companies which are 'incorporated' businesses. The proprietors of unincorporated businesses are self-employed and taxed under Schedule D.

The following matters are covered:

Self-employed individuals

(1) Current year basis
(2) Transitional provisions
(3) Capital allowance basis periods

Partnerships

(4) Special rules governing assessment of firm's profits
(5) How transitional provisions apply to partnerships
(6) Treatment of other income
(7) Qualifying loans
(8) Anti-avoidance rules

Miscellaneous

(9) Relief for trading losses
(10) Post-cessation receipts and expenses

Introduction of self-assessment and how it affects self-employed individuals

(11) Outline of new regime
(12) Penalties and interest charges
(13) Achieving finality
(14) How the system operates for 1996–97.

Annual payments, NIC etc

(15) Miscellaneous practical aspects.

SELF-EMPLOYED INDIVIDUALS

16.1 CURRENT YEAR BASIS

In broad terms, the CY basis of assessment normally means that a trader is assessed on the profits for his accounts year which ends in the tax year concerned (there are special rules for the opening years). Thus, if an individual makes up accounts to 31 August, the CY basis of assessment normally means that his tax assessment for 1998–99 will be determined by his profits for the year ended 31 August 1998.

16.1.1 Opening years

The CY basis has special rules to cope with a business during the first two tax years since there may not be an accounting year which ends in either of those tax years, or the accounting period which ends in the second tax year may be shorter or longer than 12 months. In broad terms, assessments are generally determined as follows:

- first tax year – 'actual' or 'fiscal year' basis;
- second tax year – profits of the first 12 months;
- third tax year – current year basis.

16.1.2 Example of opening years rules

A starts in business on 6 October 1996. His accounts for the year to 5 October 1997 show profits of £48,000. Profits for the year ending 5 October 1998 are £72,000. *A* will be assessed as follows:

		£
1996–97	'actual' basis ($^6/_{12}$ × £48,000)	24,000
1997–98	First 12 months profits	48,000
1998–99	Current year basis	72,000

16.1.3 No accounts for the first 12 months

The way in which the opening years rules work is more complicated where the trader does not prepare accounts for a period of 12 months ending in the second tax year. It might be that an individual starts business on 1 March 1997 and makes up his first accounts for a 16-month period ending on 30 June 1996. The assessments in such a case will be:

1996–97	$^1/_{16}$	×	profits for period
1997–98	$^{12}/_{16}$	×	profits for period
1998–99	$^{12}/_{16}$	×	profits for period

Basis of assessment under opening years rules

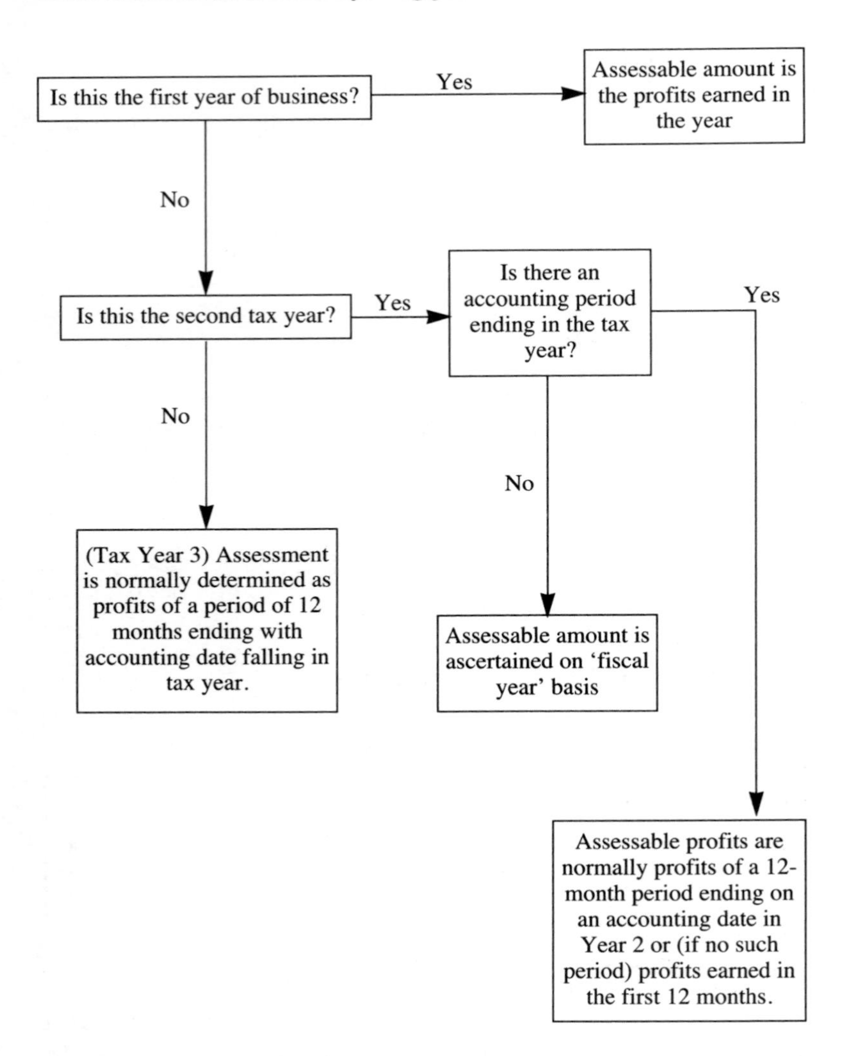

Similarly, if *X* makes up her first accounts for a six-month period ending on 30 April 1997 and then has accounts for the year to 30 April 1998, the assessments will be:

1996–97	5/6	×	profits for six months ended on 30 April 1997
1997–98	1/6	×	profits for six months ended on 30 April 1997, plus
	11/12	×	profits for year ended 30 April 1998
1998–99	profits of year ended 30 April 1998.		

16.1.4 Overlap relief

Because of the way that a new business is assessed during the first two tax years, some profits may be taxed more than once. In the last example, 11/12 of the profits for the year ended 30 April 1998 are assessed twice, once in arriving at assessable profits for 1997–98, and again in arriving at the assessment for 1998–99. To compensate for this, and to ensure that over the life of the business tax is paid only on the actual amount of profits, overlap relief is given when the business is discontinued or, for partners, when they leave the firm. In some circumstances, overlap relief may also be available if the firm's accounting date is changed (see 16.1.6).

16.1.5 Example of overlap relief

If the profits for the year ended 30 April 1996 were £36,000, 11/12 would be £33,000. This amount is carried forward and is deducted from *A*'s profits for the final year of trading. Thus, if *A* retires on 5 October 1998, and his final year's profits are £60,000, the assessment for 1998–99 will be as follows:

	£
Current year basis	60,000
Less overlap relief	33,000
Taxable profits	27,000

If the overlap relief exceeds the taxable profits for the final year, the balance may be treated as an allowable loss and either set against the individual's other income for that year or the preceding year, or carried back against Schedule D Case I profits of the last three years (see 16.9.10)

16.1.6 Effect of a change in accounting date

Where a firm changes its accounting date to one which falls earlier in the tax year, an adjustment is required to ensure that 12 months' profits are taxed as income of the year in which the change takes place.

16.1.7 Example of how a change is dealt with

B is in business. She draws up accounts to 30 June until 1997, when she changes to a 30 April accounting date. This means that her accounts which fall in 1997–98 are for a period of only 10 months.

The CY basis requires profits to be ascertained for a 12-month period which ends with the new accounting date. Suppose that the relevant figures were:

Year ended 30 June 1996	profits of £120,000
Period of 10 months ended 30 April 1997	profits of £140,000

B would be assessed for 1997–98 on £160,000 ie $\frac{2}{12}$ × profits for the year ended 30 June 1996 plus profits for the 10 months ended 30 April 1997. Once again, some profits will be taxed more than once (the period of two months ending on 30 June 1986) and therefore *B* would be entitled to increased overlap relief in due course on $\frac{2}{12}$ of the profits for the year ended 30 June 1996. The benefit of the overlap relief is enjoyed as and when the firm's accounting date is changed to a date which falls later in the tax year or *B* ceases business.

16.1.8 Moving accounting date to later in tax year

A different approach is required where a firm extends its accounts to a date which falls later in the tax year. Normally, the assessable profits are those for the entire period which ends in the tax year.

16.1.9 Example of tax treatment of such a charge

C makes up accounts to 31 December. In 1998, he extends his accounting period by three months so that the firm has a 15-month accounting period from 1 January 1997 to 31 March 1998. The whole of the profits for this period is assessed for 1997–98, but *C* can use some or all of his overlap relief. If *C* has a potential entitlement to four months' overlap relief of £20,000, and the profits for the 15 months ended 31 March 1998 are £150,000, *C* would have Schedule D Case I income for 1997–98 of:

	£
Profits for period ended 31 March 1998	150,000
Less $\frac{3 \text{ months}}{4 \text{ months}}$ × overlap relief brought forward	15,000
	135,000

16.1.10 Retirement

Where an individual retires and ceases to carry on a business, he is taxed under the CY basis on his profits for a notional period which starts immediately after the basis period for the previous tax year and ends on the date that he ceases.

16.1.11 Example of how taxable income is ascertained for final year of assessment

D makes up accounts to 30 April. Her profits for the year ended 30 April 1998 are £80,000. She ceases business on 30 November 1998 and her profits for the final six months amount to £50,000.

D's assessable income for 1998–99 is her share of profits for the period 1 May 1997 to 30 November 1988, ie £80,000 plus £50,000.

16.1.12 Accounting periods must not exceed 18 months

There is a maximum length of 18 months to an accounting period. Accounts which cover a longer period are rejected as unacceptable for tax purposes under the CY basis.

16.2 TRANSITIONAL PROVISIONS

The new rules mean that unincorporated business proprietors who are currently on the PY basis will be taxed under the CY basis for 1997–98 and future years. Thus, a sole trader who makes up accounts to 30 April 1997 will be assessed for 1997–98 as if those profits were earned wholly in that tax year. There are special provisions for 1996–97 as otherwise there would be a gap which would not be taken into account at all.

16.2.1 How 1996–97 is assessed

This depends on whether the business is assessed for 1995–96 on the PY basis. If it is presently on the PY basis, so that the 1995–96 assessment is based on profits for a period ending in the tax year 1994–95, the 1996–97 assessment is based on the average of profits for a period (called the 'transitional year basis period'). This period starts on the day following the end of the basis period for 1995–96 and ends on the day to which accounts are made up during 1996–97. Thus, if accounts are made up to 30 June, the basis period for 1995–96 is normally the year ended

30 June 1994 and the transitional basis period is the two-year period starting on 1 July 1994 and ending on 30 June 1996.

Where the transitional year basis period is 24 months, the 1996–97 assessment is arrived at by taking $^{12}/_{24}$ of the profits for that two-year period.

In some cases, the 1996–97 assessment may be based on 12 months' proportion of a period which exceeds two years. Thus, if the business has a 30 April year end at present, but it switches to 31 March during 1997, the 1996–97 assessment is based on $^{12}/_{35}$ × the profits for the 35-month period 1 May 1994 to 31 March 1997.

16.2.2 Transitional relief

The FA 1994 provides for 'transitional relief' which works like overlap relief (see 16.1.4 above). The relief represents the amount which is assessed under the CY basis for 1997–98 but which was earned before 6 April 1997. Thus, if a business makes up accounts to 5 May, the 1997–98 assessment is based on profits for the year ended 5 May 1997 and the transitional relief is $^{11}/_{12}$ of those profits.

Transitional relief is enjoyed when the accounting date is moved to be a point which is later in the tax year, or the individual ceases to carry on business (see 16.1.8–16.1.11).

16.2.3 Anti-avoidance provisions
(FA 1995, Sched 22)

The anti-avoidance rules can have no application unless 1995–96 is assessed on the PY basis and the assessment for 1996–97 is made on the profits of the transitional year basis period. This means that they may be ignored if the assessment for 1996–97 is made on the fiscal year basis because the business was started in 1993–94 and the trader elects for 1994–95 and 1995–96 to be assessed on the actual basis.

In the normal situation where a trader is presently assessed under the PY basis, the firm's 1996–97 assessment is based on a proportion of the profits for a two-year period ending in 1996–97. Thus, a business with a 30 April year end is assessed for 1996–97 on 50 per cent of its profits for the two years ending on 30 April 1996. The trader may be tempted to shift profits out of the basis period for 1995–96 (where they will be taxable in full) into the transitional year basis period (ie the extended basis period for 1996–97), where effectively only part will be taxed. There could also be a benefit if profits are shifted into the period which ends in the tax year 1997–98.

16.2.4 Conditions which must be satisfied for anti-avoidance provisions to apply

The Revenue can apply the anti-avoidance provisions where certain 'triggers' are satisfied and the taxpayer is unable to satisfy the Revenue on one of the statutory let-outs contained in the legislation. The events, etc which may trigger the application of these provisions are:

(1) a change or modification to an accounting policy;
(2) a change in business practice, for example timing of the supply or purchase of goods or services;
(3) arrangements with connected persons; and
(4) self-cancelling transactions.

Even if one of the triggers is identified, the Revenue can apply the anti-avoidance provisions only if the profits shifted into the transitional period exceed a *de minimis* figure. The rules applying the *de minimis* thresholds are as follows.

In the case of artificial shifting of business profits by an individual:

(1) the aggregate amount of profit artificially shifted into either the transitional period or the transitional overlap period is less than £10,000;
(2) the average annual turnover for either the transitional period or the transitional overlap period is less than £50,000.

16.2.5 Example 1

Suppose that a taxpayer whose business in the two years to 30 June 1996 had a turnover of £65,000 and £30,000 respectively. The average annual turnover in the transitional period is £47,500 ((35,000 + 60,000) × 50%). This is below the *de minimis* limit of £50,000 and the anti-avoidance provisions do not apply.

If turnover for the two years to 30 June 1996 had been £65,000 and £40,000 respectively then the 'appropriate percentage' of the turnover is £52,500 ((65,000 + 40,000) × 50%). This is above the *de minimis* limit of £50,000. However, the anti-avoidance provisions only apply if the taxpayer has artificially shifted profit and none of the other *de minimis* limits or let-outs apply.

16.2.6 Example 2

Suppose that a taxpayer has carried out a single artificial transaction which shifted profit of £8,000 into the transitional period. This is below the *de minimis* limit of £10,000 and the anti-avoidance provisions do not apply.

However, if the taxpayer also carried out a second artificial transaction, which shifted further profit of £4,500 into the transitional period, the aggregate amount of shifted profit would be £12,500. This is above the *de minimis* limit of £10,000. However, the anti-avoidance provisions only apply if none of the other *de minimis* limits or let-outs apply.

In the case of the artificial shifting of business profits by a partnership:

(1) the aggregate amount of profit artificially shifted into either the transitional period or the transitional overlap period is less than £7,500 × the maximum number of partners during the relevant period up to a maximum of 20. For each subsequent partner the limit is increased by £1,000 per partner.
(2) the average annual turnover for either the transitional period or the transitional overlap period is less than £50,000 × the maximum number of partners during the relevant period.

16.2.7 Example 3

If a partnership comprised the same three members throughout the transitional period the *de minimis* limit for that partnership is £7,500 × 3 = £22,500.

If, however, the maximum number of partners in the transitional period was 50 then the *de minimis* limit for that partnership is (£7,500 × 20) + (£1,000 × 30) = £180,000.

In the case of 'partnership refinancing', the aggregate amount of interest paid by a partner is less than £15,000 in the case of transitional period avoidance and less than £7,500 in the case of transitional overlap avoidance.

16.2.8 Example 4

Suppose that a taxpayer is a partner in a partnership which draws its accounts up to 31 December each year. On 1 July 1994 the partner takes out a loan of £300,000 which is advanced to the partnership to enable it to pay off a business loan. The partner pays interest and claims relief under TA 1988, s 353, as follows:

1994–95	£21,000
1995–96	£28,000
1996–97	£28,000

Interest falling in the transitional period is:

£ 7,000	(paid 1 January 1995–5 April 1995)
£28,000	(paid 6 April 1995–5 April 1996)
£21,000	(paid 6 April 1996–31 December 1996)
£56,000	

The aggregate interest paid in the transitional period (1 January 1995 to 31 December 1996) is above the *de minimis* of £15,000 and if none of the other let-outs apply a restriction of interest relief is appropriate.

In the case of the artificial shifting of interest or other income, the aggregate amount of interest or other income artificially shifted into either the transitional period or the transitional overlap period is less than £7,500.

Furthermore, there are two other statutory let-outs, although the onus of proof lies with the taxpayer. These statutory let-outs are where the taxpayer can show either:

(1) obtaining a tax advantage was not the main benefit sought by the change in accounting policy, business practice, etc; or
(2) the change was entered into solely for bona fide commercial reasons.

16.2.9 How anti-avoidance provisions operate for 1996–97

Where profits are shifted out of 1995–96 into the basis period for 1996–97, the anti-avoidance provisions mean that an additional amount will be brought into the computation equal to 25 per cent of the shifted profits. There will, however, be no adjustment to the 1995–96 assessment.

16.2.10 Example of counteraction under anti-avoidance legislation

J makes up accounts to 30 April. By changing his normal commercial practice, he diverts profits of £120,000 out of the year ended 30 April 1994 (assessable for 1995/96) into the two-year period ending on 30 April 1996. If he gets away with this, *J* has avoided tax on profits of £60,000 as only 50 per cent of the £120,000 would have been taxed for 1996–97.

If the Revenue applies the anti-avoidance rules, *J*'s taxable profits for 1996–97 are increased by 125 per cent of £120,000, ie £150,000. Of this 50 per cent is taxed so *J* pays tax on an additional 12.5 per cent. This penalty aspect is deliberate.

Where *J* is subject to 40 per cent tax, the effective rate of tax becomes 45 per cent. Against this, *J* normally enjoys a 12-month deferral, because he pays tax for 1996–97 on the profits diverted out of the 1995–96 basis period which would otherwise have been taxed for that year.

16.2.11 How anti-avoidance provisions apply to 1997–98

Where an individual presently assessed on the PY basis ceases business after 5 April 1997, he is normally entitled to transitional relief for that part of his profits which were assessed for 1997–98 but earned before 6 April 1997. Thus, if *P* makes up accounts to 31 May, his 1997–98 assessment under the CY basis is based on his profits for the year ending 31 May 1997. Approximately $^{10}/_{12}$ of these profits are earned prior to 6 April 1997 and *P* eventually receives a deduction for this proportion of his 1997–98 assessable profits. Thus, if *P*'s profits for the year ending 31 May 1997 are £72,000, his transitional relief is approximately £60,000.

The deduction for transitional relief is given for the year in which the individual ceases to carry on the relevant business or, if earlier, a year in which the accounting date is moved to later in the fiscal year. Again, there is a temptation to shift profits into the year which ends in 1997–98. In some situations this might be achieved by recognising profits earlier than normal, so that a profit which normally falls in the 1998–99 basis year falls instead into 1997–98. Accordingly, there are provisions designed to counteract this type of manipulation of profits. Where the Revenue succeeds in arguing that these provisions apply, the individual's transitional relief is reduced by an amount equal to 125 per cent of the transitional relief otherwise due on the profit which has been shifted into the basis period for 1997–98.

16.2.12 Example of restriction on transitional relief

P shifts additional profits of £30,000 into his accounting year which ends on 31 May 1997 (normal profit of £72,000). If it were not for the anti-avoidance provisions, *P*'s transitional relief would be computed as:

$$^{10}/_{12} \times £102{,}000 = £85{,}000$$

However, the Revenue can reduce this by 125 per cent of the extra transitional relief due to the profits shifted into the period and so the transitional relief becomes:

	£
	85,000
Less (£30,000 × $^{10}/_{12}$ × 1.25)	31,250
	53,750

16.2.13 Effect of cessation in 1997–98 or 1998–99

If a trader ceases business in 1997–98, the Revenue may adjust the last two years which were assessed before the introduction of the CY basis. This may mean that 1996–97 assessment will be adjusted. The assessment is no longer based on the average of the profits for the transitional year basis period (see 16.2.1) but is assessed on the fiscal year basis. The Revenue could do this only if it also adjusts the 1995–96 assessment to actual.

A similar consequence may apply if there is a cessation in 1998–99, although only 1996–97 is then affected.

16.3 CAPITAL ALLOWANCE BASIS PERIODS

16.3.1 Business on CY basis

Capital allowances are computed on exactly the same basis as profits. Normally this means that allowances are computed for the accounts year which ends in the tax year. However, there are special rules which apply for overlapping accounts.

Where there is a gap between accounting periods, the additions and disposals during the intervening period are added to the accounting period which ended before the gap.

16.3.2 Example – Overlapping periods

If a new business is commenced on 1 January 1996 and accounts are drawn up to 31 December 1996, there is an overlap of the period 1 January to 5 April 1996, as this will form part of the profits assessed for 1995–96 and 1996–97 (see 16.1.1).

If the trader spends £10,000 on plant and machinery during the first three-month period, and £40,000 during the period 6 April to 31 December 1996, capital allowances are given as follows:

		£
1995–96	$^3/_{12}$ × 25 per cent x £10,000	625
1996–97	Pool brought forward	9,375
	Additions	40,000
		49,375
Allowances ($^9/_{12}$ × 25 per cent)		9,258

PARTNERSHIPS

16.4 SPECIAL RULES GOVERNING ASSESSMENT OF FIRM'S PROFITS

Where a partnership was assessed under the old preceding year basis, the Revenue issued one assessment based on the trading profits of the whole firm. Individual partners were treated as having a share of the firm's assessable profit which reflects the way they share profits for the tax year and not the way they shared profits for the basis year. Each partner was jointly and severally liable for the whole firm's tax liability. The last year in which these rules could apply was 1996–97.

16.4.1 Transition to CY basis

The same rules apply to a partnership as to a sole trader (see 16.2 above). Thus the firm is generally assessed for 1995–96 under the PY basis, 1996–97 is based on a proportion of the profits for a period of between 24 and 35 months, and in 1997–98 the partners will be assessed separately, under the CY basis.

16.4.2 Cessations

Under the PY basis, there is a notional cessation every time a partner joins or leaves a firm, with the 'old firm' deemed to have ceased and a new firm deemed to start trading. However, it is possible to override this rule by all the partners joining in a continuation election. This election must be signed by all parties concerned, ie all the individuals previously in the partnership and any incoming partners. Moreover, the election must be submitted to the Revenue within two years of the event which would otherwise give rise to a cessation. The assessments are then made on the firm as if there had been no notional cessation. If all the partners retire from the partnership in either 1997–98 or 1998–99, there will be a cessation and the Revenue may be able to amend the assessments for 1995–96 and 1996–97 (see 16.2.13).

16.4.3 Assessment under CY basis

Where the CY basis of assessment applies, the Revenue issues separate assessments on each of the individual partners. This is the full extent of their liability; they are not jointly liable for tax payable by their partners (except, possibly, where the partner is not resident in the United Kingdom).

Because partners are assessed separately under the CY basis, the continuation election cannot apply. Each partner is dealt with as a 'separate taxable unit' and the opening and closing years rules apply separately to him.

16.4.4 Example – CY opening year rules for new partners

A and *B* have been in partnership since 1 October 1994. They share profits equally and their profits for the first two years are as follows:

	£
Year ended 30 September 1995	90,000
Year ended 30 September 1996	120,000

C joins the firm on 1 October 1996 and thereafter each partner receives one-third of the firm's profits which for the year ended 30 September 1997 amount to £150,000. *B* retires on 5 April 1997 and *A* takes over his share of profits.

The three partners are assessed as follows:

				£
1994–95	A	6/12 × 50 per cent of £90,000		22,500
	B	6/12 × 50 per cent of £90,000		22,500
1995–96	A	First 12 months profits		45,000
	B	First 12 months profits		45,000
1996–97	A	CY basis		60,000
	B	Final year (profits for period 1 October 1995 to 5 April 1997)	£85,000	
		Less overlap relief	£22,500	62,500
	C	6/12 × 1/3 of £150,000		25,000
1997–98	A	CY basis		75,000
	C	First 12 months profits		50,000

16.5 HOW TRANSITIONAL PROVISIONS APPLY TO PARTNERSHIPS

Where a firm is assessed under the PY basis, and there are either no changes in partners before 6 April 1997, or a continuation election is made (16.4.2), the firm is assessed as follows:

1995–96 PY basis

1996–97 The assessment is based on an average of the profits for the transitional year basis period, ie the period of between 24 and 35 months starting immediately after the basis

	period for 1995–96 and running on to the dates which accounts are made up in 1996–97.
1997–98	The partners are assessed on a CY basis, with the partners assessed individually.

The Revenue has the right to amend the partnership assessment if it ceases to trade in 1997–98 or 1998–99 (see under sole traders at 16.2.13). However, in this instance, the Revenue can do this only if the partnership comes to an end completely (ie all partners retire from the firm during 1997–98 or 1998–99 for the Revenue to claim that a cessation has taken place). Note that the Revenue has confirmed that even if all partners in the firm at 5 April 1997 retire during one of the two following years, it still cannot apply the cessation provisions if an individual has been admitted to partnership after 5 April 1997 and the firm continues beyond 5 April 1999.

Where a partner is assessed under the CY basis for 1997–98, part of his assessment normally relates to a period prior to 6 April 1997. The profits attributable to him for that period may be claimed as transitional relief, either when he retires from the firm or when the firm changes its accounting date to a point which falls later in the tax year.

16.6 TREATMENT OF OTHER INCOME

Where a partnership receives investment income (eg untaxed interest, miscellaneous income taxed under Schedule D Case VI or dividends), the normal tax treatment was that the income should be assessed on the individual partners. The principle that partners are jointly and severally liable for tax has never applied to investment income received by the firm.

Under the new CY basis, the way the income assessable on the partners is arrived at has changed. Instead of the income being ascertained by reference to the fiscal year, the income is assessable on the CY basis. Thus, if a firm makes up accounts to 30 April, the partners are assessed for 1997–98 on their share of partnership investment income received during the firm's year ended 30 April 1997. This rule applies even where the income actually arose prior to 5 April 1997.

16.7 QUALIFYING LOANS

Tax relief may be obtained on loan interest where the money is to provide capital into a partnership. Relief is available where the loan is applied:

(1) in purchasing a share in a partnership; or
(2) in contributing capital or advancing money to a partnership where the money advanced is used wholly for the purposes of its trade, profession or vocation; or
(3) in paying off another loan the interest on which would have been eligible for tax relief.

In addition, the borrower must be a member of the partnership throughout the period (and not just as a limited partner). He must not have recovered any capital from the partnership since raising the qualifying loan.

16.7.1 Recovery of capital
(TA 1988, s 363)

If, at any time after the application of the loan's proceeds, the partner recovers any amount of capital from the partnership, he is deemed to have used the withdrawal to repay the qualifying loan on which he is claiming interest relief. This is so whether or not he actually uses the proceeds in this manner. It is therefore advisable to segregate the partners' capital and current accounts in the partnership's books so that any withdrawal can be clearly identified.

16.7.2 Replacement capital

Where a partner has a surplus balance on either his current or capital account with a partnership and he does not already have a qualifying loan, he may withdraw the balance due to him (with the consent of his partners), use the money to pay off non-qualifying borrowings and then borrow further funds to introduce capital into the partnership with tax relief.

16.7.3 Example – Replacement capital

B is a partner in the XYZ partnership. He has a credit balance of £100,000 in his capital account. Outside the partnership, he has bought a yacht for his private use with the help of a £40,000 loan from his bank. In addition, he has a building society mortgage of £50,000.

B would withdraw £60,000 from his capital account in the partnership and use the money to make the following repayments:

	£
Yacht bank loan	40,000
Building society	20,000
	60,000

This leaves *B* with outstanding borrowings of only £30,000 with his building society on which MIRAS relief (see *Allied Dunbar Tax Handbook*) should be available. Once these transactions have been completed, *B* would borrow £60,000 as a loan (not overdraft) and use the funds to re-introduce capital into the partnership with full tax relief on the interest payable.

Professional advice should be sought in advance on such transactions.

16.7.4 Other partnership loans

Another situation where it may be appropriate to re-structure existing borrowings is where there is a partnership loan outstanding in the business's books. The loan might typically have been used to purchase goodwill or the property from which the practice/business is carried on. In this situation, each partner is required to borrow privately his share of the partnership loan and introduce the moneys raised into the partnership. The partner can then claim tax relief on the interest paid personally as a charge on his income on an actual basis.

The partnership collects the moneys raised by each partner's loan and uses the funds to redeem the partnership loan. As a result, each partner's share of profits becomes correspondingly higher because no interest is now payable by the partnership. However, overall, the situation is the same because the higher profits must be used to finance the private borrowing.

This kind of rearrangement needs considerable attention to detail and timing to be successful and tax effective, and professional advice should always be sought. This is particularly necessary during the transition to the CY basis as there is anti-avoidance legislation to be considered (see 16.8 below).

16.7.5 Purchase of plant and machinery
(TA 1988, s 359)

Where a partner incurs capital expenditure in the purchase of plant and machinery which is used for the purposes of the partnership's business, and which is eligible for capital allowances, he can claim tax relief on interest paid if the plant or machinery is financed by a loan. The relief is only available in the tax year in which the loan is taken out and the following three tax years. Similar relief is also available for employees who are required to purchase plant or machinery for use in carrying out their duties.

16.7.6 Property occupied rent-free by partnership

Where a partner takes out a loan to purchase property occupied by the partnership for business purposes and the interest is paid by the partnership, no deduction is technically due to the partnership as the interest is not its liability but the partner's. However, SP4/85, issued in February 1985, regards the interest paid as rent so that it then becomes allowable as a deduction. In the partner's hands, the rent is taxable but the interest paid is normally allowed as a deduction in arriving at his Schedule A income.

16.8 ANTI-AVOIDANCE RULES

Specific anti-avoidance provisions may apply where partners raise qualifying loans to refinance the firm. This legislation applies only in cases where the assessment for 1996–97 is based on a proportion of the profits for the transitional year basis period (see 16.5).

Where the Revenue can show that the refinancing was carried out to avoid tax, there is normally a restriction on the relief due to partners for interest paid by them during the 1996–97 basis period. Taking the normal case where the 1996–97 assessment is based on 50 per cent of the profits for a two-year period ended in 1996–97, partners are entitled to relief for only 50 per cent of the interest payments made by them during that period. Interest paid in 1996–97 after the end of the extended basis period is eligible for relief in full.

16.8.1 Example of operation of anti-avoidance legislation

A and *B* make up accounts to 30 June. Their 1996–97 assessment is based on 50 per cent of their profits for the two years ending 30 June 1996. On 1 July 1994 the partners refinanced their firm's borrowings by taking out personal loans. It is accepted that there was no commercial reason for doing this and that the anti-avoidance provisions should apply. The interest paid on the loans taken by the partners is as follows:

	£
Period 1 July 1994 to 5 April 1995	10,000
1995–96	12,000
Period 6 April 1996 to 30 June 1996	3,000
Period 1 July 1996 to 5 April 1997	9,000

If the anti-avoidance provisions apply relief for interest paid by the partners is restricted to the following amounts:

1994–95	5,000
1995–96	6,000
1996–97	10,500

As will be appreciated, each of the partners receives extra relief for 1996–97 compared with what would have happened if they had not taken out personal borrowings. The interest paid in the period 1 July 1996 to 5 April 1997 qualifies for relief in full. There will, however, be an adjustment to transitional relief (see 16.2.2) to reflect interest paid during this period. The partners' transitional relief is reduced by £9,000 each, ie by the amount of interest paid in 1996–97 but after the end of the transitional year basis period.

The effect of all this is that the partners concerned have lower taxable income for 1996–97 but have more taxable profits for the year in which they eventually retire, or in which their firm changes its accounting period, because of the reduction in transitional relief. Where partners are not particularly close to retirement and there is no real likelihood of the firm changing its year end, partners may be able to live with this. In any event, there is no punitive adjustment and so the partners will be no worse off than if they had not tried to take advantage of the transitional provisions in this way.

MISCELLANEOUS

16.9 RELIEF FOR TRADING LOSSES

Relief may be available for a loss incurred by an individual in a trade or profession. The provisions which govern the relief for trading losses are complex and there are several ways in which losses may be utilised.

16.9.1 Carry forward relief against subsequent assessments

(TA 1988, s 385)

A loss incurred by a sole trader or a partner's share of his firm's trading loss may be carried forward and deducted in assessments for later years for the same trade or profession. Where losses are carried forward in this way, they must be used against the assessable profits for the first subsequent year in which profits arise. The loss carried forward in this way may also be relieved against certain income which is connected with the trade even though it is assessed under a different schedule (for example, interest earned on temporary investment of trade receipts and dividends from trade investments). There is no limit on the number of years for which a loss may be carried forward provided that the same trade is carried on.

16.9.2 Relief against general income

(TA 1988, s 380)

Where a sole trader or partner incurs a loss and the trade was carried on with a view to profit, the loss may be relieved against his general income for the year of assessment in which it was incurred (ie his total income for the year). Prior to 1997–98 relief could also be claimed against the individual's general income for the following tax year provided that the relevant trade, profession or vocation is carried on by the individual at some time during that year. This rule changes with effect from 1997–98 so that losses are set against an individual's general income for the preceding year.

16.9.3 Relief by aggregation

Where the profits of different accounting periods are time apportioned (eg on commencement of a business) a loss may be relieved by aggregation with a profit. This situation could arise if a first period of trading is less than 12 months.

16.9.4 Example – Loss relief by aggregation

A started business on 1 January 1998. He made a loss of £9,000 for the period ended 30 September 1998 and a profit of £24,000 for the year ended 30 September 1999. Relief by aggregation would produce the following result:

Profits assessable 1997–98	NIL
Profits assessable 1998–99	NIL
Profits assessable 1999–2000	NIL

The reason for this is that the first 12 months' trading is deemed to produce a net loss computed as follows:

	£
Loss for period 1 Jan to 30 Sept 1998	(9,000)
3/12 of profit for year ended 30 Sept 1999	6,000
	(3,000)

Relief for the same loss may be obtained more than once when the loss is used by aggregation. This can produce effective relief which exceeds the loss actually incurred.

If a loss is set against other income, it cannot also be relieved by aggregation. Thus, if *A* had claimed relief for the loss that he had incurred in 1997–98, only that part of the loss for the period ended 30 September 1998 which relates to the period 6 April to 30 September 1998 could be taken into account in arriving at the profits of the first 12 months' trading.

16.9.5 Example – Loss set against other income

B commenced trading on 1 August 1997. He has a loss during the nine months ended 30 April 1998 of £36,000. He has profits for the year ended 30 April 1999 of £60,000. If the 1997–98 loss is used by its being set against *B*'s other income, the position is as follows:

1997–98		NIL
1998–99	Profits of first 12 months:	
	nine months ended 30 April 1998	NIL
	3/12 × profits for year ended 30 April 1999	15,000
		15,000
1999–2000	Profits of first 12 months	15,000

Contrast this with the situation where relief for the loss is obtained by aggregation.

1997–98		NIL
1998–99	Profits of first 12 months	NIL
1999–2000	Profits of first 12 months	NIL

16.9.6 Capital allowances and loss claims
(TA 1988, s 383)

The general principle is that where capital allowances (see 2.2) cannot be given because there are insufficient profits, the allowances must be carried forward and given in subsequent years. However, it is possible for an individual to claim for capital allowances to be treated as a deduction in arriving at the loss for the year of assessment. Capital allowances which are claimed in this way may either increase a loss or convert a profit into a loss.

The capital allowances to be taken into account are those of the normal basis period which relates to the tax year. This still applies even though the loss itself may be arrived at on the strict basis by apportioning the results of the accounting periods which overlap the relevant tax year.

16.9.7 Example – Capital allowances and loss claims

A commences trading on 6 October. His results are as follows:

	£
Year ended 5 October 1998 – profit	4,000
Year ended 5 October 1999 – profit	12,000
Year ended 5 October 2000 – profit	50,000

Assume that capital allowances are as follows:

1997–98	30,000
1998–99	38,000

If *A* claims that his capital allowances for 1997–98 should be deducted and the resultant loss relieved under s 380, the position is as follows:

		£
1997–98	6/12 × profits for year ended 5 October 1998	2,000
	Capital allowances for 1997–98	(30,000)
	Loss after deducting capital allowances	(28,000)
1998–99	6/12 × profits for year ended 5 October 1998	2,000
	6/12 × profits for year ended 5 October 1999	6,000
		8,000
	Capital allowances for 1998–99	(38,000)
	Loss after deducting capital allowances	(30,000)

The £28,000 loss for 1997–98 may be set against *A*'s other income for 1997–98 or 1998–99. The £30,000 loss for 1998–99 is available to be set against *A*'s other income for 1998–99 or 1999–2000

16.9.8 Losses in early years of a trade

(TA 1988, s 381)

In certain circumstances, relief may be claimed against an individual's general income for the three years of assessment preceding the year in which the loss is incurred. Relief is given against income for the earliest year first. The loss may be computed in the normal way, or it may be augmented by capital allowances as described in 16.9.6. There are certain preconditions for a loss to be claimed:

(1) The loss must arise during the first four tax years in which the business is carried on.
(2) Where a trade is acquired from a spouse, the four years run from the date that the spouse first commenced trading (unless the trade is taken over on the spouse's death).
(3) The trade must be carried on on a commercial basis *and with a reasonable expectation of profits*.

A claim for a loss to be relieved in this way must be made within two years of the end of the tax year in which the loss was incurred. Where a loss is carried back in this way, any repayment normally produces an entitlement to repayment supplement.

16.9.9 Relief for trading losses against capital gains

(FA 1991, s 72)

An individual who has incurred a trading loss may have the loss set against any capital gains which arise in the same year, provided he makes a claim within two years. It is not possible to claim relief for trading losses in this way without first having made a claim for relief under TA 1988, s 380 for the loss to be set against the individual's general income for the year.

It is also possible for a trading loss to be set against an individual's capital gains for the following year provided that a claim is first made under s 380(2) for the trading loss to be set against the individual's general income for that year. A precondition for a loss to be relieved in this way is that the individual has carried on the relevant trade at some time during the following tax year.

16.9.10 Terminal loss relief

(TA 1988, s 388)

Where a trade, profession or vocation is permanently discontinued, a loss incurred during the last 12 months can be deducted from the profits charged to tax in the three tax years before the final year. The relief can include a claim for the loss arising in the tax year in which the cessation takes place, and a proportion of the loss for the previous tax year.

Capital allowances for the final tax year may also be claimed, as can an appropriate proportion of the preceding year's capital allowances, representing the allowances due for the period beginning 12 months prior to the cessation.

The terminal loss may be carried back against profits from the same trade for the three tax years preceding the year of cessation. The relief is given against the latest year's profits first. If interest and dividends would have been included as trading profits (except that they were subject to deduction of tax at source), the terminal loss may be set against such income.

16.9.11 Computation of loss under PY basis

Normally, for a trader who has been carrying on business for a number of years, a trading loss incurred in an accounting year which ends in a year of assessment is treated as a loss for that year. Consequently, if a trader makes up accounts to 31 July 1994, and the accounts for that year show a loss, this is normally treated as a 1994–95 trading loss. However, this is largely a matter of practice and convention and strictly speaking the loss which qualifies for relief under s 380 is the loss incurred in a year of assessment (ie the results of two accounting periods should really be apportioned to arrive at the loss (if any) incurred in a tax year).

16.9.12 Example – Computation of loss

If *A* has a profit for the year ended 31 July 1993 of £12,000, a loss for the year ended 31 July 1994 of £48,000, and a loss to 31 July 1995 of £6,000, the strict position should be as follows:

		£
1993–94	3/12 × profits for year ended 31 July 1993	3,000
	9/12 × loss for year ended 31 July 1994	(36,000)
		(33,000)
1994–95	3/12 × loss for year ended 31 July 1994	(12,000)
	9/12 × loss for year ended 31 July 1995	(4,500)
		(16,500)

The Revenue insists on the loss being calculated on the strict basis in certain circumstances, ie:

(1) where the year of the loss is one of the first three years of assessment of a new business;
(2) where the year of assessment immediately follows a year for which a loss has been ascertained on the strict basis;
(3) where the year of loss is the fourth year that a new business has been carried on and the taxpayer has elected for his profits for years two and three to be assessed by reference to actual profits.
(4) in the tax year in which the business is permanently discontinued;
(5) in any other year of assessment if the individual so chooses.

16.9.13 Computation of loss under CY basis

The rules for computing losses under the CY basis are much simplified. They preserve most of the principles explained 16.9.1–16.9.10. The exceptions are as follows:

(1) Losses may only be relieved once. The new rules do not allow duplication of loss claims by aggregation, as is possible under the PY basis (see 16.9.4).
(2) Relief for losses can be claimed against other income of the year of loss and the preceding year. (Under the PY regime, this was the following year.) Thus a trader who makes a loss in the accounting year to 31 December 1998 will be able to claim relief against other income in 1998–99 and/or 1997–98.

(3) It is not necessary to have separate claims for surplus capital allowances to be converted into losses; under the CY rules, capital allowances are allowed as a deduction just like any other allowable business expense.
(4) The rules for claiming loss relief against future profits from the same trade are slightly modified under the CY basis so that it is not now necessary to make a claim each year when the relief is to be given. All that is required is a claim to establish the amount of the loss. Thereafter the loss is carried forward and offset every year until fully utilised, without the need for any claim.

16.9.14 Anti-avoidance provisions

Farming losses

(TA 1988, s 397)

Restrictions may apply to losses suffered by farmers. The legislation may prevent a farming loss being set against the individual's other income where he has suffered losses for each of the preceding five tax years. The only way of avoiding this restriction is for the individual to show that no reasonably competent farmer would have expected to have made a profit during the period in question.

Losses from limited partnerships

(TA 1988, s 117)

Limited partnerships were widely used in tax avoidance arrangements. The House of Lords decided in *Reed v Young* [1986] STC 285 that a limited partner could be entitled to loss relief for an amount which exceeded his actual liability under the Limited Partnership Act 1907. This led to specific legislation to limit the amount of loss relief to the capital which is 'at risk'. Any losses incurred beyond this amount have to be carried forward to be set against any future share of profits received by the limited partner from the firm.

The provisions of LPA 1907, s 117 of the 1907 Act apply to individuals who are limited partners or members of a joint venture arrangement under which their liability is limited to a contract, agreement, guarantee etc.

16.9.15 Schedule D Case V losses

(TA 1988, s 391)

Profits from a trade managed or controlled abroad are taxed under Schedule D Case V. Loss relief is calculated in the same way as for a loss incurred in a trade, profession or vocation taxed under Schedule D Case I or Case II.

Relief for such losses is given in the same way as for UK trading losses, except that where a loss is to be set against other income, a Case V loss can be deducted only from:

(a) profits from other foreign trades assessable under Schedule D Case V;
(b) foreign pensions and annuities where a 10 per cent deduction is available (see *Allied Dunbar Tax Handbook* 1997–98 at 5.16);
(c) foreign emoluments assessable under Schedule E (see *Allied Dunbar Tax Handbook* 1997–98 at 3.1.1 and 22.2).

16.10 POST-CESSATION RECEIPTS AND EXPENSES

(TA 1988, ss 103–104)

16.10.1 Post-cessation receipts

Where a person has been assessed on the cash basis (see 2.1.1) special rules apply if the trade or profession is discontinued. Subsequent receipts are normally taxed under Schedule D Case VI as income for the year in which they come in, although an election may be made for the post-cessation receipts to be treated as arising in the year of discontinuance.

Expenses may be deducted in so far as they were incurred wholly and exclusively for business and are not otherwise allowable. For example, a solicitor who had post-cessation receipts would be able to deduct premiums paid on a professional indemnity policy where the cover related to the period after the solicitor had ceased to carry on his profession.

A similar charge may arise where a change occurs in the treatment of a trader's profits so that the cash basis ceases to apply and his profits are assessed on the earnings basis. Amounts received from customers after the change which relate to invoices issued when the business was dealt with on the cash basis are treated as post-cessation receipts.

16.10.2 Post-cessation expenses

(TA 1988, s 109A)

Relief can be due for expenses incurred by a person after he has ceased carrying on a trade or profession. This relief can be due on any such expenditure incurred within seven years of the date of cessation. The following types of expenditure may qualify for relief:

(a) the costs of remedying defective work done, goods supplied, or services rendered while the trade or profession was continuing and damages paid by the taxpayer in respect of such defective work, goods or services whether awarded by a court or agreed during negotiations on a claim;

(b) insurance premiums paid to insure against the above costs;
(c) legal and other professional expenses incurred in connection with the above costs;
(d) debts owed to the business which have been taken into account in computing the profits or gains of the trade or profession before discontinuance but which have subsequently become bad;
(e) the costs of collecting debts which have been taken into account in computing the trade's profits before discontinuance.

The amount of this relief is reduced by any expense allowed as a deduction in the final accounting period which remains unpaid at the end of the year of assessment in which the relief is given. Expenditure which qualifies for the relief is set against income and capital gains of the year of assessment in which the expense is paid. Where there is insufficient income or capital gains to cover the expenditure, the unrelieved expenditure of that year cannot be carried forward under the new relief arrangements against future income or capital gains. However, the unrelieved expenditure is still available to be carried forward under the existing rules and set against subsequent post-cessation receipts from the trade or profession.

PRACTICAL ASPECTS AND INTRODUCTION OF SELF-ASSESSMENT AND HOW IT AFFECTS SELF-EMPLOYED INDIVIDUALS

16.11 OUTLINE OF NEW REGIME

16.11.1 Background

The 1997 changes amount to a fundamental change to the tax system. The Revenue no longer needs to initiate proceedings by issuing an assessment; liability for tax arises automatically.

Under the new regime, taxpayers are required to submit tax returns which incorporate a calculation of the tax to be paid (or in some cases, tax to be repaid) and payment of the amount due. In effect, instead of being required to deliver a return, the legislation requires taxpayers to make a self-assessment. This replaces the former system where a taxpayer was sent several different assessments on different sources of income and capital gains. Because of this, and because the Revenue no longer has to issue estimated assessments and amended assessments, there should be a significant reduction in paperwork.

The self-assessment form is capable of being processed by computerised scanning equipment, which further reduces the clerical work required at the Revenue's offices.

16.11.2 Liability to make self-assessments

Any person served with a notice by an Officer of the Board of Inland Revenue must file a return. Normally, the filing date is 31 January following the end of the tax year. However, if the officer is late in serving notice on an individual for him to make a self-assessment, the filing date may be extended. Basically, the officer must give the individual at least three months to make the self-assessment. Thus, if the notice requiring the delivery of a self-assessment is served after 31 October, it does not need to be delivered to the Revenue until three months later.

16.11.3 Alternative to self-assessment

Provided a return of income and chargeable gains is delivered to the Revenue not later than 30 September following the end of the tax year, the Revenue calculates the amount of tax payable and issues an assessment.

If the officer is late in issuing the notice to make a self-assessment, the 30 September deadline may be extended. The taxpayer is given at least two months in which to complete and deliver the return and so if the officer serves the notice after 31 July the deadline for filing the return is later than the normal 30 September deadline.

The Revenue has confirmed that if it receives a return by 30 September, but does not issue a notice of the tax payable by 31 December, the trigger date for interest and surcharge is 30 days after the issue of the statement of tax which is payable.

16.11.4 Inclusion of estimates

The Revenue has stated its intention that if a taxpayer includes an estimate in his return, the rest of the return becomes final within the normal timescale provided it is completed to the best of his knowledge and belief. The Revenue stated that the estimate should be corrected as soon as the missing information is reasonably available, in accordance with TMA 1970, s 97.

The need for estimates often arises in relation to CGT (eg valuations at 31 March 1982). It should be borne in mind that a valuation is not treated as an estimate, unless designated as such by the taxpayer. On the other hand, not all valuations are estimates, although they may be subject to dispute. The Revenue has agreed that it will not be able to reopen the position where no enquiry into a valuation is made within 12 months and the valuation falls within the range of bona fide valuations which could arise between valuers who were fully instructed on the facts.

16.11.5 Submission of supporting documents with self-assessment

The notice which the officer sends asking for the self-assessment may specify that certain accounts, statements and documents relating to information in the return should be filed at the same time. The Revenue will certainly continue to require business accounts for a sole trader or a partnership. Other documents which may be required include books, contracts, deeds, receipts etc.

The legislation specifies that records must be retained for a minimum period after the submission of the self-assessment, in case they are required by the officer. Personal records must be retained for 12 months after the filing date. Business records must normally be retained for a minimum period of five years after the filing date.

The FA 1994 also sets out the business records which should be retained for examination. The following need to be retained:

(a) records of all amounts received and expended in the course of the trade or profession, and the matters in respect of which the receipts and expenditure took place; and
(b) all supporting documents relating to such items.

This requirement is extremely wide and general in nature. However, the taxpayer is protected if he has preserved information in such a way that original documents can be reproduced. This means that a microfilming system is as acceptable as the retention of the original documents. Moreover, the Revenue has published guidance notes on what records should be retained. A penalty of up to £3,000 can be imposed for failure to keep records.

16.11.6 Amendments to self-assessment after it has been filed

A notice may be given to the Revenue amending the self-assessment. This notice may be given within 12 months of the filing date (ie 31 January or three months after the officer gives notice asking for the self-assessment, whichever is the later). The Revenue may also amend the self-assessment within nine months of receiving it to correct obvious errors of principle, arithmetical errors and the like (this is called 'repairing' a self-assessment).

16.11.7 Revenue enquiries and right to audit

The Revenue may start an enquiry into a self-assessment (or, where the taxpayer has filed an amendment, into the amended self-assessment). However, the officer must give written notice of his intention to make an enquiry. Furthermore, that notice must be served within a strict time limit of:

(a) 12 months after the date that the self-assessment was delivered; or
(b) where the self-assessment is delivered after the filing date, the quarter date following 12 months after delivery. For this purpose, the quarter dates are 31 January, 30 April, 31 July and 31 October. Thus, if a self-assessment which is due on 31 January is not in fact delivered until 31 March, the time limit for the Revenue starting an enquiry expires on 30 April of the following year.

Note also that the Revenue is not be allowed to institute more than one enquiry during the time limit. Once a return or an amendment has been subject to enquiry, no further notice may be given.

Where a notice of intention to enquire has been issued, the officer may issue a notice requiring the production of documents which are in the power or possession of the person on whom the notice has been served. These must be documents, etc which are reasonably required by the officer to determine to what extent, if at all, the self-assessment or amendment is incorrect. The notice may also require accounts or other particulars which he may reasonably require. The notice must give a time limit for the production of the documents, etc and the taxpayer must be allowed at least 30 days to produce the documents.

An appeal may be made to the Commissioners against such a notice. They can set the notice aside if they think that it is invalid. If they decide it is valid, the documents must be produced within 30 days of their decision. Continued failure to comply may then result in a penalty of up to £150 per day.

There is no specified time limit in which the officer must complete an enquiry but the Government has stated that a code of practice will be issued on the conduct of enquiries. One aspect to be covered in the code will be a general requirement for the Revenue to proceed with reasonable speed once it has launched an enquiry and not to drag the process out unnecessarily. The code of practice will also set other ground rules which will apply to Revenue offices when they conduct an enquiry.

Once the officer who is conducting the enquiry has completed his investigation, he must say so and state his conclusions as to the correct amount of tax which should be in the self-assessment.

16.11.8 Correction of self-assessments

There are provisions for the self-assessment to be amended by the taxpayer in accordance with the conclusions notified by the officer who has conducted the enquiry. However, if the taxpayer does not correct the self-assessment in accordance with the officer's conclusions, the officer issues a notice of amendment (in effect an assessment) against which an appeal may be made within 30 days. If the dispute cannot be settled by agreement, the Commissioners adjudicate.

16.11.9 Requirement to notify chargeability

From 1996–97 onwards an individual who is liable for unpaid tax but who has not been served with a notice requiring him to make a self-assessment must notify the Revenue within six months of the end of the tax year.

16.11.10 Payment of tax

An individual is required to pay two equal amounts on account of income tax on 31 January during the year of assessment and on 31 July following the end of the tax year. The amount of the tax payable in this way is normally equal to the total income tax assessed for the previous year. However, it is open to a taxpayer (or his advisor) to make a claim before 31 January (ie the normal filing date) for the payments on account to be reduced to 50 per cent of the tax believed to be payable for the year. The Revenue generally requires an explanation for why it is believed that the tax payable will be less than that for the previous year.

When the self-assessment is delivered on the following 31 January, any difference between the payments on account already made and the amount shown as payable for the year needs to be settled. At the same time, it is necessary to make a payment equal to the CGT liability for the year concerned.

16.11.11 Amended self-assessments

Tax is payable or repayable on the later of:

(a) 31 January following the end of the tax year; and

(b) 30 days from the date on which the amendment to the self-assessment was given.

In cases where the Revenue discovers that a source of income has not been assessed or has been inadequately assessed, the officer normally makes an assessment and the tax is payable 30 days after the assessment has been issued.

16.12 PENALTIES AND INTEREST CHARGES

16.12.1 Surcharges

Where tax is paid more than 28 days after it fell due, there may be a 5 per cent surcharge levied by the Revenue. This 28-day period applies both to the payments required on 31 January and 31 July and also to tax which is due 30 days after an assessment has been made. If the tax remains unpaid more than six months after the due date, there is a further 5 per cent surcharge.

16.12.2 Appeals against the surcharge

The Revenue may mitigate the whole or part of a surcharge where there is a reasonable excuse for the delay. In cases where there is a dispute with the Revenue over whether there is a reasonable excuse, the Commissioners can be asked to adjudicate. However, FA 1994 specifically states that inability to pay is not to be regarded as a reasonable excuse.

16.12.3 Interest

Interest is payable for periods up to the date on which payment is made and is in addition to the surcharges referred to above. This interest does not attract any tax relief.

16.12.4 Penalties

A penalty of £100 is due if the self-assessment is not delivered by the filing date. The Revenue may then appeal to the Commissioners for a continuing penalty of up to £60 per day. The starting date for this continuing penalty is the day on which the Commissioners direct that it should be imposed. It is avoided if the self-assessment is delivered before the Commissioners make their decision. However, even if no continuing daily penalty is imposed, there is a further £100 penalty if the self-assessment is delivered more than six months after the filing date.

Where the failure continues beyond 12 months the penalty, in addition to anything mentioned above, is a maximum of the tax due as shown in the return.

Penalty determinations may attract an interest charge, where the penalties are not paid promptly, as the determination is treated as if it were an assessment for the purposes of interest charged on late payment of tax.

16.12.5 Appeals

It is possible to appeal against the determination of a penalty by the inspector. However, the Commissioners may only set aside the £100 fixed penalties if there is a reasonable excuse for the taxpayer not having delivered the return throughout the period it was overdue. Where this condition is not satisfied, the Commissioners are required to confirm the penalties in full.

16.12.6 Partnerships

The basic rules are modified to take account of partnerships.

Partners' obligations to make returns

Individual partners are required to deliver self-assessments. However, the partnership is also required to make a return (not strictly speaking a self-assessment) if the Revenue serves a notice. The Revenue may serve the notice on any partner (the 'representative partner').

The notice asks for delivery of the return together with accounts and such other statements as the Revenue requires. The representative partner is required to make a return and all items relevant to the agreement of profits assessable under Schedule D Case II must be included in that return. It is not possible for individual partners to claim a deduction for expenses incurred by them unless they are shown in the partnership return. The notice requires the partnership return to include:

(a) the names, addresses and tax references of all persons who have been partners at any time during the period covered by the return; where partners have been in the firm for only part of the year, the precise period must be specified;
(b) full details of each partner's entitlement to profits (and losses) from each source of partnership income;

(c) particulars of the disposals of partnership assets as if the partnership itself (not the individual partners) were liable to tax on any chargeable gains and details of each partner's share of such capital gains;
(d) details of acquisitions of property by the partnership;
(e) the amount of annual charges borne by each partner (eg annuities paid to former partners or their dependants).

It is possible for the partnership to amend its return and for the Revenue to amend it after an enquiry.

Revenue investigations into partnership returns

The Revenue has the power to enquire into partnership returns on the same basis as they may enquire into returns made by individuals. That is to say, a notice must be issued within 12 months of the filing date or, if the return is delivered after the filing date, at the quarter date following 12 months after the delivery date.

A notice served on the partnership is deemed to include similar notices issued to the individual partners to the extent that they have actually delivered self-assessments.

Partnership returns

Each partner is liable to a £100 penalty if the partnership return is submitted late. This applies to any person who was a partner at any time during the return period. The continuing daily penalties and the six-month £100 penalty also apply to each partner.

Appeals against penalty notices imposed on partners

Where penalty determinations have been made so as to impose either the £100 penalty or the continuing daily penalty on two or more partners, appeals may be brought only by the representative partner. He then makes a composite appeal. Once again, the £100 penalty must stand unless the Commissioners are satisfied that there was a reasonable excuse which applied throughout the period of default.

16.12.7 Incorrect returns

If an incorrect self-assessment is delivered and it is wrong because of negligent or fraudulent conduct, the maximum penalty remains 100 per cent of the tax understated in the self-assessment.

A partnership return, which includes accounts and statements, and which is incorrect due to negligent or fraudulent conduct, can give rise to a penalty on each partner, with the maximum amount of the penalty being the tax under assessed on him. It is possible for this penalty to apply even though the individual partner has not completed the partnership return and has not himself been guilty of negligent or fraudulent conduct. Basically, the conduct of the representative partner who made the partnership return is all that matters.

16.13 ACHIEVING FINALITY

It has generally been accepted that any new regime should afford taxpayers the same degree of certainty that liabilities have been finalised as exists at present where an assessment is appealed against and there is a determination under TMA 1970, s 54.

The legislation specifically provides that the Revenue may make assessments to correct a loss of tax which has been discovered. However, the Act makes it plain that this may not be done where there has been an error or mistake in a return as to the basis of computing a liability but the basis which was adopted accorded with the practice generally applying at the time.

The Act makes it clear that no discovery assessment may be made where all the facts were clearly made known to the Revenue and the matter was concluded without an enquiry, or with the officer being satisfied after carrying out an enquiry. The distinction that the Revenue presently draws between points which are fundamental to the determination of the liability does not feature in the legislation for the new regime and, therefore, to that extent a taxpayer may have greater certainty once an enquiry has been concluded or the time limit for the officer to initiate an enquiry has passed.

16.14 HOW THE SYSTEM OPERATES IN 1996–97

16.14.1 Transitional rules for individuals

A special rule applies for determining the payments on account for 1996–97, which fell due on 31 January and 31 July 1997. These are computed as half the total liability for the previous year less any income tax deducted at source, but for this purpose the liability for 1995–96 is exclusive of higher rate tax on taxed investment income. The tax on this income for 1996–97 effectively falls due for payment on 31 January 1998 when the individual files his self-assessment for 1996–97 and settles the difference between his actual liability for the year and the amounts paid on account.

On the other hand, the 1996–97 payments on account are not divided equally. The tax relating to an individual's Schedule A and Schedule D Case III income is payable as part of the amount payable on 31 January 1997.

16.14.2 Partnerships

In determining the final payment due for 1996–97 on 31 January 1998, credit is given for any tax paid by a partnership on a partner's behalf for 1996–97 as if this was tax deducted at source. This provision helps to smooth over the transition from the partnership paying the tax for 1996–97 (on 1 January and 1 July 1997) to the partner paying his or her own tax by self-assessment for 1996–97, on 31 January 1998.

ANNUAL PAYMENTS, NIC ETC

16.15 MISCELLANEOUS PRACTICAL ASPECTS

16.15.1 Class 4 NICs

A deduction is available for half of the trader's liability for national insurance Class 4 contributions in arriving at the trader's income tax liability. Contributions are payable by self-employed individuals according to the level of their profits as determined for income tax purposes. For 1997–98 Class 4 NICs are levied at the rate of 6 per cent of Schedule D profits between £7,010 and £24,180.

Where an individual pays interest on a business loan or has suffered trading losses, such amounts may be set against his earnings for the purposes of assessing liability for Class 4 NICs. This situation applies even where the losses have been relieved for income tax purposes by way of offset against his other income.

16.15.2 Annual payments

(TA 1988, ss 349 and 387)

These include any annuity or other annual payment (other than interest) and any royalty or other sum paid in respect of the use of a patent. These payments are normally made out of profits or gains chargeable to income tax.

16.15.3 Example of treatment of annual payments

A has taxable profits of £20,000. He pays an annuity to a former partner of £10,000 (gross).

A cannot deduct the annuity, but he can take basic rate relief at source. This means that he pays only £7,700 to the person entitled to the annuity, ie £10,000 less 25 per cent tax. The tax withheld of £2,300 comes out of the tax that he would have paid in any event on his profits of £20,000. Furthermore, *A* may be able to secure higher rate relief on the £10,000 annuity. If, for example, his total income were £60,000 his liability for higher rate tax would be computed as follows:

	£
20 per cent and basic rate band	26,100
Gross amount of annuity	10,000
	36,100

Income subject to 40 per cent rate is:	
Taxable income	60,000
Less	36,100
	23,900

On the other hand where a person making an annual payment has an insufficient tax liability to cover the tax withheld, he must account for this separately to the Revenue. Thus if *A* had taxable income of only £8,000 (after allowances but before the annuity) his 1997–98 normal tax liability would be:

	£
Tax at 20 per cent on £4,100	820
Tax at 23 per cent on £3,900	897
	1,717

However, because he has deducted tax from an annuity of £10,000 he will instead be required to pay £2,300 to the Revenue, to cover the tax relief taken by him at source.

17

COMPANY LAW

KEITH HATCHICK, SOLICITOR, PARTNER, MARSHALL HATCHICK

This chapter gives an overview of a vast body of corporate law which affects business life, and covers the following topics:

(1) What is a company?
(2) Memorandum of association
(3) Re-registration
(4) After incorporation
(5) Directors
(6) Meetings
(7) Share capital
(8) Dividends
(9) Ultra vires
(10) Auditors
(11) Work permits
(12) Selection of administrative documents to be filed at Companies House.

17.1 WHAT IS A COMPANY?

The fundamental principle of a company is that it is a separate legal entity distinct from its members. Two important points should be noted:

(1) Property belongs to a company and not its members. Directors and shareholders can be prosecuted for theft in appropriate circumstances.
(2) A company's debts and liabilities in themselves cannot in general be enforced against that company's members.

17.1.1 Limited liability

Most companies are formed with limited liability. This means that shareholders are only obliged to pay the company such amounts that remain unpaid on any shares they hold. In the case of companies limited by guarantee (ie without a share capital – see 17.1.2 below) shareholders are only obliged to contribute the amount they have guaranteed to contribute to the company should it be wound up. Other typical characteristics of a company are:

(a) a company can be sued in its own name;
(b) a death or change in the membership does not affect its continued existence; a company continues indefinitely until wound up or dissolved;
(c) members hold shares which constitute property and can be transferred to others without affecting the company's existence;
(d) the company has power to give security for its borrowing through the creation of a floating charge over all or any part of its assets.

17.1.2 Types of company

The Companies Act (CA) 1985 provides for three types of companies:

(i) companies limited by guarantee;
(ii) unlimited companies; and
(iii) companies (either private or public) limited by shares.

Companies limited by guarantee

These are generally formed for non-trading purposes (eg charities, clubs, trade associations). Prior to the CA 1980 they could be formed with a share capital. This option was rarely used since it exposed members to liability with respect both to their guarantee in a winding-up and anything unpaid on their shares. Since the 1980 Act it has not been possible to form a company limited by guarantee with a share capital.

The memorandum of association must contain a provision stating that each member undertakes to contribute to the company's assets if it should be wound up either while he is a member or within one year thereafter. The liability is limited to a specified maximum (usually £1).

Companies limited by guarantee frequently dispense with the requirement that they should use the word 'limited' in their name. To obtain such an exemption permission must be sought from the Registrar of Companies. This is usually provided so long as

(a) the company's objects are for the promotion of commerce, art, science, education, religion and charity or any profession, and
(b) the articles or memorandum of association prohibit the payment of dividends to members, and
(c) profits, if any, are applied in promoting its objects, and

(d) on a winding-up any assets must be transferred to another similar body (ie not to its members).

Unlimited companies

These are not widely used since members, as the name implies, have no limitation on potential liability in the event that the company is wound up with debts that it is unable to pay. While the company is a going concern members can only be called upon to pay any sums that remain unpaid on their shares. Creditors of the company can, if debts owed to them remain unpaid, obtain a petition for winding up the company, but they cannot sue the members directly.

Private limited companies

The CA 1985 contains an unhelpful definition of a private company being 'one which is not a public company'. Effectively this means that a private company is one that is not allowed to offer shares to the public, eg by seeking admission on the Stock Exchange or by issuing an advertisement offering security to be issued by it. A private company is the most popular form for profit-making business entities.

Public companies

The CA 1985 contains a technical definition of a public company. The real differences between a public and a private company are:

(1) Its name must finish with the words 'public limited company' or 'plc' (for a Welsh company 'cwmni cyfyngedig cyhoeddus' or 'ccc'). A memorandum of association also needs to highlight the fact that it is a public company.
(2) There must be an authorised share capital of not less than £50,000 (this figure can be varied by the Secretary of State by statutory instrument) of which at least one-quarter and the whole of any premium has been paid up.

The advantage of a public company over a private one is that, subject to certain exceptions, a public company is entitled to issue advertisements offering securities to be issued to members of the public. The disadvantages are that public companies are subject to far more stringent controls than private ones. Public companies do not need to be and frequently are not listed on the Stock Exchange.

17.2 MEMORANDUM OF ASSOCIATION

Every company needs a memorandum of association; it acts as a company's charter and regulates the company's external affairs. Its purpose is to enable persons who invest in or deal with it to establish such facts as:

(a) its name;
(b) whether it is a private or public company;
(c) what its objects are;
(d) whether liability of its members is limited or unlimited;
(e) the location of its registered office (England, Wales or Scotland);
(f) if there is a share capital, and if so the amount and how it is divided (eg £1,000 divided into 1,000 ordinary shares of £1 each).

For a company limited by guarantee the memorandum must also state the maximum guaranteed liability of such members (see 17.1.2 above).

17.2.1 The name

The name chosen must end with the word Limited (or Ltd) or public limited company (or plc) unless a dispensation has been granted (see 17.1.2 above) or the Welsh equivalent (see 17.1.2 above) in the case of Welsh companies. It should not be the same as any other registered company or be offensive or commit a criminal offence. It should not be of a 'sensitive nature'. The Registrar keeps a list of such sensitive names and under what circumstances those names are granted. For example use of the words 'Group' or 'Holding' requires the company using the name to have at least two subsidiary companies. Use of words like 'Royal' are also restricted, normally to companies holding a royal charter.

Passing off

In forming a new company or changing the name of an existing company, attention should always be given to the name chosen since use of a similar name to an existing company may potentially give rise to a passing off action. This is where the use of a name is sufficiently similar to another as it may mislead members of the public. For example, if a company is called 'AG Honey Ltd' and a new company is formed called 'G A Huney Ltd' and both are in the same line of business (eg the extraction of honey), it may be that the first company would have an action for passing off due to its loss of goodwill. The normal action brought is one of damages, but more frequently the earlier company seeks to obtain an injunction to stop the newer company from continuing under that name. Guidelines were set down in *Warnink BV v Townend & Sons Ltd* [1979] AC 731. To establish a case there needs to be:

(a) a misrepresentation by a trader in the course of his business to a prospective customer or consumer;
(b) damage to goodwill of the existing business – it is sufficient if such damage is reasonably foreseeable as a consequence of any such misrepresentation;
(c) 'a common field of activity' – in one case a radio broadcaster failed to prevent a cereal producer from using the same name for his product (*McCulloch v May* [1947] 2 All ER 845).

17.2.2 Articles of association

The articles of association regulate a company's internal affairs, dealing with such matters as:

(a) issue and transfer of shares;
(b) alteration of share capital;
(c) holding of meetings and voting rights;
(d) directors' appointments and retirements;
(e) appointment of a secretary;
(f) declaration of dividend;
(g) accounts, auditing etc; and
(h) winding-up etc.

Both the memorandum and articles of association form a contract between the company and each member and between the members.

17.2.3 Formation requirements

The following documents should be sent to Companies House together with the relevant statutory fee (currently £20).

(1) A copy of the memorandum and articles of association. For a private company if no articles are filed Table A of the Companies (Tables A to F) Regulations 1985 automatically applies. For companies limited by guarantee the forms of memorandum and articles of association set out in Tables C and D of the same regulations must be used. These need to be signed by all members and witnessed.
(2) Form G10 – This needs to be completed by each director and the secretary. It also gives the address of the company's registered office.
(3) Form G12 – This must be completed by the solicitors engaged in the company formation (but can also be signed by a person named or a director or secretary in the Form G10). It confirms compliance with the companies legislation.

17.3 RE-REGISTRATION

At some stage during the currency of a company it may wish to convert into a company of a different form. Part II of CA 1985 anticipates that by considering four particular forms:

(a) a private company becoming a plc;
(b) a plc becoming a private company;
(c) a limited company becoming unlimited; and
(d) an unlimited company becoming limited.

17.3.1 Private company to plc

There must be the passing of a special resolution (or written resolution) that the company should be registered. The company must be able to show that it has an authorised share capital of at least £50,000 with not less than 25 per cent paid up. There are various other considerations set out in CA 1985, s 45 which may need to be considered.

A copy of the special or written resolution needs to be sent to the Registrar within 15 days of the date of the meeting (or in the case of a written resolution the date it was signed by the last member). A Form 43(3) should also be completed. This needs to be accompanied by:

(a) a printed copy of the up-to-date articles and memorandum;
(b) a statement signed by auditors that in their opinion the balance sheet shows net assets not less than the aggregate of called up share capital and undistributable reserve;
(c) a copy of the balance sheet with an unqualified auditors report. The report needs to state that if there is a qualification it is not material for purposes of determining whether (at the balance sheet date) the net assets exceeded the aggregate of its called-up share capital and distributable reserves.

A Form 53(3) should be completed and sent to the Registrar as outlined above. It contains a statutory declaration confirming that all required procedures have been complied with and the share capital requirements have been satisfied.

17.3.2 A plc to a private company
(CA 1985, ss 53–55)

A company must pass a special resolution changing the name from plc to Ltd and amend all references in the memorandum and articles accordingly.

A Form 53 needs to be completed and sent with the special resolution to the Registrar within 15 days. A shareholder is entitled to apply to court for an order of cancellation and the court will either cancel or confirm the resolution. In order for a shareholder to apply to court he or it must either

(a) hold not less than 5 per cent of the issued share capital (of any class of share);
(b) consist of not less than 5 per cent of members of a company; or
(c) consist of not less than 50 members.

Where there is a reduction of the plc's share capital which has the effect of bringing nominal value of the company's allotted shares below the authorised minimum, the company must cease to be a plc under CA 1985, s 138. A court may further order that a company shall be re-registered as a limited company and in this case it dispenses with the necessity for the company to pass a special resolution so re-registering. If a company cancels shares under CA 1985, s 146 and it results in its share capital being below the authorised minimum, the company is obliged to apply for re-registration as a limited company.

17.3.3 Unlimited companies

Under CA 1985, s 49 if a private limited company wishes to re-register as an unlimited company all members must approve that re-registration and its memorandum and articles must be altered to comply with the Act. A Form 49 must be completed and filed with the Registrar of Companies, attached to which must be a confirmation signed by each member and a statutory declaration by the director confirming that all members have agreed. On receipt of this documentation Companies House issues a revised certificate of incorporation.

If an unlimited company wishes to re-register as a private company it must pass a special resolution and complete a Form 51. If a limited company has already registered as an unlimited company it cannot again re-register as a limited company.

There are provisions in the Act enabling an unlimited company to register as a plc and a plc to register as a private unlimited company. These are very rarely used in practice, but the procedure is set out in ss 48–53.

17.3.4 Stamp duty

This is charged on any document transferring ownership of shares, debentures and other security. It is an *ad valorem* tax levied at the rate of 0.5 per cent. The minimum payable is 50p, but if for example shares are transferred for £120 stamp duty is £1 (ie it is rounded up to the nearest 50p).

Stamp duty is chargeable to the purchaser of shares. In certain cases there may be exemption from stamp duty (eg transactions involving shares in the same group of companies on a re-organisation), but this area of law is complicated and professional assistance should be sought.

Stamp duty reserved tax (SDRT) arises when there is no stampable document used (eg when a block of shares is sold on the Stock Exchange). In this case the SDRT amount paid would equal that which would arise from stamp duty.

The former Conservative Government had announced that stamp duty would be abolished with respect to shares after the Stock Exchange had introduced the TAURUS computer project. The Stock Exchange has since decided not to continue with this project, but the Government has not yet indicated how this may affect stamp duty.

17.4 AFTER INCORPORATION

When the formalities referred to above have been completed and a certificate of incorporation has been received (and also in the case of a public company a certificate confirming that the share capital requirements have been complied with) the company should hold its first board meeting. The normal business of this meeting includes the following:

(1) adoption of the company seal (an impression is normally made in the margin of the minutes);
(2) appointment of a chairman (if appropriate) and any additional directors and the approval of any service contracts;
(3) appointment of auditors;
(4) stock transfer forms transferring subscriber shares to intended members of the company;
(5) completion of the company's bank mandate form setting up banking arrangements;
(6) adoption of an accounting reference date (ARD) to which the company's accounts will be prepared (in the event that the Registrar is not notified of the ARD within six months of the incorporation the statutory ARD will apply as of 31 March).

The following company forms typically need to be filed with the Registrar following the first board meeting (and subsequently when appropriate changes are made):

(a) Form 88(2) setting out details of shares which have been allotted for cash (if there is a non-cash consideration a Form 88(3) will need to be completed);
(b) Form 288 (Appointment of any new director or secretary), which needs to be signed by each new director and the secretary resignations should also be recorded on the same form;
(c) Form 224 which is notification of the accounting reference date chosen by the company.

Any completed stock transfer form also needs to be sent to the Revenue for stamping (this is an *ad valorem* tax and is assessed at the rate of 50p per £100 or part thereof (see further below)). If there are any declarations of trust regarding the holding of such shares, such a declaration of trust form also needs to be stamped 50p.

17.4.1 Continuing requirements

In addition to notifying the Registrar about day-to-day changes (eg:

(a) the appointment or resignation of a director or secretary (Form 288);
(b) a change of accounting reference date (Forms G225(1) and (2));
(c) a change of registered office (Form 287);
(d) a change of auditor, etc,

the company also has an obligation to prepare accounts. For the first accounting reference date, the accounts must be for a period of more than six months but not more than 18 months beginning with the date of incorporation. There is no minimum duration for subsequent periods but no period may exceed 18 months.

In each financial year the company's directors must lay before the company in general meeting copies of its annual accounts and the directors and auditors report. A copy of this material needs to be delivered to the Registrar within ten months of the end of the appropriate accounting reference period for a private company, or within seven months for a public company. In the case of a first accounting period of a company which is more than 12 months, the period allowed is ten and seven months respectively from the first anniversary of the company's incorporation (or three months from the end of the accounting reference period whichever last expires). If a company fails to deliver accounts to the Registrar within those periods civil penalties are charged of up to £5,000 for a public company, and up to £1,000 for a private company.

A private company may pass an elective resolution (see 17.6.6 below) to dispense with laying the accounts or reports before the company in general meeting (see 17.6.1 below). Any such election does not relieve the company from the obligation to send copies of the accounts to all members and other people entitled to receive them (including the Registrar).

There are special provisions for dormant companies which may, by special resolution, resolve not to appoint auditors. A dormant company for this purpose means one which has not had transactions requiring entries in the company's accounting records since the end of the previous financial year (or the date of incorporation as the case may be).

17.4.2 Annual return

Each company must deliver to the Registrar on a Form 363a details made up to a date not later than the anniversary of the company's incorporation for a new company, or the anniversary of the date of the last return for other companies. The return must be delivered to the Registrar within 28 days of the relevant date.

The annual return needs to specify the following:

(1) The relevant date as it is made up.
(2) The registered office address.
(3) Details of the company's main business activities.
(4) Names and addresses of the company secretary and each director of the company. For directors, additional information is required (including nationality, date of birth, business occupation and other directorships).
(5) Where the register of members is kept (if not at the registered office).
(6) The share capital of the company and its members.

17.4.3 Borrowing

Trading and commercial companies have employed powers to borrow money for all purposes of its business and this power is invariably enshrined in a company's memorandum of association. A borrowing or loan is an agreement under which one party advances or otherwise makes available to another a sum of money in consideration of a promise, whether expressed or implied, to repay the amount advanced, whether or not at a premium and whether or not with interest. An agreement relating to borrowing must be validly entered into by the company and borrowing must not be unlawful or for some unlawful pursuit.

Borrowing takes two forms:

(a) secured debt (borrowings secured subject to a charge that has been granted on some or all of the company's property); and

(b) unsecured debt, eg bills of exchange, promissory notes and bonds etc issued by the company.

Restrictions on borrowing

Frequently articles of association limit the amount of debt in the form of borrowings which can be outstanding at any time without the shareholders' prior consent. In the case of a listed company the Stock Exchange no longer requires the articles to restrict borrowings and it is left to the company and its advisors to determine limitations; obviously they need to take a view to ensure marketability of its securities. Section 6 of Chapter 1 of The Admissions of Securities Listing (the 'yellow book') makes it a requirement of the Stock Exchange that in most cases a listed company needs to obtain the shareholders' approval to a transaction, a principle purpose or effect of which is the granting of credit (including lending money or guaranteeing the loan) by the company or any one of its subsidiaries to, or to an associate of, a director or substantial shareholder ('a class IV transaction'). 'Director' and 'substantial shareholder' includes a person who occupied that position within the preceding 12 months.

Agreements usually require the company to undertake to keep its borrowings and those of any subsidiary within a specified limit. In the event that the company fails to comply with this provision a lender would have remedies against the company for breach of contract and may also seek to bring an injunction. It may also be possible that those who authorised such offending loan may be personally liable.

17.4.4 Debentures

There is no precise meaning of 'debenture'. The broad legal meaning is that it is a document which either creates or acknowledges indebtedness. For the purposes of this section debenture is used in its banking context, ie a document signed by the company covenanting to repay all monies that may be due to the lender and creating a fixed charge over the company premises etc and a floating charge over the concern's business and undertaking.

If there is a default in the repayment of the debenture which is unsecured, the main remedy is for the holder to sue for the debts if it remains unpaid. He needs to obtain a judgment and seek distress against the company's property and possibly present a petition for the company's winding-up. In the case of a secured debenture the holder is in a far stronger position since in addition to the powers already referred to he can also appoint a receiver or administrative receiver.

17.4.5 Mezzanine finance

This is a type of debt which has in recent years become quite popular with highly geared companies. It is a form of subordinated debt which ranks behind all or certain other specified debts of the company. This type of debt may be secured by charges, but these invariably rank behind other creditors. The principal advantage to the creditor in offering this form of finance is that since the risk is high, so is the interest chargeable.

17.4.6 Charges and secured debentures

There is a temptation to use the words 'charge' and 'mortgage' interchangeably. There is an important difference between them since a mortgage arises when a property is transferred subject to a right of redemption. Conversely a charge does not transfer or convey anything but just gives the person holding the charge (the chargee) certain defined rights over the property as security or a loan.

A fixed or specific charge is one linked to either existing or future property and which attaches to that property. (For future property it attaches when that property has been ascertained.) When a fixed charge has been given relating to specific property the owner or company giving the charge is prohibited from dealing with the property without the consent of the company or individual to whom the charge was given.

A floating charge, as its name implies, floats over the relevant property until a specified event happens which would then cause it to fasten on to the subject matter of the charge. Until this occurs the relevant company can carry on its day to day activities and sell or deal with its assets without first requiring the holder's consent. If an event occurs which causes the charge to 'crystallize' (fasten), the holder of the floating charge becomes entitled to a specific or fixed charge over the property and any further dealing by the company of that property requires his or its consent. A floating charge crystallizes in circumstances including the following:

(a) upon the winding-up of the company;
(b) if an administrative receiver is appointed;
(c) if a company has sold substantially all its property and assets so that it can no longer carry on business;
(d) if possession of any assets is taken by the holder of a charge; and
(e) any other floating charge that may have been granted crystallizes or if the company granting the floating charge failed to repay money on demand.

17.4.7 Registration of charges

Section 395(1) of CA 1985 requires that if any security of a company's property or undertaking has been granted, such security shall cease to prevail unless details of the charge together with a document creating the charge has been delivered to the Registrar within 21 days. Section 396(1) lists nine types of charges to which the obligation of registration applies. The categories listed are broad, but exclude such items as fixed charges over shares which the relevant company may hold in another company and also interest under insurance policies.

To register a charge, a Form 395 must be completed as accurately as possible. To ensure that the charge is valid, full details of the nature of the charge should be set out in the form. A mistake or omission in the completion of the form can prejudice the effectiveness of that security against competing claims in the event of a winding-up. It is most important that professional assistance is sought in the drafting and registration of charges to avoid potential pitfalls. Information required to be inserted on Form 395 includes the following:

(1) Company name and number.
(2) Date of creation of charge.
(3) Description of the instrument.
(4) Names and addresses of persons entitled to charge.
(5) Particulars of property charged.

17.4.8 Failure to register a charge

If a charge is not registered within the required 21-day period:

(a) it becomes void as against the liquidator and administrator, any creditor of the company and any person who has acquired proprietary rights to an interest in assets which are subject to a charge;
(b) the money which it secures becomes immediately repayable when the time for registration expires;
(c) the company and every officer in default becomes liable to a fine under CA 1985, s 399(3);

If registration is late it is normal to execute a fresh charge, etc and duly register that within 21 days (but this may be subject to any others that may have been created in any intervening period). This second charge might also be subject to being set aside by a liquidator or administrative receiver as being a preference or possibly a transaction at an undervalue (see Insolvency Act 1986, s 244 *et seq*).

17.4.9 Foreign companies

If a company incorporated outside Great Britain has an established place of business in England and Wales, it is required to submit particulars of any charge on property in England and Wales. Charges etc created prior to an establishment of a place of business remain valid even if the charge subsequently establishes the place of business.

Where a lender takes a charge from a foreign company relating to present or future property in England and Wales he should submit particulars of the charge and relevant documentary evidence to the Registrar. Even if the particulars are subsequently returned to the sender Companies House now maintains an alphabetical index of the names of overseas companies for which charges for registration have been delivered (this is known as the Slavenburg Index after an important case involving this foreign bank).

17.5 DIRECTORS

Regulation 70 of Table A of the Companies (Tables A to F) Regulations 1985 states the general precept of company law, namely 'subject to provisions of the [companies legislation] and the articles and to any directions given by special resolution, the business of the company shall be managed by the directors who may exercise all the powers of the company'. There is broad statutory definition of 'director' since CA 1985, s 741(1) refers only to a person occupying the position of a director by whatever name called. Directors are those people who have agreed to become directors, for example by completing a company Form 288, but may also include individuals who take that role upon themselves (eg a major shareholder in a small company who meddles in day-to-day business). It could also be deemed to include a senior manager of a larger company who makes significant decisions regarding that company's day-to-day business. It is clear that just because a person is not called a 'director' may be of little importance in establishing what is for position *de facto*. Such quasi directors are normally referred to as 'shadow directors'. In *Re Tasbian Ltd No 3* [1992] BCC 358 the Court of Appeal supported the claim that in the circumstances presented to the court the company doctor, who had been required to assist in a corporate recovery case, could have been treated as a director or a shadow director in the context under the Company Directors Disqualification Act 1986.

There is no maximum number of directors that can be appointed to a company and a private company may have one director. In the case of a public company it must have at least two directors. If a private company only has one director there must be at least two people involved in the running of the company since CA 1985, s 283(2) requires that a sole director cannot also be a secretary. There is nothing to stop a director – and indeed a secretary – being another company, but this should not lead to a circumvention in the requirement that there are only two individuals involved.

17.5.1 Appointment of directors

Founding directors complete company Form G10, which must be presented to Companies House before a certificate of incorporation is granted (see 17.2.3 above). Appointment of subsequent directors is determined in accordance with the company's articles. A typical such provision appears in reg 79 of Table A of the 1985 Regulations which states that the existing directors may appoint such person who is willing to act to be a director; this could either be to fill a vacancy or due to a requirement to have additional directors. Occasionally the articles will provide special provisions relating to a director appointment and it is not unusual for the articles to require a rotating system (ie a proportion of all the main members retire and offer themselves for re-selection at each annual general meeting). Sometimes the articles also require a director to hold a number of shares in the company concerned. Such shares are frequently held on the basis that on resignation they are resold to the company's other members.

Neither the managing director nor the chairman has specific powers accorded to him by law, but regulation 84 of Table A does allow the appointment of a managing director. Each meeting requires a chairman to preside. Normally one of the directors takes this role, but larger companies appoint a specific person to fill this slot. Table A requires that the chairman ought to be a member of the board. The position of chairman is a difficult one for he is in charge of the meeting and needs to check the meeting is properly conducted. Regulation 50 of Table A gives the chairman a casting vote at meetings in addition to any other vote he may have (whether on a show of hands or a poll).

17.5.2 Non-executive directors

This has been a characteristic of larger companies for many years. It refers to a director who is not employed by a company under a service contract. Frequently he is seen as being a useful nexus between the board and the shareholders' interests and is able to offer an independent stand which may not otherwise be available at board level. Company law does not recognise any division between a director and a director's responsibilities and duties.

An executive director should have a service contract with the company. Regulation 82 of Table A provides that the director should be entitled to such remuneration as the company may by ordinary resolution determine. For a director who works without having a service contract there is a presumption that he should be paid for the work done for the company on a merit basis (*Craven-Ellis v Cannons Ltd* [1936] 2 KB 403).

17.5.3 Director meetings

The day-to-day management of a company is centred upon the decisions of the Board of Directors. Directors, unless otherwise required by the articles (or a shareholders' agreement etc), meet at such times and intervals as they feel fit. Frequently meetings, if permitted by the company's articles, are held with little formality. Notice is similarly dealt with on an informal basis, but must be given to each director. Article 88 provides that no notice need be given to a director who is absent from the UK. Table A also permits a director to appoint an alternate to represent him.

The company's articles will specify what constitutes a quorum. A sole director who can only act in limited circumstances without a meeting will usually need acts by written resolution to be effective. Each director will have a vote and in addition Table A gives the chairman a second or casting vote if votes are equal. There is little law to determine how such a casting vote should be exercised but it is recognised that it should not be exercised arbitarily or capriciously (it does not though need to be exercised in the same way as the chairman's first vote).

Meetings are increasingly being held by telephone: this is tolerated by law, but is not preferable to an actual meeting. The validity of such a meeting depends on ensuring the normal procedures are adopted. Due to the normal requirements of a meeting it is unlikely that meetings can effectively be held by e-mail.

17.5.4 Resignation or retirement

A director can at any time resign his directorship, but if in so doing he has breached a contract of service this could result in liability for damages. In the case of public companies and private companies which are subsidiaries of private companies, CA 1985, s 293 states that a director must retire from office at the AGM following his 70th birthday. This does not apply if a director's appointment has been approved by a resolution of the general meeting at which special notice giving details of the director's age has been circulated to members (at least 28 days prior to the meeting). If such notice is not practical it can take the form of a newspaper advertisement or any other method allowed by the articles, but this needs to be done at least 21 days before the meeting.

17.5.5 Disqualification

This can take two forms:

(1) The articles normally set out regulations under which a director is required to vacate office in certain circumstances (eg ceasing to hold qualifying shares (if required), becoming of unsound mind, bankruptcy etc).
(2) The Company Directors Disqualification Act 1986 sets out three circumstances:
   (a) disqualification for misconduct in relation to the company (eg if a director has been convicted of an indictable offence in connection with the company);
   (b) disqualification for unfitness (eg persistent breaches of company's legislation like failing to deliver documents or returns to Companies House on a regular basis); and
   (c) other cases of disqualification (eg if a director has participated in fraud or a breach of duty or has participated in fraudulent trading which comes to light during a winding-up).

An application may be sought for disqualification by the Secretary of State, the official receiver or the liquidator, past or present members of a company, or a creditor of a relevant company. It is within the court's discretion whether to make an order. For cases of fraud and misconduct such disqualification can be up to a maximum of 15 years, in other circumstances up to five years. Under s 6 of the 1986 Act a court must disqualify a director for not less than two years and not more than 15 years in the case where a company becomes insolvent (whether while he was a director or subsequently) and his conduct was such as to make him unfit or concerned in the management of the company. Under s 8 the Secretary of State can apply to court for a disqualification order for up to 15 years.

See *Re Sevenoaks Stationers (Retail) Ltd* (1991) Ch 164 in which the Court of Appeal set out guidelines on how the Act should be interpreted.

17.5.6 Removal of director

Section 3 of CA 1985 allows a director to be removed by ordinary resolution of the company so long as special notice of at least 28 days has been given. Such notice must be served on the company. The director affected has the right to receive a copy of the notice and be heard at the meeting whether or not he is a member of the company. He can, if he requires, oblige the company to circulate written representation to the members before the meeting (there is though a right to apply to the court to have this curtailed).

The removal of the person as a director does not deprive that person from obtaining compensation damages with respect to determination of his appointment. It may also be open to him to petition for the company's winding-up under s 122(1)(g) of the Insolvency Act 1986 on the 'just and equitable' ground. In one case the petition was held to be successful since the director had such a substantial stake in a small family company that it was felt to be based upon a personal relationship involving mutual confidence (this area of law was carefully considered by the House of Lords in *Ebrahimi v Westbourne Galleries* [1973] AC 360).

17.5.7 Directors' duties

The duties can be summarised under two heads:

(a) the duty of good faith and loyalty (more usually referred to as fiduciary duties), and
(b) the requirement to use skill and care in carrying out their duties.

Fiduciary duties

This is an individual duty imposed upon each director of a company and it is owed to the company. From this fundamental principle certain strands have developed:

(1) In exercising good faith, directors must act in what they believe to be the company's best interests.
(2) They should not prejudice their ability to make decisions or restrict how they should act.
(3) They should not place themselves in the position where their personal interests or relationships to other persons may conflict with their duties to the company.
(4) They should not use the powers placed upon them for different purposes from those with which they were conferred.

Illustrations

In *Re W & M Roith Ltd* [1967] 1 WLR 432 a controlling shareholder and director made provision for his widow under his service agreement that she should be entitled upon his demise to a pension for life. The court held that this was not binding upon the company since no thought had been given to the question of whether this provision was for the company's benefit. Here the sole object was to make a provision for the shareholder/director's widow.

In *Re Kuwait Bank v National Nominees* [1991] AC 187 the bank, which held 40 per cent of the shares in the company, had appointed two of its employees as directors, but continued to pay them for time spent in carrying out their duties. The court held that although they continued to owe a duty to the bank (ie their employers), their primary duty when acting as directors was to the company and that they should when circumstances dictated have ignored the bank's interests and wishes.

In *Re Aberdeen Railway v Blaikie Bros* (1854) 1 Macq 461 a contract was revoked between the company and the partnership since one of the directors was a partner. Lord Cranworth in discussing fiduciary duties said 'it is a rule of universal application that no one, having such duties to discharge, shall be allowed to enter into engagements in which he has, or can have, a personal interest conflicting, or which possibly may conflict, with the interests of those whom he is bound to protect . . . no question is allowed to be raised as to the fairness or unfairness of a contract so entered into . . .'.

Section 317 of CA 1985 requires a director of a company who is in any way 'whether directly or indirectly' interested in a contract or a proposed contract to declare his interest at a meeting of directors. If a director fails to declare his interest he is liable for a fine. Recent cases before the House of Lords and the Court of Appeal have been particularly interesting since in *Hely-Hutchinson v Brayhead Ltd* [1968] 1 QB 549 and *Guinness v Saunders* [1988] 1 WLR 863 both companies had in their articles of association provision that so long as the director disclosed his interest in accordance with s 317, he would be exonerated from the normal duty to account to the company for benefit resulting from such transaction. In each case the director failed to declare his interest. The courts' judgments were clear that, if the company wished, it could avoid the transactions and any such benefits received by directors would be recovered. In each case the court appeared to accept that had the interest been declared the transaction would be upheld even if it had not specifically consented to the director placing himself in a position where his duty to the company and his interests could conflict.

There are a number of examples of the use of corporate property where directors have been required to return funds which had been misappropriated. In *Guinness v Saunders*, although Mr Ward thought he was entitled to £5.2m from the company, he was required to return it.

In *Re Regal (Hastings) Ltd v Gulliver* [1942] 1 All ER 378 the directors decided to purchase two additional cinemas with the view that the company would then be sold. The directors were unable to obtain the required funds. The directors and their friends subscribed for shares in a second company, making a profit. The first company fell into different hands and brought an action against its former directors to recover profits they had made. Despite the fact that the original company would not have been in a position to make these profits it was held by the House of Lords that the directors were liable to account since they acquired their knowledge as directors while managing the original company and their actions resulted in profit.

There has been a line of cases concerned with directors who had retired to obtain remunerative work that their original companies had been denied. In each case the relevant directors have been required to account to the company for profits they made. (See further *Industrial Development Consultants v Cooley* [1972] 1 WLR 443; *Canadian Aero Service v O'Malley* [1971] 23 DLR (3d) 632.)

Section 309 of CA 1985 requires directors of a company to have regard in the performance of their functions to the interests of the company's employees in general in addition to those of its members. Section 310 states that 'any provision whether contained in the Company's articles or in any contract with the Company or otherwise which attempts to exonerate an officer (or auditor of the company) from, or indemnify them against liability for negligence, default, breach of contract, breach of trust which he may be guilty in relation to the company is unenforceable'. There is a difficulty reconciling this statutory provision with the wording in Table A, regs 85 and 86.

17.5.8 Directors' remuneration

Section 318 of CA 1985 obliges a company to keep copies of a service agreement for each director of the company or its subsidiaries. These should be kept at the registered office or at its principal place of business and must be open for inspection by any member of the company without charge.

Section 319 makes it unlawful for any provision in a director's contract which may make it last for more than five years without being terminated (ie other than through causing a breach of contract) unless the relevant term is first approved by the company in general meeting. There are special provisions relating to inspection being available without charge to members for a period prior to the meeting and at the meeting itself.

17.5.9 Substantial property transactions

Section 322 of CA 1985 requires that the company approve in advance any arrangement under which a director or person connected with such director will acquire from the company or the company will acquire from such person non-cash items of requisite value (being £100,000 or 10 per cent of the company's net assets if more than £2,000). The need for approval does not apply to intergroup transfers when the property is to be acquired by a holding company from one of its wholly owned subsidiaries or vice versa or from one wholly owned subsidiary to another of that same holding company. If a director authorises an arrangement or transaction in violation he is liable to account to the company for any gain he makes.

17.5.10 Loans to directors

Section 330(2) and (3) of CA 1985 prevents the company making a loan to a director of it or its holding company or from entering into any guarantee or providing security in connection with a loan made by any person to such director. This also covers a prohibition on 'quasi-loans' (these are when a director makes some financial benefit as a result of the company being party to a transaction), eg a gift of a holiday or some other benefit in kind. The grant of credit is also prohibited and the assignment of any rights, obligations and liability could also fall within this scope (s 330(4) and (6)).

There are certain exceptions to these rules and these should be carefully considered prior to any such potential 'loan'.

17.5.11 Directors' duties of care

Re City Equitable Fire Insurance Co [1925] Ch 407 laid down the standard of care required under three heads:

(1) In the performance of his duties a director does not need to show any greater skill than would reasonably be expected from a person of his knowledge and experience.
(2) A director's duties are of an intermittent nature and should be formed at periodic board meetings or any committee of that board on which he serves. He is not required to give continuous attention to the company's affairs.
(3) A director may rely upon agents or employees of the company not being directors to carry on day-to-day duties of the company. In particular a director can only be liable on the basis of his own personal negligence.

There are two important statutory provisions which should be noted which affect the director's duty of care:

(1) Section 214 of the Insolvency Act 1986; this provision can potentially make a director personally liable if there is 'wrongful trading' (see further 17.5.13 below)
(2) The Company Directors Disqualification Act 1986 (see 17.5.5 above).

17.5.12 Personal liability of directors

There are a number of circumstances referred to above and also with respect to the insolvency legislation in which directors can potentially be personally liable. The articles cannot relieve directors from their duty to act bona fide in the interests of a company nor can a resolution of a company in general meeting make good default, but the courts have indicated that a transaction may sometimes be validated (and the directors thereby excused from liability) if:

(a) all relevant facts are disclosed in a notice convening a general meeting or in a circular accompanying that notice;
(b) it can be shown that the resolution was 'bona fide in the interests of the company'.

In the recent case of *Williams v Natural Law* (1996) inaccurate financial projections were provided to an applicant to a franchise which persuaded him to enter into a franchise. The result was a substantial loss of money. The plaintiff had no difficulty in showing that there was gross negligence (there was clearly a duty of care to ensure projections were correct and reasonably and properly prepared). It was held that in the particular circumstances of the case the director had, since the plans were presented relying upon the personal expertise and experience of the director, effectively assumed a personal duty to the plaintiff (and was therefore personally liable). The court did however emphasise that a director who merely had control or ownership of the company in itself was not sufficient to create such a liability.

It is clear that English courts have been extending liability for directors and that a more objective test (common in Australian case-law) is beginning to be recognised (ie directors are expected to use skill and diligence and not just be enthusiastic amateurs).

17.5.13 Insurance

It has been customary for the personal liability of directors and other officers to be covered by insurance. Before CA 1989 it was unclear whether under CA 1985, s 310 such insurance was enforceable. A new provision was inserted by s 137 of the 1989 Act under which a new subs 310(3) was incorporated in the 1985 Act. This makes it clear that a company can purchase and maintain insurance for its officers if its memorandum and articles of association so allow. The normal form of cover protects past, present and future officers of a specific company (including shadow directors), but does not protect outsiders (eg an auditor or liquidator).

Indemnity insurance normally takes two forms:

(i) protecting officers of a company where an indemnity from the company is not available, and
(ii) where the company reimburses its officers for liability it would in turn make this good to the company.

It is normal for a company to protect against:

(a) paying damages and costs of any action for a 'wrongful act' (broadly defined and includes actions for wrongful trading under s 214 of the Insolvency Act 1986);
(b) legal expense incurred (except the exclusions from policy are normally limited to public policy items such as dishonesty, fraud, malicious conduct, indemnity for fines and penalties);
(c) specific risks which should be insured elsewhere (eg negligence or a breach of professional duty by an auditor or solicitor).

17.6 MEETINGS

17.6.1 General meetings

There are two types:

(a) annual general meetings (AGMs), and
(b) extraordinary general meetings (EGMs).

Every company must hold an AGM each calendar year with not more than 15 months between one AGM and the next. A newly formed company need not hold its first AGM for up to 18 months from the date of incorporation (see generally CA 1985, s 366).

An EGM is any general meeting that is held other than an AGM, and is usually convened by the company's directors when they so require. Under CA 1985, s 368 the directors are bound to convene an EGM if the holder of not less than one-tenth of the company's voting shares (or for companies without a share capital, of not less than one-tenth of voting rights) so requires. The people calling the meeting must give written notice setting out the meeting's objects and sign that notice. If the directors are requested to hold an EGM by the shareholders or those with voting rights they must fix the actual date within 28 days (ie allowing a maximum of 49 days before a meeting is actually held).

The directors of a plc are required to convene an EGM under CA 1985, s 142 if there is a serious loss of capital (where the net assets are half or less of its called-up share capital). In this instance the meeting must be convened in 28 days for a date not later than 20 days after such notice.

Before the company can hold an AGM or EGM written notice must be given to the members:

(a) for an AGM, at least 21 days' notice;
(b) for an EGM, not less than 14 days unless a special resolution is proposed, in which case it must be 21 days. In sending out the notice a company should carefully ensure that extra days are given since frequently the article requires 'clear' days' notice (eg reg 38 of Table A).

Shorter notice can be given if this is agreed by all members entitled to attend in the case of an AGM or for an EGM those holding not less than 95 per cent of the voting shares (or having such voting rights).

Notice needs to be sent to every member of a company, but frequently the articles state that accidental omission to give such notice (or non-receipt of such notice) does not invalidate proceedings of a meeting (eg reg 39 of Table A). Table A also (in reg 38) requires that the notice should state the:

(a) time and place of the meeting;
(b) general business to be transacted (eg retirement, re-election of directors); and
(c) appointment of auditors.

Where a special resolution is to be proposed the notice must set this down.

For a company with share capital, the notice must also contain the statement in reasonable prominence that a member is entitled to attend and vote and may also appoint a proxy to attend and vote in his place and that this proxy need not be a member of the company (s 372). If a company's members wish to include a resolution at an AGM and such member or members hold not less than one-twentieth of the voting rights (or 100 members entitled to vote with an average paid- up share capital of not less than £100 per member), the company must circulate:

(a) notice thereof to each member of the company that a resolution will be proposed at the AGM; and
(b) a statement of not more than one thousand words relating to the proposed resolution (s 376). The company and 'any aggrieved person' has the right to petition the court to prevent any such statement being circulated.

The court has power to call a meeting (s 371). This power is normally used if no quorum can be achieved (eg a shareholder argument) or a meeting may end in violence. An example of such use was a meeting held by the British Union for the Abolition of Vivisection: the court held that only the executive committee should meet, with all other members having a postal vote.

17.6.2 Special notice

This is required for the:

(a) appointment of a director who has attained the age of 70;
(b) removal of directors;
(c) appointment and removal of auditors.

Notice in this respect must be given to the company not less than 28 days before the meeting and the company must give notice to each of the members when it circulates a notice for the meeting (or if this is not practical through newspaper advertisement or any other form allowed by the articles not being less than 21 days before the meeting).

17.6.3 Quorum

The articles of association normally provide that a specified number of people must be present before a meeting can be held. Under CA 1985, s 370 unless the articles otherwise state, two members must be present in person for a meeting to be held. Table A, in reg 41, states that where a meeting cannot be held it should be adjourned to the same day in the following week at the same time and place (or such time and place as the directors may determine) and if after half an hour at that adjourned meeting there is no quorum the members present shall form that quorum (even if it is a single person).

A meeting can be held in more than one room at the same time provided there are audio visual links (*Byng v London Life Association* [1990] Ch 170).

17.6.4 Voting

This is normally done by show of hand with each person present having one vote, unless a poll is demanded in which case a member has a vote for each share he holds. Section 372 of CA 1985 gives the right of voting by proxy (ie appointing another person to attend and vote in his place). There are two forms of proxy:

(1) a general proxy appointing a person to vote as he thinks fit having regard to what is said at the meeting; and

(2) a special proxy where a person is required to vote for or against a particular resolution (frequently called 'a two-way proxy').

17.6.5 Minutes

Minutes should be taken of proceedings of general meetings. These are signed by the chairman of that meeting either at the end of the meeting or at the next meeting. Frequently articles state that when signed they are conclusive evidence of what took place at the meeting, but if the articles do not so provide it does not form conclusive evidence. Members are entitled to inspect the minute book at the registered office without charge; if this is refused or not made available the court can compel inspection.

17.6.6 Resolutions

There are four types of resolutions.

Ordinary resolution

Unless the company's articles or memorandum state otherwise a motion can be passed by ordinary resolution – by simple majority of votes of members entitled to vote and voting in person.

Extraordinary and special resolutions

These require to be passed by at least a three-quarter majority of the voting members entitled to vote in person at a general meeting.

Elective resolution

This was introduced by CA 1989 for use in a private company. It can be used for the following:

(a) with respect to authority of directors to allot shares;
(b) to dispense with the laying of accounts and reports for a general meeting;
(c) to dispense with the appointment of auditors;
(d) to reduce a percentage required before sanctioning short notices of meetings or special resolution; and
(e) to dispense with the holding of an AGM.

To pass an elective resolution needs at least 21 days' notice in writing. The notice needs to set out the terms of the resolution which needs to have unanimous consent of those entitled to attend and vote at the meeting (ie one shareholder can veto it). Any election can be revoked by ordinary resolution and is automatically revoked if, for example, the company becomes a plc. An elective resolution, or one revoking an elective resolution, must be registered at Companies House in the same manner as a special resolution.

17.6.7 Filing of resolution

Companies House must be sent copies of the following:

(a) special resolutions;
(b) extraordinary resolutions;
(c) elective resolutions;
(d) written resolutions;
(e) other resolutions agreed by all members (which would otherwise not be effective unless passed as a special or extraordinary resolution);
(f) a resolution passed by all members of a class of shareholders;
(g) an ordinary resolution increasing share capital.

Copies of all such resolutions must be sent to the Registrar within 15 days after they are passed or made.

The following are examples of ordinary resolutions:

(a) removal of a director (CA 1985, s 303);
(b) appointment or removal of an auditor (ss 384 and 386);
(c) increase in share capital.

Extraordinary resolution examples are few but do occur in insolvency:

(a) in sanctioning the exercise of certain powers of liquidation and a member's voluntary winding-up under the Insolvency Act 1986, s 165;
(b) for the initiation of a creditor's voluntary winding-up when the company is insolvent under s 84 of that Act.

A special resolution is required for more important situations:

(a) alterations of the objects clause in the memorandum of association (CA 1985, s 4);
(b) alterations of articles (s 9);
(c) reduction of capital (s 135).

17.6.8 Written resolutions

For some years the courts have accepted that it is not necessary that the company should always hold a meeting, and that all shareholders having a right to attend and vote at general meetings and give notice in written form constitute a binding resolution on the company. The CA 1989 now formally allows private companies to pass resolutions without holding any meeting provided all those who could have attended the meeting and voted sign such a resolution. This can only take effect when the last relevant member signs. A written resolution cannot be used to dismiss a director under CA 1985, s 303 or an auditor under s 391. The CA 1985 requires that the written resolution should be sent to the auditor who can, within seven days, notify the company that it should be considered by a formal meeting. In this case a meeting needs to be held to consider the resolution. If the written resolution in effect transacted business which would otherwise be done by special, extraordinary or elective resolutions, it must be sent to the Registrar for filing.

17.6.9 The shareholder

There is no clear definition of what a share is in law, but it is clearly recognised as being an item of property which can be bought, sold, mortgaged and approved. Normally a shareholder's rights consist of three items:

(a) dividends;
(b) in the event of a winding-up, a return of capital (also in the event of an authorised reduction of capital); and
(c) voting and attendance at a meeting.

Unless the articles state to the contrary all shares confer rights with respect to each of these characteristics.

Either a general meeting resolution or alternatively the company's articles must empower the directors to allot shares in the company (right to subscribe, convert, etc) (CA 1985, s 80). Such authority also needs to state the maximum number of shares, etc which can be issued under that power and the power can only be that for up to five years. Thereafter further authorisation must be given by the general meeting.

Sections 89–96 of CA 1985 grant pre-emptive rights to the existing shareholders, ie giving them the ability to protect the proportion of total equity that they may hold at any one stage (the provisions require that the company should not allot shares to any person unless it is first offered, on the same or more favourable terms, to each person who holds relevant shares a proportion of shares which as nearly as practicable equals his existing proportion in nominal value of his aggregate holdings of relevant shares). The difficulty with these pre-emption provisions is that they can be modified or extinguished since under CA 1985, s 31 the need to offer pre-emptive rights can be excluded in the memorandum and articles of a private company (in each case or in respect of a particular allotment).

With reference to public companies, CA 1985, s 95 empowers directors who have general authority by the articles or through a resolution at general meeting to allot shares as if the pre-emption provisions do not apply.

17.6.10 Types of shares

In a company with more than one type of share (frequently referred to as a 'class') there must be equal treatment for all holders of those shares. Frequently a company has more than one class of share with different rights with respect to

(a) dividends,
(b) return of capital,
(c) voting rights, and
(d) nominal values.

Each class of share has its own rights; this is referred to more generally at 17.6.14 below.

Preference shares

These, as the name implies, have a preferential right in comparison with ordinary shares. The preference is normally dividend or return of capital. The rights of the holder of such shares are normally set out in the articles of association. Where this share has priority with respect to dividend it normally takes two forms, either cumulative or non-cumulative. The former safeguards the shareholder in the event that a dividend is not declared since in effect it is added to the next time a dividend is paid. In the latter case, if a dividend is not paid the right is lost forever.

Ordinary shares

If there are special rights given to another class of share (eg preference shares) until these preferential rights have been satisfied claims by the ordinary shareholder are delayed. It is for this reason that ordinary shares are sometimes referred to as 'risk capital'. Sometimes such shares are themselves divided into different classes.

Employee shares

These are shares normally allotted to full-time employees under an established scheme (frequently taking advantage of tax benefits under approved option schemes; a recent government announcement (July 1995) has put the tax benefits for holders under an executive type scheme in some doubt). This may include present and past employees within the group and spouses etc. Sometimes a special class of share is created to cater for the rights of these holders, but more usually they form part of an established class with special rules regarding allotment, finance and repurchase. There is frequently also a trust document setting out various rights.

17.6.11 Debenture holder

This has sometimes been classified as a type of share, but does not really conform to the characteristics of shares discussed above. The relationship is really one of debtor creditor (frequently coupled with some form of security against some or all of the company's assets). The distinction sometimes becomes blurred, eg where a debenture holder may be able to appoint a director, obtain a share of profit (this may be irrespective of whether a dividend is declared), to attend and vote at meetings and sometimes to have the right to convert his debentures into equity shares.

17.6.12 Bonus issue

This is frequently also called a 'capitalisation' issue (and sometimes a 'scrip' issue). If a cash rich company wants to increase the network of its share capital to its shareholders it may issue them with bonus shares. It is a method of capitalising reserves by issuing new-paid-up shares to its existing shareholders (eg if a book value of a company was, say, £10m and the company had an issued share capital of 5 million shares of £1 each the shares are effectively worth £2). If a company then decides to make a one-for-one paid-up bonus issue (which is paid out of the share premium account or any free reserves) the shareholder effectively receives for each of his shares (worth £2) two £1 shares each worth £1. The sole effect is that the company can reduce the amount held in its share premium account and replace it with issued shares. Sometimes a listed company achieves the same effect by allowing shareholders to exercise an option and take shares in place of dividends.

17.6.13 CREST

After nearly ten years of work, settlement of dealing in shares can now be dealt with on a computerised basis, rather than a lengthy paper system. The CREST system was inaugurated on 15 July 1996; it is run by CRESTCo, owned by 69 institutions from various parts of the securities industry.

The computer system in its simplest form works from a computer which receives instructions for the transfer of shares and acts upon those instructions. Companies and shareholders are therefore disassociates and communicate only by electronic media through the centralised computer. Companies will continue to keep registers of members and dividends and voting remains unchanged.

CREST is a voluntary system and an issuer can choose whether to use it – even when a security is dealt with by CREST a shareholder can choose whether to hold it in a certificated or uncertificated format.

17.6.14 Class rights

Three particular types of rights are identified:

(1) Those rights which clearly attach to a class of share (eg dividend and rights to participate in surplus assets on a winding-up).
(2) Where the articles purport to confer rights on individuals not as shareholders (eg a solicitor who becomes a member of a company cannot enforce a provision that he should be the company's solicitor). Rights of this sort are clearly not a class right since it could not be said to attach to a class of share.
(3) Rights that although not attached to any particular share are nonetheless conferred upon the beneficiary in the capacity of member or shareholder of the company (eg the right of the holder of 10 per cent of the issued shares to nominate a director) (*Cumbria Newspapers Group v Cumberland & Westmorland Herald Newspaper & Printing Co Ltd* [1987] Ch 1). It was felt that this constituted class rights.

Where class rights exist they can only be varied:

(a) if the holders of three-quarters of the nominal value of the issued share of that particular class consent in writing; or
(b) a separate general meeting of holders of that class is held and an extraordinary resolution passed; or
(c) in either instant all relevant provision of a memorandum and articles of association or any agreement binding upon the shareholder is satisfied.

If variation provisions of class rights are incorporated in the memorandum and articles of association it is sufficient that variations are carried out in compliance with such provisions. If there is no such variation provision included and the rights are set out in the memorandum it can only be varied if all members of a company agree to the variation (CA 1985, s 125(5)).

Strict compliance is necessary to the length of notice to be given for any such class meeting and CA 1985, s 369 and for the holding of that meeting and voting (s 370) and the circulation of resolutions (ss 376 and 377).

Under CA 1985, s 127 a dissenting minority of not less than 15 per cent of the issued shares of a class whose rights have been varied in the manner permitted may apply to the court to have any variation cancelled. Such application needs to be made within 21 days after consent was given or the resolution passed. When such an application has been made the variation has no effect until it is confirmed by the court. If the court is satisfied the variation would unfairly prejudice the shareholder of the class represented by the applicant it will cancel the variation, but if it does not disallow the variation the court must confirm it.

17.6.15 Members' rights and duties

The company in general meeting has the power to act in place of a board if for any reason the board cannot function. For example if no quorum can be obtained for a meeting of directors or there is deadlock on the board it is well established that the company in general meeting may act instead. Similarly if the directors are in breach of duty in some circumstances this can be authorised or ratified by the company in general meeting.

There is an obligation upon directors in carrying out their duties to act for the benefit of a company as a whole, but if they are members themselves can they can vote in support of their own personal interests? This has led the courts to develop the concept of 'fraud on the minority'. Fraud in this context does not mean deceit, but refers to an abuse of power; the victim of such an abuse does not need to be a 'minority of members' – it is enough if the injured party is a company. There is a large body of cases giving examples of circumstances which have amounted to 'fraud on the minority'. In practice it is likely that a new statutory provision incorporated in CA 1985, s 459 can now be used more frequently (see 17.6.16 below).

Fraud has taken three particular forms, as follows.

Resolution permitting expropriation of property belonging to company

In *Cook v Deeks* [1916] 1 AC 554 directors diverted to themselves contracts which should have been taken up by the company and passed a resolution ratifying and approving this. The court held that the directors should hold the benefit of such contracts on trust for the company and could not be permitted to make a present of it to themselves. In *Menier v Hooper's Telegraph Works* (1874) 9 Ch App 350, those holding a controlling interest in a company compromised a pending action to their advantage (in a rival concern) which had the effect of gaining the company's assets to the exclusion of a minority. Again the court supported the minority's case.

Resolutions which relieve directors of liability

It is likely that if a director makes a full and frank disclosure to the company's members and the resolution can be shown to be bona fide in the company's interests it is unlikely that a minority is now able to successfully bring an action for fraud. Further, under CA 1985, s 35, if directors have failed to observe limitations on their power in the memorandum of association they can now be released from any liability by a special resolution.

Resolution that exappropriates members' shares

In *Brown v British Abrasive Wheel Company* [1919] 1 Ch 290 a public company was unable to buy out a 2 per cent minority so proposed by special resolution to acquire the shares. Here it was felt that the resolution could not be said to benefit the company as a whole, but only benefit the majority. An injunction was granted.

Other similar cases, though, have not followed this particular case and it is clear the courts will look carefully at the circumstances of each particular action. Further discussion on this general principle is outside the scope of this book, but a full discussion of the principles involved is discussed at length by the Court of Appeal in the influential case of *Greenhalgh v Arderne Cinemas* [1946] 1 All ER 512 (especially the judgment of Evershed MR).

17.6.16 Other remedies available to shareholders

Section 210 of the Companies Act 1948 gave protection to minorities where there had been conduct of an 'oppressive nature'. The remedy granted in the circumstances was to petition for a winding-up order on the grounds that such a remedy was just and equitable. The new law is incorporated in CA 1985, s 459 which allows a member of a company to petition a court on the ground that the affairs are being carried out or conducted in a manner which is 'unfairly prejudicial to the interests of its members generally or some part of the member (including at least himself) or that any actual or proposed act or omission of the company (including any act or omission on its behalf) is or would be so prejudicial'.

Once the court is satisfied that the petition is well founded, it makes 'such order as it thinks fit for giving relief in respect of the matter complained of'. The section goes on to give some examples:

(a) give instructions regulating the conduct of a company's affairs in future;

(b) give instructions prohibiting the company from doing an act complained of or requiring it to make an omission;
(c) authorise a company to bring in its name civil proceedings;
(d) require the purchase of shares of any member of a company either by the company itself or other members (if the company was to purchase its own shares under this head it would not need to comply with the special requirements for purchase of company's own shares) (see 17.7.5 below).

Recent cases concerned with ascertaining whether there was unfairly prejudicial conduct have indicated that there is no need to show either bad faith or a conscious intent to be unfair. It was also not essential to show a reduction in share value although that could be helpful.

In *Re Noble* [1983] BCLC 273 the judge felt that the shareholder had contributed to his own exclusion from the management of the company by showing no interest in its affairs. In *McGuinness & Anor v Bremmer plc and others* [1988] BCLC 673 it was held that a delay in holding a meeting was unfairly prejudicial even though it was within the terms of the 1985 Act.

Where a letter from the directors had deprived shareholders the chance of selling shares to the highest bidder or had reduced their chance of doing so this would also justify an action under CA 1985, s 459 (*Re a Company (No 008699 of 1985)* [1986] PCC 296).

Where a member had risked his capital in the business (a small limited company) it was justifiable that he would expect to be retained as a director. When he was dismissed it was held to be an unfairly prejudicial treatment of his interests as a member (*Re a Company (No 00477 of 1986*) [1986] PCC 372), but where a director was causing friction and difficulties his dismissal was not deemed to be unfairly prejudicial (*Re a Company (No 002470 of 1988), ex p Nicholas* [1991] BCLC 480).

In addition to a remedy from the court there remains a broad power of the Department of Trade and Industry to investigate where there is some cause of disquiet. This has led to a significant increase in publicity and the number of legal actions which have followed.

17.7 SHARE CAPITAL

The memorandum of association for a company with a share capital must declare the amount of share capital it proposes to be registered and the division of that share capital into shares of fixed amounts. For example this provision in the memorandum may state that a company's share capital shall be £1,000 divided into 1,000 ordinary shares of £1 each. The level of authorised share capital tends to be a formality and its purpose really is to prescribe the maximum number of shares which a company is able to issue without first increasing its authorised share capital. It also indicates the nominal value which it has chosen to place on shares into which the share capital is divided. In order to increase authorised share capital the company merely has to pass an ordinary resolution in general meeting. This, together with a Form 123, is then filed with the Registrar within 15 days of the passing of such resolution.

17.7.1 Issued share capital

The general rule is that shares must not be issued at a discount of a nominal par value (eg £1 shares must be issued at not less than £1). Payment does not necessarily need to be in cash; it can be made in kind and the party's valuation of non-cash consideration is usually accepted as conclusive unless the inadequacy appears on the face of a transaction or there is bad faith. Private companies are, however, required under CA 1985, s 88 to complete a return of allotment form (Form 88) reporting upon how many shares are issued and for what consideration.

There are stricter rules regarding non-cash consideration for public companies. A plc may not accept an undertaking by a person that he will work or perform services for a company in payment for shares; there are other similar rules set out in CA 1985, s 99. Further, under s 103, a plc may not allot shares as fully or partly paid up unless certain circumstances exist:

(a) the consideration needs to be valued;
(b) a report needs to be prepared for the company during the six months preceding such allotment; and
(c) a copy should be sent of this report to the proposed 'purchaser'.

17.7.2 Reductions of capital

The general rule is that a company's capital cannot be reduced without a court order being sought. Under CA 1985, s 135 a company may, if authorised by its articles, reduce its share capital so long as it has obtained court confirmation under ss 136–138. The procedure is as follows:

(1) It must pass a special resolution to reduce its share capital either by reducing or extinguishing an amount of uncalled liability on shares or cancelling any paid-up share capital which it 'lost or unrepresented by available assets', or by paying off any paid-up share capital which is in excess of the company's wants. It needs to alter reference in its memorandum of association to its share capital etc.

(2) After passing such resolution the company needs to apply to court to confirm the resolution. The court will be concerned to ensure that all creditors have been notified and given an opportunity to object. Once a court is satisfied that every existing creditor has consented or that his debt or claim has been discharged or secured, it will then make an order confirming the reduction on such terms as it sees fit.
(3) If any creditor has been overlooked or is ignorant of a reduction proceeding and the company goes into insolvent liquidation the court on the application of that creditor may order members whose uncalled liability has been reduced to contribute as if it had not been to the extent necessary to pay off the creditor.

In practice this procedure is rarely used since most companies use Companies Act procedures for the purchase of its own shares.

Just because the net asset may fall below a company's capital it does not necessarily indicate that it must cease trading. The usual effect is that the company is not able to pay dividends. In the case of a plc CA 1985, s 142 states that if net assets become half or less of its called-up share capital it must within 28 days of such becoming known to a director convene an EGM for not later than 56 days thereafter (of it becoming known) to consider what steps should be taken to deal with this problem.

17.7.3 Acquisition of own shares

Traditionally even if there was an express provision in the memorandum it has been held that a company cannot purchase its own shares since this results in a reduction of share capital. This general rule has been eroded by practical necessity over a number of years and in CAs 1980 and 1981 it was formally codified. This is now incorporated in ss 143–181 of the 1985 Act.

The general rule states that a company 'shall not acquire its own shares whether by purchase, subscription or otherwise'. Violation of it renders every officer and company liable to a fine and any purchase carried out is void. There are fives exceptions:

(a) where fully paid shares are acquired otherwise than for valuable consideration, eg where the shares were given to the company and held by a nominee for it (as was the case in *Re Castiglione's Will Trusts, Hunter v MacKenzie* [1958] Ch 549);
(b) the redemption or purchase of shares in accordance with CA 1985, ss 159–181 (see below);
(c) the acquisition of shares on a formal reduction of capital that has been confirmed by the court (see 17.7.2 above);

(d) the purchase of shares as a result of an order of court;
(e) where shares have been forfeited due to non-payment.

17.7.4 Redeemable shares

Companies have been allowed to issue redeemable shares since CA 1929. Prior to CA 1981 only preference shares could be issued as redeemable but under CA 1985, s 159 a company (if authorised by its articles) can issue shares of any class which can be redeemable or liable to be redeemed whether at the option of the company or of the shareholders. A company cannot just issue redeemable shares, but must also issue shares which are not redeemable. It also may not redeem shares until they are have been fully paid by the holders of the redeemable shares.

Normally redeemable shares can only be redeemed out of distributable profits or out of the proceeds of a fresh issue of shares made for that particular purpose. If any premium is payable this should also be made out of distributable profits.

Where shares are redeemed out of profits the amount by which the issued share capital is diminished should be transferred to a reserve called the 'capital redemption reserve' (or the proportion if partly paid out of proceeds).

17.7.5 Purchase of own shares

Up to CA 1981 a company had to issue preference shares to enable it to purchase its own shares (or required a court order).

A listed company cannot make a purchase of its own shares unless under CA 1985, s 166 it has first been authorised by the passing of an ordinary resolution. The resolution when passed needs to be filed at Companies House within 15 days. The authorisation may be a general one or limited to a class of shares and may if the company wishes be conditional. It must however state the maximum number of shares to be acquired and the maximum and minimum prices and give a date on which it expires (not later than 18 months after passing the resolution). There are various other safeguards set out in CA 1985, ss 164–169.

The situation with private companies is more straightforward and is now contained in CA 1985, ss 171–177. If the company is authorised by articles it can make a payment for the redemption or purchase of shares otherwise than out of distributable profits or the proceeds of a fresh issue of shares. It must not though exceed 'the permissible capital payment' – the amount by which available profits exceed the proceeds of any fresh issue made for the purposes of redemption. If the principal capital payment is less than the nominal value of shares redeemed or purchased the amount of the difference must be transferred to a capital redemption reserve, but if more the amount of issued share capital and undistributable reserves can be reduced by a sum not exceeding the extent of such excess.

'Available profits' is defined in CA 1985 as being those that are available for distribution under the dividend rules (see 17.8 below) and must be calculated in accordance with the usual accounting procedures used by the company's auditors. The following steps must be carried out:

(1) The directors need to make a statutory declaration in the prescribed form (Company Form 173). This needs to contain the following information:
    (a) amount of permissible capital payment;
    (b) confirmation that the directors have enquired into the affairs and prospects of the company;
    (c) it is their opinion that 'immediately following payment there will be no grounds on which the company could be found unable to pay its debt and . . . for the year following the company will be able to continue to carry on business as a going concern and to pay its debts as they fall due throughout that year'.
(2) The declaration needs to have attached to it a report by the company's auditors confirming they have enquired into the company's business and the amount stated as permissible capital payment has been properly ascertained and they are not aware of anything in the directors' statement which is 'unreasonable'.
(3) The capital payment needs to be authorised by special resolution (or one in writing) and should be passed on all within the week immediately following the making of a statutory declaration and the payment of capital must be made no earlier than five nor more than seven weeks after the date of such resolution.

There are also similar statutory protections required for public companies, eg:

(a) a member of the company whose shares are to be redeemed or bought cannot vote (if he does the resolution will be ineffective if it would not have passed without his vote);
(b) the statutory declaration and auditor's report must be available for inspection by members at the meeting;
(c) within a week of a resolution a notice must be published in the *Gazette* and also an 'appropriate national newspaper' (unless it has notified all creditors in writing); the notice must give full details of a resolution and state the creditors may within five weeks of the resolution apply to court under CA 1985, s 176 for an order prohibiting payment;

(d) on or prior to the notice's publication, the company needs to send to the Registrar the completed Form 173 and also the auditor's report (copies must also be available at the company's registered office for inspection by any member or creditor).

A member (who has not consented or voted for the resolution) and creditor may not later than five weeks after the passing of the resolution apply under s 176 to the court for cancellation. The court has wide powers under s 177 to cancel, confirm or make such an order as it thinks fit for the purchase of dissenting members' shares.

17.7.6 Financial assistance by company for purchase of own shares

Section 54 of CA 1948 became notoriously difficult to operate and the 1981 Act sought to clarify the position. The new provisions are found in CA 1985, ss 151–158. The general rule is that where a person is acquiring or proposing to acquire shares in a company it is unlawful for a company or any of its subsidiaries to give 'financial assistance directly or indirectly for the purpose of that acquisition before or at the same time as the acquisition takes place'. Financial assistance can also take the form of acquiring a liability which directly or indirectly gives financial assistance (eg gifts, loans, guarantees, waivers, indemnities etc). The definition of 'financial assistance' is very broadly worded and even if a form of financial assistance does not expressly fall within the provision it may nevertheless be unlawful if a company has no net assets or the consequence of assistance is to reduce its net assets. This section gives a particularly wide definition to the word 'liability' and seems to suggest that before a company can give any financial assistance to any person (whether or not a potential 'purchaser') it must assess that person's overall financial position before and after the acquisition and if afterwards it has deteriorated the company must refrain from any form of financial assistance which is not covered by one of the exceptions.

17.7.7 Exceptions

Section 153 sets out a number of exceptions and these include:

(a) bonus shares;
(b) lending money in the ordinary course of business;
(c) contributions to employee share schemes (public companies have an additional net asset test in this case); and
(d) lawful declaration of a dividend.

A complication exists under s 153 since it does not prohibit a company from giving financial assistance if:

(a) the company's principal purpose in giving that assistance is not for the purpose of acquisition of shares of a company or its holding company but is an incidental part of some larger purpose of a company; and
(b) the assistance is given in good faith in the company's interests.

The House of Lords has considered this wording in the important case of *Brady v Brady* [1989] AC 755 which has narrowly interpreted this wording. Advice should always be sought if seeking to fall within this exception.

Special relaxation provisions apply to private companies under CA 1985, ss 155–158. The underlying principle is that financial assistance can only be given if a company has net assets which are not thereby reduced or to the extent they are reduced assistance is provided out of distributable profits (s 155). The relaxation can only be used by genuine independent private companies (ie those not members of a group where there is a plc). The procedure is as follows.

The relevant company giving financial assistance needs to make a statutory declaration similar in terms to the one referred to at 17.7.5 above for the purchase of shares. This declaration must identify to whom the assistance is to be given and must confirm in their opinion that immediately following such assistance there are no grounds on which a company can be found unable to pay its debt and that this will apply during the preceding 12-month period or if wound up in this period it could pay its debts in full.

The declaration must have attached to it an auditors' report stating in effect that they are not aware of anything unreasonable in the circumstances in the directors' opinion.

A special (or written) resolution needs to be passed by the company giving assistance (and in the case of a subsidiary giving financial assistance to a holding company the holding company also needs to pass a special resolution). The special resolutions must be passed on or within a week of the day on which the directors make the statutory declarations and are not effective unless the declaration and auditors' reports are available for inspection by the members at the meeting.

A copy of a statutory declaration (on Company Form G155(6)(a)) and the auditors' report needs to be delivered to the Registrar within 15 days of the declaration and must be accompanied by copies of a special resolution.

Financial assistance must not be given before the expiration of four weeks beginning the date upon which the resolution was passed (or if more than one on the date of the last such resolution). This enables any member not consenting or voting in favour of the resolution to apply to court to cancel the resolution under s 157. If an application is made financial assistance must not be given until the court has given a ruling.

The financial assistance provided for must be given not later than eight weeks from the date of statutory declaration. If all members voted in favour of the resolution the assistance may be given immediately after the delivery to the Registrar of the statutory declaration and report, but must not be given after eight weeks from that date.

Application to court under s 157 needs to be made by holders of not less than 10 per cent of the company's issued share capital or if a company has no share capital by 10 per cent of the members. The court has similar rights as set out above in connection with purchase of such shares for determining the position.

17.8 DIVIDENDS

An underlying principle of company law is that the company subscribed money capital (ie issued share capital plus share premium) must be maintained. Dividends should not be paid out except from accumulated realised profits. Sections 263–281 of CA 1985 set out the position. A distribution covers any payment of the company's assets to members which is not a bonus share, a redemption or purchase of the company's own shares, an authorised reduction of share capital, or a distribution and winding-up. Distributions can only be made out of profits made available for that purpose.

The company's profits available for distribution can be summarised as being the accumulated realised profits (not already distributed or capitalised) less its accumulated realised losses not written off under the capital reduction provisions. This realised profits test applies to all companies. In addition a plc is subject to a net assets test. Thus even if it has realised profit it can only make a distribution if its net assets are less than the aggregate of its called-up share capital and its undistributable reserves and also the proposed distribution will not reduce the amount of the assets to less than that aggregate.

Net assets for this purpose is defined as being the aggregate of its assets less the aggregate of its liabilities (uncalled share capital cannot be used as an asset for determination). Special rules regarding distribution apply to companies in various particular industries (eg investment companies and insurance companies).

A shareholder who receives a distribution he knows or has reasonable grounds to believe was paid in breach of the rules must repay any amount received by the company in addition to any other liability he may have. Further a director who is knowingly a party to such payments is jointly and severally liable to the company to replace the amounts of dividends so paid with interest (ratification to bind the company is not possible). The director would however be entitled to be indemnified by each shareholder who received dividends knowing they have been paid out of capital to the extent such dividends have been received.

The procedure for declaring dividends is relatively straightforward. The articles normally provide for it. Regulation 102 of Table A states that a company is made by ordinary resolution to declare dividends, but no dividends should exceed the amount recommended by directors. It is at the AGM that a final dividend is normally declared, but an interim dividend can be paid at any date between AGMs. Article 103 of Table A states that directors may pay interim dividends if it appears to them to be justified by the profits of the company available for distribution, but must act in good faith and not incur any liability to the holders of shares conferring preferred rights etc.

The director of a company needs to carefully consider a company's assets before recommending a dividend. A declaration of dividend creates a contract to pay a debt which would have become statute barred after six years from the date of declaration. Whether a company is able to forfeit the amount held after this period depends on its articles; for example, reg 108 of Table A states that it must be unclaimed for 12 years before a dividend can be forfeited.

The articles usually also provide that dividends payable in cash can be sent by cheque through the post to a shareholder's registered address (or such other address as the shareholder may notify the company).

17.9 ULTRA VIRES

This used to be an area of some complication, but since the passing of CA 1989 the position has been simplified. The words 'ultra vires' in relation to company law are largely used to explain a situation which arises when a company's officers or employees act beyond their legal power. There are two principle elements of this rule:

(a) where the directors, officers or employees act outside their power, eg purport to bind the company when they have no authority so to do; and

(b) when the company acts beyond its objects, ie does an act which the objects clause of its memorandum of association does not extend.

The effect of the new provisions in CA 1985 (ss 35A and 35B, as inserted by CA 1989, s 108(1)) is that an innocent third party is entitled to rely upon the board of directors or a person authorised by the board and that the transaction agreed and enforceable in the normal way binds the company.

The difficulty that remains is that where a company, for example, is very small or a transaction is large a third party may have no dealings with the board and may instead be dealing with an executive of the company or a junior employee. In these circumstances the third party is unlikely to know whether the transaction has actually been authorised by the board. In this circumstance it is necessary to look at the laws of agency as interpreted by the celebrated legal case of *Royal British Bank v Turquand* (1856) 6 E&B 327. This case enunciated the rule that when a person conducts a company's affairs, in a manner which seems perfectly normal, the third parties dealing with them are not to be affected by any irregularities which may take place in the internal management of the company.

Section 285 of CA 1985 also states that the acts of a director or manager are valid irrespective of any defect which may be discovered afterwards in that director or manager's appointment or qualification.

It is unlikely that a person dealing with a company is deemed to have notice of who the true directors are, but if that third party is actually aware of the potential ultra vires problem he would no longer be said to be acting in good faith and therefore probably not be able to rely on either s 35A or 35B or the common law position. The new legislation does not though protect a third party dealing with the company through an unauthorised officer. In this circumstance the company is only bound if an unauthorised officer acts within his actual or apparent authority or the company ratifies what he has done.

Case law has recognised that where managerial powers have been delegated by the board to other officers their acts can be regarded as binding the company.

17.10 AUDITORS

Every company other than a dormant one needs to appoint an auditor. The appointment is done at each general meeting at which the accounts and reports are laid and the appointment must be from the conclusion of that meeting until conclusion of the next such meeting (this would not be the case where a private company has elected to dispense with the laying of accounts). It is to the members of the company that the auditors' report is addressed. Normally an auditor continues to be reappointed until he wishes to retire or the directors wish to appoint someone different.

For private companies which have elected to dispense with the laying of accounts, the appointment of auditors needs to be dealt with within 28 days after the date copies of the accounts are sent to members. If a private company has, by elective resolution, dispensed with the obligation to appoint auditors annually, the auditors are deemed to have been appointed for each succeeding financial year until a resolution is passed ending this appointment.

An auditor has a statutory right of access at all times to the company's books, accounts and vouchers and can require from the company's officers such explanation as he thinks necessary for the performance of his duties as auditor. In addition he is entitled to receive all notices and other communications concerning general meetings and to be heard with respect to business which concerns him.

A company can by ordinary resolution remove an auditor from office irrespective of any agreement it may have with him but such a resolution requires special notice to be given to the company of a resolution and copies have to be given to the auditor and to the person to be appointed in his place. The auditor is also entitled to make written representation and may have rights to compensation.

Under CA 1985, s 392 an auditor may resign at any stage by depositing a notice in writing to the effect at the company's registered office. This must be accompanied by a statement providing the reasons why he wishes to resign and should contain any details he feels should be brought before the members or creditors. The company must then within 14 days send copies of it to any person who is entitled to be sent copies of the accounts. The company has the right if it wishes to apply to court, but must in these circumstances notify the auditor. Where no court application is made the auditor must send a copy of the statement to the Registrar within 21 days.

17.10.1 Auditor's negligence

It is primarily the directors who are responsible for the published accounts but an auditor can be shown to be negligent in certifying the accuracy. Auditors are required to display care and skill expected from such professionals and this has led in recent years to numerous well publicised cases. The House of Lords in *Caparo Industries plc v Dickman* [1990] 2 AC 605 established:

(a) the general responsibility for preparation of accounts which should give a true and fair view of the company's position rests on the directors' shoulders;
(b) the auditors provide independent reports to members on the proper preparation of the balance sheet and profit and loss account and as to whether these documents give a true and fair view (ie their role is investigative rather than creative);
(c) auditors have a duty to obtain information from directors and officers and failure to so obtain could amount to negligence.

17.11 WORK PERMITS

17.11.1 Introduction

Decisions upon immigration are referred to the Home Office, but the position concerning work permits vests with the Department for Education and Employment (DfEE). If DfEE refuses to grant the permit there is no formal appeal against this decision (other than possibly requiring a judicial review of such decision where appropriate).

An EU citizen is permitted to enter the United Kingdom without first obtaining leave of the Home Office as this is guaranteed by the Treaty of Rome (see further EC Council Regulation 1612/68 and various directives under the Treaty). If a non-EU citizen is employed by an entity from a member state and that entity is carrying out a project in the United Kingdom it is probably also sufficient.

The rules regarding the issue of work permits are contained in parts 5 and 6 of the Immigration Rules HC395 (statement of changes in Immigration Rules). If a person requires a work permit under rule 128 he must also:

(a) 'not be of an age which puts him outside the limits of employment';
(b) be 'capable of undertaking the employment specified on the work permit';
(c) 'not intend to take employment except as specified in his work permit';
(d) be 'able to maintain and accommodate himself and any dependants adequately without recourse to public funds';
(e) if the work permit is for 12 months or less show an intention to leave the UK at the end of the approved employment.

A maximum period of time a person can remain within the United Kingdom is four years (but this can be renewed).

There are special categories and considerations applicable to post-graduate doctors and dentists, working holidaymakers, seamen, seasonal workers at agricultural camps, training and work experience persons, representatives of newspapers, journalists, news agencies and broadcasting organisations etc, sole representatives of foreign firms, diplomats and their servants, ministers of religion, overseas government employees, airport operational ground staff or for an airline.

17.11.2 DfEE requirements

Initially a potential employer must fill out a Form WP1 which should be filed as promptly as possible. An application should be made within six months before the relevant employee is required in the UK or in the case of renewal within three months before a leave expires.

Normally permits are restricted to posts requiring degree level or professional qualifications (normally with a minimum of two years' post-qualification experience). When a work permit has been issued it is the employer who becomes responsible for paying the employee and ensuring the correct tax and NIC is dealt with. An employer is required to ensure that the terms and conditions relating to such employment are equal to those UK employees doing a similar job.

17.11.3 Form WP1

This is divided into two parts. In the case of senior positions only the first part requires to be completed (eg a senior post in an international company with respect to an existing overseas employee, a board level appointment where there is no suitable alternative candidate, a post essential to investment creating jobs and capital in the UK or those occupations where there is an acute shortage nationally). This part of the form requires the following details to be included:

(a) name of proposed employer (within the UK) and proposed employee;
(b) details of job offered, period required for work permit, duties of the job and details of pay and working hours;
(c) employee's qualifications and employment record; and
(d) reasons for recruiting outside the EU and evidence which shows that there is no suitable candidate within the EU (eg details of recruitment methods, adverts etc).

Part 2 of the form needs to be completed for any other category. For such people the test is more exacting:

(1) Evidence must be shown that the need to recruit outside the EU cannot be extinguished by training an existing employee or transfer from within the EU and that the job cannot be filled by an EU worker.

(2) For key workers (ie those having technical specialist skills, knowledge or experience not readily available in the EU) evidence needs to be shown of what makes him uniquely qualified to do the job, how the business's success depends upon such recruitment and why such unique skills are essential for the job.

Employers need to supply:

(a) proof of the relevant applicant's qualification together with original references taken over the preceding two years;
(b) copies of all advertisements;
(c) if the person is in the UK and not in approved employment, his passport, the application, a copy of the employer's audited accounts and the latest annual report (this is unnecessary if an application has been made within the preceding four-year period).

With reference to the advertisement, it needs to specify the nature of the post and should have been advertised within the last six months before the application was made in a quality newspaper with national or EU circulation or alternatively in trade journals. In the case of key worker posts suitable adverts should also have been placed in each EU country.

17.11.4 Extending a work permit

This is available so long as the work permit has not lapsed and the applicant can show that his own circumstances have not changed to take him outside the requirements of rule 128 (see 17.11.1 above) and that he has the DfEE's permission to remain in employment. If the Secretary of State is not satisfied that this exists he may refuse to renew the permit.

Under rule 134 a work permit holder may stay in the UK indefinitely if he has spent a continuous period of four years there with a work permit and has complied with all requirements throughout this period and he is still required for the relevant employment. All applications for extension of work permits should be made on a Form WP5 and the applicant's passport needs to be sent in at the same time as the application is made. An application should not be made earlier than three months before the permit expires but must be made before it does so.

Indefinite leave to remain is not automatic and must be applied for after four years' continuous service. The required criteria enabling the employer to obtain a work permit for that employee must continue to exist.

17.11.5 Sole representatives

The provisions in the rules are aimed at overseas companies with no UK branch or subsidiary and which wish to appoint a sole representative there. Such an employee must:

(a) have been recruited and taken on as an employee outside the UK as a representative of the firm which has its headquarters and principal place of business outside the UK and has no branch, subsidiary or other representative there;
(b) have full authority to make operational decisions on behalf of the overseas company and establish and operate a registered branch or wholly owned subsidiary in the UK;
(c) be engaged full time in this capacity and not be a majority shareholder of that company; and
(d) maintain and accommodate himself independently and adequately without recourse to public funds and hold a valid UK entry clearance in this capacity.

The period normally granted is not more than 12 months, but this can be extended if the same conditions still apply. Any such extension can be up to three years and after four years have been completed then indefinite leave can be applied for (see 17.11.4 above). In making an application, information concerning the following must be supplied:

(a) the time and effort the representative puts into his business;
(b) what has been achieved and what can be expected to be achieved by him; and
(c) the role he plays in the overall commercial activity of the company he represents.

To show a good case the sole representative must show that there is continuous time and effort in acting for the overseas company and that his role is more than that of just a distributor or sales agent. In particular he must have authority to take operational decisions.

There are special rules applying to those people wishing to enter or remain in the UK as independent businessmen or self-employed people, investors, and creative artists; the first two categories are dealt with here.

17.11.6 Businessmen and self-employed persons

The rules require that a person intending to establish a new business must show that he will:

(a) be bringing to the country sufficient funds of his own to establish that business, and

(b) create full-time employment for at least two people already settled in the UK (rule 203).

In addition he must provide a written statement of terms under which he is to take over or join the business, audit accounts for the business in previous years and evidence that the business will result in the increase of employment as already mentioned.

Finance

The businessman is required to have no less than £200,000 of his own money under his control and disposable within the UK (this must be held in his own name and not in the form of a trust or other investment vehicle but does not need to be lodged with a UK financial institution) and he must show that he will be investing this in his business. The business must produce sufficient funds to maintain and accommodate him and any of his dependants without recourse to employment (other than his work for the business) or public funds. He must show that he is actively involved full time in the promotion and management of the business. Rule 201 contains a number of other rules of importance:

(1) His financial investment should be proportional to the interest in the business.
(2) He must have either controlling or equal interest in the business and any partnership or directorship must not amount to disguised employment.
(3) He must bear his share of liabilities.
(4) There must be a genuine need for his investment and services in the UK.
(5) He must not need to supplement his business activities by taking or seeking employment within the UK other than for work in the business concerned.
(6) He must hold a valid UK entry clearance.

Under rule 204 the DfEE has a discretion to grant permission for a person to enter the UK for up to 12 months if he is trying to establish a business on the basis that he does not take employment. The rules provide a definition of the word 'business' as being an enterprise involving a sole trader, partnership or company registered in the UK. Before trying to obtain entry in the UK an applicant must have an entry clearance. The rules' intention is that the applicant should be the controller of a business and not a sham or substitute for someone else. The business should not result in disguised employment for the individual. In one case (*Pritpol Singh* [1972] Imm AR 154) an individual received no share of profits, could be removed from the board at any time and received a salary. It was held that the arrangement was a sham and in reality the individual was an employee.

In the case of family money there needs to be an unfettered control and an ability to dispose of it in such manner as the applicant decides. In particular it has been established that an applicant cannot set up a business on borrowed money over which he has no control or ability to service a loan and the provisions are not satisfied where an applicant merely inherits a business worth in excess of £200,000 which is already established in the UK. Money invested in a freehold property may be difficult to sell and may be able to be used for other purposes so is not acceptable under this head. The rule is that the money must be immediately available for investment and the Home Office normally expects money to be invested within 12 months of admission. Where a business incurs liabilities in the ordinary course, the individual must be able to meet these.

Where a person is taking over or joining an existing business audited accounts for the business for the previous years and evidence that his services and investment will result in an increase of employment by at least two full-time employees need to be shown. The showing of accounts and employment of employees is mandatory and the mere creation of self-employment is not sufficient (*Seyed v Secretary of State for the Home Department* [1987] Imm AR 303, IAT). The evidence required to be given is the employment as a result of the investment.

A person intending to establish a new business in the UK must show that he is bringing sufficient monies of his own into this country to do so and that that investment will create at least two full-time jobs. There are various concessions relating to particular categories of people (for example lawyers, barristers and consultants in overseas law practices coming to England do not need to invest £200,000 provided he/they can show a bona fide purpose etc).

Entrance into the UK is normally limited to a comparatively short period of time (eg one year), but extensions are available. Normally, in order to justify an extension there must be evidence that investment has been made and employees engaged and that the requirements referred to above have all been satisfied. Where extensions have been granted which in some cases exceed four continuous years a person may apply for permanent settlement.

For nationals of Poland and Hungary there are EC association agreements which facilitate the establishment of a business.

17.11.7 The investor

Where an investor wishes to enter the UK he must show that he:

(a) has under his control and disposable within the UK an amount of no less than £1m;

(b) intends to invest not less than £750,000 of his capital within the UK by the purchase of UK bonds, share capital or loan capital in active and trading UK registered companies (excluding property investment and the investment by the applicant in bank or building society deposits, etc);
(c) wants to make the UK his main home;
(d) can maintain and accommodate himself, his dependants, etc without recourse to employment or public funds; and
(e) holds UK entry clearance.

Normally an investor is allowed to enter the UK for a period up to 12 months provided he can satisfy the above requirements. So long as those requirements remain constant he is able to apply for an extension and for indefinite leave to remain after he has spent a continuous period of four years there.

17.12 SELECTION OF ADMINISTRATIVE DOCUMENTS TO BE FILED AT COMPANIES HOUSE

17.12.1 Formation

(1) Copy of memorandum and articles of association
(2) Form G10 – Statement of first directors and secretary and intended situation of registered office.
(3) Form G12 – Statutory declaration of compliance with requirements on application for registration of a company (to be completed by the solicitors engaged in the company formation).

17.12.2 Capital

(1) Form 88(2) – Return of allotment of shares for cash. To be filed within one month of making the allotment.
(2) Form 88(3) – Return of allotment of shares for non-cash consideration. To be filed within one month of making the allotment.
(3) Form 123 – Increase of share capital. Filed within 15 days after passing resolution. Resolution should also be filed.

17.12.3 Directors or secretary

Form 288 – Change of directors or secretary. Notification to be given within 14 days. (Notification of interests and changes of interest in shares or debentures is to be made by the director to the company within five working days of the event.)

17.12.4 Notice of accounting reference date

(1) Form G224 – Names an accounting reference date to which statutory accounts are to be prepared. A company has nine months from the date of incorporation to file such a form.
(2) Form G225(2) – New account reference date given after the end of an accounting reference period by a parent or subsidiary undertaking or by a company subject to an administration order.

17.12.5 Annual return

Every company is required to deliver to the Registrar of Companies successive annual returns, each of which is made up to a date which is not later than the company's 'return date', that is:

(a) the anniversary of the company's incorporation; *or*
(b) if the last return lodged by the company was made up to a different date, the anniversary of that date.

The annual return must be lodged within 28 days after the date to which it is made up.

17.12.6 Registered office

Form 287 – a company can change its registered office by filing this form.

17.12.7 Charges, mortgages and debentures

(1) Form 395 – notification of particulars or charges created by a company. Filed within 21 days after the date of their creation and the relative instrument creating the charge must also be produced.
(2) Form 397 – particulars for the registration of a charge to secure a series of debentures.
(3) Form 400 – particulars of a mortgage or charge subject to which property has been acquired.
(4) Form 403a – declaration of satisfaction when a charge has been wholly or partially redeemed.
(5) Form 403b – declaration of satisfaction where the declaration relates to release of part of property or undertaking from the charge; or where the part of the property or undertaking charged no longer forms part of the company's property or undertaking.

17.12.8 Resolutions

Copies of the following types of resolution must be filed within 15 days of their being passed:

(1) Special/Extraordinary.
(2) Elective.
(3) Ordinary:
  (a) authorising increase of capital;
  (b) giving, varying, revoking or renewing an authority to allot;
  (c) shares under s 80;
  (d) revoking an elective resolution.
(4) Resolution for winding up voluntarily under the Insolvency Act 1986, s 84(3).

18

HOW COMPANIES ARE TAXED

This chapter looks at the taxation of companies under the following headings:

(1) Liability for corporation tax and how 'profits' are defined
(2) Accounting periods, rates and payment of tax
(3) Companies' capital gains
(4) Interest and other charges
(5) Dividends and advance corporation tax
(6) Losses
(7) Groups of companies
(8) Close and investment companies
(9) Double taxation relief on foreign income
(10) Controlled foreign companies and anti-avoidance legislation
(11) Forex transactions
(12) 'Pay and file'
(13) Claims and elections.

18.1 LIABILITY FOR CORPORATION TAX AND HOW 'PROFITS' ARE DEFINED

18.1.1 Liability for corporation tax

(TA 1988, ss 11 and 12 ; FA 1988, s 66)

Corporation tax is levied on the chargeable profits (see 18.1.2 below) of companies which are resident in the UK for tax purposes. A company is generally defined as meaning any body corporate or unincorporated association, but does not include a partnership, a local authority or a local authority association. The definition also extends to authorised unit trusts, the detailed provisions for which are set out in TA 1988, s 468.

Corporation tax also extends to non-resident companies carrying on a trade in the UK through a branch or agency. Such companies are chargeable to tax on any income attributable to the branch or agency and on any capital gains arising on the disposal of assets used in the UK for the purposes of the branch or agency.

A company which was incorporated in the UK is regarded as resident there regardless of where the directors exercise their management and control. However, some of the double taxation conventions negotiated with other countries override this in practice and treat a dual resident company as if it were not resident in the UK. A company which was incorporated overseas may still be regarded as UK-resident on the basis that its central management and control is exercised in this country. Questions relating to the residence status of a foreign incorporated company are usually determined by reference to the guidelines set out in SP1/90.

18.1.2 Computation of profits

(TA 1988, s 6)

A company's profits are made up of its income and chargeable gains. The computation of chargeable profits can be a very complex process because of the lengthy and detailed tax legislation and the extensive case-law. There are also a multitude of Revenue statements of practice, press releases and extra-statutory concessions which may need to be borne in mind when calculating profits upon which corporation tax is payable.

The general principles for computing taxable profits closely follow the rules for income tax and each different type of income is charged under the relevant schedule.

18.1.3 Capital allowances

(CAA 1990, s 144)

Although depreciation is not regarded as an allowable expense for tax purposes, tax relief is given for expenditure on qualifying capital assets by means of capital allowances. The principles follow very closely those which apply in the case of individuals (see 2.2) and therefore the main provisions are not covered in detail here. Capital allowances in respect of a trade carried on by a company are regarded as trading expenses for the accounting period in which they arise. They are therefore taken into account in arriving at the chargeable profits or allowable loss for the accounting period.

Capital allowances on non-trading activities are primarily deductible from the income arising from that source. Thus, if an industrial building or an enterprise zone property is acquired as an investment, the industrial buildings allowances are set first against any rental income from such properties. Any surplus allowances may be carried forward against similar source income arising in later accounting periods or deducted from any chargeable profits for the accounting period in which they arise, or the preceding accounting period. If the entitlement to allowances arises in a period of less than 12 months, the carry-back is limited to profits of a similar period. Thus if the surplus allowance arises in a three-month accounting period, the carry-back is restricted to $^{3}/_{12}$ of the profits of the preceding year.

Where capital allowances are given against chargeable profits, the allowances are deducted from profits before annual charges (see 18.1.4 and 18.4.2).

18.1.4 Interest and other annual payments
(TA 1988, s 338)

Unlike individuals, a company is liable to account to the Revenue for income tax on certain annual payments which it makes. Such annual payments (termed 'charges on income') are deductible from a company's profits in arriving at the amount assessable to corporation tax. The basic principle is that these charges on income are offset against the payer's total profits, not merely against a particular source of income with which the payment is connected. A payment counts as a charge on income only if the following conditions are met:

(1) It has been made out of the company's profits brought into charge to corporation tax.
(2) It is made under a liability incurred for a 'valuable and sufficient consideration' (or the payment is a covenanted donation to charity).
(3) The payment must not be one charged to capital or one not ultimately borne by the company.
(4) It must not be in the nature of a dividend or distribution made by the company.

Payment must actually be made in the accounting period for it to count as a charge for that period. Where there is a requirement to deduct and account for income tax on the payment, no deduction is allowed until this requirement is satisfied.

Where the total profits for an accounting period are insufficient to absorb charges on income, excess charges in respect of payments made wholly and exclusively for the purposes of the company's trade may be carried forward and utilised against the company's future trading income. Non-trade charges may not be carried forward in this manner and no further relief is available.

18.2 ACCOUNTING PERIODS, RATES AND PAYMENT OF TAX

18.2.1 Accounting periods for tax purposes
(TA 1988, s 12)

Companies pay corporation tax by reference to their accounting periods and the income included is assessed on an actual or accruals basis rather than the preceding year basis which often applies for income tax purposes. Accounting periods may straddle two financial years (which for corporation tax purposes run from 1 April to 31 March). If this is the case, the chargeable profits are apportioned on a time basis for the purposes of determining the rate of tax to apply to the overall profit. An accounting period begins for corporation tax purposes:

(1) when the company comes within the charge to corporation tax either by becoming resident in the UK or acquiring its first source of income; or
(2) when the company's previous accounting period ends without the company ceasing to be within the charge to corporation tax.

An accounting period normally runs on for a maximum of 12 months from its commencement. In some instances, the accounts year end may vary slightly for commercial reasons (for example where accounts are made up to the last Friday of a specified month). Provided the variation is not more than four days from the 'mean' date it is normally acceptable to treat each period of account as if it were a 12-month accounting period ending on the mean date.

An accounting period runs for a period of less than 12 months if the company's own accounting date falls within the 12 months; it also ends if any of the following occurs:

(a) the company ceases to trade;
(b) the company begins or ceases to be resident in the UK; or
(c) the company ceases to be within the charge to corporation tax altogether.

18.2.2 Example of how accounting period is ascertained

A Ltd is formed on 1 January 1997. It remains completely dormant until 1 February 1997 when it starts to trade. The first set of accounts are made up for a period of 15 months ending on 31 March 1998.

In strictness, there is a first accounting period of one month from 1 January to 31 January 1997. There is then a 12-month accounting period for the year ending on 31 January 1998. There is then a two-month period from 1 February to 31 March 1998 when the company makes up its accounts.

18.2.3 How profits are apportioned

Where accounts are made up for a period of more than 12 months, the income is usually apportioned on a time basis to the relevant accounting period. Thus, in the above example, if A Ltd had profits of £140,000 in its accounts for the 15 months ending on 31 March 1996, these would normally be apportioned as follows:

Accounting period ended 31 January 1997	Nil
12 months ended 31 January 1998	£120,000
Period 1 February–31 March 1998	£20,000

However, where a more appropriate basis of apportionment is available, the inspector may apply that basis instead (*Marshall Hus & Partners Ltd v Bolton* [1981] STC 18).

18.2.4 The corporation tax rates
(TA 1988, s 6)

The rate of corporation tax is fixed for each financial year which, for these purposes, starts on 1 April. The rate of tax for the financial year 1997 (ie, 1 April 1997 to 31 March 1998) is 31 per cent and the following table shows the full corporation tax rate applicable for previous financial years.

Financial year	*Rate (%)*	*Financial year*	*Rate (%)*
1989	35	1994	33
1990	34	1995	33
1991	33	1996	33
1992	33	1997	31
1993	33		

18.2.5 Small companies rates and associated companies
(TA 1988, s 13)

A reduced rate of corporation tax (known as the 'small companies rate') applies to a company's profits where those profits do not exceed a minimum level. The current rate of tax is 25 per cent and the current profit level below which the small companies rate applies is £300,000. The following table shows the small companies rate and maximum profit level for earlier financial years:

Financial year	*Rate (%)*	*Max profit level (£)*
1989	25	150,000
1990	25	200,000
1991	25	250,000
1992	25	250,000
1993	25	250,000
1994	25	300,000
1995	25	300,000
1996	24	300,000
1997	21	300,000

Where profits exceed the maximum profit limit for small companies rate purposes, an element of marginal relief is given for profits between £300,000 and £1,500,000. This relief operates on a tapered basis by charging the profits to the full corporation tax rate but gives an element of credit for the reduced corporation tax rate which would have been applicable to the initial tranche of profit.

18.2.6 Example of marginal small companies rate

B Ltd has profits for its year ended 31 March 1998 of £350,000. Its corporation tax liability is arrived at as follows:

	£
Corporation tax at 31% on £350,000	108,500
Less 1/40 × upper limit (£1,500,000 – 350,000)	28,750
	79,750

If B Ltd's profits were £450,000, the computation would be:

Corporation tax at 31% on £450,000	139,500
Less 1/40 of (£1,500,000 – 450,000)	26,250
	113,250

Thus the additional tax due to B Ltd having an extra £100,000 profits is £33,500 (33.5 per cent). Relief may be restricted if the company has franked investment income (see 18.5.1 below).

18.2.7 Restriction where there is associated company

The profit limits applicable to small companies relief are restricted, based upon the existence of any 'associated' companies which the company has during the accounting period concerned. A company is an associated company of another if they are under common control or one has control of the other. 'Control' for this purpose is defined as the ability to exercise direct or indirect control over the company's affairs and in particular:

(a) the possession or entitlement to acquire more than 50 per cent of the share capital or voting rights in the company;
(b) entitlement to receive the greater part of income distributed among the shareholders;
(c) entitlement to receive the greater part of the company's assets in the event of a winding-up.

For example, if a company has one associated company, the small companies profit limits are divided by two, ie one plus the number of associated companies. However, an associated company which has not carried on any trade or business at any time during the accounting period concerned is disregarded. Where a company's accounting period straddles more than one financial year and the marginal relief limits for each financial year differ, the 12-month period is treated as separate accounting periods for the purpose of calculating marginal relief.

18.2.8 Payment of tax

(TA 1988, s 10)

Under the 'pay and file' rules (see 18.12) corporation tax for an accounting period ending after 30 September 1993 is automatically due and payable nine months from the end of the accounting period.

18.3 COMPANIES' CAPITAL GAINS

18.3.1 Computation of gains

Capital gains made by companies are included in their chargeable profits and are subject to corporation tax. Capital gains tax (CGT) therefore does not apply to companies, although chargeable gains and losses are computed in accordance with the detailed provisions of CGT (see Chapter 3). The main differences between CGT and corporation tax on chargeable gains for companies are, first, that provisions which clearly apply only to individuals (eg annual exemption) have no application as far as companies are concerned, and secondly, that computations of chargeable gains are prepared on an accounting period basis rather than by income tax years of assessment. The total chargeable gains for an accounting period less a deduction for allowable losses are brought into charge to corporation tax in the same way as income.

Capital losses can only be offset against chargeable gains; they cannot be offset against trading or other income.

18.3.2 Roll-over relief

(TCGA 1992, ss 152–158 and 175)

Roll-over relief is available where the proceeds on the disposal of a qualifying asset used in the company's trade are reinvested in further qualifying assets (see 4.3). It provides a deferral of the corporation tax which would otherwise be payable on the chargeable gain. Relief is normally dependent upon the proceeds being fully reinvested in qualifying assets within a period of 12 months before and three years after the date of disposal.

Where the proceeds are only partly reinvested, a proportion of the gain is deferred or 'rolled over' and the balance (equivalent to the amount of proceeds not reinvested) is left in charge. The part of the gain which is deferred or 'rolled over' is deducted from the base cost of the new asset for capital gains purposes. This operates to increase the potential gain on the eventual sale of the new asset acquired, hence the term 'roll-over relief'.

Qualifying assets for this purpose are freehold and leasehold land and buildings, goodwill, ships, aircraft and hovercraft, fixed plant and machinery, satellite space stations and spacecraft, and certain agricultural quotas. Expenditure on an asset acquired from a group company (see 18.7) does not rank as qualifying expenditure for roll-over relief.

18.4 INTEREST AND OTHER CHARGES

18.4.1 Loan relationships

(FA 1996, ss 80–105; Scheds 8–12, 14, 15)

For accounting periods ending after 31 March 1996, a new 'loan relationships' regime has applied. This covers all loans made to a company (eg bank overdrafts, long-term finance etc) and all loans made by a company (eg holdings of gilt-edged securities and corporate bonds). Thus all interest paid or received by a company is brought into account on an accruals basis (so that account is taken of amounts paid in arrears and in advance – this is the normal basis of accounting for these items). Any profits or losses made on loan relationships are treated as income or expenditure on an accruals basis. Certain companies who deal in gilt-edged securities and bonds prepare their accounts on a 'mark to market' basis, and their profit or loss takes account of the market value of securities and bonds held at the beginning and at the end of the accounting period.

Profits or gains made by a company from loan relationships are taxable as trading income, to the extent that the company is a party to the loan relationships in the course of activities which are an integral part of its trade. Losses or deficits are treated as allowable deductions in arriving at the overall profit or loss of the trade. This treatment will generally apply only to financial companies.

In other cases where the loan relationship is for non-trade purposes a surplus is brought into tax under Schedule D Case III. If a deficit is suffered on loan relationships, loss relief can be claimed by:

(1) set-off against profits of the same period;
(2) group relief;
(3) carry-back against loan relationship profits of the preceding accounting period;
(4) carry-forward against non-trading profits of the next following accounting period.

18.4.2 Annual charges

(TA 1988, ss 338–339)

A company may make annual payments in respect of annuities, royalties, covenanted payments etc, which are available for offset as charges on income against the company's chargeable profits on a paid basis.

18.4.3 Income tax deduction at source

Companies must deduct and account to the Revenue for income tax on payments of charges on income. A return Form CT61 is required to be submitted on a quarterly basis detailing payments made and computing the income tax payable to the Revenue. In arriving at the income tax liability due, any income tax suffered on income received under deduction of tax may be offset. Where the income tax suffered on income received exceeds the income tax payable on annual charges, the surplus may be carried forward to the next quarterly return. If at the end of the accounting period it has not proved possible to obtain credit against income tax payable, credit may be obtained against the corporation tax liability for the accounting period (and if there is no or insufficient corporation tax liability to offset any income tax credit, a repayment may be obtained from the Revenue).

18.5 DIVIDENDS AND ADVANCE CORPORATION TAX
(TA 1988, ss 238–241)

18.5.1 Taxation of company distributions

Company distributions are defined as any dividends, and any other distribution out of the company's assets, paid by a company in respect of shares in the company. The main exception to this is that any repayment of share capital is not normally regarded as a distribution of assets. When a company pays a dividend or makes some other qualifying distribution, there is a requirement to account for advance corporation tax (ACT). Most distributions are regarded as qualifying distributions, the main exception being a bonus issue of redeemable share capital.

The current rate of ACT is 20/80 of the dividend, ie 20 per cent of the 'grossed up' amount.

UK recipients of the distribution are entitled to a tax credit corresponding to the rate of ACT paid by the company. This aggregate amount is described as a 'franked' payment and, as far as individuals are concerned, represents the gross equivalent of the dividend received. This amount is taxable income, but the shareholder may set the tax credit against his tax liability on the 'grossed-up' amount.

With effect from 6 April 1999, F(No 2)A 1997, s 30 makes changes to the treatment of dividends and other company distributions. The amount of the tax credit accompanying any dividend or other distribution from a UK company made after 5 April 1999 is to be reduced from 20 per cent of the aggregate of the distribution and the tax credit to 10 per cent thereof. Also from that date, substantially all remaining entitlements to have tax credits paid are withdrawn. The reduction of the rate of tax credit is to be matched by a reduction in the rate of the higher rate income tax charge for individuals.

Under the new rules for tax years 1999–2000 onwards there is no further tax to pay for shareholders liable at the lower or basic rate, and no increase in charge for individuals liable at the higher rate. Similar changes apply to trusts and personal representatives. The overall effect is that the double charge, to corporation tax and then to income tax, is mitigated to the same extent that it currently is.

The reason for this change is that the current system goes further than simply mitigating any double charge to tax. If a person is exempt from tax, or if the tax credits exceed their tax liability, the tax credit can be paid over to them. The payment of tax credits to certain shareholders means that profits paid out by a company can actually face a substantially lower effective tax charge than profits which are retained by the company and reinvested.

The first stage in the correction of this distortion removes the entitlement to payment for pension providers and other UK companies with effect from 2 July 1997. The second stage of the change extends the restrictions on payment and set-off of tax credits to nearly all shareholders with effect from 6 April 1999.

There is one class of shareholders who will still obtain payment of tax credits. Under the terms of some of the UK's double taxation agreements with other countries, specific provision is made, within the agreements, that tax credits can be paid to shareholders resident in that other country. These agreements have effect as long as there is any tax credit made available to UK-resident shareholders, whether that credit is payable or not. The double taxation agreements normally only pay a proportion of the tax credit, so that the effect of the reduction of the rate of tax credit is that the amount of tax credit paid will be very small.

The rates of income tax charged on dividends and similar income will be reduced, with effect from 1999–2000, to 10 per cent, while the rate charged on those who are liable at the higher rate will be reduced to 32.5 per cent.

A new 'Schedule F ordinary rate' applies to certain income of dividends and other distributions of UK companies, and equivalent foreign income. Hitherto savings income has been the top slice of income for the purposes of computing the charge to tax. Under the new rules Schedule F and equivalent foreign income will be treated as the top slice above other savings income. There will also be a new 'Schedule F upper rate' that would otherwise be chargeable at the income tax higher rate. The Schedule F upper rate is set at 32.5 per cent.

Under the new rules, in 1999–2000 on a dividend of £80 there will be a tax credit of £8.89. Taxpayers who are not liable at the higher rate will be charged to tax at the new rate of 10 per cent. So the tax due will be £8.89 (ie the total of the dividend and associated tax credit of £88.89 at 10 per cent). The liability will be matched exactly by the tax credit, leaving no tax to pay. For a higher rate taxpayer receiving a dividend of £80 in 1999–2000 the tax due will be £28.89 (ie the total of the dividend and tax credit of £88.89 at the new upper rate of 32.5 per cent). The tax credit of £8.89 can be set against the tax liability, leaving the higher rate taxpayer with £20 to pay.

Dividends received by a company from another UK company are termed franked investment income. This income is regarded as having already borne tax and does not form part of the chargeable profits of a company. However, in computing its ACT liability on distributions, a company is able to offset any franked investment income received against franked payments which it makes itself and the tax credit can therefore be utilised against the ACT liability arising on distributions made.

18.5.2 Surplus franked investment income
(TA 1988, ss 238 and 242)

Where a company incurs a loss in an accounting period and in the same period its franked investment income exceeds the franked payments made in that period, the tax credit attaching to the excess may be refunded to the company by means of a claim under TA 1988, s 242. This effectively treats the surplus franked investment income as an amount of profits chargeable to corporation tax for the purpose of obtaining relief against trading losses or charges on income in the period concerned. If relief cannot be obtained in this way, the surplus franked investment income is carried forward and treated as franked investment income received in the next accounting period for the purposes of franking distributions made by the company in that later period.

The entitlement, under TA 1988, s 242, of a company to claim to treat dividends and other distributions from a UK company carrying tax credits as if they were part of its profits, and therefore to obtain payment of the associated tax credit, when losses or other reliefs are set against them is withdrawn for accounting periods beginning after 1 July 1997. The clawback of tax credits whereby a tax credit paid is deducted from ACT available for set-off against mainstream corporation tax in a subsequent accounting period does not apply for any accounting period beginning after 1 July 1997.

Claims for accounting periods which straddle 2 July 1997 are restricted, so that franked investment income from distributions made on or after that date is not taken into account in computing surplus franked investment income.

18.5.3 Advance corporation tax
(TA 1988, s 238)

A liability to account for ACT arises when a company makes a qualifying distribution to its shareholders. As its name suggests, ACT is treated as an advance payment of corporation tax and relief is obtained by deduction from the mainstream corporation tax liability payable on the profits for the accounting period in which the distribution has been made.

The collection of ACT on dividends and other distributions made by a company is undertaken on Inland Revenue Form CT61. There is a requirement for a company to submit this return on a quarterly basis to the Revenue in respect of the ACT liability arising on dividends and other distributions made during the three-month period. ACT is due and payable 14 days after the end of the quarterly period concerned.

18.5.4 Relief for payment of ACT

(TA 1988, s 239)

The maximum relief against mainstream corporation tax for ACT paid on distributions made in an accounting period is equivalent to the ACT which would be due on a franked payment equal to the profits chargeable to corporation tax. Where the ACT exceeds this maximum, relief can be obtained in the following ways:

(1) It can be carried back to accounting periods beginning in the six years preceding the accounting period in which the surplus ACT arose, taking later years before earlier years. A claim must be lodged within two years of the end of the accounting period in which the surplus ACT arose.
(2) It may be carried forward and treated as ACT payable in respect of the next accounting period. If it cannot be utilised in the next accounting period, it is treated as surplus ACT in the following accounting period and carried forward indefinitely until utilised.
(3) It can be surrendered to a 51 per cent subsidiary company resident in the UK. It is then treated as ACT paid by the subsidiary. A claim to surrender ACT must be made within six years of the end of the accounting period in which the ACT is paid and requires the consent of the subsidiary or subsidiaries concerned.

18.6 LOSSES

18.6.1 Losses arising in the accounting period

(TA 1988, s 393)

When a company makes a trading loss for an accounting period, it may claim that the loss arising may be set off against other profits including chargeable gains arising in that accounting period. A tax loss is computed in the same manner as taxable profits, but is restricted to losses arising from trading activities carried out on a commercial basis and with a view to the realisation of profit.

18.6.2 Different ways of claiming relief for losses

There are a number of ways in which a trading loss may be relieved for tax purposes apart from being offset against other profits arising in the accounting period. The loss can be carried forward and offset against trading profits arising in succeeding accounting periods. Losses can be carried forward indefinitely in this manner for as long as the company carries on the trading activity which generated the loss. A loss may also be carried back and offset against total profits for the period of three years which ended immediately before the period in which the losses were incurred (provided the company was carrying on the relevant trade in the earlier periods). Partial relief claims are not allowed, and relief is obtained for later years before earlier years. Relief must be obtained for the loss against other profits of the accounting period before computing the balance of the loss available for carry-back.

Section 39 of F(No 2)A 1997 restricts the period against which a company may claim to carry back trading losses to set against the profits of an earlier period. The amended rules, which apply to trading losses incurred in accounting periods ending after 1 July 1997, allow a loss to be carried back only to an accounting period falling wholly or partly within 12 months of the start of the period in which the loss was incurred. For accounting periods ending before 2 July 1997 the carry-back period is three years. Losses made in periods which straddle that date are apportioned, with the new and previous rules being applied appropriately.

However, the 12-month period remains at three years in two circumstances: first, where the trading loss arose in the 12 months immediately before the company ceased to trade (a terminal loss); secondly, where the losses result from the special allowances given for the costs of decommissioning North Sea oil and gas installations.

18.6.3 Example

A Ltd makes a trading loss of £1m in its accounting period ending on 31 December 1995. If A Ltd has other income of £150,000, it can choose between the following:

(1) Carry forward the £1m loss to be set against future profits from the same trade – in this case A Ltd will have taxable profits of £150,000 for 1995.
(2) Set part of the loss against profits of 1995 and carry forward the balance of £850,000 for eventual off-set against future profits from the same trade.
(3) Set off part of the loss against 1995 profits and carry back the £850,000 against profits of the years 1994, 1993 and 1992 (in that order). Any balance can then be carried forward for off-set against future trading profits.

18.6.4 Example

A Ltd makes a trading loss of £1m in its accounting period ending on 31 August 1998. If A Ltd has other income of £150,000, it can choose between the following:

(1) Carry forward the £1m loss to be set against future profits from the same trade – in this case A Ltd will have taxable profits of £150,000 for 1999.
(2) Set part of the loss against profits of 1998 and carry forward the balance of £850,000 for eventual off-set against future profits from the same trade.
(3) Set off part of the loss against 1998 profits and carry back the £850,000 against profits of the year 1997. Any balance can then be carried forward for off-set against future trading profits.

18.6.5 Capital losses

Capital losses, like capital gains, are computed in accordance with CGT rules, although the net capital gains are subject to corporation tax as part of the overall chargeable profits for the accounting period. Capital losses may be offset against capital gains in computing net chargeable gains, and capital losses which cannot be relieved in this way may be carried forward and offset against gains arising in subsequent accounting periods without limit. The carry forward of capital losses is not dependent upon whether the company continues to carry on its trading activity, and may be offset against gains arising on trade and non-trade assets. There are, however, restrictions on pre-entry losses where a company joins a group of companies.

Certain capital losses realised by an investment company (see 18.8.5) may be set against the company's profits (see 4.2.4 on this).

18.6.6 Surplus charges on income
(TA 1988, s 393(9))

Relief for charges on income is generally given as the last of all reliefs other than group relief (see 18.7). It is given against the total profits of the period in which the charges are paid. If profits are insufficient to absorb the charges, the amount of charges paid wholly and exclusively for the purposes of the company's trading activities may be carried forward to the next accounting period and treated as a trading loss to be offset against future trading income of the company. Non-trade charges on income may not be so carried forward and therefore relief is lost.

18.6.7 Charges paid in company's final accounting period
(TA 1988, s 388)

A trading loss may be carried back and offset against profits of the previous year. A company's charges are normally ignored for this. However, charges paid wholly and exclusively for the purposes of the trade are treated as trading expenses for the purpose of computing a loss for the accounting period in which the company's trade comes to an end, and these can be carried back.

18.6.8 Changes in company ownership
(TA 1988, s 768)

There are anti-avoidance provisions designed to ensure that trading losses carried forward can only be utilised against future trading income from the trading activity which generated the losses. Losses may not be carried forward if:

(a) within any period of three years there is a change in the company's ownership preceded or followed by a major change in the nature or conduct of the trade carried on by the company; or
(b) there is a change in the company's ownership at any time after the scale of activities in a trade carried on by the company has become small or negligible, and before any considerable revival in the trade.

A 'change in ownership' means a change in more than 50 per cent of the ownership of the ordinary share capital in the company. A 'major change in the nature or conduct of a trade' includes a major change in the type of property dealt in, or the services or facilities provided in the trade, or in customers, outlets or markets. The Revenue has issued guidelines on some of the factors which will be relevant in determining whether there has been a major change in the nature or conduct of a trade or business (see SP10/91).

Similar provisions apply for surplus ACT and for excess management expenses brought forward by an investment company

18.7 GROUPS OF COMPANIES

18.7.1 Group relationships
(TA 1988, s 402)

There are special rules which apply to groups of UK-resident companies. For corporation tax purposes, a group relationship exists between two companies if one company holds not less than 75 per cent of the ordinary share capital of the other, or if both companies are 75 per cent subsidiaries of a third company. Note that these rules are quite different from those used for VAT and stamp duty purposes (see 5.41 and 6.3.8).

18.7.2 Use of losses

(TA 1988, ss 402–413)

Where one company in a group makes a loss for tax purposes, it may 'surrender' that loss as group relief to another member of the group for offset against that company's taxable profits for its 'corresponding accounting period'. For this purpose, losses available for surrender include charges on income to the extent that they exceed profits chargeable to corporation tax. For group relief purposes, the requirement for a 75 per cent shareholding relationship is extended so that the company owning the shares must also be beneficially entitled to 75 per cent or more of the profits available for distribution to equity shareholders, and of assets available for distribution in a winding-up.

Where the accounting periods of the surrendering and claimant companies do not coincide (ie 'correspond'), the amount of loss to be surrendered is restricted on a time basis reflecting the length of the accounting periods common to both companies.

18.7.3 ACT surrenders

(TA 1988, s 240)

Where a company pays ACT on a dividend distribution to shareholders, it may surrender the ACT to a 51 per cent subsidiary which is UK-resident. The 51 per cent relationship refers to ordinary share capital and the shareholding relationship must subsist throughout the whole of the accounting period during which the dividend was paid. If a surrender of ACT is made, the subsidiary is treated as if it had itself paid both the dividend and the ACT. It may therefore offset the ACT against its own corporation tax liability for that accounting period, or carry it forward to subsequent accounting periods. It is not possible to carry back surrendered ACT, although for the purpose of determining the amount of surplus ACT to be carried forward or back, surrendered ACT is offset against the subsidiary's mainstream corporation tax liability before ACT paid by the subsidiary itself.

18.7.4 Transfers of assets between group companies
(TCGA 1992, ss 171–174)

Where a trading activity is transferred from one group company to another, relief is available under TA 1988, s 343 to ensure that the company transferring the trade does not suffer balancing charges on assets which have qualified for capital allowances. The successor company takes over the assets at their written-down value for capital allowances purposes relating to those assets. It is also possible to elect under CAA 1990, s 158 that properties may be transferred between group companies at tax written-down value for the purpose of industrial buildings allowances. Where s 343 applies, any unrelieved trading losses pass across to the successor company.

Section 343 can also apply where a trade is transferred to another company which is under common control, even though it is not a member of a group.

18.7.5 Payment of dividends and interest
(TA 1988, s 247)

The payment of dividends and interest by one company to another normally requires the payer to account for ACT on the dividend and income tax on the interest payment. Where the two companies concerned are members of the same group for tax purposes, relief is available from these procedures by lodging, with the Revenue, an election under TA 1988, s 247. This is effective for as long as both companies remain UK-resident and one company beneficially owns more than 50 per cent of the ordinary share capital of the other. Dividends paid in these circumstances are termed 'group income' rather than franked investment income, and are not brought into charge to corporation tax in the hands of the recipient.

18.7.6 Capital gains and transfers within a group
(TCGA 1992, s 171)

For the purposes of capital gains, chargeable assets may be transferred from one group company to another without tax consequences. Such transfers are treated as if made at a 'no gain/no loss' price and the recipient company takes over the capital gains base cost of the asset concerned from the transferor company.

18.7.7 Example of intra-group transfers

X Ltd has two wholly owned subsidiaries Y Ltd and Z Ltd. X Ltd transfers a property to Y Ltd for its current market value. No chargeable gain arises to X Ltd on this transfer. This is ignored when working out any capital gain or loss when Y Ltd eventually disposes of the property. Y Ltd is treated as if it had acquired the property for A's original cost plus indexation (see 3.5.7) to date.

The same treatment would apply if Y Ltd transferred an asset to Z Ltd, its 'sister company'.

18.7.8 Company leaving a group after an intra-group transfer

If a company leaves a group, and it owns an asset transferred to it from another member of the group within the previous six years, a tax charge may arise under TA 1988, s 179 as if the asset had been sold for its market value at the time of the intra-group transfer.

18.7.9 Example of tax charge on company leaving a group

If X Ltd had transferred a property in 1994 to Y Ltd which was then worth £10m, and a gain of £2.5m would have arisen to X Ltd were it not for the relief under TCGA 1992, s 171 described in 17.7.6, there would be a notional disposal for Y Ltd if it leaves the X Ltd group in 1999. Basically, Y Ltd would be regarded as having made a chargeable gain of £2.5m at the time that it leaves the group

Note that the charge is based on the value at the time of the intra-group transfer and the £2.5m gain would still arise even if the property were worth £25m (or £7m) in 1999 when Y Ltd leaves the group.

18.7.10 Universal re-basing election

For assets held on 31 March 1982, it is possible for the principal company of a group (normally the holding company) to make an election on behalf of all companies in the group that assets held on 31 March 1982 should be subject to the general rebasing rule for capital gains purposes (see 3.5.4). Such an election is required within two years of the end of the accounting period in which the first disposal occurs after 5 April 1988 of an asset held on 31 March 1982 by a group company.

18.7.11 Roll-over relief and groups of companies

For the purposes of roll-over relief (see 18.3.2), all the trades carried on by group companies are treated as a single trade and therefore it is possible to roll over a gain made on qualifying assets by one member of a group against qualifying expenditure incurred by another within the appropriate timescale. Roll-over relief is generally available only for trading companies within a group although, concessionally, relief is also available for a property holding company where the properties concerned are used for trading purposes by the other members of the group.

18.8 CLOSE AND INVESTMENT COMPANIES

(TA 1988, s 13A)

18.8.1 Close companies

(TA 1988, ss 414–415)

Companies which are under the control of five or fewer persons, or under the control of their directors, are known as 'close companies'. There are special provisions which are designed to ensure that such individuals cannot take undue advantage of corporation tax legislation by virtue of their positions of influence over a company's affairs.

A person controls a company if, in fact, he is able to exercise control directly or indirectly over its affairs by owning the greater part of its share capital, voting capital, or other capital giving entitlement to more than half the assets on a winding-up. Shareholders and certain loan creditors in a close company are known as participators. Rights held by certain 'associates' are attributed to participators in order to determine whether they have control.

An associate is defined for these purposes as any relative or partner of the individual concerned, or a trustee of a settlement where the individual (or a relative) was the settlor. A relative is defined as meaning spouse, parent, grandparent, child, grandchild, brother or sister. Where the individual is a beneficiary of a trust, the trustees may also be regarded as his associate.

18.8.2 Loans to participators

(TA 1988, s 419)

Where a close company makes a loan or advances any money to a participator, or to his associate, there is a liability to account for an amount of tax equal to the ACT liability which would arise if the loan or advance were treated as a dividend payment. The tax payable under s 419 is due within 14 days after the end of period for the purposes of interest on overdue tax. The company does not receive any relief even though the tax payable is calculated in the same way as ACT.

If the loan is repaid, the tax is repaid accordingly, but if the loan is wholly or partly written off or released, the borrower is treated as receiving, as part of his total income, an amount equal to the amount so written off, grossed up at the lower rate of income tax. While no basic or lower rate tax liability arises, there may be a further liability to higher rate tax.

18.8.3 Benefits to participators

(TA 1988, s 418)

Where benefits in kind are received by participators in a close company (or their associates) and the individual is not taxed under Schedule E, the cost to the company of providing the benefit can be treated as a distribution (see 18.5).

18.8.4 Directors' defalcations

Cash diverted by a director and misappropriated by him may have to be written off as irrecoverable. However, such losses are not allowable in computing the company's profits for tax purposes.

18.8.5 Investment companies

(TA 1988, ss 75 and 130)

An investment company is any company the business of which consists wholly or mainly of the making of investments and the principal part of its income arises as a result of that activity. The expenses of managing a UK-resident investment company are deductible in computing its total profits for corporation tax purposes. Where management expenses exceed the company's chargeable income and gains for an accounting period, the surplus may be carried forward and treated as management expenses incurred in the next succeeding accounting period, and may continue to be carried forward until relieved. Surplus management expenses may also be surrendered as group relief from one group company to another. Expenses brought forward from previous periods are not available for surrender as group relief. Unrelieved management expenses of an accounting period may also be set off against surplus franked investment income by a claim under TA 1988, s 242(2), for the purposes of claiming repayment of the tax credit attaching to it.

Relief for excess management expenses and charges brought forward is not available where there is a change in the ownership of the investment company and:

(a) after the change there is a significant increase in the amount of the capital of the investment company; or
(b) within the period of six years beginning three years before the change there is a major change in the nature of conduct of the business carried on by the company; or
(c) the change in the ownership occurs at any time after the scale of activities in the business carried on by an investment company has become small or negligible and before any considerable revival of the business.

18.8.6 Close investment-holding companies

(TA 1988, s 13A)

A close investment-holding company means a close company carrying on specific investment-holding activities. For this purpose, investment-holding activities do not include the carrying on of a trade on a commercial basis, property holding, or holding shares in companies carrying on either of these activities.

A close investment-holding company does not qualify for the small companies rate of corporation tax. In addition, the Revenue has power to restrict repayment of tax credit to shareholders receiving dividends from a close investment-holding company where it appears that arrangements have been made in relation to the distribution of profits, the main purpose of which is to enable the individual shareholder to obtain the tax repayment.

18.9 DOUBLE TAXATION RELIEF ON FOREIGN INCOME

(TA 1988, ss 788–806)

18.9.1 The main reliefs

A UK-resident company may claim a credit for foreign tax paid on income or capital gains arising from any overseas source. Credit is available against the corporation tax liability payable on the same income or gains. Relief may be due either under the provisions of a double taxation agreement between the UK and the overseas country concerned, or under the general rules for 'unilateral relief' as provided in TA 1988, s 790. Where credit is due under a double taxation agreement, the relevant agreement takes precedence over UK domestic legislation.

For most types of income and gains, the full amount is brought into charge for the purpose of computing the corporation tax liability on chargeable profits for the accounting period. Any overseas tax suffered is then offset by way of credit against the corporation tax liability. The amount of credit which is available is limited to the corporation tax liability on the source of income or gain which has suffered overseas tax. No relief is due for the excess foreign tax paid.

Where double tax relief would be lost (for example, where no corporation tax liability arises for the accounting period), it is possible to obtain relief by treating the foreign tax as an expense in computing profits for the purposes of Schedule D Case I.

18.9.2 Double tax relief on dividends from foreign companies

In addition to relief for withholding or other foreign taxes suffered on payment of the dividend, relief may also be available for the foreign tax suffered on the profits out of which the dividend has been paid. This is known as 'underlying tax', for which relief is given automatically if the UK-recipient company controls, directly or indirectly, 10 per cent or more of the voting share capital in the overseas company paying the dividend. The dividend taxable in the UK is grossed up at the rate of underlying tax applicable to the profits out of which the dividend has been paid. This, together with any withholding and other taxes suffered on payment of the dividend, can then be offset against the corporation tax liability arising on the grossed-up equivalent of the dividend received (subject to the restriction that underlying tax relief cannot exceed the corporation tax liability on the same income).

18.9.3 Interaction between corporation tax and ACT

(TA 1988, s 797)

Double tax relief for overseas taxes paid and underlying tax is given by way of credit against the corporation tax liability arising on the same income. In arriving at the corporation tax liability arising on the overseas income or gains, it is possible to take account of the following:

(1) Charges on income may be allocated against other sources of income in priority to overseas income and gains which have suffered overseas tax.
(2) Double tax relief is offset against the attributable corporation tax liability in priority to ACT.

If double taxation relief cannot be obtained by way of credit against the corporation tax liability arising on the same income or gains, it may be advisable to claim the tax paid as an expense deduction in computing the profit or loss arising for Schedule D Case I purposes.

18.9.4 Unremittable income

Where an overseas source of income is taxable on an arising basis but it is not possible to remit the income due to government policy in the foreign country concerned, it is possible to make a claim to defer the corporation tax liability until such time as sufficient funds can be remitted to the UK to satisfy the liability. A claim under these circumstances may be made to the Revenue at any time within six years of the end of the accounting period in which the income arises.

18.10 CONTROLLED FOREIGN COMPANIES AND ANTI-AVOIDANCE LEGISLATION

18.10.1 Reason for legislation on controlled foreign companies

Legislation was introduced in 1984 with a view to countering the use of tax haven companies. The Government made it clear that the legislation was aimed at the following types of companies:

- 'Money box companies' (ie companies which simply accumulate investment income outside the UK);
- 'Dividend trap companies' (ie companies which are interposed between overseas subsidiaries and a UK parent company and which catch dividends before they reach the UK company and so prevent a UK tax liability);
- Offshore 'captive insurance companies';
- Sales, distribution or services companies which are used to enable profits to be put in a company which is subject to a low tax regime;
- Patent holding companies which enable royalty income to be sheltered from UK tax.

18.10.2 Definition of a CFC

A controlled foreign company (or 'CFC') is a foreign company which is controlled by UK resident persons. Basically, where a UK company has a material interest (ie normally a 10 per cent or greater entitlement to share in the profits of a non-resident company) it may be taxed on a proportion of the overseas company's income. Note that the CFC's income is computed according to normal UK tax principles. It is also worth noting that capital gains realised by such a company are not subject to tax under the CFC legislation (but see 18.10.7).

There are various escape routes which enable a UK company to avoid any tax on its share of a CFC's profits. The escape routes involve the CFC meeting one of the following:

(a) the motive test;
(b) the exempt activity test;
(c) the acceptable distribution test; or
(d) the public quotation test.

18.10.3 Motive test

The legislation provides that no tax charge arises if the Board of Inland Revenue is satisfied that the motive for forming the CFC was not to avoid UK tax. In practice, the Revenue accepts that the test is satisfied if the CFC is resident in certain countries which impose tax at a rate comparable to UK tax. Companies which are resident in the following countries are therefore outside the legislation altogether.

Australia
Austria
Bangladesh
Bolivia
Botswana
Brazil
Canada
China
Colombia
Czech Republic
Denmark
Dominican Republic
Falkland Islands
Fiji
Finland
France
Gambia
Germany
Ghana
Honduras
Hungary
Iceland
India
Indonesia
Ivory Coast
Japan
Korea, Republic of
Lesotho
Malawi
Mexico
New Zealand
Nigeria
Norway
Papua New Guinea
Poland
Romania
Senegal
Sierra Leone
Slovak Republic
Solomon Islands
South Africa (excluding the Homelands)
Spain
Swaziland
Sweden
Tobago
Trinidad
Zambia
Zimbabwe

A limited exclusion is available for certain other countries (eg Eire and the Netherlands).

Quite separately from the above, a company is not treated as a CFC if its tax liability in the country in which it is resident amounts to at least 75 per cent of the tax which would be payable if it were a UK-resident company.

18.10.4 Exempt activity test

This test requires that the CFC should have premises in the country in which it is resident and use these premises for carrying on a business. Furthermore, the exempt activity test is satisfied only if it can be shown that the CFC's business is effectively managed in the country in which it is resident and that there are a number of employees based there who are adequate to deal with the volume of the company's business.

This test cannot be satisfied where the CFC's main business consists of any of the following:

(a) the holding of securities, patents or copyrights;
(b) dealing in securities;
(c) leasing;
(d) dealing in goods for delivery to or from the UK;
(e) dealing in goods for delivery to or from a connected or associated person.

18.10.5 Acceptable distribution test

This test applies in the following way. Provided the CFC distributes an acceptable proportion of its profits within 18 months of the end of its accounting period, no tax charge can arise for the UK companies who have a material interest.

Where the CFC is a trading company, the requirement is that the CFC should distribute at least 50 per cent of its profits. Where the CFC is an investment company, the requirement is that it should distribute at least 90 per cent of its income.

18.10.6 Public quotation test

There is also an exemption from the CFC legislation where the subsidiary is quoted on a recognised overseas Stock Exchange.

18.10.7 CGT legislation on non-resident companies

Shareholders in a non-resident company may be subjected to tax on its capital gains. The legislation is contained in TCGA 1992, s 13 and applies if the company would be a close company (see 18.8) if it were a UK-resident company. Basically, any shareholder who has at least 5 per cent of the shares in the non-resident company may be charged tax as if a proportion of the non-resident company's capital gains belonged to him. The proportion is determined by the shareholder's entitlement in a winding-up.

Capital gains may not be apportioned in this way where any of the following conditions are satisfied:

(1) The non-resident company distributes the capital gain within two years, whether the distribution takes the form of a dividend, capital distribution or a payment by the liquidator etc on the winding-up of the company.
(2) The capital gain arises on the disposal of tangible property which is used (and used only) for the purposes of a trade carried on by the non-resident company wholly outside the UK.
(3) The capital gain accrues on the disposal of foreign currency where that currency represents money in use for the purposes of a trade carried on by the non-resident company wholly outside the UK.
(4) A non-resident company is charged tax on the capital gain because the gain arises on the disposal of an asset used by that non-resident company in connection with a UK branch or agency (see 18.1.1).

18.11 FOREX TRANSACTIONS

18.11.1 Outline of the basic rules

The main rules are set out in the flow-chart opposite. These rules apply to:

(1) Qualifying assets such as currency, cash or bank accounts, and debts.
(2) Qualifying liabilities, including money debts, and provisions for trading liabilities.
(3) Currency contracts involving simultaneous exchange of two currencies such as currency swaps and forward and future contracts. It includes transactions where settlement is made by a single payment instead of actual exchange of currencies.

Forex gains and losses on the above items are taxed as income on an accruals basis. Generally the accounts figures are recognised for tax purposes so long as accounts are prepared using normal accountancy practice. Transactions entered into for trading purposes are taxed as trading profits or losses under Schedule D Case I. Where this is not the case (eg where the company is an investment company) they are taxed as

New Forex regime for companies

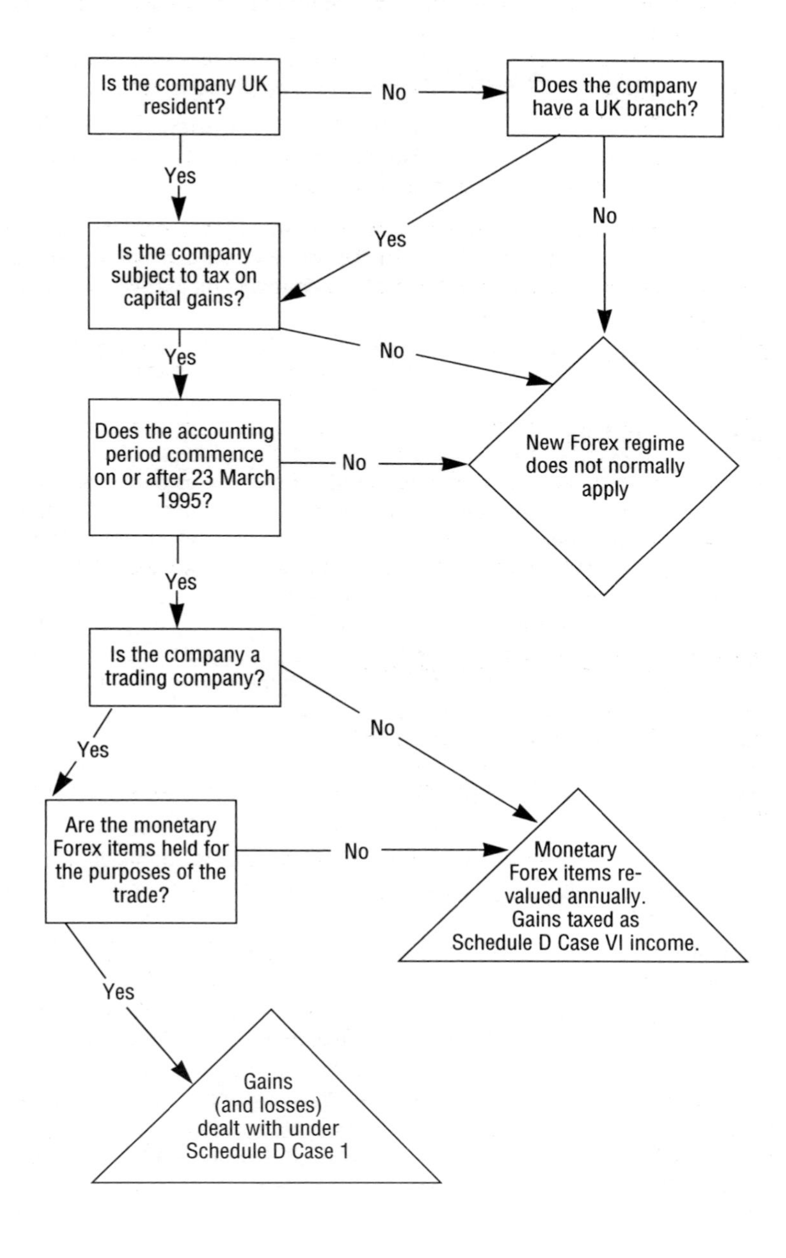

Schedule D Case VI income. Special rules provide for Forex losses arising under Schedule D Case VI to be relieved first against other Case VI profits and then:

(a) offset against other current period profits;
(b) group relieved;
(c) carried back against other Forex or Financial Instruments (FI) profits of the three preceding years;
(d) carried forward against other Forex or FI profits;

The new rules apply from a company's 'commencement date' ie the first day of its accounting period which starts on or after the 'appointed day' which was 23 March 1995. Thus the commencement date of a company will be 1 January 1996.

There are important reliefs available in respect of the above rules.

18.11.2 Matching

An election is available to match Forex gains and losses on certain borrowings and currency contracts with Forex gains and losses on certain categories of non-qualifying assets such as holdings in shares or convertible securities in non-UK resident companies, and net investments in overseas branches where a local currency election has been made (see below). The election can also be made in respect of ships and aircrafts. The effect of the election is that Forex gains and losses on the matched borrowings or currency contracts are taxed on realisation of the asset as capital gains or losses, or in the case of net investments in overseas branches are left out of account altogether. The election is irrevocable and only applies to assets and liabilities matched within the same company. This may be of concern to groups of companies where assets and liabilities are not economically matched within the same company.

18.11.3 Local currency election

Generally Forex gains and losses are calculated by reference to sterling but, in certain circumstances an election can be made to calculate *trading* profits by reference to other currencies. For example, a company which carries on an overseas trade may elect to calculate Forex gains and losses by reference to the relevant overseas currency. An overseas company with a UK trade may elect to use its 'home currency'. The effect of the election is that the trading profits or losses, including Forex gains and losses, are first computed in the local currency, then translated to sterling and adjusted for capital allowances.

18.11.4 Deferral relief

Relief is available to enable unrealised Forex gains on long-term capital assets and liabilities to be deferred for tax purposes. The amount available for deferral is the excess of the lower of either the *unrealised* Forex gains (net of losses) or *total* Forex gains (net of losses) in so far as they exceed 10 per cent of taxable profits for the period.

A claim must be made for the relief and the excess is then carried forward and included in taxable profits of the next accounting period (when a further claim may be appropriate). Where the claimant is a member of a UK group, the amount available for deferral is calculated after taking into account gains and losses of other group companies.

18.11.5 Transitional rules

There are detailed rules dealing with the transition to the new regime. These cover the following aspects:

(1) Generally speaking qualifying assets and liabilities and currency contracts in existence at commencement date are revalued as if there had been a disposal at that date.
(2) No adjustment should be required for items previously included in trading profits unless the gains and losses were previously recognised on a realisation rather than an accruals basis.
(3) Pre-commencement gains and losses on qualifying assets previously dealt with under the capital gains regime are carried forward and offset against post commencement gains and losses. Similar rules apply to pre-commencement gains and losses on trading items previously dealt with on a realisation basis.
(4) There are special rules to deal with qualifying assets and liabilities previously outside the scope of tax, such as capital borrowings. Pre-commencement Forex gains and losses arising on fixed debts are not recognised, but there is a 'kink' test to ensure that the post-commencement gain or loss does not exceed the overall gain or loss over the entire life of the debt. Fluctuating debts are 'grandfathered' for six years with the result that gains and losses are not recognised during that period. If the latter treatment is not favourable a claim can be made to include the fluctuating debts within the new regime.
(5) Currency contracts entered into prior to commencement date are dealt with by a combination of the Forex and the Financial Instrument rules (see 18.11.6 below). These are intended to ensure that gains and losses are not taxed twice under both the new rules and under pre-commencement capital gains rules.

As might be expected, there are anti avoidance rules which may deny or restrict relief for Forex losses, where the loss is the main benefit expected to accrue from the transaction, or the transactions involved are not on arm's length terms. There are also rules dealing with benefits obtained from changing the company's accounting reference date.

18.11.6 Financial instruments

The new rules which were included in FA 1994, but came into operation on the same date as the Forex rules, apply to currency contracts (eg swaps), currency options, interest rate contracts and interest rate options. The payments and receipts covered include periodic payments, premiums, fees, costs and payments for variation, termination and compensation.

The overall objective, as with Forex, is to tax the instruments as income, using the accruals or 'market to market' basis. The treatment of trading and non-trading transactions is exactly the same as for Forex transactions and the same rules apply for relief of Schedule D Case VI losses (see above).

Once again there are special transitional rules for contracts in existence at commencement date. The new rules apply to currency contracts but there are provisions to ensure that gains and losses are not taxed twice, under both the new and the old regime. Interest rate contracts and options in existence at commencement date are not dealt with under the new regime until six years after commencement date, unless the company elects to include them within the new rules.

There are anti-avoidance rules which may deny or restrict relief where a transaction is not on arms' length terms or a benefit is given by a transfer of value to an associated person.

18.11.7 Tax planning for Forex and financial instrument transactions

It is vital to review the existing position of a company before the commencement date to establish what, if any, measures need to be taken before commencement date and to assess the impact of the new legislation after commencement date. In particular, the following need to be considered:

(1) Whether existing borrowing arrangements need to be restructured to take best advantage of reliefs available and the impact of the transitional rules.
(2) Whether it is beneficial to terminate existing contracts or arrangements before commencement date.

(3) Whether matching relief is beneficial and whether relevant assets and liabilities are located and structured in the best way.
(4) Whether intra-group arrangements are affected by the new rules.
(5) Whether there is potential exposure to anti-avoidance provisions.
(6) The time limits for making the various claims and elections available, which in some cases are within 92 or 183 days of the commencement date.

18.12 'PAY AND FILE'

(TA 1988, ss 8 and 10; FA 1989, s 102;
FA 1990, ss 91–103 and Scheds 15–17)

18.12.1 Outline of the system

A new system of reporting profits and payment of corporation tax was introduced for accounting periods ending on or after 1 October 1993 which is known as the 'pay and file' system. A comprehensive return form (Form CT200–1) needs to be lodged in respect of each accounting period and this replaces the corporation tax computation previously required. The payment of corporation tax has also been streamlined with the aim of reducing the administrative costs of collection. Coupled with this is a more rigid system of penalties for delays in rendering a return form and in the assessment of interest on overdue tax and repayments of tax.

18.12.2 The pay and file return

The pay and file return is very comprehensive and requires full details of income from all sources during the accounting period, together with deductions and reliefs claimed. There is an alternative short return which may be completed if each entry on the return (including the company's *total* income) is less than £10 million. The return takes into account various deductions and credits such as ACT, double tax relief and tax payments made on account in arriving at the net corporation tax payable or repayable. A return is required to be submitted to the Revenue (together with accounts for the period and any other supporting information) within nine months after the end of an accounting period. However, a company is only required to file its return after it has received a notice to do so from the Inspector of Taxes. Such notices are expected to be issued approximately three months after the end of the accounting period. If a notice is issued more than 12 months after the end of its accounting period the return is due within three months of the date of the notice.

18.12.3 Payment of corporation tax

Under the pay and file system, corporation tax for an accounting period is due and payable nine months from the end of the accounting period. It is not necessary for the Revenue to issue an assessment to collect corporation tax since the amount shown in the pay and file return as the corporation tax liability due for the period is treated as tax charged under an assessment on the company. The Inspector of Taxes only raises an assessment upon agreement of the final liability or if there is a contentious point which needs to be decided on appeal to the Commissioners.

18.12.4 Interest and penalties

Interest on unpaid tax automatically accrues from the due date, as does any interest on corporation tax which turns out to have been overpaid (but the rate of interest on overpayments is lower than that charged on tax which is paid late). The introduction of automatic penalties for late filing of the company's accounts and Form CT200 has considerably tightened the tax regime. Penalties are calculated as shown below:

Period of delay from filing date	*Penalty*
Up to 3 months	£100
3 to 6 months	£200
Over 6 months	£200 plus 10% of tax unpaid
Over 12 months	£200 plus 20% of tax unpaid

Where there has been a delay for three consecutive accounting periods, the fixed £100 and £200 penalties for the third accounting period are increased to £500 and £1,000 respectively. There are provisions for waiving the penalty charges where the company can show a 'reasonable excuse' for its late filing but the scope to avoid penalties under this provision is extremely limited.

18.13 CLAIMS AND ELECTIONS

18.13.1 General

Throughout the Taxes Acts, there are various claims for relief from corporation tax which must be lodged with the Revenue and, in practice, are made to the Inspector of Taxes dealing with the company's affairs. Unless otherwise specified by legislation, claims must be made within six years of the end of the accounting period to which they relate. The most common claims and elections are set out below together with the time limit by which the claim or election must be made. The Inspector does not generally have discretion to accept claims made after the time limit has expired for a particular claim unless the legislation (or Revenue practice) allows otherwise.

Relief may be claimed within the normal six-year time limit against any over-assessment to corporation tax due to an error or mistake in, or an omission from, any return or statement. No relief is due where the information was not used to form the basis of an assessment, or where the assessment was made in accordance with practice generally prevailing at the time of issue. An error or mistake claim under TMA 1970, s 33 should be made to the Revenue.

For accounting periods ended after 30 September 1993, group relief and capital allowances claims are no longer made by submitting formal claims to the Inspector. Such claims are made in the pay and file return Form CT200, as are claims for repayment of tax deducted at source.

Table 18.1 Time limit for claim submission reference

Claim	*Period (years)*	*Legislation*	*Paragraph reference*
Trading losses carried forward	6	TA 1988, s 393	18.6.2
Trading losses offset against other income of accounting period	2	TA 1988, s 393A	18.6.2
Trading losses carried back	2	TA 1988, s 393A	18.6.2
Terminal loss relief	2	TA 1988, s 393A	18.6.2
Disclaimer of capital allowances	2	CAA 1990, s 24	18.1.3
Group relief	2	TA 1988, s 412	18.7
Surrender of ACT	6	TA 1988, s 240	18.7
Carry back of ACT	2	TA 1988, s 239	18.5.4
Surplus franked investment income	2 (6 for charges on income and management expenses)	TA 1988, s 242	18.5.2
Rollover relief	6	TCGA 1992, s 152	4.3 and 18.3.2
CGT rebasing at 31 March 1982	2 after the end of end of the accounting period in which the first relevant disposal is made after 31 March 1988	TCGA 1992, s 35	3.5 and 18.7.10

19

TAX PLANNING FOR SOLE TRADERS AND PARTNERS

This chapter covers some wider issues for proprietors of unincorporated businesses such as sole traders and partners. We address issues such as bringing in a partner or merging with another firm. We also describe some of the advantages (and disadvantages) which might apply if an unincorporated business were transferred to a company. Assuming that an unincorporated business has grown to the point where it should be incorporated, we set out some of the tax aspects concerning the best way in which this should be achieved. Finally, we look at some tax considerations to be borne in mind where the proprietors of an unincorporated business sell out or cease trading.

Operating as an unincorporated business

(1) Bringing in a partner (and becoming a partner)
(2) Buying out a partner.

Operating as a limited company

(3) General tax considerations
(4) Possible disadvantages
(5) Other tax aspects
(6) Transferring a business to a company.

Sale of the business and cessation

(7) Sale
(8) Cessation.

OPERATING AS AN UNINCORPORATED BUSINESS

19.1 BRINGING IN A PARTNER (AND BECOMING A PARTNER)

19.1.1 Relief for loans where new partner borrows to finance his capital

Income tax relief is available under TA 1988, s 362 for interest on personal loans taken out by partners in order to contribute partnership capital, or to make a loan to the firm (see 16.7).

19.1.2 Interest on capital

It is generally appropriate for interest to be paid on partners' capital accounts, especially where there is some disparity between the amounts of capital provided by each partner.

'Interest' paid in these circumstances is treated as an allocation of Schedule D Case I profits rather than as interest taxable under Schedule D Case III. This has the effect that the partner's relevant earnings for personal pension purposes (see 12.3.5) are likely to be higher than if the firm borrows from a bank to meet its working capital requirements.

19.1.3 Example – Treatment of partnership interest

A is a sole trader. His profits are running at the rate of £50,000 per annum. He brings in a partner and finances the practice by a loan which he raises in his personal capacity. At the end of the year, his position may be:

	£
Interest on capital	12,000
Share of profits	50,000
Interest paid on personal borrowings	(10,000)
	52,000

However, for personal pension purposes (see 12.3.5), his relevant earnings are £62,000 – ie there is no deduction for interest relieved under TA 1988, s 362.

19.1.4 Capital gains tax considerations

There is normally no CGT charge if a sole trader and his new partner each puts in capital on an equal basis – or in proportion to their profit-sharing ratios. However, it is possible that a sole practitioner may require the incoming partner to put in capital to match the value of his interest in the firm. The normal way to account for this is to re-value goodwill, and this could give rise to a capital gain.

19.1.5 Example – Valuation of goodwill

A brings *B* into partnership, sharing profits equally. *B* is required to pay £50,000 capital into the firm, but *A* does not need to pay any money into the firm, and, indeed, is free to withdraw all his undrawn profits. On the other hand, it is agreed that half of the goodwill now belongs to *B*.

A situation like this really amounts to an agreement that *A*'s goodwill is worth £50,000. After admitting *B* as a partner, he is entitled to only half of this, but he is also entitled to half of the £50,000 cash that *B* has put into the firm. So, in effect *A* has received a capital payment for a disposal of half of the goodwill and there may be a CGT charge on this.

19.1.6 Keeping certain property assets outside the firm

A sole trader may wish to retain personal ownership of the office premises etc, rather than share them with the incoming partners. This problem may be more apparent than real since there is no requirement that partners should share capital profits in the same way as they share ordinary profits. Nevertheless, many people prefer to keep the premises outside the firm altogether.

In such a situation the former sole trader can rent the premises to the firm, preferably under a formal agreement which gives the firm a tenancy or a licence. He can also charge rent, but if he does so the consequences for CGT retirement relief should be borne in mind (see 4.7–4.8).

It is also possible for the partner to forgo rent, but to receive the benefit of an appropriate adjustment in the partnership accounts, as a prior charge on profits in the same way as interest on capital is charged. If the partnership agreement is drafted correctly, this effectively converts Schedule A rental income for the partner into profits falling under Schedule D Case I. It also avoids any restriction on CGT retirement relief.

19.1.7 Admitting a partner under CY basis rules

Where the firm is already on the CY basis, either because the business was started after 5 April 1994 or because a partner retired from the firm after that date and no continuation election has been (or will be) made, matters are much more straightforward.

Basically, the partnership's profits are assessed on the CY basis (bear in mind the opening rules (see 16.1)). Each partner is separately responsible for settling his own tax; there is no principle of joint and several liability for the firm's income tax.

Where a firm is assessed on the CY basis, any changes in the partners do not give rise to a cessation as there is an automatic 'continuation' for the ongoing partners. Thus, on a partnership change under the new rules, the tax liabilities of past years are not affected because the change does not trigger a Revenue review of tax assessments for the penultimate and ante-penultimate years.

19.2 BUYING OUT A PARTNER

19.2.1 Change in status to salaried partner

Where circumstances permit, there could be some advantage for the outgoing partner to revert to salaried partner status and be taxed under Schedule E. The timing of such a change may warrant some consideration. For example, a partner expecting to retire in 1997–98 or 1998–99 may prefer to cease to be a Schedule D partner before the new regime takes effect; he does not then have to worry about the CY basis and the operation of transitional relief.

There can be other benefits in switching from Schedule D status to Schedule E. The continuing partners could undertake to fund an approved pension scheme (see 12.3.4), which in turn may enable a tax-free lump sum to be provided where the outgoing partner had previously been an employee (or a salaried partner). Benefits under an approved scheme must relate to periods of service as an employee, but there is no statutory requirement that the periods be continuous as opposed to two periods separated by a period as a Schedule D partner.

The timing of any contributions to an approved scheme may need to be carefully considered. It is less beneficial to the continuing partner if substantial contributions were to be made during the transitional basis period which determine the firm's assessment for 1996–97.

19.2.2 Consultancy arrangement

It could be that the individual agrees to retire from the firm only if he receives a 'retainer' under which the firm is committed to consult him (and pay him) for a minimum number of days over a specified period. Unless the retainer is substantial, it is unusual for the Revenue to seek to classify an ex-partner consultant as an employee, even though he may not undertake work for many other clients (if any). However, this possibility should be borne in mind and the consultancy agreement carefully drafted to avoid any suggestion of a 'master/servant' relationship (see 10.3). If there is any doubt, the partnership needs to withhold PAYE from the consultancy fees.

While it may suit the individual to be taxed as a consultant under Schedule D Case I, particularly if there are expenses that he can claim against his consultancy income (such as the cost of maintaining an office in his home, payment to a spouse for secretarial services and business use of a car), the firm must protect its position. In particular, where the consultancy fee exceeds the VAT threshold, the firm must obtain a valid VAT invoice.

During the transitional period, it may be better for the continuing partners if the retiring partner is paid an annuity rather than consultancy fees, as this may mean that greater relief is available (see below).

19.2.3 Annuity arrangements

An annuity may effectively be paid out of pre-tax income since the payer is normally entitled to relief at his marginal rate of tax. An annuity of £10,000 is satisfied if the partners pay £7,500 (ie £10,000 less basic rate tax), and they can then claim the full amount as a deduction in arriving at their total income for higher rate tax purposes.

As already mentioned, payment as an annuity may be more tax-efficient than consultancy payments during the transitional basis period. The main drawback with annuity payments is that the continuing partners cannot raise qualifying loans in order to meet these obligations.

So far as the outgoing partner is concerned, a capital sum may be preferable, especially where retirement relief (see 4.7) or roll-over relief (see 4.3) may be relevant. On the other hand, the annuity should not attract a CGT liability unless it exceeds two-thirds of his average share of profits over a period of three years which falls within the last seven years in which he is a partner.

19.2.4 Example – Annuity producing more tax relief during transitional period than consultancy fees

Richard retired from the firm on 1 May 1995 and a consultancy fee of £20,000 per annum is agreed.

Under transitional period rules (see 16.2.1), the firm may effectively receive relief only on 50 per cent of the consultancy fees paid during the firm's year ended 30 April 1996.

If Richard had received an annuity of £20,000, the partners would receive relief on the whole of the annuity payments made in the tax years 1995–96 and 1996–97.

19.2.5 Payment of a capital sum

A capital sum may be paid direct to an outgoing partner, or an adverse balance on his capital account may be written off – this is in effect a capital payment by means of a transfer from the continuing partners' capital accounts.

19.2.6 Borrowing by partners to fund the buyout

Where one or more partners raise personal loans to make a capital payment to buy out a colleague, interest normally qualifies for relief under ICTA 1988, s 362. If, exceptionally, the interest on such a loan exceeds the partnership profits, the excess may be carried forward as if it were a Schedule D Case I loss. However, it is important to bear in mind that if the buyout does not take place, and the borrower ceases to be a partner, his loan ceases to qualify for tax purposes. This has been a real problem for the proprietors of firms which have subsequently found themselves in financial difficulties.

19.2.7 Capital gains tax implications

A partner who is being bought out may have a CGT liability unless he can make use of roll-over relief or his gain is covered by retirement relief (see 4.7).

19.2.8 Splitting the practice

In some situations, the outgoing partner effectively takes over one particular office and continues to practice on his own account. This is a 'demerger' situation and the tax treatment depends on whether continuation elections are made.

19.2.9 Demergers

Where some partners buy out part of a firm's business they are usually treated as starting a new business. The partners who continue in the original firm can avoid a cessation by making a continuation election. Alternatively, it may be possible to satisfy the Revenue that a demerger consists of separating two businesses which were different businesses all along. Thus, if a firm of estate agents consists of five offices in different towns, it could be argued that one particular office was always a distinct business and its separation from the rest of the partnership does not amount to commencing a new business. This enables both the continuing partners in the main firm, and the partner(s) who have taken on the office which has demerged, to make continuation elections. Indeed it also allows the partners in the original firm to have a cessation, even though the partners who have demerged chose to make a continuation election.

Capital gains tax

The partners who have demerged will normally have disposed of their interests in the assets of the main firm and acquired enlarged interests in the assets of the demerged firm. Depending on the relative values, any capital gains may well be covered by roll-over relief (see 4.3).

VAT

As partners are jointly and severally liable for VAT, it is important to notify Customs of the departure of partners immediately the demerger takes effect. Joint and several liability continues up to the date the change is notified.

OPERATING AS A LIMITED COMPANY

19.3 GENERAL TAX CONSIDERATIONS

There is no simple answer to the question 'is it better to operate via a company?' There can be both advantages and disadvantages in carrying on business through a limited company rather than as an unincorporated business, and it is generally appropriate to take professional advice. There are commercial considerations as well as tax aspects, eg limited liability may be an important consideration, either for the current proprietors of the business or to attract finance from an outside investor. However, the apparent protection given by limited liability is often illusory, since banks or other lending institutions normally require personal guarantees from directors for any loans made to the company.

19.3.1 Lower rate of tax on profits

Having a company often means that a lower rate of tax applies to retained profits, ie profits which are not taken out as remuneration or dividends.

The small companies rate of 21 per cent (see 18.2.5) applies to profits up to £300,000 provided there are no associated companies. If there are associated companies, the threshold at which profits attract tax at either the normal 31 per cent rate, or the marginal small companies rate, is reduced. If there are no associated companies, the small companies rate can produce a substantial saving.

19.3.2 Example – Tax saving through incorporation

	£
Profits of an unincorporated business	400,000
Tax and NICs (assuming single personal allowance)	156,269
Profits of a company before director's remuneration	400,000
Less director's remuneration and NICs (say)	150,000
	250,000
Corporation tax at 21 per cent	52,500
Tax and NICs on director's remuneration	65,160
Total tax and NICs on profits of £400,000	117,660
Saving in tax through operating via a company	38,609

19.3.3 Possible ways of deferring tax

There is a useful timing difference where a business is carried on through a company in that remuneration can be deducted from the profits of the company even though it is not paid (and is not taxable income of the individuals until it is paid). Provided that the remuneration is actually paid within nine months of the company's year end, the company is normally entitled to a deduction in arriving at its profits.

19.3.4 Example – Timing of tax payments

> If a company draws up accounts to 31 March 1997, it may secure a deduction for directors' remuneration of £150,000 even though the remuneration is not paid until 31 December 1997, in which case PAYE tax does not have to be paid over until 14 January 1998 in accordance with the timetable for self-assessment payments.

19.3.5 Other tax considerations

Pension contributions

Another aspect which favours having a company is that it is possible for a company to fund pensions for directors more generously than is permitted for personal pensions. For example, if an individual is aged 44, the maximum personal pension contribution the individual may make for the year is 20 per cent of relevant earnings up to the amount of the earnings cap (currently £84,000 for 1997–98) (see 12.3.4). In contrast, a company would normally be permitted by the Pension Schemes Office to fund a pension scheme for the benefit of the individual at the rate of 100 per cent of remuneration up to the amount of the earnings cap.

Payment of remuneration may prevent personal allowances going to waste

Where an unincorporated business operates at a loss, and the individuals have no other income, the benefit of their personal allowances is lost forever. By trading through a company, it is possible to vote remuneration equal to the individuals' personal allowances, and the remuneration voted in this way increases the amount of the company's loss which can be carried forward and set against subsequent profits.

Greater scope for raising new finance

An outside investor normally prefers to be a shareholder rather than a partner. While he could in theory limit his exposure by being a limited partner, this is not familiar territory. Furthermore, a limited partner loses the protection of limited liability under the Limited Partnership Act 1907 if he takes part in the management of the firm's business. Most outside investors are therefore prepared to invest only if they can acquire shares and act as directors of a company.

Having a company also opens the way to attracting outside investment under the Enterprise Investment Scheme (see 20.10.1) or from investors who wish to secure CGT reinvestment relief (see 4.4).

19.4 POSSIBLE DISADVANTAGES

Possible disadvantages of operating through a company include the following.

19.4.1 Extra administration

Companies are subject to more statutory requirements concerning the keeping of books, filing of annual accounts, disclosure etc than unincorporated businesses. An unincorporated business does not normally need to file annual accounts at all, whereas a company needs to file accounts with Companies House, and to make an annual return.

19.4.2 Loss of privacy

A limited company must file its accounts annually, and they are available for public inspection. In contrast, an unincorporated business's accounts are a private document which need not be made available to anyone other than the proprietors and the Inland Revenue (and, possibly, the business's bankers).

19.4.3 Relief for losses

A proprietor of an unincorporated business may secure tax relief for any losses by setting them against other income. Losses suffered during the first four tax years in which a business is carried on may be carried back and set against income of the previous three years.

In contrast, losses made by a company can only be set against the company's other profits for the year (or the previous year). Any unrelieved losses may then be carried forward and can be off-set against future trading profits only.

19.4.4 Admitting future partners

If profits are retained, this may make it increasingly difficult for individuals who come up through the business to become shareholder directors. For example, if a company has 100 £1 shares in issue, and retains profits after tax of £15,000 per annum for ten years, each share is worth £1,500 more at the end of the ten years than at the start of the period. An individual seeking to acquire a 10 per cent shareholding would normally have to raise sufficient finance to pay for the shares at this increased value. The problem does not, though, arise in the case of a partnership, since the normal procedure is to allocate past profits to partners' capital accounts and then admit a new partner on the basis that he shares in future profits at a specified percentage. Having said this, the disadvantage in having a company can be over-stated. For example, if the shareholders so wished, they could arrange for the company to make a bonus issue of preference shares before allowing an incoming director to subscribe for ordinary shares. This is not always appropriate, but where it can be done, the shareholder/directors are not disadvantaged through having a company rather than a partnership and the new shareholder/director need not put in very large amounts of new share capital.

19.4.5 Tax savings may only be a deferment

The traditional analysis has been that tax generally becomes payable by shareholders on their share of retained profits, either when the shareholders sell their shares and realise a capital gain, or as and when they extract retained profits by taking a dividend. On this analysis, the saving of tax on retained profits is often little more than a deferment of tax. The validity of this view has been brought into question by the substantial increases in CGT retirement relief during recent years (see 4.7). The fact that gains may be exempt up to £500,000 if a husband and wife both qualify for the maximum retirement relief means that the traditional analysis is often no longer valid since shareholder/directors are generally able to enjoy the full value of their shares on a sale or liquidation of the company.

19.4.6 Increased liability for NI contributions

A company is required to pay Class 1 NICs on all amounts paid as remuneration. There is no ceiling akin to that which applies to employees' own contributions. This can give rise to a substantially increased burden for a company as compared with an unincorporated business. Comparing an unincorporated business owned by four equal partners with a company which has four 25 per cent shareholders (and it is assumed that in both cases the individuals will have income of £75,000 each), the national insurance bill for 1997–98 is as follows:

	Partnership		*Company*
	£		£
Class 2	319.80	Employees' Class 1	2,096.84
Class 4	1,032.20	Employer's Class 1	7,500.00
	1,352.00		9,596.84
× 4 =	5,408.00	× 4 =	38,387.36

While the benefits payable to employees are better than those received by the self-employed (a larger pension because of SERPS (see 12.3.2) and entitlement to unemployment benefit), the higher NIC costs can be a very expensive way of financing such benefits.

19.5 OTHER TAX ASPECTS

19.5.1 Work in progress

Operating via a company may mean that work in progress has to be valued and brought into account in arriving at profits. In contrast, unincorporated businesses may draw up accounts on a cash basis. There is a further problem which is particularly acute for professional firms. In principle, a professional firm should not include partner time in arriving at the cost of work in progress. This means that the figure brought into account should be lower because of this. However, if a business is carried on by a company, time put in by a director should be included when valuing work in progress.

19.5.2 Potential double charge for capital gains

Where a valuable asset is held within a company, a tax liability may arise at two stages before the shareholders can enjoy the sale proceeds. For example, if a company acquires a property at a cost of £150,000, and five years later it is worth £550,000, there might be a gain for the company (after indexation) of £400,000. The company then pays tax on this capital gain either at the marginal small companies rate or at 31 per cent. If a tax charge at 31 per cent is assumed, the company has net funds available after paying tax of £318,000, ie:

	£	
Profit for accounting purposes	400,000	
Less tax on gain	124,000	(£400,000 at 31%)
	276,000	

If the company is then wound up, and the cash distributed to the shareholders, they are likely to have a personal CGT liability on the £276,000. If retirement relief is not available, the CGT payable by them could be £110,400 (ie £276,000 at 40 per cent). This figure assumes that other assets and retained profits within the company are such that there would have been capital gains for the shareholders in any event, even if the company had not held the property concerned.

However, once again, the traditional analysis is open to question. If the company had paid a dividend in order to transmit the £276,000 cash to shareholders, their personal liability could not exceed £69,000. Furthermore, the advance corporation tax (ACT) payable by the company on such a dividend could be offset against the company's chargeable gain, with any unrelieved ACT being carried back against previous years' assessments. Consequently, while it is not generally good policy to have appreciating assets within a company, the extent of the extra tax payable is not as great as it was in the past. Furthermore, while some additional tax is likely to be payable if an appreciating asset is held within a company, this is not in itself an argument against a business operating through a company but rather an argument in favour of shareholder/directors holding such assets in their personal capacities outside the company. It should be borne in mind here that retirement relief is available to a full-time working director who disposes of a property which is used by his family company provided that a disposal is associated with a disposal of shares in the company (see 4.9.4).

19.6 TRANSFERRING A BUSINESS TO A COMPANY

Where a person transfers a business to a company (ie he 'incorporates the business'), there is a disposal of the assets which are transferred to the company. Not all the assets are necessarily chargeable assets for CGT purposes, but a gain may arise on the transfer of assets such as land, buildings and goodwill to the company. Fortunately, there is a relief which may cover such situations (TCGA 1992, s 162).

19.6.1 Nature of relief

The main relief applies only where a business is transferred to a company in return for an issue of shares to the former proprietors of the business. Where the necessary conditions are satisfied so that s 162 relief is available, the gains which would otherwise arise on the transfer of chargeable assets are 'rolled-over' into the cost of the shares issued.

19.6.2 Example – Transfer of a business to a company

A transfers a business to X Ltd in return for shares which are worth £75,000. There are capital gains of £48,000 on the assets transferred to the company. If TCGA 1992, s 162 relief applies, *A* will not have any assessable capital gain, but *A*'s shares in X Ltd will be deemed to have an acquisition cost of £27,000 computed as follows:

	£
Market value	75,000
Less rolled-over gain	48,000
	27,000

19.6.3 Conditions which must be satisfied

For s 162 relief to be available, *all* the assets of the business other than cash must be transferred to the company. It is not acceptable to the Inland Revenue for certain assets of the unincorporated business, such as trade debts, to be excluded, even though this might otherwise be desirable to save stamp duty.

Relief is available only in so far as the company issues shares rather than other consideration such as loan stock. However, some relief is still available if the business is transferred to the company in return for a mixture of shares and loan stock, or shares and cash. The formula to be used is:

$$\text{Chargeable gain} \times \frac{\text{value of shares received}}{\text{value of whole consideration received}}$$

Thus if B transfers a business to Y Ltd, and receives shares worth £10,000 and loan stock worth £200,000, only one-third of any capital gains arising on the transfer of the business assets can be rolled-over under TCGA 1992, s 162.

19.6.4 Limitations of s 162 relief

The market value of the shares issued in return for the transfer of the business must be at least equal to the capital gains arising on the transfer of assets, or there will still be a CGT charge on the transfer of the business to the company. Thus if *C* transfers a business with a net value of £400,000 to Y Ltd, a new company specially formed for the purpose, the shares in Z Ltd will have a value of £400,000. However, it may be that closer examination reveals that the business's value is depressed by heavy bank borrowings. If so, it may be that capital gains totalling (say) £490,000 arise on the chargeable assets transferred as part of the business. Section 162 relief is then limited to £400,000. The balance of £90,000 is taxable in the normal way.

19.6.5 Conditions which do not apply

(1) Relief is not confined to a transfer of a business to a company by a sole trader; the same relief is available where a partnership transfers its business to a company.
(2) The shares which are issued need not be ordinary shares.
(3) Relief is not confined to a business which is classified as a trade which falls under Schedule D Case I or II. It is arguable that the relevant business might, for example, consist of letting a group of properties.
(4) There is no requirement that the company should be incorporated or resident in the UK. It can be both of these, but relief is not prejudiced just because a foreign company is involved.

19.6.6 Alternative way of incorporating a business

It may sometimes be possible to transfer a business to a company and avoid any CGT liability by relying on the hold-over provisions for gifts (see 4.5). Thus if *A* establishes a new company, X Ltd, and he owns all the shares, he could give his business to X Ltd and 'hold over' any capital gain. If *A*'s acquisition cost was £15,000 and indexation relief (see 3.5.7) amounts to £7,000, he is deemed to transfer the business assets for £22,000 and the company takes over the assets for a notional acquisition value of £22,000. This could be a suitable way of transferring a business to a company where the proprietors do not wish to transfer all the assets to the company, as required by TCGA 1992, s 162 (eg where the proprietors wish to retain properties used in the business).

Professional advice is essential to such arrangements. Problems are particularly likely to arise if there is some consideration involved, even if it does not correspond to the market value of the business at the time of transfer.

19.6.7 Income tax consequences

Although there are specific CGT reliefs, there are no similar provisions for income tax purposes. Where individuals transfer a business to a company, they cease to carry on the business and the Schedule D closing year rules may apply.

Furthermore, the transfer of stock to the company may give rise to a taxable profit. Normally, stock is deemed to be transferred at market value in these circumstances. However, it is possible for the proprietors of the unincorporated business and the company to jointly elect for the stock to be transferred at the lower of its cost or carrying value in the unincorporated business's accounts.

The transfer of plant and machinery, and other assets which qualify for capital allowances, might give rise to a balancing charge. However, it is possible for the proprietors and the company to make a joint election so that the plant and machinery etc are deemed to be transferred at their tax written-down value.

19.6.8 VAT consequences of the transfer

The VAT legislation provides that a transfer of a business is not a taxable supply if the following conditions are satisfied:

(1) the assets transferred are to be used by the transferee to carry on the same kind of business as that carried on by the transferor; and
(2) where the transferor is a taxable person the transferee is already, or as a result of the transfer becomes, a taxable person;
(3) where part of a business is transferred, that part is capable of separate operation, ie it must have the substance of a business activity.

The above conditions are normally satisfied where a business is transferred to a limited company as a going concern. Where this happens, it is possible for the unincorporated business's VAT registration number to be taken over by the company if the following conditions are satisfied:

(1) an application on form VAT 68 must be made both by the individuals previously in business and the company; and
(2) the unincorporated business's registration must be cancelled from the date of the transfer; and
(3) the company must not already be registered, although it will of course be liable to be registered as a result of the transfer of the business to it.

The effect of such an application is that the company stands in the shoes of the proprietors of the unincorporated business and takes over all the rights and obligations of those proprietors. Thus, the company becomes liable to furnish any outstanding returns and to pay any VAT due to Customs and Excise at the date of the transfer. This includes any undetected errors in VAT returns which emerge at any subsequent VAT control visit.

19.6.9 Stamp duty on the transfer

The general principles of stamp duty in relation to the transfer of a business to a company are set out at 6.3.7. It is appropriate to go into a little more detail here, and in particular to look at possible ways of avoiding stamp duty on the transfer of land and buildings.

Land and buildings can be transferred for a consideration below market value, eg an issue of preference shares. Where this happens, stamp duty is payable only on the actual consideration which passes.

It is also possible that *ad valorem* duty could be deferred or even avoided altogether if the proprietors of the unincorporated business contract to sell the land and buildings to the company but do not complete that contract.

An agreement for the sale of an interest in land is specifically excluded from the charge to stamp duty under Stamp Act 1891, s 59 and therefore there is no stamp duty on the contract. Beneficial ownership of the property passes to the company as soon as the contract is executed and the company issues its shares as consideration. If the contract were ever completed, stamp duty is then payable. However, it may well be that the directors of the company would be safe to rely on the existence of the contract and allow the legal estate to remain in the names of the proprietors of the unincorporated business. As and when the company wishes to sell the property to a third party, the legal estate can be transferred directly from the former proprietors with only one charge to stamp duty arising, this being the duty payable by the new owner on his purchase consideration. It is essential that professional advice be taken on this.

19.6.10 Carry forward of past trading losses

(TA 1988, s 386)

Where a business has been carried on by an individual (either as a sole trader or in partnership) and the business is transferred to a company, it is possible for any unused trading losses to be relieved against the individual's income from the company in subsequent years. This relief is available only if the business is transferred to a company in return for an issue of shares and the individual has retained ownership of those shares throughout the tax year concerned. In practice, the Revenue does not withhold relief provided the individual has retained at least 80 per cent of the shares.

19.6.11 Other tax aspects

Where CGT incorporation relief is sought under TCGA 1992, s 162 (see 19.6.1 above) it is important to bear in mind that if the limited company takes over the liability of the incorporated business to pay the partners the balance on their current accounts, this counts as a form of consideration and CGT may be payable. It is generally thought advisable for the partners to withdraw the balances on their current accounts shortly before the business is transferred to the limited company. If necessary, short-term bank borrowings may be taken on to bridge the situation, with the individuals then lending money to the company after it has acquired the business. This is clearly another aspect on which professional advice should be taken.

Partners in a firm should plan ahead. Retirement relief is an important long-term consideration and there can be some pitfalls. For example, an individual who personally owned an asset used by the partnership can qualify for retirement relief on an associated disposal of the property (see 4.8.2). Directors who personally own an asset used by their personal trading company (see 4.9.4) can also claim relief on an associated disposal, but only if they work full-time for the company.

Inheritance tax should be borne in mind as well. While they were partners, the individuals would have been entitled to 100 per cent business property relief. As shareholders in a company which has taken over their business, the relief is limited to 50 per cent unless the individual concerned has more than 25 per cent of the voting shares. Thus, if five individuals who share profits equally transfer their business to a company, each of them has only a 20 per cent shareholding, and his or her entitlement to business property relief is only 50 per cent.

SALE OF THE BUSINESS AND CESSATION

19.7 SALE

19.7.1 Apportionment of sale consideration

When the proprietors of an unincorporated business dispose of it, they actually make separate disposals of different assets. The contract under which the business is sold normally allocates a specific part of the consideration to each separate asset, eg stock, plant and machinery, land and buildings and goodwill. The Inland Revenue may challenge the way in which the sale consideration is apportioned if it seems unrealistic and, if no apportionment is contained in the contract, a just and reasonable apportionment may be made. This may have income tax implications as well as CGT consequences.

19.7.2 Example – Apportionment

A sole trader sells his business for £180,000. It is decided that this sum breaks down into the following components:

	£
Stock	40,000
Plant and machinery	35,000
Leasehold property	25,000
Goodwill	80,000
	180,000

The £40,000 for stock is brought into account as a trading receipt. The £35,000 for plant and machinery needs to be set against the 'pool' balance (see 2.2.2) and there may be a balancing charge if it exceeds the pool figure. The £25,000 for the sale of the leasehold property and the goodwill may produce capital gains.

19.7.3 Transfer of business to company immediately before sale

Where a business is to be sold and the gain is likely to exceed any amount covered by retirement relief, there can be some advantage in first transferring the business to a limited company under TCGA 1992, s 162 (see 19.6), the company later selling on the business.

19.7.4 Example – Transfer to a company

Using the figures in 19.7.2, let us suppose that a disposal of the goodwill for £80,000 would produce a capital gain of £70,000. If *A* had no entitlement to retirement relief, tax of up to £28,000 might be payable.

However, if *A* transferred the entire business to A Ltd in return for an issue of shares, A Ltd's acquisition value of the business is its market value at the time of the transfer (ie £180,000). The company would have a capital gain on a sale of the goodwill etc only if the assets appreciated after being transferred to A Ltd.

A would have a capital gain if he disposed of his shares in A Ltd, but in practice he may not need to do so and could use the company for some other purpose (eg as an investment company).

19.8 CESSATION

The proprietors of an unincorporated business may not be able to sell it to anyone else and may simply have to terminate the business themselves. A number of tax points arise in this connection.

19.8.1 VAT

Where assets such as stock or plant and machinery are still held by the business at the date that it ceases to make taxable supplies, there is a deemed supply and the assets are treated as if they have been sold. VAT is then due to Customs based on the open market value (except in the situation where the value is less than £250).

There are minor exceptions to this rule, ie there is no deemed supply where the goods retained by the proprietors are motor cars or goods obtained under a second-hand scheme.

19.8.2 Redundancy costs

Payments made to former employees on the cessation of a business do not qualify for relief under TA 1988, s 74 as the payments are not made for the benefit of the trade but are expenditure incurred in bringing that trade to an end. However, TA 1988, s 90 allows a deduction for payments of up to three times the statutory redundancy payments which are due.

19.8.3 Post-cessation expenses

(TA 1988, s 109A)

Relief is available for expenses incurred by a person after ceasing to carry on a trade or profession provided it is incurred within seven years of the date of cessation. The following types of expenditure may qualify for relief:

- the costs of remedying defective work done, goods supplied, or services rendered while the trade or profession was continuing, and damages paid by the taxpayer in respect of such defective work, goods or services, whether awarded by a court or agreed during negotiations on a claim;

- insurance premiums paid to insure against the above costs;
- legal and other professional expenses incurred in connection with the above costs;
- debts owed to the business which have been taken into account in computing the profits or gains of the trade or profession before discontinuance but which have subsequently become bad;
- the costs of collecting debts which have been taken into account in computing the profits of the trade before discontinuance.

The relief is reduced by any expense allowed as a deduction in the final accounting period which remains unpaid at the end of the year of assessment in which the new relief is given.

Expenditure which qualifies for this relief is set against income and capital gains of the year of assessment in which the expense is paid. Where there is insufficient income or capital gains to cover the expenditure, the unrelieved expenditure of that year is not eligible to be carried forward under the new relief arrangements against future income or capital gains. Any unrelieved expenditure is then available to be carried forward under the existing rules and set against subsequent post-cessation receipts from the trade or profession.

20

TAX AND THE COMPANY PROPRIETOR

In this chapter, we look more closely at tax planning for proprietors; points to bear in mind when buying a company; the treatment of shareholder directors, and the way in which they are assessed on benefits received by them (and by members of their family); how cash may be extracted from the company in the most tax-efficient manner; and the tax implications of various transactions with the company. The topics covered are:

(1) Buying a company
(2) Corporation tax planning
(3) Treatment of remuneration for PAYE and NIC purposes
(4) Benefits in kind
(5) Dividends
(6) Loans to the company
(7) Loans by the company
(8) Sale and purchase of assets by the company
(9) Self-administered pension schemes
(10) Raising business finance
(11) Purchase of own shares
(12) Demergers
(13) Longer term capital gains tax planning
(14) Anti-avoidance legislation
(15) Sale of the company.

20.1 BUYING A COMPANY

There are several points to bear in mind where an individual or group of individuals are purchasing an existing company.

20.1.1 Relief for financing costs

Where an individual finances such a purchase through a qualifying loan, the interest payable on the loan may qualify for income tax relief under

TA 1988, s 360. The conditions which need to be satisfied for a loan to be a qualifying loan are:

(1) The loan must be a formal loan and not merely an overdraft.
(2) The loan must be used to acquire ordinary share capital of a close trading company or ordinary share capital of a company which is the holding company of a trading group or to make a loan to such a company.
(3) The borrower must have a material interest in the close company or be employed full-time by the company at the time the interest is paid.

As can be seen from the above, it is a requirement that the company is a close company and that the individual has a material interest. Close companies are defined at 18.8.1 above. An individual is regarded as having a material interest if he owns more than 5 per cent of the ordinary share capital of the company. In fact, the 5 per cent test applies to the individual taken together with his associates, so that if an individual held 4 per cent personally and his wife owned 2 per cent, he is deemed to have a material interest.

The requirement that the individual should have a material interest does not apply if he works full time for the company. Working full-time means that the individual works for the greater part of his time in the management of the company, and he must therefore be a director or a person who has a wider management role that affects the company as a whole and not merely a particular department within the company.

20.1.2 Income tax relief for capital losses

As explained at 4.2, a UK-resident individual who has subscribed for ordinary shares in an unquoted company may be able to claim income tax relief for any loss realised on a disposal of those shares. This contrasts with the normal position where capital losses may be set only against an individual's capital gains and not against income.

In practice, where an individual or group of individuals are considering purchasing an existing company, they may be better advised to form a new company, subscribe for shares in that company, and have that company ('Newco') purchase the target company. If Newco has no assets or activities apart from holding shares in the target company, there would be a very close relationship between the value of the shares in Newco and the shares in the target company. If the target company fails, the shares in Newco are likely to become worthless and this produces a capital loss. Because the individuals will have subscribed for shares in Newco, and the other requirements of TA 1988, s 574 are satisfied, it should be possible for them to secure income tax relief (see 4.2).

20.1.3 Checklist of tax points when buying a company

(1) Establish whether the target company has any assets which have been the subject of a roll-over relief claim (see 4.3).
(2) Ensure that none of the company's assets have been transferred to it from another group company within the past six years as this could give rise to a tax charge on the company under TCGA 1992, s 179 (see 18.7.8).
(3) Obtain appropriate indemnities against any tax payable for back years because of failure to make PAYE and NIC deductions, failure to make correct end of year returns, problems in operating the sub-contractors scheme, or interest or penalties payable under the VAT legislation following an investigation.
(4) Take professional advice if the vendors are to receive compensation for loss of office or *ex-gratia* payments, as these payments are not always an allowable deduction for corporation tax purposes.
(5) Take professional advice on possible ways to minimise stamp duty (see 6.3).

20.2 CORPORATION TAX PLANNING

20.2.1 Maximising benefit of small companies rate

There can be a tax penalty where there is more than one associated company (see 18.2.7) and the profits of the two companies are not equally distributed. Even though the combined amount may fall within the limits which would apply for small companies rate if there were only one company, the way in which the rules work can produce a situation where one company's profits suffer tax at the full 31 per cent rate.

20.2.2 Example – Adverse tax position

A Ltd and its wholly owned subsidiary B Ltd may have total profits of £300,000 which would attract corporation tax at only 21 per cent if they arose within A Ltd and A Ltd had no associated companies. If, however, A Ltd has profits of £250,000 and B Ltd has profits of £50,000, the total corporation tax payable is as set out below.

A Ltd	£
£250,000 at 31%	77,500
Less: Marginal relief $1/40$ × (£750,000 – £250,000)	12,500
	65,000

B Ltd	
£50,000 at 21%	10,500
Total corporation tax payable	75,000

The effect in this particular case of having two companies rather than a single company is that the overall rate of tax is increased from 21 per cent to 25.17 per cent.

20.2.3 Commercial considerations

Tax is not, however, the only consideration. There may be good commercial reasons why the directors prefer to keep certain trading operations in a separate company. For example, this may be a way of ensuring that valuable properties within a holding company are not put at risk if those trading operations result in insolvency.

It is sometimes possible to have the small companies rate computed on the basis that a company is left out of account. In particular, if the company is a pure holding company which has no business operations apart from holding shares in one or more subsidiary companies, or holding property used by such subsidiary companies, and the holding company has no profits for corporation tax purposes, it may be left out of account.

20.2.4 Companies controlled by associates

The Revenue also operates a concession where there is no trading interdependence or connection between two companies and they are technically associated companies only because the individuals who control each of the companies are associated with one another (eg an individual controls company A and his brother controls company B). This is an area where professional advice should be taken in the light of the precise wording of ESC C9.

20.2.5 Avoiding disallowable expenditure

If it is decided to have a group of two (or more) companies or associated companies (ie companies which are under common control but are not parent/subsidiary), each company should avoid incurring expenditure which is partly or wholly for the benefit of the other company's trade. Such expenditure is not allowable in computing profits for corporation tax purposes.

20.2.6 Managing a group's tax affairs

It is most important that the necessary elections are in place to enable interest and other annual payments to be paid from one member of a group of companies to another, and for any dividends to be paid within the group, without the company which declares the dividend having to account for ACT. Bear in mind that such elections do not take effect automatically. The proper procedure is to submit the elections to the Inspector of Taxes. They then take effect after three months, or at some earlier date if the Inspector gives notice that he agrees that the elections are valid.

Care is needed if any shares in a subsidiary company are held by outside shareholders. Certain reliefs, and specifically group relief, are dependent on the holding company being entitled to at least 75 per cent of the ordinary share capital of subsidiaries. Other tests also have to be satisfied and group relief might not be available if an outside investor holds preference shares or convertible loan stock, which might mean that less than 75 per cent of the subsidiary's profits, or assets available for distribution on a winding-up, would belong to the holding company (see 18.7.2).

Group relief is available only to cover profits of a corresponding accounting period. It cannot be carried back and set against a subsidiary's profits for an earlier accounting period. There may also be problems where a subsidiary has a different accounting date from that of its parent company.

Some of the above points would be dealt with by the company's tax advisors, but a prudent director will wish to understand the statutory requirements and to ensure that the advisors are on top of the matter. The following checklist may be of assistance in this connection.

20.2.7 Checklist of tax considerations for group of companies

(1) The position should be monitored to identify cases where a subsidiary may have a loss for tax purposes. It may be possible to maximise tax relief if certain action is taken before the end of the accounting period in which the loss will arise. Professional advice is appropriate.
(2) The company's accountant should be consulted before a subsidiary company pays a dividend.
(3) A valid group dividend election should be in place. It is also worth checking with the group's accountant that it will not be more beneficial for the dividend to be paid outside the group election.
(4) Annual charges such as interest should actually be paid by the company's year end as no tax relief is otherwise available.

(5) Advice on the tax implications of any transfers of assets between group companies should be taken. Tax on a gain which is covered by TCGA 1992, s 171 may become payable if a subsidiary leaves the group within six years (see 18.7.8).
(6) The deadlines for submitting formal claims to the Inspector of Taxes, explained below, should be kept in mind.

20.3 TREATMENT OF REMUNERATION FOR PAYE AND NIC PURPOSES

In essence, shareholder directors are treated in the same way as all other directors and P11D employees (see 11.3.1) in that their remuneration is taxed under Schedule E, and the same rules govern the tax treatment of benefits in kind. However, directors who are also significant shareholders in the company are likely to be affected more by certain aspects of the legislation.

20.3.1 How receipts basis applies to shareholder/directors

Where remuneration is deemed to have been received, PAYE must be accounted for and it is assessable as income in the year of receipt.

Special provisions define the date on which an individual is deemed to receive remuneration, as the earlier of:

(1) the date when payment is actually made; and
(2) the time when the employee becomes entitled to payment.

In the case of directors, the date can be earlier than above, in that payment is deemed to take place on the earliest of (1) and (2) and

(3) the date that income is credited to the director in the company's accounts or records; and
(4) the date when the accounts of income for a period is determined.

20.3.2 NIC in respect of company directors

Remuneration paid to a company director is normally assessed for NICs as if it arose on a yearly basis. This means that a payment of fees or a bonus in a lump sum may attract the maximum contributions for a year, rather than the maximum contributions for one week or one month.

20.3.3 Example – Assessment on lump sum payments

A company director receives remuneration of £30,000 paid in a single sum. The liability for contributions is the liability for the year, ie

	£
52 × (£465 – £62) × 10 per cent ie	2,095.60
plus 52 × £62 × 2 per cent ie	64.48
	2,160.08

It is not simply the maximum for one week's earnings, ie 2 per cent of £62 and 10 per cent of £403.

20.3.4 NIC problem areas

One major problem concerns directors' drawings. The DSS takes the view that where a director arranges for a personal liability to be settled by his company and charged to his drawings account, the payment constitutes earnings for national insurance purposes unless the drawings account is in credit. Thus, payments are treated as earnings for PAYE purposes if:

- payment has actually been made;
- the individual has become entitled to payment;
- the individual is a director;
- the money has been credited to the director's account with the company; and
- the amount of income for a period has been determined.

20.3.5 Example – Directors' drawings

A has a drawings account with his company which is £60 in credit. The company pays a personal bill for *A* of £100 and debits his drawings account with £100, thus turning the credit balance into an overdrawn balance of £40.

The Contributions Agency takes the view that £60 of the payment of the £100 bill is a repayment of a loan and attracts no national insurance liability, but the balance of £40 is a payment of earnings and the grossed up amount is subject to NICs.

20.3.6 Loans by the employer

Curiously, the Contributions Agency takes the view that if an individual arranges for a loan from his employer and the loan is used to settle a personal liability, there is no liability for NICs unless (and until) the loan is written off by the employer.

There is clearly a need for considerable care in dealing with any documentation and structuring the arrangements to minimise liability for NICs on payments of this nature. It should, though, be borne in mind that in general it is unlawful under the Companies Acts for an individual to be given a loan from a company of which he is a director.

20.4 BENEFITS IN KIND

20.4.1 Benefits for a director's family

(TA 1988, s 154(1))

A tax liability may arise even though the director or employee has not personally received a benefit in kind, as where a benefit is made available to a member of the director's or employee's household by reason of his employment. The Revenue may say that substantial benefits in kind enjoyed by a director's family are provided by reason of that person's employment even though the recipient may also be a company employee. The Revenue is especially likely to argue this where a director's spouse is employed by the company and receives abnormally large benefits in kind for employees of that category.

20.4.3 Benefits for 'participators'

(TA 1988, s 418)

The legislation also covers a slightly different situation where shareholders receive benefits because they are shareholders, or associates of shareholders, rather than by reason of their own or anyone else's employment. The legislation applies only to *close* companies (see 18.8) and effectively treats the individual as if he or she had received a dividend equal to the value of the benefits as measured for Schedule E purposes (see 11.6–11.11). This is a complex subject on which professional advice should be taken.

20.5 DIVIDENDS

The usual reason why directors take cash from their company in the form of dividends rather than remuneration is because of the national insurance savings. Where the company is subject only to the small companies rate (see 20.2.1) there can be a considerable saving by taking dividends.

20.5.1 Example – Dividends rather than remuneration

A Ltd has profits for corporation tax purposes of £250,000. If *A* takes £100,000 as remuneration, he is left with £60,000 after tax at 40 per cent and this costs the company £82,650, ie:

	£
Remuneration	100,000
Additional employers NICs	10,200
	110,200
Less: corporation tax relief at 21 per cent	23,142
	87,058

In contrast, it generally costs such a company only £80,000 to provide the shareholder with the same net income by means of a dividend. The figures work out as follows:

	£
Dividend	80,000
Add: tax credit 20 ÷ 80 =	20,000
	100,000
Less: basic and higher rate tax	40,000
Net amount retained by *A* after tax	60,000

The above comparison is based on the assumption that the company is subject only to the small companies rate. If it is subject to corporation tax at the full rate of 31 per cent, it is generally less advantageous to pay a dividend.

20.5.2 Possible drawbacks

There are other aspects to bear in mind, in particular the potential effect on the director's pension entitlement. Where the director is within ten years of normal retirement date, his final remuneration may have to be determined as the average of the three best consecutive years' remuneration. Taking dividends rather than remuneration may have the effect of reducing the individual's potential pension benefits.

20.6 LOANS TO THE COMPANY

20.6.1 Qualifying loans to the company

Where an individual borrows from a bank (other than under an overdraft) and then lends the money on to a company, he is entitled to income tax relief on the interest paid on the borrowings, provided:

- the company concerned is a close company (see 18.8) and the individual is a full-time director or employee involved in the management of the company's business; or
- the company concerned is a close company and the individual has a material interest in it (normally this means having more than 5 per cent of the ordinary share capital); or
- the company is 'employee controlled' and the individual is a full-time employee.

However, the interest ceases to qualify for tax relief to the extent that the individual recovers capital from the company.

20.6.2 Example – Effect on a qualifying loan recovering capital

A has a 'material interest' in a close trading company. He borrows £150,000 from the bank and lends this money to the company for use in its business.

In year one, all the interest that *A* pays to the bank is an allowable deduction in arriving at taxable income. In year two, *A* withdraws £70,000 as part repayment of the loan to the company, but uses this for personal expenditure and does not clear his bank borrowings. From this point, only part of the interest payable on the bank loan qualifies for income tax relief.

20.6.3 Consequences if the company fails

Where an individual has raised a qualifying loan, his entitlement to income tax relief ceases when the company ceases to qualify. Thus, if an individual has borrowed £100,000 to finance his investment in a close trading company, and the company is wound up, the individual is not entitled to relief for any interest paid after the company ceased trading. If he is unable to repay the borrowings, he is left with having to pay interest which does not qualify for any tax relief whatsoever.

20.7 LOANS BY THE COMPANY

In the past, many companies operated on the basis that a director drew sums from the company in anticipation of bonuses or other remuneration which would be voted after the end of the company's year, perhaps when draft accounts were available. In many cases, the directors' account was effectively overdrawn at the year-end, and was restored to credit only because of the bonus approved after the year-end at the company's annual general meeting.

The Revenue normally maintains that bonuses should be treated as having been credited to a director only when the accounts were approved at the annual general meeting, and not at the company's year-end. It is generally difficult to resist such an argument since a director normally becomes entitled to a bonus only when the accounts are approved, and credit for such a bonus should not be applied retrospectively.

Where a director's loan account is effectively rewritten and is found to be overdrawn at the year-end, the Revenue is likely to seek to assess a benefit in kind as if the director had received a beneficial loan (see 11.9). Furthermore, there may be a liability on the company under the provisions of s 419 (see 18.8.2).

20.8 SALE AND PURCHASE OF ASSETS BY THE COMPANY

Where a director, or some other person connected with the company (eg a shareholder or an associate of a shareholder) purchases an asset from a company, there may be an income tax charge on any benefit enjoyed by the purchaser. Furthermore, the CGT legislation often requires the company's capital gain to be calculated if the company had disposed of the asset for its market value.

The company law aspects also need to be borne in mind. The purchase of an asset by a director normally needs to be disclosed in the company's annual accounts. It may be necessary, or at the very least advisable, for the transaction to be approved by the members of the company in a general meeting.

20.8.1 Purchase of assets by a director

Where a director (or other employee) acquires an asset from the company, the Revenue needs to be satisfied that the price paid is market value. If, in fact, the asset has been purchased at less than market value, the undervalue is treated as a benefit subject to income tax under

Schedule E (see 11.3). Thus, if *A* acquires a property from A Ltd for £150,000, but its market value is £250,000, he is charged income tax on a benefit of £100,000. The fact that the buyer has purchased the property at an undervalue needs to be disclosed on form P11D (see 11.9).

In addition to the above, TCGA 1992, s 18 means that the company is deemed to have disposed of the property at its market value (ie £250,000). Thus, the company may have a tax charge based on value which it has not in fact received.

In the past, the Revenue made matters worse in such cases by resisting a claim by the company for a tax deduction in arriving at its profits. It is thought that this is not correct, and in the above example A Ltd ought to be entitled to a deduction of £100,000 (ie matching the amount assessed on *A* under Schedule E). However, the position remains uncertain and problems of this type are best avoided if at all possible.

20.8.2 Purchase of assets by associate of a director

Much the same treatment applies if, in the above example, the property had been purchased by *A*'s wife rather than by *A* himself. In general, the Revenue normally argues that a benefit obtained by a close relative or other associate of a director should be treated for tax purposes as if the director had enjoyed the benefit himself.

20.8.3 Capital gains tax treatment of the director

Where a director etc has acquired property from his company, and has been assessed under Schedule E on any undervalue, he should be able to deduct the property's market value at the time of acquisition in arriving at any capital gain when he eventually disposes of the property.

20.8.4 Example – Value of capital gain

If *B* acquires a property worth £300,000 from his employer but pays only £180,000, he is assessed to income tax under Schedule E on £120,000.

If he later sells the property for £350,000, his capital gain is £50,000 (before indexation), and not £170,000.

20.8.5 Acquisition of property by shareholder

An individual who is a shareholder in a company, but not a director or employee, may likewise purchase an asset at an undervalue. In this situation, the amount of the undervalue is treated as if it were a distribution (ie dividend). The company needs to account for ACT on the amount of the undervalue. Moreover, the company's capital gain is once again calculated as if it had in fact received market value.

Thus, if *B* in the above example had been not a director or employee, but a shareholder, the company may need to account for ACT on £120,000, and *B* would be treated as receiving £150,000 income, less tax at the basic rate.

20.8.6 Sales of assets to the company

Much the same considerations arise where a director or shareholder sells an asset to the company. If the company is deemed to pay too much, the amount of the overvalue is treated as subject to income tax.

20.8.7 Capital gains aspects

Where an individual gives an asset to a company or sells it at an undervalue, he is often treated as if he were making a disposal to a connected person. This is particularly likely where the individual controls the company, or he and his associates, when taken together, have control. In such a case, TCGA 1992, s 18 normally requires the individual's capital gain to be calculated as if he had in fact received market value.

Where the asset concerned is a business asset, however, used either by the individual in a trade carried on by him personally, or by the company in the course of its own trade, it is possible for any gain to be avoided by the two parties making a joint election under TCGA 1992, s 165 (see 4.5 on hold-over relief).

20.8.8 Example – Transfer for no consideration

C is the main shareholder in C Ltd. He owns a warehouse used by C Ltd which is currently worth £1m. His original cost was £100,000, the 31 March 1982 value is £300,000, and indexation relief amounts to £200,000. If *C* transferred the warehouse to C Ltd for no consideration, and an election were made under TCGA 1992, s 165, *C* would not have a capital gain and C Ltd would be deemed to acquire the property for £500,000.

20.8.9 Sale at an undervalue

The treatment is slightly different in the case of a sale at an undervalue. The excess of the amount paid to the transferor over the unindexed cost must be deducted in arriving at the amount of the gain which is eligible for hold-over relief. Thus if, in the example above, *C* had sold the warehouse to C Ltd for £700,000, the hold-over relief would be limited to £300,000 and *C* would have a chargeable gain of £200,000.

20.8.10 Interaction with retirement relief

Retirement relief (see 4.7) is mandatory, ie it does not have to be claimed. Thus, if *C* met all the conditions in relation to the disposal described in 20.8.8, his held-over gain would be reduced by £375,000 retirement relief and this relief is not then available to cover gains on any other disposal.

20.8.11 Company law aspects

The Companies Acts contain many provisions intended to ensure that directors do not obtain personal benefits at the expense of their companies. The main safeguards which apply where a director buys or sells an asset are contained in CA 1985, s 320. This provides that the company may not enter into an arrangement for the purchase/sale of a non-cash asset of the 'requisite value' unless the arrangement is approved in advance by the company's shareholders. The requisite value is 10 per cent of the company's net asset value, subject to a minimum of £1,000 and a maximum of £50,000. The CA 1985 also requires such transactions to be disclosed in the company's accounts.

There are specific rules which preclude a public company from entering into a 'credit transaction' with a director or connected person. A credit transaction is defined as including the sale of an asset on terms such that payment may be deferred. Thus, where a public company sells an asset to a director or connected person, it is normally necessary for full payment to be made at the time the purchase contract is entered into.

20.9 SELF-ADMINISTERED PENSION SCHEMES

In the past, one way in which directors arranged their affairs to best advantage was by having the company form a small self-administered pension scheme, with the trustees making loan-backs to, or other investments in, the company. In effect, a company could secure tax relief while still having the use of the money paid into the pension scheme. There are now, however, special rules which apply to small self-administered schemes (ie schemes which have fewer than 12 members). The Revenue is particularly anxious to monitor such schemes to ensure that they operate as pension schemes and not for the benefit of the directors or as a way of financing the company.

The Revenue requires one of the trustees to be a pensioneer trustee, ie an individual or body widely involved in pension scheme work and having regular dealings with the Pension Schemes Office (PSO). A pensioneer trustee is required to give an undertaking to the PSO not to acquiesce in any arrangements which are considered by the PSO to be inconsistent with a scheme operating as a *bona fide* pension scheme.

20.9.1 Prohibition on loans to members

Loans to scheme members, or anyone connected with a scheme member, are specifically prohibited. Moreover, there are restrictions on the purchase of assets from scheme members.

20.9.2 Loans to the company (and associated companies)

There is a general rule that not more than 25 per cent of the self-administered pension fund's assets may be lent to the company within the first two years. Moreover, the 25 per cent rule applies to the value of the fund contributed by the company (and the members), and does not include any value arising from a transfer to the fund from another approved scheme. After the first two years, the proportion of the fund which may be invested in this way increases to 50 per cent.

Even where a loan is not barred by the above rules, there are other conditions which need to be satisfied. The money must be lent to the company for business purposes and not for a purely speculative purpose such as the purchase of shares or other investments. Any such loan must be for a fixed period and on arms' length terms. The Revenue has indicated that in general such loans must carry a commercial rate of interest, equivalent to clearing bank base rate plus 3 per cent.

20.9.3 Investment in shares in the company

This is another area where the Revenue has tightened the rules. The 50 per cent ceiling referred to in 20.9.2 applies to both loans to the company and investment in its shares. Moreover, there is a separate limit in that a self-administered pension scheme's investment in any unlisted company must not exceed 30 per cent of the shares in that company. Furthermore, where a self-administered scheme purchases shares from a director, it is normally advisable to seek prior clearance, and, indeed, for the directors to seek clearance under TA 1988, s 707 (see 20.14.1). This is very much an area where specialist advice is required.

20.9.4 Investment in property used by the company

The PSO is less difficult where a small self-administered pension scheme acquires a property to be used by the company. The relevant memorandum issued by the PSO states:

> it is not for the Inland Revenue to interfere in the way the trustees invest trust monies, except where tax avoidance is in point, or where the investment appears to be irreconcilable with the *bona fides* of the scheme having regard to its cash needs for purchasing annuities. Investment in land or buildings may be a good long term investment for a scheme where the members are many years from retirement, but even so, questions would need to be asked if the property purchased appeared to be an important part of the employers own commercial premises, and thus potentially difficult to realise.

One particular point is that the PSO does not normally sanction a situation where the trustees take on borrowings which exceed three times their equity in the property.

There is a specific prohibition for residential property. The PSO Memorandum states that investment in residential property is prohibited except where it is for occupation by:

- an unconnected employee as a condition of employment (eg a caretaker), or
- someone unrelated to the members of the scheme (or to a person connected with a scheme member) in connection with his or her occupation of business premises (eg the occupier of a shop with an integral flat above) where the business premises are held by the trustees as a scheme asset.

20.9.5 Overall limit on borrowings by trustees

The Revenue has a well established rule that any borrowings by the trustees should not exceed 45 per cent of the market value of the investments held by the trustees plus three times the ordinary annual contributions payable by the employer.

20.10 RAISING BUSINESS FINANCE

A successful private business often finds itself prevented from fully developing and expanding its business because of lack of finance. There may be a limit on the finance available from a bank in the form of medium-term loans, and in practice many companies survive on overdraft. The proprietors may come to see that they can develop the company to its full potential only if they can attract new equity finance.

There are various commercial aspects to raising new business finance and directors should take professional advice from an accountant and a solicitor who are experienced in venture capital work. From a tax point of view there are three major aspects to bear in mind.

20.10.1 Enterprise Investment Scheme

It may be possible to raise new equity finance from business 'angels' by issuing shares which qualify under the Enterprise Investment Scheme (EIS). An individual who invests at least £500 under the EIS may secure 20 per cent income tax relief, and may also be able to secure CGT deferral relief which may be worth another 40 per cent.

The provisions governing EIS relief which apply to an investor are set out in the *Allied Dunbar Tax Handbook 1997–98* at 11.6. From the company's point of view, the following provisions are relevant in determining whether the company can issue shares which qualify under the EIS.

20.10.2 Qualifying companies

A qualifying company is defined as an unquoted company which either:

(1) exists wholly for the purpose of carrying on one or more qualifying trades 'or which so exists apart from purposes capable of having no significant effect (other than in relation to incidental matters) on the extent of the company's activities'; or
(2) has a business which consists wholly of:
    (a) the holding of shares or securities of, or the making of loans to, one or more qualifying subsidiaries of the company; or
    (b) both the holding of such shares or securities, or the making of such loans, and the carrying on of one or more qualifying trades.

There are also certain other conditions which need to be satisfied if it is to be a qualifying company:

(1) The company's share capital must not include any issued shares that are not fully paid up or would not be fully paid up if any undertaking to pay cash to the company at a future date were disregarded.
(2) The company must not control another company apart from a qualifying subsidiary, either on its own or together with a connected person, and there must not be any arrangements in place under which the issuing company can acquire such control.
(3) The company must not be under the control of another company or under the control of another company and persons connected with it, and once again there must be no arrangements in place whereby such a company may acquire control of the issuing company.

20.10.3 Qualifying trades

There are certain trades which are excluded under TA 1988, s 297, ie the company's business must not consist to any substantial extent of any of the following:

(1) dealing in land, in commodities or futures or in shares, securities or other financial instruments;
(2) dealing in goods otherwise than in the course of any ordinary trade of wholesale or retail distribution;
(3) banking, insurance (but not insurance broking), money-lending, debt-factoring, hire-purchase financing, or other financial activities;
(4) oil extraction activities;
(5) leasing (except for certain short-term charters of ships) or receiving royalties or licence fees;
(6) providing legal or accountancy services;
(7) providing services or facilities for any trade carried on by another person (other than a parent company) which consists to any substantial extent of activities within any of paragraphs (1)–(6) above and in which a controlling interest is held by a person who also has a controlling interest in the trade carried on by the company.

20.10.4 Wholesale and retail distribution trades

Wholesale and retail distribution trades qualify only if they are 'ordinary' trades. Section 297(3) states that a trade does not qualify as an ordinary trade of wholesale or retail distribution if:

(1) it consists to a substantial extent of dealing in goods of a kind which are collected or held as an investment; and
(2) a substantial proportion of those goods are held by the company for a period which is significantly longer than the period for which a vendor would reasonably be expected to hold them while endeavouring to dispose of them at their market value.

The following are taken as indications that a company's trade is a qualifying trade:

(1) The goods are bought by the trader in quantitites larger than those in which he sells them.
(2) The goods are bought and sold by the trader in different markets.
(3) The company incurs expenses in the trade in addition to the costs of the goods, and employs staff who are not connected with it.

The following are 'indications' that the trade is not a qualifying trade:

(1) There are purchases or sales from or to persons who are connected with the trader.

(2) Purchases are matched with forward sales or vice versa.
(3) The goods are held by the trader for longer than is normal for goods of the kind in question.
(4) The trade is carried on otherwise than at a place or places commonly used for the type of trade.
(5) The trader does not take physical possession of the goods.

The above are only indications and are not conclusive that a company's trade is or is not a qualifying trade, but it will be difficult to persuade the Revenue that a trade qualifies if there are a number of indications to the contrary.

20.10.5 Qualifying subsidiaries

A qualifying subsidiary is one in which the issuing company or one of its subsidiaries holds at least 90 per cent of the share capital (TA 1988, s 308(2)). In addition, the company must meet one of the following tests:

- it must be carrying on a qualifying trade; or
- it must exist to hold and manage a property used by the parent company, or by a fellow 90 per cent subsidiary, for the purposes of a qualifying trade; or
- it must be dormant.

20.10.6 Three-year period

EIS relief is withdrawn if a company, having initially satisfied the requirements set out in 20.10.2–20.10.5, ceases to satisfy them within three years.

20.10.7 Individuals excluded from EIS relief

A qualifying investor is defined as an individual who is not 'connected with the company'. This means that he must not own more than 30 per cent of:

- the issued ordinary share capital of the company, or any of its subsidiaries;
- the loan capital and issued share capital of the company or any subsidiary; or
- the voting power in the company or any subsidiary; or
- any loan capital in a subsidiary of the company.

An individual is also connected with the issuing company if he directly or indirectly possesses, or is entitled to acquire such rights as would, in the event of the winding-up of the company (or any of its subsidiaries), mean that he is entitled to receive more than 30 per cent of the assets available for distribution to equity holders of the company.

Rights of 'associates' need to be taken into account. For these purposes, an 'associate' means partner, spouse, parent, grandparent, great grandparent, child, grandchild, great grandchild and certain family trusts.

20.10.8 Individual must not be previously 'connected with the company'

An individual is also deemed to be connected with the company if he is:

- a paid director of the issuing company or any of its subsidiaries;
- an employee of the issuing company or any of its subsidiaries;
- a partner of the issuing company or any subsidiary; or
- an associate of someone who is a director or an employee or a partner of the issuing company, or any of its subsidiaries.

An individual is disqualified if he falls into any of the above categories during the two years prior to the date that the EIS shares are issued. Furthermore, an individual does not qualify for EIS relief if he is connected with the issuing company at the time the shares are issued, unless he is a business angel who qualified for EIS relief on his original investment and is now acquiring additional shares and he is connected only because he is a paid director.

20.10.9 Five-year period

EIS relief is withdrawn if the individual breaches the 30 per cent limit within a period of five years.

20.10.10 Purchase of own shares/redemption of shares

There may be a partial withdrawal of EIS relief if the company (or a subsidiary) purchases its own shares or redeems shares within the five-year period. See further, *Allied Dunbar Tax Handbook 1997–98* at 11.6.12.

20.10.11 Approved investment funds

As well as seeking investment from business angels and other private individuals, it is possible for a company to issue shares to an approved EIS fund which operates in a similar way to a unit trust. From the point of view of the directors of the company which issues the shares, the same requirements apply as for shares issued to individuals direct.

20.10.12 Venture capital trusts

It may also be possible for an unquoted company to attract new equity finance from a venture capital trust (see *Allied Dunbar Tax Handbook 1997–98* at 11.7). The following parameters apply in determining whether a venture capital trust may invest in a company.

(1) The company must exist wholly for the purpose of carrying on wholly or mainly in the UK one or more qualifying trades (defined as for the EIS).
(2) Venture capital trusts may count annual investments of up to £1m in total any one qualifying unquoted company as a qualifying holding.
(3) The gross asset of the unquoted company must not exceed £10m, immediately prior to the investment by the venture capital trust.

20.10.13 The Alternative Investment Market

The Stock Exchange introduced a new market to replace the Unlisted Securities Market (USM). The new market, the Alternative Investment Market (AIM), provides smaller companies, including companies which have only recently been set up, with a way of raising new equity finance. AIM shares qualify for the following reliefs:

- income tax relief under the EIS;
- CGT reinvestment relief;
- income tax relief for capital losses realised by an individual who subscribed for shares in an AIM company;
- CGT hold-over relief for gifts of shares;
- IHT business relief, provided the shares have been held for at least two years.

In addition, the Revenue has announced that venture capital trusts are permitted to invest in AIM securities.

In practice the availability of CGT reinvestment relief and IHT business relief are the most important tax incentives for investors. EIS relief is not available for investment in *all* AIM companies, only those carrying on qualifying trades and having no quoted securities. Thus, shares dealt in on AIM do not qualify for EIS relief if the company has preference shares or loan stock which are quoted on the main market. Where the necessary conditions are satisfied, however, investment in an AIM investment could qualify for 60 per cent tax relief.

20.11 PURCHASE OF OWN SHARES

Since 1980, it has been possible for a company to purchase its own shares. The tax legislation contains specific provisions covering such transactions.

The general rule is that any amount paid by the company in excess of the amounts originally paid for the issue of the shares may be treated as a distribution (TA 1988, s 209). Where certain strict conditions are satisfied, however, it is possible for an unquoted trading company to buy in its own shares without the payment being treated as a distribution.

20.11.1 Conditions for capital treatment to apply

The following conditions need to be satisfied if a purchase by a company of its own shares is not to be treated as giving rise to a distribution:

(1) The company must be an unquoted company.
(2) It must be a trading company or the holding company of a trading group.
(3) The vendor shareholder must be resident and ordinarily resident in the UK.
(4) The vendor must have owned his shares for at least five years.
(5) The vendor's interest in the company must be substantially reduced.
(6) The company must purchase its own shares to benefit its trade.

20.11.2 Definition of unquoted company

For these purposes, a company is regarded as a quoted company if any of its securities are quoted on the Stock Exchange. On the other hand, the fact that shares are dealt in on the USM or the AIM does not make the company a quoted company.

20.11.3 Ownership of shares for five years

The legislation provides that the vendor shareholder must have owned his shares throughout a period of five years ending with the purchase. There are exceptions to cover situations where an individual acquired the shares by a gift from his or her spouse, or inherited them.

Section 220(6) of TA 1988 provides that an individual may count any period of ownership by his spouse towards the five-year period, provided they are not separated or divorced at the time the company purchases its own shares.

Section 220(7) of TA 1988 reduces the five-year period to three years in cases where the shareholder inherited his shares. Moreover, it is also possible to include the period during which the shares were owned by the person from whom he inherited them.

20.11.4 Substantial reduction

The legislation states that a shareholder shall be regarded as substantially reducing his interest in the company only if his interest is reduced by at least 25 per cent. Furthermore, in looking at an individual's interest in the company, it is necessary to take account of his interest as a loan creditor (ie someone who has lent money to the company) as well as a shareholder. Although the legislation refers to a minimum reduction of 25 per cent, the Revenue normally expects a much greater reduction.

20.11.5 Benefit to the company's trade

The legislation states that a purchase of own shares by a company is regarded as a distribution unless the purchase is made wholly or mainly for the purpose of benefiting a trade carried on by the company or by any of its 75 per cent subsidiaries. The legislation also requires that the purchase must not be part of a 'scheme or arrangement' the main purpose of which is to enable the individual to avoid tax or to participate in the profits of the company without receiving a dividend.

20.11.6 Advance clearance procedure

It is possible to submit details of the commercial reasons for a proposed purchase of own shares with a view to securing confirmation from the Revenue that the purchase will be treated as a capital transaction and not as a distribution. The basic information required by the Revenue is set out in Statement of Practice SP2/82.

20.11.7 Distribution treatment more beneficial

Where an individual cannot benefit from retirement relief, and his shares are bought back by the company, it may be more beneficial for him if the company is treated as making a distribution. This is because the amount received by him is treated as carrying a tax credit just as if it were a dividend. He is then liable only for any higher rate tax liability.

20.11.8 Example – Purchase of shares: distribution

A acquired 10,000 £1 ordinary shares in 1989 by subscribing for them at par. It is now proposed that these shares be bought back for £11 per share.

If the company applies for clearance that the transaction should not be treated as a distribution, and if that clearance is forthcoming, *A* will have a capital gain of £100,000 (before indexation relief). If *A* has substantial other income, his rate of tax is 40 per cent and so, ignoring indexation (which is trivial) he may have a tax liability of £40,000.

If the transaction is treated as a distribution, the company needs to account for ACT of £25,000 (see 18.5), but this may be off-set against the company's tax on its profits, and in many cases it is not an additional tax liability but merely means that tax is paid earlier than it would otherwise have been paid.

A is then treated as if he had income (including a tax credit) of £125,000 and the maximum tax he has to pay is then £25,000, ie

	£
Tax at 40% on 125,000	50,000
Less tax credit	25,000
	25,000

20.11.9 Position where a shareholder has not subscribed for the shares

The calculation becomes more complex where a person has purchased shares from an existing shareholder. Thus, if A had acquired his shares in 1989 by purchasing them from his father for £5, his CGT computation is as follows:

Position if Revenue gives clearance

	£
Sale proceeds	110,000
Less cost	50,000
Gain before indexation	60,000
Indexation relief (say)	28,000
Capital gain	32,000

Position if buy-back is treated as a distribution

	£
Sale proceeds	110,000
Less assessed as income (see 20.11.8)	100,000
	10,000
Cost	50,000
Allowable loss for CGT purposes	40,000

There is still an income tax charge as set out in 20.11.8.

20.11.10 Trustee shareholders

The position is yet more complex where trustees have their shares bought back by the company. In general, the distribution treatment is likely to be more favourable than where an individual has his shares bought back, since any income arising from the fact that the repurchase is treated as a distribution is confined to the 20 per cent tax credit and there is normally no liability for the additional rate (which applies to discretionary trusts), or for higher rate tax (in the case of an interest in position trust). Where the settlor is a beneficiary of the trust, the tax treatment may be less favourable.

It is important to obtain professional advice where trusts are involved.

20.12 DEMERGERS

It often happens with family companies that different members of the family wish to develop the business in different directions. If the founding generation has passed control to their children, a company may be run by two cousins or more distant relatives who have markedly different ideas and ambitions. There is a way in which the businesses can be separated in a tax-efficient way so that each of the different sides of the family can have a separate company with a distinct business.

Demergers are not confined to family companies and may also be appropriate where individuals who have been business partners wish to go their separate ways.

20.12.1 Form of the demerger

Demergers may take one of three forms, but they all involve the distribution of assets to shareholders out of distributable profits. The three types of transaction are as follows:

- distribution of shares in a subsidiary company to shareholders (ie the holding company declares a dividend);
- transfer of shares in a subsidiary to another company ('Newco') in return for its issuing shares to the shareholders of the holding company;
- transfer of a business to another company (again Newco) in return for that company's issuing shares to the shareholders in the holding company.

Where the Revenue gives approval to a demerger, the value transferred to the shareholders in one of the above three ways is not subject to income tax or CGT.

20.12.2 Conditions which must be satisfied

Demerger relief is available only where the purpose of the demerger is to separate two distinct trading activities. Relief is not intended to be available where the purpose is to separate trades from investments or other assets. It is also necessary to show that the purpose of the demerger is to benefit the trade being demerged. This condition is normally satisfied if it can be shown that the directors have irreconcilable differences as to business policy and the trade of the company to be demerged is being inhibited or held back because of these policy differences.

The demerger reliefs are not available where the demerger forms part of a scheme or arrangement where the main purpose is either:

- the avoidance of tax, or
- the acquisition by any person other than a shareholder of the distributing company of control of that company or any other company involved in the demerger.

20.12.4 Advance clearance

It is possible to secure advance clearance from the Revenue that a proposed demerger qualifies for the tax reliefs. In practice, it is necessary to make out a case to the Revenue that there are good commercial reasons for the demerger and there is no immediate likelihood of one of the demerged companies being sold.

20.12.5 Informal demergers

It may sometimes be possible to achieve a demerger which separates assets from trading activities, but this is not possible under the above rules for statutory demergers.

Informal demergers are a type of reconstruction which relies on Revenue Statement of Practice SP5/85. Specifically, the transactions involved are normally as follows:

(1) the company's ordinary share capital is re-classified so that A shares carry the right to participate only in the profits of one trade or business and B shares carry similar rights over another business;
(2) the company is put into liquidation;
(3) the liquidator transfers the assets and undertakings which relate to the A shares to a company ('Newco') which issues its share to the A shareholders. The process is repeated in relation to the B shareholders.

In some circumstances it is shares in a subsidiary which are transferred to the new company, which issues shares to the A and B shareholders.

The transfer of the business or undertaking to Newco A and Newco B does not normally give rise to a tax charge for the transferor company because this is specifically covered by TCGA 1992, s 139. Similarly, the issue to the A and B shareholders of shares in Newco A and Newco B does not normally give rise to a CGT charge because of reliefs available under TCGA 1992, s 136. However, both these sections apply only where the transactions are carried out for *bona fide* commercial reasons and not for the avoidance of tax.

Once again there is a clearance procedure, which clearly should be contemplated only after taking appropriate professional advice.

20.13 LONGER TERM CAPITAL GAINS TAX PLANNING

Inevitably, medium- to long-term CGT planning depends upon a person's particular circumstances, and the following are merely suggestions to be borne in mind.

20.13.1 Should investments be held by trustees?

There is a major distinction between capital gains realised by an individual and gains made by trustees of an interest in possession trust. An individual's capital gains are effectively added to his taxable income and, if the aggregate amount exceeds £24,300, the gains are subject to 40 per cent tax (see 3.1.4). In contrast, where gains are realised by trustees, the rate of CGT is 25 per cent, regardless of the amount of the gain. It follows that if an individual is a beneficiary of an interest in possession trust, whether this be a trust created by another person's Will, or a settlement created by a relative etc, then it may well be more appropriate from a tax point of view if the trustees, rather than the individual himself, hold shares in a private company.

20.13.2 Example – Shares held by trustees

A has 500 shares in X Ltd. His brother does not have any shares but is the life tenant of a trust created by his father which owns the remaining 500 shares.

If X Ltd is taken over and *A* and the trustees both have a capital gain of £400,000, *A* pays tax of £160,000, but the trustees are liable for CGT of only £100,000.

20.13.3 Special rules where settlor or spouse a beneficiary

The treatment described in 20.13.2 does not apply if the settlor or his spouse can benefit. If so, the trustees' gain is taxed as if the settlor had realised it himself.

20.13.4 Forward planning for retirement relief

Both spouses may qualify for the full measure of retirement relief (see 4.7 and 4.9) provided they meet the conditions for that relief. In practice, this means that both husband and wife should hold at least 5 per cent of the voting shares for a period of ten years up to the time of a disposal, and they should both be full-time officers or employees of the company.

20.13.5 Example – Maximising retirement relief

A and his wife both work full-time for their private company, X Ltd. *A* holds 99 per cent of the shares and his wife holds only 1 per cent.

In due course, a capital gain of £1m arises on the sale of the company. *A*'s share is £990,000 and his tax is as follows:

	£
Capital gain	990,000
Less exemption	250,000
	740,000

Less 50 per cent exemption	370,000
	370,000

If he has used his annual exemption elsewhere, the tax normally amounts to £148,000.

If *A* and his wife had each held 50 per cent of the shares, the tax would instead have been calculated as follows:

	£
Capital gain for both husband and wife	500,000
Less exemption	250,000
	250,000
Less 50 per cent exemption	125,000
	125,000

The maximum tax payable would then be £100,000 (ie £50,000 each).

20.13.6 Assets owned privately but used by personal company

In many situations, the company concerned is not particularly valuable and the proceeds which are likely to arise on a disposal are insufficient to allow retirement relief to be taken up in full. On the other hand, the individual may have charged rent for making a valuable asset (eg a property owned by the director concerned) available to the company for use in its business. A gain on the disposal of the property does not qualify for retirement relief at all if a market rent has been charged (see 4.9.4), so retirement relief may go to waste.

One solution may be for the individual to transfer the property to the company by way of a gift, or a sale at an amount equal to his acquisition value. There should be no problem from the point of view of IHT provided all the shares in the company are held by the individual and spouse. The overall effect is that the individual realises a larger gain on the eventual disposal of his shares and this should qualify for retirement relief in full.

In some situations, it may also be possible for the individual to sell the property to the company for full consideration and to cover any capital gain which arises by using the sale proceeds to subscribe for new shares in the company concerned. Such an investment should qualify for reinvestment relief (see 4.4) and this should mean that no CGT is payable on the disposal of the property. In due course, when the shares and the company are sold, retirement relief should be available to cover any capital gain (subject to the normal limits).

20.14 ANTI-AVOIDANCE LEGISLATION

20.14.1 Transactions in securities

Section 703 of TA 1988 enables the Revenue to treat certain capital sums as if they were income. This section has particular application to a sale of shares in a private company.

For the Revenue to invoke s 703, one of the five prescribed circumstances set out in TA 1988, s 704 must apply. Several of these prescribed circumstances refer to an abnormal dividend and it is therefore particularly dangerous for a person to sell shares as part of a series of transactions under which another person (eg the purchaser) receives an abnormal dividend. However, s 704D can also apply to a series of transactions which does not involve an abnormal dividend but has the effect of extracting cash which could have been distributed as dividend.

There is an exemption for transactions which are carried out for bona fide commercial reasons or in the ordinary course of making or managing investments. However, it needs to be shown that none of the transactions was entered into with the main object, or one of the main objects, of obtaining a tax advantage.

Fortunately, TA 1988, s 707 provides an advance clearance procedure whereby a taxpayer may require the Revenue to state whether s 703 would apply to a proposed transaction. The taxpayer must set out all the material facts in his application. If the Revenue is not satisfied that clearance can be granted, or if it requires further information, notice must be given within 30 days. Once the Revenue has given clearance, an assessment cannot be made under s 703 unless it can be shown that the application did not fully and accurately disclose all the proposed transactions.

20.14.2 CGT anti-avoidance provisions

There are two anti-avoidance provisions in respect of CGT, both relating to value shifting.

20.14.3 Controlling shareholders

Section 29 of TCGA 1992 can apply where a controlling shareholder takes actions (or refrains from action) so as to cause value to pass out of his shares and into shares held by some other person with whom he is connected. Section 29 allows the Revenue to treat such a controlling shareholder as if he had disposed of his shares for their value at the time when he exercised his control to shift value into the other shares.

20.14.4 Example – Value shifting

> *A* holds 51 per cent of the ordinary shares in X Ltd and his son holds the remaining 49 per cent. *A* arranges for the company to offer ordinary shareholders the option of converting their shares into preference shares. *A* accepts this offer but his son does not. This means that control of the company shifts from *A* to his son since, after the conversion of ordinary shares into preference shares, all the ordinary shares are held by his son. If the Revenue invokes s 29, it will assess *A* as if he had disposed of his 51 per cent shareholding at its market value before the shares were converted into preference shares.

20.14.5 Section 30 of TCGA 1992

This legislation can apply to a scheme or arrangement under which the value of an asset which has been transferred has been materially reduced and a tax-free benefit has been obtained. Fortunately, there are specific exemptions for the following transactions:

- disposals between husband and wife;
- disposals by personal representatives to legatees;
- disposals within a 75 per cent group of companies.

Nevertheless, this anti-avoidance section is important in connection with any transactions which may affect the balance of control within a family over a private company. Proprietors of companies should therefore take appropriate professional advice.

20.14.6 Share exchanges and take-overs

The exchange of shares or securities in Company A for shares in Company B which is making a take-over bid or acquiring a 25 per cent shareholding in Company A can give rise to a CGT liability for shareholders in Company A unless they had no more than 5 per cent of Company A or advance clearance had been obtained (see 3.4.5). This legislation therefore needs to be borne in mind where shareholders in an unquoted company take shares or loan stock issued by an acquiring company.

20.15 SALE OF THE COMPANY

Once again, the purpose of this section is to outline some of the more common ways in which CGT may be mitigated.

20.15.1 Pre-sale dividends

Vendors of a private company may have a choice. They can sell their shares for a capital sum or they can take a pre-sale dividend and a reduced amount on the sale of their shares. Provided that the company can secure full relief for the ACT payable on its dividend, there may be a significant benefit if the shareholders organise a pre-sale dividend.

20.15.2 Example – Dividend paid before sale

A holds all the shares in X Ltd. He can sell them for £500,000 or take a pre-sale dividend of £100,000 and sale proceeds for the shares of £400,000. Assume that *A*'s acquisition value plus indexation amount to £300,000:

Sale for £500,000

A's tax liability is likely to be £80,000 (ie 40 per cent CGT on a capital gain of £200,000).

Position if A receives a pre-sale dividend of £100,000

In this situation, *A* has to pay higher rate tax on a dividend of £100,000. This may give rise to tax payable of £25,000.

A also has a capital gain on the disposal of his shares for £400,000. However, his maximum liability is £40,000.

Overall, *A* makes a tax saving on the amount extracted as a dividend. The saving is effectively the difference between 40 per cent CGT and the higher rate tax, which in this case represents 25 per cent of the amount received by him.

20.15.3 Using CGT hold-over relief

Where an individual makes a gift of shares in an unquoted trading company, it may be possible to secure hold-over relief. The conditions which must be satisfied are basically that:

- the company is an unquoted company;
- it is a trading company or the holding company of a trading group;
- the recipient of the gift is UK resident;
- the recipient joins in a hold-over election.

A restriction on hold-over relief may apply where the company has chargeable assets which are investment assets. (See 4.5.)

Where hold-over relief is obtained, the person transferring his shares does not normally have a capital gain but the recipient of the gift takes over his acquisition cost for the purposes of CGT.

Where substantial amounts are involved, it may be worthwhile for an individual to use this relief to make gifts to his children, or to a settlement for the benefit of his children.

20.15.4 Example – Hold-over relief

> *A* receives an offer for his shares in X Ltd and stands to realise a capital gain of £2m. If he transfers a quarter of his shares to an interest in possession trust for his children, and makes a hold-over election, the trustees take over his CGT acquisition value. The position on the sale to the third party is that *A* now realises a gain of £1.5m and the trustees realise a gain of £500,000. Their rate of tax is 25 per cent rather than 40 per cent so *A*'s family saves £75,000 at the Revenue's expense.

20.15.5 Taking loan notes or other paper from the acquirer

Where a public company is acquiring an unquoted company, it may be attractive for the vendors to take loan stock (or other securities) issued by the quoted company. Provided that clearance has been obtained under TCGA 1992, s 138 (see 3.4.7 and 20.14.6) no capital gain arises to the extent that the vendors take such consideration. They do, however, realise a capital gain as and when they dispose of the loan stock or other securities.

Taking loan stock can be attractive where the vendors anticipate that they may subsequently cease to be resident or where they can cash in the loan stock in stages, so as to realise modest gains in different tax years to take advantage of the CGT annual exemption for those years.

20.15.6 Consideration payable by instalments

One potential problem area is where a person sells shares (or any other asset) with the sale consideration being receivable in instalments. The CGT legislation requires the full amount to be brought into account for the year in which the disposal takes place. In some cases this might cause hardship in that a vendor is assessed for CGT but does not yet have sufficient cash to cover this liability. The legislation caters for this by allowing payment of CGT to be made by instalments over a period of up to seven years. However, this is not automatic and the basis on which payment may be made by instalments needs to be negotiated with the Inspector of Taxes.

Where it subsequently transpires that not all the consideration is actually received, the CGT assessment may be reduced.

20.15.7 Contingent liabilities

If a person sells shares (or any other assets) but is under an obligation to return part of the money in certain circumstances, the legislation requires that his capital gain should be computed without reference to the contingent liability. However, if and when the contingent liability becomes an actual liability, the CGT assessment is then adjusted to reflect this (see 3.5.2).

20.15.8 Earn-outs

It is also possible for a person to sell his shares for an amount in cash, plus a further amount based on the future result of the company's business. The House of Lords decision in *Marren v Ingles* [1980] STC 500 has established that such a vendor must be deemed to have received two types of consideration at the time of his disposal: the cash amount, plus the contingent right to receive further sums in the future. The technical term for the right to receive sums in the future is a *chose in action*. The House of Lords decided that CGT must be charged on the cash received plus the market value of the *chose in action*.

20.15.9 Example – Tax treatment of earn-out transaction

A sells out for £1.5m plus a contingent right to receive up to another £1m if his company achieves profit targets.

The present value of this contingent right or chose in action is £450,000 and so *A* is assessed as if he had received £1.95m. If the full amount of £1m is eventually received, he then has a further gain in the year that this is paid out. His gain in that year is:

	£
Proceeds	1,000,000
Less market value of chose in action when acquired	450,000
Capital gain before indexation	550,000

TCGA 1992, s 138A deals with the above problem and states that where the earn-out consideration consists only of shares or other securities to be issued by the acquiring company, those securities may be treated as if they were securities issued by the acquiring company on the take-over.

20.15.10 Example

> If the sale contract in 20.15.9 provides that *A*'s further £1m consideration must be satisfied by an issue of shares by the acquiring company, he would then be taxed only on the £1.5m cash, and tax would not be payable on the *chose in action* or on the issue of the shares, but only as and when he disposes of those shares.

20.15.11 Qualifying corporate bonds

Some caution is required where a private company is being disposed of and the vendors are offered a share exchange involving the issue of qualifying corporate bonds (QCBs). A QCB is a special type of loan stock (see 3.3.2). It is called a *qualifying* corporate bond because no capital gain may normally arise on its disposal (similarly, no allowable loss normally arises on its disposal).

However, where a company has been taken over, and the acquiring company issues a security which is a QCB, the legislation provides that the vendors' capital gain may be deferred only until such time as the QCB is disposed of.

This can cause real problems if the acquiring company gets into financial difficulty and cannot redeem the QCB. The deferred gain may become chargeable, as a disposal is deemed to take place when the acquiring company is wound up, and there is no relief for the loss due to the QCBs becoming worthless. This is an area where a potential vendor should obtain professional advice.

21

INHERITANCE TAX AND BUSINESS PROPERTY

Inheritance tax (IHT) is a combined gift tax and death duty. It applies to certain gifts and deemed gifts made during a person's lifetime and to the estate on death. The first £215,000 of chargeable transfers (the nil rate band) is free of IHT. Cumulative transfers in excess of this, which take place either at death or within seven years before death, are taxed at 40 per cent (though the overall impact may be reduced on transfers that take place more than three years before death). On all other occasions when IHT is payable, the rate is 20 per cent.

This chapter covers the following topics:

(1) Persons subject to IHT
(2) When a charge arises
(3) Transfers of value
(4) Gifts which are not transfers of value
(5) Exempt transfers
(6) Potentially exempt transfers
(7) Reservation of benefit
(8) Business property
(9) Agricultural property
(10) Computation of tax on lifetime transfers
(11) Computation of tax payable on death
(12) Handing on the family business/company without attracting IHT.

21.1 PERSONS SUBJECT TO IHT

A UK-domiciled individual is subject to IHT on all property owned by him, whether it is located in the UK or overseas. In contrast, a person who has a foreign domicile is in general subject to IHT only on property situated in the UK. Foreign nationals and individuals with family connections overseas should refer to the *Allied Dunbar Tax Handbook 1997–98* at 22.1 and 22.16 for further details. This chapter concentrates on the position of individuals domiciled in the UK.

21.2 WHEN A CHARGE ARISES

Inheritance tax can apply in the following circumstances:

- on a gift made by an individual during his lifetime;
- on a lifetime transfer of value which is regarded as a 'chargeable transfer';
- on death.

A person who has an interest in possession under a trust or settlement is normally regarded as entitled to the capital. When the beneficiary dies, the full value of the trust property is treated as part of his estate for IHT purposes (see 21.11.1).

Figure 21.1 overleaf indicates the circumstances under which a gift may be a chargeable transfer for IHT purposes.

21.3 TRANSFERS OF VALUE

21.3.1 Transfers which do not amount to gifts

(IHTA 1984, s 3)

The legislation refers mainly to *transfers* rather than gifts. The reason is that all gifts are transfers of value but not all transfers of value are gifts. For example, where a person deliberately sells an asset at less than market value, he may not be making a gift but he is certainly making a transfer of value. Similarly, deliberately omitting to exercise a right can also be a transfer of value, but this is not a gift in the normal sense of the word. To give a third example, a transfer can feature property which is not even owned by the person making it since the IHT legislation deems that a person has made a gift if his interest in possession under a trust comes to an end (see *Allied Dunbar Tax Handbook 1997–98* at 18.4.15).

21.3.2 Gratuitous intent

(IHTA 1984, s 10)

IHT does not normally apply to a transaction unless there is an element of 'bounty' (ie a deliberate intention to make a gift). An unintentional loss of value (eg a loss made on a bad business deal) is not subject to IHT because there was no intention to pass value to another person. On the other hand, it may be difficult to satisfy the Capital Taxes Office that there was no gratuitous intent to benefit a relative or connected person if the terms of the transaction seem unusually favourable.

Figure 21.1 – Chargeable or exempt transfer

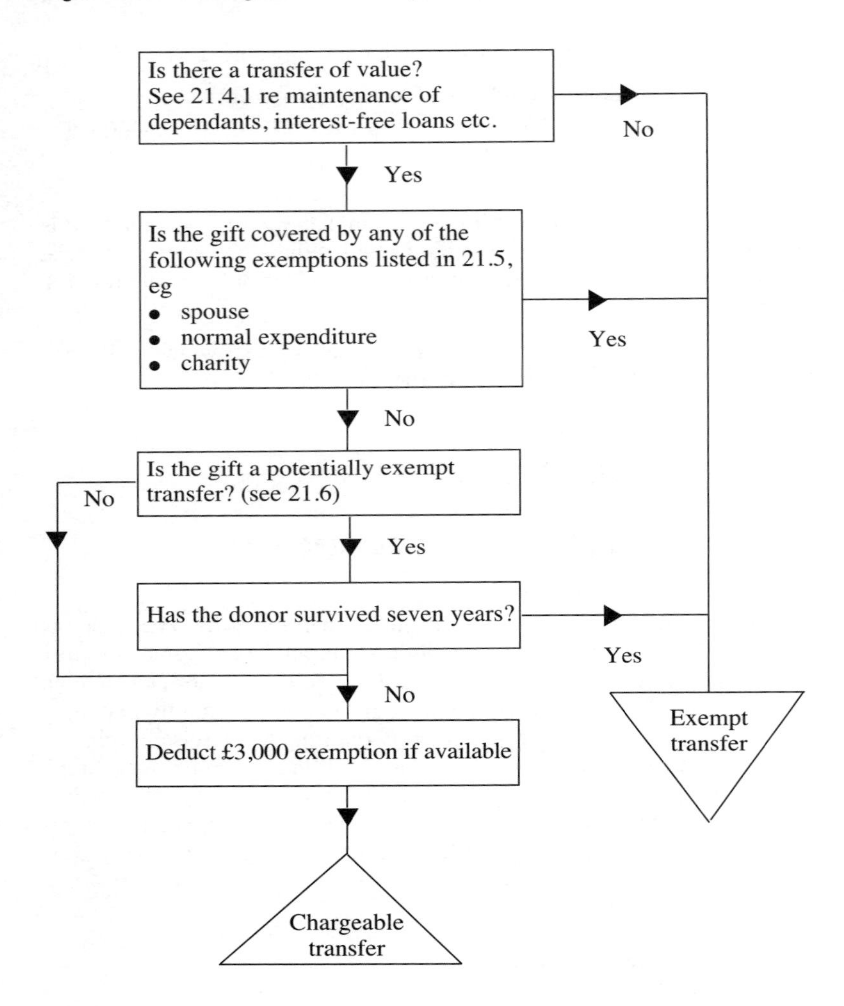

21.3.3 Calculating the value of a transfer

(IHTA 1984, s 3)

The amount of any transfer of value is determined by the reduction in the donor's wealth. This is not necessarily the same as the increase in the recipient's wealth.

This can be illustrated by considering the situation where a person owns 51 out of 100 shares in a company. He has control because he has the majority of the shares. If he were to give two shares to his son, he would relinquish control of the company and his remaining 49 shares might be worth disproportionately less because of this. The two shares given to his son might not be worth particularly much in isolation, and the son may not have acquired a particularly valuable asset, but the father's estate would have gone down in value by the difference between the value of a 51 per cent shareholding and the value of a 49 per cent shareholding. Contrast the way that market value is ascertained for CGT purposes (see 3.6.4).

21.4 GIFTS WHICH ARE NOT TRANSFERS OF VALUE

Certain gifts and other transactions are not regarded as transfers of value so the issue of whether they are chargeable transfers simply does not arise. These include:

- maintenance of family, dependants etc
- waivers of dividends
- waivers of remuneration
- interest-free loans
- disclaimers of legacies
- deeds of variation.

21.4.1 Maintenance of family, dependants etc
(IHTA 1984, s 11)

The legislation specifically provides that the following lifetime payments are not transfers of value:

(1) Payments for the maintenance of a spouse or former spouse.
(2) Payments for the maintenance, education or training of a child or stepchild under the age of 18.
(3) Payments made to maintain a child over 18 who is in full-time education or training.
(4) Reasonable provision for the care or maintenance of a dependent relative, ie someone who is incapacitated by old age or infirmity from maintaining himself, or a widowed, separated or divorced mother or mother-in-law.

21.4.2 Waivers of dividends
(IHTA 1984, s 15)

A waiver of a dividend is not regarded as a transfer of value provided certain conditions are satisfied:

(1) The dividend must be waived by deed.
(2) The deed must not be executed more than 12 months before the right to the dividend has accrued.
(3) The deed waiving the dividend must be executed before any legal entitlement to the dividend arises.

There is a difference in the treatment of interim and final dividends, as the time at which entitlement may arise can be different.

Interim dividends

A shareholder has no enforceable right to payment before the date on which the board declares that a dividend shall be payable. Therefore, a deed waiving a dividend should be executed before any board resolution is passed.

Final dividends

A company might declare a dividend without stipulating any date for payment. In such circumstances, the declaration creates an immediate debt and it is therefore too late to execute a waiver.

In other cases where a final dividend is declared as being payable at a later date, a shareholder *may* waive his entitlement but must do so before the due date for payment.

In practice, a final dividend requires the shareholders' approval; an individual shareholder may therefore waive a dividend provided that the deed is executed before the company's annual general meeting.

21.4.3 Waivers of remuneration
(IHTA 1984, s 14)

There is a specific provision that a waiver of remuneration does not constitute a transfer of value. The terms of this exemption are based on income tax treatment. In practice, the Revenue normally accepts that remuneration is not subject to income tax under Schedule E if it is waived, and the Schedule E assessment has not become final and conclusive, provided:

(1) the remuneration is formally waived (usually by deed), or, if it has already been paid, it is repaid to the employer; and
(2) the employer's assessable profits are adjusted accordingly.

21.4.4 Interest-free loans
(IHTA 1984, s 29)

The IHT legislation specifically provides that an interest-free loan is not to be treated as a transfer of value provided that the loan is repayable on demand.

This exemption would not cover a situation where a loan was made for a specific period, with the lender having no legal right to call for repayment before that time has expired. The grant of such a loan could be a transfer of value. The Revenue would assess the value of the transfer as the difference between the amount of the loan and the present market value of the loan if it were to be assigned.

21.4.5 Disclaimer of legacies
(IHTA 1984, s 142)

If a person becomes entitled to property under a Will or on an intestacy, or under a trust (for example, a life tenant's death), he may disclaim his entitlement. Where such a disclaimer is made, the legacy or other entitlement is not treated as a transfer of value provided that:

(1) no payment or other consideration is given for the disclaimer, and
(2) the person has not already accepted his entitlement, either expressly or by implication.

21.4.6 Deeds of variation
(IHTA 1984, s 142)

A deed of variation may be entered into where a person has died leaving property to a beneficiary, the effect being to redirect the property. Where the necessary conditions are fulfilled, the revised disposition is treated as having taken place on the deceased person's death. Once again, a person who gives up an entitlement is not treated as making a transfer of value.

The following conditions need to be satisfied:

(1) The deed of variation must be executed within two years of the death.
(2) The deed must be in writing and must specifically refer to the provisions of the Will etc which are to be varied.

(3) It must be signed by the person who would otherwise have benefited, and anyone else who might have benefited.
(4) Only one deed of variation in respect of a particular piece of property can be effective for IHT purposes.
(5) No payment or other consideration may pass between beneficiaries to induce them to enter into the deed of variation (except that a variation which consists of an exchange of inheritances and a cash adjustment is permitted).
(6) The deed must be submitted to the Capital Taxes Office within six months of its being executed.

21.5 EXEMPT TRANSFERS

Even if a transfer takes place, it does not attract IHT if it is an exempt transfer. The full list of exempt transfers is as follows:

(1) Gifts to spouse
(2) Normal expenditure out of income
(3) Small gifts of up to £250
(4) Gifts of up to £3,000 a year
(5) Marriage gifts
(6) Gifts to charities
(7) Gifts for national purposes
(8) Gifts for public benefit
(9) Gifts to political parties
(10) Certain transfers to employee trusts.

21.5.1 Gifts to spouse
(IHTA 1984, s 18)

There is normally an unlimited exemption for transfers between husband and wife. For this purpose, a couple is regarded as husband and wife until a decree absolute has been made. The exemption covers outright gifts, legacies and transfers of property to a trust under which the spouse has an interest in possession. (The transfer may be either a lifetime transfer or a transfer which takes place on death.)

The exemption is restricted where a UK-domiciled individual makes transfers to a foreign domiciled spouse. In this situation, the exemption is limited to £55,000 (see *Allied Dunbar Tax Handbook 1997–98* at 17.5.1).

21.5.2 Normal expenditure out of income
(IHTA 1984, s 21)

A lifetime gift is exempt if it is shown that it was made as part of the donor's normal expenditure and comes out of income. The legislation requires that the gift should be 'normal', ie that the donor had a habit of making such gifts or must have intended to make a series of such gifts. The legislation also requires that by taking one year with another, the pattern of such gifts must have left the donor with sufficient income to maintain his normal standard of living.

Gifts which take the form of payments under deed of covenant or the payment of premiums under life assurance policies written in trust frequently qualify as exempt because of this rule.

21.5.3 Small gifts
(IHTA 1984, s 20)

Any number of individual gifts of up to £250 in any one tax year are exempt. But where gifts to any one individual exceed £250, the exemption is lost completely.

21.5.4 Annual exemption
(IHTA 1984, s 19)

This exemption is available to cover part of a larger gift. The exemption is £3,000 for each tax year. Furthermore, both husband and wife have separate annual exemptions.

If the full £3,000 is not used in a given year, the balance can be carried forward for one year only, and is then allowable only if the exemption for the second year is fully utilised.

21.5.5 Gifts in consideration of marriage
(IHTA 1984, s 22)

Gifts made to a bride or groom in consideration of their marriage are exempt up to the following amounts:

Gifts made by	*Maximum exemption*
Each parent	£5,000
Grandparents	£2,500
Bride or groom	£2,500
Any other person	£1,000

21.5.6 Gifts to charities
(IHTA 1984, s 23)

Gifts to charities which are established in the UK are exempt regardless of the amount. A charity may be established or registered here even though it carries out its work overseas and the exemption covers gifts to such charities. However, donations made to a foreign charity which is established abroad do not normally qualify.

21.5.7 Gifts for national purposes
(IHTA 1984, s 25)

Gifts to certain national bodies are totally exempt. These bodies include colleges and universities, the National Trust, the National Gallery, the British Museum and other galleries and museums run by local authorities or universities.

21.5.8 Gifts for public benefit
(IHTA 1984, s 26)

This exemption covers gifts of eligible property such as historic buildings, land of outstanding scenic, historic or scientific interest, works of art and collections of national, scientific, historic or artistic interest. It is necessary to clear the position in advance with HM Treasury if the exemption is to be available.

21.5.9 Gifts to political parties
(IHTA 1984, s 24)

Gifts to 'qualifying political parties' are exempt only if certain conditions are satisfied. A political party qualifies if it had at least two MPs returned at the last general election, or if it had at least one member and more than 150,000 votes were cast for its candidates.

21.5.10 Certain transfers to employee trusts
(IHTA 1984, s 28)

Transfers by an individual to an employee trust of shares in a company can be exempt provided all the following conditions are satisfied:

(1) The beneficiaries of the trust must include all or most of the persons employed by or holding office with the company.
(2) Within one year of the transfer:

   (a) the trustees must hold more than 50 per cent of the company's ordinary share capital and have voting control on all questions which affect it as a whole; and
   (b) the trustees' control must not be fettered by some other provision or agreement between the shareholders.
(3) The trust deed must not permit any of the trust property to be applied at any time for the benefit of:
   (a) a participator in the company (ie a person who holds a 5 per cent or greater interest);
   (b) any person who has been a participator at any time during the ten years prior to the transfer; or
   (c) any person connected with a participator or former participator.

A further restriction may apply where a company makes a transfer to an employee trust.

21.6 POTENTIALLY EXEMPT TRANSFERS

(IHTA 1984, s 3A)

21.6.1 Definition

Irrevocable gifts made during an individual's lifetime may, provided certain conditions are satisfied, be 'potentially exempt transfers' (PETs). These gifts become actually exempt only if the donor survives for seven years. If the donor dies during that period, the PET becomes a chargeable transfer. The tax payable depends on the rates of IHT in force at the date of death. The donee is liable to pay the tax.

The main conditions to be satisfied for a gift to be a PET are that:

(1) the gift is made to an individual; or
(2) the gift is made to a trust for a disabled person (see *Allied Dunbar Tax Handbook 1997–98* at 18.7);
(3) the gift is made to an accumulation and maintenance trust (see *Allied Dunbar Tax Handbook 1997–98* at 18.6).

A gift which is subject to a reservation of benefit (see 21.7) cannot be a PET. Furthermore, a gift to a discretionary trust is a chargeable transfer (see 21.10).

21.6.2 Taper relief

(IHTA 1984, s 7)

Where an individual makes a PET and dies within the seven-year period, taper relief may reduce the amount of tax payable. The tax payable on the transfer which has become a chargeable transfer is subject to the following reduction:

Years between gift and death	*Percentage of the full charge*
Three to four	80
Four to five	60
Five to six	40
Six to seven	20

21.7 RESERVATION OF BENEFIT

(FA 1986, s 102 & Sched 20)

21.7.1 Introduction

Property which has been gifted may still be deemed to form part of a deceased person's estate unless:

(1) possession and enjoyment of the property was *bona fide* assumed by the donee; and
(2) the property was enjoyed virtually to the entire exclusion of the donor and of any benefit to him by contract or otherwise.

The reference under (2) above means that for all practical purposes this is an 'all or nothing' test. The Revenue view is that the exception is intended to cover only trivial benefits, for example, where the donor of a picture enjoyed the chance to view it when making occasional visits to the donee's home.

The term 'by contract or otherwise' is meant to embrace arrangements which are not legally binding but which amount to an honourable understanding. This might arise where a person gives away a house but remains in occupation. A reservation of benefit would arise even if there is no legal tenancy and the donee could, in law, require the donor to vacate the property at any time.

21.7.2 Two specific exemptions

The legislation specifically states that occupation of property or use of chattels does not count as a benefit provided a market rent is paid by the donor. The legislation also provides for the benefit enjoyed by a donor who occupies property he has given to another where the donor's financial circumstances changed drastically for the worse after the gift was made.

21.7.3 Ending of reservation of benefit

Where a person makes a gift and initially reserves a benefit, but then relinquishes that reservation, the donor is treated as making a PET at the time that he gives up the reserved benefit. The amount of the PET is governed by the market value of the property at that time.

21.7.4 Example – Giving up reservation of benefit

> *A* gives property worth £150,000 in July 1990 but reserves a benefit. The benefit is relinquished in July 1995 when the property is worth £220,000. *A* dies in October 1996.
>
> If no benefit had been reserved, the gift would have been completely exempt by August 1997 (ie seven years after the gift), but because a benefit was retained until July 1995, the seven-year period starts only from that date.
>
> The full £220,000 (ie the value at July 1995 when the reservation of benefit came to an end) would form part of *A*'s estate for IHT purposes.

21.7.5 Settlements and trusts

The Revenue has confirmed that a settlor may be a trustee of a settlement created by the settlor without this constituting a reservation of benefit. Also, where the settled property includes shares in a family company, the settlor/trustee may also be a director of the company and may be permitted under the trust deed to retain his remuneration provided it is reasonable in relation to the services rendered.

The position is less clear where a person has sought to reserve the *possibility* of a benefit, eg where an individual has created a settlement and is a potential beneficiary. It is the Revenue's view that a benefit is reserved where the settlor creates a discretionary trust and is a member of a class of potential beneficiaries. This would also apply where the settlor may be added to a class of potential beneficiaries. However, the Revenue has confirmed that no reservation of benefit arises where a person creates a settlement and is a contingent or default beneficiary. This might apply, for example, where property is put into trust for the settlor's children but would revert to the settlor if the children die or become bankrupt.

The legislation does not require that the donor's spouse should be excluded from benefit, and where a discretionary settlement is created it would be possible to include as a potential beneficiary the donor's spouse, any future spouse or widow/widower. However, if property were to be distributed to the donor's spouse from the trust and that property were then to be applied for the benefit of the *settlor,* the Revenue might well take the view that, looked at as a whole, there had been a reservation of benefit.

21.8 BUSINESS PROPERTY
(IHTA 1984, ss 103–114)

21.8.1 Basic requirements

A special deduction from liability to IHT is given in respect of value of business property where the following conditions are satisfied:

(1) The property must have been owned during the previous two years; or it must have been inherited from a spouse and, when the spouse's period of ownership is taken into account, the combined period of ownership exceeds two years.
(2) The property must not be subject to a binding contract for sale.

There is no requirement that the business should be carried on in the UK.

21.8.2 Rates of business property relief

Unincorporated businesses

A sole proprietor's interest in his business qualifies for a 100 per cent deduction. A partner's interest in his firm also qualifies for 100 per cent relief. A 50 per cent deduction is available in respect of an asset owned by a partner but used by his firm.

Shares and debentures

Business relief on shares is available only where the company concerned is a trading company or the holding company of a trading group.

The 100 per cent relief is available on shares and debentures in an unquoted company where the transferor had voting control before the transfer. Relief of 100 per cent is also available for a controlling interest in a quoted trading company.

The 100 per cent relief is also available for a transfer of shares in an unquoted trading company provided that the transferor had control of more than 25 per cent of the voting rights before the transfer. Specific legislation on 'related property' means that where a husband and wife's combined shareholding exceeds 25 per cent, the 100 per cent relief is available even though neither spouse has more than 25 per cent when looked at in isolation. A 100 per cent deduction is given for other shareholdings in unquoted trading companies. Shares dealt in on the USM or the AIM are regarded as unquoted shares.

Relief of 50 per cent is available where a controlling shareholder transfers an asset which is used by his company, or where such an asset passes on his death.

21.8.3 Businesses which do not qualify

Business relief is not normally available where the business carried on consists wholly or mainly of dealing in securities, stocks or shares, or land or buildings, or in making investments.

Where the transfer is of shares, business relief may be restricted if the company owns investments. The legislation refers to such investments as 'excepted assets', which are defined as assets which are neither:

(1) used wholly or mainly for the purposes of the business, nor
(2) required for the future use of the business.

21.8.4 Example – Restriction on business property relief

A dies holding shares in X Ltd, and X Ltd's balance sheet shows the following assets:

	£
Investments	750,000
Factory	1,000,000
Stock	300,000
Debtors	200,000
Cash	1,250,000

Only part of the value of the shares qualify for business relief. The part which would not qualify is normally:

$$\frac{\text{Investment} \quad 750{,}000}{\text{Total assets} \quad 3{,}500{,}000}$$

If the cash were excessive in relation to the likely needs and requirements of the business, there could also be a restriction on this count.

21.8.5 Test normally applied on a 'consolidated basis'

Where a company has subsidiaries, it is necessary to look at the group situation (ie shares in subsidiaries may have to be treated as excepted assets if the subsidiaries are investment companies). The Capital Taxes Office has confirmed that business assets held by subsidiaries of subsidiary companies should qualify for business relief.

21.9 AGRICULTURAL PROPERTY

(IHTA 1984, ss 115–124B)

Relief is available on the agricultural value of farmland in the UK, Channel Islands or Isle of Man.

21.9.1 Land occupied by the transferor

Relief is available where the individual had occupied the farmland for the two years prior to the date of the transfer. Where a farm has been sold and another farm acquired, the replacement farm normally qualifies for agricultural property relief provided that the owner occupied the two farms for a combined period of at least two years in the last five years. Agricultural property relief is also available for land owned by an individual but occupied by a firm of which he is a partner, or by a company of which he is the controlling shareholder for the two years preceding the date of the transfer.

21.9.2 Tenanted land

To qualify under this head, the individual must normally have owned the land for at least seven years.

A 100 per cent deduction is available on land which is not occupied by the owner provided he has (or had at the date of his death) the legal right to regain vacant possession within a period not exceeding twelve months.

A 100 per cent deduction is available for tenanted farmland where the owner cannot obtain vacant possession within twelve months. This is generally the case where the land is let under an agricultural tenancy.

21.10 COMPUTATION OF TAX ON LIFETIME TRANSFERS

In practice, IHT is likely to be paid during a person's lifetime only for chargeable transfers made by him to a discretionary trust or on transfers effected through a gift of assets to a company.

The IHT is computed as follows:

Table 21.1 IHT payable on lifetime transfers

Initial calculation		
Chargeable transfers made during the preceding seven years		A
Add	Amount of chargeable transfer	B
		C
Deduct	Nil rate band	D
		E

Table 21.1 ***Cont.***

	IHT thereon at 20 per cent	[X]
Deduct	IHT on a notional transfer of [A] minus [D] as if it took place at the same time	[Y]
	IHT payable in respect of the chargeable transfer	[Z]
Position if the donor dies within three years		
Chargeable transfers made during the previous seven years		[A]
Add	Potentially exempt transfers caught by the seven year rule	[B]
		[C]
Add	amount of chargeable transfer	[D]
		[E]
Deduct	Nil rate band	[F]
		[G]
	IHT thereon at 40 per cent	[H]
	Deduct IHT at 40 per cent on a notional transfer of [A] minus [F]	[I]
		[J]

The donee is liable to pay additional IHT of [J] minus the amount already paid under [Z] above.

21.11 COMPUTATION OF TAX PAYABLE ON DEATH

21.11.1 Normal basis

The charge on death is normally computed as shown in the figure overleaf:

Figure 21.2 IHT payable on death

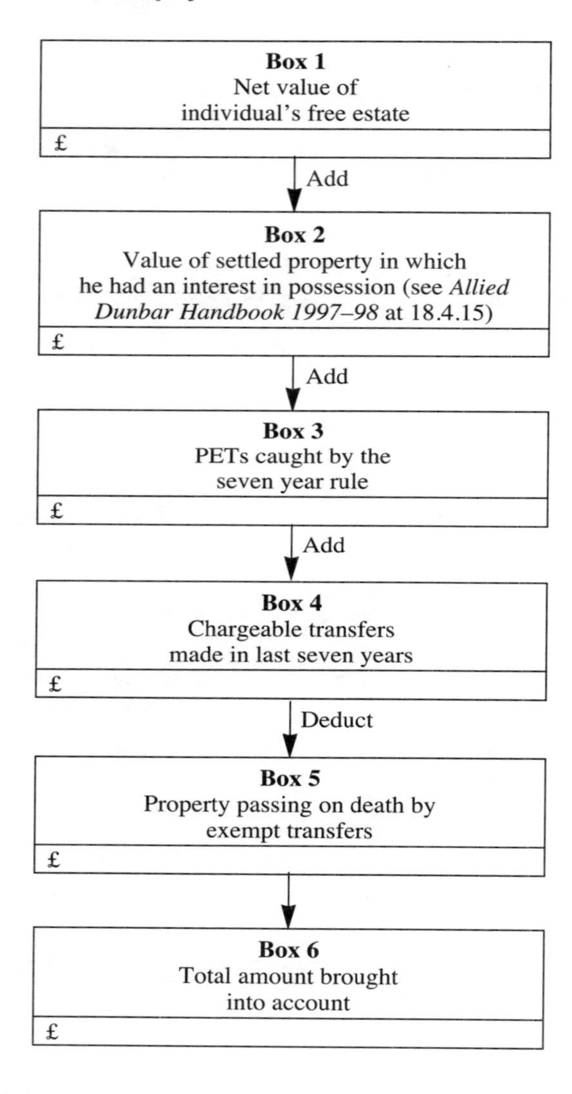

The IHT is the tax on the figure in box 6, minus the tax payable on a normal transfer equal to the amount in box 4 as if the notional transfer took place immediately prior to the death. Some taper relief may be due on the PETs caught by the seven-year rule, see 21.6.2.

A number of special reliefs may be available.

21.11.3 Sales of land at a loss

(IHTA 1984, ss 190–198 as amended by FA 1993, s 199)

Relief is due where land and buildings are sold at a loss within four years of death, provided the loss is at least £1,000 or 5 per cent of probate value (whichever is less). The net proceeds are substituted for the value at the date of death and the IHT is re-computed. However, this relief applies only where the property is sold to an arms' length purchaser rather than to a connected person.

The period was three years rather than four in relation to deaths before 16 March 1990.

21.11.4 Debts which may be disallowed

(FA 1986, s 103)

As a general rule debts are not deductible where the deceased made a capital transfer to a person who subsequently made a loan-back to the deceased. This rule applies only to loans made after 18 March 1986 but there is no such time limit on the capital transfers. A debt may be disallowed because the deceased had made a capital transfer to the lender even though that capital transfer took place before 18 March 1986. Nor is it of any help that the loan was made on normal commercial terms and a market rate of interest was payable.

21.11.4 Treatment of gifts caught by seven-year rule

(IHTA 1984, s 113A)

Tax on a PET which becomes a chargeable transfer because of the transferor's death is payable by the recipient of the gift.

Business relief is available on a PET that becomes a chargeable transfer only if the conditions in 21.8 are satisfied both at the time of the gift and at the time of death.

21.11.6 Examples – Business relief on PETs

(1) *A* owns all the shares in a family company. He gives his son a 24 per cent shareholding. Three years later, the company is sold and the son receives cash for his shares. One year after that *A* dies.

Business relief is not normally available as the necessary conditions are not satisfied by the donee at the time of *A*'s death. If the son had reinvested the proceeds in another private company, business relief might have been available after all.

(2) In this case the basic position is as in (1), ie *A* has made a gift to his son of a 24 per cent shareholding. However, this time, the son retains his shares, but by the time *A* dies, the shares are quoted. No relief is due as the son does not control the company and his shares are quoted shares.

(3) The basic position is as in (1) but, in this case, the son retains the shares and they are still unquoted at the time of *A*'s death. The shares attract the 100 per cent relief and this is not lost even if the son disposes of the shares shortly after *A*'s death.

21.11.7 Replacement property

Where a donee has disposed of business property but acquires replacement property, the PET may yet attract business relief. The replacement property must be acquired within three years.

21.12 HANDING ON THE FAMILY BUSINESS/COMPANY WITHOUT ATTRACTING IHT

21.12.1 General strategy

Many proprietors are reluctant to transfer ownership of their businesses or family companies to the next generation. There may be good reasons for this: perhaps the proprietor's children are too young to take on the responsibility or they may not appear to have much aptitude for business. Experience is that most proprietors wish to retain control during their lifetime, but are equally anxious that their work should not go to waste, and often wish to take appropriate steps to avoid heavy death duties on the business.

The best way for a proprietor to plan varies according to the particular circumstances, although the following general strategy suits most situations:

(1) A proprietor should endeavour to provide himself with a guaranteed 'income stream' which is not dependent on the family business/company. Once he has secured this (eg by funding a personal pension plan) he is in a position to contemplate gifts.
(2) Effective use of insurance and pension arrangements can help to cover the position in the short and medium term.
(3) The benefits of business property relief or agricultural relief should be maximised. It is particularly important to make sure that no action is taken which jeopardises these very valuable reliefs.
(4) The proprietor should draw up a Will in the most tax-efficient way.

(5) It usually makes sense for gifts to be made sooner rather than later, especially if the business is growing in value. Ideally, such gifts should be PETs.
(6) Transferring property to a trust may enable the individual to mitigate IHT without relinquishing control of the capital during his lifetime.

21.12.2 Pension arrangements

The tax advantages of funding a pension scheme cannot be overstated. An individual who funds a personal pension plan will secure income tax relief at his marginal rate. Where a company funds a pension scheme for a director, the company normally secures relief against its corporation tax liability, thus saving tax at either 33 per cent or 25 per cent (or in exceptional circumstances, at 35 per cent, see 18.2.6).

The pension which results from such contributions confers a degree of financial independence so that the individual relies less on income from his business or family company and is therefore more able to consider giving away part or all of his interest in that business.

Furthermore, most pension arrangements provide death-in-service cover which means that a lump sum may be paid out, free of IHT, if the individual dies before drawing his pension. The existence of such cover (which in the case of company directors may be up to 400 per cent of the individual's salary and other remuneration) means that funds should be available to cover any IHT liability which may arise if the proprietor should die in the short term.

21.12.3 Maximising business relief

It is crucially important that any loans are secured on non-business assets. The reason for this is that business (and agricultural) relief is due only on the net value after deducting any loan secured against the property.

21.12.4 Example – Securing loans

> *A* owns a business worth £500,000. The business assets include a factory which is subject to a £300,000 mortgage. If *A* should die, business relief is due only on £200,000. In contrast, if *A* had borrowed against other assets, business relief might have been due on the full £500,000.

It may be possible to secure the best of both worlds. Income tax relief on interest is available where a loan has been raised for a particular purpose, regardless of how the loan is secured. Thus, it seems possible in principle for a person to borrow for a qualifying purpose but secure the loan against another asset (eg his main residence) so that business relief is not restricted on death.

21.12.5 Avoiding buy/sell clauses

In the past, many partnership agreements included a clause intended to protect the widow and family of a deceased partner. Typically, such agreements contained a clause (often called a buy/sell clause) requiring that on the death of a partner the surviving partners purchase the deceased's interest in the firm. Similar arrangements were often contained in shareholder agreements entered into by working shareholder/directors in private companies. While such arrangements are commercially sensible, there is a problem in that the Revenue regards them as amounting to a binding contract for sale and so not eligible for business property relief at all (see 21.8.1).

This problem can be avoided. It is possible to have a legally enforceable agreement which has almost exactly the same consequences as a buy/sell agreement but which does not jeopardise business relief. The recommended arrangement involves options. Each partner or shareholder/director grants his colleagues an option and his colleagues grant him an option. The options are exercisable on death and enable the deceased's executors to require the surviving partners/shareholder/directors to buy them out at a fair price.

The Revenue has specifically confirmed that the existence of such options does not preclude availability of business relief or agricultural relief; see Statement of Practice SP12/80.

21.12.6 Assets owned by a partner but used by the firm

Where a partner owns an asset (eg a building) which is used by the partnership for its business, business relief is available at the rate of 50 per cent. In some family situations, it may be appropriate for the asset to be brought into the partnership so that on the death of the owner 100 per cent business property relief, rather than 50 per cent, is available.

21.12.7 Assets owned by shareholders

Similarly, a shareholder may own an asset which is used by a private company in which he is a shareholder. Unfortunately, no business property relief is available unless he is a controlling shareholder. It follows that a minority shareholder should carefully consider giving away such an asset (see 21.6 on PETs). Alternatively, it could make sense from this particular point of view to add to his shareholding so that he becomes a controlling shareholder.

21.12.8 Tax-efficient Wills

It is usually desirable for a proprietor to fully utilise the nil rate band rather than leave his entire estate to his spouse. However, this is general advice and the best way of drawing a Will depends upon the individual's particular circumstances.

In some cases, it is likely that property which qualifies for business property relief may be sold after the individual has died. If this property passes in the first instance to the individual's widow, it means that IHT is payable in the long term, when she dies. In a case such as this, it may be appropriate for the individual to draw his Will so that business property passes into a discretionary Will trust. No IHT should be payable if 100 per cent business property relief is available, and the burden of IHT is much reduced in a situation where 50 per cent relief is available. Property held in a discretionary trust will not form part of the widow's estate on her death, even if she is one of the beneficiaries of the Will trust, and in fact receives most of the income. There may be a charge on property held by the trustees once every ten years, but the rate is relatively modest compared with the normal 40 per cent rate which applies where an individual owns non-business property or has an interest in possession.

21.12.9 Example – Planning a Will

A is the managing director and a substantial shareholder in X Ltd. His shares qualify for 100 per cent business property relief on his death. However, his children are not involved in the business and the executors sell the shares for £1m.

If *A* had left the shares to his children, the IHT position would be satisfactory in that no charge would arise on *A*'s death or on Mrs *A*'s death.

If *A* left the whole of his estate to his widow, an IHT charge would eventually arise on capital of £1m, and additional IHT of £400,000 might be payable on Mrs *A*'s death.

If *A* left the shares to a discretionary will trust, Mrs *A* could benefit during her lifetime but there would be no IHT charge on her death. The trustees may be liable for the periodic charge every ten years but the maximum rate at present is 6 per cent (see *Allied Dunbar Tax Handbook 1997–98* at 18.5.12).

21.12.10 Property which cannot attract business property relief on widow's death

An individual may be a partner in a business which the widow cannot take over, eg the individual may be a doctor, dentist or solicitor. If he owns an asset used by the firm (eg the business premises) there is 50 per cent business property relief if the property passes on his death to someone other than his widow. However, there is no business property relief if the property is left to the widow and then forms part of her estate on her death.

21.12.11 Double business property relief

It is sometimes possible to obtain business relief twice. For example, B dies owning non-business assets worth £2m and a 26 per cent shareholding in an unquoted trading company worth £1m; his Will leaves all the non-business assets to his widow and the 26 per cent shareholding to a discretionary Will trust. The position is:

	£
Will trust	1m
Less business relief	1m
Chargeable transfer for IHT purposes	NIL

If the Will trustees then buy £1m of the non-business assets from the widow and sell the 26 per cent shareholding to her, it may qualify for business property relief on her death (provided she survives two years). The position is then:

	£
Will trust (no charge on widow's death as it does not form part of her estate)	1m
Widow's free estate	2m
Less business property relief	1m
IHT payable on	NIL

21.12.12 Deeds of variation

Even if an individual's Will is not drawn up in the most tax-efficient way, it may be possible for the family to reorganise matters during the two years after his death by taking advantage of the provisions on deeds of variation (see 21.4.6).

21.12.13 Family trusts

One advantage for an individual who makes a gift into a settlement is that he may be a trustee and can therefore continue to control the way in which the capital is used.

The Revenue has specifically confirmed that the fact that a settlor is the first named trustee and can therefore exercise voting rights attaching to shares which he has put into trust does not mean that he has reserved a benefit. The Revenue has also confirmed that an individual may include his or her spouse as a potential beneficiary without the trust being caught by the gift with reservation rules. However, this may have adverse income tax consequences in that any income arising to the trustees is taxed as if it were the settlor's income. Accordingly, settlements are usually drawn up so that the spouse cannot benefit during the settlor's lifetime, but can benefit as the settlor's widow. Where the trust deed is worded in this way, the adverse income tax consequences do not arise.

GLOSSARY

Actual basis of assessment This describes the situation where a person carrying on a trade or profession is assessed according to the profits which he has actually earned during the tax year concerned.

Accounting reference date The date to which accounts are made up for a company. In practice, when a company is formed, the accounting reference date is normally the last day of the month in which the anniversary of its incorporation falls.

Ad valorem duties Duties which are charged as a percentage of the value of the asset concerned, particularly stamp duty.

Administrator An officer appointed by the court who takes charge of the company's affairs on insolvency and one of whose aims is to secure the company's survival.

Advance corporation tax Tax payable by companies on dividend payments, etc, which may be offset against the company's mainstream corporation tax liability.

Agricultural buildings allowances A form of capital allowance given for expenditure on buildings used for agricultural purposes.

Agricultural property relief A relief given for inheritance tax purposes. The relief is either 50 or 100 per cent of the value of agricultural land. To qualify, the land must be situated in the UK, Channel Islands or Isle of Man.

Alternative Investment Market The Stock Exchange launched the AIM in June 1995 to enable investors to deal in shares in unquoted companies. The AIM replaces the Unlisted Securities Market, a market for dealing in unquoted shares which is now closed to new entrants.

Annual charges Certain payments made by a company are allowable in computing its corporation tax liability. Such payments include interest and payments under deed of covenant. In general, when the company makes an annual payment it must deduct tax at the basic rate and account for this at the end of the quarter on form CT61.

Annual exemption An individual is entitled to an annual exemption for CGT purposes of £6,000. There are two types of annual exemption for IHT. An individual may give away up to £250 to any number of people in a tax year. This is generally called the 'small gifts exemption'. Separately from this, an individual is allowed to make chargeable transfers of up to £3,000 per annum which are treated as exempt.

Arrival A VAT term used for imports from other EU member states, particularly in connection with reporting trade statistics.

Articles of association A company's regulations which govern its procedures, day-to-day operations and the members' relationship between themselves.

Associated companies Companies controlled by the same person or groups of persons.

Business property relief This is a deduction of either 50 or 100 per cent which is made from the value of business property when it is assessed for IHT purposes.

Buy/sell clause A legally binding agreement under which two shareholders agree that in the event of certain things occurring in the future, one shareholder will offer the other his shares and the other will be required to buy them.

Capital *Authorised or nominal* – The limit of capital to which the company can go to in issuing new shares without passing a resolution to increase its capital.

Issued or allotted – The amount of shares actually issued by the company to its members.

Paid up – The amount of issued or allotted share capital paid up by the members.

Capital allowances These are allowances given for plant and machinery, industrial buildings and commercial property in enterprise zones. In general terms, capital allowances represent a form of relief which corresponds to depreciation.

Capital expenditure This is expenditure of a once and for all nature to achieve an enduring benefit for a trade. It is not a cost which may be deducted in arriving at profits for tax purposes, although capital allowances may be available. Contrast revenue expenditure.

CFC legislation There is special legislation on controlled foreign companies (CFCs). A UK-resident company which has an interest in a CFC may be taxed on a proportion of the CFC's profits.

Charge Security for the payment of a debt or performance of an obligation. In property law the most common charge is by way of legal mortgage. In company law a charge can be fixed on a particular asset or a floating charge.

Chargeable transfer A gift or other transfer of value made by an individual which is not covered by any of the various exemptions and which is therefore a transfer for IHT purposes.

Class rights Rights attaching to different classes of shares in the articles.

Closing years' rules Under the Schedule D preceding year rules basis, a firm is assessed on the actual basis for the tax year in which it ceases to carry on business. Furthermore, the Revenue has the right to adjust the assessments for the two preceding years so that those years may also be assessed on the actual basis if this produces higher assessments than under the preceding year basis.

Condition Under English contract law, a condition is a term of a contract of such importance that if a party to the contract breaches it the other party may repudiate the contract.

Conditional sale A type of contract for sale which does not become legally binding until some condition is satisfied.

Consideration In general, a contract becomes legally binding under English law only if it is entered into for consideration, ie for money or monies worth.

Constructive dismissal Under employment law, an employee who has resigned because of unfair action taken by an employer may argue that the employer has broken the contract of employment and thus constructively dismissed the employee.

Continuation election This is an election which may be made in respect of a change in partners prior to 6 April 1997. Unless the election is made, such change is generally treated as giving rise to a cessation of the firm for tax purposes whereas the effect of a continuation election is that the change in partners is disregarded and the firm's business is treated as a continuing business.

There is a strict time limit for the submission of a continuation election: basically the election needs to be in the hands of the Inspector of Taxes within two years of the change in partners.

A continuation election needs to be signed by all parties, ie all individuals who were partners before the change and all individuals who were partners immediately afterwards.

Contingent liabilities A contingent liability to make a payment, or return part of sale proceeds, if certain events occur (ie if contingencies occur).

Copyright The exclusive right of printing and copying a published literary work or other original material and the right to prevent all others of doing so.

Corporation tax This is a tax levied on companies' profits. The full rate is 31 per cent but many companies qualify for the small companies rate (see below).

Covenant An obligation which is contained is a deed and can be negative or restrictive on the one hand and positive (ie requiring some act or payment) on the other.

Current year basis This is the new Schedule D basis of assessment introduced by FA 1994, whereby an individual is assessed on his profits for the firm's year which ends in the tax year. It came into effect from 1996–97 onwards (unless the business started after 5 April 1994 in which case it applies from commencement).

Debenture A document evidencing a loan to a company. Such a document often enables the lender to have a charge over the company's property.

Deeds of variation A lease can be varied by agreement. In addition it is a special term for IHT purposes. Where the provisions of a person's Will are varied by the beneficiaries' mutual consent, and the necessary deed of variation is executed within two years of the relevant death, IHT may be computed as if the deceased's Will had contained the revised provisions from the outset. A similar treatment may apply where a person has died without making a valid Will, and the individuals who would benefit under the intestacy rules mutually agree to vary the position.

Deep discount bonds These are loan stocks issued by a company. A loan stock is a deep discount bond if it is issued at a discount of more than 15 per cent or more than 0.5 per cent for each year of the bond's life. Thus, if the company issues loan stock at a price of £94, and the loan stock is repayable in ten years time, the loan stock is a deep discount bond as the £6 discount represents more than 0.5 per cent for the ten-year period during which the loan stock exists.

A company may secure tax relief for discount as if it were interest payable on the loan stock. The investor may be charged tax on the discount which has accrued during his period of ownership, as if it were interest.

Deep gain securities These are loan stocks issued by companies. A deep gain security is similar to a deep discount bond except that the overall rate of return cannot be precisely computed. In such circumstances, the investor may be taxed on any gain when the security is redeemed. However, there is no relief to the company when it redeems the deep gain security.

De-registration De-registration occurs when a trader who has been registered for VAT purposes is permitted to deregister. Once the trader has deregistered, he must not charge VAT on any supplies subsequently made by him in the course of his business.

Despatches A VAT term used for exports in EU trade.

Directive EU legislation which must be implemented in the national legislation of each of the member states.

Dispensations An employer is required to make annual returns of payments and benefits provided to employees (form P11D). A dispensation may be negotiated with the Revenue whereby certain expenses and other payments need not be reported on form P11D.

Distribution A distribution of a company's assets to its members (ie shareholders), for example a payment of a dividend. Distributions may also be made by a liquidator. Where assets are distributed to members of the company during the course of a liquidation, there is said to be a distribution *in specie*.

Dividends A dividend is a cash amount paid to a member of a company according to the number of shares held by him. Dividends may only be declared out of distributable profits.

Earnings basis Accounts should be prepared so as to reflect a trader's earnings for a year rather than just cash received. Thus, accounts should include debtors, ie bills which have been issued but which have not been paid by the year end.

Election to waive exemption A VAT term used in commercial land and property transactions. Otherwise known as the option to tax. A landowner has the option to make what would otherwise be an exempt supply into a taxable supply. Formal notification to Customs is required.

Enhancement expenditure This is a term used in the context of CGT. In computing a person's capital gain, it is possible to deduct the costs incurred in acquiring the asset and any enhancement expenditure on improvements etc which is reflected in the state of the asset at the date of disposal.

Enterprise Investment Scheme This is a scheme launched by the Government on 1 January 1994 under which individuals may receive income tax and CGT relief when investing in qualifying unquoted trading companies.

Enterprise zones The Government has designated certain areas as enterprise zones. Designation normally lasts for a period of ten years. During that period, a person carrying on a business within the enterprise zone is exempt from business rates. There is also considerable freedom from planning controls.

Expenditure on commercial buildings situated in an enterprise zone qualifies for capital allowances. The acquisition of an unused commercial building, or a building which has been let only during the preceding two years, attracts a 100 per cent allowance.

EU The European Union comprises Austria, Belgium, Denmark, Finland, France, Germany, Greece, Ireland, Italy, Luxembourg, the Netherlands, Portugal, Spain, Sweden and the UK.

Exempt supplies Supplies which are not liable to VAT. A person who makes only exempt supplies cannot recover input VAT suffered by him.

Exempt transfers The following transfers are exempt from inheritance tax: gifts to spouse; normal expenditure out of income; £250 small gifts exemption; annual £3,000 exemption; exemption for marriage gifts; gifts to charities; gifts for national purposes; gifts for public benefit; gifts to political parties; certain transfers of employee trusts.

Ex-gratia A person makes an ex-gratia payment when he does so without admitting liability.

Fiduciary duties A director is under a duty not to let his own interests conflict with those of the company.

Floating charge This is a type of charge or security that may be granted to lenders. A floating charge differs from a fixed charge in that it does not apply only to a specific asset or assets but rather applies to a class of assets.

Forex Extensive new tax legislation came into effect for companies in respect of accounting periods starting on or after 23 March 1995. The legislation deals with foreign exchange gains and losses as recognised for tax purposes. The Forex regime may result in a tax liability on certain profits which are recognised for accounting purposes but are unrealised profits in that no disposal has occurred during the accounting period concerned.

Form CT61 A quarterly return required for a company in respect of dividends and annual payments made under deduction of tax.

Form P11D An annual return made by employers of expenses payments and benefits in kind provided for an employee.

Full-time working directors and managers This is a concept which applies for the purposes of CGT retirement relief. A person selling shares in a company qualifies for retirement relief only if he is a full-time worker or manager, ie someone who is required to spend the greater part of his time working for the company in a managerial capacity.

Groups of companies There are various different rules under which companies may be regarded as part of a group.

A parent company may have subsidiaries, ie other companies in which the parent company has a majority shareholding. The companies constitute a group for company law purposes.

The conditions which need to be satisfied for companies to form a group for tax purposes vary, but in general the parent company needs to have a 75 per cent interest in its subsidiaries.

Group registration for VAT purposes Companies which are under common control may register for VAT purposes as a single unit or VAT group. Where this happens, all supplies between the companies concerned are disregarded for VAT purposes. VAT is charged only on supplies outside the group.

Hold-over relief This is the relief given to a donor or other transferor of business assets. Where an individual etc is entitled to hold-over relief, his gain is not charged but is deducted from the asset's market value in determining the transferee's acquisition value for CGT purposes.

Indemnity A collateral contract or security which prevents one person from suffering loss from the act or a default of the other.

Indexation This is an adjustment made for CGT purposes to allow for inflation. The adjustment is computed by reference to the increase in the retail price index between the month of acquisition (or March 1982 if later) and the month of disposal.

Industrial buildings Buildings which are occupied for the purposes of a qualifying trade may qualify as industrial buildings. The significance of this is that a person who incurs expenditure on an industrial building may claim industrial buildings allowances. Normally, allowances are given at the rate of 4 per cent per annum over a 25-year period.

Industrial tribunal This is a body set up to hear complaints concerning statutory employment rights such as unfair dismissal, redundancy etc.

Inheritance tax Inheritance tax is a combination of a gift tax and death duties. Tax is payable on chargeable transfers made by an individual during his lifetime and on his estate at the time of his death.

Input VAT The VAT paid to suppliers of goods and services. Where a person has paid for such goods and services and he is himself VAT registered, he may recover input VAT by offsetting the tax paid by him against tax charged on his own supplies.

Insolvency This is the situation where a person or business is unable to pay his or its debts in full.

Intrastats Statistical returns which record EU arrivals and dispatches. Commonly known as SSDs.

Investment companies An investment company is a company which exists wholly or mainly for the purpose of carrying on a business of managing investments.

Joint and several liability Applies where two or more persons enter into an obligation jointly and severally so that each is liable separately and all are liable jointly. A creditor may choose to sue one or more severally or all jointly.

Know-how Certain expenditure by a person carrying on a trade to acquire information required to carry out certain industrial or manufacturing processes may qualify for a form of capital allowances.

Lien The right to hold the goods or property of another as security for the performance of a particular obligation such as an unpaid invoice.

Liquidator A person who presides over and administers the winding-up or dissolution of a company.

Mainstream corporation tax Corporation tax payable on a company's profits.

Market value rule Where an asset is transferred to a person by way of a gift or some other disposal which is not an arm's length transaction, CGT may be charged as if the person making the disposal had in fact received market value.

Members of a company Shareholders.

Memorandum of association This is a document setting out a company's constitution and in particular giving its name, the objects for which the company was formed, terms under which shares are issued etc.

Misrepresentation A statement or act which conveys a false or wrong impression.

National insurance contributions These are Social Security Contributions. Class 1 contributions are payable by an employer and employees. Class 2 and Class 4 contributions are payable by self-employed individuals. The national insurance system is administered by the Department of Social Security.

Opening years rules Under the Schedule D current year basis, there are special rules for computing the assessable profits for the year in which the business commences, and the subsequent tax year.

Options Legally binding contracts under which one party to a contract is bound to buy or sell an asset to the other party. A call option is an option under which the person granting the option agrees to sell an asset to the other party if he exercises his option. A put option is where a person has the right to require the other party to buy an asset from him.

Output tax The VAT chargeable on goods or services supplied in the UK. The trader must account for VAT charged on such supplies by completing a VAT return, normally on a quarterly basis.

Outworkers Some industries have outworkers who work on their own premises. However, depending on the circumstances, outworkers may be regarded as employees and not as self-employed individuals. This means that payments made by the person using the outworkers' services may be subject to PAYE and employers' national insurance contributions.

Overlap relief Under the new Schedule D current year basis of assessment, there are special provisions to cover the way in which profits are assessed for the opening years. The general principle is that the total amount of profits which are assessed over the life of the business should precisely equal the actual profits earned by the business. Overlap relief covers situations where a particular year's profits are assessed more than once (usually under the opening years' rules) and is effectively an adjustment to ensure that this does not result in excessive amounts being assessed overall.

Overlap relief is given by way of a deduction from an individual's profits when he ceases to carry on his business or profession, or when the firm's accounting date is changed to a date which falls later in the tax year.

Partially exempt traders This is a VAT concept. A partially exempt trader is a person who makes a mixture of standard-rated or zero-rated supplies and supplies which are exempt for VAT purposes.

A partially exempt trader may not be able to claim full credit for his input tax.

Partnership The relationship which subsists between persons carrying on business with a view to profit.

Patent The exclusive use and benefit of a new invention.

Pay as you earn (PAYE) This is a compulsory system for deduction of tax at source from cash payments to employees. There are different rules for PAYE and national insurance contributions and an individual's earnings may be different for the purposes of these two systems.

Personal pension scheme An approved pension scheme run by an insurance company, bank, building society or unit trust group. An individual who is self-employed or who is in non-pensionable employment may make contributions to a personal pension scheme.

Plant and machinery Plant and machinery attract capital allowances if used by a person in the course of a business carried on by him. There is no statutory definition of plant and machinery although certain rules have evolved through decided cases.

Preceding year basis Under the present Schedule D system, which applies for an individual who commenced business prior to 6 April 1994, the normal basis of assessment for a tax year is the preceding year basis, ie the assessment for the tax year 1994-95 is based on the firm's accounts for a period which ended during the tax year 1993-94.

Prescribed accounting periods A VAT term for periods covered by VAT returns. Normally periods are of three months' duration ending on the dates notified in the certificate of VAT registration.

Potentially exempt transfers (PETs) An outright gift made by one individual to another or to an interest in possession or accumulation and maintenance trust is a PET. This means that the gift is exempt from IHT provided the donor survives seven years. If the donor does survive for that period the PET becomes an actually exempt transfer. If he dies during the period the transfer proves not to have been exempt.

Pre-emption The right to purchase property before or in preference to other property eg shares or premises.

Pre-sale dividends Where a group of people are about to sell their shares in a private company, it may be more tax efficient for them to extract part of the value from the company by taking a dividend immediately before the sale takes place.

Pre-trading expenditure Certain expenditure incurred in connection with a trade which is about to be carried on may qualify for tax relief once the trade is commenced.

Premium A lump sum payment to a landlord to obtain a lease is regarded as a premium for tax purposes. Where the lease is for a period of less than 50 years, part of the premium is normally treated as income for the landlord.

Private company Under company law, this is a company which is not a public company. The Financial Services Act 1986 prohibits a private company from issuing any advertisement under which the public may invest in its securities.

Privity of contract This is a rule under English contract law that only a party to a contract may sue under the contract.

Public company A company which uses the suffix plc and which has a minimum share capital of £50,000, at least a quarter of which is paid up, and which observes certain requirements under the Companies Acts.

Purchase of own shares A company may purchase its own shares. A public company is normally permitted to do so only in so far as it has distributable profits or the purchase of own shares is being funded by the proceeds from an issue of new shares. A private company may purchase its own shares out of capital.

In all situations, there is a set procedure which must be followed for the purchase to be in accordance with company law. A special tax treatment may apply where a private trading company purchases its own shares.

Qualifying corporate bonds A loan stock issued by a company may be an exempt asset for CGT purposes (ie it qualifies for exemption). On the other hand, any loss realised on a disposal of a QCB is not normally allowable for CGT purposes.

Qualifying loans An individual who is a partner is entitled to relief for interest paid on qualifying loans, ie loans used to acquire an interest in the firm or loans which have been taken to enable the individual to make a loan to his firm for use in the ordinary course of the firm's business. Shareholders in a close company may also be able to raise qualifying loans to acquire shares or make loan capital available to the company.

Quiet enjoyment The right of a tenant of premises to occupy the premises without any lawful interruption or disturbance by the landlord or his agent.

Rebasing This is a technical term for CGT purposes whereby an individual who held an asset at 31 March 1982 may have his capital gain computed as if his cost were the market value of the asset at that date.

Receiver An official appointed by the court or by a debenture holder to take charge of the company's affairs and realise its assets. Following the Insolvency Act 1986, the proper term is an administrative receiver.

Relevant earnings Schedule D profits and earnings from a non-pensionable employment. An individual may make contributions into a personal pension scheme based on a percentage of his relevant earnings for a tax year.

Relief for reinvestment in unquoted shares CGT relief may be obtained where an individual or trust invests in a qualifying unquoted trading company within three years of the date of a disposal which gave rise to a capital gain.

Rescission The revocation of a contract eg where the seller rescinds a contract relating to land where the purchase raises an objection in the title.

Reservation of benefit This is an IHT term. Where a person makes a gift but reserves a benefit, the transaction is not regarded as a PET. The asset remains part of the individual's estate for as long as he continues to reserve a benefit. If he has not relinquished his reserved benefit by the time of his death, the asset's market value is brought into account for IHT purposes just as if he still owned the asset.

Resolution A decision of a company's members at a general meeting or of directors at a Board of Directors meeting.

Retirement annuity These are similar to personal pension schemes. In effect, they are approved contracts under which a person who was self-employed or in non-pensionable employment could provide for their retirement prior to the introduction of personal pension schemes in July 1988. Many retirement annuity policies make provision for premiums to be paid in subsequent years and, whilst no new retirement annuity policies are now issued, contributions under existing policies thus continue to attract relief for some years to come.

Retirement relief This is a special relief for CGT purposes which applies where an individual aged 55 or over disposes of his business or an interest in a business (eg an interest in a firm).

Revenue expenditure Expenditure which is deductible in arriving at a company's profits. Contrast capital expenditure.

Reverse charge A VAT charging mechanism which obliges the customer to account to Customs for VAT on the price charge for goods or services. The VAT charged is recoverable as input VAT, subject to the normal rules.

Roll-over relief This is a CGT relief which applies where an individual disposes of a business or an asset used in a business and spends the proceeds on acquiring replacement assets during a qualifying period (normally up to one year before and up to three years after the date of disposal of the original asset).

Romalpa clause A term under a sale contract under which the vendor reserves legal title over the assets which have been sold until he receives payment.

Salaried partner An individual subject to the supervision and direction of equity partners and who is therefore no more than a very senior employee. Salaried partners are assessable under Schedule E rather than under Schedule D.

Scientific research allowances Certain expenditure incurred by traders on scientific research may attract allowances. Revenue expenditure is allowed in full. Capital expenditure may attract 100 per cent capital allowances.

Self-administered pension scheme A pension scheme with no more than 12 members where one or more of the members is a trustee or the company which established the scheme is a trustee.

Schedule D A self-employed person's profits are assessed under Schedule D.

Schedule E Directors and employees are assessed under Schedule E. The normal basis of assessment for Schedule E income is the receipts basis, ie an individual is assessed according to remuneration received by him during the year.

Share capital See Capital.

Shares valuation division A specialist section of the Capital Taxes Office which negotiates valuations of unquoted shares where such a valuation is required for tax purposes.

Small companies rate Corporation tax is charged only at 25 per cent unless the company concerned has profits in excess of the lower limit (at present £300,000 provided that there are no associated companies). If there are associated companies, the lower limit is divided by the number of associated companies.

Sole traders An individual is a sole trader if he carries on business on his own account rather than in partnership or through a company.

Specific performance An order for a party who has defaulted to carry out the obligations that he has entered into under a contract.

Stamp duty A duty payable at 0.5 per cent on transfers of shares and at 1 per cent to 2 per cent on transfers of property.

Table A Table A of the Companies (Tables A to F) Regulations 1985 (SI No 805), a standard form of articles of association which are adopted in many companies' articles.

Target company Where it is intended that a company should be purchased, the company concerned is often referred to as the 'target company'. This helps to distinguish it from other companies such as where the person making the acquisition is itself a company.

Tax invoice An invoice issued by a supplier which must show specific information. It is the docuement on which VAT accounting and control procedures are based.

Tax point The time at which a transaction is regarded as taking place for VAT purposes, and when VAT becomes payable or recoverable.

Title The right of ownership in property.

Time apportionment basis Where an asset was owned at 6 April 1965, and no universal rebasing election has been made, it is sometimes possible for a capital gain to be computed on the time apportionment basis. This means that only a proportion of the gain achieved over the total period of ownership is brought into charge.

Tort A civil wrong committed against another party, eg negligence or trespass. This is different from a liability under a contract since a person may be liable under the law of tort where there is no contractual relationship.

Transitional relief Where a firm has been assessed on the PY basis for 1995–96, the firm is normally assessed under the transitional basis for 1996–97. In practice, this normally means that the assessment for 1996–97 is based on 12 months' share of the profits for a period commencing immediately after the end of the basis period for 1995–96 and ending on the date to which accounts are drawn up during the tax year 1996–97.

Ultra vires A doctrine in company law that a company must keep within its registered objects.

Unfair dismissal A dismissal of an employee contrary to the Employment Rights Act 1996.

Unfair prejudice In company law, a minority shareholder may have a claim against the company's directors if they exercise their powers unfairly to the prejudice of minority shareholders.

Unincorporated businesses A company is an incorporated business.

Businesses carried on by a sole trader or by a partnership are unincorporated businesses.

Universal rebasing election An irrevocable election which may be made under which the 31 March 1982 value of assets held by that person is treated as if it were the original cost.

Venture capital loss relief Where an individual has subscribed for shares in an unquoted trading company, any losses may be set against the individual's income for the year in which the loss is realised. This is known as venture capital loss relief.

Venture capital trust A new type of investment trust established under the Finance Act 1995 provisions. VCTs must invest in unquoted trading companies with net assets of no more than £10m.

Vicarious liability Where a party is liable for the acts of others even though that party did not commit the act or omission.

Warranty In contract law, a term of a contract which is breached entitles the injured party to sue for damages but not to repudiate the contract.

Wasting assets A wasting asset is an asset with an expected useful life of less than 50 years.

Wrongful dismissal A term in employment law describing a situation where an employee is dismissed in breach of contractual rights under common law.

Zero-rating A VAT term for a sale on which no VAT is charged. A person making zero-rated supplies may nevertheless still be able to recover input VAT.

INDEX

(All references are to paragraph number.)

Accounts,
  accounting periods, 18.2
  debtors, inclusion in, 2.1.1
  earnings basis, 2.1.1
  incorrect, penalties for, 2.4.6
  Inland Revenue. *See* Inland Revenue
  principles, adherence to, 2.1.2
  work-in-progress, 2.1.1
Agricultural buildings,
  capital allowance, 2.2.25
Agriculture,
  flat rate VAT scheme, 5.7.6
  tenancy, 9.2.1
  trading losses, 16.9.14
Annual payments, 2.1.11, 16.15
Assets,
  bought in year, 2.2.9
  cars. *See* Cars
  cost of acquiring, 2.1.3
  destruction of, 3.4.10
  kept separately, 2.2.4
  long life, 2.2.11
  negligible value, becoming of, 3.4.10
  plant & machinery. *See* Plant and machinery
  short life, 2.2.10
Auditors, 17.10
  negligence, 17.10.1

Bad debts,
  provisions for, 2.1.8
Benefits in kind,
  assets,
    free use of, 11.5.9
    ownership of, 11.5.11
    transfer of, 11.5.10
  beneficial loans, 11.6
    de minimis exemption, 11.6.3
    qualifying purpose, used for, 11.6.2
    types of, 11.6.1
    written off, 11.6.4
  car parking spaces, 11.5.7
  cars. *See* Company cars
  Christmas parties, 11.8.6
  club subscriptions, 11.8.4
  company vans, private use of, 11.4.7
  council tax, 11.8.1
  dining facilities, 11.3.4
  discount goods and services, 11.8.9
  end of year returns, 11.9
  entertaining expenses, 11.4.6
  functions, 11.8.6
  general rules, 11.3.1
  legal fees, 11.8.7
  living accommodation, 11.7
    assessable amount, reduction in, 11.7.5
    charge for, 11.7.2
    foreign properties, 11.7.5
    generally, 11.7.1
    holiday, 11.7.5
    properties owned for more than six years, 11.7.3, 11.7.4
  long service awards, 11.3.4
  luncheon vouchers, 11.3.4
  medical insurance, 11.8.2
  mobile telephones, 11.5.8
  non-P11D employees,
    benefits capable of being converted to cash, 11.3.2
    credit tokens and vouchers, treatment of, 11.3.2
    living accommodation, charge for, 11.3.2
    personal liabilities, payment of, 11.3.2
    tax charge for, 11.3.2
    transport vouchers, treatment of, 11.3.2
  not taxable, 11.3.4
  nurseries and creches, workplace, 11.3.4
  outplacement counselling, 11.8.8
  pool cars, 11.3.4
  profit-related pay. *See* Profit-related pay
  profit sharing. *See* Profit sharing
  relocation expenses, 11.3.4
  representative accommodation, 11.3.4

Benefits in kind – *continued*
retirement benefits, 11.3.4
retraining, 11.3.4
sandwich courses, 11.3.4
shares. *See* Shares
sports facilities, 11.3.4
staff canteen, 11.3.4
subsistence expenses, 11.4.2
spouse, of, 11.4.4
treatment of, 11.4.2
suggestion scheme awards, 11.3.4
tax and financial advice, 11.8.5
telephone rental, 11.8.3
termination payments. *See* Termination payments
travelling expenses, 11.4
home and work, between, 11.4.1
mileage allowances, 11.4.1
overseas, 11.4.3
overseas employees, family visits, 11.4.5
spouse, of, 11.4.4
Bonus payments, provision for, 2.1.9
Bribes. *See* Illegal payments
Building,
enterprise zones,
capital allowances, 2.2.19
disposal of building, 2.2.20
located in, 2.2.18
expenditure on, 2.2.14
industrial buildings 2.2.21
allowance, 2.2.15
definition of, 2.2.23
disposal, 2.2.22
refurbishment, 2.1.22
repairs and renewals, 2.1.23
second-hand buildings, 2.2.17
Business,
cessation, 19.8
expenses post, 19.9.3
redundancy costs, 19.8.2
VAT on, 19.8.1
sale of, 19.7
apportionment on, 19.7.1, 19.7.2
transfer to status of company, 19.7.3, 19.7.4
Business finance, cost of raising, 2.1.13
Business premises,
alienation, 9.3.1
alterations, 9.3.1
covenants,
implied and express, 9.3.1
user, 9.3.1
keeping, 9.3
occupation, requirements of, 9.3.1
repair, 9.3.1
Business tenancies,
authorised guarantee agreement, 9.2.4
bank guarantees, 9.2.11
defining a, 9.2.1
easements, 9.2.2
generally, 1.7
Landlord and Tenant (Covenants) Act 1995, 9.2.6
landlord's incentives, 9.2.12
fitting out, 9.2.12
rent free periods, 9.2.12
reverse premiums, 9.2.12
tenant-only break clauses, 9.2.12
leases,
application to court for a new tenancy, 9.3.3
compensation, 9.3.4
expiry of, 9.3.2
full repairing and insuring, 9.2.4
landlord's notice, 9.3.3
tenant's response to, 9.3.3
privity of contract in, 9.2.5
renewal, landlord's opposition to, 9.3.3
right to renew, 9.3.2
tenant's request for a new tenancy, 9.3.3
leaving business premises, 9.4
disposal options, 9.4.3
tenant's notice to determine, 9.4.1, 9.4.2
licence to occupy, 9.2.1
occupation, 9.2.1
outside the 1954 Act, 9.2.3
personal guarantees, 9.2.8
premises,
defining the, 9.2.1
taking, 9.2
rent,
deposit, 9.2.9, 9.2.10
fixed increases, 9.2.12
free periods, 9.2.12
index-linked, 9.2.12
reviews, 9.2.13
turnover, 9.2.13
tenancy at will, exclusion of, 9.2.1
tenant, occupied by, 9.2.2
tenant's covenant, 9.2.7
Business transactions,
business property, 1.19
definition of, 4.5.2
hold-over relief for, gifts of, 4.5, 4.5.1, 4.5.6
restriction on, 4.5.3, 4.5.5
shares, hold over relief on, 4.5.4
hold over relief, clawback of, 4.5.8
inheritance tax,
hold over relief and, 4.5.7

Business transactions – *continued*
loan guarantees, payments under, 4.1.3
loans to,
companies, 4.1.2
private businesses, 4.1
unincorporated businesses, 4.1.1
losses on unquoted shares, 4.2
companies, relief for, 4.2.4
relief, nature of, 4.2.3
subscribers, special relief for, 4.2.1, 4.2.2
reinvestment in unquoted shares, relief for, 4.4, 4.4.1
EIS investments, 4.4.4
eligible shares, 4.4.2
qualifying trades, 4.4.3
venture capital trusts, 4.4.5
roll-over relief. *See* Roll-over relief

Capital allowances,
accounting for, 16.3.1
assets,
bought in year, 2.2.9
kept separately, 2.2.4
long life, 2.2.11
short life, 2.2.10
cars, 2.2.6
current year basis, 16.3.1
disposal proceeds, 2.2.4
doubling of, 2.2.3
generally, 2.2.1
unincorporated businesses, 16.3
writing down, 2.2.3
cars, 2.2.7
Capital expenditure,
definition of, 2.1.3
training as, 2.1.3
Capital gains tax,
chargeable assets, 3.3
exemptions, 3.3.2
gains on, 3.3.1
chargeable gain,
assets, compulsory acquisition of, 3.4.7
company takeovers, 3.4.6
compensation payments, 3.4.8
conditional sale, 3.4.2, 3.4.3
examples of, 3.4
gifts, 3.4.9
insurance policy, proceeds under a, 3.4.8
option, exercise of, 3.4.4
outright sale, 3.4.1
property, exchange of, 3.4.5
share exchanges, 3.4.5, 3.4.6
computation of, 3.5, 18.3.1
acquisitions,
incidental costs, of, 3.5.2
values, other, 3.5.6
assets acquired via inheritance, 3.5.6
companies, groups of, 3.5.4
contingent consideration, 3.5.1
contingent liabilities, 3.5.1
costs allowable, 3.5.2
deduction for amounts charged as income, 3.5.1
deemed acquisition value, 3.5.6
disposals, incidental costs of, 3.5.2
disposal value, amount brought in as, 3.5.1
enhancement expenditure, 3.5.2
family trusts, 3.5.6
foreign currency, 3.6.8
foreign property, 3.6.6
gifts, 3.6.5
assets, of, 3.5.4
held over gain, 3.5.5
improvements, expenditure on, 3.6.1
indexation, 3.5.7, 3.5.8
land and buildings, 3.6.1
market value, 3.5.1
married persons, 3.5.4
minority shareholdings, 3.6.4
part disposals, 3.5.2, 3.5.3
rebasing, 3.5.4
receipts, small capital, 3.5.3
restoring assets, capital sums applied in, 3.5.3
sale at arm's length, 3.5.1
shareholdings,
unquoted, 3.6.4
valuing, 3.6.5
short lease, disposal of, 3.6.2
time apportionment, 3.6.2, 3.6.3
transfer of assets, prior to 6 April 1988, 3.5.5
exemption, annual, 3.1.1
generally, 1.2
liability for, 3.2
losses, 3.1.3
outline of, 3.1
payment of, 18.3
roll-over relief, 18.3.2
tax rate,
companies, for, 3.1.5
individuals, for, 3.1.4
transfers between spouses, 3.1.2
Close companies, 18.8.1
close investment-holding companies, 18.8.6
directors' defalcations, 18.8.4
investment companies, 18.8.5
participators,
benefits to, 18.8.3
loans to, 18.8.2

Companies House,
  documents to be filed at, 17.12
    accounting reference date, 17.12.4
    annual return, 17.12.5
    capital, 17.13.2
    charges, mortgages and debentures, 17.12.7
    directors, 17.12.3
    formation, 17.12.1
    registered office, 17.12.6
    resolutions, 17.12.8
    secretary, 17.12.3
Company, establishing a,
  deferring tax, 19.3.3
  disadvantages of, 19.4
  income tax considerations, 19.6.7
  incorporating a business, 19.6.6
  losses, carry forward of, 19.6.10
  operating as a, 19.3
  profits, lower tax on, 19.3.1
  stamp duty, 19.6.9
  tax considerations, 19.3, 19.3.3, 19.5
  transferring business to, 19.6
    conditions on, 19.6.3, 19.6.5
    relief on, 19.6.1, 19.6.4
  value added tax and, 19.6.8
Company cars, 11.5
  benefits, 11.5.1
  capital allowances, 2.2.6, 2.2.7
  chauffeur, provision of, 11.5.6
  employee contributions, 11.5.2
  fuel benefit, 11.5.5
  parking spaces, 11.5.7
  returns to Inland Revenue, 11.5.4
Company law,
  annual return, 17.4.2
  articles of association, 17.2.2
  borrowing, 17.4.3
  charges, registration of, 17.4.7
    failure to register, 17.4.8
  foreign companies, 17.4.9
  formation requirements, 17.2.3
  directors. *See* Directors,
  generally, 1.15
  company,
    types of, 17.1.2
    what is a, 17.1
  conversion, 17.3
  debentures, 17.4.4
  dividends, 17.7
  incorporation, 17.4
  limited liability, 17.1.1
  meetings. *See* Meetings
  memorandum of association, 17.2
  mezzanine finance, 17.4.5
  operating as, 19.3
  re-registration, 17.3
  share capital. *See* Share capital
  stamp duty, 17.3.4
  ultra vires, 17.9
Company proprietor,
  anti-avoidance legislation, 20.14
    capital gains tax provisions, 20.14.2
    controlling shareholders, 20.14.3
    disposals and capital gains, 20.14.5
    securities, transactions in, 20.14.1
    share exchanges, 20.14.6
    take-overs, 20.14.6
    value shifting, 20.14.4
  assets, purchase of,
    associate, by, 20.8.2
    capital gains on, 20.8.3, 20.8.4
    company law and, 20.8.11
    director, by, 20.8.1
    undervalue, 20.8.5
  assets, sale of,
    capital gains, 20.8.7
    company, to, 20.8.6
    company law and, 20.8.11
    retirement relief and, 20.8.10
    transfer without consideration, 20.8.8
    undervalue, sale at, 20.8.9
  benefits in kind, 20.4
    director's family, for, 20.4.1
    participators, benefit for, 20.4.3
  business finance, raising, 20.10
    enterprise investment scheme, 20.20.1, 20.10.7
      alternative investment market, 20.10.13
      approved investment funds, 20.10.11
      five year period, 20.10.9
      qualifying companies, 20.10.2
      qualifying persons, 20.10.8
      qualifying subsidiaries, 20.10.5
      qualifying trade, 20.10.3
      retail distribution trades, 20.10.4
      shares, purchase of own, 20.10.10
      three year period, 20.10.6
      venture capital trusts, 20.10.12
      wholesale trades, 20.10.4
  buying a company, 20.1
    capital losses, relief for, 20.1.2
    checklist, 20.1.3
    financing costs, relief for, 20.1.1
    income tax relief, 20.1.2
  capital gains tax planning,
    assets used by company but owned by family, 20.13.6
    investments held by trustees, 20.13.1
    retirement relief, planning for, 20.13.4, 20.13.5

Company proprietor – *continued*
capital gains tax planning – *continued*
shares held by trustees, 20.13.2
special rules, 20.13.3
corporation tax planning, 20.2
adverse tax position, 20.2.2
commercial considerations, 20.2.3
companies controlled by associates, 20.2.4
disallowable expenditure, avoiding, 20.2.5
small companies rate, maximising, 20.2.1
demergers, 20.12
advance clearance, 20.12.4
conditions on, 20.12.2
form of, 20.12.1
informal, 20.12.5
dividends, 20.5
drawback of, 20.5.2
group of companies,
checklist of tax considerations, 20.2.7
managing tax of, 20.2.6
loans by company, 20.7
loans to company,
consequences on company failure, 20.6.3
qualifying loans, 20.6.1, 20.6.2
pension schemes, self administered, 20.9
borrowings by trustees, overall limit on, 20.9.5
investment in property used by company, 20.9.4
investment in shares in the company, 20.9.3
loans to associated companies, 20.9.2
loans to company, 20.9.2
loans to members, prohibition on, 20.9.1
remuneration, treatment of, 20.3
director's drawings, 20.3.5
lump sum payments, 20.3.3
national insurance, 20.3.2, 20.3.4
receipts basis, 20.3.1
sale of the company, 20.15
capital gains tax, hold-over relief, 20.15.3
consideration paid by instalments, 20.15.6
contingent liabilities, 20.15.9
loan notes from acquirer, 20.15.5
pre-sale dividends, 20.15.1
qualifying corporate bonds, 20.15.11
shares, purchase of own, 20.11
advance clearance procedure, 20.11.6
applicable conditions, 20.11.1
benefit to company's trade, 20.11.5
distribution treatment, 20.11.7
ownership of, 20.11.3
shareholder not subscribing for shares, 20.11.9
substantial reduction , 20.11.4
trustee shareholders, 20.11.10
unquoted company, definition of, 20.11.2
Company taxation, 18.1
advance corporation tax, 18.5.3, 18.5.4
annual charges, 18.4.2
capital gains. *See* Capital gains
charges paid in final accounting period, 18.6.7
company distributions, taxation of, 18.5.1
company ownership, changes in, 18.6.8
corporation tax. *See* Corporation tax
franked investment income, surplus, 18.5.2
generally, 1.16
groups of companies. *See* Groups of companies
income, surplus charges on, 18.6.6
income tax, deduction at source, 18.4.3
interest and other charges, 18.4
loan relationships, 18.4.1
losses,
accounting for, 18.6.1
capital, 18.6.5
claiming relief for, 18.6.2–18.6.4
roll-over relief. *See* Roll-over relief
Consumer protection, 14.52
Contract law,
acceptance, 7.2
certainty of terms, 7.2.6
communication of, 7.2.2
contract to make a contract, 7.2.5
contractual intention, 7.2.7
method of, 7.2.3
post, by, 7.2.4
advertisements, 7.1.2
affirming the, 7.9.1
breach of, 7.9
anticipatory, 7.9.4
both parties, by, 7.9.3
consideration, 7.3
agreement not to sue, 7.3.2
past consideration, 7.3.1
counter offers, 7.1.4
cross offers, 7.2.1
duress and undue influence, 7.6, 7.6.1, 7.6.2
economic, 7.6.1
effect of, 7.6.1

Contract law – *continued*
exemption clauses, 7.8
burden of proof, 7.8.2
liability for negligence, 7.8.1
statutory control, 7.8.4
third party, from, 7.8.3
frustration, 7.10
benefit acquired under the contract, 7.10.3
consequences, 7.10.3
delay, 7.10.1
excluding the act, 7.10.3
exclusion, 7.10.3
sale of goods, 7.10.2
serving part of the contract, 7.10.3
generally, 1.5
invitation to treat, 7.1.1
lapse of time, 7.1.5
misrepresentation, 7.5, 7.5.4
constructive notice, 7.5.2
damages for, 7.5.3
fraudulent, 7.5.3
innocent, 7.5.3
negligent, 7.5.3
non-disclosure, 7.5.1
mistake, 7.4
identity, in, 7.4.3
mutual mistake, 7.4.1
unilateral mistake, 7.4.2
non est factum, 7.4.4
offer, 7.1
rejection of offer, 7.1.4
repudiation, 7.9.2
sale of goods. *See* Sale of goods
termination of offer, 7.1.3
terms of, 7.7
collateral contracts, 7.7.6
conditions and warranties, 7.7.3
conflict of, 7.7.2
extrinsic evidence, 7.7.5
implied term, 7.7.7
incorporation of, 7.7.1
meaning and construction of, 7.7.4
standard form of, 7.7.1
Unfair Contract Terms Act 1977, 7.8.4
unfair, meaning, 7.8.4
Unfair Terms in Consumer Contracts Regulations 1994, 7.8.4
Contract of employment, 10.5
continuity of employment, 10.8
periods without a contract, 10.8.2
weeks which count, 10.8.1
weeks which do not count, 10.8.3
deductions from wages, 10.7.4
employee duties, 10.5.1
employer's duties, 10.5.1
express terms, 10.5.1
implied terms, 10.5.1
intellectual property rights, 10.6.3
non-competition covenants, 10.6.1
non-solicitation covenants, 10.6.2
restraint of trade, 10.6
terms of, 10.5.1
unfair dismissal. *See* Unfair dismissal
written particulars of, 10.7
changes to, 10.7.1
employees working overseas, 10.7.2
remedies for failure to provide, 10.7.4
unlawful terms, 10.7.3
Controlled foreign companies, 18.10
acceptable distribution test, 18.10.5
definition of, 18.10.2
exempt activity test, 18.10.4
legislation, reason for, 18.10.1
motive test, 18.10.3
non-resident companies, legislation on, 18.10.7
public quotation test, 18.10.6
Corporation tax, 18.1
accounting period, 18.2.1
associated companies, 18.2.5, 18.2.7
capital allowances, 18.1.3
interest and other annual payments, 18.1.4
liability for, 18.1.1
payment of, 18.2.8
profits,
apportionment, 18.2.3
computation of, 18.1.2
rates, 18.2.4
small companies, 18.2.5, 18.2.6

Debtors, accounts, inclusion in, 2.1.1
De minimus, provisions, 2.2.11
Depreciation, relief for, 1.1
Directors, 10.4.4, 17.5,
appointment of, 17.5.1
disqualification, 17.5.5
duties of, 17.5.7
duties of care, 17.5.11
insurance, 17.5.13
loans to, 17.5.10
meetings of, 17.5.3
non-executive, 17.5.2
personal liability of, 17.5.12
property transactions, 17.5.9
removal of, 17.5.6
remuneration of, 17.5.8
resignation of, 17.5.4
retirement of, 17.5.4
Disability,
definition of, 10.18.1

Disability – *continued*
  discrimination,
    on grounds of, 10.18
    types of, 10.18.2
  exemptions, 10.18.5
  reasonable adjustments, employer's duty to make, 10.18.3
  remedies, 10.18.4
Dismissal. *See* Unfair dismissal
Dividends, 17.8

Employee, 10.4
  bonus payments to, 2.1.9
  compensation, 1.9
  directors, 10.4.4
  guarantee payments, 10.14.2
  medical suspension, 10.14.1
  part-time, 10.4.3
  pay statements, itemised, 10.15
  pension contributions for, 2.1.10
  seasonal, 10.4.2
  statutory payments, 10.14.1
  temporary, 10.4.1
  wages, payment of, 10.16
    deductions, 10.16.1
    retail workers, 10.16.2
    unlawful deduction, remedy for, 10.16.3
Employment law,
  contract of service or contract for services,
    tests for, 10.3.1
  EC law, impact of, 10.2
  generally, 1.8, 10.1
  worker's status, 10.3
Enterprise Investment Scheme, 20.20.1, 20.10.7
  alternative investment market, 20.10.13
  approved investment funds, 20.10.11
  five year period, 20.10.9
  qualifying companies, 20.10.2
  qualifying persons, 20.10.8
  qualifying subsidiaries, 20.10.5
  qualifying trade, 20.10.3
  retail distribution trades, 20.10.4
  shares, purchase of own, 20.10.10
  three year period, 20.10.6
  venture capital trusts, 20.10.12
  wholesale trades, 20.10.4
Enterprise Zone,
  buildings in, 2.2.18
  capital allowances, 2.2.19
  disposal of building in, 2.2.20
Entertaining, 2.1.4, 2.1.6
Equal pay, 10.19
  comparator, 10.9.4
  equal value, 10.19.3
  like work, 10.19.1
  material factor defence, 10.19.5
  remedies, 10.19.6
  work rated as equivalent, 10.19.2
European Economic Interest Groupings (EEIGs), 15.9
Expenditure,
  disallowed for tax purposes, 2.1.2
  mixed purposes of. 2.1.4
  pre-trading, 2.3
  provisions for future costs, 2.1.2
  wholly for the business, 2.1.4
Expenses,
  fines. 2.1.7
  mixed purposes of, 2.1.4
  removal expenses, 2.1.4

Family companies. *See* Company proprietor
Fines, 2.1.7
Fire,
  regulations, 13.5.12
  safety equipment, 2.2.16
First aid, 13.8.6
Fixtures & fittings,
  allowances on, 2.1.15
  expenditure on, 2.2.13
  landlord's and tenant's, 2.2.15
Foreign exchange (Forex),
  basic rules of, 18.11.1
  deferral relief, 18.11.4
  financial instruments, 18.11.6
  local currency election, 18.11.3
  matching, 18.11.2
  regime of, 18.11.1
  tax planning for, 18.11.7
  transitional rules, 18.11.5
Foreign income,
  corporation tax and ACT, 18.9.3
  dividends, 18.9.2
  double taxation relief, 18.9.1
  unremittable income, 18.9.4

Gifts, customers, to, 1.1, 2.1.6
Goodwill, purchase of, 2.1.3
Groups of companies, 18.7
  advance corporation tax surrenders, 18.7.3
  assets, transfer of, 18.7.4
  capital gains and transfers, 18.7.6
  dividends, payment of, 18.7.5
  interest, payment of, 18.7.5
  intra-group transfers, 18.7.7
    company leaving after, 18.7.8, 18.7.9
  losses, use of, 18.7.2

Groups of Companies – *continued*
relationships, 18.7.1
roll-over relief, 18.7.11
universal rebasing election, 18.7.10

Health & safety,
At Work Act 1974, 13.2
codes of practice, 13.2.10
computers and display screen equipment, 13.9
eye tests, 13.9.2
information on use, 13.9.3
training, 13.9.3
workstations, 13.9.1
defective equipment, 13.8.3
employees,
duty of, 13.2.4
information for, 13.8.5
employer's duty,
employees, to, 13.2.1
other people, 13.2.2
enforcement, 13.2.7
equipment, charges for, 13.2.5
European regulation, 13.3.3
Factories Act, 13.3.1
fire safety. *See* Fire
first aid, 13.8.6
fumes and hazardous substances, 13.7
fumes, 13.7.2
dangerous substances, 13.7.1
explosive substances, 13.7.2
flammable substances, 13.7.2
generally, 1.11, 13.1
improvement notices, 13.2.8
injuries, reporting, 13.8, 13.8.2
insurance, 13.8.1
interference, 13.2.5
liability, 13.2.6, 13.4
civil, 13.4.2
criminal, 13.4.1
vicarious, 13.4.3
lifting & carrying, 13.8.4
machinery, 13.6
hoists and lifts, 13.6.2
lifting methods, 13.6.3
protective clothing, 13.6.5
protective equipment, 13.6.5
safety of, 13.6.1
steam boilers, 13.6.4
manufacturers,
materials, duty for, 13.2.3
substances, 13.2.3
misuse, 13.2.5
Offices, Shops and Railways Premises Act 1963, 13.3.2
prohibition notices, 13.2.9
regulations, 13.2.10
reporting,
dangerous occurrences, 13.8.2
diseases, 13.8.2
injuries, 13.8.2
working conditions, 13.5
changing facilities, 13.5.8
cleanliness, 13.5.2
clothes storage, 13.5.8
drinking water, 13.5.7
floors, 13.5.3
humid factories, 13.5.11
lighting, 13.5.1
overcrowding, 13.5.2
passages, 13.5.3
rest areas, 13.5.9
safe access, 13.5.3
seating, 13.5.4
stairs, 13.5.3
temperature, 13.5.1
toilets, 13.5.5
underground rooms, 13.5.11
ventilation, 13.5.1
washing facilities, 13.5.6
women, 13.5.10
workstations, 13.5.4
young persons, 13.5.10
Health insurance, permanent, 1.10, 12.4
companies, 12.8.3
partners, 12.7.3
sole trader, 12.6.3
use of, 12.5
Hire purchase, 2.1.16
adjustment for, 2.1.17
Hotels, 2.2.24

Illegal payments, 2.1.7
Inducements. *See* Illegal payments
Inheritance tax,
agricultural property, 21.9
land occupied by transferor, 21.9.1
tenanted land, 21.9.2
annual exemption, 21.5.4
benefit, reservation of, 21.7
business property, 21.8
basic requirements, 21.8.1
groups of companies, 21.8.5
non-qualifying businesses, 21.8.3
relief,
rates of, 21.8.2
restriction on, 21.8.4
deeds of variation, 21.4.6
dividends, waiver of, 21.4.2
exempt transfers, 21.5
normal expenditure out of income, 21.5.2

Inheritance tax – *continued*
potentially, definition of, 21.6.1
taper relief, 21.6.2
family business, passing on the, 21.12
assets,
owned by partner, 21.12.6
owned by shareholder, 21.12.7
relief, maximising, 21.12.3
generally, 1.19
gifts,
charities, to, 21.5.6
marriage, in consideration of, 21.5.5
national purposes, for, 21.5.7
political parties, to, 21.5.9
public benefit, gifts for, 21.5.8
small, 21.5.3
spouse to, 21.5.1
interest free loans, 21.4.4
legacies, disclaimer of, 21.4.5
liability for charge, 21.2
lifetime transfers, computation of, 21.10
maintenance of family, 21.4.1
pension arrangements, 21.12.2
persons subject to, 21.1
remuneration, waivers of, 21.4.3
settlements and trusts, 21.7.5
tax payable on death, computation of, 21.11
seven year rule, 21.11.4
transfers to employee trusts, 21.5.10
transfers of value, 21.3
calculating value of 21.3.3
gifts, not amounting to, 21.3.1, 21.4
gratuitous intent, 21.3.2
wills, tax efficient use of, 21.12.8–21.12.13
Inland Revenue,
Collector's audit division, 11.18.1
Schedule E compliance unit, 11.18.2
work of, 11.18
Insolvency,
employer of, 10.20
occupational pension schemes, 10.20.2
redundancy payments, 10.20.1
remedy, 10.20.3
Insurance,
broker, 14.4.1
business interruption, 14.5.4
compulsory requirements, 14.3
consumer protection , 14.5.2
cover,
arranging, 14.4, 14.4.2
need for, 14.1
types available, 14.5
credit insurance, 14.5.5
employers' liability insurance policy, 14.5.2
fidelity insurance, 14.5.5
fire and special perils, 14.5.1
generally, 1.12
income derived from, 2.1.5
inspection for, 14.3.3
legal expenses policy, 14.5.5
legislation, 14.3.1
liability insurances, 14.5.2
loss of profits, 12.6.1
money, loss of, 14.5.1
motor insurance, 14.5.3
policies, types of, 14.6
package, 14.6.2
single risk, 14.6.1
product liability policy, 14.5.2
property and buildings, 14.5.1
professional indemnity, 14.5.2
protection, 14.2
public liability policy, 14.5.2
redundancy payments, for, 12.6.1
Road Traffic Act 1988, 14.3.2
security for loans, 12.6.2
theft policy, 14.5.1
transit insurance, 13.4.2
Interest, treatment of, 2.1.12
Investment companies, 18.8.5, 18.8.6

Know-how, expenditure on , 2.2.26

Leases,
business tenancies. *See* Business tenancies
cars, 2.1.15
finance, 2.1.14
premiums,
relief for, 2.1.20
treatment of, 2.1.21
rentals, 2.1.14
Legal fees, 2.1.18
Life assurance, 12.2
chargeable event,
gain on, 12.2.6
taxable gains on, 12.2.7
companies, 12.8.1
generally, 1.10
non-qualifying policies, 12.2.3
partners, 12.7.1
policy, types of, 12.2.1
qualifying policies, 12.2.3
advantages of, 12.2.4
sole traders, 12.6
tax treatment, 12.2.5
traditional policies, 12.2
unit linked policies, 12.2
use of, 12.5

Loans,
business transactions. *See* Business transations
interest on, 2.1.12
security for loans, 12.6.2

Maternity rights, 10.12
ante-natal care, 10.12.1
dismissal,
protection from, 10.12.7, 10.12.8
written reasons for, 10.12.10
health & safety, 10.12.11
maternity allowance, 10.12.6
maternity leave, 10.12.2
maternity protection, 10.12.11
notice requirements, 10.12.3
redundancy and, 10.12.9
return to work, right to, 10.12.4, 10.12.8
sex discrimination law, interaction with, 10.12.12
statutory maternity pay, 10.12.5
Medical insurance. *See* Health insurance
Meetings,
general meetings, 17.6.1
minutes, 17.6.5
quorum, 17.6.3
resolutions, 17.6.6
filing of, 17.6.7
written, 17.6.8
shareholders, 17.6.9
special meetings, 17.6.2
voting, 17.6.4
Mobile phones, 11.5.8

National insurance, 11.2
annual payments, 16.15.2
anti-avoidance rules, 11.2.5
class 4, 16.15.1
contributions,
employees', 11.2.2
employer's, 11.2.3
liability to deduct, 11.2.1
earnings, definition of, 11.2.4
Negligence, provision for, 2.1.24

Partnership,
agreements, 15.7
existence of, 15.3
good faith, 15.7.1
management and control, 15.7.2
what is a, 15.1
anti-avoidance rules, 16.8
assessment of, 16.4
cessations, 16.4.2
current year basis, 16.4.1
other income, treatment of, 16.6
qualifying loans, 16.7
transitional provisions, 16.5
bringing a partner. *See* Sole trader
buying out a partner,
annuity arrangements, 19.2.3, 19.2.4
borrowing to fund the, 19.2.6
capital gains tax implications, 19.2.7
capital sum, payment of, 19.2.5
change to salaried partner, 19.2.1
consultancy arrangement, 19.2.2
practice, splitting the, 19.2.8
capital gains and, 4.6
acquisition value, 4.6.1
assets held at 31 March 1992, 4.6.2
change of partners, 4.6.7
gains, divisible among partners, 4.6.3
new partner, introduction of, 4.6.6
partner leaving after roll-over relief secured, 4.6.8
rebasing, 4.6.2
retirement of a partner, 4.6.5
revaluations, 4.6.4
capital,
recovery of, 16.7.1
replacement, 16.7.2, 16.7.3
demergers, 19.2.9
disputes, settling, 15.7.4
dissolution of, 15.8
profits, sharing of, 15.8.4
valuation of assets, 15.8.2
EEIGS, 15.9
financial provisions, 15.7.5
generally, 1.13
goodwill, 15.8.3
insolvency, 15.8.5
liability, 15.6
inter se, 15.6.2
third parties to, 15.6.1
limited, 15.2
loans, taken by partners, 2.1.12, 16.7.4
losses. *See* Trading losses
meetings, 15.7.3
partner,
change of, 15.7.6
salaried, 15.4
plant and machinery, purchase of, 16.7.5
receiver, appointment of, 15.8.1
third parties and, 15.5
winding up of, 15.8
Pay and file, 18.12
claims and elections, 18.13
corporation tax, payment of, 18.12.3
interest and penalties, 18.12.4
outline of, 18.12.1
return for, 18.12.2

PAYE, 11.1
  accounting to Revenue for, 11.1.2
  end of year returns, 11.1.3
  operation of, 11.1.1
Payments,
  future, 2.1.26
Pensions, 12.3
  changing arrangements, 12.3.6
  companies, 12.8.2
    employees of, 12.8.2
  contracting in, 12.3.3
  contracting out, 12.3.3
  contributions,
    employees, for, 2.1.10
    tax deductible, 1.1
  Directors, 12.8.2
    spouses of, 12.8.2
  generally, 1.10, 12.3.1
  occupational pension schemes, 12.3.4
  partners, 12.7.2
    employees of, 12.7.2
  personal pensions, 12.3.5
  post-cessation,
    expenses, 16.10.2
    receipts, 16.10.1
  sole trader, 12.6.2
    employees of, 12.6.2
    spouse of, 12.6.2
  state pension scheme, 12.3.2
  use of, 12.5
Plant & machinery, 2.2.12
  assets
    not qualifying as, 2.1.14
    qualifying as, 2.2.14
  disposals, 2.2.15
  election to treat as fixture, 2.2.15
  fixtures and fittings. *See* Fixtures and fittings
  industrial buildings allowance, 2.2.15
Professional fees, 2.1.18
Profit-related pay, 11.10
  income tax, exemption from, 11.10.1
  profit sharing. *See* Profit sharing
  registration, conditions on, 11.10.2
  shares. *See* Shares
Profit sharing, 11.13
  disposals, 11.3.1

Race discrimination,
  Commission for Racial Equality, 10.17.9
  direct discrimination, 10.17.4
  discrimination, types of, 10.7.2
  genuine occupational qualification, 10.17.6
  indirect discrimination, 10.17.4
  liability for, 10.17.7
  recruitment, 10.17.1
  remedies, 10.17.8
  victimisation, 10.17.5
Redundancy,
  checklist, 10.10.4
  consultation and notification requirements, 10.10.3
  insolvency, 10.20.1
  payments, 2.1.26, 11.17.1
    calculation of, 10.10.6
    claim for, 10.10.5
    insurance for, 12.6.1
  provision for, 2.1.24
  qualifying conditions, 10.10.1
  selection process, 10.10.2
  termination of employment. *See* Termination of employment
  unfair dismissal and, 10.9.8, 10.10
Refurbishments, 2.1.23
Rent, payments, 2.1.19
Repairs and renewals, 2.1.22
Retirement relief,
  directors, full-time, 4.9, 4.9.1
  disposal, date of, 4.7.2, 4.7.3
  employees, full-time, 4.9, 4.9.1
  example of, 4.7.1
  ill health, retirement due to, 4.7.4
  limited relief, 4.7.6
  managers, full-time, 4.9.1
  partners, for, 4.8.2, 4.8.3
  premises used by company, sale of, 4.9.4
  restriction, 4.8.3, 4.9.2, 4.9.3
  sole trader, 4.8.1
  time limits, 4.7.5
  trustees, for, 4.7.7
  unincorporated traders, 4.8
Roll-over relief, 4.3, 4.3.1, 18.3.2
  assets,
    owned by employee or office holder, 4.3.13
    used by personal trading company, 4.3.12
  conditions on, 4.3.2
  freehold, acquisition of, 4.3.10
  full relief, availability of, 4.3.3
  old assets, 4.3.4, 4.3.5
  partners, 4.3.11
  reinvestment of non-wasting assets, 4.3.8
  replacement assets,
    bringing into use of, 4.3.9
    wasting of, 4.3.6, 4.3.7
Royalties, 2.1.11

Sale of goods,
  acceptance, 8.10.2
  buyer, remedies, 8.12, 8.12.4

Sale of Goods – *continued*
consumer protection,
cancellation rights, 8.8.1
defences, 8.8.2
product liability, 8.8.2
delivery, 8.10.1, 8.12.1,
delay in, damages for, 8.12.2
description, 8.2
fitness for purpose, 8.3.1
generally, 1.6
goods, rejection of, 8.12.4
money, recovery of, 8.12.4
non-delivery, damages for, 8.12.1
performance, 8.12.4
property and risk, passing of, 8.9, 8.9.2
quality, 8.3.2
defective, damages for, 8.12.3
Romalpa clauses, 8.9.1
sale by sample, 8.4
seller, remedies of the, 8.11
terms implied into contract for, 8.1
breach of, 8.6
exclusion of, 8.5
time, stipulations of, 8.7
title, retention of, 8.9.1
Scientific research,
expenditure on, 2.2.27
fixtures and fittings, 2.2.15
plant & machinery, 2.2.15
Self assessment, 16.11
amended, 16.11.11
amendments after filing, 16.11.6
alternative to, 16.11.3
chargeability, requirement to notify, 16.11.9
corrections of, 16.11.8
estimates, inclusion of, 16.11.4
finality, achieving, 16.13
incorrect returns, 16.12.7
operation of, 16.14
partnerships, 16.12.6
penalties and surcharges, 16.12
appeals against, 16.12.2, 16.12.5
interest, 16.12.3
penalties, 16.12.4
revenue enquiries, 16.11.7
right to audit, 16.11.7
supporting documents, 16.11.5
tax, payment of, 16.11.10
Self-employment, taxation of,
accounting date, change of, 16.1.6–16.1.9
accounting periods, length of, 16.1.12
anti-avoidance provisions, 16.2.3–16.2.13
assessing 1996-97, 16.2.1
capital allowances. *See* Capital allowances
current year basis, 16.1
final year assessment, 16.1.11
first twelve months, 16.1.3
losses. *See* Trading losses
opening years, 16.1.1, 16.1.2
overlap relief, 16.1.4, 16.1.5
post-cessation,
expenses, 16.10.2
receipts, 16.10.1
retirement, 16.1.10
self assessment. *See* Self assessment
shifting income, 16.2.4–16.2.13
transitional provisions, 16.2
relief, 16.2.2
Sex discrimination,
Equal Opportunities Commission, 10.17.9
direct discrimination, 10.17.4
discrimination, types of, 10.7.2
genuine occupational qualification, 10.17.6
indirect discrimination, 10.17.4
liability for, 10.17.7
recruitment, 10.17.1
remedies, 10.17.8
victimisation, 10.17.5
Share capital, 17.7
issued, 17.7.1
reductions in, 17.7.2
Shares,
acquisition of own, 17.7.3, 17.7.5
assistance by company to buy, 17.7.6
exceptions, 17.7.7
bonus issues, 17.6.12
business transactions. *See* Business transactions
capital gains tax. *See* Capital gains tax
class rights, 17.6.14
company proprietor. *See* Company proprietor
CREST, 17.6.13
debenture holder, 17.6.11
dividends. *See* Dividends
gift of, 11.11
members' duties and rights, 17.6.15
options, 11.12
employer, return by, 11.12.6
exercise of, 11.12.3
other employee schemes, 11.12.5
residence status of, 11.12.4
option schemes, 11.14
approval of, 11.15.1
executive, 11.15
SAYE options, 11.14.2
redeemable, 17.7.4
shareholders,
meaning, 17.6.9
remedies available to, 17.6.16

Shares – *continued*
  special employee shares, 11.16
    dependent subsidiary, in, 11.16.1
  types, of, 17.6.10
Sick pay, statutory
  amount payable, 10.13.3
  medical suspension payment, 10.14.1
  payment, period of, 10.13.2
  qualifications for, 10.13.1
Sole trader,
  life assurance, 12.6.1
  loss of profits, 12.6.1
  partner, bringing in a, 19.1
    assets, keeping property outside of firm, 19.1.6
    capital gains tax, 19.1.4
    capital, interest on, 19.1.2
    current year basis, 19.1.7
    goodwill, valuation of, 19.1.5
    loans, relief for, 19.1.1
    partnership interest, 19.1.3
  redundancy payments, insurance for, 12.6.1
  security for loans, 12.6.2
  tax planning for, 19
Stamp duty,
  avoiding or reducing, 6.3
    company reconstructions, 6.3.3
    depositary receipts, 6.3.2
    intra group transfers, 6.3.8
    loan stock, 6.3.4
    sale of business assets, 6.3.6
    sale of land and buildings, 6.3.5
    sale of shares, 6.3.1
    transfer of a business to a company, 6.3.7
  business assets, sale of, 6.1.8
  contract, sale of, 6.1.7
  debts , sale of, 6.1.8
  documents liable to, 6.1
  generally, 1.4, 6
  goodwill, sale of, 6.1.8
  land and buildings, sale of, 6.1.2
  lease, grant of, 6.1.3, 6.1.4
  partnerships, 6.1.9
  sanctions for non-payment, 6.2
  securities, sale of, 6.1.1
  shares, ale of, 6.1.1
  sub-sales, 6.1.6
  unstamped documents, status of, 6.2
  VAT and, 6.1.5
Stock, valuation of, 2.1.25

Taxable profits,
  computation of, 1.1, 2.1
  earnings basis, 2.1.1
Taxation,
  company proprietor, 1.18
  employees, of. *See* PAYE
Tax planning,
  generally, 1.17
Termination of employment, 10.11
  damages for, 10.11.4
    accelerated receipt, 10.11.6
    interest, 10.11.7
    mitigation, 10.11.5
    payment in lieu of notice, 10.11.8
  exempt amounts, 11.7.3
  ex gratia payments, 11.17.2
  foreign service, 11.7.4
  lawful methods of, 10.11.1
  loss of office, compensation for, 11.17.3
  redundancy. *See* Redundancy
  restrictive covenants, 11.17.5
  taxation of, 11.17.4
  written reasons for dismissal, 10.11.2
  wrongful dismissal, 10.11.3
    claims procedure, 10.11.9
    damages for, 10.11.4
    mitigation, 10.11.5
Trading losses,
  aggregation, relief by, 16.9.3, 16.9.4
  anti–avoidance provisions, 16.9.14
  capital allowances, 16.9.6, 16.9.7
  capital gains, against, 16.9.9
  carry forward relief, 16.9.1
  computation of, 16.9.11–16.9.14
  early years of a trade, 16.9.8
  farming losses, 16.9.14
  general income, relief against, 16.9.2
  limited partnerships, 16.9.14
  relief for, 16.9
  Schedule D Case V, 16.9.15
  terminal loss, 16.9.10
Transfer of undertakings, 10.21
  application of, 10.21.1
  business transfers, 10.21.4
  collective agreements, 10.21.8
  economic, technical or organisational reasons, 10.21.4, 10.21.5
  immediately before the transfer, 10.21.3
  operation, 10.21.2
  redundancy payments, 10.21.6
  references, 10.21.10
  regulations, avoiding the, 10.21.7
  summary, 10.21.11
  trade union,
    consultation with, 10.21.9
    recognition, 10.21.8
  unfair dismissal, 10.21.4
Travelling expenses. *See* Benefits in kind

Unfair dismissal, 10.9
automatically unfair dismissals, 10.9.5
claim for, basis of, 10.9.1
compensation, 10.9.11
constructive dismissal, 10.9.1
contravention of an enactment, 10.9.9
dismissal,
employer, by, 10.9.1
grounds for, 10.9.6
procedures, 10.9.7
fairness, defence of, 10.9.4
fixed term contracts, expiry of, 10.9.1
illness, 10.9.6
misconduct, 10.9.6
qualifying period, 10.9.2
reasons for dismissal, 10.9.3
redundancy. *See* Redundancy
reinstatement, 10.9.11
remedies, 10.9.11
settlement, 10.9.12
substantial reason, 10.9.10
termination by employer, 10.9.1
Unincorporated business
generally, 1.14
self-employed. *See* Self-employed

Value added tax,
administration of, 5.1
accounting for, 5.4.3
Act of 1994, 5.2.1
agricultural flat rate scheme, 5.7.6
annual accounting, 5.7.4
anti-avoidance measures, 5.6
buildings, 5.6.3
business splitting, 5.6.1
reverse charges, 5.6.3
sales to connected parties, 5.6.2
self supplies, 5.6.3
stationery, 5.6.3
transfer of a business, 5.6.4
appeals, 5.10
departmental reviews, 5.10.2
tribunals, 5.10.1
bad debt relief, 5.4.4
business entertainment, 5.4.5
cash accounting, 5.7.3
Customs notices and leaflets, 5.2.4
de-registration, 5.4.2
EC directives, 5.2.5
enforcement, 5.8
interest, 5.8.2
late registration, 5.8.2
late returns, 5.8.2
misdeclaration, 5.8.2
penalties, 5.8.2
visits, 5.8.1
exempt, 5.3.1
exports outside of EU, 5.5.2
fraud,
civil, 5.9.1
criminal, 5.9.2
generally, 1.3
harmonisation, 5.1
imports of non-EU goods, 5.5.1
introduction of, 5.1
invoices, 5.4.4
legal authorities, 5.2
legislation, 5.2.1
motor car, 5.4.5
operation of, 5.1.1
output, 5.4.4
partial exemption, 5.4.6
principles of, 5.3
recovery of, 5.4.5
registration, 5.4.1
retail schemes, 5.7.1
scope of, outside the, 5.3.1
second-hand schemes, 5.7.2
single market, transactions within, 5.5.3
special schemes, 5.7
supply on, 5.3.1
admission to premises, 5.3.2
business, in course of, 5.3.2
charities, 5.3.2
clubs and societies, 5.3.2
consideration, 5.3.4
taxable person, 5.3.3
statutory instruments, 5.2.2
tax points, 5.4.4
tour operators, margin scheme, 5.7.5
Treasury orders, 5.2.3
zero-rated supplies, 5.3.1

Work in progress,
accounts, inclusion in, 2.1.1
valuation of, 2.1.25
Work permits, 17.11
businessmen, 17.11.6
DfEE requirements, 17.11.2
extending, 17.11.4
investor, 17.11.7
self-employed persons, 17.11.6
sole representatives, 17.11.5
WP1, 17.11.3